The Euro at 10

The Euro at 10

Europeanization, Power, and Convergence

Edited by
Kenneth Dyson

OXFORD
UNIVERSITY PRESS

OXFORD
UNIVERSITY PRESS

Great Clarendon Street, Oxford OX2 6DP

Oxford University Press is a department of the University of Oxford.
It furthers the University's objective of excellence in research, scholarship,
and education by publishing worldwide in

Oxford New York

Auckland Cape Town Dar es Salaam Hong Kong Karachi
Kuala Lumpur Madrid Melbourne Mexico City Nairobi
New Delhi Shanghai Taipei Toronto

With offices in

Argentina Austria Brazil Chile Czech Republic France Greece
Guatemala Hungary Italy Japan Poland Portugal Singapore
South Korea Switzerland Thailand Turkey Ukraine Vietnam

Oxford is a registered trade mark of Oxford University Press
in the UK and in certain other countries

Published in the United States
by Oxford University Press Inc., New York

© The several contributors 2008

The moral rights of the authors have been asserted
Database right Oxford University Press (maker)

First published 2008

British Library Cataloguing in Publication Data
Data available

Library of Congress Cataloging in Publication Data
The euro at 10 : Europeanization, power, and convergence / edited by Kenneth
Dyson.
   p. cm.
   ISBN 978-0-19-920886-9
1. Euro.   2. Euro area.   3. Europe–Economic integration.   4. Economic and
   Monetary Union. 5. European Union countries–Economic policy. I. Dyson,
   Kenneth H. F.
HG925.E86785   2008
332.4'94–dc22   2008016930

Typeset by SPI Publisher Services, Pondicherry, India
Printed in Great Britain
on acid-free paper by
CPI Antony Rowe, Chippenham, Wiltshire

ISBN 978-0-19-920886-9

1 3 5 7 9 10 8 6 4 2

Preface and Acknowledgements

By general consent, the Euro Area represents a historic event for European unification and for EU member states. Its effects on Euro Area insiders, temporary outsiders, and semi-permanent outsiders are a matter of great topical and academic interest. This study is more than a second edition of *European States and the Euro* (OUP), which appeared in the early stage of the Euro Area's existence. The difference resides in the time period. The first book retains historical value in dealing primarily with how European states were responding to the conditions for entering into European monetary union—the effects and legacies of 'accession' Europeanization rather than of 'membership' Europeanization. It focused on EMU's effects as a historical process stretching back through the Exchange Rate Mechanism (ERM) into the 1970s.

This book is concerned with what has happened to member states since monetary union on 1 January 1999—after which they faced a 'one-size-fits-all' monetary policy and devaluation no longer remained a policy instrument—and currency union on 1 January 2002, when over 300 million Euro Area citizens began to use a single set of euro banknotes and coins. Not least, businesses now operated in a new context where exchange-rate risk was no longer present. This book deals with European states in stage three of EMU, facing the European Central Bank (ECB) and its single monetary policy for the new Euro Area, the constraining fiscal rules of the Stability and Growth Pact, and new challenges to coordinate domestic economic reforms in the so-called Lisbon process. Both 'insiders' and 'outsiders' were engaged in an intensified competition of ideas. The substance of the first edition forms the context and initial conditions for this volume, which deals with the first decade.

A word of caution about 'the first decade' is in order. This book appears in time for the tenth anniversary of the euro. However, the logistics of production schedules and the dated and incomplete nature of reliable statistics mean that, in reality, the timescale is less than a decade. Timely publication for the anniversary and the time period of a decade are difficult to reconcile. The editor's introduction makes plain the problems of coming to firm assessments. They include a timescale in which the main effects of the euro have yet to fully reveal themselves: for instance, trade effects, market-based adjustments, and changes in institutional capacities to deal with risks to financial stability and with asymmetric euro exchange rate, growth, and inflation shocks. The full scale of adjustment problems from anaemic productivity growth, persisting high inflation, booming property markets, an appreciating euro, or lax prudential supervision of financial institutions may take more than a decade to manifest themselves. Effects unfold at different speeds across states, as well as in discrete forms in particular sectors.

Further complications arise from the difficulties of disassociating euro effects from other contextual factors, international, European, and domestic; its embeddedness in other EU projects like the single market and the Lisbon process for economic reform; and the challenge of discriminating direct and indirect effects, material and ideational effects, and of weighing their individual significance. Assessments have inexorably a provisional and tentative character. Underlying economic, political, and ideational structures can be mapped; state-specific and function-specific biases identified; and certain spatial and temporal patterns discerned, albeit often crosscutting. However, in seeking patterns the complicating roles of different domestic historical legacies, specific institutional arrangements, varying economic structures, leadership, and unanticipated consequences remain salient. A further complicating factor is the changed character of the EU polity between the Amsterdam Treaty and the Lisbon Treaty and the effects of EU enlargement from 15 to 27 on diversity.

A second note of caution relates to this book's character as a political economy of the euro. It derives from the focus, questions, and approaches typical of political science in addressing comparative political economy. This book is about Europeanization, power, and legitimacy, and convergence in institutions and policy processes. It deals with ideas, institutions, discourse, and party and electoral strategies, and how they mediate the effects of the euro on states. These effects relate to the polity, politics, and policies. They are captured in the notion of Europeanization. At the same time, a key theme is the limits of Europeanization as a concept for capturing processes of change associated with the euro, especially comparative advantage and the role of firms.

The final note of caution relates to the terms 'Economic and Monetary Union' (EMU), the 'Euro Area', and the 'euro'. The euro is the name of the single currency and is a phenomenon of stage three of EMU, post-1999. The Euro Area comprises those EU states that have adopted the euro and for whom a single monetary policy is conducted by the Governing Council of the European Central Bank. EMU's effects began in stages before 1999, as defined by the EU: stage one from July 1990 dismantled all internal barriers to the free movement of capital within the EU; stage two from January 1994 established the European Monetary Institute to prepare stage three, prohibited the financing of the public sector by central banks, prohibited privileged access of the public sector to financial institutions; and required the avoidance of excessive government deficits. In these respects, EMU applies to all EU states. More broadly, EMU included macroeconomic policy coordination exercises that were developed with and after the Maastricht Treaty: like the Broad Economic Policy Guidelines, the European Employment Strategy, the Lisbon process, and the ongoing single market programme. Additionally, monetary union had its antecedents in the Exchange Rate Mechanism (ERM), 1979–99, and its post-1999 successor, ERM II, through which states peg their currencies to the euro.

Hence, EMU has effects for states that have not adopted the euro (as for the new EU member states in 2004 and 2007). For EU states without a formal opt-out from the euro and with a political commitment to euro entry, EMU is a process of 'accession' Europeanization. For Euro Area states, EMU is a process of 'membership' Europeanization. This book deals with 'membership' Europeanization in the Euro Area and with 'accession' Europeanization principally in the context of the first decade of the euro. The key point is that being outside the Euro Area still means being part of EMU, minus the stage three obligations of using the euro as the single currency and the single monetary policy.

This book was made possible by the generosity of the British Academy in funding a major conference in May 2007 and of the EU-CONSENT Network of Excellence in funding a preparatory workshop in May 2006 in Cardiff. Along with a further workshop for authors of the thematic chapters, these events provided an invaluable opportunity for authors to present drafts of their chapters for discussion. Particular thanks are due to Angela Pusey at the British Academy for the courteous, patient, and efficient way in which she and her team organized the conference and to the Public Understanding and Activities Committee of the British Academy for its financial support.

In addition, the final revision of chapters benefited greatly from the comments of all contributors, who served as discussants on each other's papers at the British Academy conference. Further debts of gratitude are owed to Professor Charles Goodhart (LSE), Professor Jack Hayward (Hull), Professor Ivo Maes (Catholic University of Louvain), and Professor Jim Rollo (Sussex).

Not least, the editor would like to thank Dominic Byatt and his team at Oxford University Press for their encouragement and support at every stage and to the contributors for their unfailing good humour, dedication to the project, and the cooperative team spirit that they displayed. The commitment of OUP and of contributors lightened the editorial load. Any shortcomings in the final product remain, of course, the responsibility of the editor.

Kenneth Dyson

Cardiff University, January 2008

Contents

Contents

Contents

List of Figures

List of Figures

List of Tables

List of Tables

Notes on Contributors

Joshua Bridwell is a Graduate Student at Emory University. His research interests include political economy and European politics.

Jim Buller is Lecturer in Politics at the University of York. He has written widely on the subject of Britain's relations with the European Union, including recent articles in the *British Journal of Politics and International Relations* and *West European Politics*. He is currently completing a book entitled *The International Sources of British Politics*.

Benjamin J. Cohen is Louis G. Lancaster Professor of International Political Economy at the University of California, Santa Barbara. A specialist in the political economy of international money and finance, he is the author of 12 books, including *Global Monetary Governance* (Routledge 2008) and *International Political Economy: An Intellectual History* (Princeton University Press 2008).

Kenneth Dyson is Research Professor in European Politics at Cardiff University, Wales. He is a Fellow of the British Academy and an Academician of the Learned Society of the Social Sciences. In 1996 and 2001, he chaired the Higher Education Funding Council research assessment panels for European Studies. His books on EMU include *Elusive Union: The Process of Economic and Monetary Union* (Longman 1994); *The Road to Maastricht: Negotiating Economic and Monetary Union* (with Kevin Featherstone, Oxford University Press 1999); *The Politics of the Euro-Zone: Stability or Breakdown?* (Oxford University Press 2000); *European States and the Euro* (Oxford University Press 2002), and *Enlarging the Euro Area: External Empowerment and Domestic Transformation in East Central Europe* (Oxford University Press 2006). He was adviser to the BBC2 series 'The Money Changers' on the making of EMU. His main research interests are in German policy and politics, European economic policies and politics, and the EU. He is co-editor of the journal *German Politics* and co-edited in 2003 with Klaus Goetz *Germany, Europe and the Politics of Constraint* (Oxford University Press) and in 2006 with Stephen Padgett *The Politics of Economic Reform in Germany* (Routledge).

Kevin Featherstone is Eleftherios Venizelos Professor of Contemporary Greek Studies at the London School of Economics. He has written extensively on EU and Greek politics. A book on Greece and structural reform (with Dimitris Papadimitriou) will appear in 2008. Recent books include *The Road to Maastricht* (with Kenneth Dyson), *Politics and Policy in Greece* (edited, 2005), and (co-edited with Claudio Radaelli) *The Politics of Europeanisation* (Oxford University Press 2003).

Magnus Feldmann is a Ph.D. candidate and Research Fellow at the Weatherhead Center for International Affairs and affiliated to the Minda de Gunzburg Center for European Studies at Harvard University. He has published various articles and book chapters on economic policy reform, post-socialist transition, and European politics.

Paul Furlong is Professor of European Studies and Head of the School of European Studies at Cardiff University. He has written widely on Italian politics and public policy, focusing especially on the role of Parliament and on political economy. Most recently, he has also published on the Bologna process and higher education reform in Europe.

Andrew Gamble is Professor of Politics at the University of Cambridge. He is a Fellow of the British Academy and joint editor of *The Political Quarterly* and *New Political Economy*. His books include *Between Europe and America: The Future of British Politics*, which was awarded the W. J. M. Mackenzie prize. In 2005 he received the Isaiah Berlin prize for lifetime contribution to political studies.

Béla Greskovits is Professor of International Relations and European Studies at the Central European University, Budapest. He is author of *The Political Economy of Protest and Patience. East European and Latin American Transformations Compared* (Central European University Press 1998). His most recent articles on the political economy of policy reform and the diversity of post-socialist capitalism have appeared in *Studies in Comparative and International Development, Labor History, Orbis, West European Politics, Competition and Change*, and *Journal of Democracy*.

Mark Hallerberg is Professor of Political Economy and Public Management at the Hertie School of Governance. He also maintains an affiliation in the Political Science Department of Emory University. He is author of one book, co-author of a second, and co-editor of a third. He has published over 25 articles and chapters on fiscal governance, tax competition, exchange-rate choice, and European politics.

Colin Hay is Professor of Political Analysis in the Department of Politics at the University of Sheffield. He is the author, co-author, or editor of a number of books including, most recently, *Why We Hate Politics* (Polity 2007), *European*

Politics (Oxford University Press 2007), *The State* (Palgrave 2006), *Developments in British Politics 8* (Palgrave 2006), and *Political Analysis* (Palgrave 2002). He is founding co-editor of the journals *Comparative European Politics* and *British Politics*.

David Howarth is Senior Lecturer in Politics at the University of Edinburgh. He is the author of the *French Road to European Monetary Union* (Palgrave 2001), (with Peter Loedel), *The European Central Bank* (Palgrave 2003 and 2005), and (with Georgios Varouxakis) *Contemporary France* (2003). He has written several articles and book chapters on French economic policy and policymaking and Economic and Monetary Union.

Johannes Lindvall is the Samuel Finer Post-Doctoral Fellow in Comparative Government at the University of Oxford. He studies economic and social policy making in comparative perspective. His work has appeared in *Comparative Politics*, *Scandinavian Political Studies*, and *West European Politics*.

Huw Macartney is an ESRC Postdoctoral Fellow at Nottingham University. He has recently completed his Ph.D., *Transnational Social Forces, Variegated Neo-liberalism and Financial Market Integration in the EU,* at the University of Manchester and has a forthcoming article in the *British Journal of Politics and International Relations*.

Martin Marcussen is Associate Professor of Politics at the University of Copenhagen. He specializes in global governance, European integration, and the role of ideas in public policy. He is author of *Ideas and Elites: The Social Construction of Economic and Monetary Union* (Aalborg University Press 2000).

Michael Moran is W. J. M. Mackenzie Professor of Government at Manchester University. He has written extensively on the politics of market regulation. His most recent book is *The British Regulatory State: High Modernism and Hyper-Innovation* (Oxford University Press, 2nd edn., 2007).

Nick Parsons is Reader in French in the School of European Studies at Cardiff University. He has published extensively on employment policy and industrial relations as well as French politics and society. His recent books are *French Industrial Relations in the New World Economy* (Palgrave 2005) and (co-edited with Yuan Zhigang) *Economic Globalization and Employment Policy* (Beijing 2005).

Philippe Pochet is director of the Observatoire social européen. He is Adjunct Professor, Griffith University (Australia), invited lecturer at the Catholic University of Louvain and affiliate at the Centre of European Studies (Free University of Brussels). He is the Digest Editor of the *Journal of European Social Policy*. His main research fields are social impacts of the monetary union, social dimension of the European Union, and new modes of governance.

Notes on Contributors

Lucia Quaglia is Senior Lecturer in Politics and Contemporary European Studies at Sussex University. In addition to numerous articles in journals and chapters in edited volumes, she has published *Central Bank Governance in the EU: A Comparative Analysis* (Routledge 2008).

Jari Matti Riiheläinen undertook his Ph.D. research at the University of Birmingham. His research examined legitimacy discourses surrounding the Economic and Monetary Union in national parliaments and print media in Austria, Finland, and Ireland, focusing on the debates on the effect of EMU on the welfare state.

Nicola J. Smith is Lecturer in Political Science at the University of Birmingham. She has published various articles and book chapters on Irish politics and economics and is author of *Showcasing Globalisation? The Political Economy of the Irish Republic* (Manchester University Press 2005).

Gaby Umbach is senior research associate at the Jean Monnet Chair for Political Science, University of Cologne. Her main fields of research and expertise include European integration and governance and Europeanization studies. Her doctoral thesis is on the Europeanization of British and German employment policies and policymaking structures.

Amy Verdun is Professor of Political Science, Jean Monnet Chair and Director of the Jean Monnet Centre of Excellence at the University of Victoria, Canada. She is the author or editor of 10 books and has served as guest editor of six special issues of peer-reviewed journals. She has published in peer-reviewed journals such as *British Journal of Politics and International Relations, Journal of Common Market Studies, Journal of European Public Policy, Journal of Public Policy*, and *Review of International Political Economy*.

Matthew Watson is Associate Professor (Reader) in the Department of Politics and International Studies at the University of Warwick. He is the author of two monographs with Palgrave Macmillan: *Foundations of International Political Economy* (2005) and *The Political Economy of International Capital Mobility* (2007).

Daniel Wincott is Professor of European and Comparative Politics at the University of Birmingham. His research interests include European integration, especially social policy, law, and integration theory, as well as comparative social policy, particularly the political economy of social aspects of citizenship and of territoriality (at and below the State level, as well as supranationally). He is co-author (with Colin Hay) of *Welfare in the New Europe* (Palgrave 2008).

Wolfgang Wessels holds the Jean Monnet Chair for Political Science at the University of Cologne. In 2007, he received the European Award 'Jean

Monnet' in Gold. He is chair of the Executive Board of the Institut für Europäische Politik (Berlin) and of the Trans European Policy Studies Association (Brussels), as well as coordinator of the EU-CONSENT Network of Excellence. Recent publications include *Economic Government of the EU. A Balance Sheet of New Modes of Policy Coordination* (co-edited by Ingo Linsenmann and Christoph O. Meyer 2007).

Radoslaw Zubek is Postdoctoral Research Fellow in the European Institute at the London School of Economics. His main research interest is in the comparative study of executives and parliaments in Europe. He is author of *Core Executive and Europeanization in Central Europe* (Palgrave Macmillan 2008) and has published in *Journal of European Public Policy, West European Politics*, and *Journal of Legislative Studies*.

1

The First Decade: Credibility, Identity, and Institutional 'Fuzziness'

Kenneth Dyson

The story of the first decade of the euro centres on the European Central Bank (ECB), a new European institution whose challenge was to establish the credibility of a new currency, the euro, in the unpropitious setting of a 'weak', incoherent, and potentially indecisive European polity and of 'strong', opaque, and potentially volatile financial markets. The ECB was not anchored in the traditional context of a sovereign nation state with its associated authority and claims on identity. It operated in a European polity characterized by institutional 'fuzziness' and 'thin' identity. This novel historical circumstance for a central bank created an incentive for the ECB to give a sharply pronounced emphasis to its own independence in the service of a clear, narrowly defined mandate of price stability and to adopt a 'hawkish' attitude to inflation.

In negotiating this complex politico-institutional environment, the ECB had to face the additional difficulty of the weak empowerment of the Euro Area to secure financial stability in the fast-changing context of highly dynamic, innovative, risk-taking, globally integrating financial markets and new, opaque forms of 'endogenous' liquidity creation. This combination of market opacity and volatility with inadequate instruments to influence lending meant that the ECB faced serious challenges in claiming a central bank leadership role. Its decisive contribution, at least until the end of 2007, was to deliver price stability, to lock in expectations of low inflation and— consequent on a single currency—to help shield its member states from previously painful currency instabilities consequent on market turbulence. However, the ECB remained poised uneasily between a 'weak' polity and 'strong' markets. Its capacity to sustain its poise depended on a broad political consensus around the principle of central bank independence and in particular stout defence of this principle by German governments. This defence remained intact.

The relationship between European states and the euro over the first decade was defined by a series of interwoven economic and political problems. On the economic front, the Euro Area experienced a low rate of economic growth (an annual average of 1.4 per cent, 2001–5); declining labour productivity and high long-term unemployment; a low employment participation rate, especially amongst young and older people; and between 1999 and 2007, a decline in annual rate of growth of real disposable incomes whilst corporate profits rose as a share of Gross Domestic Product (GDP). Politically, the Euro Area faced collective action problems in fiscal policies (notably the crisis of the Stability and Growth Pact in November 2003) and in economic reforms (especially in labour markets), where responsibility remained at the national level; the lack of positive emotional engagement of public opinion; and weak ownership of the euro project by domestic political leaders.

This combination of low, even declining public enthusiasm with historic and comparative relative weaknesses in economic performance and collective action problems made the euro a potentially dangerous area for domestic political engagement, both for Euro Area 'insider' political elites and for 'outsider' EU states. Though the Euro Area expanded from 11 to 16 members (with entry of Greece, Slovenia, Cyprus, Malta, and Slovakia), it failed to attract British, Danish, or Swedish entry. The Baltic States, the Czech Republic, Hungary, and Poland deferred entry to 2012–14 and even beyond, signalling strengthening reservations about entry. In short, despite an improved growth and employment performance in post-2005 led by Germany, the Euro Area's gravitational pull remained weak.

Internal conflict over the Iraq War in 2003 and, even more seriously, Dutch and French rejection of the European Constitutional Treaty in referenda of 2005 and Irish rejection of the Lisbon Treaty in 2008 underlined the euro's failure to act as a catalyst for strengthening European identity in the Euro Area's core. The euro continued to lack the protective political umbrella of a sovereign European political power. This deficit in political union meant continuing weaknesses and vulnerabilities in capacity for international representation of common interests (e.g. in the International Monetary Fund), for fiscal action through a collective budget, and for prevention and management of potentially contagious cross-national banking and financial crises (again including the provision of federal funding for meeting the costs). The main achievement in the successive Amsterdam (1997), Nice (2001), and Lisbon (2007) treaties was to preserve the essential features of the Maastricht monetary 'constitution', notably the principle of an independent central bank whose mandate was limited to price stability.

Before examining the core questions and concepts that unify this book, this chapter outlines the euro's key effects on public opinion, political elites, and expert elites; its sources of fragility and its 'fuzziness' that relate to the unfinished business of Economic and Monetary Union (EMU); and its balance sheet of performance. It concludes by highlighting the difficulties in tracing its effects on European states.

Publics, Political Elites, and Experts

EMU is a classic example of an elite-driven process of integration, reliant on a 'permissive' public consensus in favour of European unification. It represented an historical conjunction of political leadership driving the process, notably from the French President and the German Chancellor, of co-option of expert elites in European central banks and finance ministries into the process, and of these expert elites providing the policy content (Dyson and Featherstone 1999). EMU functioned paradoxically as a catalyst in promoting further European unification (financial market integration is one example; successive treaty revisions might be another), in unleashing new debates about the integration process, and in generating unanticipated consequences for political elites. These debates and unanticipated consequences challenged how permissive the public consensus was for elites. EMU has been simultaneously depoliticizing—above all, as an engine for change in empowering independent central banks in European macroeconomic management and discourse—and politicizing—with new public debates about the direction and agenda of European integration, especially around neo-liberalism, its variants, and the nature and sustainability of the European social model.

First and foremost, the consolidation of the single monetary policy and single currency, and its ramifications for macroeconomic coordination and for European financial markets, preoccupied expert elites in and around the central banks of the 'Eurosystem' (the ECB and the national central banks of the Euro Area), the national finance ministries, and the European Commission. The European Central Bank (2007b) claimed successes in organizing a smooth transition from national currencies to the euro in 2002; in delivering low inflation (averaging just over 2 per cent per annum); in locking in market expectations of low inflation consistent with its price stability target; and in acting as a catalyst in financial market integration, especially in European money and bond markets and, to a lesser extent, equity markets. More problematic were slower progress in integrating retail banking and retail payments and still untested risk of inadequate institutional capacity to manage cross-national and contagious banking and financial crises. Nevertheless, the ECB gained legitimacy from the close coordination of its stability-oriented discourse with financial market players and with fellow central bank and monetary economics professionals. The ECB had effectively cultivated professional and market credibility by demonstrating its independence and acquiring formidable technical competence in economic research and analysis. Stability-oriented policies were shifted to the centre of EU and domestic debates, with central bankers—equipped with an impressive intellectual edifice of supportive theory—acting as 'monetary missionaries' (Dyson 2000*b*). Expert elites—in the Eurosystem, the Economic and Financial Committee and the Economic Policy Committee—'owned' the euro and strengthened their European identity in the process (Dyson and Quaglia 2007).

In contrast, domestic political elites shied away from the discursive challenge of crafting a positive and persuasive narrative about the euro. Their incentive was reduced by problems of communication with suspicious publics. Public opinion had been made brittle by widespread experience and perception of the euro's introduction as inflationary and then anxious by painful adjustment challenges from an appreciating euro, low growth, and high unemployment. Political elites were anxious to keep the euro off the agenda of domestic reform. In consequence, and in contrast to euro accession, the cutting edge of the euro as an external discipline was blunted. There were occasional critiques of the ECB for not doing more to tackle growth and employment problems, notably from France and Italy; of fiscal failures to abide by the Stability and Growth Pact, notably from small states like Austria and the Netherlands; whilst in 2005 the Italian Prime Minister Silvio Berlusconi referred to the euro as a 'disaster' and a minister called for euro exit. As in the Italian elections of 2006 and 2008 and the French elections of 2007, these critiques were in part attributable to short-term centrist tactics of drawing the sting from populist attacks on the euro from the Left and Right extremes of the political spectrum. The potentially high economic and political risks of euro exit, associated with the dense web of interdependencies in which the euro is embedded, and the complex technical uncertainties of currency conversion, continued to make 'loyalty' and 'voice' preferable strategies (Eichengreen 2007).

To the extent that the attitudes of Europe's citizens can be accurately and reliably captured by public opinion surveys, the euro appears to be simultaneously viewed as a major historical event for Europe and as an unloved offspring of the European integration process. According to Gallup Europe (2006: 73), five years after its introduction 66 per cent of those polled in the EU-12 identified the euro as a major event in European history (29 per cent disagreed). Support for this view exceeded 50 per cent in all states, being highest in Italy (80 per cent) and lowest in Germany (52 per cent) and Austria (55 per cent).

More ominously, the percentage evaluating the euro as 'advantageous overall' fell steadily from 59 per cent in September 2002 to 48 per cent in September 2006. Correspondingly, the score for 'disadvantageous overall' climbed from 29 to 38 per cent. By 2006, the percentage viewing the euro as 'disadvantageous overall' was higher than those seeing it as advantageous in Greece, Italy, and the Netherlands (Gallup Europe 2006: 29–30). When it came to effects on feelings of 'being European', Gallup Europe (2006: 42–3) results were similarly modest. Nineteen per cent claimed that the euro had made them feel 'more European' (though only 2 per cent reported to feel 'less European'). Seventy-eight per cent indicated no effect, with the least effects in Germany (85 per cent), the Netherlands (83 per cent), and Austria (82 per cent). The biggest effects were in Ireland (73 per cent reported themselves to feel 'more European'). Between 2002 and 2006, enthusiasm for the euro declined, whilst in terms of European identity the overwhelming majority reported no change. The FT/Harris poll (Financial Times 2007a) suggested that more than two-thirds in France, Italy, and Spain, and over half in Germany, believed that the euro had harmed their national economies and preferred their former currencies (though, with the exception of the French, more saw gains than losses to the EU economy as a whole). This poll confirmed the 'unloved' quality of the euro, especially in France and Italy, complementing the Gallup Europe (2006) picture of it as 'unloved' in Greece, Italy, and the Netherlands.

The precarious hold of the euro on public opinion across the Euro Area placed centrist political elites in Euro Area member states and in potential entrants in a difficult position. Dissatisfaction with the euro was a standing incentive to political elites on the extreme Left and Right to instrumentalize it for a populist Euro-sceptic politics. Hence, centrist political elites hesitated between avoidance of the euro issue and occasional defensive position taking to neutralize the issue. They had little incentive to employ it as an external discipline to legitimate economic reforms. At the same time, centrist elites had much to lose from challenging a project in which so much political capital had been sunk, especially from the negative effects of undermining the credibility of the new currency and thereby incurring accusations of irresponsible political conduct. Higher ECB interest rates in response to declining market confidence could only exacerbate growth and employment problems; whilst unravelling European integration in one of its core areas was rife with unanticipated, destabilizing economic and political consequences (Eichengreen 2007).

The barriers to Euro-sceptic political mobilization around the euro were higher in domestic contexts where generalized support for European political unification and for economic stability was firmly entrenched. This context helps explain why German opposition to losing the D-Mark did not translate into the euro as a catalyst for growth of a more general Euro-scepticism. However, threats to economic stability—whether from a perceived inflationary bias or from perceived incapacity to manage banking and financial crisis in the Euro Area (or, most ominously, both simultaneously)—would offer new incentives to question both the euro and European political unification.

The stalemate between political elites and publics was anchored in the way that the Euro Area shielded its member states from crisis, at least in the short to medium term. The painful and politically humiliating sanction of foreign exchange market crisis for national currencies under the ERM, like the

French franc in 1983, 1987, and 1992–3 and the Italian lira in 1992, had been removed and, with it, an external discipline that forced economic and fiscal reforms onto domestic agendas. A major pressure valve powering domestic reforms had been closed, so that for many, mainly larger, states the pace of reforms slowed rather than speeded with the euro (Duval and Elmeskov 2006). Fiscal 'sinners' like Greece and Italy no longer had to pay a significant premium to borrow with the convergence of yields on government bonds.

On the other hand, the Euro Area served as a new catalyst for crisis. German-led reduction of unit labour costs accentuated competitive pressures for economies like Italy, Portugal, and Spain. States could no longer opt for ERM realignments or ERM exit to offset the accumulated effects of relatively high unit labour cost growth. Removal of the veils provided earlier by domestic exchange-rate and interest-rate adjustment highlighted structural weaknesses in economies. Simultaneously, the euro removed former sources of external discipline and developed new internal disciplines.

In part in consequence of this lost external discipline, and in part because of foregone policy instruments of adjustment with the euro, political leaders had to assume an increased responsibility for the domestic temporal management of economic reforms. Their political skills in the timing, sequencing, and pacing of economic reforms involved a difficult balancing of risks: domestic risks of pursuing reforms in the face of a fragile public opinion on the euro and in the context of often complex and crowded domestic electoral calendars and generating a popular backlash; and the European and domestic economic and political risks from precipitating a crisis of the euro through failure of timely reforms. The euro made more transparent not just the temporal management skills of political leaders but also the domestic veto points and partison veto players that they faced. The result was a harsher critical environment for domestic political leadership. The euro was a project in danger of crisis from failures in domestic temporal management of reforms. Domestic political ownership of the euro was the missing magic ingredient. This ingredient mattered because, as Cohen (2000) noted: 'In a world of sovereign states . . . nothing can be regarded as truly irreversible.'

'Fuzziness', Fragility, and Power to Deliver: Collective Action Problems

The Euro Area's historical novelty as a 'monetary union without a state' lent a quality of precariousness to the euro. It was an incomplete project under construction, characterized by two main asymmetries: between centralized monetary policy making and decentralized banking and financial market supervision; and between a supra-national monetary pillar and an economic pillar in which states retained the central attributes of sovereignty, not least in fiscal and in economic reform policies. As a monetary union, it was stronger and more sustainable than predecessors like the French-led Latin Monetary Union and the Scandinavian Monetary Union of the nineteenth century in being embedded in a much broader and deeper web of interdependencies (Dyson 1994).

However, the Euro Area had the fragility of a monetary union without the protective umbrella of a sovereign political power. Its asymmetries of design and quality of fragility reflected the ambivalent relationship of EMU to the European state. On the one hand, as with earlier projects of European integration, the incentive to pursue a single currency rested on perceptions of the weakness of European states (cf. Milward 1992). These perceptions were grounded in experience both of their vulnerability to exchange-rate volatility and crisis and of the trade constraints from high transaction costs associated with multiple currencies. A further incentive was to manage the difficulties raised by German monetary power in Europe. On the other hand, in the process, European states sought to tightly define their loss of sovereignty. The development of EMU and the Euro Area became, in consequence, bound up with the domestic political leadership problems and policy choices in European states. As this book shows, the weak states that created EMU did not suddenly become capable of endowing it with the strength to deliver the performance in securing price stability and higher growth and employment that their citizens expected.

The Euro Area demonstrated a hierarchy of collective action problems, which affected even its capacity to deliver economic stability. Economic stability rests on two components: price stability and financial stability. In using monetary policy to secure price stability, the Euro Area's collective action problems were relatively low. The central bankers in the Eurosystem enjoyed an 'extreme' treaty-based form of independence, including defining their own price stability target. They were united by an impressive corpus of monetary theory that offered guidance on appropriate policies (Dyson 2000b). In contrast, neither supra-national authority to organize crisis management nor a similar body of shared theory existed in financial stability policies. Financial instability threatened to compromise monetary policy and highlighted a collective action problem at the heart of Euro Area economic stability (and more generally in central banking). Collective action problems were even greater in fiscal policies. The Euro Area lacked a fiscal union for the purpose of economic stabilization. The fiscal rules of the Stability and Growth Pact faced problems of domestic compliance as governments attended to varying domestic electoral calendars and divergent economic interests. Collective action problems were even starker in economic reforms, where post-2000 the Lisbon process of coordination foundered.

The Euro Area, like the EU in which it nested, had a 'fuzzy' character. It lacked the fundamental attributes of a polity: coherence between authority, function, and identity (Bartolini 2007). The EU's 'fuzzy' character was exemplified in its simultaneous existence as an 'actor' with authority in monetary policy (in the Euro Area) and in competition policy and as an 'arena' for dialogue in tax policy, economic reform policies, and banking supervision. The Lisbon process of coordinating economic reforms illustrated the 'fuzziness': it talked the language of an actor but, outside single market measures, behaved as little more than an arena. This 'fuzziness' was also apparent in the coexistence of ECOFIN, with all 27 EU member states, and the informal Euro Group of Euro Area finance ministers who coordinated, without legal authority, in areas like fiscal policy and economic reforms. Notably, financial market integration remained an EU-level rather than Euro Area–level matter. Neither the TARGET2 electronic wholesale payment system nor the Single Euro Payment Area (SEPA) remained solely Euro-Area matters. For purposes of payment systems, competition, fiscal policies, and single market matters, the Euro Area lacked independent authority and clear identity. It had neither its own 'council' at finance minister level nor its own council of heads of state and government. Outside monetary policy the Euro Area was even 'fuzzier' than the EU. In this sense, it fell short of being a 'core' Europe. As the debate on the Constitutional Treaty showed, the Euro Group failed to act as an engine for creating 'core' Europe.

In consequence of this lack of sovereign political power and institutional 'fuzziness', the ECB risks exposure to rising political demands for accountability and for revision of its mandate when growth and unemployment problems deepen, and awkward policy dilemmas arise. 'Output' legitimacy is inherently contingent on performance (Scharpf 1998), and becomes problematic as 'stagflation'—simultaneous risks from rising inflation and recession—increases economic and political costs of securing price stability and produces more controversial trade-offs. In the context of these economic 'bad' times, more vocal political challenges to ECB independence could readily translate into diminished credibility. In addition, the absence of a sovereign European political power aggravates problems of applying rules of fiscal discipline through the Stability and Growth Pact. Fiscal sanctions against sovereign states lack credibility. An absent sovereign European power also means an inability to develop the EU budget as a large-scale fiscal stabilization mechanism to ease adjustment problems through resource transfers. Not least, the European taxpayer cannot be called on in the event of a cross-national banking crisis. This gap further exposes the ECB to risk in case of contagious financial crisis.

The succession of treaty revisions—Amsterdam, Nice, the abortive Constitutional Treaty, and the prospective Lisbon Treaty—fell short of creating a sovereign political power at the European level to bolster domestic fiscal discipline, create cross-national fiscal stabilization, or strengthen institutional capability to secure banking and financial stability. The failure of the

Constitutional Treaty highlighted that the Euro Area lacked the stabilizing ballast of a common European identity across mass publics and expressed in a shared willingness to collectivize these financial and fiscal risks and ease problems of adjustment.

Born in the 'good times' of historically unprecedented global economic expansion, downward pressure on manufacturing prices from the economic rise of Asia, and low real interest rates, the Euro Area had the reward of a lucky early life. However, it was simmering potentially multiple crises. Once 'bad times' began, it was unclear precisely in what form, how, and where crises were most likely to manifest themselves; how skilled its political leaders would prove in managing them; and at what point, and again where, the balance might tip domestic strategy in one or more states from loyalty and voice towards exit. The record up to early 2008 offers no clear guidance. However, notable sources of fragility include a combination of euro appreciation, low growth, high unemployment, and relatively high unit labour costs in states like Italy and Portugal; high public debt, unemployment, and unit labour costs in Greece (shared with Italy); and euro appreciation, rising unit labour costs and the consequences of a credit-induced housing and property boom in Ireland and Spain. This fragility matters when one considers that between 2002 and 2006 Ireland and Spain contributed 26 per cent of Euro Area GDP growth.

A Balance Sheet of Performance: Living with a Hegemonic Discourse and the Contingencies of Good Times and Bad

Underpinning debate about Euro Area performance is a global hegemonic discourse of economic statisticians using GDP-based, macro-economic measures of welfare and anchored in international institutions like the IMF and the OECD as well as in economic think tanks and investment banks. These measures imply judgements about significance, most fundamentally that GDP advances are the precondition for enjoying the moral as well as material benefits of living in a liberal, tolerant society that offers opportunity (cf. Friedman 2005). They form the basis of international league tables that define images of success. However, GDP measures may have little to do with people's subjective experience of work and life, including economic insecurity, aversion to personal greed and flawed compensation practices in the financial sector, job-related stress, environmental degradation, urban breakdown, and crime and delinquency. They hide key features of economic as well as social and cultural life and risk distorting public debate. There are also issues surrounding the reliability of the underlying figures, including differences in reporting practices (e.g. in taxation), in how output is calculated (e.g. in financial services), and in measuring output where there are often no market prices (e.g. education and health). However, since the Euro Area is, first and foremost, an economic construct, it can expect to be judged in terms of this dominant global discourse of GDP measures.

Strengths, Difficulties, and Vulnerabilities

When measured in terms of official league tables, and largely against the United States, the Euro Area exhibited serious, albeit largely inherited GDP-related difficulties. They included anaemic overall real GDP growth (averaging 1.4 per cent per annum 2001–5), with persisting dispersion (Germany and Italy performing below average between 1996 and 2005); steady decline in labour productivity growth in historic terms and compared to the United States over the period 1996–2005 after a long period of catching up, with the decline most evident in using new technologies in the retail, wholesale, and financial service sectors; persistently higher inflation rates in the service sector than the US high levels of long-term unemployment and relatively low labour force participation rates by older and younger persons (though not in the 30–50 age group); persisting inflation differentials (with Greece, Ireland, Portugal, Slovenia, and Spain well above average); slower price adjustment to changing economic conditions than in the United States; and problems of sustainable public finances with accumulated gross government indebtedness since the 1970s rising to 68.6 per cent of GDP in 2006 (with Greece and Portugal at highest risk).

These interpretations of failure need to be contextualized. In some significant areas the Euro Area led the United States: job creation between 1999 and 2006; gross saving, especially by households; aggregate fiscal deficit; exports of goods and services and current account balance; and various measures of income distribution, child poverty, deaths from preventable diseases, and delinquency and crime (cf. Panic 2007). On this range of measures, the Nordic states and the Netherlands, followed by France and Germany, most notably outstripped the United States. When set aside price stability and low average annual wage growth, and along with a comparatively strong aggregate fiscal position, they represented a solid set of economic and social foundations. Average inflation performance, job creation and aggregate fiscal performance were strengthened over the first decade of the euro.

Perhaps more fundamentally, absolute levels matter as much as the relative rates of change measured in official league tables. These tables do not measure the gains in extra leisure time and a less stressful life from shorter working hours and more congenial working conditions, especially in Austria, France, Germany, and the Netherlands, nor from preserving (even if 'unproductive') a 'small-shop' culture. They also do not account for the effects of tighter spatial constraints than in the United States on planning laws and retail organization. Moreover, league tables do not compare the overall gains from a low rate of change in GDP growth in economies at high absolute levels of GDP with those from high rates of change at low absolute levels. The Euro Area was enviable in its combination of public and private affluence, the quality of its economic and cultural infrastructure, and its attractive quality of life, which tempted many to relocate for retirement from 'Anglo-Saxon' economies. Absolute levels and opportunities to choose life styles mark out the Euro Area, especially its core, as affluent, liberal, and open societies that retain a model quality.

Even so, as a monetary union the Euro Area presented particular difficulties. It lacked the credibility that stems from close approximation to the classic features of an 'optimum currency area': labour mobility, flexible labour markets, fiscal transfer mechanisms, and synchronization of business cycles (Dyson 2000). Hence, doubts persisted about the Euro Area's capacity to adjust efficiently to asymmetric shocks. Institutional and policy design faults, notably the absence of a European fiscal insurance mechanism and a European mechanism for anticipating and tackling cross-national financial crises, added to the list of potential weaknesses. The more weakly business cycles were correlated, the greater the internal adjustment pressures within the Euro Area (Sadeh 2006: 47). These adjustment pressures were a reminder of the problematic character of the Euro Area in terms of conventional optimum currency area theory.

The Euro Area's vulnerability was increased by the combination of lack of a sovereign European political power to tackle financial, fiscal, and competitiveness crises with pronounced internal diversity in economic structures, trade intensity, and business cycle synchronization. Internal differentials in productivity growth, alongside persisting inflation differentials, accentuated risk of internal and protracted crises in the absence of exchange-rate adjustment. In particular, sustained wage moderation and intensive firm-level restructuring led to the increasing competitiveness of German firms and consequent increasing long-term adjustment pressures in states like Italy and Spain. To this potentially lethal cocktail was added the differing 'misfits' of the new 'one-size-fits-all' ECB monetary policy to domestic business cycles. One result was credit-fuelled housing booms in Ireland and Spain through lower interest rates, leading to higher inflation and property bubbles. Meanwhile, from 2003, the appreciation of the euro vis-à-vis the US dollar added a further ingredient of differential economic pain. Differentials in price inflation, in unit labour cost development, and in exposure to extra-Euro Area trade added to adjustment pressures in the Euro Area.

Also, the ECB inherited far-reaching structural changes in financial markets that intensified in its first decade. 'Disintermediation', the shift from a bank-based to a market-based financial system, revealed the weak international collective action problems of central banks in averting systemic risk and 'market gridlock'. By 2007, irresponsible lending practices culminating in the

US sub-prime mortgage crisis had created a crisis in credit markets, potentially spreading to bond insurance and consumer credit, and pushed financial stability to the forefront of the ECB agenda. These structural changes included: a new 'originate-and-distribute' business model through which, by passing on credit risk, banks created extra scope for new lending; new, highly complex and weakly regulated financial instruments like collateralized debt obligations (CDOs) and credit default swaps (CDS); a growing role for new players such as hedge funds, private equity firms, sovereign wealth funds, and—designed to keep risks off the balance sheets of banks—Asset-Backed Commercial Paper Conduits and Structured Investment Vehicles (SIVs). Finally, but not least, increasingly close international financial integration meant that shocks, like the US sub-prime mortgage market, were more rapidly transmitted as financial institutions straddled currency regions and markets. The result was the endogenous creation of liquidity as the markets themselves expanded and contracted liquidity and blunted the effectiveness of the classic central bank interest-rate instrument of the ECB.

Credit creation has increasingly been funnelled through complex 'vehicular' finance, producing an opaque 'shadow' banking system. The 'credit-crunch' crisis led to a huge shrinkage of this system. The Euro Area was vulnerable because bank lending accounted for some 60 per cent of private-sector liabilities (as opposed to only 20 per cent in the United States, where the main vulnerability was to equity and debt markets). Hence, the banks were the most likely transmission mechanism for crisis. The rapid action of the ECB in coming to the rescue of the money markets in 2007 suggested that it understood well this source of particular vulnerability. However, though banking regulation and supervision was a clear source of serious vulnerability, the Euro Area had no sub-prime crisis of its own, no mono-line insurers, and no pandemic of overstretched borrowers.

The ECB was not alone in facing declining transparency, loosening credit standards, weak internal bank risk management systems, and new hidden liquidity risks in financial markets. Unlike in monetary policy, there was no international consensus in financial stability policies either on the appropriate analytical framework for measuring risk or on the most appropriate policy instruments to ameliorate risk. There was no single, quantifiable goal to target, no agreed index for measuring market stability, and even more serious data problems than in monetary policy. Central banks also had fragmented liquidity management policy regimes that created arbitrage opportunities for investors. The 2007 'credit crunch' and banking crises highlighted the weak collective action capacity of central banks vis-à-vis globally integrated financial markets as bubbles burst simultaneously in property and in credit markets. Central banks in general lacked adequate policy instruments that could relate capital adequacy requirements to rates of growth in bank lending and asset prices. Indeed, in 2007, the ECB displayed high technical skills in fine-tuning money market operations, inviting favourable comparisons with other central banks. Nevertheless, despite these skills and the shared problems, the Euro Area's institutional capacity to manage cross-national banking and financial crisis remained problematic in the absence of a sovereign European political power to organize speedy rescues.

The Political Economy of Good Times (1999–2005)

Against this background, there was much material from which sceptics could weave pessimistic narratives about, and scenarios for, the euro. Suspension of judgement seems appropriate when one considers the global political economy of the euro. Bearing in mind that 'good' and 'bad' times are relative, the euro had been born into the political economy of good times. In addition to longer-term challenges in financial market and banking developments, there were early problems to address: the year 2000 threat of disruption to computer systems; the burst of the bubble in technology stocks in 2000; the 9/11 terrorist crisis in 2001; huge oil price increases; and, more seriously, the 'credit crunch' crisis in 2007 as money markets seized up in the wake of the US sub-prime mortgage crisis and insolvencies threatened.

Seen in a longer-term perspective, however, the period 1999–2005 was characterized by a historically benign conjunction of factors: sustained high rates of global growth bolstered by rising US consumption and corresponding indebtedness; a continuing flow of technological changes that generated new products, product improvements, and production efficiency gains; and the entry of India and China into the global economy, with a huge expansion in the supply of cheap labour and subsequent downward pressures on prices. In short, the ECB, like other central banks, could deliver historically low real interest rates and conduct overall an accommodating monetary policy for growth and employment. It was flanked in doing so by substantial decline between 1995 and 2005 in average wage growth per hour worked (2.6 per cent) and in annual growth of unit labour costs (1.4 per cent) in the Euro Area, as well as relative improvement in the aggregate fiscal position.

From 2005, this benign global context began to erode, for internal and external reasons. The ECB faced evidence from its monetary analysis of mounting inflationary pressures from credit-induced property booms in some Euro Area economies like Ireland and Spain and more generally from buoyant credit creation. Moreover, it entertained continuing doubts that economic reforms had increased the potential non-inflationary output growth of the Euro Area. These doubts were reinforced in late 2007 when the German Grand Coalition—prompted by electoral challenge to the Social Democratic Party from the new Left Party—signalled an interest in introducing minimum wage policies and reversing elements of the earlier Schroeder government labour-market reforms. More seriously, global imbalances—defined by US fiscal and personal indebtedness and current account deficit levels and by mounting huge Chinese surpluses—began to unravel. The falling US dollar exposed Euro Area states to an appreciating euro, not least vis-à-vis the Chinese and other currencies, which were tied to the dollar. In addition, India and China began to generate inflationary effects as they bid up international energy and food prices. The ECB faced a heightened risk of 'stag-inflationary' conditions as the global political economy of 'bad times' manifested itself in dilemmas of monetary policy: whether to raise interest rates to pre-empt increasing inflationary risks and strengthen credibility through vigilance in delivering its price stability mandate; or to lower rates to prevent liquidity crisis in the banking sector, to counter euro appreciation—especially if the US Fed cut aggressively, and to offset negative effects on the 'real' economy of growth and jobs.

Against this background, a definitive assessment of the Euro Area is impossible. Though stressing its continuity with pre-EMU monetary policy, the ECB remains—compared to the Bundesbank earlier—a young institution that has yet to be fully tested by policy dilemmas, especially the conjunction of mounting inflationary risks, cross-national financial crisis, an appreciating euro and threats to growth and jobs. In this kind of context, external political pressures and internal dissension are likely to mount. Nevertheless, the ECB showed signs of its 'coming of age' as an international central bank. It delivered a solid inheritance through its professional discipline in securing its mandate of price stability, in communicating with markets, and in dealing with the onset of the 2007 credit crisis, as well as through promoting financial market integration. The early years of the Euro Area were associated with credibility gains for companies and states in lower real interest rates and debt servicing costs; a heightened political consciousness of the need for supply-side reforms; and a greater transparency in domestic reform processes about governance issues and veto points.

Price Stability: Official and Perceived Inflation

Though the ECB failed to deliver its price stability goal of 'below but close to' 2 per cent since January 1999, a record of just over 2 per cent remained a creditable achievement in the face of the explosion in oil prices and other shocks like international terrorism. Average annual official inflation during 1999–2006 was 2.05 per cent (2.2 per cent during 2001–6). This figure was below the long-term average for the D-Mark, which was 2.8 per cent (though this includes the period of high international inflation in the 1970s). It compared favourably with an average of 2.4 per cent for the Euro-11 states between 1991 and 2000. Moreover, using both survey-based and financial market-based measures, up until 2007 the ECB fostered medium-term inflation expectations for the Euro Area broadly consistent with its price stability goal. In terms of its official measure (the Harmonized Index of Consumer Prices, HICP), the ECB dealt effectively with significant price shocks. They included a huge increase in oil price, from $12 a barrel in 1999 to over $70 by 2006 and approximating to $100 by November 2007. However, by end-2007, rising food and energy prices were pushing monthly inflation to 3.1 per cent and, more seriously for credibility of monetary policy strategy, driving up medium-term inflation expectations to about 2.5 per cent (European Central Bank 2007*f*: 52–5).

More problematic than official HICP performance was the heightened consumer price awareness with the euro cash changeover in January 2002, the public's association of the changeover with price increases (notably in food, petrol, and personal services), and the long-lasting impact of this experience on consumer inflation perceptions. The European Commission Consumer Survey showed that 'perceived' or 'experienced' inflation peaked in January 2003 and stabilized from late 2004 at a level higher than in 2001 (European Central Bank 2007*f*). The Brachinger 'index of perceived inflation', which was developed with the German Federal Statistical Office and gave a higher weighting to goods of daily purchase like food and petrol, estimated a 'perceived' inflation rate of approximately 11 per cent in Germany in January 2002. In September 2007, it showed a gap between an official German inflation rate of 2.4 per cent and a 'perceived' rate of 5.8 per cent (Bernau 2007). German debate about the '*Teuro*' was matched across the Euro Area and figured as a central public fear in states that sought euro entry. The association of Slovenian entry in 2007 with rapid inflation sent a further negative signal to east central European states. The euro stimulated debate about the distinction between official, measured inflation— which seeks to be representative of aggregate consumer expenditure—and subjective, 'perceived' inflation. Behavioural economics pointed to the greater stickiness of memories of price increases than of decreases in the public mind.

The ECB combined a hawkish definition of price stability with flexibility in pursuing its monetary policy strategy. The scope for flexibility was implicit in the pragmatism of its 'two-pillar' monetary policy strategy. Following the 'clarification' of its 2003 review, this strategy rested on a broadly defined 'economic' pillar of various indicators (like fiscal policy, wages, exchange rate, forecasts) with cross-checking to the analysis of longer-term trends in the 'monetary' pillar. In behavioural terms, the ECB's monetary policy decisions were fairly consistent with taking account of output as well as inflation. However, it was strategically rational for the ECB to signal clearly that it had a strong anti-inflation bias; as a new central bank, it had a special challenge to build credibility. This game of being simultaneously hawkish and flexible was relatively easy to play in the conditions of 1999–2007, but showed signs of becoming more difficult.

International Role

Whilst the ECB did not ignore the euro exchange rate (which was an element in the 'economic' pillar of its monetary policy strategy), overall it practised benign neglect. However, its broad preference was for a 'hard' currency, in part to subdue imported inflation, and in part to foster confidence in holding assets denominated in the euro and, in the long term, to strengthen its role as an international currency. In this respect, the period 1999–2002 was difficult with negative news reporting in Germany contrasting the 'weak' euro with the historic image of the 'strong' D-Mark. The euro's record low was reached on 26 October 2000 at US$0.8225. Thereafter, it climbed beyond its initial value to reach 1.47 in November 2007. The lack of serious damage to Euro Area export performance owed much to a lower appreciation of the euro on a trade-weighted basis (i.e. measured against the currencies of its 22 major trading partners) and in Germany, the motor in goods exports, to a less price-sensitive export sector. However, by late 2007, euro appreciation was emerging as a potentially sensitive political issue in states with more price-sensitive export sectors, like France and Italy.

The euro's appreciation was not, however, associated with its displacement of the US dollar as the dominant international currency, for reasons outlined in Chapter 2 by Cohen (like inertia and incumbency advantages and the lack of British membership). There was some evidence of international strength. The euro had by 2007 overtaken the US dollar in value of its notes in circulation and as the main denomination of international debt issues. It dominated the European region, where its gravitational pull was most pronounced. In most Euro Area states, more than 50 per cent of extra-Euro-Area-exports of goods were invoiced in euro (in Germany over 60 per cent). However, though taking over the international role of the D-Mark, the euro did not move much beyond being the sum of its past prior currencies. More modestly, as reserve currency held by central banks—according to IMF data in 2007—the euro's known share rose from 18 per cent in 1999 to 26 per cent; the US dollar fell from 71 to 63.8 per cent. At least until the end of 2007, the evidence supported the contention that central banks, sovereign states, and market players were reluctant to diversify away from the US dollar, whether as an exchange-rate peg, as an element in reserves, or as the currency denominator for key goods like oil.

Financial Market Integration

The euro made a substantial contribution to the integration of European financial markets. The more closely market segments were related to the single monetary policy, the tighter the integration. The most pronounced integration effects were in European money markets, in consequence of the

ECB's reserve requirements, its open market operations and its operation of the inter-bank electronic payments system TARGET. Indeed, the efficiency of the monetary transmission mechanism depended on tightly integrated money markets. As the credit crisis in 2007 revealed, the ECB played a key role in reducing volatility in these markets through fine-tuning operations. Significant effects were also apparent in euro-denominated bond markets, more so in the public sector than corporate bonds; whilst equity markets showed a euro effect from the elimination of exchange-rate risk with a small increase in diversification of equity portfolios. Integration of equity markets in the Euro Area exceeded global integration. Similarly, the influence of shocks from elsewhere in the Euro Area on national equity markets grew more strongly than that from global/US shocks. The result of these new opportunities to borrow abroad was a substantial increase in risk sharing across Euro Area states and reduced dependence on domestic economic and financial developments.

In contrast, retail banking markets were fragmented and slower to consolidate on a Euro Area basis despite some headline deals, notably in 2005 (like Unicredit/HVB and ABN AMRO/Banca Antonveneta). Banking systems, as in Germany and Italy, exhibited distinctive national and regional characteristics, and consolidation was more marked within domestic markets than across the Euro Area. In fact, cross-border acquisitions by Euro Area banks were more striking in east central Europe, in part predating the euro. This fragmentation was reflected in the continuing dispersion of interest rates in retail banking across the Euro Area (European Central Bank 2007e: 43–8).

The policy challenge for the ECB was to help promote a market-led process of integration through developing a new financial market infrastructure of central bank services, through acting as a catalyst for a Single Euro Payments Area (SEPA), and through bank product standardization through the so-called Lamfalussy process (Macartney and Moran). It had a vested interest in this process of financial market integration for three reasons: inadequately integrated financial markets impaired the functioning of the monetary transmission mechanism; closely integrated financial markets contributed to financial stability; whilst, in addition, they supported economic growth. Hence, the ECB was actively involved in four key projects: TARGET2—launched in November 2007 to replace the earlier TARGET—offered a single shared platform for 'in-time' cross-national payments and settlement in central bank money with a uniform pricing structure; the TARGET2-S proposal sought to extend this computer platform to European securities payment and settlement; a further Eurosystem project sought joint central bank collateral management for monetary policy operations; whilst SEPA, rolled out from 2008, sought to ensure smooth, efficient, and low-cost European-wide retail transactions. These projects were costly and long term in providing the necessary infrastructure to enable the Euro Area to realize its potential as an integrated financial market. In realizing this potential, the benefits also seep to EU and non-EU states outside the Euro Area.

Trade Creation

This same externalization of gains from the euro is apparent in trade-creation effects (on which see Chapter 20 by Dyson). Baldwin's (2006a) comparison of estimates suggests substantial trade effects, especially in the old 'D-Mark-Zone' core, with the prospect that these effects will increase over time. Through the EU single market, euro 'outsiders' are able to participate in these gains, especially if they sustain stable exchange rates with the euro. These seepage effects—in financial markets as well as trade—reduce the incentive to seek early euro entry; gains can be made without euro entry, whilst retaining the options of domestic interest-rate and exchange-rate adjustment (Baldwin 2006b). Trade effects are differential inside the Euro Area (greater for the old core) and not confined to Euro Area members.

Overall, the euro reduced the capital costs of firms with the convergence of long-term interest rates on the lower German level and eased problems of financing budget deficits. The result was a potentially more robust economy that could benefit from the growing depth and liquidity of Euro Area financial markets and was better able to withstand economic shocks and become less dependent on the United States. However, much depended on how willing and capable firms and governments proved in making effective use of these opportunities. Here, as Dyson shows in Chapter 20, there was substantial divergence in patterns of behaviour that related to such diverse factors as comparative advantage, 'gravity', domestic governance mechanisms, and political temporal management of economic reforms.

The uncertain balance sheet of the euro is the product not just of the complexity of parameters—economic, financial, fiscal, and monetary—but also of the contingency and temporality of economic performance. The resurgence of Germany as a manufacturing exporter after years of painful post-unification adjustment illustrates how strengths can be masked and can reassert themselves. Equally, states like Ireland and Spain, which contributed disproportionately to aggregate Euro Area growth on the basis of cheap money and credit, breed potentially excessive risk-taking, and exposure to default by lenders. 'Models' have their own vulnerabilities, rooted in their functional specificities: in over-commitment to the property sector in Ireland and Spain and to manufacturing exporting in Germany as engines of growth. The outcomes depend on the robustness of these different dependencies: consumption-led growth in the former and export-led growth through unit cost reduction in the latter. Britain's vulnerabilities were to house prices and to high commitment to financial markets and business services. In exposing these contrasting vulnerabilities, shifting events underline the contingency of models of economic performance.

Europeanization, Power, and Convergence: Core Concepts and Questions

This book focuses on a set of core questions about the euro that derive from political science literature on Europeanization, power, and convergence. To what extent, and in what ways, has the euro 'Europeanized' states in terms of its impacts on domestic policies, politics, and polities? Two outcomes of this Europeanization process are examined. First, has euro accession, euro membership, or remaining 'outside' strengthened or weakened the power of states to shape economic policy outcomes (cf. Milward 1992)? How has it transformed the relative power of domestic actors? Second, to what extent, and in what ways, has the euro produced convergence in that states come to resemble each other more? These questions about Europeanization, power, and convergence give overall coherence to this book.

Prima facie, the centrality of the euro as a European project leads on to the expectation that states that actively seek Euro Area accession or are insiders will display pronounced Europeanization. Europeanization is most likely where there is a clear European policy template with which there is a domestic 'misfit' and states are obliged to comply (cf. Cowles, Caporasa and Risse 2001). This 'top-down' process is most evident in central bank independence, monetary policy (where central bankers are empowered), and money and bond markets. Amongst Euro Area 'insiders' and 'temporary outsiders', central banking emerges as an island of Europeanization. In turn, empowerment of central bankers involves substantial convergence pressures.

However, these 'top-down' processes of Europeanization are less evident in banking supervision where a single European policy template is lacking and various types of domestic policy regime coexist (see Chapter 17 by Macartney and Moran). Similarly, the Stability and Growth Pact is not prescriptive about domestic fiscal institutions, and again various regimes coexist (see Chapter 4 by Hallerberg and Bridwell). In economic reforms more generally, there is no pressure from 'misfit' with specific European templates, whilst (as Marcussen shows) even benchmark models are contingent and contested. Hence, Europeanization processes vary across policy areas. This variation reflects not just the different pressures from 'misfit' but also a 'bottom-up' form of Europeanization. Domestic policy makers use the new opportunities offered by euro entry or membership to strengthen their own power over economic change and reframe debates about reform. Central bankers engage more actively in pressing the case for major structural reforms to liberalize product, services, financial and labour markets; finance ministries seek

19

enhanced power over domestic budgets. In short, EMU becomes bound up in domestic power games, including the reframing of debates.

Both Europeanization processes are explored in these chapters. The picture that emerges is of variegated Europeanization, varying with policy area, with scale of the problems of 'misfit' before entry, with whether a state is seeking accession or is a member, and—not least—with the nature and range of domestic veto points and partison veto players that reformers face in different states.

Prima facie, the treaty-based nature of the Euro Area and its intergovernmental negotiation as 'high' politics by member states lead to the expectation that the euro was designed to strengthen both the power of states *to* shape economic policies and the power of some domestic actors *over* others. It reflects both the weaknesses of states in meeting the expectations of their citizens and the power of some domestic actors over others in exploiting this weakness. These two dimensions of power—power 'to' and power 'over'—are connected. Power to produce socially desirable outcomes like price stability depends on power over others to alter behaviour in desirable directions, for instance, in wage negotiations. This ambiguity surrounds attitudes to the power of central bankers in the Euro Area. The euro empowers central bankers to safeguard price stability through a radical form of central bank independence; at the same time, the implications for relative power—a 'Euro Area for central bankers'—sparks political concerns, especially where—as often in east central Europe—power is seen in personalized terms. In fiscal policies, executives are empowered over legislatures, and central governments over regional and local authorities, in order to safeguard sustainable policies. More generally, party and electoral competition functions in a more constrained monetary and fiscal environment. The scope for party ideology to shape policy economic policy outcomes is diminished. Parsons and Pochet's Chapter 18 shows how trade unions have embraced productivity-oriented wage formulae in collective bargaining, whilst Wincott focuses on how employability, 'activation', and social investment have moved to the centre of welfare-state discourse. These developments illustrate that the euro has contributed to a shift in the location of 'who has to adjust, and how'.

These general patterns in effects on domestic power hide variegation according to the extent to which the power of particular domestic actors is institutionally anchored. In some states, for instance, employer and trade union organizations have an entrenched commitment to sector-wide collective bargaining or, more broadly, to 'social pacts' (see Chapter 18 by Parsons and Pochet). Trade unions are, in consequence, better placed to shape economic policy outcomes around the concept of social solidarity. Similarly, strong presidencies, majoritarian parties, or ideologically connected, numerically manageable coalition governments are better placed to give a stronger political direction to economic policies. All, however, operate in the context of the shift in structural power represented by the euro, which itself is part of a larger global power shift towards financial markets and stability-oriented monetary policies, flanked by supportive fiscal, employment, and wage policies.

Prima facie, one might expect the euro to produce convergence. However, variegation in Europeanization processes and in domestic power effects suggests that convergence itself will be limited, contingent, and not necessarily a one-way process. The euro generates some powerful convergence pressures, not least in and through the single monetary policy. The effects are seen in convergence in central banking amongst 'insiders', in money markets and in bond markets, but less in retail banking. In contrast, as Chapter 4 by Hallerberg and Bridwell and Chapter 17 by Moran and Macartney show, domestic banking supervision and fiscal institutions have not converged on a single European template. Institutional and policy patterns, not to mention outcomes, are even more diverse in wages policies and in welfare-state policies.

Convergence pressures are more effective in reshaping behaviour and outcomes to be more alike, the closer a policy area is to the single monetary policy. Overall, however, these pressures do not translate automatically into convergent institutions, policies, or outcomes. They face domestic institutional 'stickiness' and powerful 'path dependencies'. Also, as the chapters on financial markets, wages, and welfare states illustrate, powerful functional specificities and dynamics mediate the effects of the euro in promoting convergence in different areas. In terms of outcomes, since 1999 convergence has been less striking than stable dispersion in real GDP growth rates (though some smaller states have moved closer to the average), labour productivity, inflation rates, and retail banking interest rates (European Central Bank 2007b).

In addressing these questions about Europeanization, power, and convergence, this book stresses not just the mediating effects of domestic state institutions and traditions but also the powerful differentiating effects of comparative advantage, economic structures, trade patterns, and business cycle synchronization. Europeanization processes and effects on power and convergence are embedded in the political economy of dominant sectors and firms and how intra-industry or inter-industry trade affects business cycle synchronization. The differential trade effects of the euro are a key factor in explaining the nature and limits of Europeanization, power shifts, and convergence.

This book is structured with four objectives: to contextualize the euro and thereby to try to ward off the risk of theoretical prejudgement of its significance; to offer an in-depth examination across a representative range of states with different relationships to the euro; to examine convergence on a cross-national, thematic basis; and, more ambitiously, to ask whether patterns exist in the relationship of European states to the euro.

Domestic Effects of the Euro: Analytical and Explanatory Challenges

Analysis and explanation of the effects of the euro on European states encounters some serious difficulties, the most serious of which is the risk of attribution bias.

Specifying the Independent Variable: The 'What'

What kind of regime change does EMU represent for European states? This question highlights three difficulties: isolating the independent variable; discriminating changes in material realities caused by the euro from the embedding of change in discursive constructions of EMU; and its 'nested' properties. At one level, EMU functions as an independent variable in providing a distinct structure of new material incentives for domestic changes. At another, EMU involves different discursive constructions about what it means for member states, including the relationships between 'stability-oriented' policies, globalization, and the European social model. These constructions, especially when embedded in Euro Area institutions, raise questions about the shaping power of ideas as a constitutive element in domestic changes. They also raise problematic issues of 'fit' with traditional, institutionally embedded discourses at the domestic level (explored in the country chapters).

MATERIAL CHALLENGES

The new material incentives for domestic change comprise the loss of classic domestic instruments of economic adjustment to asymmetric shocks; new EU 'rules-based' constraints on domestic fiscal policies; increased opportunities for the corporate sector to capture trade-creating effects through competitive unit cost reduction, notably wage moderation and more flexible working time and conditions; and differential international effects from the euro.

In addition, the euro offers new incentives to intensify EU-level reforms to financial market regulation and supervision and to use the EU to expedite reforms to product, services, and labour markets (e.g. to capture the inflation-containment effects of market competition). In short, its effects work through, and in tandem with, the single European market agenda and the Lisbon process, adding to the difficulties of discriminating effects. The euro increases the incentives for market-oriented reforms, most visibly in the banking and financial sectors and also for more painful, longer-term reforms to labour, product, and services markets (Belke, Herz, and Vogel 2005). However, the scope and pace of reform is conditional on domestic economic and political structures and dynamics.

The euro involves the loss of official short-term interest rates and exchange rates as instruments of macroeconomic adjustment for its member states. Any remaining semblance of monetary policy autonomy gives way to a 'one-size-fits-all' ECB monetary policy that focuses on delivering price stability for the Euro Area 'as a whole'. As ERM members had effectively renounced this autonomy already, only Germany as anchor of the ERM gave up substantial monetary policy autonomy. In addition to this divergence of experience for Germany, member states differed in the length of time that they had been 'training' for EMU in the ERM.

States faced the challenges of different types of pro-cyclical, destabilizing effects from the 'one-size-fits-all' monetery policy on growth and inflation. Real interest rates (nominal interest rate minus inflation) were either too high for the domestic economy (notably Germany in 2001–5) or too low (e.g. Ireland and Spain). They threatened to reinforce and prolong domestic stagnation or induce credit-fuelled booms. A deterrent to British entry in 1997–8 was the prospect of a politically unwelcome and untimely fiscal policy contraction to prevent an inflationary shock from lower real interest rates on entry. As Enderlein (2004) emphasizes, states face different challenges of 'misfit' between the single monetary policy and domestic economic conditions and hence different adjustment pressures.

Also, states face risks of 'real' exchange-rate shocks. With euro entry, states had renounced nominal exchange-rate adjustment, through which it had been earlier possible to restore lost competitiveness—whether by staying outside the ERM, seeking ERM realignment, or ERM exit. Differentials in domestic inflation rates and in productivity growth now meant shifts in real effective exchange rates, with direct effects no longer mediated by potential nominal exchange-rate adjustment. Nominal exchange rates no longer functioned as a buffer for dealing with destabilizing effects from asymmetric, country-specific shocks and for speedily correcting adverse internal developments in costs by exporting adjustment to others. The risk of subsequent drawn-out shocks rises for states like Italy that have been prone to rely on this policy instrument to avoid internal adjustment. Without this buffer, states became more dependent on the endogenous capacity of the corporate sector to contain unit costs through wage moderation, non-wage cost containment, and higher productivity growth.

New challenges from differences in unit labour cost development, spearheaded by Germany, replaced earlier threats of competitive devaluation and highlighted emerging imbalances for Greece, Italy, Portugal, and Spain. In short, as real exchange rates adjust, risk shifts from one form of 'beggar-my-neighbour' policy to another. This risk of major accumulating internal imbalances is linked in part to persisting inflation differentials, with the largest increases recorded by Greece, Ireland, Portugal, and Spain; and, in part, to differences in 'total factor productivity' (TFP), which measures technical progress and efficiency gains. In TFP Finland, the Netherlands and Slovenia excel; Germany, like Austria and France, is brought down by its business services sector; and Italy and Spain perform weakly.

In addition, EMU is accompanied by a shift to 'hard' coordination in fiscal policies. Within the framework of the Stability and Growth Pact states face increased peer pressure for domestic fiscal policy consolidation. Also, there is the ultimate threat of sanctions for persisting excessive deficits: financial for Euro Area members and withdrawal of Cohesion Funds for post-2004 EU member states. Fiscal policy is at the centre of domestic democratic politics. Hence, new tensions arise between pressures to respect EU-wide rules on budget deficits and public debt (designed to flank and support the ECB) and the incentives and constraints that derive from the specificities of domestic electoral cycles and political preferences for policies to promote social solidarity and high levels of public investment. Governments face the prospect of politically painful 'misfits' between EU fiscal rules and domestic electoral exigencies. Their problems in applying EU fiscal rules are further complicated by potential 'misfit' with the economic cycle (especially when faced with stagnation) and with 'real' convergence in GDP in the case of new member states. These issues of fiscal 'fit' touch on the fundamental question of the political sustainability of EMU. Fiscal policy reveal most glaringly the problems of domestic political ownership of EMU.

EMU's effects are also expressed in trade creation (Frankel and Rose 1998, 2005; Rose 2000). Though their scale is contested, the broad consensus remains that the trade effects are substantial (some 5–15 per cent), if differentiated by sector and spatially (Baldwin 2006a, 2006b). They derive from the removal of exchange-rate risk, lower transaction costs of doing business, and price and cost transparency in a monetary and currency union. In consequence, the euro offers an incentive for export-oriented firms to press for a reform agenda aimed at ensuring that fiscal, welfare-state, labour-market, and wage policies are focused on sharpening competitiveness through relative reductions in unit labour costs. However, this incentive is less where, as in Greece, there is a low degree of trade openness, where inter-industry trade dominates, and where firms look to the state to protect market position and power rather than to liberalize trade. Trade-creation effects are most concentrated around a cluster of essentially old 'D-Mark-Zone' states that are closely linked by growing intra-industry trade (Baldwin 2006a, 2006b).

The euro has three main effects on the international context of European states. First, Euro Area-level institutions, especially the ECB, have an incentive to seek changes in European representation in international economic institutions, like the IMF, to ensure a single unified voice in international monetary, financial, and exchange-rate policies. In the context of wider debates about broadening global representation, the large EU states are forced to reconsider whether defence of their traditional 'big power' role is compatible with a new global leadership role for the Euro Area. In short, the Euro Area raises issues about how best to organize external political projection and what this means for large and small states.

Second, Euro Area member states gain a margin of domestic manoeuvre from the loss of direct international financial market sanctions on their domestic fiscal policies. With their national currencies gone, their exchange rates are no longer a vulnerable target. They can shelter under the umbrella of the euro. For this reason, a rules-based system of sanctions on excessive deficits assumes an extra importance in regime change.

Third, Euro Area member states differ in the nature and degree of their exposure to extra-Euro Area trade and hence in vulnerability to movements in the euro exchange rate and to foreign shocks. This trade exposure is highest for Finland and Ireland, effectively outliers. Though Belgium and the Netherlands are also exposed, intra-Euro Area trade remains more significant for them (Baldwin 2006a). However, domestic competitiveness and market share are also affected by trends in unit labour costs and by technological innovations. These trends may offset the effects of differential exposure to euro exchange-rate depreciation (1999–2001) and appreciation (2002–). There was in practice little correlation between extra-Euro Area trade exposure and developments in price competitiveness between 1999 and 2005. Austria, Finland, France, and Germany improved their export price competitiveness. In this respect, they formed a distinct cluster, united by the dynamism of firm-led, 'bottom-up' change (see Chapter 20 by Dyson). In contrast, Belgium lost ground, along with Greece, Spain, and Italy, to form a separate cluster; whilst a third cluster—Ireland, the Netherlands, and Portugal—remained essentially unchanged (European Central Bank 2005c).

At the same time, the euro had little effect on reducing exposure to risk of contagion from extra-European financial shocks, especially in the US core of the world financial system. Here, vulnerability to excessive risk taking by banks straddling currency regions was more acute and shared than in trade and capable of spilling over into the real economy. The key variables determining vulnerability were the effectiveness of national financial supervisory authorities in monitoring financial risk and the competence of banks in managing their exposure to risk. This competence was placed in question by the 2007 'credit-crunch' crisis. With the euro, the locus of risk shifted from exchange-rate shocks to financial shocks through insolvency crises. 'Insider' states faced a paradox: they had decoupled from exchange-rate crises but remained exposed to financial shocks through globally integrated markets with weak collective action capacity in cross-national financial crisis management.

DISCURSIVE CONSTRUCTIONS: A DISCIPLINARY DISCOURSE

The challenges of 'misfit' that face Euro Area member states are also bound up in the discursive constructions of EMU that underpin the monetary and fiscal policy positions of Euro Area institutions, notably the ECB. Domestic actors respond differently to the dominant ways in which EMU is perceived, communicated, and legitimated. For many on the political Left and some on the nationalistic, social conservative Right, the euro is narrowing and constraining debate about macroeconomic policies, notably in relation to demand management and coordination of euro exchange rate, fiscal, monetary, and wages policies. A dominant construction of EMU in the ECB, rooted in German 'Ordo-liberal' thinking on firm rules of 'sound' money and finance, sits with difficulty alongside many domestic constructions of economic policy. This difficulty is observable in insider members like France, disposing politicians to voice criticisms of the ECB, and amongst outsiders, disposing politicians to defer entry.

At the Euro Area level, dominant discursive constructions—rooted in a 'sound money and finance' paradigm—take a strongly disciplinary form (Dyson 2000). As articulated by the ECB, they rest on a fundamental normative belief in economic stability and in fostering a supportive 'stability culture', along with a shared belief in the fundamental and overriding importance of central bank independence. The 'sound money and finance' paradigm involves a set of interrelated causal beliefs: that inflation is a monetary phenomenon; that money is neutral with respect to growth and employment; that stability is a matter of anchoring expectations of inflation amongst economic agents through the credibility and reputation of the central bank; that this credibility is best secured by central bank independence; that macroeconomic coordination is best achieved *ex post* through the clear assignment of responsibilities for price stability, growth, and employment to different actors; and that growth and employment require 'structural', 'supply-side' reforms by governments, employers, and trade unions that boost market flexibility in responding to shocks.

The disciplinary character of this discourse is enshrined in two concepts— potential output growth and the 'non-accelerating inflation rate of unemployment' (NAIRU). The ECB, the European Commission, and other international institutions use them to justify a tight policy constraint. The Euro Area potential output growth is defined as the level of output that does not generate inflationary or deflationary pressures. The European Commission, the OECD, and the IMF estimates converge around the notion of a decline in Euro Area potential output growth from closer to 2.5 per cent in 1981–90 to nearer to 2 per cent in 1995–2005. The lower level of real GDP growth is explained by reference to declining labour productivity growth and, to a lesser extent, by labour utilization (i.e. the persons employed per head of population). Notably the ECB projected a downward trend because of unfavourable demographic developments (lower growth in working age population) unless structural reforms encourage higher participation rates, especially for women (European Central Bank 2005*b*). Though noting structural reforms by 2005, the ECB remained reluctant to raise the estimate of potential output growth (ibid. 2005*a*). Its estimates created a bias to raise interest rates when faced by increasing growth.

The NAIRU is defined as the level of the unemployment rate that does not put pressure on inflation. A similar broad consistency with European Commission, OECD and IMF estimates is to be found with respect to NAIRU. The Euro Area NAIRU appears to have gradually declined from around 9.3 per cent in 1995 to around 8 per cent in 2006 (ECB 2005*b*: 46–9). This decline is attributed to labour-market reforms and wage flexibility. The earlier increase in the NAIRU from the 1970s to the mid-1990s had reflected a combination of adverse shocks with rigid labour markets and resulting increases in structural unemployment. The two notable exceptions were Germany, where from the mid-1990s to 2004 the NAIRU increased, and the Netherlands, where the NAIRU had decreased between the early 1970s and the mid-1990s (also, the UK where it decreased from the mid-1980s). The ECB traced the high level of the NAIRU to country-specific variations in the extent and timing of labour-market reforms. NAIRU estimates also underpinned a tough message to Germany about the need for deep structural reforms before interest rate reductions are possible.

'NESTED' PROPERTIES OF EMU

The specification of EMU as an independent variable becomes more difficult in that it is intimately bound up in a complex dialectical relationship with other EU projects: the objective of 'completing' and more firmly securing the Single Market (in the rationale 'one market, one money'); the Lisbon agenda of economic reforms; and, in particular, the so-called Lamfalussy process in financial market integration. EMU creates new pressures for EU-wide liberalization of product, services, financial, and labour markets to enable a smoother, more efficient adjustment to asymmetric shocks. The ECB—and the European Commission—has a particular vested interest in ensuring that institutional arrangements are in place to avert threats to financial stability and to ensure efficient and integrated financial markets to support the single monetary policy (see Chapter 17 by Macartney and Moran). EMU also exists in a complex relationship with the post-2000 Lisbon agenda that aims at promoting growth, employment, and innovation. Lisbon's effects are even more difficult to trace, not least because it seems an introverted process of 'Brussels talking to Brussels'. In contrast to the 'sound money and finance' paradigm, which is zealously promoted by the ECB, the intergovernmental

Lisbon process is notably lacking in domestic ownership by those who are supposed to promote it, testament again to the 'fuzzy' character of the EU polity (Pisani-Ferry and Sapir 2006).

Dating Regime Change: The 'When'

The second main question relates to when to date regime change. The obvious answers are January 1999 (de jure monetary union) and January 2002 (currency union). In particular, a shift to Euro-Area-wide considerations in monetary policy formulation was a significant regime change (Angeloni and Dedola 1999: 11). In terms of market expectations, the key date was May/June 1997, when the Stability and Growth Pact was agreed. At this time, market actors firmed up their expectations that there would be a monetary union in 1999. This change was associated with rapid convergence of long-term interest rates (Frankel 2006) and discernible trade effects (Baldwin 2006a, 2006b). Nevertheless, as Angeloni and Dedola (1999) note: the Euro Area was 'a step in an ongoing process, not a one-time regime change'. Its evolutionary character and endogenous processes complicate the task of identifying causal links.

The question of dating regime change becomes more complex when one shifts to individual states as the unit of analysis. The timing of regime shift varies in terms of when they entered (if at all in some cases) a de facto monetary union with Germany through a credible decision to adopt a 'hard' exchange-rate peg with the D-Mark (and stick with it for good), usually in the ERM—though Austria did this outside the ERM. A group of states appears to have entered a de facto monetary union before the Maastricht Treaty was agreed in 1991: Austria (not then an EU member), the three Benelux states, Denmark, France, and Germany. They comprise the so-called D-Mark-Zone cluster. Indeed, Austria, Denmark, and the Netherlands were in a de facto union with Germany for 20 years before currency union.

States that were late, often very late, entrants into de facto monetary union—Greece, Ireland, Italy, Portugal, and Spain—proved the most problematic members in terms of trade integration, business cycle synchronization, and domestic adjustments (Baldwin 2006a, 2006b; Boewer and Guillemineau 2006). Most importantly, their earlier reliance on nominal exchange-rate adjustments made them vulnerable to shifts in unit labour costs and in 'total factor productivity'. The result is that they are prime candidates for debate about exit. As Chapter 20 shows, the temporal variable of timing of accession helps to identify different patterns of 'fit'/'misfit' with EMU. The 'D-Mark-Zone' cluster retains a discernible identity within the Euro Area, as well as within the wider EU, and suggests an underlying historical continuum of a cluster of states.

Tracing and Interpreting Effects: The 'How'—Constructing a 'Moving Picture'

The third set of questions involves tracing and interpreting processes of change and their effects over time. They reflect wider problems of contextualization and of temporality in studies of Europeanization: how much weight to ascribe to EMU compared to other global, EU, domestic, and sector-specific drivers of change; and how to capture an evolving process? They also reveal a risk of an attribution bias in Europeanization studies: not just in too readily attributing significance to EU-level variables but also in stressing state institutions and giving too little weight to political economy variables (see Chapter 20 by Dyson).

EMU is caught up in vortex of domestic and global drivers of change; in Europe's relative economic decline with the international economy vis-à-vis other power centres; in global imbalances and potential crises within the international political economy; in long-term individual dynamics within policy sectors like financial markets, wages, and welfare states; in different discursive constructions of EMU that are endogenous to states; and in domestic policy failures. A satisfactory account has to contextualize EMU whilst focusing on its distinctive effects as a variable.

A key part of this context is the political economy of economic structure and the variable endogenous capacity of sectors and firms, whether as agencies of institution shaping (as in Germany) or as protectors of the status quo (as in Greece). 'Top-down' reforms by governments are one mechanism through which the effects of EMU express themselves. Another is a 'bottom-up' process that is firm-centred and sector-specific. Whether 'top-down' or 'bottom-up', both processes of change combine dynamics that are larger in scale and longer in timescale than EMU.

Tracing the effects of the euro on states is made difficult because cause–effect relations are obscured by the 'endogeneity' and temporality of change. EMU is a product of, and embedded within, a series of EU integration projects as it evolved over time (like the customs union, the Single Market, the Lisbon process, and the 'old' pre-euro ERM). As well as unleashing its own direct and indirect effects (Frankel and Rose 1998), for instance, through trade creation, the Euro Area is caught up in the complex time-lagged effects of these related projects. Hence, for instance, it is unclear whether significant trade effects, identifiable in 1998/9 and 2001/2, are attributable to the euro or to other delayed and differential effects over space and time from pro-trade Single Market directives working their way through. These aspects of endogeneity and of temporality are captured in Baldwin's (2006a: 42) characterization of the Euro Area as an historic continuum, distinguishing the tight integration amongst the 'D-Mark-Zone' cluster from the rest of the Euro Area. Similarly, Mongelli, Dorrucci, and Agur (2005) stress the dialectical relationship between trade and successive integration projects like the euro. The relationship between European states and the euro is better captured as a 'moving picture' than just 'snapshots' (Pierson 2004).

To add to the complexities, processes that are endogenous and specific to individual states—especially reforms that predate the Single Market and EMU and that bear no clear relationship to the ERM—shape and constrain effects from EMU. Domestically originated arrangements to secure a stability culture reduce the benefits from, and incentives to join, the Euro Area (as in Britain and Sweden), unless entry is seen as a means to lock in a potentially fragile domestic stability culture (see Chapter 12 'Baltic States' by Feldmann).

An additional problem is that the experience of de jure monetary union (1999) and currency union (2002) on which we can draw is limited. Reliable and comparable data is too scarce for more than rudimentary formal modelling. In particular, many effects that might prove most important—for instance, trade effects or even effects on intensity of structural reforms—operate with a long time lag so that we are unable to capture them empirically. In any case, formal economic modelling does not capture much of the historical and political processes and effects that are relevant to understanding European states and the euro.

Problems of interpretation are also bedevilled by the different discursive constructions of EMU that are held by analysts themselves. Analysts rarely escape their specific contexts of thought and discourse. A further problem stems from uncertainty. One source of uncertainty surrounds the question of whether EMU is associated with convergence. It is difficult to be sure whether observed convergence represents a long-term structural trend or a captured moment in shorter-term and more volatile cyclical fluctuations. Uncertainty also attaches to attribution. Business cycle synchronization might be attributable to EU variables like the Single Market, the ERM, and the euro. Reference to these variables can be used to explain why there is a specific Euro Area cycle—longer and shallower than that of the United States. Alternatively, business cycle synchronization might be attributable to 'globalization', helping to explain why Euro Area and EU business cycle synchronization is part of a wider OECD process, in which the United States leads and the Euro Area cycle lags (Artis and Zhang 1999; Artis, Krolzig, and Toro 2004; Giannone and Reichlin 2006: 17). As we saw above, contextualization of the euro is fraught with disagreement about selecting, specifying, and weighting variables.

Specifying the Dependent Variable: Policies, Politics, and Polity

The final difficulty relates to the dependent variable. This book's intellectual roots in political science are reflected in the interest in the effects of the euro on policies and more broadly on the polities and politics in which they are embedded. In short, the scope of effects is defined broadly.

This breadth of definition of dependent variables invites a series of difficulties. First, it is difficult to specify dependent variables in a form that avoids serious disagreement, for instance in measuring 'structural' reforms—which matter most?—and in handling 'soft' political data about changes in power. Second, there are varying time lags in effects. Macro-economists have tended to narrow their focus to 'hard' data, explaining 'top-down', 'structural reform intensity' of governments. In the process, they miss 'bottom-up', firm-led processes of change. Conversely, political scientists are attracted to discursive constructions of policies and agenda setting, to how policy change is legitimated, to institutional channels that shape reform trajectories, and to structures of political competition. Grounded in political science, this book opts for the difficulties of a wider definition of effects. It grapples with the problems of handling and interpreting 'soft' data.

Even a narrow policy focus on measuring state 'structural reform intensity' encounters disagreements about what to measure and how. 'One-size' policy prescriptions may not fit all. Domestic context matters. Similar structural reforms may not offer the same rates of return in different institutional contexts; whilst small reforms in product, financial, or labour markets may generate large effects in particular contexts. More fundamentally, rankings of states are contingent on the choice of weights attached to scores in specific policy types. In working with OECD definitions (cf. Duval and Elmeskov 2006), one must remain aware of these weaknesses, and their openness to contest. On the one hand, they represent an authoritative and influential construction of an economic policy model against which states are assessed. On the other, they invite critical deconstruction.

In addition, the time period of the first decade may not capture major impacts on policies, polities, and politics. A 20-year perspective is likely to yield a very different picture by uncovering longer-term effects. It is more likely to capture both learning and socialization processes at corporate and at state and EU levels and complementarities between fiscal, product, service, financial, and labour-market reforms. In some states—Germany is a possibility—acceleration of 'structural' reforms may follow, and ratify, a 'bottom-up' process of firm-led change. By 2005, for instance, the European Central Bank (2005a, 2005b) was noting an increase in the pace of labour-market reforms in France, Germany, and Italy; whilst in 2007, the Bundesbank (2007a) raised its estimate of Germany's growth potential by a (modest) 0.25 per cent.

Conclusion

The euro is the history of a politically driven process that is entangled in highly technical issues of central banking, financial and fiscal policies, and economic reform: a work of 'visionaries and plumbers' (Norman 2007). It history is rich in unanticipated consequences for the political elites that have driven it and is beset by bemusing paradoxes. Early 'pace-setters' in euro entry and in economic reforms become 'laggards' and vice-versa; credibility gains from euro entry can be exploited to advantage or squandered; vulnerability of states to shocks shifts from exchange rates to contagious cross-national banking and financial crises; economic stability is imperilled by differences in collective action capacity in monetary policies for price stability and in financial stability policies; whilst euro-related convergence pressures coexist with institutional 'stickiness', path dependency, and consequent divergence in domestic policies and with persisting divergence in outcomes like real GDP growth, inflation, and labour productivity. Above all, domestic politics continues to matter.

The euro also reveals some of the political complexities and inconsistencies thrown up by 'differentiated' European integration. Though arguably the most advanced project in 'differentiated' integration, as a group of states moves ahead of others, the euro remains embedded in the wider EU, especially the single market. Hence, in core areas for a currency and monetary union, like financial market regulation, payment systems, banking supervision, fiscal policies, and employment and wages, the Euro Area lacks its own authority, functions, and identity. It is too institutionally 'fuzzy' to represent 'core' Europe, in part because the specific character of certain functions suggests a wider framework of integration than just currency and money. The Euro Area is even less of a polity than the EU. It has a few but delimited set of institutional and policy templates of its own to 'download' to its member states. Hence, 'direct', 'top-down' Europeanization is constrained. In this context, a 'large economy' perspective has been slow to take root outside monetary policy; provincial introspection triumphs over global ambition and reach.

Though a politically driven and technocratic project, the euro is also an economic project that is embedded in a global context of crises, in processes of firm-led, market-based adjustment, and in a hegemonic discourse of GDP-based international league tables. In revealing vulnerability and creating opportunity for change, economic crises have left an enduring set of historical imprints on EMU and the Euro Area. The 1983, 1987, and 1992–3 ERM crises highlighted exchange-rate vulnerability of states and created opportunity for fixing exchange rates in EMU to rise to the top of the agenda. The Great Inflation of the 1970s gave centrality to price stability in the design of EMU; whilst the 1987 crash highlighted the importance of strengthening the central bank role in securities settlement systems and shaped the prominent role given to liquidity-providing repurchase operations (repo) in the ECB monetary policy

(Norman 2007). During the first decade of the euro, the 2007 credit crunch was critical in revealing the vulnerability of the Euro Area to banking crisis and pushing banking regulation and supervision and liquidity management to the top of the agenda. The dependency on bank lending, as opposed to equity and debt markets, increased this vulnerability when tied to the incentives for banks to be active in global financial integration and seek gains from asset-price bubbles.

In addition, the euro has been associated with different forms of market-based changes that affect the room for manoeuvre and potential power of states in different ways. The triggers for these changes are trade-creation and interest-rate effects and potentially contagious banking and financial crises. One form of adjustment is through different rates of growth in unit labour costs as companies in the trade-related sector restructure, moderate wage increases, and change working conditions. This adjustment has been led by German firms and unleashed new pressures on the Italian and Spanish corporate sectors and hence on their states. A second form of adjustment has been through 'house-price' Keynesianism in Ireland and Spain, where sharp reductions of interest rates with euro entry prompted credit-induced property booms and boosted domestic consumption as a motor of growth. German competitive disinflation and export-led growth coexisted with credit expansion and consumer-led growth in Ireland and Spain. For different reasons, these states were gainers, though Germany only visibly after 2005. However, they also had their distinctive vulnerabilities: Germany to anaemic consumption and weak development in the services sector, Ireland and Spain to asset-price bubbles and rising unit labour costs.

Overshadowing these developments was an ongoing process of global financial market integration. Its epicentres were outside the Euro Area in the United States and the City of London (which was the de facto 'offshore' financial capital of the Euro Area) and in the evolving China/US relationship. Not least, the Euro Area had not internalized the major European international financial centre. In short, the underlying drivers of the direction and pace of change remained external to the Euro Area. European political elites had to deal with the unanticipated consequences of 'euro-ization' and also, more fundamentally, larger historical transformations in power in the world economy that accompanied its birth, notably the rise of Asia. By 2008, it remained unclear whether the Euro Area would prove able to significantly enhance the power of European states to secure the twin components of economic stability—financial and price stability—and take resolute collective action to secure growth and employment in a less benign global environment. Its 'fuzzy' character and fragility suggested a distinctively difficult set of collective action problems.

The Euro Area was also embedded in a hegemonic global discourse of economic statisticians using GDP measures of welfare to rank states. On these measures, the Euro Area performed relatively weakly in key areas. It remained, nevertheless, strong in its absolute GDP level and relatively strong across a range of economic indicators—like gross savings, current account balance, inflation, and aggregate fiscal position—and, no less crucially, major social and cultural indicators of quality of life.

Part I

European and Global Contexts and Challenges

2

The Euro in a Global Context: Challenges and Capacities[1]

Benjamin J. Cohen

The birth of the euro in 1999 was expected to create a new power in international monetary relations. Even without the participation of Britain and some other European Union (EU) members, the Euro Area would constitute one of the largest economic units in the world, rivalling even the United States in terms of output and share of foreign trade. Consequences for the geopolitics of finance promised to be momentous. Europe's Economic and Monetary Union (EMU) would become a major player on the monetary stage. Europe's new money, building on the widespread popularity of Germany's old Deutschmark (D-Mark), would pose a serious threat to the predominance of America's greenback as an international currency.

A decade later, how have matters turned out? The purpose of this chapter is to evaluate the experience of the Euro Area to date in a broad global context. The central question is: How has the creation of the euro affected the power of participating states to cope with external challenges?

International monetary power, as I have suggested elsewhere (Cohen 2006), may be understood to have two dimensions, internal and external. The internal dimension has to do with the ability to exercise policy independence—to act freely, insulated from outside pressure. A useful synonym for this meaning of power is *autonomy*. The external dimension has to do with the ability to shape the actions of others—to exercise leverage or enforce compliance. A common synonym for this meaning of power is *influence*. Challenges for the Euro Area encompass both dimensions.

With regard to the dimension of autonomy, two key issues are involved. One is the global macroeconomic environment, including especially the evolution of exchange rates and regional payments imbalances. Though Europe

[1] I am indebted to Kenneth Dyson and Jim Rollo for useful comments. The research assistance of Heather Arnold is gratefully acknowledged.

itself has remained relatively close to payments equilibrium in relation to the rest of the world, EMU cannot help but be affected by any stresses created by broader global imbalances or the risk of contagious debt defaults. How well equipped is the Euro Area to deal with any threat of financial instability? The other issue is the potential competition with the greenback for use as an international currency. Perhaps the greatest benefit of an international currency is the ability to finance external deficits with one's own money, thus enhancing internal policy flexibility (Cohen 2004). Can the euro compete effectively with America's dollar in global markets? With regard to the dimension of influence, the key issue has to do with institutional participation. Does membership in the Euro Area enable EU governments to play a more authoritative role in the International Monetary Fund (IMF) or other financial forums?

Overall, this chapter concludes, EMU has failed to live up to expectations. Though exposure to exchange-rate disturbances has obviously been reduced inside Europe, member states remain vulnerable to fluctuations of the euro's exchange rate vis-à-vis outside currencies. The Euro Area is largely a passive participant in global payments developments and, if anything, has become even more exposed to threats of financial instability. Likewise, the euro has failed to mount a significant challenge to the dollar and the bloc continues to punch below its weight in monetary diplomacy. The fundamental problem lies in the mismatch between the domain of EMU and the jurisdictions of its member governments. The euro is a currency without a country—the product of an interstate agreement, not the expression of a single sovereign power. Hence EMU's power to cope with external challenges is structurally constrained. It is difficult to become a major player when speaking with many voices.

Financial Stability

In one key respect, EMU has clearly enhanced the autonomy of its members. With a single joint money replacing a plethora of national currencies, participants no longer have to fear the risk of exchange-rate disturbances inside Europe. For a continent long plagued by currency instability, that is no small accomplishment. But in other respects vulnerability remains considerable, particularly in relation to the world outside Europe. The Euro Area is largely a passive participant in global payment developments, leaving members critically exposed to fluctuations of the euro's exchange rate vis-à-vis the US dollar and other major currencies. Moreover, even though European states could hardly expect to be unaffected should a crisis hit the broader financial system, the Euro Area remains remarkably unprepared to cope with any major disruption in banking or credit markets.

A Bystander

To date, the Euro Area has been something of a bystander in global monetary affairs, more reactive than active. For the newly created European Central Bank (ECB), the highest priority was to establish its own anti-inflationary credentials, consistent with its narrowly drawn mandate under the Maastricht Treaty, EMU's founding document. Policy was targeted almost exclusively on the domestic price level. The balance of payments and exchange rate were left largely to their own devices.

As measured by the current account (the balance on trade in goods and services plus unilateral transfers), EMU's external position has been very near balance throughout the period since 1999, varying from mild deficits in 1991–2001 to small surpluses in most succeeding years. Imbalances in either direction have never exceeded 1 per cent of the Euro Area's gross domestic product (GDP) and in most years have amounted to a mere fraction of 1 per cent, adding little to global disequilibrium.

Variations in the euro exchange rate have been greater but have largely reflected the fluctuating fortunes of the US dollar. Born at a time of substantial dollar strength, Europe's fledgling currency first depreciated sharply, dropping from an initial value just above \$1.18 to a low near \$0.82 in October 2000 before settling around 90 cents for the remainder of 2000 and 2001. Then, when a weakening trend began to afflict the greenback, the euro came roaring back, passing \$1.00 in mid-2002 and peaking in late 2004 at above \$1.36. In 2005, the euro again declined modestly as US interest rates rose, languishing around \$1.20 until mid-2006. In the latter half of 2006, a new ascent began, surpassing \$1.35 by mid-2007. Rates in relation to other major currencies have largely mirrored the euro's movements in relation to the greenback. Overall, the trade-weighted ('effective') exchange rate of the euro has differed little from its bilateral dollar rate (Zestos 2006: ch. 5).

An appreciation of some 40–60 per cent from the euro's lows in 2000–1 was a source of some satisfaction to the ECB, which had been worried about the effect of the currency's initial depreciation on the credibility of Europe's grand monetary experiment. 'I welcome the recent appreciation of the euro', declared the Bank's first President, Wim Duisenberg (quoted in *The New York Times*, 10 January 2003: C11). Many Europeans experienced a surge of pride when their new currency left the greenback in its wake. But there was also an obvious downside—the dampening effect that a more expensive euro might have on economic growth. In the words of one commentary: 'A stronger euro may give Europeans bragging rights, but it has also hobbled their exports' (Landler 2004). By one common rule of thumb, a 5-per cent rise in the euro's trade-weighted exchange rate would be expected to have the same negative impact on growth as an increase of 1 per cent in interest rates (*The Economist*, 10 May 2003: 66). Predictably, appreciation brought an anguished chorus of complaints from European exporters. Jean-Claude Trichet, the ECB's second President, called the rise 'brutal'.

Particularly distressing to many Europeans was the knowledge that the appreciation had more to do with dollar weakness than with euro strength. Confidence in the greenback, already undermined by America's persistent payments deficits, had been shaken by the Wall Street slump and consequent recession of 2001–2, as well as by war fears prior to the invasion of Iraq in 2003. Later came the bursting of America's real estate bubble and the sub-prime mortgage crisis in 2007. And compounding it all was a distinct change of tone by the US government, especially once John Snow took over as Treasury Secretary two years into the administration of George W. Bush. Gone was the 'strong dollar' rhetoric of the previous Clinton administration. Instead, Snow now spoke of the benefits of a 'modest realignment of currencies', suggesting that some depreciation of the greenback would not be at all unwelcome in Washington as a means to improve US trade competitiveness. In effect, America seemed to be 'talking the dollar down' at Europe's expense, rankling many Europeans. Declared the chief economist of Germany's Deutsche Bank: 'The U.S. has always had the philosophy, "the dollar is our currency, and your problem". We have to come to grips with that' (quoted in *The New York Times*, 25 May 2003: WK5).

But Europe could not come to grips with that. Except for one brief episode in the fall of 2000, the ECB has studiously avoided any manner of direct intervention in the foreign-exchange market. Partly, this is because the anti-inflationary impact of a rising currency is welcome to the Bank's management. But mainly it reflects an understanding that any attempt to reverse the rise abroad, via sales of newly issued euros, would simply undermine the battle against inflation at home. In practice, the Euro Area can do little but remain passive witness to its currency's appreciation.

As a group, therefore, members remain critically exposed to damaging fluctuations in the euro's exchange rate—though, individually, effects are likely to vary considerably. For the bigger participants, such as Germany and France, the negative consequences of a prolonged appreciation are regrettable but manageable. For some smaller members, by contrast, impacts could be much more painful, possibly more than offsetting the evident benefits of the new currency stability within Europe. Countries like Finland or Ireland, with their more open economies and greater dependence on trade outside the Euro Area, appear to be at particular risk.

Coping with Instability

Worse, European states seem remarkably unprepared to cope with any wider instability that might erupt in international finance. The Euro Area's prevailing rules are not at all clear about who, ultimately, is responsible for management of a monetary crisis, should one occur.

Two central issues have dominated the global macroeconomic environment over the last decade. One is the huge gap in America's balance of payments, matched by corresponding surpluses in East Asia and among energy-exporting nations. The world has never seen such a massive monetary disequilibrium. The other is the continuing vulnerability of emerging or transition economies to the kind of financial disruptions that struck Asia in 1997–8 or Argentina in 2001. Though market conditions have been relatively benign in more recent years, the risk of instability remains an ever-present threat. At any moment, global imbalances or a debt default could explode into a full-fledged crisis, destabilizing asset prices and possibly spreading illiquidity or insolvency among financial institutions. EMU, however, does not seem well equipped to maintain stability in the event of such rude shocks.

According to the Maastricht Treaty, the ECB has no specific powers to deal with any disruptions that might occur. Financial integration among EMU members has bourgeoned since the euro's birth; as a result, the risk of contagion within the bloc, should troubles hit, has clearly grown. In the words of the European Central Bank (2007a: 74): EMU has 'led to broader and deeper systemic inter-linkages between Member States, increasing the likelihood of potential financial market disturbances in one Member State spreading across borders'. Yet the ruling principle of the Euro Area remains decentralization, otherwise known as subsidiarity—the notion that the lowest level of government that can efficiently carry out a function should do so. Formal authority for crisis management continues to reside at the national level, as it did before EMU. Each central bank is charged with responsibility for the financial institutions and markets based within its own borders.

There is only one exception. General language in the Maastricht Treaty does appear to empower the ECB to backstop TARGET, the large intra-European clearing system, in the event of a payments gridlock or other difficulties. One of the basic tasks of the ECB (Article 105: 2), declares the Treaty, shall be 'to promote the smooth operation of payment systems'. But for any other contingency, such as a sudden wave of illiquidity in the banking sector, the Treaty is as uncommunicative as the Oracle of Delphi. Nothing is said about any authority for the ECB to act as a lender of last resort. Economist Garry Schinasi (2003: 3) says that this silence makes the ECB the 'ultimate "narrow" central bank'. The ECB has a mandate for price stability but not for financial stability.

The Treaty's silence in this regard has been a source of much debate. Some specialists interpret it as a form of 'constructive ambiguity'—an indication that, in practice, the ECB's crisis-management powers could be enhanced if and when needed. As one legal commentator puts it: 'The wording of the

41

subsidiarity principle leaves the door open for a possible Community competence' (Lastra 2003: 57). But others disagree, arguing that, because the responsibility has not been specifically delegated, it must remain at the national level. The Treaty's language is seen as restrictive rather than permissive. In practice, as in pre-EMU Europe, the lender-of-last-resort function has been left to the individual central banks. In September 2007, EU officials again declined to fix rules in advance on how to bail out banks that have cross-border operations within the union. No one, it appears, is directly accountable for the stability of the Euro Area as a whole.

Can such a decentralized arrangement be counted on to ensure smooth operation of the overall system? The European Central Bank (2007a: 84) remains optimistic, emphasizing the extent to which member states, by a variety of measures, have sought to provide 'a comprehensive, multi-layered and flexible framework... with the potential to adapt to the specific challenges that a crisis situation may pose'. But there is certainly room for doubt.

What would happen, for instance, if in a given country a large financial institution with extensive cross-border business were to find itself in trouble? Would the national authorities be evenhanded in their response, fully recognizing the interests of claimants elsewhere in the Euro Area? Or would they act protectively, even at the risk of conflict with the regulatory authorities of partner countries? We have no way of knowing. The scheme 'may work well', observes Schinasi (2005: 119–20), 'but this still remains to be seen.... It is [not] obvious that national supervision in Europe would tend, as a first priority, to focus on European priorities.... It is difficult to imagine the national supervisor pursuing European interests first and national interests second.' The International Monetary Fund (2007a: para. 12) echoes this concern in a recent review of Euro Area policies: 'Progress on the ground is being held back by the governance framework. The core problem is the tension between the impulse toward integration, on the one hand, and the preference for a decentralized approach, on the other.... This setting rules out efficient and effective crisis management and resolution.'

In short, the possibility that central banks might work at cross-purposes, aggravating a crisis, is certainly not outside the realm of possibility. There is no Invisible Hand for public agencies. Decentralized decision-making among sovereign governments without some form of coordination is potentially a recipe for disaster.

Competition with the US Dollar

At the time of EMU's birth, many predicted a bright future for the euro as an international currency. Though the dollar had long reigned supreme in monetary affairs, Europe's new currency was expected to quickly assert itself as a major competitor. If the Euro Area could be the equal of the United States in output and trade, why should it not be America's equal in monetary matters, too? Typical was the view of Robert Mundell (2000: 57), a Nobel laureate in economics, who expressed no doubt that the euro 'will challenge the status of the dollar and alter the power configuration of the system'. In the oft-quoted words of Jacques Delors, when he was President of the European Commission, *'le petit euro deviendra grand'*.

In reality, however, Europe's little euro has not become big—and for good reason. The currency clearly did start with many of the attributes necessary for competitive success, including a large economic base, unquestioned political stability, and an enviably low rate of inflation, all backed by a joint monetary authority, the ECB, that was fully committed to preserving confidence in the money's future value. But, as I have argued previously (Cohen 2003), the euro is also hampered by several critical deficiencies, all structural in character, that dull its attractiveness as a rival to the greenback. These include limited cost-effectiveness, a serious anti-growth bias, and, most importantly, ambiguities at the heart of the monetary union's governance structure. Only in the EU's immediate neighbourhood, where trade and financial ties are especially close, does the euro enjoy any special advantages. That is EMU's natural hinterland—'the euro's turf', as Charles Wyplosz (1999: 89) calls it. Elsewhere, Europe's money is at a distinct disadvantage.

Cost-Effectiveness

The first problem is the cost of doing business in euros. Transaction costs directly affect a currency's attractiveness as a vehicle for exchange transactions or foreign trade. From the start, it was clear that the dollar would continue to be favoured unless euro transaction costs, which began high relative to the widely traded greenback, could be lowered to a more competitive level. The same-scale economies and network externalities that encourage use of a money such as the dollar in the first place are also responsible for what economists call 'hysteresis' or 'ratchet' effects. Switching costs can be steep. Hence, international adoption of a new currency like the euro tends to be resisted unless the money can be expected to be truly cost-effective.

Could the euro become sufficiently cost-effective? That, in turn, depended directly on what might be done to improve the structural efficiency of Europe's financial markets (see Chapter 17 by Macartney and Moran). In practical terms, much has indeed been accomplished to knit together previously segmented national markets, particularly in short-term money-market instruments, syndicated bank lending, credit derivatives, and the corporate bond sector. Though numerous obstacles remain—including significant differences in clearing and settlement systems, tax structures, and accounting and business conventions—the EU seems well on its way to creating the largest single-currency capital market in the world. In turn, costs have shrunk considerably as measured by spreads in bond markets or the market for foreign exchange. Costs have not shrunk enough, however, to overcome the greenback's natural advantages of incumbency.

The core problem is evident. The euro is condemned to remain at a disadvantage vis-à-vis the dollar so long as EMU is unable to offer a universal financial instrument that can match the US Treasury bill for international investor liquidity and convenience. This is a deficiency that will be impossible to rectify so long as the Euro Area, with its separate national governments, lacks a counterpart to the federal government in Washington. As Ben Bernanke (2005: 187), chair of the Federal Reserve Board of Governors, has observed: 'The European government bond market . . . has not attained the liquidity of the US Treasury market (and may never do so). . . . The fundamental difference [is] that eurozone debt is the debt of 12 sovereign entities rather than one, as in the United States.' The best the Europeans could do was encourage establishment of selected benchmark securities for investors. Gradually, 3 euro benchmarks have emerged: the German Bund at 10 years, the French bond at 5 years, and the Italian bond at 2 years. But such a piecemeal approach falls far short of creating a single market as large and liquid as that for US government securities.

Admittedly, yield differentials in the public debt market have shrunk since the euro was born, suggesting that interchangeability among national issues has increased considerably. But the convergence of yields is hardly complete. Investors continue to treat the obligations of EMU governments as imperfect substitutes, mostly owing to differences in perceived default risk. And these differences of perception could eventually be compounded as a result of a decision by the ECB in November 2005 to limit the collateral it will accept in refinancing ('repo') operations with European commercial banks. Previously, the ECB had accepted all Euro-Area government bonds indiscriminately, as if the debts of EMU member states were all of equal creditworthiness. Now, however, the Bank is more selective. Bonds must have a single A-rating or better from at least one of the three main rating agencies (Moody's, Standard and Poor's, and Fitch). Observers predict that this decision will lead commercial banks, in turn, to be rather more selective in their choice of issues, accentuating yield spreads.

On balance, therefore, segmentation of the public debt market is proving difficult to overcome; and that, in turn, means that the cost of doing business in euros is likely to remain a drag on the currency's appeal for years to come. Though, to date, efficiency gains in financial markets have been substantial, they clearly have not, on their own, been enough to make the euro more cost-effective than the dollar. The greater liquidity and convenience of the US Treasury bill market continues to give an advantage to the greenback.

Anti-Growth Bias

A second critical factor inhibiting the internationalization of the euro is a serious anti-growth bias that appears to be built into the institutional structure of EMU. By impacting negatively on yields on euro-denominated assets, this bias directly affects the currency's attractiveness as a long-term investment medium.

When EMU first came into existence, eliminating exchange risk within the European region, a massive shift was predicted in the allocation of global savings as compared with holdings of European assets in the past. Yet, as the European Central Bank (2007b) has ruefully noted, international portfolio managers have actually been quite slow to commit to the euro. Liquid funds have been attracted when there was a prospect of short-term appreciation, as in 2002–4. But underlying investor preferences have barely budged, in good part because of doubts about prospects for longer-term economic growth in the Euro Area. Many factors contribute to these doubts—aging populations, which limit manpower increases and stress old-age pension systems; rigid labour markets, which hinder economic adaptability; and extensive government regulation, which can constrain innovation and entrepreneurship. Europe's monetary union, regrettably, adds yet one more brake on growth.

The core problem here lies in EMU's institutional provisions governing monetary and fiscal policy, two key determinants of macroeconomic performance. In neither policy domain is priority attached to promoting output expansion. Rather, in each, the main emphasis is on other considerations that tend to tilt policy towards restraint, producing a distinct anti-growth bias to the Euro Area as a whole. As *The Economist* (29 April 2006: 38) laments, the euro 'has provided currency stability but has done little to promote growth'. Opportunities for future investment returns thus are even more limited than they might be otherwise.

On the monetary policy side, the ECB, unlike many other monetary authorities, was created with just one policy mandate—to maintain price stability. Moreover, the ECB is formally endowed with absolute independence, largely insulating it from political influence. Legally, the ECB is free to focus exclusively on fighting inflation, even if over time this might be at the cost of stunting growth. In practice, naturally, the ECB is not wholly insensitive to growth concerns. Nonetheless, the overall orientation of ECB priorities is clear. Since EMU's start, the bias of monetary policy has mainly been towards restraint, not expansion. Summarizes Hannes Androsch (2007: 48), formerly finance minister of Austria: 'The ECB is obliged to focus on fighting inflation, not promoting general economic development, and they are overdoing it.... We are not fully using the growth potential I think Europe has.'

Similarly, on the fiscal policy side, Euro-Area governments have formally tied their hands with their controversial Stability and Growth Pact (SGP). The SGP, first set up in 1997, was intended to implement the 'excessive deficit procedure' called for by the Maastricht Treaty (Article 104c). The Pact's key provision is a strict cap on national budget deficits at 3 per cent of GDP. That tight restraint makes it difficult for elected officials to use budgetary policy for contra-cyclical purposes, to offset the anti-growth bias of monetary policy.

The Pact is not air-tight, of course. In reality, we know, practice has increasingly diverged from principle, with a number of EMU's original members—including, most notably, France and Germany—repeatedly missing the 3 per cent target. We also know that little has been accomplished to make the Pact more effective, apart from some limited reforms in 2005. To many, these facts mean that the SGP has no 'bite'. But as Chapter 4 by Hallerberg and Bridwell indicates, empirical evidence clearly demonstrates that overall the Pact has in fact exercised a significant discipline, with an especially strong impact on most of EMU's smaller members. Moreover, can anyone doubt that in most cases deficits might be even larger in the absence of the SGP? Historically, many EMU governments routinely ran deficits in excess of 3 per cent; most had to struggle to qualify for membership in the first place. De facto, if not de jure, the SGP straitjacket remains a constraint on Euro-Area states, perpetuating an anti-growth bias in fiscal policy, too.

Is it any wonder, then, that the anticipated shift of global savings has turned out to be largely illusory? Is it any wonder that many politicians, including France's new President Nicolas Sarkozy, have been calling for improvements of EMU's 'economic governance'? EMU's built-in tilt towards restraint exacerbates an already serious growth problem in Europe. Dim prospects for returns on euro-denominated assets inevitably discourage use of the currency for investment purposes.

Governance

Finally, there is the governance structure of EMU, which for the euro's prospects as an international currency may be the biggest handicap of all. The basic question is: Who is in charge of monetary policy? From the start, uncertainty has reigned over how decisions are to be made in EMU's core agency, the ECB.

The problem goes back, once again, to the institutional provisions of the Maastricht Treaty. Practical operational control of monetary policy was to lie in the hands of the ECB's Executive Board, made up of the President, Vice-President, and four other members. Overall managerial authority, however, was formally lodged in the Governing Council, which in addition to the six-member Executive Board would include the heads of the central banks of all participating states, each with the same voting rights. Evidently, the drafters of the Treaty were not overly concerned that the large size and mixed representation of the Governing Council might be inconsistent with efficient governance.

The flaw is obvious. Even before the EU's recent enlargements in 2004 and 2007, the Governing Council—with the 6 Executive Board members and 12 (now 15) national governors—was already significantly larger than the top managerial unit of any other central bank in the world. With the entrance of a dozen new countries into the EU, bringing total membership to 27, the size of the Council threatened to become utterly unwieldy as the Euro Area enlarged. Upon joining the EU, all new members immediately gain observer status on the Council, with voting rights to follow once they adopt the euro. Cyprus, Malta, and Slovenia have already made the jump to full participation. The number could thus grow to as many as 30, with even more governors to be added down the road as other candidate governments successfully negotiate their way into the club (or if Britain, Denmark, or Sweden ever decide to adopt the euro). A gaggle of three dozen or more strong willed individuals could hardly be considered conducive to efficient decision-making. With so many bodies around the table, discussions would undoubtedly be time-consuming and complicated. As one source commented sarcastically, enlargement would leave the Council with 'too many to decide on where to go to dinner, let alone agree on how to run monetary policy for more than 400 million people' (Baldwin 2001). In short, the ECB had a 'numbers problem'.

To their credit, Europe's leaders did come soon to recognize the problem and sought to provide a remedy. In March 2003, a reform was approved, restricting votes on the Council to a smaller total on a rotating basis. Membership of the Council will continue to include the Executive Board and all national central bank governors; moreover, all six members of the Executive Board will retain their individual votes. But voting rights of national governors are now to be limited to no more than 15 and will rotate among governors according to a specified formula, taking explicit account of the diversity among member states.

The remedy, however, may be worse than the disease. On the one hand, the reform leaves intact the large number of bodies at the table. Every national governor, as well as the six Executive Board members, will continue to participate in all policy discussions, with full speaking rights. The approach has been defended on the grounds that it is vital to promoting the legitimacy of the euro enterprise. No other EU institution denies representation to any member state. In addition, it is argued, full participation may be expected to facilitate consensus building and contribute to a better flow of information. But the approach can also be criticized for perpetuating all the inefficiencies of the

ECB's numbers problem. As one astute observer puts it, the Governing Council will remain 'more like a mini-parliament than a decision-making body' (Gros 2003: 124).

On the other hand, the reform may well deepen rifts within the Governing Council, since the rotation model is so unabashedly state-based. Votes are allocated strictly along lines of national identity. In principle, governors are supposed to be fully independent professionals operating in a personal capacity, making monetary policy objectively for the Euro Area as a whole. In practice, however, they may now be forgiven for thinking first of their own countries rather than in terms of collective interests. In the words of a prominent German economist: 'The reform proposal does not meet the rationale of an integrative monetary policy.... It re-nationalises European monetary policy' (Belke 2003: 122). The dollar's advantage in this regard is obvious.

A Regional Destiny

For all these reasons, it should be no surprise that the euro's experience as an international currency to date has been underwhelming, even allowing for the characteristic stickiness of monetary preferences. In most categories of cross-border use, adjusting for the elimination of intra-EMU transactions, the euro has managed roughly to hold its own as compared with the past aggregate shares of EMU's 'legacy' currencies. This means that Europe's joint money has smoothly taken its place as successor to Germany's old D-Mark, which among international currencies had already attained a rank second only to the dollar. But that is about all. After an initial spurt of enthusiasm for the new currency, use in most market segments has leveled off or even declined in recent years. Moreover, since its birth, the euro's only enduring gains have been among neighbouring states with strong regional or political ties to the EU—what might be described as EMU's natural hinterland. In the European Central Bank's words (2007c: 7), a 'strong institutional and regional pattern continues to characterise the internationalisation of the euro'. Beyond the European region, the euro remains very much in the dollar's shadow.

For example, in the foreign-exchange market, according to the European Central Bank (2007c), the euro entered on one side of just 39 per cent of all transactions in the period from mid-2005 to end-2006—less than half the dollar's share (93 per cent). That was higher than the share of the D-Mark, which had appeared in 30 per cent of transactions in 1998 (its last year of existence) but lower than that of all euro's legacy currencies taken together (53 per cent) and actually down from a high of 41 per cent in the preceding 12-month period from mid-2004 to mid-2005. Only in the Nordic states and East-Central Europe, where commercial ties are largely concentrated on the EU, is the euro the favoured vehicle. Likewise, evidence from the IMF on trade invoicing (Bertuch-Samuels and Ramlogan 2007) suggests that at best the euro has been able to maintain the D-Mark's share of world exports—roughly 15 per cent, less than one-third the dollar's share. It has yet to show any sign of increase except, again, in neighbouring European states.

There has been some new use of the euro as a vehicle for lending. Once the new currency was born, outside borrowers were attracted by the opportunity to tap into the much broader pool of savings created by the consolidation of EMU financial markets. Overall, the euro's share in the stock of international bonds and notes rose strongly, from roughly a fifth in 1999 to nearly half by the end of 2005, before falling back by a few percentage points in 2006. But again, most of the increase came from immediate neighbours (mainly recent or prospective EU members). Borrowers in Asia and Latin America continue primarily to use the dollar. Moreover, these developments represent growth only in the *supply* of euro-denominated assets. On the demand side, as indicated, foreign portfolio managers have been slower than anticipated to add to their holdings of euro-denominated claims, despite the greater depth and liquidity on offer. Most issues have been taken up by investors inside Europe itself, making them in effect 'domestic'. Outside EMU, the euro's overall share of portfolios has changed little from the previous aggregate of legacy currencies. Similar patterns have also prevailed in international banking markets (European Central Bank 2007c).

Only in official reserves has there been a sustained increase of use as compared with the D-Mark and other legacy currencies. From its birth in 1999 to end-2006, the euro's share of currency reserves advanced from 18 per cent to nearly 26 per cent. It is noteworthy, though, that as much as half the growth came at the expense of Japan's yen and miscellaneous 'other' currencies rather than the dollar. Moreover, much of the increase vis-à-vis the greenback has been the result of exchange-rate shifts rather than deliberate dollar sales. Direct conversions from the greenback to the euro have been cautious and slow. As economists Edwin Truman and Anna Wong (2006: 36) conclude: 'The available evidence suggests that the amount of *active* diversification of countries' foreign exchange reserves has been limited to date' (emphasis in the original). The dollar's share of reserves is still two and a half times that of the euro.

None of this, therefore, adds up to a serious challenge to the greenback. The dollar's appeal may be eroded by America's persistent payment deficits. But that by itself does not ensure success for the euro so long as the new currency's own deficiencies remain uncorrected. The euro clearly does have a future as an international currency. But its allure is not unqualified and, worse, seems limited mainly to the EU's own backyard. The currency's destiny appears to be regional, not global.

Institutional Participation

Finally, there is the issue of institutional participation. With a population presently exceeding 300 million and a GDP rivalling that of the United States, the Euro Area was expected to start playing a major role in international monetary diplomacy. Joined together in EMU, it was widely thought, members would surely have more bargaining leverage than if each acted on its own. Europe's voice would be amplified on a broad range of macroeconomic issues, from policy coordination or crisis management to reform of the international financial architecture. Yet, here too, experience to date has been underwhelming. In practice, membership in EMU has not enabled EU governments to play a more influential role in the IMF or other global forums. Europe's voice has been muted at best.

The Problem

The problem is that no one knows who, precisely, speaks for the Euro Area. Here too the Maastricht Treaty is regrettably uncommunicative. No single body is formally designated to represent EMU in international discussions. Instead, the text simply lays down a procedure for resolving the issue of external representation at a later date, presumably on a case-by-case basis (Article 109). Some sources excuse this on the grounds that it achieves a balance between the need to convey a common position and the prerogatives of member states. But that seems too kind. In fact, it was a cop-out, a diplomatic formula to mask failure to reach consensus.

At a minimum, therefore, the Treaty compounds confusion about who is in charge. At worst, it condemns the Euro Area to lasting second-class status, since it limits its ability to project power on monetary matters. EMU, laments Fred Bergsten (2005: 33), a euro enthusiast, 'still speaks with a multiplicity, even a cacophony, of voices... Hence it dissipates much of the potential for realizing a key international role'.

At the IMF, for example, the Euro Area's 13 members in 2007 were split up among no fewer than 8 different constituencies. France and Germany each has a single chair on the Fund's 24-member Executive Board. The other 11 are all part of diverse constituencies that include non-EMU states as well as EMU members and in some cases are led by non-EMU governments. Belgium, for instance, provides the elected Executive Director for a constituency that includes four EMU countries, three non-EMU members of the EU, and three non-EU states. Italy, similarly, leads a constituency with three EMU countries, one non-EMU member of the EU, and three non-EU states. The Netherlands heads a group that includes not a single other EMU country, while Finland, Ireland, and Spain all are minority members of constituencies led by non-EMU governments. Collectively, EMU's membership accounts for some

23 per cent of total voting power at the Fund. But, because representation is so fragmented, it is difficult for the Euro Area to exercise a commensurate influence on decision-making or even to develop common policy positions.

Likewise, in the influential Group of Seven (G-7), which with nearly half of all IMF voting power plays a decisive role in Fund decision-making, only the three biggest EMU states—Germany, France, and Italy—are formally included. Each speaks for itself alone. Other EMU governments have no direct voice at all.

The result is a lack of coherence that saps much of the authority that the Euro Area might otherwise be expected to exercise. Informally, efforts have been made to address the problem through tactical cooperation among the Euro Area's members on an ad hoc basis (Bini Smaghi 2004). At the IMF, for example, EMU's representatives all stand together on issues related directly to the Euro Area and its single monetary and exchange-rate policies. But, in the absence of a strategic commitment to achieve and defend common positions, backed by genuine political agreement, such actions are bound to lack impact. The point has been best put by political scientists Kathleen McNamara and Sophie Meunier (2002: 850): 'As long as no "single voice" has the political authority to speak on behalf of the Euro Area, as the US Secretary of the Treasury does for the American currency, the pre-eminence of the US in international monetary matters, as in other realms, is likely to remain unchallenged.' EMU will continue to punch below its weight.

A Single Voice?

Is there any way to provide that single voice? In principle, any of several bodies might be designated to represent the Euro Area internationally. In practice, however, none is fully up to solving the problem.

One possibility, for example, might be the ECB. As the Euro Area's only truly collective institution, the ECB would in fact seem to be the most natural candidate to speak for EMU on global monetary issues. But this choice runs up against the tradition that in most such settings, states are normally represented not by central banks but by finance ministers—officials with the political clout to speak for their respective governments. The ECB obviously cannot claim that kind of authority. Indeed, it is difficult to imagine the elected governments of Europe ever delegating such a fundamental power to an institution that has been deliberately designed to be as free from political influence as possible.

Alternatively, some have suggested the appointment of a single individual with sufficient credentials and legitimacy to act as the equivalent of a finance minister for the Euro Area (McNamara and Meunier 2002)—a Mr. (or Ms.) Euro, as it were. Precedent exists in the realm of foreign and security affairs, where EU members already agreed a decade ago to name a single High Representative to stand for them all—a Mr. Europe (presently Javier Solana of Spain). But experience has shown that Mr. Europe's ability to speak authoritatively for the entire EU can be easily hamstrung by policy differences among individual governments. A single appointed official cannot ignore or overrule the preferences of diverse sovereign states.

A third possibility would be a collective one, centered on the informal committee of EMU finance ministers that has emerged since the birth of the euro—what has come to be known as the Euro Group. Like comparable EU institutions, such as the Council of Ministers or European Council, the Euro Group can be represented at any given time by its chair; the chairmanship itself, as with those other institutions, rotates periodically among members. This appears to be the Euro Area's preferred route to date. Already, in 2005, the Euro Group chair began attending meetings of the G-7, albeit with no specified responsibilities. Likewise, when issues related to the euro are discussed at the IMF, the chair is invited to make a statement on behalf of all EMU members. But here too the authority of EMU's voice can be easily constrained by underlying policy differences. In no venue is the Euro Group chair permitted to negotiate on behalf of EMU as a whole.

The underlying obstacle is of course the lingering influence of national allegiance. Though EMU members share a joint money, their interests are hardly identical. Thus, however advantageous a single voice might be for the group, any effort to consolidate the Euro Area's institutional participation is bound to run into resistance from at least some individual participants. As Jeffry Frieden (2004: 262) observed, any such reform 'requires that member states weigh the potential benefits of a common policy against the potential costs of a policy that is not to their liking. . . . There is a clear trade-off between the advantages of scale and the disadvantages of overriding heterogeneous preferences.' Divergent preferences make members reluctant to give up the right to speak for themselves. Even after a decade of living with the euro, national identity still trumps collective interest.

Conclusion

Overall, the conclusion seems clear. For all its undoubted success in other respects, EMU has failed to improve the power of participating states to cope with external challenges. Neither the autonomy nor the influence of the bloc has been significantly enhanced. The reason seems equally clear. Based as it is on an agreement among sovereign states—what one scholar calls a 'sovereignty bargain' (Litfin 1997)—the Euro Area lacks the clean lines of authority traditionally associated with the management of money by individual states. Its founding document, the Maastricht Treaty, is full of artful compromises and deliberate obfuscations, reflecting unresolved disagreements among governments at the time of negotiation (Dyson and Featherstone 1999). In the decade since the euro's birth, the Treaty's ambiguities have persistently clouded understandings about decision-making and the distribution of competences and responsibilities. As long as it remains a sovereignty bargain rather than a genuine federal union, EMU will always be at a structural disadvantage in the geopolitics of finance.

3

The Changing European Context of Economic and Monetary Union: 'Deepening', 'Widening', and Stability

Gaby Umbach and Wolfgang Wessels

From the outset, the idea of supranational monetary policymaking and the establishment of Economic and Monetary Union (EMU) with the Maastricht Treaty was a project of highest political relevance. In addition to its economic rationale, EMU was perceived as a political project, a major step towards deeper European integration and eventual 'political unity' (Single European Act: Article 1; cf. Krägenau and Wetter 1994: 73). Like earlier milestones in European economic integration that formed 'first steps' (cf. Schuman 1950) in the evolution of the EU's political system, the provisions of EMU were conceived as an instrument to smooth the way for a 'political union' (Bundesregierung 1991: 85) and the creation of 'an ever closer union among the peoples of Europe' (Preamble Treaty on European Union Nice/Lisbon). Hence, the creation of EMU followed essential elements of what is generally known as the 'Monnet method' (cf. Wessels and Faber 2007).

At the same time, the relationship between EMU and political union was not one-sided, as EMU is seen as strongly dependent on the EU's political stability as a major precondition of the system's performance (cf. Wessels 1994: 107). As a consequence, the adaptation of EMU members' domestic institutions and policies to the challenges and constraints of EMU depends on the overall perception and performance of the EU.

Taking these reflections as its starting point, this chapter examines the changing European context of EMU over the first decade of the euro. It focuses on the European constitutional, institutional, and policy contexts of EU 'deepening' and 'widening' in which the relationship of states to EMU is embedded. Given the predominant role of the European Central Bank (ECB), especially in shaping European monetary policy, this chapter highlights its role and functions within EMU. As part of the analysis of the European macroeconomic policy context, it also examines policy developments and changes in policy coordination. At the same time, as Dyson stresses in Chapter 1, the first decade of the euro might yet turn out to be too short a period to identify all relevant developments concerning mutual effects of EMU and political union.

The European Constitutional Context: Stability of EMU in an Evolving Constitutional Architecture

The first decade of the euro took place in the context of considerable evolution and adaptation of the EU's constitutional basis (the polity in which EMU institutions operate) in general and of some related modes of governance in particular. It began with the difficult ratification of the Nice Treaty and terminated in the signature of the Lisbon Treaty, which the EU heads of state and government declared to be the final stage of constitutional 'deepening' of the EU for the 'foreseeable future' (European Council 2007: 2).

Moderate Constitutional Adaptation Through EU 'Deepening'

Contrary to the evolving constitutional basis of the EU's overall political system, the first decade of the euro was characterized by a considerable constitutional stability of EMU-related objectives, competences, and institutional provisions. A robust ECB remained at its institutional core (Dyson 2000). Against the trend of redesigning the allocation of competences, as well as of reformulating tasks and functions of major EU institutions (cf. Wessels 2005) in the Lisbon Treaty, the essential institutional features of EMU were left untouched. In particular, as far as the overall monetary policy objective of price stability is concerned, neither the Nice nor the Lisbon Treaties introduced any changes to the Maastricht and Amsterdam Treaty provisions. Only towards the end of the first decade of the euro did the Lisbon Treaty terminate this period of constitutional stasis by some moderate amendments to secondary elements of the institutional framework of EMU.

Even so, with respect to the allocation of competences within the EU, the Lisbon Treaty ties in with the existing treaties, locating European monetary policymaking for Member States whose currency is the euro in the area of 'exclusive competences' (Article 3 TFEU). The—slightly rephrased—provisions on the coordination of economic policies are listed in a rather undefined article (Article 5 TFEU) that is located between the provisions on 'shared' and 'supporting competences'. With this new constitutional design—which is in line with the results of the European Convention's working group on economic governance (Norman 2003: 124)—the existing treaty patterns of competence allocation regarding core EMU activities are reiterated. No major changes are to be found in the basic division of tasks between national and EU levels.

The Lisbon Treaty makes moderate amendments to the EMU institutional provisions related to the European Commission. In the case of the Broad Economic Policy Guidelines, Article 99 empowers it to issue warnings to Member States that breach the guidelines by domestic economic policies. Also, the co-decision procedure applies to the adoption of rules on broad guidelines of economic policies. In addition, the Commission has the opportunity of warning, and making proposals for possible sanctions, in case of domestic excessive deficits (Article 104).

The European Parliament also sees moderate changes to its influence under Articles 101–3 and 106, shifting its involvement from cooperation to consultation; and in Article 105, from assent to consultation. The co-decision procedure and partially qualified majority voting (QMV) applies in decisions on the amendment of the ECB Statute (Article 107). Moreover, via the co-decision procedure, the European Parliament is also involved in the adoption of legislation regarding the use of the euro as single currency (new Article 111).

Other changes include the option of emergency economic measures in energy policy (Article 100); the adoption of legislation on surveillance of excessive deficits for Eurosystem members (new Article 114); the adoption of measures regarding international aspects of EMU (new Article 115a); and the adoption of recommendations on new Member State's accession to the Eurosystem by Eurosystem members (Article 117; Peers 2007: 2).

Additionally, the Lisbon Treaty contains amendments related to 'countries whose currency is the euro'. These amendments make references to the Stability and Growth Pact, the Broad Economic Policy Guidelines, and the Euro Group, enhancing their visibility and strengthening aspects of coordination of the European macroeconomic policy context of the euro (see below). With these amendments, the Lisbon Treaty—after a long period of constitutional 'fuzziness'—officially institutionalizes the existence of the Euro Group by integrating a protocol into the treaties in order to 'lay down special provisions for enhanced dialogue between the Member States whose currency is the euro' (Protocol No. 3 TEU/TFEU). By doing so, after nearly 10 years of the euro, it establishes a treaty basis for the institutional aspects of the Euro Group's informal meetings, including the participation of the European Commission and the ECB as well as the election of a president of the Euro Group for a two-and-a-half-year term. Moreover, it clarifies and structures the 'links between Member States who have adopted the euro...in order to provide greater co-ordination with regard to their economic, budgetary and fiscal policies' (Fondation Robert Schuman 2007: 18). By a qualified majority, the Euro Area states may adopt new measures to bolster the coordination and surveillance of their budgetary discipline and to set out specific policy guidelines for its members. Decisions on non-compliance with the Stability and Growth Pact and the Broad Economic Policy Guidelines will be taken only by Euro Area states, without the member state directly concerned.

In terms of EU 'deepening', the Lisbon Treaty also touches upon the position of the ECB. Despite the critical intervention of its president Jean-Claude Trichet (Trichet 2007), it officially integrates the ECB into the institutional framework of the EU (Article 13 TEU). This new provision could for the first time change its constitutional position and 'deprive' the ECB of its special treaty-based character as an institution outside the EU's institutional architecture 'that, because of its specific institutional features, ... needs to be differentiated from the "Union's institutions"' (Trichet 2007: 2; Frankfurter Allgemeine Zeitung 2007). At the same time, this change could lead to a certain 'upgrading' of the perception of the ECB as a 'real and normal' EU institution, distinguishing it more clearly from, for instance, the European Investment Bank. It remains difficult to predict whether this new position in the treaties will lead to changes of the ECB's independence, a greater visibility of the institution within the European political process or a stronger integration of the ECB into the European macroeconomic policy context of EMU. Given the relevance of macroeconomic policy coordination under the Lisbon Strategy, among the three options, the third scenario should be reflected on in more in-depth (Marcussen, this volume).

The Lisbon Treaty also introduces changes in the procedure to establish and decide upon the EU's external representation in the macroeconomic realm (Article 115a TFEU). It tries to harmonize external representation by avoiding the past rather incoherent picture of the EU as an international financial actor. The Lisbon Treaty states that the 'Council, on a proposal from the Commission, may adopt appropriate measures to ensure unified representation within the international financial institutions and conferences. The Council shall act after consulting the European Central Bank' (Article 115a(2) TFEU). In decision-making on these issues, only member states whose currency is the euro may vote.

Limited Constitutional Adaptation Through EU 'Widening'

As with formal steps of treaty revision, the accession of 12 new EU Member States in 2004/07 had—at first sight—little direct impact on the European constitutional context of EMU. Yet, as one obvious consequence, EU 'widening' necessitated and motivated the reform of voting rules in the ECB's Governing Council. In order to avoid endangering the operations of the Eurosystem, this reform was embedded in the Nice Treaty before formal accession of new members to the Euro Area (Berger 2006; Eijffinger 2006). The constitutional changes define new voting rules for the point in Eurosystem 'widening' when the Governing Council consists of more than 21 members (Article 10(2) Protocol No. 18 TEC). Thereafter, only 15 voting rights are attributed to the national central bank (NCB) governors, who are members of the Governing Council. The six members of the Executive Board will keep one vote each. Special rotation rules are applied to the exercise of the voting rights by the NCB governors, who are divided into several groups (Article 10 Protocol No. 18 TEC). These different groups are defined by 'a ranking of the size of the share of their national central bank's Member State in the aggregate gross domestic product at market prices and in the total aggregated balance sheet of the monetary financial institutions of the Member States which have adopted the euro' (Article 10 Protocol No. 18 TEC).

Compared to the tough negotiations on the voting powers in the Council of the EU that took place during the negotiations on the Nice and the Lisbon Treaties, and regardless of the dominant cleavage between large and small EU economies in it, the above agreement was achieved without major public controversies.

The European Politico-Institutional Core: The ECB and Supranational Monetary Policymaking

As linchpin of the Euro Area's institutional core, the ECB holds an outstanding position in supranational monetary decision-making (Dyson 2000*b*). It is exclusively and independently responsible for monetary policymaking (Article 105(2) TEC; Begg 2007: 36). Possessing legal personality (Article 107(2) TEC), it additionally holds a special position among the members of the European System of Central Banks (ESCB) as it is to be consulted in the case of—and can issue opinions on—Community proposals in the field of its competences as well as proposals 'by national authorities regarding any draft legislative provision in its fields of competence' (Article 105(4) TEC). It is, hence, given the competence to interfere in and to influence economic policies not only at supranational level but also at national level in the EU member states.

Both the ECB and the ESCB are legally anchored in Articles 8 and 105–24 TEC as well as in Protocol No. 18 to the TEC ('Statute of the European System of Central Banks and of the European Central Bank'). Article 8 established the treaty-based position of the ECB as the core supranational institution of monetary policymaking located outside the institutional architecture of the European Community that is, its *sui generis* character. This position underlined and protected the ECB's particular independence within European monetary policymaking. Similar protection was provided by the lack of discretionary power of any other EU institution or member state governments over the

ECB and the NCBs of the Euro Area member states (Article 108 TEC). The independence of the ECB is additionally underlined by the treaty provision that the President of the Council of the EU (ECOFIN), who can also 'submit a motion for deliberation' (Article 113 (1) TEC), and a member of the European Commission are allowed to participate in Governing Council meetings but do not hold voting rights (Article 113(1) TEC). The Lisbon Treaty's changes to the position of the ECB outside the EU's institutional framework—analysed above—belong to the few formal changes to the ECB's constitutional context of EMU during the first decade.

In this period, changes to the composition of the ECB's Executive Board (Article 112(2b) TEC) were decided smoothly and uncontroversially after the puzzle about the de facto duration of tenure of the ECB's first president was solved in 2002. A certain continuity of nationality of Executive Board members reflected a predominance of the Euro Area's four largest states— France, Germany, Italy, and Spain (Selmayr 2006: 125, 2007: 123). Nevertheless, the decisive factor for appointment was the expertise and professional experience of the candidates. This pattern of institutional stability does, however, underline the strong national interest of these four big EU member states in a more stable and permanent influence within the ECB, hoisting the national flag.

In terms of fulfilment of tasks, the ECB Executive Board remained the dominant technocratic body. Due to its responsibility for Euro Area monetary policy, as well as its competence to give necessary instructions to the NCBs and to prepare the meetings of the Governing Council, the Executive Board is the key guarantor of the implementation of the Eurosystem's tasks. Its dominant position derives from the fact that it not only implements monetary policy decisions but also possesses considerable agenda-setting power (McNamara 2006: 175).

By connecting itself to the European macroeconomic policy context of the euro (see below), the ECB used the treaty provisions to establish institutional ties to other EU institutions. It also actively engaged in administrative networks of a plethora of EU committees and decision-making bodies which ECB officials attended, notably the two 'top administrative bodies' (Wessels and Linsenmann 2002: 68)—the Economic and Financial Committee (EFC, Article 114 TEC) and the Economic Policy Committee (EPC).[1] These two pivotal committees of European macroeconomic governance (see below) gather senior civil servants 'dealing with confidential matters and operating in an environment that privileges discretion' (Dyson and Quaglia 2007: 1). As central administrative 'chambers' at the institutional core of EMU, and main

---

[1] ECB officials interviewed for this chapter highlighted elements of informal information gathering and sharing as positive in the context of the ECB's integration into macroeconomic and structural policymaking.

preparatory bodies assembling the 'masterminds of administrations' (Puetter 2007: 26) engaged in macroeconomic decision-shaping, they form quite special cases among the Council's preparatory committees (Linsenmann and Meyer 2003: 125). With the increasing relevance of macroeconomic policy coordination and the Lisbon agenda, the EPC became the main coordinating body to improve European structural policies aiming to enhance growth and job creation within the EU. It lays strong 'emphasis on policy reflection exercises, economic analysis and policy advice as regards more fundamental challenges' (Puetter 2007: 27). While the EPC is not closely involved in financial policy and central banking topics, the EFC holds an outstanding position in this area. As the main arena for central bankers and national finance ministries, the EFC was characterized by a high level of institutional and constitutional stability over the first decade of the euro. Preparing the work of the Euro Group and laying the ground for decision-making within ECOFIN, it had a strong influence on sensitive aspects of problem-solving in European macroeconomic policymaking. Additionally, the EFC monitored the budgetary and economic development of EU member states in the framework of the Broad Economic Policy Guidelines (see below).

A major arena for the ECB to connect with the political level is the Euro Group. Since its first meeting in 1998, the Euro Group, designed in 1997, formed the central body for informal exchange among Euro Area members' finance ministers, the European Commission and the ECB as well as for Eurosystem decision-shaping. In the course of the European Convention's deliberations on the Constitutional Treaty, the Euro Group was subject to reform debates about whether and how to strengthen its position in EMU. Among the reform suggestions was, most prominently, the 2002 contribution by Joschka Fischer and Dominique de Villepin that proposed a strengthening of cohesion of the Euro Area by reinforcement of the Euro Group and the decision-making capacity of the Euro Area. It foresaw the integration of a protocol on the Euro Group into the treaty; the establishment of a two-year presidency of the Euro Group to improve its visibility; and the need for EU member states whose currency is the euro to take decisions within ECOFIN among themselves on topics related to the euro (European Convention 2002: 3). The Convention's plenary sessions underlined the will to strengthen the Euro Group's institutional position (Norman 2003: 124). The three proposals presented by Fischer and de Villepin were taken up in the protocol on the Euro Group attached to the Constitutional Treaty establishing a two-and-a-half-year presidency, and in Article III-88 to 96 TCE on the differentiation between 'member states which are part of the Euro Area' and 'member states with a derogation', which also entered the Lisbon Treaty (see above). Even without ratification of the Constitutional Treaty the Euro Group presidency proposal was implemented in September 2004 when Jean-Claude Juncker was elected by the finance ministers of the Eurosystem to officially preside over the Euro Group for a two-year term starting on 1 January 2005.[2]

The institutional links of the ECB went beyond the participation of its President and officials in other EU institutions' policymaking processes. The ECB also cultivated more informal links to the EU institutions, ranging from 'rather close and intensive' in the case of the European Parliament to 'less intensive and more formalised' in the case of the European Commission and the Council.[3] In addition, the ECB had intensive reporting obligations to the European Council, the ECOFIN, the Commission, and the European Parliament (Article 113(3) TEC). The ECB annual reports on the ESCB activities and on monetary policymaking, as well as the ECB monthly bulletins and quarterly reports (Article 15 Protocol No. 18 TEC) formed important information tools in this context.

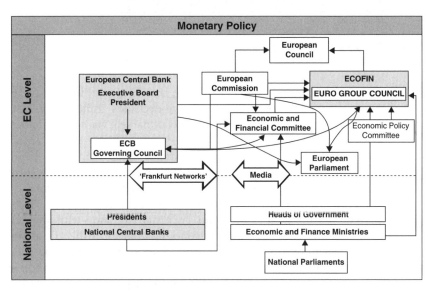

Figure 3.1. European monetary policymaking

Source: Adapted version of Wessels and Linsenmann (2002: 58) (arrows mark participation rights and/or formal cooperation provisions).

ECB Activities and Monetary Policy Strategy

In pursuing its tasks, the ECB has been quite active over the first decade. Its main output consists of guidelines, recommendations, and opinions at the request of EU institutions, followed by decisions and regulations on European

---

[2] On 6 September 2006, his tenure was extended until 31 December 2008.
[3] According to ECB officials interviewed for this chapter.

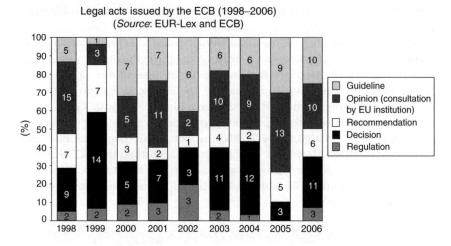

Figure 3.2. ECB activities (1998–2006)

Source: Compilation by Tobias Kunstein, Jean-Monnet Chair Prof. W. Wessels, Cologne, 2008.

monetary policy (cf. Figure 3.1). Thematically, these activities focused on its monetary policy strategy, concrete interest-rate decisions, inflation forecasting, money supply, and stabilization of financial markets via money market operations (Figure 3.2).

ECB elaboration of its monetary policy strategy was shaped by a key constraint in the economic and politico-institutional context of the euro: the argument that an 'efficient single market require[s] monetary stability' (Collignon 2007: 163). Thus, its main focus was on price stability. Treaty provisions required the ECB to maintain price stability and—without prejudice to this primary goal—to support economic policies of the EC, as the core objective of European monetary policymaking (Article 105(1) TEC). Its stability-oriented monetary policy paradigm influenced other macroeconomic policies as it provided the key reference point for policy development.

This shaping influence of the ECB over the first decade of the euro points to the predominant and autonomous position of the ECB in developing its two-pillar approach to its stability-oriented monetary policy strategy. Initially, pillar one was money-supply growth; pillar two, economic and financial indicators. Critiques of this policy strategy broadly focused on the lack of transparency of ECB monetary-policy decision-making in a complex, two-pillar approach (cf. Deutsche Bank 2001); on the imprecise definition of the price-stability target (initially 'under 2 per cent', then 'below but close to 2 per cent') and its asymmetric nature (suggesting that inflation was a greater risk than deflation); and the need for a more integrated framework of macro-economic policy coordination (cf. Howarth 2005: 1). Critics sought a shift from the focus on price stability towards more attention to, and competences in, areas such as fiscal policy and broad economic policy development (cf. Kunstein 2007: 29). They wished to transform ECB 'stability policy' into a real 'stabilization policy' (cf. Rochon and Rossi 2006: 93).

ECB monetary policy strategy and its underlying paradigm remained stable during the first decade of the euro. Over the first four years, the ECB stuck to the two-pillar approach of its stability-oriented monetary strategy (Schill and van Riet 2000; Schill and Willeke 2001; Selmayr 2002, 2003). However, its monetary policy strategy was not exempted from change. In 2003, the ECB 'clarified' its definition of price stability as 'below but close to 2 per cent' as its medium-term goal and newly accentuated its two-pillar strategy by making the 'economic' pillar the first pillar and using the second 'monetary' pillar to cross-check for longer-term inflationary risks. As a consequence, the communication of ECB Governing Council decisions from 2003 onwards no longer started with the development of money supply but with the economic analysis of short-to-medium-term risks to price stability. The Executive Board was keen to stress that this was not a strategy reversal and relaxation but a 'clarification'. In 2005–7, critique mounted of the 'monetary' pillar of the strategy, given that the 4.5 per cent reference value for the broad monetary aggregate M3[4] had been constantly exceeded since early 2001. Critics argued that this volatility and overshoot proved the benefit of changing the ECB's monetary policy strategy towards focusing on price development rather the money supply and further relaxing monetary policy (Selmayr 2003: 118f, 2008: 100).

The Evolving Practice of European Macroeconomic Policy: The Changing Context of Interlinked Modes of Governance

Given that EMU is 'not a single-rule exercise' (Wessels and Linsenmann 2002: 56; Begg, Hodson, and Maher 2003: 71), it is strongly interlinked to other macroeconomic policies. The interaction between these different policy areas is necessary to achieve the EU's self-set Lisbon Agenda targets of sustainable economic growth and job creation that are mirrored in the EU's objectives newly defined in Article 3 of the Lisbon Treaty, that is, sustainable development, balanced economic growth, price stability, and a highly competitive social market economy aiming at full employment and social progress (Collignon 2007: 155; Heise 2006: 303; Marcussen, this volume).

[4] Comprising intermediate money (M2: deposits with maturities of up to two years plus deposits redeemable at notice of up to three months including narrow money (M1: currency and balances immediately convertible into currency or used for cashless payments)) and marketable instruments issued by the Monetary and Financial Institutions' (MFI) sector.

Hence, the challenge of macroeconomic policy coordination also character-ized the European macroeconomic policy context of the euro. So, in addition to supranational policymaking in monetary policy (Article 105–10 TEC), two other policies and modes of governance add to the polyvalent character of this policy context. These two other modes of governance are 'hard' policy coordination in fiscal policy (Article 104 TEC; Stability and Growth Pact) and 'soft' policy coordination in economic and employment policies (Article 99 TEC; Broad Economic Policy Guidelines and Article 125–30 TEC; European Employment Strategy, EES).

The above observations about the overall stability of the European con-stitutional context of EMU would be misleading if this chapter ignored the evolution of the European macroeconomic policy context of the euro. This evolution has been in the political practice of EMU. Key elements in this evolution of the two other modes of governance over the first decade of the euro were

- The establishment, experience, and 'reform' of the Stability and Growth Pact (Hallerberg and Bridwell, this volume).

- The establishment and reform of the Lisbon agenda (Marcussen, this volume), including the evolution of the 'open method of coordination', the overhaul of the Broad Economic Policy Guidelines and their merger with the Employment Guidelines and the Internal Market Strategy (IMS) into the new Integrated Guidelines for Growth and Employment.

A decisive milestone in this evolution of political practice in the European macroeconomic policy context—highlighting once again the relevance of the European Council in shaping the European context of EMU—was the decision of the 2005 spring European Council on the reform of the Lisbon Strategy and the Stability and Growth Pact (European Council 2005). Below the level of formal constitutional change, this reform responded to perceived shortcom-ings in the coordination of macroeconomic policy coordination processes. It was the most important and influential adaptation in political practice, marking a certain 'sea change' towards 'Lisbonization' of governance in which the Lisbon strategy came to act as a big umbrella for other macroeconomic policies.

During the first decade of the euro the 'inability to find a satisfactory way of formulating discretionary fiscal policy as an implementable rule and a set of practical institutions to support that rule . . . had made . . . [member states] sceptical of attempts to use discretionary fiscal policy to stabilize the business cycle' (Collignon 2007: 164). Additionally, breaches or threats of breach of rules have been frequent phenomena, damaging the overall efficiency and reputation of the Stability and Growth Pact (Collignon 2007: 166; de la Porte and Pochet 2003: 55; Hallerberg and Bridwell, this volume). Despite the option of 'hard' financial sanctions, the implementation of fiscal policy under the Pact revealed serious problems from 2001 onwards and highlighted the unresolved question of the legitimacy of European fiscal policy (Collignon 2007: 166). Because of this record of non-compliance, '[c]onfidence in the Pact's substantive rules has been severely shaken since the launch of EMU by the fiscal performance of four member states. Portugal breached the deficit ceiling in 2001, France and Germany followed suit in 2002, and Italy...in 2005' (Hallerberg and Bridwell, this volume; Hodson and Maher 2004: 799).

After this difficult period of non-compliance, the temporary waiver of the excessive deficit procedure by ECOFIN in November 2003, followed by the overruling of the ECOFIN decision by the European Court of Justice in 2004, led to the 'painstaking reform' (Heipertz and Verdun 2005: 986) of the Stability and Growth Pact, endorsed by the European Council in 2005. As Chapter 4 by Hallerberg and Bridwell shows, this reform involved increasing flexibility in assessment 'of medium-term budgetary positions as well as [in] the imposition of sanctions by reviewing the "concept of exceptional excess over the reference value resulting from a severe economic downturn" (Council of the European Union 2005a: 5, 2005b)' (Umbach forthcoming) and by more scope to claim exceptions. Thus, in practice, the 'hard letter' of the Pact was transformed into 'soft' policy coordination, providing member states with considerable flexibility in implementation (Heipertz and Verdun 2005: 994; Hodson and Maher 2004: 800f; Schäfer 2005: 172).

With respect to the second mode of governance of the macroeconomic policy context of the euro, the lack of legal authority of the Broad Economic Policy Guidelines and the absence of the opportunity to sanction non-compliance damaged their intended strong position in the first decade of the euro. This weakness in supporting the stable performance of EU member states under EMU became evident when 'the recommendation to Ireland about pro-cyclical policies had no real effect, as the Irish government disregarded the Commission's arguments' (de la Porte and Pochet 2003: 36). The Lisbon Treaty partially responded to this problem with its amendments to the Guidelines (see above).

Regarding the European Employment Strategy, two reform steps reshaped 'soft' employment policy coordination over the first decade of the euro. In 2003, the Strategy was reformed. It was simplified in terms of horizontal and vertical priority areas and streamlined with the Broad Economic Policy Guidelines to increase policy coherence between the two 'soft' policy coordination processes as well as to avoid overlaps and contradictions (Employment Taskforce 2003: 59; European Commission 2003a, 2006b). The initial annual coordination cycle was extended to three years and made parallel with the time frame of the Broad Economic Policy Guidelines and the Internal Market Strategy. With this reform step, the evaluation of the different processes was presented at the same time of the year to provide input into the spring European Council. This temporal streamlining exercise sought to emphasize 'the role of the BEPGs as an overarching economic policy coordination instrument and the leading role of the EES in giving direction to and ensuring co-ordination of the employment policy priorities to which Member States should subscribe' (European Commission 2003*a*: 7). In 2005, the spring European Council welded the different processes and integrated the Broad Economic Policy Guidelines and the Employment Guidelines into one single document (cf. European Commission 2005*a*: 7, 2005*b*: 3). By doing so, one single economic policy coordination cycle was created, fusing the two modes of governance and related coordination cycles into the 'Integrated Guidelines'.

Conclusion: Stability and Evolution Revisited

During the first decade of the euro, EMU became a core part of the EU polity not merely because Euro Area member state citizens got used to life with the euro. In addition, EMU developed particular patterns of governance not echoed in other areas of the EU polity: it developed a life apart from the evolving political system of the EU. The evolution of EMU's European context of 'deepening' and 'widening' was characterized by first, an odd coexistence of EMU's formal stability and an overall constitutionally and institutionally evolving EU system; second, a dominant role of the ECB as the core actor of the Euro Area's institutional architecture (Dyson 2000*b*); and, third, a major evolution of practices in the European macroeconomic policy context of the euro below the level of formal treaty revisions.

The constitutional continuity of EMU is an indicator of EMU's institutional stability in the interests of reinforcing the credibility of its core actor, the ECB. Contrary to pessimistic projections of EMU that painted a picture of gloom and doom in the 1990s (like Hasse and Hepperle 1994), the ECB made effective use of the treaty provisions on EMU to become the core actor of its politico-institutional context.

The ECB proved an effective operator in supranational monetary policy-making, showing clear signs of autonomy and paradigm-shaping power. Nevertheless, reform debates intensified and continue to centre on the two-pillar approach of the ECB monetary policy strategy; aspects of ECB independence and accountability; the interaction of the ECB with other EU institutions such as the Euro Group and ECOFIN; and the institutional framework of macroeconomic policy coordination, including the involvement of the ECB. The ECB's strong independence remains a topic of reform debates as over the first decade of the euro, it was critically assessed to have created an 'economic order [that] is radically independent from the political order' (Le Heron 2007: 156). As a consequence, accountability problems in the case of the non-compliance of the ECB with treaty-based obligations are viewed as unresolved. These unresolved problems were reinforced because the European Parliament has no opportunity to make the ECB accountable within the 'quarterly monetary dialogue' (ibid.: 157).

However, merely focusing on the acknowledged moderate degree of constitutional change within formal treaty revisions, or linked to EU enlargement, turns a blind eye to adaptation below, or beyond the level of formal constitutional evolution. This adaptation has taken place within the European macroeconomic context of the euro. In consequence, EU 'deepening' and 'widening' have had a greater impact than the formal continuity of the constitutional context indicates and might in the long run affect citizens' identification with the 'political community' (Easton 1965) of the EU more deeply. In the most positive scenario, it might create additional trust in EMU, exceeding the mere belief in the functionality of treaty provisions or market operations.

So, taking up the initially stated interlink between the two dimensions of EMU and political union, the overall stability of EMU and the Eurosystem has the potential to positively affect the overall stability of evolution of the EU's political system. Indirectly, it might pave the way for further system change, accompanied by formal treaty revisions. However, during the first decade, this interlink between EMU and political union was not forcefully influenced by a strong Euro Group, which—beyond its original policy field—had not developed into the constitutional 'core' or 'pioneer group' (see Juppé 2000; Schäuble and Lamers 1994), 'avantgarde' (Chirac 2000) or 'centre of gravity' (Fischer 2000) that it was initially envisaged to become by some political actors.

Explanations for the failure of the Euro Group to shape the overall evolution towards political union include increasing heterogeneity of the Euro Group due to enlargement of the Euro Area, loss of power of the formerly hegemonic Franco-German tandem, failed referenda in two core Euro Area states (France and the Netherlands), and the development towards a form of 'semi-permanent variable geometry' in European integration (i.e. different sectoral integration of groups of 'insiders' and 'outsiders', with certain opt-out elements for the members of the different groups).

The overall constitutional stability of the EMU treaty framework over the first decade does not, nevertheless, necessarily point to the unchanged appropriateness of European provisions. It also documents, first, the fact that the heads of state and government assembled in the European Council did not identify a particular and generally shared need to change the constitutional basis for the overall division of competences, including the rules for policy coordination; and, second, the force of the persuasive ECB argument that its credibility as a new central bank was a paramount need in successfully establishing the new currency and must not be put in jeopardy. Hence, challenges and constraints of EMU for domestic economic and fiscal policies have not led EU member states to take explicit treaty reshaping action, which would have eroded the wisdom of their decisions taken in the Intergovernmental Conference leading towards the Maastricht Treaty.

Given existing difficulties and problems of member states' performance under EMU, this insight is both astonishing and counter-intuitive. Governments did not use the formal opportunities of treaty change to remedy the shortcomings that they were confronted with during the first decade of the euro. Instead, they opted largely for adaptation of the institutional framework of EMU below the level of treaty revision. Additionally, with the Lisbon Treaty, and after the abortive Constitutional Treaty, energy and enthusiasm for fundamental treaty changes seem to be exhausted, at least for this generation of European leaders.

Apart from stable monetary policymaking with a strong ECB steering the supranational policy paradigm, the European macroeconomic policy context of EMU has shown considerable signs of 'below-treaty-revision' evolution. Reform of the Stability and Growth Pact and increasing interlinkage of economic, internal market, and employment policy coordination at the European level resulted in the synchronization and welding of macroeconomic policy processes. At the level of policy paradigm, a durable focus on price stability can be found in European monetary policymaking over the first decade of the euro. It influenced not only supranational monetary but also other macroeconomic policies. Additionally, due to the merger of European economic and employment policy coordination, the macroeconomic policy realm was further integrated to enhance coherence of policy coordination. Whether this evolution will in the long run lead to an 'optimal policy mix' in the European macroeconomic policy context of the euro remains an issue for future analysis, alongside the outcome of co-evolution of EU 'deepening' and 'widening' and EMU after the Lisbon Treaty.

4

Fiscal Policy Coordination and Discipline: The Stability and Growth Pact and Domestic Fiscal Regimes

Mark Hallerberg and Joshua Bridwell

Has the Stability and Growth Pact improved fiscal discipline in European Union states? Simple comparisons of means for budget deficits suggest that the SGP *has* had a beneficial effect. The average budget deficit for the eight years after the signing of the Treaty of Maastricht (1991–8) among members of the Euro Area was 3.9 per cent while it was 0.60 per cent for the eight years after the introduction of the euro (1999–2006).[1] If one compares years of weak or negative growth, or 1992–4 with 2002–4, the differences are even greater, with the average in the earlier period 5.5 per cent and in the later period 1.5 per cent (AMECO May 2007).[2] While more evidence will be presented later, there has been a clear convergence, and clear improvement, of fiscal performance since the introduction of the euro.

Yet, if one reads both the popular and academic press, one would think that the Pact has been a failure. The reason is that these authors judge the success of the Pact on the Pact's own guidelines. One of the most prominent goals is to keep states from running 'excessive deficits', which roughly correspond to general government deficits below 3 per cent of GDP (the exact details follow). States with excessive deficits are expected to take remedial action. In practice, several states failed to keep their general government budget deficits below 3 per cent. In 2005, 6 of the 12 Euro Area states had excessive deficits, and those states together represented almost 80 per cent of Euro

---

[1] Because Slovenia joined the Euro Area only on 1 January 2007, this chapter focuses on either the EU-12 that constituted the Euro Area as of 2006 or the EU-15.

[2] The performance in the latter period is also noteworthy compared to Japan and the United States where deficit levels were higher or, for 2004, 3.5 per cent of GDP for the federal level in the United States (Office of Management and Budget 2006) and close to 6 per cent of GDP for Japan (AMECO 2006).

Area GDP (Stéclebout-Orseau and Hallerberg 2007, based on AMECO figures). This outcome would not necessarily be problematic if the excessive deficits were temporary. However, two core members of the Euro Area, France and Germany, had excessive deficits beginning in 2003 and 2002, respectively, and those excessive deficits were to last through 2006. While the press has focused on these breaches of the Pact, several states have healthy budget balances and have not come close to the reference value. Fitting with the themes of this book, it appears that there has been a 'clustered' divergence in fiscal policy outcomes.

This discussion begs the question: why has there been such clustering? One possibility is differences in external economic shocks: some states may have simply gotten 'lucky', while others experienced negative economic shocks.[3] In fact, this view motivated states to revise the Pact in spring 2005 to include more 'exceptional' circumstances that should be taken into consideration before a given state is found to have an 'excessive' deficit. While the official focus has been on economic shocks, political 'shocks' like elections may have also affected budgetary outcomes.

A second possibility focuses on fiscal rules and institutions at the domestic level. The states have had fiscal policies for a long time. There are clear differences in how states formulate and execute budgets, and these domestic institutional differences could be driving the results.

The third possibility, and perhaps of most interest for this book, is the interaction between European and domestic rules. There are two different ways this interaction can play out. First, EMU could encourage domestic reforms that centralize the budget process. Second, and more directly, the European rules could reinforce certain domestic rules so that the interaction between the two is more beneficial than either independently.

In fact, both of these factors are important in explaining the two stylized facts of this chapter, namely that overall fiscal performance has improved but that there is 'clustered' divergence under the Stability and Growth Pact. We argue that a general improvement of fiscal institutions among the EU-15 (partly due to EMU, partly not) explains the general improvement of fiscal policy. At the same time, the interaction between European and domestic institutions explains the partial success of the Stability and Growth Pact in preventing 'excessive' deficits. In particular, the Member States that together make up the ECOFIN Council determine whether to punish other states, and there are reasons to believe that Council members will not always apply them. Indeed, in our empirical section, we find that the 'rules of the game' at the EU level are not applied equally to all states, suggesting a partial answer to the question of 'clustered' divergence in fiscal policy.

---

[3] This is how some states that experienced excessive deficits perceived what happened (at least in public).

The first part of this chapter provides a brief review of the European framework and how it applies to fiscal policy. The second part considers the literature on domestic fiscal institutions. It also develops an argument about the relationship between the domestic and European-level institutions. The third part provides data on our two stylized facts about fiscal performance. In addition to budgetary outcomes, we have collected data on the comments of both the European Commission and ECOFIN on the Stability and Convergence Programmes that all member states must submit. We use this data to consider under what conditions the European level has made official recommendations to Member States, whether the Council has consistently weakened the Commission's recommendations (and presumably thereby weakened the Stability and Growth Pact), and whether the states in turn have complied.

The European Framework

The Maastricht Treaty provided the road map to create a single currency and an independent central bank to regulate it. While fiscal policies were to remain the domain of Member States, the treaty anticipated the need for some sort of macroeconomic policy coordination. As Article 99(1) of the treaty stated: 'Member states shall regard their economic policies as a matter of common concern and coordinate them in the Council.' The initial institutional tool was the Broad Economic Policy Guidelines, which the Commission would draft and the Council would pass.

The EMS crises in 1992–3, however, combined with a general worsening of budget deficits across the Union, heightened concerns about how states would perform once stage three of EMU began. Two of the so-called Maastricht criteria focused on fiscal policy and set reference values of a general government deficit no larger than 3 per cent of GDP and general government debt burden no larger than 60 per cent of GDP. The Commission used these values, in turn, to judge whether countries met the requirements to join the Euro Area (stage three). In practice, the emphasis in the run-up to the introduction of the euro was on the deficit figure, and Member States had to get their deficits at or below 3.0 per cent if they wanted to adopt the euro. However, there were only vague provisions for what to do once the euro was created.

Article 103 of the Maastricht Treaty is judged as a 'no bail-out clause' because it stated that neither the Community nor the other Member States were liable for the commitments of other governments. There was concern, however, that this position was not credible. A state with a fiscal crisis could hurt all members of the Euro Area, and the remaining states could subsequently find it in their best interest to bail out this state. Consequently, there seemed little to prevent states from relaxing their fiscal stances once they joined.

These concerns led to the creation of the Stability and Growth Pact, which the Member States agreed at the Dublin Summit in December 1996.[4] The details of the Pact's operation are important in assessing whether the Pact has been successful in improving fiscal discipline and in coordinating the fiscal policies of the Member States. At its core, it has both preventive and corrective mechanisms. The preventive mechanism focuses on detailed monitoring of what Member States are doing. While states submitted some information to the Commission beginning in 1994, the contents of those reports were not well specified. States would now have to write either convergence (non-euro members) or stability programmes (euro members) and update those programmes roughly at the end of each year. All states were expected to have budgets that were 'close to balance' or in surplus over the medium-term. The Commission then had the responsibility of reviewing each programme and making recommendations to the ECOFIN Council on whether the programme met European goals and whether the goals set in the programmes were realistic, given domestic conditions. The Commission could also recommend that a state receive an 'early warning' that it would run an excessive deficit if immediate action were not taken, which the ECOFIN Council would subsequently have to approve in order for the warning to become official.

The corrective arm followed from the Commission's assessment of a given state's domestic policy. If it judged both that an 'excessive' deficit existed and that a state had not made any progress in eliminating it, the Commission could recommend to the Council that the state make a non-interest-bearing deposit with it of up to 0.5 per cent of GDP, depending on the size of the deficit. If the Member State continued to neglect necessary reforms, the deposit could become a fine. The Commission is further charged with considering 'exceptional' circumstances in its assessment, which would be automatic if there were an economic contraction of at least 2 per cent of GDP; if economic growth were to drop into the 'box' 0.75–2 per cent of GDP, the existence of 'exceptional' circumstances would be determined by Commission recommendation and subsequent ECOFIN vote. In practice, this meant that zero growth years were not 'exceptional'.

We will provide detailed data below on compliance under this framework, but there is more to the story that requires some explanation. France and Germany had problematic deficits beginning in 2002. The Commission recommended an 'early warning' to Germany in 2002, but the ECOFIN Council did not pass it, and an informal agreement reached with Germany meant that Chancellor Gerhard Schröder avoided getting such a warning in an election year. In autumn 2003, the Commission judged that the deficits in France and Germany were excessive and that they would continue, and it attempted to begin the sanctioning process against each Member State. The ECOFIN

---

[4] See Heipertz and Verdun (2004) for more detail about the Pact's creation.

Council, however, balked at following the Commission's recommendation. The Commission's response in January 2004 was to take ECOFIN to the European Court of Justice. In its judgment, the Court ruled that the Council could not suspend a procedure without the Commission's recommendation. (European Commission 2004*b*; Morris et al. 2006: 17–18).

There was a clear sense both in the academic and policy communities that something was wrong with the Pact, resulting in a slew of reform proposals (e.g. Begg et al. 2004; Schelkle 2005; Schuknecht 2004).[5] The Member States agreed to a concrete reform in March 2005. Under the revised Excessive Deficit Procedure (EDP), more factors are now explicitly considered when determining whether a state has an excessive deficit, such as whether spending fosters international solidarity or promotes the unification of Europe.[6] Member States also set their own medium-term objectives, which can include the future fiscal effects of major structural reforms in their calculations. Even if a state is found to have an excessive deficit, it may receive extended deadlines so that it has more time to correct the deficit than before the revision. States experiencing negative growth are now exempt, whereas the previous requirement for automatic exemption was a decline in economic output of 2 per cent of GDP.

Though these changes weaken the Commission's position vis-à-vis Member States, the Commission does have a new mechanism that supplements the previous 'early warning' system: the ability to issue policy advice directly to Member States without prior Council approval. The 'early warning' mechanism remains, but it is meant to be used only when it is likely that a state will exceed the 3 per cent deficit limit without further action.[7]

In summary, the process under the Stability and Growth Pact is more complex than a simple 3 per cent deficit rule. Critically, there is an interaction between the Commission, on the one hand, and the Council that includes the Member States, on the other. For example, the European Commission must initiate an excessive deficit process against a state. That process only results in an 'excessive deficit' label for a state if the ECOFIN Council agrees with a qualified majority. This process is generally true for other parts of the Pact as well. The Commission is supposed to evaluate every Stability and Convergence Programme and issue recommendations for changes where it finds that the Member States have not taken actions it deems necessary. These recommendations, however, have to be approved by the Council, and

---

[5] See Fischer, Jonung, and Larch's (2006) appropriately titled paper '101 Proposals to Reform the Stability and Growth Pact. Why so Many?'

[6] The clause on 'international solidarity' was widely seen as a way to mollify France, which wanted defence spending to be exempt, while 'European unification' would allow Germany to include the costs of German unification.

[7] An excellent review of the changes in the Pact appears in Morris, Ongena, and Schuknecht (2006).

the Council can (and does) change them. Conveniently for our purposes, the various recommendations at the different stages of the process on the programmes are public. In the empirical section, we will consider concretely the Commission's actions against states and whether ECOFIN followed the Commission recommendation. We also ask whether there are systematic biases in the types of recommendations the Commission makes and whether the Council accepts them. Before moving to the data, however, it is important to consider the domestic context.

The Domestic Context

There is a growing literature that considers the effects of domestic fiscal institutions on fiscal outcomes (e.g. Von Hagen 1992; Wehner 2007; Wildavsky 1975). In this section, we summarize one version of this literature, which focuses on forms of fiscal governance and their application to EU states.

The 'forms of fiscal governance' approach contends that the decision-making rules for making budgets have an effect on budgetary outcomes. In game-theoretic terms, all governments face a common pool resource (CPR) problem. This problem arises whenever the decision-makers consider the full benefits of spending but only part of the tax burden. A centralization of the budget process that forces the actors to internalize the full tax externality leads to lower spending and, over multiple periods, lower budget deficits (e.g. Velasco 2000*a*, 2000*b*).

How the CPR problem is solved in practice is the subject of recent research (e.g. Hallerberg 2004; Hallerberg, Strauch, and von Hagen 2009; von Hagen and Harden 1994). Forms of fiscal governance are packages of rules, norms, and institutions that structure the budget process. Two ideal forms of fiscal governance can provide the needed centralization. The first, known as *delegation*, exists when the players delegate powers on the budget to one central player, typically the finance minister. This minister considers the full tax burden, may have agenda-setting and veto powers during the formulation of the budget, has docile parliaments that do not overturn key provisions of the government's budget draft, and has the ability to make unilateral cuts during the execution of the budget. This form of fiscal governance establishes a principal–agent relationship between the cabinet members, the principal, and the finance minister, the agent, and it works well only when the preferences of the various actors are essentially the same. As the preferences diverge, the ministers will not delegate to the finance minister in the first place. If one assumes that preferences are fairly uniform in a one-party government but diverge in multi-party governments, *delegation* is most appropriate to one-party governments or governments where the ideological conflicts are low (e.g. France under an RPR–UDF government in the 1980s).

When ideological differences increase, a second form of fiscal governance is most appropriate. In coalition formation, parties can negotiate fiscal contracts. This *contracts* approach means that the parties make a political, or sometimes even legal, commitment to fiscal targets for every ministry for the life of the coalition. Such contracts also usually include provisions for what to do if there are shocks, such as weaker economic growth or lower revenue than expected. Because all coalition parties are involved in the negotiations for each ministry, the full tax burden is considered. Ministers then effectively become managers of ministries that already have their spending mandates predetermined.

Hallerberg, Strauch, and von Hagen (2009) present a rich data-set of fiscal institutions, norms, and rules for the EU-15 for the time period 1985–2004. It is based upon successive surveys, in-person interviews in capital cities, and correspondence with policymakers. They create two indices that aggregate the decision-making rules based on whether they are consistent with *delegation* or *contracts*. They also compare the fiscal performance of countries based upon their expected form of fiscal governance—those with low ideological distance among the players needed to pass the budget are expected *delegation* states while those with high ideological distance are expected *contract* states.[8]

Two relevant questions remain: did domestic institutions improve since the Treaty of Maastricht; and, if they did improve, is the EMU process at the European level responsible for the change? The answer to the first question is clearly 'yes'. Table 4.1 reproduces data from Hallerberg, Strauch, and von Hagen (2009) according to three dimensions: a delegation index, a contracts index, and the expected form of fiscal governance for each state. The respective indices range from a score of 0, which means that a state has none of the fiscal institutions, norms, and rules consistent with a given form of fiscal governance, to a score of 1, which means that it has all of them.

Table 4.1 indicates a clear improvement on both indices, with a bigger jump for the 'contracts' index than for the 'delegation' index. Moreover, there are differences according to the expected form of governance. Expected delegation states have more delegation 'rules' on average in 2000, or 0.70 on average versus 0.57 for expected contract states. The differences for the 'contracts' index, however, are not as great, with expected delegation states at 0.73 and expected contract states at 0.76. Hallerberg, Strauch, and von Hagen find that centralization according to a given index matters only if the respective form of governance is expected for a given state. That is, strengthening multi-annual planning in an expected delegation country like France does not improve

---

[8] The concept of ideological distance is based on Tsebelis (2002). In practice, it is coded both according to the data-set Tsebelis provides on his website as well as using data from the Manifesto Project.

Table 4.1. Delegation and contracts indices: expected form of fiscal governance

Country	Delegation		Contracts		Expected governance	
	1991	2000/4	1991	2000/4	1991	2000/4
Austria	0.38	0.62	0.59	0.91	C	D
Belgium	0.23	0.44/0.51	0.12	0.75	C	C
Denmark	0.59	0.58	0.37	0.66	C	C
Finland	0.37	0.52	0.69	0.69	C	C
France	0.9	0.81/0.77	0.46	0.78	D	D
Germany	0.58	0.62	0.77	0.73	D	D
Greece	0.23	0.75	0.49	0.75	D	D
Ireland	0.35	0.77	0.58	0.75	C	D
Italy	0.27	0.73/0.69	0.34	0.66	C	D
Luxembourg	0.53	0.64	0.25	1	C	C
The Netherlands	0.56	0.47	0.44	0.49/0.67	C	C
Portugal	0.49	0.54/0.60	0.19	0.69	D	D
Spain	0.27	0.58	0.23	0.53	D	D
Sweden	0.32	0.71	0.03	0.69	C	C
UK	0.74	0.87	0.52	0.74	D	D
Average	0.45	0.64/0.65	0.40	0.73/0.74		

Data are from Table 3.7 of Hallerberg, Strauch, and von Hagen (2009). The delegation index is composed of four measures for the formulation of the budget, four measures for parliamentary passage, and six measures for implementation. The contracts index is composed of four measures for the formulation of fiscal targets and two measures for implementation.

French fiscal performance, but it does improve fiscal discipline in an expected contracts country like The Netherlands.

The second question, namely whether EMU contributed to the overall improvement of domestic fiscal institutions, is more complex. In case studies for every Member State but Luxembourg, Hallerberg (2004) finds that EMU was used explicitly in government discourse to justify fiscal institutional reforms in some states, such as Belgium, Greece, and Italy. At the same time, it was consciously ignored in other states, including most prominently the 'outs' of Denmark, Sweden, and the United Kingdom, for fear that mentioning EMU would lead to more public opposition to the reforms. In still others, policymakers felt that they had enough pressing domestic need for reform that the EU level was either not critical enough or even superfluous (i.e. Finland). Finally, a set of states began reforms well before Maastricht, and indeed Maastricht cannot explain why some states have high scores in 1991 and others do not.

There are, however, some direct effects of the EMU process on these scores. The Stability and Convergence Programmes require multi-annual plans according to common accounting standards that are linked to clear macroeconomic assumptions. EMU therefore forces an improvement in the 'contracts' index for all states. The key distinguishing feature across states is whether they make either political or legal commitments to the fiscal targets that they present to Brussels. Such commitments are common in expected contract states but generally unheard of in delegation states.[9]

This discussion suggests that there is an asymmetric relationship between the European-level requirements and domestic fiscal institutions. In places where fiscal contracts are expected, the EU rules are useful reinforcements to the domestic rules. In places where delegation is expected, the EU rules have no effect. We would therefore anticipate that expected delegation states will have the most trouble complying with the Stability and Growth Pact.

There is a second hypothesis that we will test. The Council approves a series of items, from recommendations on member state Stability and Convergence Programmes to whether or not sanctions should be proposed. While states are not supposed to vote on their own cases, it is reasonable to expect that the big states will have more weight than the smaller states.[10] Specific hypotheses appear below, but we anticipate that the Stability and growth Pact may be more effective in restraining small states than large ones (with large states defined as those with 10 votes under the Treaty of Amsterdam voting rules in the Council).

Convergence and Clustered Divergence

The first task of this section is simply to document fiscal performance over the period from the agreement in Maastricht to 2006. Figure 4.1 presents the performance of the EU-15 over this time frame with respect to the most important reference value, the budget balance. It presents 'box and whisker' plots. The middle line for each year is the median, the box is bounded by 25 per cent either way, and the whiskers indicate the 95 per cent confidence intervals. Any circles outside the 95 per cent intervals are beyond two standard deviations and can, according to convention, be thought of as outliers. The figure indicates a clear improvement in budget balances over the time frame, and especially since 1997. It also indicates that the distance between the whiskers has decreased somewhat, which suggests some convergence.

[9] In Spain in 2000, the multi-annual stability programme was written in a different ministry than where the budget was formulated, and there was no evidence offered to one of the current authors at the time that the staffs even spoke to each other, let alone that the annual budget used figures from previous Stability Programmes for planning purposes.

[10] The size of the country could also affect the degree of fiscal institutional reform in the run-up to Economic and Monetary Union; Duval and Elmeskov (2006), find that labour market reforms were more likely in European small states. We run a correlation between population and the change in either its delegation or fiscal contract institutions as coded by Hallerberg, Strauch, and von Hagen (2009). The correlation between the change in the delegation index and country size (measured as size of the population) is −0.25 while the correlation between the contracts index and country size is −0.31. These correlations are in the expected negative direction, but they are low.

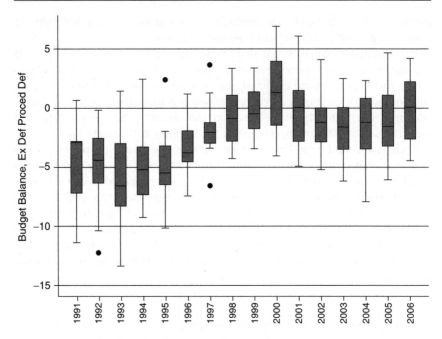

Figure 4.1. Budget balances in the EU-15, 1991–2006
Figures from the Spring 2007 AMECO forecasts.

The second task of this section is to consider how the Stability and Growth Pact has been applied to Member States as well as how frequently states have run 'excessive' deficits. We first examine variation between Commission assessments and Council opinions of the Stability and Convergence Programmes between 1998–9 and 2006–7. We then consider which states received 'excessive' deficit labels. We finish with a comparison of Commission recommendations for explicit action on the part of a Member State and Member State compliance. The states in the study consist of the EU-15 only.

For the assessment, we code contrasts between Commission assessments and Council opinions as falling into one of the following three categories:

- 'No change'—no noteworthy or substantial variation
- 'Weakening'—the Council Opinion places less stringent demands or in general is less critical of a state programme than the Commission assessment
- 'Strengthening'—the Council Opinion has placed more stringent demands or in general is more critical of a state programme than the Commission assessment.

A few words about coding are in order. Statements that are substantively similar yet vary in level of detail are not generally considered significant.[11] Omissions in the Council statement are considered significant if the Commission holds a state to a specific outcome but the Council does not. Treatment of omissions is especially relevant because there is variation in the length and detail in various reports. For instance, Commission assessments are publicly available in extended summary format only prior to the 2003–4 round of updates.[12] If summarized/full-length version comparisons of later years are any guide, the extended summaries capture the significant points. However, we cannot be sure this is true. Finally, we do not record a distinction in the magnitude of weakening or strengthening; if there is a perceived change in one direction or the other, we simply record it as such. Commission and Council documents are recorded as having a weakening or a strengthening (or both) in a given year. Table 4.2 provides examples from each.

Given these provisos, our data-set includes 133 annual Commission and Council reports on member state programmes.[13] There were 42 instances of the Council opinion weakening the Commission assessment. This amounts to ~32 per cent of the observations. There were also seven instances of the Council opinion strengthening the Commission assessment (or about 5 per cent of observations). Especially striking is the clustering of weakened Council reports. The Commission's fight with France and Germany certainly got the most press in autumn 2003, but most states received lighter Council recommendations that year than what the Commission first proposed. Also noteworthy is that at least two states received a weaker report in every year but 2006. The lack of cases of weakening in the most recent year may reflect the steady convergence of text between the Commission and Council reports starting in 2004–5. Indeed, the texts are nearly verbatim in recent years.

There is also notable variation when the numbers are examined by state. Total number of cases of weakening, for instance, varies from a high of five (France and Germany) to a low of zero (Ireland and Spain). Collectively,

[11] For Greece 1998–9, the Commission indicated that 'structural reform is needed in order to improve the efficiency of the Greek economy, particularly in its large public sector'.

The Council's response was: 'The Council welcomes the structural reforms included in the programme which are geared towards the labour market, the social security system and the wider public sector. The Council urges the Greek Government to implement them as scheduled and pursue further the reform effort in order to enhance the potential and efficiency of the Greek economy.' This case was coded 'no significant change'.

[12] The Europa website states that Commission statements are released in full only since the 2003–4 updates. See: http://ec.europa.eu/economy_finance/about/activities/sgp/ca_en.htm.

[13] We drop one observation for Denmark in 2002–03 because the Commission posts the UK assessment in its place on the Europa website. We have been unsuccessful in getting the Commission assessment, but given good fiscal performance of Denmark we would expect 'no change'.

Table 4.2. Example of Commission and Council assessments of stability and convergence programmes

Examples	Country and year	Commission assessment	Council assessment
No change	Italy (2002–3)	8 January 2003: 'Given Italy's high debt, large primary surpluses will be required for many years.'	21 January 2003: (A) 'Given Italy's high debt, primary surpluses on the order of 5% of GDP will have to be maintained for many years.'
Strengthening	The Netherlands (2005–6)	22 February 2006: 'With regard to the sustainability of public finances, The Netherlands appears to be at low risk on grounds of the projected budgetary costs of ageing populations.'	14 March 2006: 'With regard to the sustainability of public finances, The Netherlands appears to be at medium risk on grounds of the projected budgetary costs of ageing populations.'
Weakening	United Kingdom (2004–5)	16 February 2005: (A) 'Deficit projections to 2006/2007 have been revised upward relative to the previous update despite an essentially unchanged macroeconomic outlook, while . . .' (B) Paragraph concerning possibility of crossing 3% deficit rule (see Council cell); (C) 'For 2004/05, evidence of significant progress remains unconfirmed in outturn data and there is a high degree of uncertainty over both expenditures and revenues, leaving the risk noted above of a deficit higher than 3% of GDP.'	8 March 2005: (A) 'Relative to the 2003 update, deficit projections for both this financial year and the next have been revised upwards; beyond . . .' (B) In a paragraph warning of UK's potential to break 3% rule, Council adds the following sentence: 'However, given the decreased volatility of the UK economy in recent years and the cautious approach on the growth assumptions underlying the public finance projections, the risk appears small in the outer years.' (C) 'There is a clear risk that the budgetary outcome could be worse than projected in the programme in the short term.'

France and Germany had nearly 24 per cent of all cases of weakening, despite constituting around 14 per cent of the data-set. If one compares the large states (i.e. 10 votes in the Council most of the period) with the small ones, they had 38 per cent of the 'weakenings' but were 27 per cent of the sample. While this relationship is in the expected direction, the surprise is that many states received lighter comments from the Council. The 'out' states of Denmark, Sweden, and the United Kingdom seemed to be treated like the others; while they constitute 21 per cent of the 'weakenings', they also represent 20 per cent of the cases. Finally, there is no difference between expected delegation and contract states—expected delegation states represent 60 per cent of the sample and have 62 per cent of the 'weakenings'. When it comes to the strengthening of recommendations, the sample here is much smaller: Spain has the highest amount with two, whereas the majority of states have a total of zero.

We next consider instances where the Commission has issued a concrete, unambiguous recommendation to a member-state government, and whether the respective government complied. Our definition of recommendation has several requirements:

- The Commission must make explicit reference to a specific, clearly measurable economic goal to be reached by a particular date. It should, in other words, be an unmistakable tripwire set up by the Commission.[14]

- The Commission must employ language indicating that it expects action on the part of the member-state government. In contrast, instances where the Commission mentions aspects of a state programme and notes that such plans 'are justified' are not considered a recommendation in our study.[15]

- We include instances where the Commission notes Council statements that satisfy the conditions of a strict recommendation.[16]

With a clear definition of what constitutes a recommendation, one can code compliance. Most of the required economic information on annual budget deficits comes from the European Union's online AMECO—'Annual

---

[14] For example, as in the Commission assessment of the French economic programme of 2005–6, in which the Commission recommended that France 'bring the general government deficit below 3 per cent of GDP in 2006'. This qualifies as a recommendation. If the Commission assessment had written 'bring the general government deficit below 3 per cent of GDP as soon as possible' it would not be specific.

[15] For example, 'high government surpluses are justified in view of future expenditure pressures posed by a rapidly ageing population ...' is not considered a recommendation by our strict coding.

[16] For example, for The Netherlands 2004–5, the Commission notes the Council decision that an excessive deficit existed in the country, and further restated the Council's recommendation that the excessive deficit be corrected by 2005 at the latest.

macro-economic database'.[17] For compliance, we code as 'no information' those instances where the Commission has issued a recommendation but state compliance cannot be assessed given the time frame.

Once again, we consider whether EU institutions treat large states differently and/or whether their governments behave differently relative to the rest of the EU member states. We have four predictions:

- The Commission issues fewer recommendations to large member states.

- The Commission should issue recommendations most often to countries currently in excessive deficit. If larger states are being treated differently in the system, we should see large states receiving no/fewer Commission recommendation(s) despite being in excessive deficit.

- We should see larger states complying less often than other member states with the Commission recommendation.

- It is possible that member-state governments in general are under more pressure to comply with Commission recommendations if they have an 'excessive deficit' label. We should therefore see large states complying less often with Commission recommendations despite being in excessive deficit.

The fifth and sixth predictions come from the fiscal governance literature:

- Delegation states have more flexible fiscal policy and do not rely on hard multi-annual fiscal targets found in contract states. They should be more likely to face difficulties avoiding excessive deficits.

- Contract states find European-level recommendations most useful for domestic purposes. They should therefore be more likely to comply with Commission recommendations.

Before examining these hypotheses, some interesting patterns deserve discussion. First, the distribution of Commission recommendations is clearly non-random. There is a statistically significant relationship (χ^2 p-value below 0.05) between the variables for Commission recommendation and state as well as Commission recommendation and year. There is also a statistically significant relationship (χ^2 p-value below 0.001) and high correlation ($r = 0.59$) between a Commission recommendation and excessive deficit. Commission

---

[17] Some codings for compliance are judgement calls concerning what constituted compliance on 'correcting' an excessive deficit by a certain year. We coded positive compliance by a member state if its annual budget deficit fell below 3 per cent of GDP within/by a given period of time mentioned in the Commission recommendation. Thus, it is possible for a country to be coded as complying with a Commission recommendation to correct its excessive deficit by a given year, even though the Council may not yet have abrogated the excessive deficit procedure. This does not affect other codings, however, such as for the variable for whether a country is in excessive deficit. This value is determined by the Council opinion.

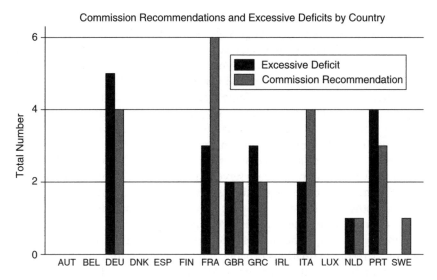

Figure 4.2. Number of years with Commission recommendations and years in excessive deficit by state (1999–2007)

Note: Chart uses United Nations ISO country abbreviations.

recommendations are typically issued to a state when it is undergoing the excessive deficit procedure or in the preceding year. In other words, the Commission only makes concrete suggestions when the reference value has either been violated or is about to be violated.

Moreover, it is when the state is in most trouble, and after it receives a strong Commission recommendation, that it will also get a report weakened in the Council. There is a strongly significant relationship (χ^2 p-value= 0.005) between the existence of a weakening in the Commission assessment by the Council and whether the Commission assessment includes a recommendation. In cases where the Commission assessment included an explicit recommendation, nearly 57 per cent of the time (or 13 of 23) the Council issued an opinion with weakened language.

Going directly to the five hypotheses, there is strong evidence that— contrary to expectations—large states receive a greater share of Commission recommendations. Large states constitute 16 of 23 (nearly 70 per cent) of recommendations despite making up only 27 per cent of the sample. The reason for this pattern is likely behaviour: large states are simply more inclined to have excessive deficits. As Figure 4.2 indicates, all four large states had an excessive deficit at some point, while 7 of 11 small states did not.

There is noteworthy support for hypothesis 2. Large states obtained 8 of the 14 recommendations (about 57 per cent) issued to states in excessive deficit; but they received 7 of the 9 (about 78 per cent) of the recommendations issued to states that were not in excessive deficit. While this outcome seems to support the hypothesis of large state bias in the Commission, it is more likely due to the variation in when states are declared to be in excessive deficit by the Council. Specifically, the strong correlation between the issuance of a Commission recommendation and existence of an excessive deficit weakens noticeably when applied to large states. As Figure 4.2 illustrates, in the majority of large state cases there is a lag between the Commission issuing recommendations and Council declaration. For instance, the Commission issued recommendations to the French government for three years prior to the Council's eventual declaration of excessive deficit. Thus, rather than revealing bias in the Commission, the data serve to illustrate foot-dragging on the part of the Council to declare large states as having excessive deficits.

For hypothesis 3, the evidence suggests that large states are more likely to ignore concrete recommendations. We code compliance as 1 if the member state followed the specific recommendation and 0 if it did not. There are a total of 21 recommendations capable of being assessed for compliance, with 16 of them going to the four largest Member States. In 11 of the 16 cases (about 69 per cent), the large Member State failed to comply, while only in one of the five cases (20 per cent) for small Member States did the given state (Portugal) fail to comply.[18] The divergence in compliance rates persists when restricted to states experiencing an excessive deficit: large states fail to comply in four of nine instances (44 per cent) and small states in zero of five instances.

The numbers for delegation and contract states are even more striking. Six of the seven states with excessive deficits are expected delegation states. The one expected contract state with an excessive deficit, The Netherlands, corrected it the following year.[19] The divergence between delegation and contract states extends to compliance with Commission recommendations. While contract states demonstrated 100 per cent compliance in the two instances such states received recommendations, delegation states complied in only seven of 19 instances (around 37 per cent).

What is surprising is that there are not more concrete Commission recommendations to contract states (only The Netherlands and Sweden get them, and each state only in one year). We anticipated that concrete recommendations from the Commission could prove useful for coalition parties to make explicit necessary trade-offs. Such recommendations, however, may not be necessary. Stability and Convergence Programmes are generally repeating the terms of the domestic fiscal contracts. Moreover, the European level is adding monitoring of the domestic contract. It therefore provides a role that may

[18] The divergence in compliance rates could narrow in the near future if Portugal's fiscal performance does not dramatically improve.

[19] See also Annett's (2006) analysis where he compares the effects of country size and form of fiscal governance in a more sophisticated regression analysis. He finds that form of fiscal governance is a better predictor of fiscal behaviour under the Stability and Growth Pact.

Table 4.3. Strengthening and weakening by year

Year	Weakening	Per cent of total	Strengthening	Per cent of total
1998–9	3	7.1	0	0.0
1999–2000	2	4.8	0	0.0
2000–1	4	9.5	0	0.0
2001–2	8	19.0	0	0.0
2002–3	5	11.9	0	0.0
2003–4	11	26.2	0	0.0
2004–5	5	11.9	3	42.9
2005–6	4	9.5	3	42.9
2006–7	0	0.0	1	14.3
Total	42	100	7	100

improve fiscal discipline, but concrete recommendations outside of a given fiscal contract may not have much effect (Tables 4.3 and 4.4).

Conclusion

This chapter considered the fiscal policy context of EMU. It argued that the effects of the Stability and Growth Pact have been asymmetric. It serves a useful function in fiscal contract states, where it reinforces the domestic fiscal institutions based on fiscal targets. It has no real effect, however, on delegation states. Such states were more likely to have excessive deficits and to ignore explicit Commission recommendations.

This chapter also found that large states were more likely to have excessive deficits and not to comply with explicit Commission recommendations on

Table 4.4. Variations by strengthening and weakening by state

Country	Weakening	Per cent of total	Strengthening	Per cent of total
Austria	3	7.1	1	14.3
Belgium	3	7.1	0	0.0
Denmark	1	2.4	0	0.0
Finland	4	9.5	0	0.0
France	5	11.9	0	0.0
Germany	5	11.9	0	0.0
Greece	4	9.5	0	0.0
Ireland	0	0.0	0	0.0
Italy	2	4.8	1	14.3
Luxembourg	1	2.4	1	14.3
The Netherlands	2	4.8	1	14.3
Portugal	4	9.5	0	0.0
Spain	0	0.0	2	28.6
Sweden	4	9.5	1	14.3
United Kingdom	4	9.5	0	0.0
Total	42	100	7	100

changes. However, this size difference did not have a big impact on the likelihood that the Council weakened Commission recommendations. Most states 'benefited' from weaker Council statements.

At the same time, one should be aware of the relevant yardstick when considering the fiscal performance of EU states. Compared to the period prior to 1999, or the beginning of stage three of EMU, states clearly have tighter fiscal discipline. The reason for this change is to be found in the domestic institutions that the governments had in place, not pressure from the EU per se. If the European level were largely responsible for the improvement, one would expect compliance with European regulations. We find that those regulations matter when they reinforce domestic institutions and not otherwise.

5

The Lisbon Process and Economic Reform: Learning by Benchmarking?

Martin Marcussen

The Three European Reform Discourses

A set of Europe-wide reform discourses underpins the institutions and policies that comprise European economic governance.[1] One major example is the *stabilization discourse* promoting the European stabilization state (Dyson 2002*b*: 251ff). A key element of this discourse is a perceived division of function between the market and the state. By engaging in excessive or misdirected intervention, so the argument goes, state actors risk destabilizing market balances. Therefore, measures should be taken to shelter markets from what is seen to be short-term- and narrow-minded politicians. These measures include de-politicizing key policy areas by establishing autonomous regulatory agencies that help to ensure long-term stability, foster credibility on the financial markets, and guarantee regularity in the private sector's planning environment. Indeed, certain policy areas and functions are entirely privatized. In policy content, this discourse argues for stability-oriented macroeconomic policies based on sound money (low inflation and stable exchange rates), sound finances (budget surplus and low external debt), and sound institutions (independent central banks). Clearly, the German-inspired, ECB-centric EMU project with its convergence criteria, Stability and Growth Pact, and inbuilt asymmetry between monetary and economic policymaking fits well with the overall thrust of the stabilization discourse (see Dyson's Chapter 7 and Chapter 3 by Umbach and Wessels).

[1] For help, encouragement, and inspiration in writing this chapter, the author is extremely grateful to Kenneth Dyson, the members of the Center for Democratic Network Governance at Roskilde University, Denmark as well as Colin Hay.

A second European reform discourse is the compensation or *redistribution discourse*, which promotes the European welfare state as compensation for the costs of economic adjustment (Dyson 2008*a*). Again, the market and the state are seen as two fundamentally different spheres of governance. Contrary to the stabilization discourse, this discourse holds that markets on their own will not help to ensure a desirable level of prosperity and equality in society. They need to be regulated in order to minimize the potential negative consequences of unrestricted competition. As a result, a certain extent of politicization of key policy areas is deemed to be necessary since it cannot be assumed that markets alone provide for optimal policy outputs. Market failures will occur as a result of which political intervention is required to compensate for, and repair externalities. By providing protection, distribution, and growth, policymakers insulate some areas of activity from market forces. In other areas, however, the market is promoted by business regulation (competition rules), by co-opting labour movements into corporatist processes, by reducing barriers to international trade, and by imposing controls on 'speculative' international movements (embedded liberalism). At the European level, some degree of fiscal federalism in the form of cross-regional and cross-sectoral redistribution through structural fund policies resonates well with this redistribution discourse.

A third European reform discourse focuses on competition, innovation, and flexibility. This *innovation discourse* promotes the idea of a European competition state (Cerny 1997). The clear distinction between the state and the market makes less sense in this perspective because the state is seen as the engine and steering mechanism of political globalization and so-called global markets. Markets cannot be conceptualized in isolation from the 'market-maker' state. The state is seen as a complex set of institutions whose functioning can be optimized through planning and innovation. State and market institutions must be complementary to foster innovation, adaptability, and knowledge creation. International competitiveness goes together with, and is conditioned by, institutional competitiveness, which can be achieved through the ongoing optimization of society-wide institutions with a view to delivering public purpose in the broadest sense (Marcussen and Kaspersen 2007). Thus, enterprise, innovation, and profitability are promoted through active political entrepreneurship and institution building and maintenance (Crouch 2005). A central feature of the innovation discourse is that key policy areas and functions are a-politicized. They are simply removed from the contested sphere of politics (Hay 2007). Through a technocratic process of rationalization, knowledge elites are empowered in policymaking. With its ambition of making the EU the most competitive region in the world by 2010, and its inbuilt 'soft' governance mechanisms, including benchmarking, persuasion, and learning, the post-2000 Lisbon process goes well with the idea of a European competition state.

These three main European reform discourses constitute 'meta-frames' that encapsulate and shape institution and polity building in Europe (Radaelli 2003*b*: 19). They help political elites to make sense of problems, opportunities, and priorities in European economic governance. In its own way, each reform discourse promotes (different) 'success' economies as models for emulation and learning. Thus, the stabilization discourse has promoted the German model (the German monetary 'anchor') as the key point of reference; the redistribution discourse has the Swedish welfare state (the 'Northern Light') at the centre; while the innovation discourse promotes various forms of liberal and coordinated competition states such as Ireland (the 'Celtic Tiger'), the Netherlands (the 'Dutch Miracle'), and Denmark (the 'Great Danes'). These different meta-frames and their favourite models may coexist, and sometimes be in contradiction with each other, or they may, as fashions change, replace each other over time.

This chapter is particularly interested in studying the innovation discourse, the reform processes and mechanisms enshrined in this discourse, and the way in which the Lisbon process has unfolded in Europe since 2000. It identifies the innovation strategy enshrined in the original Lisbon process (Lisbon 1); it analyses some of the tensions built into the kind of benchmarking exercise that it employs; and it describes the alternative mechanism for fostering innovation embarked on since 2005, one that emphasizes decentralized innovation processes and 'regulated self-regulation' (Lisbon 2).

Another feature of European economic governance is the number and types of governance mechanisms in use (Scharpf 2001). There are five main regulatory instruments:

The *supra-national/hierarchical mode of governance* involves unilateral imposition by supranational actors such as the ECB (see Chapter 3 by Umbach and Wessels).

The *intergovernmental mode of governance* implies consensus among EU member states' governments, for instance in the operation of the Stability and Growth Pact (see Chapter 4 by Hallerberg and Bridwell).

The *joint decision mode of governance* typically involves some kind of qualified majority voting in the Council of Ministers, as in banking legislation (see Chapter 17 by Macartney and Moran).

Regulatory competition implies mutual adjustment by individual governments, for instance in the area of taxation (see Chapter 19 by Wincott).

Various sorts of EU-induced *learning*.

This chapter focuses on this last category of European governance mechanisms: the Open Method of Coordination (OMC). More specifically, the crucial role of benchmarking in the Lisbon process will be spelled out, with particular attention to some of its problems and inbuilt tensions that may have contributed to the limited success of the Lisbon process so far.[2]

Benchmarking and the Lisbon Process: The Kok Report

Benchmarking was first applied in the private sector at the company level or at the level of an industrial sector as a mechanism to induce innovative change. With the diffusion of 'New Public Management' ideas worldwide, private-sector management and organizational techniques were transferred to the public sector, and benchmarking gained a footing at all levels of public governance. As the innovation discourse took hold among political elites, it seemed logical to introduce comparison and identification of best practices into the public sector as governance mechanisms in their own right.

Benchmarking as an instrument of governance has gained ground across the various areas of European economic governance. It takes many different forms. In the internal market, for instance, the European Commission registers the records of member states in transposing the various directives and publishes the results annually as a league table. This simple implementation score shows which states have been insufficiently efficient in their implementation activity, and which states stand out as the most eager 'transposers'. With regard to EMU, member states aspiring to adopt the euro have to meet a set of nominal convergence criteria. Once part of the Euro Area, they will be evaluated, on a continuous basis, on their ability to respect the criteria enshrined in the Stability and Growth Pact.

Thus, benchmarking as a tool of regulation in European economic governance is neither new nor unprecedented. Following the Amsterdam Intergovernmental Conference in 1997, it came to the fore in the area of employment policy under Article 118 and the subsequent Luxembourg process for the development and implementation of national action plans for employment (today referred to as National Reform Programmes for growth and jobs); in the Cardiff process comparing structural reforms in product and capital markets; and in the Cologne process instituting consultation on macroeconomic policy between the European Central Bank, the social partners, and the European Commission (Arrowsmith, Sisson, and Marginson 2004: 318).

Common to these cases of benchmarking is that the EU has regulatory competence in the affected areas of economic governance and that different degrees of financial and/or legal sanctions are attached to the exercise. In this respect, benchmarking in the Lisbon process is quite different.

---

[2] Clearly, the Lisbon process is not only about soft governance. It is also about developing common standards and providing for regulatory competition, for instance. In that sense, the Lisbon process reflects the complexity that characterizes European economic governance (see Chapter 3 by Umbach and Wessels).

At the Lisbon European Council in March 2000, the presidency conclusions formulated the overall objective of making the EU 'the most competitive and dynamic knowledge-based economy in the world, capable of sustaining economic growth with more and better jobs and greater social cohesion'. This ambitious objective was to be achieved by way of a new form of policy coordination among the member states, the so-called open method of coordination (OMC), which involves policy guidelines for the EU as a whole, with short-, medium-, and long-term goals; quantitative and qualitative indicators for benchmarking national performance against the best in the world; and periodic monitoring, evaluation, and peer review of member states. The consequence was a rolling programme of yearly planning, monitoring, examination, and re-adjustment. It was based on a list of well over 100 indicators in numerous areas of priority action, such as improving employability; developing entrepreneurship; encouraging adaptability in businesses and their employees; and strengthening policies for equal opportunities (Arrowsmith, Sisson, and Marginson 2004: 319). This programme will be referred to as the 'Lisbon 1' process.

The dominant discourse in the OMC presents benchmarking as the ideal application of the principle of subsidiarity. However, the Lisbon Council conclusions were ambiguous. On the one hand, they emphasized that OMC should be conceived as a learning process for all, which should respect national diversity. On the other hand, the conclusions stipulated that the OMC is a means of spreading best practice and of achieving greater convergence (de la Porte, Pochet, and Room 2001: 6). In other words, there seems to be an endemic tension or contradiction at the heart of the process (Radaelli 2003b: 27). The question is whether this 'tension between the recognition of the coexistence of specific national innovation systems and the frequent reference to the need to diffuse "best practice" among member countries' can be reconciled (Lundvall and Tomlinson 2002: 227).

At the Spring 2004 Brussels European Council, EU governments and the European Commission painted a dire picture of results in economic growth, employment, and social cohesion. Though not much had been achieved over the preceding four years, the Presidency conclusions reaffirmed that the process and goals of the Lisbon programme remained valid. However, 'the pace of reform needs to be significantly stepped up'. Consequently, governments appointed the former Dutch Prime Minister, Wim Kok, to head a high-level expert group to come up with suggestions for giving new impetus to the Lisbon strategy.

The Kok Report, *Facing the Challenge*, was presented to the European Commission and the European Council in early November 2004. It held that 'there are no grounds for complacency. Too many targets will be seriously missed. Europe has lost ground to both the United States and Asia and its societies are under strain' (Kok 2004: 11). These disappointing results from the Lisbon 1 process can be explained by an overloaded agenda, poor coordination, and conflicting priorities. As regards the *overloaded agenda*, 'the Lisbon strategy has become too broad to be understood as an interconnected narrative. Lisbon is about everything and thus about nothing. Everybody is responsible and thus no one. The end result of the strategy has sometimes been lost' (Kok 2004: 16). The complexity of the issues at stake seems to be insurmountable. Achievement of the Lisbon ambitions implies action on many different, interdependent levels, involving coordinated action by a variety of actors. In addition, the scale of change needed is enormous. To become the most competitive society in the world by 2010 requires large-scale transformation in Europe on many dimensions and in many sectors.

As regards, the *conflicting priorities*, the report made a direct reference to the operation of the Stability and Growth Pact, which did 'not sufficiently support growth-enhancing macroeconomic policies' (Kok 2004: 10). The Kok Report directly supported the 'flexibilization' of the SGP (Kok 2004: 16). In other words, member states had been busy complying with stability-oriented macroeconomic policy requirements within the EMU framework (the stabilization discourse) rather than actively dealing with growth and competitiveness (the innovation discourse), making it harder to implement the Lisbon strategy.

Finally, *poor coordination* follows from the interdependency between states, levels of administration and sectors, which requires that an immense effort is put into 'top-down' management of the innovation process. This requirement has a direct bearing on the form and use of the OMC, which 'has fallen far short of expectations' (Kok 2004: 42). The Kok Report proposes a radical reformulation of the OMC, simplifying the process of measuring success by replacing the more than a hundred indicators that have been associated with the Lisbon process with a more limited framework of 14 targets and indicators. This simplification aimed to offer the opportunity for the European Commission to improve the working of the instrument of peer pressure. Annually, the Commission should publicly provide updates on these key 14 Lisbon indicators in the format of league tables with rankings 'praising good performance and castigating bad performance—naming, shaming and faming' (Kok 2004: 43).

In short, midway towards the objective of creating the most competitive region in the world by 2010, the Kok Report concluded that the Lisbon 1 process has been disappointing as regards the willingness and ability of the member states to realize the overall objective; that there was a potential clash between two parallel reform discourses—the stabilization discourse and the innovation discourse; and that the criteria applied in the 'soft' benchmarking exercises should be tightened. In line with the practice in the rest of the EMU process, the report recommends fewer and clearer criteria, with harder and more explicit sanctions tied to them. Whereas monetary union and the internal market contain clear 'top-down' benchmarking exercises, the Lisbon process was originally conceived as an alternative benchmarking philosophy that included 'bottom-up' processes of innovation as well as imposing, 'top-down', a uniform model of innovation on the EU member states. The Kok Report attempted to resolve this endemic tension between the two types of benchmarking in favour of the 'top-down' version.

The comprehensive reforms of the Lisbon process proposed by the European Commission in February 2005 largely neglected the Kok Report's emphasis on being tough on poorly performing member states (Commission of the European Communities 2005*b*, 2005*c*). In sharp contrast, the Commission envisions a role for itself, not as a school master and lecturer that names and shames, but rather as a coach and partner that facilitates and advises (ibid. 2005*d*). Its rationale was that structural heterogeneity among EU member states does not call for a 'one-size-fits-all' prescription or model. Rather, it requires flexibility and pragmatism. In addition, in order to be effective, structural reforms necessitate that each individual member state systematically involves all concerned parties in the formulation of regular National Reform Programmes. To work as intended, and not least to be considered as necessary and legitimate, radical reforms need to be 'owned' by the individual member states. This new approach will be referred to as the 'Lisbon 2' process.

The preceding discussion about the formulation, use, midterm evaluation, and reform of the OMC illustrates the central point that it is possible to distinguish between two kinds of benchmarking: one focused on the measurement of output and performance (Lisbon 1); and the other more interested in comparing learning processes (Lisbon 2). According to the first 'output-oriented' form of benchmarking, this particular governance mechanism is first and foremost a tool for improvement, achieved through comparison with other organizations recognized as the best within the area. A model is being selected, and other systems of innovation, partly or entirely, copy elements from this model with a view to catching up. The expected outcome of such an exercise will almost inevitably be increased levels of *institutional convergence* across states and sectors.

On the other hand, the 'learning-oriented' version of benchmarking— 'bench-learning'—holds that the essence of benchmarking is to learn how to improve activities, processes, and management. According to this approach, the overall objective of the benchmarking exercise is not that organizations and states should mirror each other. Rather, the purpose is that each sector- and state-specific production and innovation system is supposed to exploit and develop its unique potentials through transformative processes of learning. 'Bench-learning' may underpin and even accentuate *institutional divergence*.

The Danish, Dutch, and Irish Models of Economic Reform: Uses and Misuses of Benchmarking

'Top-down' benchmarking of the type associated with the Kok Report is more often than not evaluated in sceptical terms. A main point of criticism is that, when we are talking about many, interrelated criteria involving micro-actors and their learning capability, we cannot take much inspiration from previous benchmarking exercises in the EMU and internal market contexts. 'A few simple indicators, imposed top-down as a set of goals to which all are committed, may be appropriate in the monetary field, or for the removal of the remaining barriers to the single market. They are less applicable elsewhere, if policy learning is the goal' (Room 2005: 128). 'Bottom-up' 'bench-learning' offers a more intelligent, if potentially slower, way of progressing in economic reforms by allowing for diversity and flexibility.

Innovation system research has long recognized that 'top-down' bench-marking is associated with a number of problems (Lundvall and Tomlinson 2002). First, the idea that there is *one single practice* that can be referred to as *the* benchmark is valid only under some very specific circumstances. For instance, in recent years, the OECD (2006*a*: 3) has praised the Danish model:

The Danish economy is performing very well, reaping the benefits of 25 years of well-managed economic reform that have produced sound macroeconomic policies, a flexible labour market and a competition-friendly regulatory environment.

In a similar vein, a recent Lisbon Scorecard concludes that Denmark is the 'Hero' in the Lisbon process and that:

Denmark's winning combination of fast growth, high employment and high standards of social security has attracted so much attention that economists across the EU are now debating how to copy 'the Danish model' (Wanlin 2006: 7).

It is not only in Europe that Danish institutional competitiveness ranks high. Over the last couple of years, the World Economic Forum's *Global Competitiveness Index*, the UNCTAD's *Innovation Capability Index*, the World Bank's *Ease of Doing Business Ranking*, The Economist Intelligence Unit's *Business Environment Ranking*, among others, praise the Danish model. Adding up the rankings of these indexes in a so-called meta-ranking we find that, on a global level, Denmark performs second only to the United States.

Although a series of independent league tables place Denmark as *the* success model in Europe on the performance measures listed in the Lisbon strategy, it seems problematic to draw direct lessons from such a benchmarking exercise. If we look at the top of this world ranking, which is constituted by both large and small states, it is clear that there is more than one way to success (see Table 5.1). For instance, to be a role model neither EU nor Euro Area

94

Table 5.1. Meta-ranking—the ultimate beauty contest

Country	The Lisbon league table, 2006	The WEF Growth Competitiveness Index, 2006	The UNCTAD Innovation Capability Index, 2001	The World Bank Ease of Doing Business Ranking, 2006	EIU's Business Environment Ranking, 2005	Average ranking
1. USA	—	6	3	3	3	4
2. Denmark	1	4	4	8	1	4
3. Finland	6	2	2	13	7	6
4. Sweden	2	3	1	14	11	6
5. United Kingdom	4	10	8	9	8	8
6. Norway	—	12	5	5	17	10
7. Switzerland	—	1	13	17	9	10
8. The Netherlands	5	9	10	24	6	11
9. Japan	—	7	11	10	28	14
10. Ireland	7	21	21	11	10	14
11. Germany	10	8	18	19	14	14
12. Belgium	13	20	9	18	12	14
13. Luxembourg	9	22	—	—	—	16
14. Austria	3	17	17	32	20	18
15. France	8	18	16	44	13	20
16. Estonia	16	25	25	16	—	21
17. Spain	21	28	20	30	21	24
18. Lithuania	20	40	29	15	—	26
19. Czech Republic	12	29	36	41	24	28
20. Portugal	18	34	28	42	23	29
21. Latvia	19	36	34	26	—	29
22. Malta	27	39	—	—	—	33
23. Hungary	15	41	32	52	25	33
24. Slovak Rep.	22	37	39	37	30	33
25. Slovenia	11	33	23	63	—	33
26. Cyprus	14	46	43	—	—	34
27. Poland	26	48	31	54	29	38
28. Italy	23	42	27	70	27	38
29. Greece	17	47	30	80	34	42
30. Bulgaria	24	72	38	62	36	46
31. Romania	25	68	47	78	38	51

membership seems to be a sufficient or a necessary requirement. The top-ten is constituted by several states that take part in none of these forms of cooperation (Norway, Switzerland, Japan, United States), and key EU member states that are actually doing quite well in institutional competitiveness are the North-European Euro Area 'outsiders' (Denmark, Sweden, and the United Kingdom). Only three Euro Area 'insiders' make it into the top-ten states (Finland, the Netherlands, and Ireland).

In addition, so-called coordinated (Germany, Japan), negotiated (Denmark, Norway, Sweden, the Netherlands, Switzerland), and liberal (United States, United Kingdom, Ireland) market economies have established an optimal constellation of institutions that fosters competitiveness, innovation, and growth. Also, there are no clear-cut messages about the kinds of state models that are

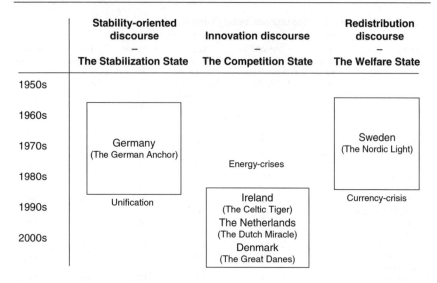

Figure 5.1. European reform discourses

conducive to success. Both federal and unitary, centralized and fragmented, corporatist and pluralist state structures can overcome decision-making traps and institutional gridlocks, make reforms and enhance their institutional competitiveness. In short, the narrow focus on the top of the ranking misses the important lesson that success can be achieved in many different ways.

This finding cautions against an overly naive application of benchmarking. More generally, it points to the danger of applying 'top-down' benchmarking in a *de-contextualized* fashion. It is highly problematic to neglect the local, regional, and national contexts when selecting and introducing new ways of doing things (Lundvall and Tomlinson 2002: 209). By focusing only on the top of the league table, and trying to export exactly that model to other places and contexts, there is a danger that the whole socioeconomic system of institutions and values that define and precondition success is ignored. Economic reform requires 'context-sensitive lesson drawing' (Radaelli 2003b: 42).

A second reason why 'top-down' benchmarking is a doubtful approach for fostering innovation is that *lesson-drawing cannot be politically neutral* (Rose 1993: 22). The political nature of benchmarking is reflected in the fact that the very criteria and standards of success tend to alter as a result of the dominant world view at the time. As discussed earlier in this chapter, European reform discourses are meta-narratives that express ideas whose time has come. The problem is that, studied over a longer period of time, the 'fashionability' of benchmark criteria and targets tends to be a product of the dominant reform discourses (see Figure 5.1). As a consequence, 'some of the [states] characterized as parading "excellence" one year may be treated with disdain the next'

(Lundvall and Tomlinson 2002: 208). Over time, it should not be forgotten that various states have been stressed as models for others to emulate, and then entirely forgotten (Rose 1993: 107–8).

EMU can be said to be directly inspired by the German stability ethos, and it used to be common practice among European policymakers to refer to the 'German anchor' (see Dyson's Chapter 7). In a similar vein, but within the framework of a completely different reform discourse, Sweden, the so-called Nordic Light, seems to have played a large role over a number of decades, exemplifying a particularly interesting welfare state model (Olson 1990). For decades, the Scandinavian model (read: the Swedish model) was central in the study of corporatism. In this respect, no mention was made of Denmark, for the obvious reason that Denmark did not deliver.

During the 1990s, however, a new set of states competed for attention in Europe. Ireland was referred to as the 'Celtic Tiger' (see Chapter 9 by Hay et al.), due to amazing rates of growth, and the Netherlands as the 'Dutch miracle' (see Chapter 11 by Verdun), referring to the successful turn-around of the economy by the end of the 1980s and beginning of the 1990s (Becker and Schwartz 2005). References were also found outside Europe. It appears to have been the concern with global competitiveness that has been an important driver behind initiatives for further market integration in Europe (Room 2005: 117). Negative integration during the 1980s led to the creation of the internal market in an attempt to measure up to the United States and Japan. During the 1990s, positive integration and the establishment of EMU with a world currency also contained a large measure of competition with the United States. Towards the latter part of the same decade, with the United States enjoying sustained economic expansion in the 'new' economy, competitive anxieties in Europe focused increasingly on technological innovation and human investment. These concerns were at the top of the agenda in the Lisbon European Council, March 2000.

Thus, model status in a benchmarking exercise is fundamentally politically defined and depends on the meta-narratives of the time. However, benchmarking is also political in another sense. When establishing criteria and targets used in benchmarking exercises, some criteria are highlighted, whereas others are suppressed. In the Danish case, the evaluation of Danish institutional competitiveness within the framework of the Lisbon process concerns 'innovation' (Internet access, new technologies, patents, R&D spending); 'liberalization' (competition in telecommunications, gas and electricity markets, transport sectors, and financial services); 'legal and financial conditions for SMEs' (start-up environment, regulatory burden, subsidies and state aid); 'employment and social inclusion' (workforce participation, upgrading skills, social protection); and 'sustainable development' (greenhouse gas emission, renewable energy sources, public transportation, ozone emissions, natural resource management).

This set of indicators is already ambitious. Nevertheless, a more complete picture of the relative successes and failures of the Danish model of innovation might include Denmark's high levels of social unrest, measured as working days lost as a result of labour disputes (*The Economist* 29 April 2006: 96). In addition, Denmark is not performing outstandingly in life-expectancy rates (Juel, Bjerregaard, and Madsen 2000), the quality of primary education (Andersen et al. 2001), the comparatively modest amount of foreign direct investment (UNCTAD 2005: 22, 2006), and the number of citizens on early retirement schemes (*Børsen* 16 March 2006). All these indicators have either direct or indirect consequences for the innovative capacity of the Danish model and, consequently, for an overall evaluation of Danish institutional competitiveness.

A one-sided application of benchmarking criteria can make almost all states look favourable in international comparison. This point is also valid with regard to other contemporary competition states that have attracted considerable attention in recent years: Ireland and the Netherlands. Ireland topped A. T. Kearny's and Foreign Policy's globalization index (www.foreignpolicy.com) as the most globalized state in the world. Kenichi Ohmae, an ardent proponent of globalization, held that: 'If I had to pick one country as a harbinger of the coming shift in national economies, it would be Ireland' (cited in Kirby 2004: 208).

During the 1990s, Ireland went through a process of transformation that gained worldwide attention. The state earned its nickname 'Celtic Tiger' as a result of its average GDP growth rate of 7.6 per cent between 1990 and 2001, which was only equalled by states like Singapore and China. Over the same period, more than half a million new workers entered the work force, resulting in a remarkable increase in employment. In addition, unemployment fell from about 15 per cent of the workforce at the beginning of the 1990s to about 4 per cent around 2000. Living standards and private consumption increased and now equal the EU average. At first glance, therefore, Ireland has done what a decade ago seemed to be impossible: it has turned an underdeveloped, peripheral, and poor European developmental state into a modern, high-growth, globalized, competition state.

However, a closer analysis that goes beyond narrow 'top-down' benchmarking reveals a 'sharp contrast between economic success and social failure' (Kirby 2004: 219). Whereas Denmark is an example of a 'coordinated' competition state, Ireland is an example of a neo-liberal competition state that has managed to contain wage development while cutting personal taxation and decreasing public expenditures. A key issue in Ireland's future capacity to innovate is investment in research and education. Figure 5.2 shows that Ireland seems to be lagging far behind the other two model competition states in Europe, Denmark, and the Netherlands, and that the Lisbon target

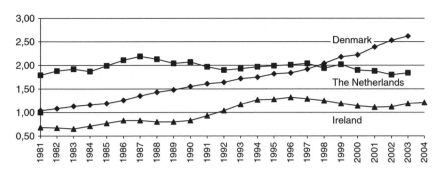

Figure 5.2. Gross domestic expenditures on R&D (as a percentage of GDP)
Data retrieved from OECD (2006*b*).

of 3 per cent of GDP for public and private investment in R&D is far off achievement.

In the continued development of the human resources needed to foster innovation, Ireland, once ahead of the Netherlands in relative terms in 1995 in overall spending on education, seems to have been overtaken by the two other model economies by 2002. It even lags behind its own 1995 level (see Table 5.2).

Finally, the OECD points to the need to upgrade the level of social services in Ireland in order to create social cohesion and health (Figure 5.3). In all three model economies, the amount relative to GDP spent on social services seem to be dropping, partly as a result of the higher employment levels and the lower levels of spending on unemployment benefits. However, the OECD (2005*a*) argues that in Ireland the level of social services does not enable the country to supply the most basic services needed in any comparable welfare state.

In the case of the Netherlands, the 1970s was the era of the 'Dutch disease', characterized by high inflation, public budget deficits, and unemployment. However, the 1980s and the beginning of the 1990s saw a 'Dutch miracle'. By

Table 5.2 Expenditure on educational institutions for all levels of education (as a percentage of GDP)

	1995			2002		
	Public	Private	Total	Public	Private	Total
Denmark	6,1	0,2	6,3	6,8	0,3	7,1
Ireland	4,7	0,5	**5,3**	4,1	0,3	**4,4**
The Netherlands	4,5	0,4	4,9	4,6	0,5	5,1

Data retrieved from OECD (2006*b*).

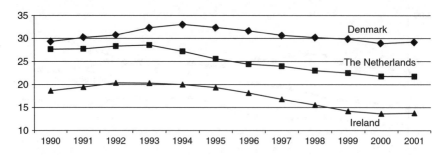

Figure 5.3. Public social expenditure (as a percentage of GDP)
Data retrieved from OECD (2006*b*).

the end of the 1990s, the then Prime Minister Wim Kok reaped the harvest of the 1982 Wassenaar agreement, where the trade unions, chaired by Kok, agreed with the government to moderate their wage claims in exchange for a reduction in working hours. The Netherlands attracted attention from all over Europe for its combination of a currency firmly linked to the D-Mark, wage moderation, low inflation, reduced budget deficits, falling taxes and high social contributions, and huge trade surpluses (Becker and Schwartz 2005). It was hailed as a prime example of the so-called Third Way by the US President Bill Clinton and the UK Prime Minister Tony Blair and emulated by the new SPD-led government of Gerhard Schröder in Germany. Kok travelled the world to spread the word about the so-called Polder model, referring to policymaking by consensus between the government, unions, and employers. The IMF declared that the Netherlands used 'textbook policies' and had gained broad public support to sustain economic growth and to create jobs. The Netherlands had entered a virtuous circle (International Monetary Fund 2000: 4–6).

By 2001, however, economic growth suddenly came to a halt, unemployment rapidly increased to 5 per cent, inflation reappeared, and the volume of exports fell for the first time since 1982. Among the reasons mentioned for the sudden, and for many analysts unpredicted, 'hard' landing of the Dutch economy were an overheated labour market leading to large wage increases and a tumultuous political climate rocking the very basis of consensual decision-making (see Chapter 11 by Verdun). Even during the 1990s, when the Polder Model was characterized as a 'miracle' in various league tables, a closer look at a larger and more varied number of indicators would have presented a more nuanced picture of its vices and virtues (Becker and Schwartz 2005). One example was the Dutch employment rate that kept going up during the 1990s (Figure 5.4). By focusing on that single indicator, one cannot avoid being positively surprised by the capacity of the Dutch economy to integrate newcomers.

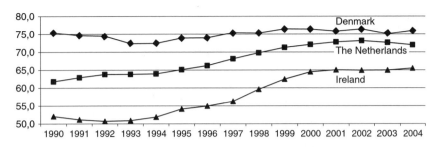

Figure 5.4. Employment rate (share of persons of working age [15 to 64 years] in employment)

Data retrieved from OECD (2006*b*).

However, the reality behind the steep increase in the employment rate offers another picture, which probably would not contribute to placing the Netherlands among the model economies (OECD 2005*b*; Salverda 1998). Employment rates were boosted by employing people in part-time jobs (Figure 5.5). Overall, the Netherlands came close to an OECD record in the low number of hours worked by persons in the labour market (Figure 5.6).

In summary, an analysis of the three European competition states—Denmark, Ireland, and the Netherlands—indicates that the identification of a model through benchmarking is based on politically selected criteria that resonate well with the most dominant reform discourse of the time and that ignore, even within the given meta-frame, a whole set of alternative, potentially relevant indicators.

In addition, 'top-down' benchmarking suffers from the fact that it is *a historical*. League tables take a picture of the state of the economy at a given time. They tend to be blind to performance over a longer period of time. The sustainability of a model does not appear clearly from 'top-down' benchmarking.

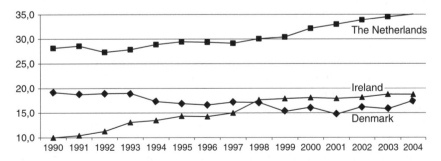

Figure 5.5. Part-time employment rates (as a percentage of total employment)

Data retrieved from OECD (2006*b*).

101

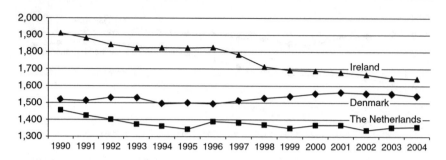

Figure 5.6. Actual hours worked (hours per year per person in employment)
Data retrieved from OECD (2006*b*).

Finally, from an innovation system perspective, 'top-down' benchmarking has been criticized for not promoting learning. Attempts to impose convergence on national innovation systems ignore the fact that *innovation processes always require diversity*. Too much 'top-down' induced copying is problematic for the workings of a system of innovation. If all innovation takes the form of borrowing from other organizations, sectors and states (external inspiration), then the innovating entity has no incentive to develop processes that cultivate reflection, analysis, and research that challenge established wisdom or practices (internal inspiration). The process of copying may itself undermine the dynamic capabilities of the industry, sector or state by simply rendering truly innovative learning processes irrelevant (Lundvall and Tomlinson 2002). Copying will lead either to emulation of best practices abroad or, in the best case, to hybrid structures and processes in the copying state, that is, institutional 'bricolage' (Campbell 2004). But it will never lead to anything entirely new.

In addition, copying seems to be backward-oriented rather than oriented towards the future. When a process of copying is initiated, attention is directed towards the practices and structures of a state that has cultivated its institutional competitiveness under certain conditions. In copying these practices, policy makers may fail to note that, in the model state itself, these practices may already be considered to be antiquated and out of touch with forthcoming challenges. In both Denmark and Finland, for instance, systematic analysis has been undertaken in recent years to embark on so-called second-generation reforms in which various dimensions of globalization play a central role. This new reform debate is the result of a general perception in these states that existing institutions are poorly adapted to a truly globalized world. The paradox is that, while Denmark and Finland are fundamentally transforming their own institutions to maintain a high level of institutional competitiveness, their old institutions are being subject to emulation in the rest of Europe.

Finally, copying induced by 'top-down' benchmarking may result in a damaging lemming-like behaviour among prospective innovators. By blindly following a lodestar, the trend-followers run the risk of being led down an entirely wrong track. As we have seen, very few, if any, model economy has lasted for more than a couple of decades. At some point, model economies top their performance curve and have difficulties in maintaining success rates, either because they simply do not deliver the expected output any-more or because the criteria established to measure success have changed. This pattern has happened before and will recur. If all European economies go in one direction, gradually eradicating their institutional diversity, then there will be no distinct alternative European way to go if, at some point, the selected European model goes down. Therefore, in Europe, institutional diversity should be seen as an innovative potential rather than something that should be eradicated (Lundvall and Tomlinson 2002: 208). In the final section, attention is directed at the alternative form of benchmarking, 'bottom-up' 'bench-learning', which cultivates diversity and regulated self-regulation.

Self-Regulation and Meta-Governance—A Way Forward?

A distinction has been drawn between 'top-down' benchmarking, the most prevalent form of soft governance included in the Lisbon 1 process, and 'bottom-up' benchmarking, which is central to the Lisbon 2 process. A further distinction can be made based on the *type* of challenges handled through soft law: whether societal problems are relatively easy to understand, identify, and diagnose or whether they are more composite phenomena involving a large set of interconnected dimensions that influence one another in multiple ways. This distinction raises the issue of how concretely and narrowly the benchmark criteria can and should be formulated.

The question 'what counts as a success story?' is much more difficult to answer if the problems faced by the EU are complex and badly understood. Under such circumstances, clear quantitative criteria for benchmarking can-not be formulated. If, on the other hand, there is broad consensus about what the problem is, and how we would recognize success when we see it, it is much easier to formulate quantitative criteria as measures of success.

A further distinction can be made based on the *level* on which reforms need to be implemented with a view to achieving success. Some reform processes require that a number of comprehensive decisions need to be made at the cen-tral level of government. The classical decision-making structures are activated in the benchmarking exercise, and central authorities interact on the basis of prescribed procedures. Other reform processes, however, are dependent on the voluntary contributions of multiple change entrepreneurs. Whereas the first form of reform processes relies on existing bureaucratic structures and

Table 5.3. Benchmarking in European economic governance

	Straightforward problems and solutions and clear criteria for success (*e.g. High inflation is the problem and low inflation is an indication of success*)	Complex problems and solutions and unclear criteria for success (*e.g. The problem is that the EU is lacking behind USA. If the EU can become the most competitive region in the world by 2010 it will be a seen as a success story*)
Central decision-makers with will and legitimacy to make decisions need to be involved (*e.g. Central bankers, ministers and parliamentarians*)	Simple dirigisme: Top-down bench-marking by setting quantitative targets and imposing sanctions (*e.g. Stability and Growth Pact—this kind of bench-marking comes close to the suggestions made in the Kok Report*)	Complex *dirigisme*: Top-down bench-marking by enthusing convergence around politically selected success models (*e.g. Lisbon 1, 2000–5*)
Independent, society-level actors with skills and capacity to engage in self-governance need to be involved (*e.g. Scientists, SMEs, trade unions, and finance*)	Simple voluntarism: Bottom-up bench-marking by providing criteria for receiving public goods (*e.g. Applying for structural funds, research funds, etc.*)	Complex voluntarism: Bottom-up bench-marking by providing a framework for learning and fostering a sense of ownership, and by acting as facilitator and idea-generator (meta-governance) (*e.g. Lisbon 2, 2005*)

procedures, the second kind relies on self-governance and initiatives at the level of society. Combined, these two distinctions give rise to four types of benchmarking (Table 5.3).

In the first quadrant—'simple *dirigisme*'—the procedures related to the Stability and Growth Pact exemplify 'top-down' benchmarking, which is premised on the idea that it is easy to distinguish success from failure, and that it is easy to make a limited group of individuals accountable for the reform processes. As we have seen, the Kok Report recommended that similar kinds of premises should be applied in the Lisbon process. A speed up in reform processes required more centralized coordination, a reduction and clarification of the number of indicators and, in general, more 'top-down' control.

In the second quadrant—'complex *dirigisme*'—the problems faced and the goals established by EU decision-makers are very complex. The number of measures of reform progress are numerous and difficult to quantify. Nevertheless, in Lisbon 1, an attempt was made to do so. Protracted reporting procedures were organized, systematic comparisons and scorecards were established, and laggards and leaders were nominated.

Both kinds of 'top-down', *dirigiste* benchmarking exercises would, if successful, induce increasing institutional convergence in Europe. An explicit success criterion for the EMU is that inflation rates have come down to the same low level all over the Euro Area. Some institutional convergence would also result from the Lisbon 1 process because it was explicitly constructed to foster institutional emulation across borders.

In the third quadrant—'simple voluntarism'—problems are well understood. In this case, however, successful implementation of a programme needs an active and continuous contribution from civil society. To exemplify, the EU would have no structural policy to talk of if nobody cared to apply for Structural Fund money. To make a successful application for this funding, a certain set of criteria (partnership and additionality, for instance) needs to be observed. This does not mean, however, that all Structural Fund projects respecting these criteria are similar in shape, form, and purpose. On the contrary, the criteria allow for a very large extent of institutional divergence, although the procedural requirements are the same for all applicants.

The last quadrant—'complex voluntarism'—covers cases where the challenges faced by the EU are enormous and involve a very large and diverse set of actors. It corresponds to the benchmarking model suggested by the European Commission and endorsed by the European Council for the revised Lisbon 2 strategy. The assumption is that innovation requires complexity, diversity, and uncertainty and that management cannot be imposed from above. Innovation requires the involvement and participation of change agents such as the social partners, private entrepreneurs, and scientists as well as national governments. Lisbon 2 seems to acknowledge that Lisbon 1 has suffered from government failure as a consequence of the 'ungovernability' of European micro-processes of innovation (Mayntz 1993). An alternative route for the Lisbon process recognizes that innovation processes cannot possibly be governed hierarchically from above. In contrast, in order to enhance the 'governability' of society, the European Commission's role is to facilitate the work of self-regulating innovation networks.

Consequently, the movement from hierarchical government to network governance does not mean that the EU abdicates its role; its role is to promote 'self-regulation in the shadow of hierarchy' (Scharpf 1994), 'meta-governed reflexive self-organization' (Jessop 1998), 'organized decentralization' (Traxler 1995), or 'space sharing' (Crouch 1993). Just as government as well as market failures occur, so governance failures occur. These failures leave an open space to be filled by the EU. Since 'bottom-up' benchmarking associated with Lisbon 2 consists in providing a framework for learning, and in acting as facilitator and idea-generator promoting true innovation, the role of the EU will not, as suggested by Kok and his expert group, be substantial coordination and control (simple *dirigisme*). It will consist of 'meta-governance' (regulated self-regulation) that upholds the conditions under which change entrepreneurs can interact with relative autonomy ('complex voluntarism').

Following this model for promoting economic reform, the EU provides and guarantees the legal framework for self-regulation. It establishes the ground rules for network governance, that is, a regulatory order in and through which change entrepreneurs can pursue their aims. In this sense, the EU keeps decentralized innovation processes on track by providing a 'shadow of hierarchy' (Scharpf 1994: 40). The EU can establish criteria for deciding who can take part in network governance, and it can re-balance power asymmetries in governance networks by strengthening weaker forces in the interests of social cohesion. The EU can also provide the framework and physical infrastructure for ongoing dialogue and coordination between change entrepreneurs and between sector- and state-specific innovation systems. The EU can act as a 'meta-governor' by injecting knowledge and information into innovation processes in governance networks. In addition, it can handle disputes arising in the process of innovating.

Lisbon has been a learning process from which emerges the notion of the EU as an *organizing state* that is less keen on running things 'from above' through 'top-down' benchmarking and more interested in enabling and monitoring self-regulation. This role is consistent with the complex world of European governance of economic reforms in which the pursuit of innovation is dependent on mobilizing various kinds of resources among private change entrepreneurs and in which decentralized innovation processes need to be monitored with a view to serving the larger public.

Conclusions

Economic reforms are undertaken everywhere in Europe, and at all levels of governance. Some of these reforms are induced by the EMU process, particularly in meeting the convergence criteria for euro entry; others result from member states trying to upgrade their institutional competitiveness in the wake of globalization. But hitherto few of these reforms directly emanate from the Lisbon process. As a result of this flawed relationship between the Lisbon process and European innovation, European Council conclusions and Commission white papers and programmes have in more recent years put new impetus on economic growth, employment and social cohesion 'from below'.

This chapter argues that, contrary to the fiscal and monetary policy reforms that were undertaken as part of the EMU process, the micro-processes associated with fostering innovation require a different role for EU institutions in European economic governance: one as a 'meta-governor' or 'organizer state'. This role implies that, in fostering innovation, classical hands-on, 'top-down' governance is being replaced by 'encouraging hand-shakes'. Emphasis is put on the provision of a framework that supports, consolidates, and coordinates interaction between autonomous change entrepreneurs in self-regulating governance networks that transcend sectors and borders. 'Meta-governance' also implies that a large measure of institutional diversity is not only accepted but also encouraged in European economic governance. 'Bottom-up' processes of innovation thrive on the border between order and anarchy and lead in all sorts of directions, exploiting existing institutional capabilities as well as developing entirely new institutions. At the same time, self-regulation may fail to occur or to deliver. It may also have normative implications as a result of the exclusion or inclusion of certain concerned parties. Hence, the EU role of a 'meta-governor' is one of monitoring and embedding decentralized innovation processes. Whether it will work remains to be seen.

Part II

Domestic Political and Policy Contexts in Euro Area Member States

6

France: The Political Management of Paradoxical Interests

David Howarth

French participation in the Euro Area is to be seen principally as a *self-imposed* 'semi-sovereignty game'. From the creation of the European Monetary System (EMS) in 1979, French political leaders have seen a European monetary constraint as a tool to reinforce domestic economic restructuring. In this sense, President François Mitterrand's March 1983 decision to keep the franc in the Exchange Rate Mechanism (ERM) represented the final decision to end socialist reflation, embrace market integration in the EC, and conform largely to the German economic standard.

Yet the French pursuit of Economic and Monetary Union (EMU), and the policies of various French governments on EMU reform since the signing of the Maastricht Treaty in December 1991, must also be seen in terms of loosening the external constraint on French monetary and fiscal policies. The tightness of this constraint was blamed for a serious decline in French economic output and rise in French unemployment, particularly in the period following German reunification in 1990. The operation of the EMS resulted in French policymakers having to follow German monetary and fiscal policies or risk speculation against the franc. EMU was thus supported because it eliminated both the need to follow German monetary policy and speculative pressures against the currency.

The fiscal policy constraints of the convergence criteria of the Maastricht Treaty and the Stability and Growth Pact (Stability Pact) have still allowed considerable government margin of manoeuvre, which has been used by French governments struggling with low economic growth since 2001. At the same time, the return to relatively high real interest rates in France—albeit still far below those under the ERM—undermines the claim that the move to EMU would result in a more accommodating monetary policy than under the EMS. It thus appears that France suffers from its position as one of the lowest inflation states in the Euro Area: in third place below only the Netherlands and Finland in the first half of 2007 and, at 1.4 per cent, significantly below the Euro Area average of 1.8.

The first section of this chapter briefly explores the context and initial conditions of EMU in France. The pursuit of low inflation through the external constraint of the EMS and then EMU reflected real economic needs linked to developments in French capitalism and notably financial market liberalization. The discursive/ideological structure underpinning and shaping the impact of EMU involved a dialect between a conservative liberalism—in the ascendant given the economic constraints reinforced by monetary integration—and a rearguard interventionism that is bolstered by widespread public hostility to economic liberalism and globalization. The decision to embrace EMU should furthermore be seen in terms of French strategy to increase monetary policymaking power in relation to both the Germans and the Americans (Howarth 2001), though this is of limited significance to the politics of EMU in post-1999 France.

The following sections examine substantive reforms to, respectively, the French polity, politics, and policies in terms both of this domestic dialectic between conservative liberalism and interventionism and of Europeanization. EMU embodies a paradox for French policymakers. The project can be seen in terms of meeting long-standing French macroeconomic goals of achieving competitiveness through disinflation, the elimination of the German-centred EMS, and sheltering France from speculative pressures. Yet EMU also involves an institutional framework and rules that ostensibly decrease policymaking margin of manoeuvre. The third and fourth sections are, in effect, studies of the French political management of this paradox.

Context: Reforming French Capitalism and Competitiveness as Legitimating Formula

The Decline of French State-led Capitalism and EMU

French interest in monetary integration was reinforced by the perceived need to reform French capitalism—thus 'bottom-up' Europeanization. The operation of the EMS and the move to EMU reinforced processes of liberalization, privatization, and budgetary restraint in France, developments that contributed to the decline of the state-led model of capitalism. Initially, President Valery Giscard d'Estaing saw in the EMS a mechanism to contain the inherently inflationary effects of the *circuits de trésor* system, in which French businesses depended principally upon state-allocated credit. Subsequently, the deflationary effects of the EMS supported the drive to reform the 'overdraft' economy (Loriaux 1991; Mamou 1987) through financial market liberalization started in 1984 by Pierre Bérégovoy as Minister of Finance with the creation of the MATIF (the French futures market). Financial market liberalization was encouraged by EMS membership—the search for non-inflationary sources of finance. Liberalization also reinforced continued EMS membership because it increased the need for monetary stability to attract foreign capital. The challenge of controlling inflation also provided a useful logic that helped overcome the institutionally rooted reluctance to accept financial liberalization in the powerful Treasury division of the Ministry of Finance, which had blocked previous reform attempts (Loriaux 1991).

Financial market liberalization in turn reinforced the ERM constraint and increased the logic of moving to EMU. The limited development of French institutional investors resulted in the rapid growth of French dependence on foreign-held—largely American-held—debt, which amounted to roughly 40 per cent of total debt by the early 1990s, far higher than any of the larger EU member states. In consequence, French governments had to be particularly cautious about the perceived strength of the franc and attractiveness of French interest rates (Reland 1998). Liberalization created new controlling interests—American pension funds, which increased the importance of shareholder value and discouraged interventionist strategies that were inconsistent with this value. Increased reliance on foreign capital reinforced the interest of the large-scale (principally CAC-40) business constituency in the 'sound money' goals of the EMS and EMU. Foreign capital needs and the desire to build Paris as a financial centre also undermined the economic logic underpinning French capital controls. In consequence, France had less to lose from capital liberalization, which the German government had established as a precondition for discussions on EMU.

The pursuit of low inflation in France—principally to achieve national competitive advantage—has also been closely connected to support for monetary integration. The apparent success of the policy of 'competitive disinflation'—measured in terms of the record French trade surplus during the second half of the 1990s and impressive productivity gains in many French companies—helped bolster support for EMU amongst policymakers, despite the perceived price of high unemployment and slower economic growth. Support has been potentially undermined by the return to French commercial and current account deficits from 2003 (24 billion euros in 2005, a level not attained since 1982), combined with several years of poor economic growth below the Euro Area average and well below the EU-25 average, and persistently high levels of unemployment hovering just below the 10 per cent figure.

Reinforcing the Conservative Liberal Agenda

The French politics of EMU is shaped by the dialectic between 'conservative liberalism' in the ideological ascendance and a rearguard interventionism, supported by French public opinion. Conservative liberalism is a label—albeit one never used explicitly in France—that describes the dominant economic ideology in the Treasury division of the Ministry of Finance, the Bank of France, and the Financial Inspectorate, the *grand corps* that forms the leading part of the French financial administrative elite. The influence of this ideological framework has always been limited by its fragmentation and weakness in French party politics (Dyson, Featherstone, and Michaelopoulos 1994: 35; Hazareesingh 1994). The creation of the EMS in 1979 corresponded to the hitherto rare predominance of conservative liberalism in government under President Giscard d'Estaing and Prime Minister Raymond Barre.

Conservative liberalism was inspired more by the German model of low inflationary economic growth than Anglo-American liberalism (Dyson 1994; McNamara 1998). Neo-liberalism has few adherents in either political or policymaking circles in France. Anglo-American economic arguments opposed to both the EMS and the EMU project had little presence in national debates on monetary integration (Rosa 1998), even if many of the economic reforms adopted since the 1980s that have been linked to European monetary commitments, such as privatization, can be described as neo-liberal.

Conservative liberals uphold the self-adjusting nature of market mechanisms and reject state-led reflation. They also seek exchange-rate stability, low inflation, balanced budgets, and current account surpluses—none of which are liberal economic goals per se. Conservative liberals embraced the EMS and EMU as useful means to import German 'sound' money policies and budget and wage discipline. Core conservative liberal economic ideas formed the bedrock of 'competitive disinflation', the major French macroeconomic policy from the mid-1980s (Fitoussi 1992, 1995). The value of 'sound' money was linked to the idea that the weakening competitive position of French exports was due to structural problems that could not be resolved through competitive devaluations. Conservative liberals also respect technical expertise in economic policy and the maintenance of a measure of autonomy from political interference in the formulation and implementation of economic policy—which serves the interests of the Treasury and the Bank of France. EMU reinforced conservative liberalism through the convergence criteria and the transfer of monetary policy to technocratic control in the Bank of France and the ECB.

In decline since the 1960s with the opening of the French economy to international markets, *dirigiste* strategies have been restricted in the context of the operation of the EMS and the EMU project. *Dirigisme* reflects a strong mistrust of market mechanisms, the economic utility of which is nonetheless accepted. It insists on the need for active state intervention in the economy, labelled *volontarisme*. *Dirigisme* has influenced a wide spectrum of French political and public opinion to different degrees, notably the Gaullist/neo-Gaullist parties on the Right, the Socialist Party on the Left, in addition to the elite technical corps of the French state. Politicians that are widely labelled as liberal frequently pursue interventionist strategies. Giscard and Barre nationalized steel companies and sought to avoid financial market liberalization by prolonging the existing credit system by making it less inflationary (Loriaux 1991). *Dirigistes* tend to prefer the conservative liberal goals of a strong currency, monetary stability, and a trade surplus, although normally for different reasons. These goals are secondary to state-led economic growth. *Dirigistes* also seek to place constraints on the operation of international financial markets and speculative capital.

In the 1980s and 1990s, both the neo-Gaullists and the Socialists rejected many elements of *dirigisme*. At the same time, electoral constraints—the public sanctioning of perceived excessive liberalism and expectation of robust state interventionism—forced both parties to continue to emphasize state-led action. There have been active government responses to the challenges of 'modernization' in industrial, social, and employment policies. The idea of regulating and controlling markets in the context of what Prime Minister Lionel Jospin (1999) labelled a 'modern socialism' was an important element of Socialist Party discourse in dealing with the constraints of globalization and Europeanization (Cambadélis 1999; Marian 1999). Even conservative liberals like Edouard Balladur, Edmond Alphandéry, and Alain Juppé have made a spirited defence of French public services against European competition rules. Since 2002, centre-Right Gaullist (UMP) governments intervened in a range of areas, under the banner of 'economic patriotism', blocking foreign takeovers of French companies, insisting on the need to restrict foreign ownership in a range of economic sectors, providing state subsidies illegal under EU competition rules, and foot-dragging on the privatization of state-owned gas and electricity firms and the liberalization of the energy sector required by EU-level agreements.

EMU and French State Reform

Adjusting to Independent Monetary Authority

In polity reform, the EMU project functioned as 'top-down' Europeanization. Its role as an independent variable was seen in the imposition of central bank independence, sought by few French policymakers and politicians, and opposed by many. Compared with other central banks, the Bank of France was normally considered to be one of the more 'dependent', with monetary power concentrated in the Finance Ministry (Goodman 1992). Efforts to increase central bank autonomy were blocked. The conservative liberal admiration of the 'German model' did not necessarily extend to support for central bank independence (Howarth 2001). The rapid move to independence in

1994—the start of Stage Two of EMU—was justified in terms of building confidence in the franc in the context of vulnerability to record levels of speculation, revealed in the French-centred ERM crisis of 1993, and of the possibility of a rapid move to Stage Three, not the desirability of independence per se.

From 1994, the Bank of France accommodated itself to a more active and public role in promoting a 'stability' culture in France. Jean-Claude Trichet, the first governor of the independent Bank of France, made several thinly veiled attacks on presidential and government economic and monetary policy statements and economic policy decisions that appeared to menace the pursuit of 'sound' money policies, the move to EMU, and respect for the Stability Pact (Aeschimann and Riché 1996; Milesi 1998). This very public role of the Bank was short-lived. Since the start of EMU's Stage Three, there has been a significant cut in the Bank's staff total and closure of two-thirds of its branches in France. In 2006, its Monetary Policy Committee was replaced by the smaller Monetary Council. However, the Bank has also developed or been assigned new roles (Howarth 2008). The Bank has slowly strengthened its position as an independent source of economic expertise—although its research capacity still lags behind other large central banks in the Euro Area. The bank has also been given an important new role in banking supervision which it shares with the Treasury and other bodies. The Governor of the Bank of France chairs the Banking Commission and is one of six voting members, while the Bank of France provides the Commission's General Secretariat with most of its staff members and resources. The Bank also shares with the Treasury a role monitoring competition in the financial sector and regulating credit institutions and investment firms. Efforts by supportive politicians and elements of the administration to extend to the Bank complete control over banking supervision and competition in the financial sector—and thus eliminating direct Treasury influence—have not yet been successful.

As an independent variable, EMU was a catalyst for several reforms directly affecting the powers of the Treasury. The Treasury's loss of control over monetary policy contributed to the further decline in its power caused by financial market liberalization, privatization, and the imposition of European competition rules. Yet, the influence of the Treasury in the context of domestic policymaking increased, consequent on reinforced EU-level surveillance of fiscal policies, the medium-term stabilization plans required by the Stability Pact, and the Lisbon process, which largely corresponded to conservative liberal reform priorities. With persistently high French public spending deficits, and the repeated failure to meet medium-term targets, the Ministry of Finance plays the central galvanizing role in governments' efforts to contain state spending. It leads, for example, the annual conference on the national budget that was launched in 2005 by Thierry Breton, the minister of finance.

The French Politics of EMU

We can apply Radaelli's (2000) analytical framework which examines Europeanization in terms of the scope of domestic change by reference to the concepts of transformation, accommodation, absorption, retrenchment ('negative' change), and inertia (resistance) (also Cowles, Caporaso, and Risse 2001; Héritier and Knill 2001). The possibility of retrenchment was strongest between 1992 and 1996, when record high real interest rates, sluggish economic growth, and rising unemployment, combined with republican and nationalist opposition to EMU, made the government's support for EMU problematic (Howarth 2001). Yet public opposition at that time was due principally to the perceived negative economic implications of EMS asymmetry and the EMU convergence criteria. Polls showed that a majority of French voters supported the core elements of EMU (Figure 6.1), and, unlike in some states, the mainstream French press was on the whole supportive of EMU (Balleix-Banerjee 1999). The normally acquiescent business community began to turn against the ERM constraint from 1992, although the leading peak association of large-scale companies—the *Conseil national du patronat français* (CNPF), renamed from 1998 the *Mouvement des enterprises de France* (MEDEF)—continued to support EMU (Aeschimann and Riché 1996).

Both the centre-Left and centre-Right were significantly divided over the desirability of the EMU project, and all French political parties sought to manipulate frustrations with EMU-linked constraints against opponents. No party collapsed over the issue of monetary integration, despite the strong opposition of Euro-sceptics in the Gaullist Rally for the Republic (RPR), including the large majority of the party's National Assembly deputies and leading members Philippe Séguin and Charles Pasqua. The surprise election victory of the 'Plural' Left in 1997 created the threat of retrenchment, but the promises of creating a more 'social euro' and an end to budget cutting proved to be only temporary. Since the start of EMU's Stage Three, opposition to EMU in the Socialist Left and the Gaullist Right dwindled to the extent that no leading members call for French withdrawal. Rather, frequent criticism has instead been directed at the design of EMU and ECB monetary policies (discussed below). The Socialist Party has justified its support for EMU along similar lines to its defence of the Single Market Programme from the mid-1980s: as a mechanism to make the economy more competitive, while preserving the relatively generous French social security system and working conditions (*les acquis sociaux*).

The EMU constraint was manipulated explicitly by the candidates and parties in the 1995 presidential and 1997 legislative elections. During the 2002 presidential and legislative election campaigns, the principal economic policy differences between Jacques Chirac and Jospin and between the UMP and Socialist Party camps related to tax and the European constraint (Howarth

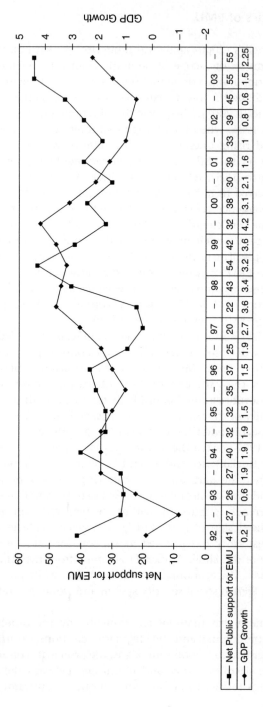

	92	–	93	–	94	–	95	–	96	–	97	–	98	–	99	–	00	–	01	–	02	–	03	–
Net Public support for EMU	41	27	26	27	40	32	32	35	37	25	20	22	43	54	42	32	38	30	39	33	39	45	55	55
GDP Growth	0.2	–1	0.6	1.9	1.9	1.9	1.5	1	1.5	1.9	2.7	3.6	3.4	3.2	3.6	4.2	3.1	2.1	1.6	1	0.8	0.6	1.5	2.25

Figure 6.1. French public support for EMU and GDP growth

Public support for EMU figures from Eurobarometer polls; GDP growth figures from the OECD.

2004). On the one hand, Chirac and the UMP played the more traditional tune of the Right, promising significant cuts in taxes on income (a third in the life of the next government and 5 per cent immediately), corporate (to the EU average), and value-added taxes (on CDs and the hotel sector). On the European constraint, Chirac and the UMP took a more ambiguous line: accepting the need for budgetary restraint and accepting the desirability of the goal of balanced budgets, while refusing to commit to the balanced budget goal of 2004, to which the Jospin Government had agreed. There was a marked element of rebellion in Chirac's policy: challenging the constraints of the Stability Pact if these constraints made the fulfillment of his promises on tax cuts and government spending unrealistic. On the other hand—and this was the most significant irony of the 2002 campaign—Jospin and the Socialists found themselves in the completely reverse position from where they had been in the spring of 1997: defending the constraining rules of EMU and the Stability Pact and presenting themselves as more financially responsible than the conservative opposition.

Between 1994 and the start of EMU's Stage Three, French government and opposition leaders regularly used the Bank of France and notably its governor, Trichet, as scapegoats. Once independent, the Bank was blamed for the high interest rates needed to keep the franc in the EMS. With the transfer of monetary policy to the ECB, the target of scapegoating shifted. Since the start of the economic down-turn in 2001, French political leaders—including Presidents Chirac and Nicolas Sarkozy—engaged actively in attacking the ECB for being excessively hawkish in its singular pursuit of low inflation and challenged both the goals and independence of the bank. Sarkozy—as finance minister, UMP presidential candidate, and then President—regularly criticized the ECB's monetary policy, calling for it to adopt a US Federal Reserve-style target that includes economic growth (*Financial Times*, 11 June 2004; *Le Monde*, 23 February 2007). Several leading French politicians—including Chirac, Sarkozy, Prime Minister Dominique de Villepin (2004–7) under Chirac, and Ségolène Royal, the Socialist Party's candidate in the 2007 presidential elections—also made both veiled and direct attacks on the ECB's goal-setting independence (e.g. *Le Monde* 9, 19, and 22 December 2006).

An Ambiguous Public and the Euro

French public opinion on EMU and the EU fluctuated markedly over the past 15 years with virtually no correlation to levels of economic growth (a standard correlation of 0.073) (Figure 6.1). Broadly negative political discourse on the institutional framework of EMU and ECB monetary policy—the most consistently negative in any Euro Area member state—must contribute to negative perceptions. Yet, French support for EMU has also been amongst the highest in the Euro Area—with France consistently placed in fifth place in

Eurobarometer polls in terms of net support ('Is the euro globally positive for one's country?') and only Luxembourg, Belgium, Italy, and the Netherlands higher. Net support since 1999 was, on average, higher than support prior to Stage Three and the percentage of those in favour of the euro averaged at just below 73 per cent.

Despite these findings, there are indications that the persistently mediocre levels of economic growth from 2001 contributed to rising public concern about the impact of EMU. Responses to specific polling questions demonstrate more nuanced public opinion. In December 2003, a Sofres poll conducted for the centre-Left magazine, *le Nouvel Observateur* (no. 2044, 8 January 2004) showed that a growing minority (over 40 per cent) were of the opinion that the introduction of the euro 'was a bad thing' for France. Moreover, according to this poll, 45 and 50 per cent believed that the euro had a negative effect on, respectively, the economy and employment, while 56 per cent felt that the euro had a negative effect on their own personal situation. Only 1 per cent thought that the euro was advantageous to French citizens versus 52 per cent who thought that the financial markets were the main beneficiaries. A September 2006 Gallup Poll for the European Commission recorded that only 51 per cent found the euro to be 'broadly advantageous' with 30.9 per cent saying that the inconveniences outweighed the gains (Gallup for the European Commission, *Le Monde*, 30 December 2006). However, in late 2006, two polls recorded majorities (52 per cent) of the opinion that the introduction of the euro 'was a bad thing' for 'France, economic growth, employment and them' (TNS Sofres, *Le Monde* 26 December 2006), with only 46 per cent finding it to 'be a good thing'. The results follow four years of poor economic growth, suggesting that the legitimacy of the EMU is linked to its perceived economic output. Curiously, these findings run counter to the Eurobarometer polling that indicate consistently high public support for EMU. Poorer socio-economic categories were particularly negative on the impact of the euro.

Policy Regime Reform

Policy regime reform represents principally 'bottom-up' Europeanization, in that the EMS and EMU operated as intervening variables shaping the operation of the French state and French policies to achieve economic 'modernization' (Alphandéry 2000; Boissonnat 1998). Prior to 1999, successive governments used the EMS constraint and the EMU project to justify a range of reforms: budgetary, welfare-state, administrative, labour-market, and privatization. Yet, the extent to which EMU has itself brought about 'transformation' in France—as argued by Schmidt (2002*b*)—should be qualified. The 'transformation' disguises developments that worked to increase government margin of manoeuvre rather than decrease it. Rather

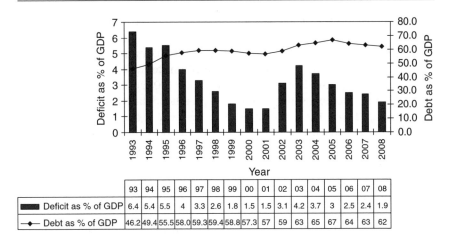

Figure 6.2. French public deficit and debt

Source: INSEE, http://www.insee.fr/fr/indicateur/cnat_annu/base_2000/secteurs_inst/xls/t_3341.xls; accessed 2 July 2007.

than restricting the macroeconomic framework in which French governments must operate, EMU in some respects decreased constraints on French governments.

There is greater margin of manoeuvre in fiscal (and other macroeconomic policies) despite (or even because of) the Stability and Growth Pact. As EMU removes the possibility of speculation against national currencies, greater deficits are less problematic in the short-term for governments in the management of their macroeconomic policies as they are effectively sheltered by the single currency. The Pact—created ostensibly to restrain the spending of profligate governments—in fact increased adjustment time for governments. The clearest manifestation of this margin of maneouvre is the persistently high French public sector deficits since the start of EMU (well above the pre-1992 average) and the rise of public debt to record levels (Figure 6.2). When respecting the Maastricht Treaty's fiscal policy rules became politically difficult from 1993, French governments tried to relax their application to determine EMU entry. They then opposed automaticity in Stability Pact sanctions and a very tough definition of exception from sanctions sought by the Kohl Government (Heipertz and Verdun 2004; Milesi 1998).

After the start of EMU's Stage Three, it became possible to flout and then change the rules (with the March 2005 Stability Pact reform) to ensure continued margin of manoeuvre. Since the creation of the Stability Pact in 1997, no French governments respected the medium-term target of a budget that is balanced or in surplus. Thus, 'transformation' in the realm of monetary policy has, at best, allowed for 'accommodation' and 'absorption' in fiscal and macroeconomic policies and at worse 'retrenchment'—higher budget deficits and debt load—and 'inertia'—failure to engage in structural reform.

The most politically difficult feature of the EMU project for French governments was respecting the short and medium-term fiscal policy goals of the Pact. In 2005, the European Commission (2005*b*) placed France in the category of EU member states with unsustainable public finances. Prior to the start of Stage Three, the justification of budget cutting by both conservative and Left-wing governments involved a reinvention of discourse appealing to the preoccupation with unemployment: a lower deficit could result in lower taxes which would result in job creation. For the Left, this reinvention was particularly challenging, with Finance Minister Dominique Strauss Kahn announcing that there was nothing 'Socialist' about public spending deficits.

When politically convenient, French governments deliberately sought to link policy reform to the pressures created by EMU. This connection was made most prominently in the 1994 Minc Report, *La France de l'an 2000*, one of the most comprehensive packages of public-sector reform recommendations in the history of the French Fifth Republic. EMU as a justification for reform was the central message of Chirac's public U-turn on economic policy on 26 October 1995, the Juppé Plan of the following November, and the shift in the Jospin government's budget policy in the summer 1997. At the time of the 2002 elections, Prime Minister Jospin justified the limited margin of manoeuvre in Socialist Party tax and spending policies in terms of Stability Pact rules. While the UMP government led by Jean Pierre Raffarin (2002–4) was willing to break these rules, emphasizing the general goal of debt reduction rather than the specific deficit rule, the de Villepin and François Fillon (2007) governments raised debt-cutting to the highest echelon of government priorities and renewed their commitment to the Pact's medium-term goals. However, the ability of the Fillon government to respect French commitments remains to be seen.

EMU as a justification for reform has run up against competing values. Ideologically inspired political opposition to reforms has combined with labour-union opposition to modifications to social security regimes and the privatization of public services, both of which are seen as disadvantaging public-sector employees. The result has been some degree of inertia—to which the sheltering effect of EMU has likely contributed. French public-sector spending as a percentage of GPD has been consistently one of the highest in the EU (after Sweden and Denmark). It has risen over the past 15 years when there has been a decline in most of the other EU member states (Figure 6.3) and is forecast to reach the top position in 2007 at 53.2 per cent of GDP (European Commission 2007*a*).

Improved budget management came on to the agenda as another example of 'bottom-up' Europeanization. The Juppé centre-Right government (1995–7) brought about institutional changes to extend some parliamentary

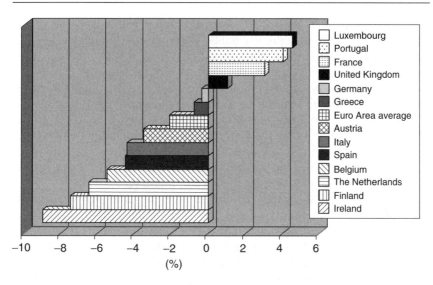

Figure 6.3. Ratio of French public expenditure to GDP (change from 1991 to 2006)

Source: OECD (2006). 'OECD Economic Outlook: Statistics and Projections', online database; Accessed 4 July 2007. The ratio of public spending to GDP is calculated in cyclically adjusted terms as the share of cyclically adjusted current disbursements and net capital outlays of the government sector in potential GDP.

(and thus government) control over the operation of the semi-autonomous social security budgets, controlled hitherto solely by the social partners—employers' representatives and trade unions. Decrees were also adopted to reform hospital administration and to control more effectively medical practitioners' standard consulting fees.

In 1998 the Jospin government introduced a medium-term budgetary strategy based on the setting of a target for the cumulated increase in real government expenditure over a three-year period. In practice, real expenditure was planned to increase more slowly than potential real GDP. The strategy was created to enhance the transparency of the budgetary framework and help form expectations. However, as it failed to lead to expected results, and initial targets were missed by a large margin, attempts have been made to modify the strategy.

Debt reduction came to assume a leading position in UMP government discourse. Thierry Breton, minister of finance from February 2005 to May 2007, called himself the 'anti-debt' crusader. In 2006, he introduced the annual national conference on public finance under his chairmanship with the presence of the Prime Minister, as a device to reinforce efforts to cut spending in government departments. Breton also held press conferences every quarter with the participation of all the central government department directors. The Balladur government had commissioned the well-known

French business leader, Alain Minc, to prepare a report with high public profile that could then help to legitimize public-sector reform through the guise of non-administrative business expertise (Minc 1994). Similarly, Breton hired the services of Michel Pébereau, Président de BNP Paribas, who chaired the commission which prepared a report on French debt (Pébereau 2005) which he presented to Prime Minister de Villepin in December 2005. In response, de Villepin presented a five-year plan to reduce French debt to the 60 per cent threshold and meet the medium-term goal of the Stability Pact by 2012. President Sarkozy claimed to be personally engaged in the struggle to lower French debt. He attended the July 2007 meeting of the Euro Group, promising to do everything he could to meet this medium-term goal.

With the failure of the Jospin government to make sufficiently large cuts to the budget, the economic slow-down from 2001 resulted in the rapid rise of the deficit towards the 3 per cent figure, exceeding this figure for four years in a row from 2002 before dropping below in 2006 (Figure 6.2). The Raffarin government's prioritization of tax cutting over deficit reduction in the context of an economic slow down exacerbated matters. French debt exceeded the 60 per cent figure in 2003, rising to 66.2 in 2005 before dropping to 63.9 in 2006. With the 'early warning' and then excessive deficit procedures against France, and the stubborn refusal to move rapidly to cut the deficit, President Chirac and the Raffarin government called for a temporary 'softening' of the Stability Pact (*Le Monde*, 14 July 2003) and even a rethink on the Pact. Repeated German failure to meet the 3 per cent deficit figure from 2002 gave the French greater political margin of manoeuvre on the Pact rules and the two states demanded the suspension of the excessive deficit procedure at the 25 November 2003 ECOFIN meeting (ECOFIN 2003; Howarth 2007; Schwarzer 2007).

The restriction of interest-rate and exchange-rate policies in the EMS and their loss with EMU, combined with the intensified wage competition in the Euro Area, reinforced pressures on French governments to modify labour-market policies and increase wage flexibility. Governments attempted to undertake reform in a context of high structural unemployment. The lack of centralized wage bargaining in France makes negotiated solutions to labour-market rigidities more difficult. Gaullist-led governments sought to respond to these rigidities by relaxing rules on hiring. They allowed greater scope for the creation of jobs of a limited duration—*contrats de durée déterminé, CDD*—the non-enforcement of rules that standard wages (as under *contrats de durée indéterminé*, CDI) apply to these jobs, and the toleration of a significant increase in part-time work, not remunerated at SMIC (the minimum monthly wage).

The de Villepin government failed in its efforts through the CPE to extend existing provisions for limited duration contracts for younger workers from SMEs to all companies. This followed the failure—over a decade earlier in 1994—of the Balladur Government to introduce a young persons' SMIC to address high youth unemployment. The Jospin government created the possibility for greater flexibility in the context of the 35-hour week policy. It allowed companies, in collective bargaining on the implementation of the 35-hour week, the possibility of freezing wages, and spreading the calculation of the 35-hour week over the period of a year. President Sarkozy and the Fillon government sought to increase further the flexibility in the 35-hour week policy by adopting a law allowing companies to pay staff for supplementary hours without the imposition of income tax. President Sarkozy also achieved a significant breakthrough in overcoming traditionally conflictual relations between the 'social partners' who were told in September 2007 to reach agreements on mutually acceptable labour market reform or face government imposed legislation. On 11 January 2008, the 'social partners' reached an agreement on a range of labour market reforms and notably increased flexibility which will form the basis of forthcoming legislation.

French companies have taken full advantage of the fixed duration contract, 35-hour week provisions and holes in French labour law to increase competitiveness in the context of the Single Market and EMU (see Hancké 2002*b* for an overview of firm-led adjustment in France). The percentage of full-time salaried workers on CDD rose from 1.4 per cent in 1983 to 10.8 per cent in 2000 (although dropping to 8.3 per cent in 2006), with higher percentages for younger workers (14.3 in 2006 of those aged 15 to 29) (Blanchard and Landier 2002; Insee 2008*a/b*). The estimated percentage of part-time employees as a percentage of total salaried workers increased markedly in the period prior to EMU when French unemployment reached particularly high levels. It rose from 11.9 per cent of salaried workers in 1990 to just below 18 per cent in 2006 (Insee 2008*a*). French temporary employment rates have been below the EU25 and Euro Area averages (14.5 and 16.2 per cent respectively in 2005) and similar to those in Germany (13.3 per cent versus 14.2 in 2005) but are well behind those in Spain at about 30 per cent (Eurostat 2006). In 2006, French part-time employment rates were just below the EU27 average but fell far below those in Germany (25.8 per cent in 2006) and well behind those in the Netherlands (46.2 per cent in 2006) (Insee 2007). The 35-hour week policy allowed company-level negotiations to fit hours worked per week with business needs.

The Pursuit of EU-level 'Governance Economique'

All French governments since 1991 emphasized counter-balancing the 'sound' money bias of EMU and the power of the ECB in the Euro Area by strengthening European 'economic government', and by reinforcing European social and employment policies. Yet the desire for tightened EU-level coordination (the implication at the supranational level of the interventionist legacy) is contradicted by consistent French insistence upon national margin of manoeuvre.

Because of this contradiction, French policymakers have been unable to spell out very clearly what they mean by EU economic governance (Howarth 2007). Their pronouncements on the subject take on a variety of meanings, from effective policy mix, to interventionism, to enhancing EMU and ECB credibility and legitimacy but also to directly challenging ECB independence. For domestic political consumption, French governments repeatedly exaggerated the importance of institutional and policy developments at the EU level for the process of constructing an economic government: the creation of the Euro Group, the informal intergovernmental gathering of Euro Area finance ministers and its reinforcement; the creation of the new Economic and Financial Committee (*Libération,* 13 January 1999), consisting of EU treasury and central bank officials; the Cologne Macro-Economic Dialogue and the Lisbon process more generally.

Regular French initiatives on interventionist EU strategies demonstrate the extent to which French governments, be they on the Left or Right, still feel the need to call for deficit spending in order to stimulate the economy. Yet no such initiatives—principally infrastructural programme proposals—resulted in EU-level agreements that involve significant spending on programmes. Some of these projects were presented as Franco-German joint initiatives. The Franco-German growth initiative of 18 September 2003 attacked the Commission for being excessive in its drive for budget cutting and 'anti-industry', pledging further tax cuts in both countries and 10 major jointly funded infrastructural projects (*Le Monde,* 19 September 2003). In April 2006, Chirac joined with Chancellor Merkel to launch a 'Europe of grand projects', which involved the allocation of €1.7 billion French funding. In June 2006, Chirac and Merkel announced additional joint projects to focus on areas such as education, research, and energy policy.

'Economic government' as expressed through the creation of a substantial EU employment policy and reinforced social policy was of particular importance for the 'plural Left' government as a reinforcement and legitimization of activist domestic employment policies. The Socialists placed emphasis on the construction of 'social democracy' at the European level as a means to counterbalance the monetary power of the ECB and to 'manage' the effects of globalization. Jospin reached a compromise with the Germans that involved the creation of the EU employment chapter, the resolution on growth and employment, and the formulation of a European employment strategy. The resolution involved only vague objectives. The employment chapter involved no additional spending or obligatory measures but focused on information sharing, pilot projects, and benchmarking, as agreed at the Luxembourg and Cardiff jobs summits. French Socialist ministers consistently stressed, if not exaggerated, the significance of EU policy developments in this area (Howarth 2002).

Since 2002, UMP governments were considerably less activist in these areas. However, in the context of challenging opposition to the Draft Treaty Establishing a Constitution for Europe, and then building support for the Lisbon Treaty, successive UMP-led governments nonetheless placed emphasis on EU-level social and employment policies as a buffer against the perceived liberalizing bias of European integration. Prime Minister Raffarin listed the Draft Treaty's provisions on employment and social policy and the goals of 'employment and social progress' as forming one of the most important reasons for voting 'yes' in the June 2005 referendum (*Le Monde*, 5 March 2005). Opinion polls in the aftermath of the referendum 'no' vote further demonstrated the importance of social policy considerations for French voters (Eurostat 2005).

Modifying the terms of the Stability and Growth Pact was another constant objective of French governments. President Chirac and the Juppé and Jospin governments very reluctantly accepted the creation of the Stability Pact to meet the demands of the Kohl government and to counter strong public and political opposition to EMU in Germany (Milesi 1998; Schor 1999). Following the November 2003 suspension of the excessive deficit procedure, the Raffarin government presented reform proposals that sought a more flexible application of the Pact by officially taking into consideration the economic situation facing a participating member state. In practice, these proposals allowed more scope for political bargaining and thus margin of manoeuvre for French (and other) governments in the determination of excessive deficits. The Raffarin government wanted a reformulated Pact to take into consideration deficit spending on public investment, contributions to the EU budget, and defence—eliminating them for total public deficit considerations (*Le Monde* 3 December 2004).

Conclusion

On EMU institutional design and fiscal policy rules, 'misfit' has been long emphasized by both governments and the political opposition. 'Misfit' was tolerated because of the perception of real economic gain in the context of EMU, reinforced by relatively strong economic growth at the start of Stage Three, and the corresponding perception of ECB policy aligning with French economic preferences. From 2002, UMP-led governments blamed the strong euro for France's commercial and current account deficits and low economic growth.

Yet French public support for the euro remains consistently high. This high level of support is all the more remarkable given the persistently low public confidence in the French economy and in government economic management (Figures 6.4, 6.5, and 6.6). At the same time, the growing perception

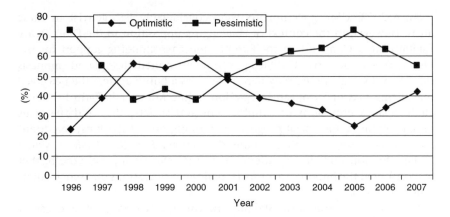

Figure 6.4. French public opinion on the national economic situation

Question asked: 'Regarding the evolution of the economic situation in France in the next six months, are you very optimistic, quite optimistic, very pessimistic or quite pessimistic?' Poll CSA/ LA TRIBUNE, 29–30 2007; http://www.csa-fr.com/dataset/data2007/opi20070830-les-francais-et-la-rentree-economique.htm; Accessed 23 September 2007. This poll is taken at the end of August / start of September at the end of the summer vacation.

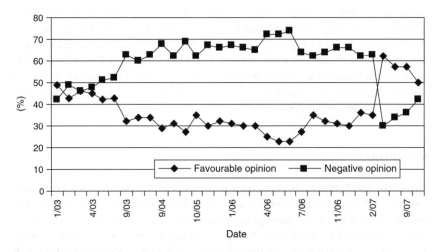

Figure 6.5. Popularity of the French government's economic policy

Question asked: 'Would you say that the economic policy of the current government is very good, rather good, rather bad or very bad?' The favourable results combine very good and rather good; and the negative results combine very bad and rather bad.

Le baromètre économique-Vague 19-BVA-BFM-Les Echos, June 2007; http://www.bva.fr/data/ sondage/sondage_sondage/572/sondage_fichier/fichier/barobfm-lesechosv19_a1e86.pdf; Accessed 10 September 2007.

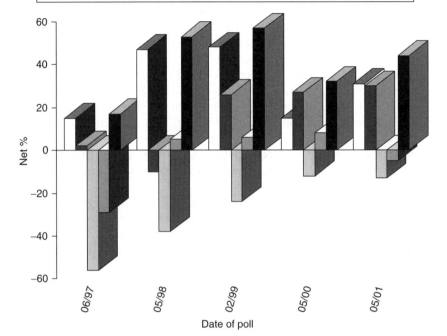

Figure 6.6. French public support for the euro and public confidence

Source: IPSOS France; http://www.ipsos.fr/CanalIpsos/poll/image/807-m-Diapositive18.gif; Accessed 10 September 2007.

that EMU has had a negative impact on the French economy and the financial situation of individual citizens contributes to the generally weak economic policy reputation of French governments. In the years leading to 2002, one of the consistently positive public impressions of government managerial competence concerned the introduction of euro notes and coins (Figure 6.6), which suggests that EMU membership bolstered confidence in the government. However, in following years, the almost universal opinion that the introduction of euro notes and coins had significant inflationary effects (TNS Sofres, *Le Monde* 26 December 2006) contributed to negative impressions of government competence.

There has been no politics of retrenchment in France to date because of monetary integration. Strong growth from 1997 to 2001 made it politically easier for French governments to respect the deficit criterion of the Maastricht Treaty and Stability Pact. The low economic growth of the past half-decade increased the possibility of retrenchment. However, the unexpected flexibility of the EMU project and notably the application of Stability Pact rules gave recalcitrant UMP-led government's fiscal policy room to manoeuvre.

Europeanization as transformation has been seen principally in institutional reform—central bank independence—and in budget management, which reinforced the position of the Ministry of Finance in government policymaking. With EMU participation allowing France more fiscal policy margin of manoeuvre, persistently high deficits and a rising debt load, it can be argued that EMU has contributed to inertia in public-sector and social-security reforms. Yet, the fiscal policy rules of the Pact remain a very important ostensible constraint that governments use to justify reform.

It is problematic to claim any clear impact of EMU on French state power. Debt itself created greater constraints on state power and resulted in a new sense of urgency that both encouraged French governments to initiate reform and forced a strategic engagement with trade unions and expert opinion to bring about reform.

EMU contributed to the impressive productivity gains in the French private sector. These gains follow in part from the policy of competitive disinflation, the effects of which persisted after 1999 because comparatively low inflation means that real interest rates in France have been higher than in most other Euro Area member states. The record level of profits of the ten largest French companies in 2005—a year of sluggish French growth—was due to sales and activities outside France. Many French companies responded to the gradualism of French governments on labour-market reform by making full use of short-term and irregular contracts, just as many took full advantage of flexibility provisions in the 35-work week legislation to match hours worked with cyclical needs. Unemployment remains high in France due to the combination of productivity gains and the sluggishness of the state on labour-market and public-sector reform.

French governments are engaged in the political management of a paradox. On the one hand, their credibility has been bolstered by the creation of an EMU project that was embraced to facilitate particular macroeconomic goals. On the other hand, this project has created a constraint that has frequently been politically inconvenient. EMU is a project that has failed to meet economic and political expectations. French governments responded by insisting on national margin of manoeuvre (in fiscal and other policies) and engaged keenly in 'scapegoating' the ECB. In so doing, they risk undermining the legitimacy of EMU and, in turn, their own reputation for governing competence to the extent that French governments are seen to cooperate in a maligned system.

French governments also sought to qualify the 'sound' money policies of EMU through active state responses to the challenges of the single European market and globalization, in social, employment, and interventionist industrial and infrastructural policies, at both the domestic and EU levels.

Most French efforts to build EU economic governance were frustrated not only by German and other member-state opposition but also by contradictions within French policy, given the repeated refusal to accept binding European constraints. The very limited success of French governments in their pursuit of these policies potentially further undermines their reputation for governing competence.

7

Germany: A Crisis of Leadership in the Euro Area

Kenneth Dyson

German elite and public opinion has continued to view the euro as a fundamentally political project: as an indispensable part of completing and making 'irreversible' European unification, not least around German leadership
on the single market and economic stability. Despite the anxieties that it
provoked, the euro was seen as securing vital, long-term national interests
in a peaceful and prosperous Europe. The contentious issues in German
debates about the euro were functional, spatial, and temporal. Functionally,
the euro's creation and operation had to be on terms that met fundamental,
historically conditioned German concerns about firmly anchoring economic
stability in Europe. This issue was delegated to the German Bundesbank,
in which public opinion retained high confidence, and framed around the
central Ordo-liberal principles of price stability, central bank independence,
and firm fiscal rules. Spatially, the euro had to comprise a 'stability' community of 'convergent' economies that shared core policy beliefs (especially in
stability-oriented monetary and fiscal policies) and economic requirements
(cyclically convergent). Finally, the launch of the euro had to take place
at an 'appropriate' time in the integration project, at least in parallel with
political union so that monetary union was also anchored in a 'solidarity
community'.

The first decade of the euro did not quell German concerns about these
three sources of risk: about whether the conditions for a 'stable' and 'strong'
euro were secure; whether convergence was adequate and sustainable; and
whether monetary union was premature and should have come at a later stage
in the integration process (according to the so-called coronation theory as the
final step in political union). Nevertheless, the underlying politics of the euro
were not in dispute. Experience of living with the euro, with its attendant
stresses and strains, did not erode this basic German belief in the fundamental

'rightness' of the euro as a political project. This enduring shared core belief across elite and public opinion shaped how politicians responded to the association, between 2001 and 2005, of the euro with economic stagnation and a palpable sense of weakened German leadership in the Euro Area.

The close symbiosis of German interests and the euro is manifested not just in its role as a core political project for Germany but also in the dependence of the Euro Area's reputation on German performance. Accounting for 27.5 per cent of total Euro Area GDP and 37.25 per cent of external trade in goods in 2006, Germany could claim to be the centre of gravity of the Euro Area economy (Deutsche Bundesbank 2007*b*: 36). Relative economic size alone created opportunities for a German leadership role in European economic governance.

However, in the period 1999–2005, Germany's magnetic attraction as leader of the Euro Area was in decline and, with it, the reputation of the Euro Area as a whole suffered. Germany's average GDP growth in 2001–5 was bottom of the Euro Area league table, alongside Italy and Portugal (0.6 per cent) and less than half the average; its share of total Euro Area unemployment reached 33.9 per cent in 2006; growth in household disposable income and in consumer spending remained weak; whilst its structural fiscal balance deteriorated, especially on the revenue side (public debt climbing from 60.3 per cent of GDP in 2002 to 67.5 in 2006) (Deutsche Bundesbank 2006). The Euro Area's performance mirrored that of its main engine, the German economy.

Similarly, from 2006 the upswing in the German economy reversed Euro Area fortunes and reopened scope for German leadership, for instance in fiscal policy and debates about competitiveness in the traded-goods sector. In 2006 for the first time it exceeded the Euro Area average growth rate in achieving 2.7 per cent; whilst in 2007 it achieved its second only public-sector budget surplus since unification in 1990, employment rose by 650,000 to the highest level since unification, and the Bundesbank spoke of a 'solid' export-powered upswing.

This chapter examines the central paradoxes in Germany's relations with the euro since 1999 before analysing the euro's effects on the German polity, its policies, and its politics. It argues that these effects have been secondary to—and essentially reinforcing—those flowing from German unification, EU enlargement to east central Europe, and newly emerging economies outside Europe, notably China and the rise of Asia; that German politicians have sought to 'de-centre' the euro in domestic institutional and policy debates about economic reforms (to avoid a 'blame-shifting' to the EU that could be risky for larger German interests); and that the brunt of responsibility for managing these, and related, effects has fallen to the corporate trading sector, flanked by supportive—but politically cautious—governments. The result has been a paradox of active, painful, corporate-led, market-based accommodation with a politics of Europeanization combining inertia and slow transformation.

The Paradox of Arduous Market-Based Adjustment with Enduring Political Inertia and Slow Transformation

The early years of the euro were characterized by a festering sense of domestic political inertia and crisis about fiscal policies and economic and welfare reforms. There was a mounting sense that the once much-envied 'semi-sovereign' German state, with its power sharing and consensus-building, was no longer fit for purpose in delivering timely policy change and in supporting a continuing leadership role for Germany in the Euro Area.

The period 2003–5 witnessed a new clarity of direction and pace of reform, spurred by Chancellor Gerhard Schröder's bold but belated 'Agenda 2010' reform package in March 2003, especially reforms to unemployment benefits. However, it generated internal Social Democratic Party (SPD) turmoil, electoral setbacks, and the engineering of early federal elections. Similarly, Angela Merkel failed as Chancellor candidate of the Christian Democratic Union/Christian Social Union (CDU/CSU) in 2005 to win a federal majority for an even bolder new centre-right programme of market liberalization and radical tax reforms. A combination of stagnation in disposable incomes with heightened economic insecurity made for weak public support for reforms.

CDU/CSU electoral reversal, coupled with SPD trauma, dissuaded the subsequent Grand Coalition of the two main parties under Merkel from embracing radical proposals for domestic economic reforms (other than fiscal consolidation and raising the pension age to 67). Agenda 2010 was a spike in a slow-moving reform process. A Grand Coalition political discourse of 'improving' reforms hid cross-party tendencies to retrenchment (Rürup 2007). A key factor in this retrenchment in economic reforms was new electoral threat to the SPD in the west from the Left Party, formed in 2006 from a merger of SPD defectors with the Party of Democratic Socialism (PDS, the successor to the ruling Socialist Unity Party of the former German Democratic Republic). Correspondingly, Merkel had an incentive to shift policies in order to occupy the opening in the political centre. By 2007 the SPD led party competition to lengthen unemployment benefits for older workers, to introduce new high statutory minimum wage in the postal sector, to advocate a high national minimum wage, and to support substantial wage increases. The former SPD Economics and Labour Minister, Wolfgang Clement, spoke of 'gambling away the dividends of past reforms' (*Financial Times* 2008).

Germany's record as a reform 'laggard'—though reversed in the short period 2003–5—suggested a failure of domestic political 'ownership' to embrace the 'logic' of EMU. Its leaders seemed unwilling or unable to act on the acknowledgement that renouncing domestic interest-rate and exchange-rate policies required economic adjustment by radical fiscal reforms and by market liberalization, especially in services and labour markets (Duval and Elmeskov 2006). Even if increased by reforms, the annual output growth potential remained only 1.5–1.75 per cent by 2007 (Deutsche Bundesbank 2007a).

However, this judgement of domestic political and policy failure needs qualification. First, the cautious domestic political management of economic reforms, and their framing in terms other than the euro, helped protect the euro project, and wider German interests in Europe, from incipient populist mobilization of domestic 'losers' as a consequence of painful economic adjustment. It reduced the political risk that 'soft' Euro-scepticism about the economic costs of the euro to Germany could harden into a principled opposition to European integration. German political leaders delivered public continuity in support for the euro as a political project, if at a price in reforms.

Second, the powerful trade-exposed German corporate sector proved robust in correcting the competitive disadvantages that Germany faced on euro entry (including the legacy of lost competitiveness consequent on German unification and then the high conversion rate into the euro) and bringing down the real effective exchange rate. 'Bottom-up', market-led change by firms as they restructured their operations, refocused their businesses and improved their cost base, assisted above all by wage moderation, produced the major reduction in unit labour costs that had not been delivered through government reforms to labour markets and the welfare state. Political inertia and limited transformation of products, services, and labour markets were complemented by major sustained behavioural accommodation in the corporate sector. Its benefits began to become apparent from 2005, notably in employment, tax revenues, and fiscal policy. The corporate traded-goods sector delivered a renewed German leadership role in competitive disinflation within the Euro Area by consistently large increases in productivity that exceeded wage increases. Though by 2006 there were signs that productivity growth was beginning to trail wage growth, this change was in part at least due to other changes in the labour market.

Finally, the German labour market offered evidence of accommodation as well as rigidity. Rigidity through high regulation remained in large areas of the service sector and in utilities but was matched by very high internal flexibility inside the trade-exposed manufacturing sector. It was also complemented by the growth of new forms of very flexible temporary and part-time employment outside the framework of collective bargaining agreements. Its growth prompted in 2007 a new internal Grand Coalition debate about statutory general versus sector-specific minimum wages and SPD party competition to set the rate high. A process of retrenchment was evident. Nevertheless, the development of a more complex, differentiated set of labour markets boosted employment and reflected both corporate-led adjustment and governmental reforms. By 2006, they had altered prospects for the German economy and potentially for the Euro Area as a whole and produced a faster employment growth than previous post-unification economic upswings (Deutsche Bundesbank 2007, 2007a: 40).

Context and Initial Conditions

Over the first half decade, Germany's relationship to the Euro Area was marked by paradox. On the one hand, the 'uploading' of German policy preferences and institutional arrangements into the design of the Euro Area manifested German leadership in Europe based on 'ideational' power. It created an over-riding impression of continuity, of 'path dependence', in German European power. German and European economic and monetary ideas resonated more easily than, for instance, French and European ideas. If institutional and policy convergence was at work, it was on German terms through the agency of the 'Germanic' ECB and 'flanking' rule-based fiscal policy coordination insisted on by Germany. These presumed initial conditions of ideational 'fit' suggested an underlying accommodative relationship.

Euro Area membership was associated with unanticipated policy 'misfits' that challenged this presumption. These misfits emerged in fiscal policy (most strikingly, the German-centred Stability and Growth Pact crisis of November 2003); in monetary policy (an ECB monetary policy that proved less 'accommodating' for Germany than for other Euro Area states, at least until 2005); and in Germany's reputation as a laggard in economic reforms. In consequence, Germany shed its image of 'model pupil' (*Musterknabe*). Until 2005–6 German 'soft' power eroded.

Path dependence in German relations with the euro derived from her leading role in defining the initial conditions in the Euro Area, namely in a 'rules-based' approach to securing stability-oriented fiscal and monetary policies. This approach was rooted in a powerful indigenous post-war economic ideology of 'Ordo-liberalism', whose epicentre was the Bundesbank but which dominated the German economics profession. Drawing on historical lessons from the economic and political costs of Weimar hyperinflation and of Nazi tyranny, Ordo-liberalism called for a limited but strong state. The state's responsibility was to deliver the two collective goods of economic stability and open, competitive markets. Uploading of 'Ordo-liberalism' into EMU was secured by the Bundesbank's activism in preparations for the euro, especially the design of the ECB and its monetary policy, and by German sponsorship of the Stability and Growth Pact. In consequence, its key ideas had been institutionalized in EMU. EMU 'locked-in' a set of pre-commitments. They not only defined the scope and trajectory of German economic policy development but also 'fit' ascendant post–war German economic thought.

Moreover, they resonated in German public opinion, which showed continuing strong support for the exclusive price stability mandate of the ECB and for the Stability and Growth Pact as the necessary bases for a strong and stable euro (Eurobarometer 2006). This support narrowed the EU policy options for German governments.

Emerging institutional and policy 'misfits' challenged German governments. Institutional 'misfit' was exhibited in the lack of a national stability pact to bind in the federal states and local authorities to EU fiscal commitments and equivalent to the arrangements at the EU level or to comparable cases like Austria and Belgium. Policy 'misfit' was manifest in a crisis of the Stability and Growth Pact in November 2003 whose epicentre was Germany. The subsequent EU-level reform of the Stability and Growth Pact in 2005 (enabling more external fiscal flexibility) and domestic constitutional reform to the federal system in 2006 (supporting internal fiscal tightening) helped reduce, but by no means eliminate, this fiscal 'misfit'. Policy 'misfit' between domestic economic stagnation and ECB interest rates was, however, not open to similar re-negotiation. It faced the high hurdles not just of Treaty amendment but, more fundamentally, of domestic elite and public opinion that remained deeply averse to any risks to economic stability.

The terms of euro entry had two further widely unanticipated disciplinary effects for Germany that reinforced domestic sources of stagnation. First, the larger-than-anticipated membership of the Euro Area in 1999 generated the potential for 'misfits' in monetary policy. In sharp contrast to the previous Exchange Rate Mechanism (ERM), Germany experienced the highest real interest rates in the Euro Area (Deutsche Bundesbank 2007b: 40). With interest rates no longer set by the Bundesbank for Germany as a European benchmark or 'floor', Germany lost its earlier interest rate advantage. The ECB set them for the Euro Area as a whole, and the Euro Area contained a number of states with persistently higher inflation than Germany. At least up to 2005–06 critics could argue persuasively that ECB interest rates had deflationary effects (Aherne and Pisani-Ferry 2006; Enderlein 2004).

However, the Bundesbank countered this critique by stressing that real interest rates were at an historic low in Germany and that the stimulus from lower real interest rates in other Euro Area states acted as a 'positive shock' for the Euro Area and benefited German exports and thus the potential for a German export-led expansion. German capital goods exports were also able to benefit disproportionately from the infrastructural investment boom in east central Europe associated with EU enlargement.

In addition, the entrenched institutional power of domestic Ordo-liberalism, and the strength of public support for price stability, meant that there was no incentive for federal governments (SPD/Green 1998–2005 and CDU-CSU/SPD Grand Coalition 2005–) or main opposition parties to try to exploit any unanticipated policy 'misfit' by challenging the independence of the ECB. Against this background the strategic option of Franco-German leadership in developing an economic policy 'counterweight' to the ECB was a non-starter for German governments. Merkel (CDU) and Finance Minister Peer Steinbrück (SPD) were united in rebutting President Nicolas Sarkozy's attacks on the ECB's independence, calls for a stronger Euro Group, and proposal for a special Euro Area 'summit' as unnecessary and divisive. Merkel favoured building on the Lisbon economic reform process of the EU-27 to capture the wider benefits of completing the single market over strengthening the Euro Group.

Secondly, there was widespread support for the view that Germany had entered the Euro Area at too high a conversion rate. It had not taken account of the loss of competitive advantage consequent on German unification. German negotiators had been keen to put in place an external discipline to compensate for the economic risk entailed in loss of the Bundesbank as a reliable domestic discipline. Critics argued that this decision had entrenched a loss of competitiveness, further compounding the effects of German currency unification in 1990.

Both the conversion legacy and relatively high real interest rates compared to other Euro Area states challenged domestic policymakers and employers and trade unionists to rethink how this loss of competitiveness could be tackled by changes in taxation, in financing the welfare state, in wage bargaining, and in working arrangements. EMU did not act as a primary, let alone the single cause of the aggressive 'bottom-up', firm-led adjustment in the traded-goods sector, which—though it intensified after 1999—can be traced back to 1995. However, it served as a strong reinforcement to processes already catalysed by German unification, prospective EU eastern enlargement, and a powerful new 'globalization' discourse. German unit labour costs displayed a downward curve from 2003 and, over the period 1998–2006, rose by over 16 per cent more quickly in the Euro Area (excluding Germany) than in Germany (Deutsche Bundesbank 2007*b*: 44). Germany's terms of trade with her Euro Area partners, calculated on the basis of export and import price indices, fell by 7 per cent over this same period, with especially large surpluses with Austria, Belgium, France, Italy, and Spain (ibid.: 37).

For Germany, the Euro Area had paradoxical implications for power over policy. Above all, it meant the loss of the institutional authority of the Bundesbank, the most visible symbol of German economic power in Europe and internationally and—alongside the Federal Constitutional Court—the most respected and trusted German institution. It had served not just as the main domestic embodiment and guardian of Ordo-liberal economic ideology but also as the epicentre of European monetary policies via the D-Mark-centred ERM. In combination, these two roles had endowed the Bundesbank with extraordinary disciplinary power over domestic and European economic policies and with power to set the agenda of European monetary integration.

The symbolism of the location of the ECB in Frankfurt could not compensate for this loss of substantive institutional power over monetary policy. A central institutional component of the German 'semi-sovereign' state had been fully Europeanized. In consequence, as we shall see below, the Federal Finance Ministry was unleashed from the constraint of having to 'bind-in' the Bundesbank to its European policies.

The paradoxical effect was a strengthening of German Ordo-liberalism by its export upwards to the institutional design of the Euro Area on principally German terms. In parallel, mainstream German 'Ordo-liberal' academic economics, partly led by the Bundesbank, evolved away from a critical distance from EMU to a reframing of EMU in an Ordo-liberal discourse. This reframing legitimated the euro as a disciplinary instrument of overdue domestic market liberalization, empowering domestic change agents. The discursive focus shifted from the risks of importing economic problems from 'irresponsible' partner states in EMU to the euro as 'logic' for accelerating German reforms, especially for weakening the ideology and practice of 'social partnership' in corporate governance and in labour markets. This shift also focused attention on the problems of the 'weak' semi-sovereign German state in delivering reforms. Ordo-liberalism had always extolled the merits of the limited but strong state for safeguarding competitive markets and economic stability.

A further paradox lay in the successful export of German 'semi-sovereign' state characteristics to the EU at the same time as the forms of the German state were subjected to heightened domestic critique. The birth of the Euro Area was predated by, and in turn contributed to, a discursive shift about the German 'semi-sovereign' state. It figured more as liability than asset (Green and Paterson 2005). Initially, the 'semi-sovereign' state had been seen as an exemplar of a consensual, incremental policy style and durable, well-designed outcomes. It shared powers amongst political parties and federal and state levels and with powerful courts, para-public institutions like the Bundesbank, the Federal Labour Office and the Council of Economic Experts, and strong centrally organized employer organizations and trade unions. Reforms were slow but, because they embodied consent, effectively implemented (Katzenstein 1985).

By 1997 German political discourse was fixated on 'reform blockage' (*Reformstau*), whilst academic analysis focused on 'decision traps'. The semi-sovereign state was pictured as harbouring multiple powerful veto players: internal party factions like the 'social' wing of the centre-right CDU/CSU or 'traditionalists' in the SPD (both wedded to the defence of social entitlements), the Bundesrat (the location for a frequently different and varying federal majority from that supporting the federal government in the Bundestag), organizations that defended traditional labour-market and welfare-state entitlements (notably the traditionally powerful trade unions), and the ambivalence within public opinion about reforms (Koenig 2006). In particular, the reform process was complicated by the domestic electoral calendar, which was notably crowded, with 1 federal and 16 state elections spread over every four years. State elections had the capacity to directly change federal majorities in the Bundesrat. Hence reforms faced multiple sources of uncertainty. The question was whether institutional constraints on taking decisive state action translated into an inability to take significant and well-prepared reforms which, even if in small steps, embodied a coherent logic.

The particular complexity of domestic political opportunity structures meant that German political elites had compelling incentives to calculate the costs and risks of domestic reforms as especially high and to proceed with great caution. As discourse stressed the multiple urgent challenges of globalization, technological change, the EU single market, EU enlargement, and the euro, Germany's image became that of a state of institutional veto players that lacked a capacity for political and policy innovation. This image was fortified by the failure of the Schröder government's Alliance for Jobs (*Bündnis für Arbeit*) to establish Germany as a plausible Dutch-style model of macro-level neo-corporatism in engaging employer and trade-union organizations in economic reforms and by its belated adoption of a bold reform programme in 2003 (Dyson 2006a). The birth of the Alliance for Jobs in 1998 coincided with the Euro Area; its protracted demise followed in February 2003 with very few reforms to its credit and much mutual recrimination.

A further paradox was the shift in the intellectual centre of gravity in domestic policy: from 'exporting' German economic governance to the Euro Area to 'benchmarking' best practice elsewhere. The political incentive to pursue 'benchmarking' stemmed from the incentive to appeal to a technocratic legitimation for domestic reforms in politically sensitive areas like labour-market, taxation, health, and pensions policies where veto points made change difficult. Also, benchmarking ideologically attractive states like the Netherlands and the Nordic states opened up opportunities to reframe domestic debates, notably in the SPD and the trade unions, and to tilt the domestic balance of forces towards acceptance of more market liberalization. This discursive shift reflected in part a loss of intellectual self-confidence, consequent on poor growth and employment creation records and on fiscal problems. It also illustrated the efforts of the Schröder government to craft an appropriate 'evidence-based' economic policy discourse that would 'bind in' potential domestic veto players to a reform agenda. The Schröder government played a leading role in the EU agenda shift in 1999–2000 from monetary union (which had been achieved) to the model of a 'knowledge-society' Europe. In seeking to fill the new German-supported Lisbon process with content, debate moved from 'Model Germany' to the Nordic model. By the 2005 federal elections the Nordic model had become a legitimating focus for inter-party consensus, though the CDU and the SPD drew different conclusions on policy lessons.

The most striking paradox was that this loss of intellectual confidence and a reputation as a 'laggard' in economic reforms and in fiscal responsibility was accompanied by an assertive corporate leadership in a painful and protracted domestic economic adjustment inside the trade-exposed sector. Market share in Euro Area, EU, and world trade was increased by cutting German unit labour costs through wage moderation, corporate restructuring, and flexible working practices (with average weekly working time rising from 38.5 to 41 hours). Restructuring focused on high-quality capital goods that were complementary to Chinese exports, and on 'off-shoring' production to cheaper locations (so that the import content of German exports rose and domestic employment generation through exports weakened). By 2003 Germany had returned to its position as the world's top exporter of goods, whilst its current account surplus climbed from return to balance in 2001 (for the first time since unification) to some 5 per cent of nominal GDP in 2006 (Deutsche Bundesbank 2007*b*: 38). Germany's share of exports of Euro Area goods rose from 32.75 per cent in 1999 to 37.25 per cent in 2006 (ibid.: 36).

Strong corporate-sector leadership in strengthening price competitiveness offset problems of the 'weak' state. When the federal government was emboldened to reform, the outcomes typically ratified a strong corporate-led agenda. This process was apparent in business tax reforms, like relief of capital gains tax on the sale of cross-shareholdings, and in pensions and health reforms (and VAT reform in 2007) designed to lower employer contributions. These moves enhanced the freedom of manoeuvre of key firms in the trade-exposed corporate sector.

The German Polity and the Euro: Changing Opportunity Structures

The creation of the Euro Area unleashed new opportunities for institutional reforms to the German state in three main areas: the organization of the federal executive; intergovernmental relations in the federal system; and the roles and structure of the Bundesbank. Euro-related reforms focused on the Federal Finance Ministry and the Bundesbank whose relative powers were transformed. The Federal Finance Ministry sought to strengthen its roles in economic policy coordination within the federal executive and in fiscal policy coordination within the larger federal system. The Bundesbank attempted to carve out new roles to compensate for its loss of monetary policy. Though both actors were only partially successful in these strategies, the Federal Finance Ministry was the net gainer. Reforms to German banking and financial market supervision—as well as the management of the Stability and Growth Pact crisis—revealed a weakened Bundesbank. Reforms to the internal governance of the Bundesbank illustrated the centralizing implications of the disempowerment of the *Land* central banks in monetary policy.

The Federal Core Executive

The main mechanism of Europeanization of the federal core executive through EMU was its use in coalition formation and in intra-party contests for power over policy. Traditionally, economic policy has been shared between the Federal Economics Ministry and the Federal Finance Ministry. Under Ludwig Erhard (CDU) 1949–63, and Karl Schiller (SPD) 1966–72, the Economics Ministry had retained the pre-eminent role as intellectual powerhouse in German economic policy. This power rested on its prestigious policy division (*Grundsatzabteilung*) where Hans Tietmeyer (Bundesbank president 1993–9) began his career, its 'money and credit' division, and its key coordinating role in European policy. After the 1972 federal elections Helmut Schmidt used the SPD's increased weight in the social-liberal (with the Free Democratic Party, FDP) coalition to shift the 'money and credit' division to his Finance Ministry. However, over the subsequent 25 years the 'kingmaker' coalition role of the small liberal FDP, and its determination to retain a strong Economics Ministry, meant that under SPD-led coalitions and then the CDU/CSU-led coalitions (1982–98) it prevented the Finance Ministry from extending its macro-economic coordinating role.

In 1998 the coincidence of imminent euro entry with a new SPD/Green coalition government, in which the Greens lacked a similar 'kingmaker' role to the FDP, offered the SPD an opportunity to strengthen its grip on economic policy. Its powerful party chair and new Finance Minister, Oskar Lafontaine, used the new challenges of macro-economic coordination with euro membership to argue for a stronger Finance Ministry to match other Euro Area states, not least France. He secured a transfer of key functions from the Economic Ministry in economic policy and in European policy, establishing a new, strengthened European Division. This 'Europeanization' reform was made possible by two political factors: in 1998 the SPD was the 'median' party (it was indispensable to coalition formation) and could take both the Economics and the Finance Ministries; whilst Lafontaine, the SPD chair, was determined to exercise power over economic policy rather than share it with a Schröder 'ally' in Economics. He also wished to use the Finance Ministry as a vehicle for radical change towards a neo-Keynesian, demand-led, and employment-policy-focused approach to European-level macro-economic policy coordination.

This core executive arrangement survived Lafontaine's abrupt resignation in 1999 and the associated failure to embed these neo-Keynesian ideas. It was, however, subject to the vagaries of his successor Hans Eichel's domestic reputation. Following the 2002 federal elections and the continuing crisis in German public finances, Eichel was on the defensive. Key functions in economic policy slipped back to a new 'super' Federal Ministry of Economics and Labour Affairs under Wolfgang Clement. This development served as a barometer of the stronger standing of Clement in the coalition and in the SPD, and a signal of Schröder's desire for a stronger political profile for his government's economic policies.

With the Grand Coalition in 2005 the Finance Ministry was in a paradoxical position. The SPD remained 'median party', though without the Chancellorship. Hence, the new SPD Finance Minister, Steinbrück, was able to defend Finance Ministry prerogatives with some success, in consequence dissuading the CSU chair, Edmund Stoiber, from accepting the invitation to become Federal Economics Minister. However, Steinbrück was not able to translate the Grand Coalition political commitment to prioritize fiscal consolidation into a coalition fiscal contract that would bind federal ministers 2009. As the two parties manoeuvred for partisan advantage before the 2008 state elections and the scheduled 2009 federal elections, he could not count on firm backing from Merkel.

Europeanization of the federal core executive under EMU did not produce a linear development of stronger macro-economic policy coordination. The ambitions of officials in the Finance Ministry's European Division to strengthen their positions vis-à-vis other federal ministries and the federal states were frustrated rather than fulfilled. A key part of the explanation is to be found in the relatively lower weight of euro-related issues in the career incentives and strategic calculations of political leaders during government formation, portfolio allocation, and policy decision-making than in those of officials. The result was a complex rebalancing of economic powers within the federal executive that reflected changing electoral fortunes of parties. The one constant was a low-profile coordinating role for the Chancellor and her or his economic policy division. Another source of frustration for the European Division derived from the constraints posed by the federal system.

The Federal System

The creation of the Euro Area challenged the federal system in two ways. First, from 2001 increasing problems of delivering fiscal discipline to fulfil commitments under the Stability and Growth Pact pointed to flaws in what had been traditionally seen as a 'unitary' federal state of 'cooperative' federalism. These problems of fiscal compliance provided an incentive for the Federal Finance Ministry, backed by the Bundesbank, to resurrect the idea of a national stability pact. This idea had surfaced in 1996–7 when Germany had fiscal difficulties in meeting the Maastricht criteria for euro entry. Second, the combination of the euro with the single market encouraged in particular the richer southern states like Bavaria, Baden-Württemberg, and Hesse, and, to some extent, North-Rhine Westphalia to seek a more competitive form of federal system. They sought more freedom to invest in infrastructure to strengthen their attraction as locations for investment. The resulting mix of contrasting 'top-down' fiscal and 'bottom-up' competitive pressures, simultaneously for 'tightening' and for 'loosening' of coordination, complicated the politics of federal reform. Europeanization was an ambivalent process.

The Financial Planning Council, which had been created in 1967, was the institutional fulcrum of federal-state–local authority fiscal policy coordination. Paradoxically, given German Finance Ministry leadership on the Stability and Growth Pact and stress on firm fiscal rules, 'automaticity', and sanctions, this body represented little more than a 'soft' coordination mechanism. The states asserted the primacy of their sovereign rights. They argued that, in the context of a strongly embedded stability culture in Germany, trust in the fiscal self-discipline of state governments was sufficient. Given that the bulk of expenditure was accounted for by the states, the federal government was vulnerable in delivering on EU-level fiscal commitments. Consequently, in 1997 Finance Minister Theo Waigel linked the Stability and Growth Pact to a domestic initiative for a new law on a national stability pact that would emulate the good practice that Germany had insisted on from others. He called for clear and binding commitments on deficit and debt from states and sanctions on individual states if they failed to comply. Despite his threat of future appeal to the Federal Constitutional Court, the states rejected this proposal. In particular, the conflicts of view between rich and poor states about how deficits might be distributed amongst them proved irreconcilable. Waigel's own state, Bavaria, was most insistent that its sovereignty should not be further eroded. Indeed, it promoted an agenda of greater autonomy in an integrating Europe. As chair of the Bavarian CSU, Waigel was too politically vulnerable to press this issue.

The painfully slow process of Europeanization of the Financial Planning Council gained momentum in 2001–2 when public finances deteriorated sharply and the European Commission criticized German failures in fiscal consolidation. Eichel agreed with the states a reform of the Budgetary Principles Law, notably a new section 51a dealing with budget discipline within EMU that aimed to strengthen coordination. Though the states committed to the principle of balanced budgets, they agreed no clear timetable (implementation was deferred until 2005), no rules for distributing the deficit across federal, state, and local levels or amongst states, and no sanctions mechanism.

Eichel's position was strengthened in January 2002 when the European Commission threatened Germany with a request to ECOFIN for a formal warning under the Stability and Growth Pact. In order to avert this threat in a federal election year, the Finance Ministry committed in ECOFIN to strengthen fiscal coordination with the states. The subsequent 'national stability plan' of March 2002, hammered out in a special meeting of the Financial

Planning Council, brought forward implementation of the new budgetary principles to 2002 and agreed that the three levels of government would achieve a total budget position of 'close to balance' by 2006. Though there was a new commitment to immediately reduce public expenditure in 2003–4, the plan fell well short of the Commission's recommendation of a national stability pact with numerical deficit ceilings. The main advance was agreement on a ratio for distributing the total deficit between the three levels. State reluctance was overcome by the argument that such rules would serve to protect them from future federal government expenditure commitments.

The Federal Finance Ministry's European Division remained unhappy about the very limited Europeanization of the Financial Planning Council and its implications for Germany's capacity to deliver on fiscal policy commitments. Its preferences for clear rules for individual states and for 'hard' sanctions were stoutly resisted by states. The idea of a national stability pact in accordance with these provisions made no headway in the work of the Federalism Commission of 2003–4, which in any case ended in failure to achieve overall agreement on how competences might be reallocated (Scharpf 2006). It did, however, resurface with the Grand Coalition's constitutional reforms to the federal system in 2006 and formed the central issue in the Federal-State Commission for Federalism Reform II. In addition to trying to unblock reforms by a clearer allocation of competences between federal and state levels, the 2006 reform introduced an obligation on the states to meet 35 per cent of any sanctions imposed on Germany. In effect, it drew them into the EU sanction's regime (Gunlicks 2007). However, it remained a limited concession. The richer states were aggravated by the unwillingness of the federal government in the 2006 federalism reform to significantly increase their fiscal flexibility on the revenue and expenditure sides. The result was a structure of federal state fiscal relations that failed to satisfy the European Division of the Federal Finance Ministry. The domestic fiscal reforms showed little signs of impact on budgetary processes at state levels, notably in increasing accountability of individual states.

In 2007 the new Federal-State Commission considered two main proposals to constitutionalize clearly defined limits on deficits and debt with sanctions in a new Article 115. Incorporation of the Stability and Growth Pact rules in the constitution was preferred by the Bundesbank and the CDU/CSU; whilst the SPD and the Council of Economic Advisers preferred more tightly specifying the existing 'golden rule' (deficits not to exceed investment) through a more narrowly defined investment concept. The SPD states rejected sanctions. Though there was consensus on constitutional rules to facilitate reduction of the structural budget deficit, there were big internal differences between CDU/CSU states on whether to prohibit new debt, with Bavaria and North-Rhine Westphalia the main supporters. The Federal Finance Ministry was itself divided on which of the two options to support.

Federalism reform debates in 2003–4 and 2005–6 revealed another aspect of EU-level effects. EU enlargement to east central Europe, the single market, and the euro provided incentives for the rich states to pursue more assertively a model of 'competitive' federalism. This model argued for more competences for the states, revenue sources to match, and greater fiscal flexibility to compete to attract and retain inward investment. It stressed the 'subsidiarity' principle in allocating economic policy competences. This discursive shift produced new political tensions and conflicts with both the poorer states (especially in the east), which depended on federal aid, and the federal government, which wanted to use the Lisbon process to strengthen its role in economic reforms (notably the SPD in education). The euro was not so much a stand-alone factor as an additional contribution to this debate. It was especially relevant to those rich Western states that had borders with other Euro Area states (like Bavaria, Baden-Württemberg, and North-Rhine Westphalia). Their frame of reference was competition on the European level to be the most advanced 'knowledge-based' economies. In terms of the Lisbon process Europeanization did not mean tighter federal coordination.

The Bundesbank

The biggest institutional loser in the EU from EMU was the Bundesbank. It underwent a difficult process of radical adjustment in functions and structure: a crisis of lost power, status, and morale gathered momentum in 2002–4 and culminated in the humiliating resignation of its President Ernst Welteke over an expenses scandal; whilst Axel Weber (2004–) consolidated its position. The Bundesbank's changed role and diminished significance were symbolized by its presidents: Tietmeyer, a high-profile international figure, was replaced by Welteke, a more provincial figure; Weber, an academic macro-economist, reflected a new focus on sharpening the profile of the Bundesbank as partner in the Eurosystem through strengthening the research dimension of its various functions, including its contribution to monetary policy formulation in the ECB Governing Council. Jürgen Stark, its pugnacious vice-president, represented the main thread of continuity with the 'old' Bundesbank. However, this thread was severed with his move to the ECB in 2006.

The changes were above all substantive. Unlike other European central banks in the ERM, the Bundesbank's work had been intensively focused on monetary policy. This focus derived from the combination of its mandate under the 1957 Bundesbank Act 'to safeguard the currency' with an unrivalled independence in interest-rate policy amongst its ERM peers and, above all, with its role in setting the terms of monetary policies across the ERM area. Correspondingly, the Bundesbank council had been the European epicentre of monetary policy, its deliberations watched with acute market and political interest. In discharging its monetary policy responsibilities, the Bundesbank was deeply embedded in German society. The majority of Bundesbank council members were the presidents of the state central banks, so that it was umbilically linked to the federal structure. Other central banking functions were secondary, notably its role in financial stability and in promoting the German financial markets. Both functions were seen as potentially in conflict with its monetary policy mandate. In this sense it was a reverse image of the pre-1997 Bank of England.

Once the Maastricht Treaty was ratified, the Bundesbank refocused its resources and energies on shaping the design of the monetary policy strategy and instruments of the future ECB. Its capacity to exercise power over these issues derived from the pressing requirement of EU and German actors to 'bind in' the Bundesbank at all stages of the transition to EMU. The 'long arm' of the Bundesbank seemed to be manifest in the appointment of its chief economist, Otmar Issing, as the first chief economist of the ECB (1998–2006) and the clear imprint of his thinking on ECB monetary policy strategy, especially the importance attached to its 'monetary' pillar and to longer-term refinancing operations that suited the interests of the German savings banks. The appointment of Stark as Issing's successor (though shorn of the research portfolio) was seen as confirmation that this imprint would continue.

The creation of the euro represented a radical role shift for the Bundesbank. With stage three of EMU, the Bundesbank ceded its monetary responsibility to the ECB, its president reduced to sharing in decision-making as just one member of its Governing Council. The Bundesbank council—not least its powerful state central bank presidents—was excluded from monetary policy. In this context currency union in January 2002 provided a timetable for an urgent re-examination of both the functions and the structure of the Bundesbank. It sought out new and enhanced roles to replace the loss of monetary policymaking, especially in financial stability, banking supervision, and payment and settlement systems. They were legitimated by reference to the increasingly close and complex interface between operational aspects of monetary policy and financial markets, boosted by the euro, its superior competence and local presence in banking supervision, and the vital importance of modern efficient infrastructure to interconnect central banks, the banking industry, stock markets, and financial markets.

The Bundesbank's increased interest in financial stability and efficient, integrated market operations was manifest in its leading role in developing cashless individual electronic payment and securities settlement systems around a single shared computer-based platform for the Eurosystem (TARGET2). With the Banca d'Italia and the Banque de France, it assumed responsibility for developing and operating this platform, including the legal framework and business organization. The Bundesbank was responding to the fact that the largest group of users was German, and German interests required that it be one of the first states to switch to TARGET2. The same three central banks, along with the Banco de Espana, cooperated in the T2S initiative that would use the TARGET2 platform for securities settlement in central bank money.

Given this role change, the Bundesbank directorate argued that a smaller, more centralized, and streamlined structure was required, that the nine *Länder* central banks could no longer be justified, and that the Bundesbank council should be abolished. Frictions arose with the Bundesbank president when presidents of the state central banks—who were Bundesbank council members—offered public opinions about ECB monetary policy though he, and not they, was responsible as the ECB governing council member. Hence, EMU triggered a complex and difficult structural reform of the Bundesbank. It involved substantial staff cuts mainly through cuts in the branch network: 11,773 core staff in 2006 represented a fall of nearly 30 per cent since 2001.

In January 2001 Finance Minister Eichel presented two interrelated legislative reform proposals. Though in part they offered what the Bundesbank directorate sought, they were also a surprising setback to its ambitions. In his proposed amendment to the Bundesbank Act, Eichel accepted the directorate's idea of a small, centralized, and single-tier governing board (to be federally nominated) and the replacement of the state central banks by regional offices of the Bundesbank. This attack on the federal principle underpinning the structure of the Bundesbank triggered the fierce opposition of state governments, notably Bavaria. The proposal involved abolition of the executive boards of the state central banks, the removal of their autonomous powers, and an end to the remaining tasks of the Bundesbank council.

However, in a separate but linked reform, Eichel proposed that responsibilities for supervision of banking, insurance, and securities markets—which had been divided—should be amalgamated in a single new Federal Financial Supervisory Authority (*Bundesanstalt für Finanzaufsicht*, BaFin) under the tutelage of the Federal Finance Ministry. Modelled on the British Financial Services Authority, this proposal had the strong backing of the big commercial banks. The Bundesbank, which was taken by surprise, gained ECB support for its view that it was risky to separate central banking from banking supervision.

Eichel legitimated these interlinked reform proposals in terms of simultaneously strengthening the European role of the Bundesbank by centralizing authority and reinforcing Germany's role as a financial centre by a modern supervisory system that recognized the closer integration of markets. Faced with political opposition from state governments in the Bundesrat, the federal government made concessions to secure the passage of the two bills in March 2002. The rights of the Bundesbank to share in banking supervision with BaFin were more clearly recognized, especially in its detailed operational aspects (which would grow with Basel II reforms). Also, the new single-tier governing board of the Bundesbank was to be slightly larger (eight rather than six) and to be nominated half by the federal government and half by the Bundesrat. This return to a plurality of nominating bodies represented a concession to the states and was justified as better securing the Bundesbank's independence. More serious for the Bundesbank was that it was thwarted in its ambition to gain full responsibility for banking supervision or at least bring the federal agency responsible for it to Frankfurt. The blow was exacerbated by Eichel's leading role in promoting supervisory convergence and cooperation at the EU level through the new Committee of European Banking Supervisors (CEBS). The loser was the Banking Supervision Committee of the ESCB, which was chaired by Edgar Meister of the Bundesbank. The Bundesbank had to share power with BaFin in the EU domain.

Further setbacks were threatened in 2007 when Steinbrück proposed to further weaken the Bundesbank's role in banking supervision by bringing this function more firmly under the tutelage of the Federal Finance Ministry. The Bundesbank rejected this proposal on the grounds that it undermined central bank independence. The proposal foundered on the opposition of the CDU/CSU and on the loss of reputation that BaFin suffered in the wake of the two bank rescues of IKB and Sachsen Landesbank in August.

The Bundesbank sought to consolidate around strengthening its research capacity and the international dimension of its remaining functions in the context of overall substantial staff cuts. This task was made difficult not just by the competition of the ECB for talented staff but also by the federal government cutting the special Bundesbank salary premium. Weber took personal responsibility for research and monetary policy to increase the impact of the Bundesbank in the ECB Governing Council (especially in refining the 'monetary' pillar). The allocation of banking supervision to the new vice-president in 2006 was of symbolic importance, along with staffing increases there to deal with the new Basel II rules.

Above all, the Bundesbank profiled itself as having a special responsibility for safeguarding stability in the Eurosystem. This led it to adopt tough positions, until 2006 fronted by its vice-president Jürgen Stark, on such matters as opposition to reform of the Stability and Growth Pact and to provisions in the draft European Constitutional Treaty that were seen as jeopardizing central bank independence.

However great its legacy of domestic prestige, the Bundesbank struggled to be heard in domestic economic policy. It had success in extending its role in technical areas like euro payment and settlement systems and liquidity management and also defended its role in the operational aspects of banking supervision. However, it confronted key obstacles in the strengthening macro-economic research expertise of the ECB in the Eurosystem; in the effective competition of the City of London in frustrating the development of Frankfurt as the German and European financial centre; and in shared powers with BaFin in banking supervision, frustrating its ambition to be the lead actor in banking and financial market supervision. In macro-economic research it was overshadowed by the ECB (though the appointment of Axel Weber as president in 2004 strengthened its reputation); compared to the Federal Finance Ministry, it had few levers of power to assist Frankfurt as a financial centre; whilst Eichel seized the initiative to sweep banking supervision into a new integrated financial services authority on the British model. Central banking talent tended to drift away to the ECB. The prestige of the Bundesbank as a privileged economic policy adviser to government had fallen.

Crucially, post-1999 the Federal Finance Ministry no longer had the same incentives to bind in the Bundesbank to its economic policy proposals. This newly found freedom of the federal government was apparent in the powerlessness of the Bundesbank's opposition to the Schröder government's support for a more flexible Stability and Growth Pact and the assertiveness of the Federal Finance Ministry in financial and banking supervision.

German Public Policies and the Euro

Perhaps the most striking instance of the power of EMU over domestic policy was the failure of Lafontaine's attempt to use the new (and, in the history of the Federal Republic, first) centre-left government to engineer a domestic and EU-level discursive shift to neo-Keynesianism in 1998–99. This shift was frustrated both at EU and at domestic levels. In contrast to Lafontaine, Schröder emphasized micro-economic supply-side reforms, to be agreed in cooperation with employer and trade union organizations, over ideas of demand-led, coordinated macro-economic policies. Schröder's approach was symbolized in the idea of economic reforms through 'government by commission', above all in the tripartite Alliance for Jobs (1998–2003), the Hartz Commission on labour-market reforms (2002), and the Rürup Commission on health and pension reforms (2002–3). This 'commission' approach to reform was constructed discursively around the ideas of consensus and cooperative capitalism. For Schröder it also served a more instrumental strategic function in 'binding in' the traditionalists in the SPD and in narrowing down the options for parliamentary opposition (Dyson 2006*a*, 2008*b*).

Fiscal Policy: Exporting Neo-Keynesian Practice

Despite the discursive demise of a demand-oriented neo-Keynesianism after Lafontaine's departure, and the stress on a stability-oriented policy of fiscal consolidation and debt reduction under Eichel, the Schröder government's fiscal policies exhibited a pragmatic combination of demand- and supply-side elements to support growth and employment rather than a rigid Ordo-liberal orthodoxy. This pragmatism was evident in the combination of the fiscal consolidation in the *Zukunftsprogramm* 2000 (which aimed at balance after 2003) with the phased tax reform and the investment programme of 2000 and in later opposition to pro-cyclical fiscal consolidation. These programmes were framed not so much around EMU as in terms of domestic Social Democratic social justice arguments about intergenerational equity as a moral basis for debt reduction. However, deficit and debt dynamics, which eluded control of the federal government, forced Eichel and Schröder to address the EMU context.

The unwillingness of Eichel to pursue a rigorous Ordo-liberal application of fiscal rules was evident in how the government responded to the sharp deterioration in public finances in 2002–3, dealt with the threats of the European Commission to ask ECOFIN to invoke a formal warning to Germany, and ignored the warnings and advice of the Bundesbank. This unwillingness was strongly motivated by electoral concerns, with the federal elections due in October 2002, and by the constraints of internal SPD opposition to accompanying painful structural reforms of labour markets and welfare policies with further deep expenditure cuts. It also reflected a neo-Keynesian view that budgetary policy should not be pro-cyclical. The mounting deficit after 2000 and breach of the 3 per cent rule in four consecutive years (2002–05 inclusive) reflected the underlying effects of a sharp fall in revenues from profit-related taxes, from income tax, and from social contributions with rising unemployment and wage moderation, and from tax cuts. Expenditure cuts only partly offset these revenue shortfalls (Deutsche Bundesbank 2006: 61). In the process public debt rose from 60.3 per cent of GDP in 2002 to 67.5 per cent in 2006.

The crisis in Germany's relationship to the Stability and Growth Pact deepened between January 2002 and November 2003 over the European Commission's recommendation of an early warning to Germany about its increasing deficit ratio. The German government's position—opposed by the Bundesbank but supported by the French government—was that it should be allowed flexibility in hard times to adjust budgetary policy to the economic cycle; that major reforms to labour markets and the welfare state (like Agenda 2010 in March 2003) should be taken into account in assessing the state of public finances because of their effects on long-term potential growth and employment; and that, if existing rules did not allow recognition of individual circumstances and Germany was being required to engage in ever more pro-cyclical savings, the rules needed to be renegotiated to make them more credible. The stimulus to renegotiate came from the crisis of November 2003 when both Eichel and Schröder lobbied at the highest levels to ensure that ECOFIN vetoed the Commission's proposal for an early warning to France and Germany. The Schröder government was further dissuaded from compliance by the severe domestic political problems it faced with Agenda 2010.

The resulting reformed Pact of March 2005 met Eichel and Schröder's requirements in adapting the fiscal rules to legitimate German fiscal policy practice since 2001. This practice involved a neo-Keynesian emphasis on avoiding pro-cyclical fiscal policies and prioritizing structural reforms to raise long-term growth and employment potential in the interests of revenue generation and expenditure reduction. Politically, it reflected a fundamentally transformed relationship between the Bundesbank and the federal government since the negotiation of the Stability and Growth Pact in 1995–7. Pursuing EMU in the 1990s created an incentive for the federal government to adopt a strategy of 'binding in' the Bundesbank by aligning itself with the central bank's Ordo-liberal orthodoxy. However, once this constraint was relaxed after 1999 the federal government had more freedom of manoeuvre both in domestic fiscal policies and in renegotiating fiscal compliance.

The Grand Coalition of CDU/CSU and SPD in 2005 gave top priority to fiscal consolidation for three main reasons: to restore lost German prestige and reassert a German leadership role in EMU, consistent with Merkel's recognition that domestic constraints made European policy a critical domain to display her governing competence; as a response to the need to forge common ground against the background of the electoral message that voters were not attracted by radical ideas of more supply-side reforms; and to take advantage of clear signs that from 2003 a new economic cycle had begun and tax revenues were increasing. The deficit declined markedly to 1.6 per cent in 2006 on the basis of strong growth of tax revenues (especially profit-related taxes) and social security contributions (before the 3 per cent increase in VAT, raising the retirement age and reducing tax exemptions took effect). Again, the Bundesbank criticized the lack of ambition in debt reduction, the focus on tax increases rather than expenditure reduction, and the need to target a reduced share of public expenditure in GDP (Deutsche Bundesbank 2006). Like the previous SPD/Green government, the coalition agreement lacked a clear and detailed 'fiscal contract' that bound individual ministries to specific spending targets and thereby strengthened the hand of the Federal Finance Minster. Whilst the Grand Coalition could take political comfort from a striking improvement in Germany's relative fiscal position, the Bundesbank feared complacency in putting public finances on a long-term sustainable path and excessive dependence of fiscal consolidation on the economic upswing. However, its voice carried relatively little weight, at a time when the stipulations of the revised Stability and Growth Pact were less precise and onerous and the government continued to avoid medium-term detailed fiscal targets.

Labour Market, Wage, and Welfare State Policies: not in the Euro's Name

The year 2003 represented a 'tipping point' in the German process of economic reform. From the inception of the Schröder government in 1998 the focus had been on the role of the Chancellor in organizing and mediating a process of reform through cooperation between employer and trade union organizations. This role was reflected in his efforts to persuade both sides to engage in longer-term, productivity-oriented wage bargaining in the interests of restoring competitiveness, and notably in the Alliance for Jobs, which was coordinated in the Chancellery. Reforms were prepared in commissions that brought together a range of interests and experts, as in labour markets (Hartz) and health and pensions (Rürup). However, the Alliance for Jobs served more as an instrument for vetoing reforms (like the creation of a low-wage sector in 1999) than as an engine of reforms. It reflected the lack of substantive economic policy ideas in the new SPD/Green government, other than the reversal of previous reforms of the Kohl government (e.g. in sickness pay and pensions), eco-taxation, and imposition of social contributions on lower-wage employment (Dyson 2002).

In practice, key reforms were routed outside the Alliance for Jobs: from fiscal consolidation and tax reform, through pension reform, to reform of works councils and changes in wage bargaining. The limitations of the Alliance for Jobs became more obvious as the economy deteriorated, and mutual recriminations gathered pace. Instead, Schröder resorted to other specialized commissions to deal with labour markets and health and pensions rather than using the infrastructure of the Alliance for Jobs (Dyson 2006a).

The 'tipping point' derived from the acrimonious failure of the Alliance for Jobs in 2003 to coordinate views on a reform agenda, and Schröder's decision to abandon it and assume personal responsibility (Dyson 2005). In March 2003 his Agenda 2010 package of labour-market and welfare-state reforms aimed to increase incentives for work through benefit reductions and new flexible low-wage forms of employment, to reduce non-wage costs on employment, and to provide efficient job placement services. In effect, it marked an abandonment of the search for cooperation with employer and trade-union organizations and reliance on them for reform ideas. The search for cross-party cooperation in the Bundestag and Bundesrat replaced that for cooperation with organized interests: in effect, *de facto* grand coalition began before *de jure* in 2005. The Grand Coalition continued this practice of sidelining the organized employer and employee interests.

However, neither the periods 1998–2003 nor the 'tipping point' itself and post-2003 economic reforms had EMU as a central point of discursive reference. EMU figured little in Agenda 2010 compared to 'globalization'; it played only a minor role in the Hartz and the Rürup reports. This unwillingness to frame economic reforms around EMU 'requirements' reflected a broadly shared elite fear of provoking a political backlash against a project that the public already saw as very questionably in Germany's best economic interests. 'Globalization' offered a less clear institutional target for voter frustrations. On the other hand, these processes of economic reform were substantially informed by comparative European 'benchmarking' of good practice, notably in the Netherlands and in the Nordic states, whether in employment or welfare-state policies. In this way government commissions and the federal government sought to clothe their reforms in a 'halo' effect. EMU did not offer a 'halo' effect for domestic reforms. This comparative referencing was a substantial feature of German economic reforms.

The main focus of reforms remained unit cost reduction, reflecting a competitiveness discourse whose roots were in the enormous political and economic power of the exposed traded-goods sector (Dyson 2008a, 2008b). This discourse drove tax reforms under the Schröder and the Grand Coalition governments (like the large VAT increase in 2007), welfare-state reforms (to pensions and to health), and labour-markets reforms (more scope for part-time and temporary working). Its also underpinned changes in collective bargaining, notably productivity-oriented wage bargaining and flexibility clauses that de facto empowered firm-centred works councils on wages and working time. The results included the slow onset of systemic change in the welfare state away from a cost on employment (the Bismarckian welfare state) to general taxation and private contributions. More immediate was a new complexity and flexibility in the labour market. This change was in part attributable to employer-led initiatives in the trade-exposed sector to entrench wage moderation, productivity-focused and flexible wage bargaining, and more flexible forms of working. It also reflected government reforms to create new forms of part-time and temporary working (especially in personal services) and incentives for people to seek these forms of employment. Again following employer best practices, the Grand Coalition examined ways of encouraging profit sharing with employees. Labour-market rigidity remained primarily a problem in the traditional service sector where craft traditions remained strong and where the CDU/CSU has a powerful constituency.

Political Parties and the Euro: Systemic Disincentives to Mobilize Opposition to the Euro

The political parties cultivated neither Euro-scepticism around the euro nor a climate of support for linking major domestic reforms to the euro. The strategic environment of the German party system shaped the domestic political effects of the euro. It produced a lack of incentives for party leaders to exploit and mobilize Euro-scepticism around the specific issue of the euro. It also led to a significant gap between party elites and public opinion on the euro. The euro was significant for what it was not, namely a 'critical juncture' in party system development. In this sense monetary union in 1999 and currency union in 2002 were unlike 1983 and 1990, when respectively the Greens and the Party of Democratic Socialism, PDS, entered the Bundestag. Euro entry was not equivalent to German unification in effects on party system development.

The euro was born against the background of a pre-existing shift from a pre-1983 process of party system concentration—that had benefited the two big *Volksparteien* ('catch-all' parties) to one of fragmentation. A two-and-a-half party system (CDU/CSU, SPD, and the small 'kingmaker' FDP) had given way to a five-party system: CDU/CSU, FDP, SPD, and—to the left of the SPD—the Greens and the PDS (later Left Party). Party fragmentation was, above all, a phenomenon of the political Left. It involved a shift in ideological range of the party system, in strength of territorial cleavage, and in the centre of ideological gravity towards the Left, as well as a declining capacity for a small party like the FDP or the Greens to play the 'kingmaker' role in coalition government formation (Lees 2005). The effects were revealed with, and after, the 1998 federal elections. The euro was linked neither to this fragmentation in the party system caused by new parties nor to splits, or threats of splits, in existing parties.

The conjunction of the September 1998 federal elections with EU decisions in May to go ahead with stage 3 on 1 January 1999 as a large Euro Area of 11 member states, including Italy, seemed to offer optimal timing for the euro to impact on party policies and campaigning and on the party system. Poll data show that for a short period Europe ranked as issue number two after unemployment. In February 1998, 70 per cent viewed the introduction of the euro as 'not good' and 46 per cent as bringing on balance disadvantages, with only 15 per cent seeing it as advantageous (Bundesverband deutscher Banken 2001). However, by election time it was no longer in the top 10 issues. The loss of vote attributable to the pro-European policy of the Kohl government was estimated to be 'below half a percentage point' (Pappi and Thurner 2000: 435). The outcome of the 1998 federal elections and structural change in the party system had no direct link to euro.

The absence of linkage between the euro and structural change in the party system is illustrated by the electoral failures associated with attempts to exploit Euro-scepticism around the loss of the D-Mark. In the campaign for the March 1996 Baden-Württemberg state election the SPD leadership opted to tolerate a tactic of criticizing the Kohl government's euro strategy, arguing for delay and a tougher, more rigorous approach. To the extent that the issue had any resonance it benefited the far-right Republican Party, not the SPD whose share of the vote dropped (Rheinhardt 1997). The SPD leadership drew the lesson that this kind of tactics could produce a negative image of cynical and opportunistic behaviour, benefit the extremes of politics (with which there was no ideological affinity), and split rather than unite the party before the federal elections. Even so, in his capacity as *Ministerpräsident* of Lower Saxony, Gerhard Schröder continued up to 1998 to express a preference for delay.

In addition, the euro was the catalyst for the formation of two new parties: the Bund Freier Bürger—Offensive für Deutschland (BfB) by Manfred Brunner in 1994 and the Initiative Pro D-Mark (Pro-DM) by Bodo Hoffmann in 1998. Both positioned themselves as defenders of the D-Mark and the independence of the Bundesbank and argued that the euro would destroy European unity. In linking this issue to right-wing policies, personnel, and networks, they reduced the appeal of their anti-euro message. The BfB gained 0.2 per cent in the 1998 federal elections and dissolved in 2000. The Pro-DM achieved 0.6 (2.2 in East Germany), ceased to campaign on restoring the D-Mark, and redefined 'DM' as *Deutsche Mitte* ('German centre'). The far-right Deutsche Volksunion (DVU), the NPD, and the Republicans wrapped their opposition to the euro in a 'harder' Euro-scepticism that rejected the integration project but similarly failed to make a sizeable impact; whilst the PDS, which had been the only party to vote against euro entry in the Bundestag, gained an additional five seats in the Bundestag.

The results of the 1996 Baden-Württemberg elections and the 1998 federal elections served as a caution to party elites about the electoral risks of trying to use the euro issue to mobilize Euro-sceptic opinion. Public opinion had come to see the EMU process as irreversible by 1998 (other than at high political and economic costs), remained overwhelmingly resistant to nationalist appeals and was prone to contextualize and hence qualify opposition to loss of the D-Mark in a generalized support for European integration (Schumann 2003). Though public opinion had shifted to a fall in support for further European integration below the EU average, and hence the passive consensus was more fragile, 'hard' Euro-scepticism had failed to find a broad support (Gallup Europe 2002: 53).

With the exception of the PDS/Left, the five-party system remained united in a pro-euro and a pro-European integration consensus. Opinion polling in November 2001 suggested that clear majorities of those expressing a party preference for the SPD, the Greens, and the FDP believed the euro was 'good': a narrow majority thought not in the case of those supporting the CDU/CSU (49 per cent to 47 per cent), whilst those attached to the PDS were overwhelmingly negative (60 per cent to 33 per cent) (Bundesverband deutscher Banken 2001). The PDS position correlated with the much higher levels of opposition to the euro in East than West Germany: 71 per cent opponents to 29 supporters in the East to 53 per cent opponents to 47 supporters in the West (Maier, Brettschneider, and Maier 2003: 56).

The historical legacies of a constrained ideological space especially to the far right (and to associated 'hard' Euro-scepticism) and the strategic environment of the party system (including the 5 per cent clause as a barrier to representation) reduce incentives to party fragmentation and in particular to mobilize around Euro-sceptic appeals on issues like the euro (Lees 2002, 2006; Smith 1976). Even if under more strain, the politics of centrality proved proof against the temptations of pursuing populism around the euro (Padgett and Poguntke 2001). Opposition to the euro has not helped the far right to find its way into the mainstream of German politics. These parties, including the PDS on the far left, were never well embedded enough in state governments to find an effective platform to oppose the euro in the Bundesrat. Hence, the federal and territorial base of German politics did not offer a venue for institutional opposition to the euro, even in the eastern states (the only state to abstain in the Bundesrat against the euro in 1998 was CDU-led Saxony). The CSU in Bavaria was constrained from extending its forays into 'soft' Euro-scepticism to the euro by the presence of its party chair, Theo Waigel, as Federal Finance Minister (1989–98). Adoption of a hard line against the euro by the far right served as a disincentive to embrace this issue for fear of guilt by association.

The core to understanding the relationship between the euro and party policies in government lies in the nature of the 'median' party: the 'kingmaker' in coalition government formation without which an 'ideologically connected' majority cannot be found (Lees 2002, 2006). In the period 1969–98 this role was played by the relatively small, strongly pro-European FDP: its Foreign Minister was the key domestic agenda setter in getting EMU back on the EU agenda in 1988 (Dyson and Featherstone 1999). After 1998 the SPD emerged as 'median' party, initially in government with the Greens under Schröder and then from 2005 in the Grand Coalition under a CDU Chancellor Merkel. This development went along with a party system shift to the Left, with first the Greens (from 1983) and then the PDS (from 1990) competing for votes in this part of the spectrum (Lees 2005). In consequence, from 1998 the SPD remained decisive in any coalition games about EMU, not least reflected in its holding top relevant ministerial portfolios (under Red–Green economics, finance, labour, and social policy; under the Grand Coalition foreign, finance, labour, and social policy).

The 'median' party role of the SPD helps to understand the broad policy style of the German government on the euro after 1998. On the one hand, reflecting the views of its supporters, it was reluctant rather than enthusiastic, compared to the Greens (whose supporters, typically better educated, were more likely to approve of the euro). However, the position of the Greens was weaker than that of the FDP in the previous Kohl government. On the other hand, the SPD kept away from the more radical critiques of the euro, associated with the PDS. To the extent that there was a radical critique from within the SPD it came from Oskar Lafontaine (party chair and finance minister in 1998); by 2005 he was campaigning alongside the PDS and anathema to the SPD leadership. Caught between a lack of enthusiasm and the disincentive to develop a radical critique, the SPD brought very little intellectual capital into office on this core policy area (on why see Dyson 2006a). Its main policy platform on the euro drew on the public's number one issue, unemployment: the euro was to be given an employment policy dimension. Precisely how this was to be achieved remained unclear.

Public Opinion and the Euro: A Loveless Second Marriage

Seen in the aggregate German public opinion has learned to live with, but not to love, the euro. Five years after the launch of euro notes and coins, Germany remained entrenched below the EU-12 average. German attitudes reflected in part an opposition to EMU on the part of some two-thirds going back to the 1970s (Bulmer and Paterson 1987; Eckstein and Pappi 1999). As late as 1996–8 only some 30 per cent welcomed the euro (Brettschneider, Maier, and Maier 2003: 49). Especially after currency union in 2002 German attitudes also reflected some negative associations linked to practical experience with the euro: initially the falling value of the euro vis-à-vis the US dollar, then widespread perceptions of inflation associated with the conversion in 2002 (especially in retail and catering where people were making frequent purchases), and post-2001 economic stagnation and rising unemployment. Attitudes to the euro reflected more general negative views about the economic situation in Germany (of stagnation and decline), even if professional economists did not attribute significant causal connections between the euro and Germany's economic problems (Maier, Brettschneider, and Maier 2003; Schumann 2003).

Flash Eurobarometer figures offer a clear picture. They show that there was on balance a positive view of the management of the currency transition (Table 7.1).

However, questioned one year after currency union, 68 per cent of Germans expressed themselves as 'unhappy' with the euro and 33 per cent as 'very unhappy', in both cases hugely out of line with other member states (Table 7.2). Austria was closest with 39 per cent 'unhappy' and the Netherlands with 16 per cent 'very unhappy'. The EU-12 average for 'unhappy' was 39 per cent and for 'very unhappy' 16, showing how much Germany depressed the average (Gallup Europe 2002: 75).

Table 7.1. Did the introduction of the euro go well or badly?

	Generally	
	Very or fairly well	Very or fairly badly
Germany	82.5%	8.2%
EU-12 average	81.6%	9.9%
	Personally	
	Very or fairly pleased	Not at all pleased
Germany	55.2%	37.4%
EU-12 average	60.4%	28.1%

Source: Gallup Europe (Eurobarometer 2002b): http://ec.europa.eu/ public opinion/flash/.

Table 7.2. Are you happy that the euro is our currency?

	Germany	EU 12 average
Very happy	3.0%	9.2%
Quite happy	24.8%	40.5%
Quite unhappy	35.1%	22.4%
Very unhappy	32.7%	16.3%
Neither	4.0%	11.1%

Source: Gallup Europe (Eurobarometer 2002*a*): ibid.

Similarly, one year after currency union, 52 per cent of Germans believed the euro was a disadvantage, contrasted with 39 per cent viewing it as advantageous: the only state in which negative opinions were in a majority (Table 7.3; Gallup Europe 2002).

In November 2005 the percentage taking this negative view (48 per cent) still outnumbered those seeing it as an advantage: with the Dutch, and second only to the Greeks (Gallup Europe 2005: 34). By November 2006, more positive economic sentiments were reflected in a slim majority (46 per cent to 44 per cent) for those seeing the euro as advantageous, placing Germany just below the EU 12 average (48 per cent) and ahead of Portugal, Italy, the Netherlands, and Greece (Gallup Europe 2006: 30).

Continuing negative sentiments towards the euro came out in other Eurobarometer results. Ninety per cent of Germans believed that the euro had had a negative effect on prices, even though officially Germany had the second lowest average inflation rate (1.6 per cent) over the period 2001–5 (Gallup Europe 2006: 34). Germany had the highest proportion (29 per cent) that viewed the euro as lacking international status, whilst German respondents were the least persuaded that it had reduced price differences amongst states (Gallup Europe 2006: 39).

The Germans reported the least effects on their feelings of being European, with 89 per cent answering in the negative (only 8 per cent positive) in 2002 and 83 per cent negative in 2006 (when they were matched only by the Dutch) (Table 7.4; Gallup Europe 2002: 71; ibid. 2006: 46).

When it came to the question on whether the euro was a major event in European history, the lowest percentage in the EU 12 answering 'absolutely'

Table 7.3. Is the adoption of the euro beneficial overall?

	Yes	No	Neither
Germany	38.8%	51.7%	5.0%
EU-12 average	53.9%	31.7%	7.3%

Source: Gallup Europe (Eurobarometer 2002*a*): http://ec.europa.eu/ public opinion/flash/.

Table 7.4. Do you feel more or less European because of using the euro?

	Germany	EU-12 average
A little more	8.3%	17.6%
A little less	1.8%	1.6%
No change	88.6%	79.9%

Source: Gallup Europe (Eurobarometer 2002*a*): ibid.

was in Germany (14.7) and the highest answering 'not a lot' (27) and 'not at all' (19.5) (Gallup Europe 2002). In 2006, 47 per cent still answered in the negative; the EU 12 average was 29 (Table 7.5; Gallup Europe 2006: 73).

As we saw above, the high proportion of negative sentiments did not translate into a significant growth either of 'hard' or of 'soft' Euro-scepticism partly because of systemic disincentives for party leaders to pursue populism on this issue. Two additional factors were at work: populist strategies were inhibited by a paradox at the heart of German public opinion towards the euro and by a generally supportive media reporting and lack of critiques from the Bundesbank and the commercial banks, with the result that popular anxieties were not fuelled by negative commentary from professional elites in banking and media.

In one sense, public opinion on the D-Mark and the Bundesbank was defined by their enormous symbolic importance because of their association with the 'economic miracle'. The D-Mark's status as a strong and stable currency, and experience of it as successful, endowed it and the Bundesbank with historical legitimacy as symbols of post-war identity in the wake of memories of the catastrophic effects of hyperinflation in the Weimar Republic. Unsurprisingly, the D-Mark's demise in favour of an untried euro elicited a compound of anxiety, distrust, and fear.

In this context of uncertainty two factors emerged as critical in 1998–2002 in qualifying public opposition to the euro: a generally favourable press and television reporting on European integration in general (Maier, Brettschneider and Maier 2003) and the endorsement of EMU from the leading banks and the

Table 7.5. Is the introduction of the euro a major event in European history?

	Germany	EU-12 average
Absolutely	14.7%	24.8%
To some extent	37.0%	41.3%
Not a lot	27.0%	16.9%
Not at all	19.5%	12.4%

Source: Gallup Europe (Eurobarometer 2002*a*): ibid.

lack of an opposition of principle from the Bundesbank. Both conservative and liberal newspapers shared a strong support for European integration in which occasional negative comments about the euro were embedded (Voltmer and Eilders 2003: 194–5). At the national level at least there was no Euro-sceptic press seeking to drive an anti-euro agenda. In order to align itself with the principle that the euro must be at least as stable as the D-Mark, the federal government's strategy had been to 'bind in' the Bundesbank and the commercial banks at every point in the euro entry process (Dyson and Featherstone 1999). This strategy was critical in the context of public uncertainty and anxiety. It defused the potential for tension and crisis between public opinion and party leadership.

At another level German public opinion was defined by the symbolic importance that the euro acquired in the process of European economic and political unification, which was associated with post-war peace and prosperity and had been traditionally supported by a passive consensus. This passive consensus endowed German political elites with a wide room of manoeuvre to play a leadership role in European unification, including even in abolishing the valued D-Mark. Germany lacked the kind of strong nationalist sentiments that could translate distrust of the new currency into a more generalized Euro-scepticism (Schumann 2003). Germans could position the euro within a generalized support for European integration: though this connection was less clear in the East (Maier, Brettschneider, and Maier 2003: 225–7, 229). The euro tested this tension in German political culture to its limits.

Conclusion: Domestic Power and Euro Leadership

The early years of the Euro Area were dominated by a weakening German leadership role that reflected the critical conjunction of severe domestic challenges from the protracted burdens of German unification for wage and non-wage costs, the EU enlargement process to the east, the emergence of China and India, and new technologies. The euro added to these challenges. From the mid-1990s to the mid-2000s Germany's leadership role waned. Paradoxically, it was sustained through the 'Germanic' Eurosystem more than through the behaviour of German governments. 2003–5 represented a turning point in the form of the reformed Stability and Growth Pact and Agenda 2010. This turning point—together with the performance of the traded-goods sector—enabled the Grand Coalition to embark on a stronger leadership role. By 2007 the *Financial Times* (2007b) was choosing Steinbrück as Euro Area finance minister of the year.

In formally depriving Germany of fiscal and monetary policy autonomy, and increasing pressure to adjust through market liberalization, EMU made transparent the relative lack of power of federal governments over structural

161

reforms to product, services, and labour markets and to the welfare state. It also provided incentives to strengthen this power through making the Stability and Growth more flexible, through resorting post-2003 to informal and then formal 'grand coalition' in reforms, and through constitutional reforms to unblock reform capacity (notably in the federal system). Nevertheless, the overriding impression was of 'bottom-up' change, driven by a powerful traded-goods sector, flanked by supportive governmental action. This mismatch of corporate and governmental performance in engineering change reinforced the image of a state in the grip of political inertia and slow transformation. EMU's indirect effects mediated through markets proved more potent than direct effects on the German political process.

Overall, the euro was not seriously detrimental to the reputation for economic competence of federal governments. It undermined the governing parties' reputation, but only marginally relative to other factors, like the mismanagement of German unification and 'globalization'. From the 1994 federal elections successive federal governments' reputations for economic competence declined, to the cost of Chancellor Helmut Kohl (in 1998) and Chancellor Schröder (in 2005). This decline contributed decisively to the erosion in electoral support for the two main 'catch-all' parties (Volksparteien), the CDU/CSU and the SPD, from 77.8 per cent of the vote in 1994 to below 70 per cent in 2005. Public perceptions both of general economic conditions and of unemployment became overwhelmingly negative or indifferent, especially in the East (Kellermann and Rattinger 2006). In particular, voters identified unemployment as overwhelmingly the top issue in the 1998, 2002, and 2005 elections; inflation only figured significantly in 2005, and then below social security (Wüst and Roth 2006: 446).

There was continuing public association of the euro with price rises, with 'perceived' inflation at times more than double official figures (cf. 5.8 per cent and 2.4 per cent in September 2007) (Bernau 2007). In consequence, the guiding shared principle of German euro strategy—that the euro must be 'at least as stable as the D-Mark'—appeared not to be fully convincing. However, price rises were not a significant issue for voters. By 2007–8 escalating food and energy prices and the erosion of consumer purchasing power threatened to produce 'second-round' effects through an end to tolerance of wage moderation. A rise in official inflation to over 3 per cent threatened to create a new dynamics in the German political economy.

Three factors account for the surprisingly low profile and impact of the euro—given the scale of public opposition to loss of the D-Mark. First, Germany lacked an emerging, let alone intractable domestic inflation problem, at least before 2007–8. Secondly, the public did not attribute responsibility to the ECB for the most pressing economic problems. Thirdly, differences of public attitude to the euro cut through, rather than between, the two main 'catch-all' parties. To the extent that the German public attributed responsibility to the euro for this decline in economic competence, it is for additional price increases (75.9 per cent) rather than for lower growth and higher unemployment (4.1 per cent), for loss of competitiveness (4.8 per cent), or for too rigid an approach to public expenditure (1.2 per cent) (Gallup Europe 2006: 89–91). In fact, 3.9 per cent of Germans polled believed that the euro had improved growth and employment (giving a net deficit of only 0.2 per cent), and 73 per cent thought that the Stability and Growth Pact was 'a good thing' because it makes the euro a strong and stable currency (ibid.: 62 and 88).

In addition, electoral incentives were stacked against exploiting partisan cleavage to shape and mobilize public opinion against the euro when the lines of division cut through each of the two main political parties. In consequence, their party leaders were discouraged from developing a legitimizing discourse for rejection of the euro and no sustained attempt was made to shape Euro-sceptic preferences around the euro issue. Given the shared historically grounded commitment to defend European unification as in vital German interest, the parties had an incentive to collude informally to ensure that measures to strengthen the euro (like the Stability and Growth Pact) were consensually supported. They had a shared interest in avoiding public and electoral blame for a policy failure that struck at the roots of German national interest. In short, the euro exhibited 'cartel-like' features in German party behaviour. Party leaders colluded in a 'blame-avoidance' strategy in relation to potential problems with the euro.

Equally, because of widespread public opposition to the euro, party elites were very reluctant to use Euro Area membership to legitimate major domestic fiscal, labour-market, and welfare-state reforms or exploit opposition to these reforms by attributing responsibility to the euro. These reforms were in their own right fraught with domestic difficulties: in part, rooted in defence of the private entitlements created by the Bismarckian welfare state and, in part, in the entrenched strength of institutional veto players in the German polity. It did not make strategic political sense to try to harness an unpopular project, the euro, to legitimate or to oppose unpopular reforms. Such an association would have deepened the crisis between political elites and public opinion. Hence party elites colluded to keep the euro off the agenda and away from legitimating discourses of reform. This lack of scapegoating of the euro in the search for an external cause to which to attribute German economic problems has its roots in the elite and public consensus on the euro as a fundamentally political project in Germany's vital national interests.

What about the images of rigidity and inertia that the euro helped make more transparent? Germany retrieved its leadership role in EMU from 2005 onwards, in a process that began in 2003 with the Agenda 2010 reforms and the first signs of recovery from stagnation. By 2007 the entrenched image of Germany as caught in a straitjacket of political inertia and rigid labour markets was due for revision. A long-standing and arduous process of market-based adjustment that was led by the exposed traded-goods sector offered the prime explanation for this reversal of fortunes. German governments facilitated and supported this process in a way that underlines the power of this corporate sector in pursuing a competitiveness agenda. It also suggests a critique of the image of political inertia. 'Inertia' is politically constructed: it suggests 'failure' to make certain changes, for instance in defending forms of corporate governance that stress long-term commitments and make corporate control by new financial market players difficult (Eichengreen 2006) and in seeking to reduce exposure to short-term financial market dependence. Nevertheless, through a combination of legislative changes (Agenda 2010 reforms based on the Hartz and Rürup reports) and firm-led adjustment in the traded-goods sector, labour markets have been made much more flexible and employment growth generated. Politically painful labour-market and welfare-state reforms and major tax reforms, again over a protracted period, demonstrated that 'consensus' democracies have a capacity for change on their own terms. This capacity involves the reconfiguration of how consensus operates rather than its demise and replacement by new governance mechanisms.

8

Greece: A Suitable Accommodation?

Kevin Featherstone

The participation of Greece in the evolving Euro Area has entailed a series of significant and varied domestic political effects. Indeed, it has been more potent than any other EU policy in this period or any since the immediate post-accession transition. Economic and Monetary Union (EMU) involved a contrasting mix of domestic effects. It has been variously determinant, facilitating, and ineffective; permanent and temporary; and both penetrating and shallow. Accordingly, the effects need to be differentiated—they eschew simple generalizations.

This chapter seeks to establish a number of themes by examining, first, the context and conditions for monetary policy prior to euro entry; then examining the impact of EMU on the polity, politics, and policies of Greece. The extent of these impacts will be gauged in terms of the 'Europeanization' literature on transformation, inertia, and retrenchment. Overwhelmingly, the experience of EMU in Greece has had a 'top-down' character, with the downloading rather than uploading of policies.

The Greek System Before EMU

Greece was obliged to play 'catch-up' on EMU from the beginning. It did not even join the ERM until 1998; at the same point, it was deemed to be unready to participate in the initial group of 11 EU states preparing for the single currency. The understanding was that Greece would join the transition group a little late, provided that current progress was maintained. By 1999, Greece was judged to have achieved the required nominal convergence, and by March 2000 it had satisfied the two-year ERM membership stipulation. The Feira European Council in June 2000 congratulated Greece on its progress with convergence as a result of its 'sound economic and financial policies'. Greece joined the Euro Area on 1 January 2001.

Yet, EMU caught Greece by surprise. The emergence of EMU on the then European Community agenda occurred at a time when the Greek political scene was confused and distracted (Featherstone 2003). Little attention was given to its implications, and as a result the process of domestic adjustment was delayed. As a process of Europeanization, EMU was more an imposed choice than one in which Greece was able to make any substantive input into its content and design.

Economically, Greece was also experiencing deep failure. Jacques Delors, as Commission President, had written an unprecedented letter to Xenophon Zolotas, the then Greek premier, warning that the deteriorating economic situation in Greece was 'a serious concern for all of us'. Delors also saw Greece as not having honoured the terms of an EC loan made in 1985, though the Mitsotakis government managed to secure an emergency loan from the EC of some ECU 2.2 billion in January 1991, albeit with stringent new conditions and a monitoring of domestic reforms.

In principle, EMU offered the Greek monetary authorities the opportunity to build a new stability culture. Whilst the objective of Euro Area membership was accepted across the major parties, the strategy for entry and the position of Greece in relation to the EMU rules became a basis for exceptional domestic conflict.

The Impacts on the Greek Polity

The institutional impact of EMU on the Greek polity involved the effects of benchmarking; disputes over the accuracy of official data; and the enhancement of the relative position of both the Ministry of Economy and Finance and the Bank of Greece, the central bank. These impacts stem directly from Euro Area participation. Each has had some transformative quality in their impact.

Maastricht and the SGP provided a set of clear policy benchmarks, seemingly independent of domestic manipulation. The Greek approach to the criteria had shown some scepticism as to their definition; it also varied with changes of government (Featherstone, Kazamias, and Papadimitriou 2000). Much domestic attention was paid to the specifications of the Maastricht criteria in the 1996–2000 period and to Greece's approximation to them. When the Feira European Council accepted that Greece had qualified for euro entry, the Simitis Government basked in the political achievement. Yannos Papantoniou, the highly respected Minister of National Economy, said that Greece's entry had been 'historic' and Greece had joined the group of the 'strong' in Europe. The symbolism was powerful and attractive to the domestic audience.

The Feira Council had accepted Greece's convergence on the basis of official Greek data, verified by Eurostat. However, with the change of government in 2004, this same data soon became a political football. The 'rights' and 'wrongs' of how the Greek data had been calculated became somewhat obscured beneath the technicalities of accountancy rules. Yet, it also became clear that Eurostat, as the relevant EU agency, had frequently raised concerns with the Athens's authorities about the basis of their data. Indeed, it had done so more frequently than for any other member state. Eurostat defended its own role in the matter by stressing that it had no legal power to control the national data. With the political change in Athens, Giorgos Alogoskoufis, the new Minister of Economics and Finance, initiated an audit. This was a highly charged act, challenging the key economic achievement of the Simitis government. The audit led the Greek authorities in September 2004 to significantly adjust the data that had been reported just before the election (see Table 8.4). These adjustments were taken up by Eurostat (2004) and reported to the Commission and ECOFIN.

Such a revision of the data was exceptional: the new deficit was 4.6 per cent of GDP, well above the 3 per cent limit of the SGP, rather than a virtuous 1.7 per cent. The figures for 2001 and 2002 had also been revised by more than two percentage points. Following a further investigation by Eurostat and the Greek authorities, it was also reported that the deficits and debt levels for the previous three years (1997–9) had also to be revised upwards significantly. Tellingly, Greece had never met the 3 per cent rule on the public deficit in the relevant reference period. In hindsight, Greece's euro entry appeared misjudged, even fraudulent.

The response of PASOK was one of fury, as evident in the parliamentary debate on 21 December. The next day a letter was published from Simitis (2004) in the *Financial Times*, decrying the fact that the Alogoskoufis's audit had not involved any independent agency and that it had 'bent previously accepted rules'. He argued that the main reason why the figures diverged was because of 'the retroactive application of a new method for estimating defence expenditure'. Simitis noted that the effect was to shift expenditure from the future to the past, easing the current government's position prior to the next elections. A few days later, the head of Eurostat, Guther Hanreich, replied in the same newspaper, denying that there had been a retroactive application of new rules (28 December 2004). Indeed, the Greek problem was due to 'a clear under-reporting ... of military expenditure irrespective of the accounting method used, an over-reporting of revenues from social security and an incorrect treatment of a significant amount of capitalized interest on government bonds'. As a result of the Greek case, the Commission rapidly brought forward (in December 2004) a set of proposals to strengthen the position of Eurostat and to bolster the independence and accountability of statistical institutes. Eurostat carried out a special review of the Greek data and, on 23 October

2006, declared that it was now satisfied with the compilation of the deficit and debt figures.

Greece was now subject to the 'excessive deficit procedure' (EDP), due to its weakened position. The general government deficit in 2004 was set at 7.8 per cent of GDP. An ECOFIN notice of 17 February 2005 signalled the action expected from Greece. The 2006 Greek budget set a target of 2.6 per cent for the deficit, with 2.4 per cent projected for 2007, and a balanced budget by 2012. In the event, in April 2007, Eurostat reported that Greece's deficit in 2006 had indeed been 2.6 per cent of GDP, pending further examination, and the following month ECOFIN agreed to lift the EDP from Greece. The public debt level was also projected to fall beneath 100 per cent of GDP—to 91.3 per cent by 2009, though in 2006 it still stood at 104.6 per cent. Alogoskoufis—an internationally renown economist—argued that his projections were realistic on the basis of high growth, rising primary surpluses (containing spending and improved tax efficiency), falling debt, and higher proceeds from privatization. The Greek stability programme of 2006 received a very positive endorsement by ECOFIN on 6 February 2007, as had the government strategy from the IMF on 25 January.

The economic position had been boosted earlier by a remarkable upward revision of GDP data on the part of the National Statistical Service of Greece (NSSG). Its head, Emmanuel Kontopyrakis, had conducted a review in accordance with EU rules. The previous revision had been undertaken in 1994. The new review led to an upward revision of Greek GDP by over 20 per cent. It took into account new survey information and the most recent census, enabling a more accurate picture of economic activity in the services sector (especially wholesale and retail trade, transportation, construction, and tourism). The foreign press highlighted the fact that the upgrade was due to new estimates on the black economy, including money laundering and prostitution (*Financial Times*, 29 September 2006). The higher GDP figure was to be reviewed by Eurostat. If accepted, the new GDP data would have meant that the government deficit in 2006 would be 2.1 per cent (not 2.6) and in 2007 it would be 1.9 per cent (not 2.1). More strikingly, given the higher GDP level, public debt would be reduced from 107.5 to 85 per cent (*Financial Times*, 29 September 2006) or 83 per cent (International Monetary Fund 2007*b*). At a stroke, Greece's relative performance in the Euro Area would be significantly improved. In the event, Eurostat agreed an upward revaluation of 9.6 per cent in early October 2007 (Eurostat 2007*b*). This was still a significant shift, altering Greece's relative position in the EU.

In no other Euro Area state have the national data for EMU been the source of so much revision and dispute. Alogoskoufis proclaimed a new transparency and accuracy in the statistics, and these improvements have been praised by the EU. Earlier, Simitis and his economics ministers—Yannos Papontoniou and Nikos Christodolou—had prided themselves on their achievements and maintaining a break from the past reputation for fiscal laxity. Never had accountancy offered such political prizes. Statistics legitimized policies and built reputations.

An unrelated issue reinforced the contest over government financial management when in March 2007 it emerged that there had been some suspect dealings over the sale of a government bond. JP Morgan, the US investment bank, had arranged a 'structured bond' for the Greek government (worth €280m) to fund some military expenditure (*Financial Times* 2007b). The clear loser had been the pension funds, with the government as a major beneficiary. The political damage was that it looked as if the government had profited by means of political pressure on the pension funds, and the matter raised questions about how the sale process had been coordinated across government. PASOK and the rest of the opposition charged the government with corruption and incompetence.

At an operational level, the prospect and reality of Euro Area membership also changed the context in which the Ministry of National Economy and the Bank of Greece acted. The 'vertical' adjustment was profound for the Ministry, which engaged many more personnel in EU-level processes of networks, reports, and meetings.[1] The cultural impact was significant as ministerial personnel witnessed new methods of working and faced new technical demands in environments of considerable peer pressure. The contrast was with the long-term tradition of the public bureaucracy in Greece, marked by low-paid, low-skilled staff with low morale. Little rectification was available to this problem, as legislation prevented flexible recruitment to administrative posts at the higher levels. Moreover, the Ministry enjoyed a major structural enhancement in its 'horizontal' relations across government. The profile and status of its leading personnel heightened, and the ministerial office received a major boost, as did the Council of Economic Advisers (SOE).

EMU also provided the trigger to the granting of full, formal independence to the central bank. This was enacted by legislation in December 1997 (Law 2609/1998) and April 2000 (Law 2832/2000). In reality, though, the Bank of Greece had enjoyed considerable de facto independence on a long-term basis. Despite the context of, at times, a highly charged and conflictual party system, successive governments had respected the institutional interests and policy management of the Bank. EMU thus sanctified the Bank's position at home, further insulating it from any risk of political interference. The biggest change was to place the Bank under the instruction of the ECB. Institutionally, this opened a new world for the central bank. It also created a new body, the Monetary Policy Council, a six-member body chaired by the Governor. According to its statutes, the Council is to discuss the implications

---

[1] Based on comments with a former senior ministerial official given in a confidential interview.

of the monetary policy formulated by the ESCB (without compromising the independence of the Governor), and it reports to Parliament twice a year.

The Impacts on Greek Politics

The impact of EMU on Greek politics has to be placed in the context of the more general discourse on the position of Greece within 'Europe'. This discourse has been structured around a long-term foreign policy imperative of placing Greece at the core of the integration process. EU entry secured the return to democracy. It also brought economic benefits, notably, substantial development aid. Public opinion recognized these benefits and became overwhelmingly in favour of European integration. Political elites saw in EU membership a lever for 'modernization' and in EMU the prospect of creating a stability culture in monetary and fiscal policy.

Yet, with the basic benefits secured, and new challenges ahead, new public concerns arose, involving something of a limited cultural backlash against perceived threats to Greek identity and a renewed sense of distance from the 'West'. At the same time, support for the single currency fell as popular criticism of its inflationary impact occurred. By 2007, the two dimensions of a cultural threat and of an economic irritant had not yet merged into a more substantial anti-EU shift, but they have created a more complex structure in the prevailing discourse.

Public opinion in Greece has long been amongst the most supportive of European integration, though it has become noticeably more fickle. The original turning point occurred in the 1980s, after accession, when both voters and PASOK switched to a more positive stance on basic issues of membership—cause and effect here between party and public being difficult to fully determine. By the time of the EMU negotiations, a large majority of Greek voters favoured a single currency. The 'Eurobarometer' public opinion surveys indicate an interesting pattern. In December 1990, some 64 per cent of Greeks were recorded as supporting a single currency, with only 10 per cent against, a level of support bettered only in Italy. In April–May 1995, the level of support had increased: 67 per cent were in favour (19 per cent against), bettered only by Ireland. On the eve of the launch of the euro, support had crept up to 70 per cent (21 per cent against), though that in Italy, Luxembourg, and Belgium was higher.

Following the introduction of the new currency, however, another turning point occurred: Greek support went into a steep decline. By October–November 2003, only 33 per cent supported the euro, with 64 per cent against, a pattern that was sustained precisely in February–March 2004. Support had recovered somewhat by June 2006: 46 per cent were reported as supporting EMU. Clearly, however, as elsewhere in the Euro Area, public attitudes had

Table 8.1. Greek attitudes towards EU/EC membership 1980–2005 (%): *I feel that my country has benefited from EU membership*

Country	1985	1990	1995	2000	2005
LU	69	72	73	70	75
IRL	67	84	87	86	86
NL	67	75	68	61	61
IT	70	65	52	49	49
GR	42	78	72	72	67
EC-12	53	58			
EU-15			46	47	
EU-25					52

Sources: (1) European Commission (1985*a*), Eurobarometer No. 24, December; (2) European Commission (1990). Eurobarometer No. 34, December; (3) European Commission (1995), Eurobarometer No. 43, Autumn; (4) European Commission (2001*b*), Eurobarometer, No. 54, April; (5) European Commission (2006*c*), Eurobarometer No. 64, June.

moved against the currency—probably in the belief that it had been used as an excuse by retailers and suppliers to raise prices.

Attitudes towards EMU must be seen in a wider context, however. Public support for EU membership remains relatively high, but the trend is somewhat negative. Overwhelmingly, the electorate feels that Greece has benefited from EU membership. In 1985, just 42 per cent believed this; but in 2005, 67 per cent did so (see Table 8.1). This represented a decline from the 78 per cent of 1990. The number believing membership has been a 'good thing' fell from 75 per cent in 1990 to 54 per cent in 2005 (Table 8.2).

At the same time, the public discourse on 'Europe' shifted. The eruption of the identity card issue in 2000 signalled a populist backlash against a European imposed modernity. In May, the Simitis Government had instigated a reform by which a Greek citizen would no longer be obliged to state his

Table 8.2. Greek attitudes towards EU/EC membership 1980–2005 (%): *I think EC/EU membership is a good thing*

Country	1985	1990	1995	2000	2005
LU	83	76	80	79	82
IRL	53	76	79	75	73
NL	77	82	79	71	70
IT	72	77	73	59	50
GR	45	75	63	61	54
EC-12	57	69			
EU-15			56	50	
EU-25					50

Sources: (1) European Commission (1985*b*), Eurobarometer No. 23, June; (2) European Commission (1990), Eurobarometer No. 34, December; (3) European Commission (1995), Eurobarometer No. 43, Autumn; (4) European Commission (2001*b*), Eurobarometer, No. 54, April; (5) European Commission (2006*c*), Eurobarometer No. 64, June.

or her religion (if any) on the national identity card. The new Archbishop of Greece, Christodoulos, strongly opposed the move. It was a threat to 'Greekness', a Western usurpation of national distinctiveness. The Archbishop led an extensive, populist campaign with major rallies in Athens and Thessa-loniki in June 2000 and gathering just over three million public signatures—a third of the electorate—to demand a referendum on the issue. President Stephanopoulos refused the request.

The emergence of the new far-right LAOS party paralleled the appeal of the Archbishop to cultural nationalism. Earlier, public opinion had sided with Milosevic in Serbia in his confrontation with the West (Michas 2002). The theme was consistent: the West threatened Orthodoxy, who 'we' are. Moreover, Greek society has undergone a remarkable change over the last decade and more. Almost a million migrants have settled in Greece since 1991. Greece has become a net importer of labour for the first time in its history, with migrants contributing about 1.5 per cent of GDP per annum (*Kathimerini* 26 January 2007a). One of the most homogeneous states in Europe has now had to confront new issues of 'multiculturalism'.

The emergence of a brand of Euro-scepticism within Greek society is a remarkable shift, given the earlier popular craving for all things 'European'. It remains a minority concern, however, isolated within the party system. LAOS obtained just 2.8 per cent in the 2004 national elections and no parliamentary seats. In the September 2007 national elections, its significance rose—it had 10 MPs—though still only 3.8 per cent (Table 8.3). Moreover, the party system remains anchored in support for the EU and EMU. Only the Communist Party (KKE) opposes the EU. New Democracy under Constantine Karamanlis (the elder) took Greece into the (then) EC in 1981 and remained a self-proclaimed Europeanist party. The shift of PASOK from opposing entry in the 1970s to

Table 8.3. Greek electoral results 1996–2007

Party	22 September 1996		9 April 2000		7 March 2004		16 September 2007	
	%	Seats	%	Seats	%	Seats	%	Seats
PASOK	41.5	162	43.8	158	40.5	117	38.10	102
ND	38.1	108	42.7	125	45.4	165	41.83	152
POLAN	2.9	—	—	—	—	—	—	—
KKE	5.6	11	5.5	11	5.9	12	8.15	22
SYNASPISMOS	5.1	10	3.2	6	3.3	6	—	—
SYRIZA	—	—	—	—	—	—	5.04	14
DIKKI	4.4	9	2.7	—	1.8	—	—	—
LAOS	—	—	—	—	2.19	—	3.80	10
Others	2.2	—	2.1	—	0.91	—	3.08	—
Total	100.0	300	100.0	300	100.0	300	100	300

Sources: (1) Ministry of Interior, http://www.ekloges.ypes.gr/pages/index.html, accessed 14 October 2007; (2) Nicolacopoulos (2005), p. 49.

its 'renegotiation' and scepticism of the early 1980s and, finally, its embrace of Europeanism by the 1989 elections was the crucial change. It was accompanied by an ideological reorientation from a loosely defined populist and nationalist socialism to a modernist social democracy. In addition to LAOS, minor, breakaway parties have been more critical of EU constraints: Politiki Anoiksi on the Right over FYROM and Dimocratiko Koinoniko Kinima—DIKKI on the Left over economic policy. But EU membership and EMU specifically face no significant challenge at the level of party elites. The EU Constitutional Treaty, for example, was ratified by the single-chamber Greek Parliament with overwhelming ease—by a majority of 268 to 17 votes on 19 April 2005.

The re-election of the Karamanlis government on 16 September 2007 gave only a modest boost to an agenda of liberal economic reform, however (Table 8.3). Voters swung against the two major parties: PASOK obtained its lowest vote in 30 years, New Democracy slipped over three percentage points, in favour of smaller, more extreme parties. In addition to the success of LAOS, the Communist Left scored its largest vote since 1974. The tragic forest fires of the summer had shaken the voters' faith in the competence of the Karamanlis government, whilst there was much criticism of PASOK's 'confused' campaign. The government's majority had been reduced, and the parliamentary support for economic reform lessened.

Within the domestic polity, Greek governments face relatively few formal veto points (Héritier and Knill 2001). Both its constitutional structure (a unitary and largely centralized state, with a politically limited head of state and a unicameral legislature displaying weakness in relation to the executive) and the tradition of unitary and single-party government create executive power. Yet, it is in the wider structures of the polity where entrenched informal veto points severely constrain this power. This 'paradox of governance' has been explored elsewhere (Featherstone and Papadimitriou 2008).

The Impacts on Greek Policies

Reform capacity in Greece is crucially determined by the nature of state-economy relations: specifically, the ability of government to lead and to negotiate support with the key business and labour actors. This context provides the intervening variables between the EMU stimulus and the domestic policy response.

The Greek model of capitalism is difficult to identify with the typology of varieties of capitalism set out by Hall and Soskice (2001: 21), as they themselves acknowledged (Featherstone and Papadimitriou forthcoming). It fits neither the 'liberal market' economies of the UK type nor the 'coordinated market' economies of the German kind. Both downplay the centrality of the

Table 8.4. Greek economy 1997–2007

	1997	1998	1999	2000	2001	2002	2003	2004	2005	2006	2007
GDP growth (%)	3.6	3.4	3.4	4.5	4.5	3.9	4.9	4.7	3.7	4.2	3.9
Inflation (consumer price indices—% change from previous year)	5.4	4.5	2.1	2.9	3.7	3.9	3.4	3.0	3.5	3.3	2.8
General government debt (% GDP) as reported by Greek Govt. in March 2004	108.2	105.8	105.2	106.1	106.6	104.6	102.6				
General government debt (% GDP) as reported by Greek Govt. in September 2004	114.0	112.4	112.3	114.0	114.7	112.5	109.9				
General government debt (% GDP) as reported currently by Eurostat	108.2	105.8	105.2	114.0	114.4	110.7	97.9	98.6	98.0	95.3	n.a.
General government deficit as reported by Greek Govt. in March 2004 (% GDP)	4.0	2.5	1.8	2.0	1.4	1.4	1.7				
General government deficit as reported by Greek Govt. in September 2004 (% GDP)	6.6	4.3	3.4	4.1	3.7	3.7	4.6				
General government deficit as reported currently by Eurostat (% GDP)	6.0	4.2	3.3	4.0	4.9	5.2	5.6	7.3	5.1	2.5	n.a.
Labour productivity (% change from previous period)	4.2	−0.7	3.4	4.6	5.2	1.9	2.3	3.6	2.1	1.8	2.2
Labour cost (% annual growth)	7.5	7.1	2.4	0.2	0.2	6.3	2.6	1.1	3.5	7.5	n.a.
Unemployment (% of labour force)	8.7	10.4	11.4	10.8	10.3	9.8	9.3	10.0	9.4	8.4	8.1

Notes: (*) OECD index of relative unit labour costs indices 2000=100.

Sources: (1) OECD (2007*a*), Economic Outlook No. 81: Annex Tables, http://www.oecd.org/document/61/0,2340,en_2825_32066506_2483901_1_1_1,00.html, accessed 13 November 2007; (2) OECD (2007*b*), Statistics database, http://stats.oecd.org/wbos/default.aspx?DatasetCode=ULC_QUA, accessed 13 November 2007; (3) Eurostat (2004) 'Report by Eurostat on the revision of the Greek Government Deficit and Debt Figures' 22 November 2004; (4) Eurostat (2007*c*), Economy and Finance, Main Economic Indicators, Public Finance–Excessive Deficit Procedure Statistics, http://epp.eurostat.ec.europa.eu/portal/page?_pageid=0,1136173,0_45570701&_dad=portal&_schema=PORTAL, accessed on 26 November 2007.

state and neglect the importance of other forms of non-market relationship, such as patronage and clientelism. Both models exaggerate the position of Greek firms to lead processes of economic adjustment. The tradition of state-driven development in southern Europe is central to Greece's economic history (Diamandouros 1994: 11, 1993; Pagoulatos 2003: 47). Yet, whilst the state was omnipresent, it was also fundamentally weak. 'Its pervasive influence', notes Tsoukalis (1997: 169), 'is intimately related to a clientele system, which it has been precisely intended to serve.'

The structure of the contemporary Greek economy is marked by very few large firms and very many micro- and small firms. Thus, the state's relations with the private sector reflect this juxtaposition. On the one hand, there is the pre-eminence of a small number of enterprise networks, and especially their individual heads, who possess a strong public profile and have privileged access to, and influence over, the 'party-state', which in turn affects the policy, planning, and allocation decisions of relevance to their particularistic interests. By contrast, there is the relative political weakness of the vast majority of Greek enterprises vis-à-vis the state and the 'heavy' impact of the latter in terms of the regulation and availability of resources.

State-economy relations are structured by this contrast and affect the reform capacity of the system and, in particular, the constituency for liberal economic reform. Lavdas (1997: 17) depicted the Greek system of interest mediation as one of 'disjointed corporatism' in which there is 'a combination of a set of corporatist organisational features' with a prevailing political environment that cannot sustain the necessary patterns of reciprocity 'and remains incapable of brokering social pacts'.

The political style is defensive, marked by short-termism, and based on distorting structures of representation of particular groups of firms and of workers.

This background of political economy mediates the pressures of EMU. As elsewhere, the crucial differentiation in EMU impacts has been between the core areas of monetary and fiscal policy, on the one hand, and other albeit contiguous policy sectors. In the core areas, executive authority is high and relatively effective. By contrast, in the wider policy areas, government must negotiate and build support. As a result, unsurprisingly, adjustment in core monetary and fiscal policies has been relatively significant and successful, whereas in the wider sectors adjustment has been highly contested and modest [see below].

The Greek economy performed relatively well under both the previous PASOK and the post-2004 New Democracy governments (Table 8.4). The Simitis administration sustained economic growth above the EU average for eight consecutive years from 1996, finishing on 4.7 per cent in 2004. This advantage was sustained under Karamanlis: growth in Greece in 2005 was 3.7 per cent (EU25: 1.7 per cent), in 2006 4.1 per cent (EU25: 2.8 per cent), and in 2007 likely to be 3.8 per cent (EU25: 2.4 per cent), with the relative trend continuing in 2008 and 2009 (*Kathimerini* 27–28 January 2007*b*). However, growth had not produced many jobs. Unemployment remained amongst the highest in the EU: 10.5 per cent in 2004, 9.9 per cent in 2005, 9.0 per cent in 2006, and estimated at 8.8 per cent in 2007. This major black spot reflected labour-market rigidities and unprecedented inward migration.

The Greek growth trajectory raises questions, however, about the goodness of fit of ECB monetary policy for the domestic economy. This is the opposite concern to that outlined by Enderlein (2004) for euro powerhouses like Germany (cf. Hay et al. this volume). The Bank of Greece in its monetary policy report for 2000–1 indicated that it did not share such fears (Bank of Greece 2001: 84). It argued that the inflationary impact was likely to be 'rather limited' for several reasons: the decrease in interest rates in 2000 was gradual, whilst for some loans it had started earlier; the impact would be offset by 'the fact that annual net income from interest will be less than in 2000'; the decrease in interest income coincided with the drop in the current value of shares, restraining domestic consumption; and a 'considerable part of the increase in demand' would be oriented to imports, easing the pressure on the prices of Greek products. In the event, inflation rose from the lows of 1999 and 2000, though its causes are disputable.

Arghyrou (2006: 3) argued that 'the single monetary policy reinforced, instead of controlling, the existing inflationary pressures'. He calculates that Greece's nominal interest rates would likely have been substantially higher than those set by the ECB. This incompatibility between the 'one-size-fits-all' single monetary policy and Greece's macroeconomic fundamentals overheated the domestic economy. The effect was to highlight the contrast between nominal convergence and real convergence—and the problems of Greece in making significant 'supply-side' reforms. Later, the Bank of Greece (2007: 7, 19) noted that the sharp falls in interest rates associated with euro entry were associated with increases in consumption and investment. These falls had contributed to generating excess demand that had, at least in part, been behind inflationary development. Again, however, there was an uncritical reporting of ECB monetary policy. Indirectly, the signal was clear: ECB policy had had an inflationary impact, yet the gains for Greece in other respects (e.g. in stable, credible policies) outweighed it. Euro Area membership was not questioned; rather, the objective was to make domestic adjustments to accommodate its implications.[2] Moreover, relatively little public attention was given to the ECB's policy stance or even the appropriateness of the SGP. Instead, domestic criticism of the euro dwelt far more than in 2000–1 on the perceived inflationary effect of the actual introduction of the new currency.

[2] See speech by Governor Nikos Garganas, 'Does One Size Fit All? Monetary Policy and Integration in the Euro Area'; Santiago, Chile, 12 October 2007.

This issue, like many others, was enveloped in a discourse that accepted Greece's participation in core EU policies as the top priority and recognized the implications for domestic adjustment as being of an overwhelmingly positive nature. The Greek discourse was crystallized in the political campaign of Costas Simitis for 'modernization'. Here, 'modernization' was defined in a manner that made it synonymous with 'Europeanization', in the sense of approximating Greece as closely as possible to EU policies, norms, and practices. The interests of Greece were bound up with the future development of the EU. Greek 'participation in the integration process was the strongest lever for our exit from a reality of developmental deficits and social backwardness' (Simitis 2005: 125). Greece had to become a credible partner in the EU, shifting from always seeking more and more aid. The faction within PASOK associated with Simitis—the so-called modernizers—in the 1990s saw their task as bringing about a wide-ranging set of domestic reforms, explicitly couched within a European setting. The requirement was structural economic reforms to introduce greater flexibility and competitiveness: an agenda that foreshadowed, in inspiration, that of the EU Lisbon 2000 project. The overall thrust was a modernization project, couched in the frame of contemporary social democracy. Whilst the state's economic role had to be leaner and more efficient, it had a basic responsibility to strengthen social solidarity. Simitis referred to a 'new social state', a theme that was shared elsewhere in Europe: not least in Romano Prodi's Italy.

As early as the 1980s, Simitis was associated with budget stability and reform. EMU reinforced that agenda. In the 1990s, he broadened the perspective to incorporate wider aspects of structural reform. Similar notions had been signalled by Delors' White Paper of 1993 and then by a sequence of European Council initiatives between 1997 and 2000, which notably in the Lisbon 2000 programme strengthened Simitis's agenda. He was clearly in line with European thinking, and his position was bolstered when the EU formulated its new commitments. There was a straightforward accommodation between the two: it would be inaccurate to describe the EU agenda as simply being 'imported' as Simitis and his supporters were already predisposed to it (Simitis 2005). The timing of the EU initiatives were crucial, nevertheless, as the domestic momentum was defined in terms of Greece's European commitment and would have been even more vulnerable without it.

Market liberalization and social solidarity marked the Simitis project. EU initiatives sought the opening-up of markets and the breakdown of state monopolies and legitimized state sell-offs. Privatization arrived in Greece with the Mitsotakis government (1990–3), but the return of Andreas Papandreou was in part based on successful campaigns against the programme. Simitis then revived the momentum—delicately crafting the discourse behind it— from 1996 onwards. The EU factor was repeatedly relevant. Financial market liberalization had started in the late 1980s and was deepened in 1991 and

1994 (Bank of Greece 1995; Pagoulatos 2005). The operating framework and the rules governing banking services had been changed radically. With respect to ownership, privatization in the banking sector began with the Bank of Piraeus in 1991 and the Bank of Athens in 1993, followed by a swathe of banks in 1998–2000 and continuing. This unleashed a wider dynamic: EU capital adequacy standards after 1992 'forced banks to widen their capital base and privatize most of their (predominantly loss-making) industrial subsidiaries in order to limit their non-financial investments' (Pagoulatos 2005: 367).

EMU provided a clear fiscal incentive for privatization, as it allowed revenues to be raised—easing the government's deficit—without politically costly increases in taxation. Pagoulatos (2005) notes that Greece raised funds equivalent to approximately 12 per cent of GDP during the 1990s from privatization, placing it amongst the leaders in the EU-25. The 1998 European Electricity Directive (96/92/EC), for example, liberalized the EU market. Though the EU directive did not require privatization, by July 2002, DEH (Public Enterprise of Electricity) was operating to all intents and purposes as a private-sector, profit-making company, even though the state still owned 85 per cent of its shares (Burnes, Katsouros, and Jones 2004). The company's organizational structure and orientation had changed. Burnes, Katsouros, and Jones (2004) argue that the EU commitment to liberalized markets was crucial to the privatization of DEH, which generates 97 per cent of Greece's electricity needs and is the country's largest employer. In short, EU pressures mattered for privatization in Greece.[3]

Yet, the reach of EU-inspired liberalization is far from clear. The core Greek strategy was to 'float' or offer shares in the companies, partially privatizing their ownership. At first, only minority stakes were offered for sale, but this was then lifted above 49 per cent for OTE, the telecoms corporation, Hellenic Petroleum and Olympic Airways (the latter unsuccessfully). However, the depth of change in the relationship between the government and partially privatized Greek corporations remains open to serious doubt.

Moreover, the implementation of the privatization programme has repeatedly proved problematic. The extreme case was Olympic Airways, the loss-making national flag-carrier. EU directives liberalized the air transport sector in three packages (1987, 1990, and 1992) with the freedom of EU companies to operate routes anywhere in Europe from 1997 onwards (Featherstone and Papadimitriou 2007). In addition, the company's huge losses were a drain on the government's budget in the context of EMU and clashed with the EU's strictures on state aids. Yet, successive attempts to reform the airline have achieved very little. The Papandreou government agreed with the

---

[3] Pagoulatos (2005: 360) argues that the shift to privatization resulted from a mix of motivations and pressures, but that 'these were associated with either the EC/EU or globalisation in general'.

Commission in October 1994 to end political interference in the company: this proved unobtainable. Moves to bring in a strategic partner, to sell off part of the firm, and to create a new company free of past debts all came to nought. Union pressures were intense, but the company also appeared unattractive. The post-2004 Karamanlis government struggled to find a buyer for the entire company. Previously, the creation of a new 'Olympic Airlines' company by the Simitis government in 2004 was successfully challenged by the Commission in the European Court of Justice, which ruled in May 2005 that it constituted illegal state aid (Featherstone and Papadimitriou 2007).

The challenge to established interests and practices was also evident in the reform of employment in the labour market. The stimulus to reform had both external and domestic aspects. The overriding objective of gaining Greek participation in the euro was connected to the specific agenda of labour-market reform when the latter was raised by some of Greece's EU partners in the context of the negotiations over the drachma's entry into the ERM. Despite enjoying high economic growth, Greece suffered continuing high unemployment. This combination highlighted a problem of labour-market rigidities (Sabethai 2000).

The Simitis government invested heavily in labour-market reform, but its stake yielded only a limited return and involved high political costs. The impact of the 1998 and 2000 reforms was limited and attempts of social dialogue had highlighted inconsistency of strategy and mistrust.

This was a difficult legacy for the Karamanlis government after 2004. It appeared, however, to show more conviction and tactical guile. It neutralized opposition by bringing forward package deals with mixed incentives and proved willing to face down opposition from its own allies. This was evident in its two reform packages of 2005, affecting the opening hours of shops (Law 3377/05) and a new labour market law (3385/05). The government then moved on to labour practices in state enterprises: in December 2005 Economics Minister Giorgos Alogoskoufis introduced a new law (3429/05) that ended lifelong security for all *new* employees in such enterprises and required new employment codes for loss-making firms. The package was a bold liberal move and seemed designed to prepare the enterprises for privatization. Again, there was much opposition from the unions and within parliament. Yet, reform from 'within' had been achieved, despite the troublesome past and without firm EU levers.

Such boldness was not to be repeated on pension reform. In Greece, pension reform *is* welfare reform—given that other forms of social security are minimal by comparison. Again, EMU produced a relevant fiscal constraint, and the Lisbon Agenda (and the Open Method of Coordination) provided new EU-level coordination on welfare policy. Reforms were made, but on a small, incremental basis, tackling immediate fiscal crises and making modest adjustments of provision. Bolder reforms were repeatedly thwarted by opposition from those with current privileges, despite gross inequities in provision. Attempts at resolving the reform problem via consultation and 'social dialogue' in 2001–2 broke down amidst recriminations about government deceit and the absence of trust on the part of the unions. A set of 'softly, softly' reforms was introduced by Dimitris Reppas, the relevant Minister, in June 2002. They actually increased the cost to the government in the long-term, with a government guarantee to secure the fiscal health of the main pension fund (IKA). The Karamanlis government kicked the issue of pensions into touch for its first term by asking a 'committee of wise men' in April 2006 to prepare yet another report. Despite EU stimuli to act, domestically pension reform remained too hot to touch politically.

Conclusions

EMU raises questions of a systemic nature. The leverage for the Simitis government proved limited. The imperative of remaining within Europe's core 'necessitated' structural economic reforms, alongside a 'modernization' of the social state. Yet, fiscal adjustment meant priority to state sell-offs of public corporations. These were done on a piecemeal basis, for reasons of political sensitivity and opposition, rather than as a new venture of popular capitalism. Indeed, the interventionist culture of government politicians into the partially privatized corporations remained intact in many respects.

EMU—and the Lisbon 2000 agenda more particularly—exposed the limits to the reform capacity of the Greek state. There was a marked contrast between the improved macroeconomic performance of relatively high growth (with falling inflation and deficits), on the one hand, and the unfulfilled promises of 'supply-side' reform. The contrast appeared to be related to differences in the nature of the policy process and implementation. For monetary policy, the policy process was relatively self-contained, and leadership was available to state authorities, often opaque to the wider public. By contrast, the policy process on pensions and the labour market was far more open, with powerful domestic actors intent on protecting sectional interests and armed with their own knowledge of current practice. EU leverage proved insufficient on the wider domestic landscape of employment and welfare interests, with much structural unemployment and evidence of public concern over EMU.

The Greek economic and social 'model' affects the rational interests of voters, who in the context of very limited unemployment benefits are induced to seek the preservation of job security. The engrained culture of 'clientelism' creates its own political constraint on state–society relations. The problems of reform capacity in Greece are truly systemic, rather than the simple result of union opposition or of the 'wrong' party or leader in office.

The Greek political economy has undergone a number of long-term changes in the last two decades or more. According to Pagoulatos (2003, 2004), Greece has made the transition from a weak and incomplete 'development state' (dependent on state-controlled finance) to a fully fledged 'stabilization state', operating in the context of EMU and financial liberalization. Particularly, for Greece, increased competition under EMU creates a strong external push for advancing liberalization in the product, services and labour markets, including greater flexibility in wage and employment conditions to offset the loss of control over monetary policy' (Pagoulatos 2003: 208–9). The external stimuli also encouraged neo-corporatist social pacts at home. However, the reality, fell well-short of these projections on all accounts. Structural reforms were limited, pacts elusive. Moreover, unlike in other EU states such as Belgium, wage negotiation has not adopted external benchmarking. Fundamental features of the Greek 'system' remain undisturbed by EMU and provide the domestic constraints on reform capacity.

The contrasting Greek performance was also related to differences of 'commitment device' emanating from the EU—the 'hard' constraints of EMU and the 'soft' constraints of Lisbon. A 'window of opportunity' of leverage from euro entry may have been squandered, as reform initiatives proved modest. After entry and with the Lisbon agenda, the strategic empowerment was far less. Public opinion had shifted from 'statism', but remained anxious over the consequences of reform. Moreover, after euro entry popular attitudes towards the EU showed a notable negative shift. The earlier idealized image of 'Europe' was now challenged by fears of cultural encroachment. The public discourse was now far more complicated. The issue raised in this context is of how far Greece can reform without the leverage of an effective EU constraint. It was notable, for example, that Nikos Christodoulakis, when Minister of National Economy, failed to join in the chorus of criticism from Prodi and others directed at the SGP in 2003. It seemed to signal an appreciation of the existing fiscal constraint. The default option is a strategy of gradualism: of government seeking consensus and shifting perceptions. The Karamanlis government claims to be following such a path and has scheduled pension reform as a priority in its second term. Given the uncertain will of the EU to pursue a more focused and vigorous agenda, such a strategy may prove just enough to satisfy Greece's core foreign policy interest.

EMU entry has highlighted key questions of governance and of external adjustment for Greece. Paradoxes abound. Greece adjusts gradually, is much less the black sheep, and remains part of the core. There are no imminent threats. A syndrome is set.

9

Ireland: The Outlier Inside

Colin Hay, Jari Matti Riiheläinen, Nicola J. Smith,
and Matthew Watson

Ireland inhabits a unique position within the Euro Area. It is an outlier in
almost every relevant respect, being the sole liberal market economy within
the Euro Area, the most distant geographically of the Northern European
members from the heart of the Euro Area, the most heavily dependent in
terms of trade and investment on non-Euro Area economies (in particular
the UK and the USA), and one of only three members that are not part
of the continental land mass. Partly as a consequence, its business cycle
(at least on entry) was not at all closely aligned with that of the core
Euro Area economies, and, owing to its trade dependence on the Anglophone economies in particular, its economy was characterized by relatively
low levels of intra-industry Euro-Area trade. On the face of it, it had less
to gain from Euro-Area membership than other prospective participants
in EMU. The relative size of the anticipated microeconomic advantages—
principally, reduced transactions costs, more effective price signalling mechanisms and the elimination of exchange rate uncertainty with its Euro
Area trading partners—was always likely to be less than for other member states. And, in macroeconomic terms, it arguably had much to lose—
in adapting itself to a sub-optimal interest rate setting and to the loss of
competitiveness in key export markets that might arise from an appreciating
currency.

The Irish case thus poses a series of interesting political and political economic questions. Has EMU worked, and can it continue to work, for Ireland?
Are the potential gains for the 'outlier inside' greater than those for economies
closer to the core? Is Ireland's seemingly good economic performance in
recent years attributable to EMU in any way or has the latter been a drain
on growth and the sustainability of its growth trajectory? And what effect has
Euro Area membership had on the embeddedness of the Irish economy within
the European Union and Euro-Area?

These are the principal concerns of this chapter. Its argument unfolds in three sections. In the first of these, we consider the domestic debate over the merits and demerits of Irish membership of the Euro Area in the period before and subsequent to entry. In the second, we turn directly to Ireland's performance within the Euro Area since 1999 and to the contribution of EMU to that performance. Finally, in the third, we raise more prospectively some concerns about the viability of the growth trajectory on which the Irish economy is currently embarked in the context of the Euro Area by reflecting in some detail on the contribution of the housing market to the Irish economy's peculiar and distinctive growth trajectory in recent years.

Debates about EMU in Ireland

It has often been noted that Ireland's decision to join the EMU was principally motivated by political rather than economic considerations (e.g. Fitz Gerald 2001; Honohan 2000; Lane 2006; Smith 2005). Indeed, our own interviews with policymakers consistently highlight how membership of the euro was seen as attractive primarily because it offered Ireland the opportunity to operate (or to continue to operate) at the heart of the EU decision-making process.[1] Yet, in public debates, it appears that the rationale for joining EMU was articulated rather differently. Claims that acceptance of the Treaty of Maastricht (and by implication EMU) would be beneficial politically were certainly expressed. Yet a detailed examination of Dáil Éireann debates reveals that this was by no means the most pervasive discourse. Rather, the most common argument was that the economic policy entailed by the Treaty of Maastricht convergence criteria (budget deficit below 3 per cent, public debt below 60 per cent of GDP) represented 'good economic policy' to which there was no sensible alternative. Quite simply, EMU made good economic sense.[2] What is more, this was not merely a government view—there was strong consensus among the major parties on the issue.[3] The economic character of that consensus is also reflected in the fact that the second most frequently cited

[1] We refer to 28 interviews with senior policymakers, economic advisers, and opinion formers conducted by Nicola J. Smith in 2002 and 2005. Interviewees were carefully selected to reflect a range of perspectives within and outside the Irish government and all were semi-structured and open rather than tightly structured and closed. Interviewees have requested that quotations are not directly attributable (in part due to concern about future social partnership negotiations) but a full list of names is available from Nicola Smith. We are indebted to the Economic and Social Research Council for funding this research (project grant RES000220780).
[2] This argument was found in 80 speeches out of 218 that were examined during the period between 1992 and 2003.
[3] Such discourses appeared in 45 speeches from Fianna Fáil, 16 from Fine Gael, and 16 from Labour, in addition to three from the Progressive Democrats.

Table 9.1. Irish policymakers' attitudes to the benefits of EMU membership

	'Membership of EMU is good for Ireland's economic performance'			'Membership of EMU increases Ireland's influence in Europe'		
	Strongly agree/ agree (%)	Neither (%)	Strongly disagree/ disagree (%)	Strongly agree/ agree (%)	Neither (%)	Strongly disagree/ disagree (%)
Civil servants	95.4	2.3	2.3	71.1	21.4	7.4
Members of the Dáil	92.0	4.8	1.6	74.2	14.5	9.7
Fianna Fail	92.0	4.0	4.0	72.0	12.0	12.0
Fine Gael	100.0	0.0	0.0	85.7	14.3	0.0
Labour	100.0	0.0	0.0	100.0	0.0	0.0

argument in favour of EMU was that it would promote economic stability.[4] The centrality of an economic logic to the EMU discourse of Irish policymakers is also supported by our own more recent survey data.[5] This shows that nearly all (93.7 per cent) of Irish policymakers believe that membership of EMU is beneficial for Ireland's economic performance. A significantly lower, if still substantial, majority (72.7 per cent) feel that EMU enhances Ireland's influence in Europe. In terms of EMU's overall benefits, just 2.9 per cent of Irish policymakers opposed Irish membership (see also Table 9.1).

The attitudes of the Irish public have also been strongly positive. A survey undertaken prior to the adoption of the euro found that Irish citizens (at 64 per cent) were the second most likely in the Euro Area (after Luxembourg, at 66 per cent) to agree with the sentiment that the euro would be personally advantageous to them (Eurobarometer 2001b: 46). Since joining, overall support for EMU amongst Irish citizens has remained high, fluctuating at levels between 72 and 75 per cent in the period 2002–6 (see also Figure 9.1).

However, when asked to identify the specific benefits and drawbacks of Ireland's EMU membership, Irish citizens reveal a rather different view from that of their policymakers. While they saw EMU as making travel easier and cheaper, and also making prices easier to compare, they do not appear to

---

[4] For example, as Minister of State at the Department of Finance, Martin Cullen (Fianna Fáil), argued to the Dáil Éireann in 1998: 'EMU . . . will increase the efficiency of the Single Market through the elimination of the exchange rate risk and improved transparency and competition. It will also provide a new environment of price stability and sound public finances. These will, among other things, reduce the uncertainties that impede investment decisions and should, therefore, provide a solid basis for future growth and employment generation' (Cullen 1998).

[5] This survey consisted of a postal survey sent to all Members of the Dáil and a random sample of 500 senior and middle-ranking civil servants (out of which 286 policymakers—or 42.5 per cent responded). The questionnaire comprised 37 questions of identical answer formats ('strongly agree', 'agree', 'neither', 'disagree', or 'strongly disagree') that through earlier qualitative analysis had been carefully selected to reflect a range of perspectives regarding globalization and European integration. For further details, see Smith and Hay (2007).

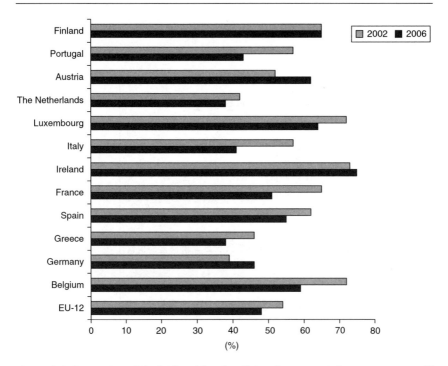

Figure 9.1. Proportion of the Irish public identifying the euro as 'advantageous overall' for their country, 2006

Source: Adapted from Eurobarometer (2002, 2006).

accept the broader economic and political benefits that Irish policymakers have been so keen to emphasize. Instead, they pointed to the key drawbacks of EMU as being 'more unemployment, less growth', and 'loss of sovereignty' (see Table 9.2). Thus, while Irish citizens consistently express themselves positively towards EMU, their reasons are rather different from those articulated in Irish public policy discourse (Table 9.3).

While the degree of support for EMU amongst Irish policymakers and the general public is striking, the Irish media have been somewhat more circumspect. Whereas the *Irish Independent* has on the whole been pro-EMU, more consistently critical voices have been expressed in the *Irish Times*— most notably, prior to membership. Cliff Taylor is representative of this view in arguing that 'loss of economic independence and rising unemployment may be the price Ireland pays for EMU ... As a small open economy, Ireland's policy independence is already restricted. Joining the single currency would impose a much tighter strait-jacket' (*Irish Times*, 20 October 1995). This view was shared by a number of prominent Irish economists, who pointed to the profound constraints on Ireland's national policymaking autonomy that

185

Table 9.2. Main advantages of the adoption of the euro—Irish public opinion, 2006

	More stable prices (% = 'yes')	Reinforce place of Europe in the world (% = 'yes')	Improve employment growth (% = 'yes')	Easier/ cheaper to travel (% = 'yes')	Easier to compare prices (% = 'yes')	Lower interest rates, less debt charges (% = 'yes')	Sounder public finances (% = 'yes')
EU-12	11.2	27.2	5.2	45.9	30.2	4.2	4.7
Belgium	14.3	22.5	5.8	60.8	52.1	2.2	1.7
Germany	9.8	17.3	3.9	46.7	33.2	1.0	2.4
Greece	17.8	29.9	8.2	24.6	17.3	1.0	10.6
Spain	9.0	25.0	6.4	51.5	16.9	1.3	4.1
France	5.5	27.9	3.6	37.4	16.3	2.6	2.6
Ireland	22.4	16.8	11.3	63.1	47.5	27.6	18.3
Italy	19.1	35.1	6.4	42.8	39.4	10.9	8.5
Luxembourg	14.3	22.2	7.7	71.8	59.6	2.3	3.7
The Netherlands	7.4	18.4	3.9	34.0	28.9	1.0	2.7
Austria	12.9	16.7	6.9	57.0	51.5	8.1	4.4
Portugal	17.5	25.8	9.7	66.1	53.3	8.1	5.1
Finland	7.4	9.7	1.9	57.6	38.8	8.7	16.1

Source: Compiled from Eurobarometer (2006: 87–8).

Table 9.3. Main disadvantages of the adoption of the euro—Irish public opinion, 2006

	Low interest rates (% = 'yes')	Too rigid for public spending (% = 'yes')	Loss of competitiveness (% = 'yes')	Price rises (% = 'yes')	Loss of sovereignty (% = 'yes')	More unemployment, less growth (% = 'yes')
EU-12	3.0	1.9	5.2	81.4	5.0	7.0
Belgium	4.0	6.6	10.2	89.2	2.6	12.6
Germany	0.6	1.2	4.8	75.9	6.4	4.1
Greece	1.6	0.9	2.5	82.2	2.9	6.0
Spain	0.6	0.8	1.5	85.9	1.2	3.0
France	0.3	0.0	5.1	64.4	6.6	5.0
Ireland	6.6	6.3	6.5	22.1	24.0	58.3
Italy	8.8	3.5	5.3	95.9	3.1	10.6
Luxembourg	2.0	3.0	16.5	85.4	11.0	11.3
The Netherlands	2.1	1.1	5.9	85.7	2.7	4.0
Austria	4.0	4.2	8.2	92.7	7.4	11.7
Portugal	4.7	5.1	16.7	91.8	9.0	22.2
Finland	0.8	5.5	7.4	64.9	16.8	1.5

Source: Compiled from Eurobarometer (2006: 89–90).

EMU represents (e.g. Barry 2001; Leddin and Walsh 1998; MacCoille and McCoy 2002). That said, some commentators took the view that—whatever the constraints posed by EMU—the dangers of opting out would be more severe (not least due to the macroeconomic uncertainty it would create for foreign investment, which had accelerated in the early 1990s due to the establishment of the Single European Market) (e.g. Baker, Fitz Gerald, and Honohan 1996). With the Irish economy performing relatively well since entry, Irish economists have tended to express optimism, albeit qualified, about Ireland's future prospects (e.g. Honohan and Leddin 2006; Traistaru-Siedschlag 2007).

Business representatives, too, expressed some initial concern about the impact of EMU on Ireland. In particular, there were fears that Ireland's decision to join without its closest trading partner, Britain, could leave it vulnerable to sterling volatility and (especially) sterling weakness. This could, in turn, lead to a loss of competitiveness in sterling-sensitive sectors. However, given that the most dynamic sectors in the Irish economy (such as electronics and pharmaceuticals) are not sterling-sensitive, such anxieties have not translated into a generalized resistance towards EMU across the business community. Quite the contrary: the bulk of business representatives welcomed the prospects for sustained low inflation, reduced interest rates, the elimination of currency transaction costs and exchange-rate uncertainty and increased price transparency and stability (IBEC 2000). One survey by the Irish Business and Employers' Confederation (IBEC 1999) found that over two-thirds of its members anticipated that EMU would impact positively on their business (with the remainder more indifferent than negative). On the whole, then, the business community in Ireland welcomed EMU.

In sum, then, Irish attitudes to EMU entry, both public and amongst political elites, were, and by 2007 remained, extremely positive. Moreover, they have not altered decisively with the experience of membership. Yet, there have been dissenting voices—and the substance of their concerns has been consistent. For a number of academic commentators and certain sections of the business community, EMU entry *without Britain* has posed for Ireland a significant exchange-rate risk for producers, particularly those in the most sterling-sensitive sectors. To that concern has now been added additional anxieties about the potential loss of price competitiveness in the US market, with the appreciation of the euro against the dollar (see Chapter 2 by Cohen). On the macroeconomic side, consistent concerns have been expressed, again largely by academic sceptics, about the costs of adjustment of the Irish economy to a sub-optimal interest rate set in Frankfurt for the entire Euro Area economy rather than in Dublin for the Irish economy. It is to the direct evidence of the Irish experience within EMU that we now turn in an attempt to gauge the legitimacy of such concerns.

The Outlier Inside's Experience within the Euro Area

Membership of the Euro Area has undoubtedly had a considerable impact on macroeconomic governance in Ireland. Although all states within the Euro Area were required to relinquish formal control of monetary policy to the ECB, the implications for Ireland are potentially more severe. This is because the Irish economy cycles is out of phase with that of the core continental states in the Euro Area due to its heavy export and investment dependence on the UK and USA. Such misalignment between the Irish and Euro Area business cycles means that Ireland's interest rate demands are unlikely to be met by the ECB. With currency devaluation no longer an option, EMU leaves Ireland less able to adjust to country-specific shocks. Yet the principal measure through which Irish policymakers might adjust to such shocks—fiscal policy—is itself constrained by the 3 per cent budget deficit limit imposed by the Stability and Growth Pact. Since EMU results in the loss of important policymaking instruments, setting the exchange rate and interest rate, the pressure for adjustment falls on the labour market.

The Political Dimension

In a political economy characterized by its social partnership arrangements, this might well have been expected to politicize EMU. Yet it has not served to generate significant opposition to EMU, nor has it become a significant tension between the social partners. It is interesting to consider why.

In interviews, Irish policymakers consistently identified the constraints of the Stability and Growth Pact on their policymaking autonomy as 'huge'. That said, there was also some recognition that these constraints might sometimes be invoked for strategic reasons. As one very senior civil servant suggested: 'I think maybe we're inclined to invoke Europe...when actually the lines of policy are what we would do anyway'.[6] Indeed, while Ireland has never broken the terms of the Pact, tensions between Ireland and the European Commission emerged in 2001. The budget of 2001 promised to represent the 'biggest tax and social welfare package in the history of the State', and an 'unprecedented opportunity' to spread Ireland's wealth more evenly (Ahern 2001: 4). In response, the European Commission issued a formal reprimand to Ireland on the grounds that the budget was 'inappropriately expansionary' and inconsistent with the Broad Economic Policy Guidelines (European Commission 2001*a*: 38). The Irish government refused to alter its budgetary policy, with the Minister of Finance declaring: 'It is no accident that in all European countries, there is growing support for people who want to step back' (cited in *Irish Times*, 8 May 2002).

Yet Ireland's membership of EMU has not become a highly politicized issue; quite the contrary, the most striking characteristic is the *absence* of political debate about EMU.[7] Rather, EMU has been—and continues to be—articulated as a non-negotiable external constraint (Hay and Smith 2005). For example, as Fianna Fáil and the Progressive Democrats stated in their 2002 programme for government (p. 7): 'The EU Stability and Growth Pact provides the overriding framework for our budgetary policy. Under the pact Ireland has given a sovereign commitment to keeping the finances of general government close to balance or in surplus.' This view has been reflected in successive social partnership agreements between the government and key economic and social interests, which have characterized Irish macro-economic policymaking since 1987. As the latest agreement, *Towards* 2016, states:

With monetary policy set by the European Central Bank, macroeconomic policy is now essentially concerned with management of the public finances, incomes policy and structural reform. The key principles referred to, particularly sustainability and prudent fiscal policy, will guide the management of the public finances (Government of Ireland 2006: 16).

[6] Interviews conducted by Nicola J. Smith (2002, 2005).

[7] For example, the view of the National Economic and Social Council—the body responsible for coordinating social partnership negotiations—has tended to be that 'there is little value in active discussion of macro-economic matters, or in agonising over the transition to, or terms of, European monetary union' (O'Donnell 2001: 3).

Above all, EMU is understood by the social partners to heighten the need for budgetary and wage restraint (e.g. MacCoille and McCoy 2001).[8]

Nor can EMU be seen to have had much of a direct impact on electoral politics in Ireland.[9] Ireland's strong economic performance since the late 1990s certainly contributed significantly to Taoiseach Bertie Ahern's decade-long tenure in office. Moreover, the impression that EMU is responsible to a significant extent for that performance has served to consolidate further the pre-existing cross-party and social partner consensus on the subject. Yet, Fine Gael and the Labour Party mounted strong challenges in the 2007 election, bringing up social problems, unequal wealth distribution and housing problems resulting from the economic boom. This was successful, in that Fine Gael gained 20 seats, but it was not enough for them to overtake Fianna Fáil. While there was some evidence of dissatisfaction with the government among citizens, EMU and its effects on the Irish economy did not feature in the debate.

The Economic Dimension

Turning to the economic impact of EMU on Ireland, the principal concern amongst the Irish business community prior to entry was that the loss of control of the exchange rate, when set in the context of the anticipated strength of the euro on international markets, might damage Irish (price) competitiveness in key non-Euro Area export markets. If we are to gauge the legitimacy of such concerns, it is important to track exchange-rate movements both before and after EMU entry.

Figure 9.2 shows the punt–sterling exchange rate prior to EMU entry and the euro–sterling exchange rate following entry. Figure 9.3 presents similar data for the punt–dollar and subsequently euro–dollar exchange rates. Both graphs also display least-means-square trend lines for the periods 1990–9 and 1999–2007, and a standardized punt exchange rate for the entire period.

---

[8] It should be noted that Irish social partnership, which was first introduced in 1987, was borne out of a sense of economic crisis and initially focused on the need to control Ireland's spiralling public finances through public borrowing and expenditure cuts and through wage restraint. While the Republic's subsequent economic boom meant that the emphasis soon shifted from managing crisis to managing growth (Hardiman 2000), the need for budgetary and wage restraint has remained a central theme in macroeconomic policy that has only become strengthened under EMU.

[9] If one examines the 10-year period between elections in 1997 and 2007, the picture looks relatively stable. After all three elections (1997, 2002, and 2007), the government has been formed by Fianna Fáil and Progressive Democrats, which are both pro-EMU parties, with the addition of the Green Party to the government in 2007, when the two parties were not able to form a majority coalition between them. During this period, Fianna Fáil's popularity has been relatively stable, with 77 seats in 1997, 81 in 2002, and 77 in 2007, being clearly the largest party in Ireland. Their coalition partner, the Progressive Democrats, has had more change in their electoral support, from four seats in 1997, to eight in 2002, and suffering a loss in 2007, only managing two seats. But the largest pro-EMU party, Fianna Fáil, has continued to have strong support.

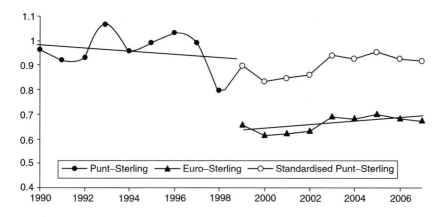

Figure 9.2. Punt–sterling exchange rate, 1990–2007
Source: Irish Central Statistics Office; European Central Bank, authors' own calculations.

Any appreciation in the value of the punt/euro against its anglophone trading partner equivalents (an upward trend) indicates a loss of simple price competitiveness; conversely any depreciation (a downward trend) represents a gain in simple price competitiveness.

The picture that this data paints is relatively clear, and seems to add some substance and plausibility to the sceptics' case. The euro appreciated

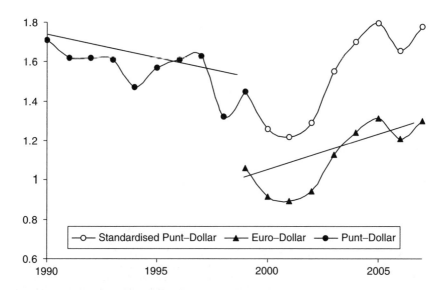

Figure 9.3. Punt/euro–dollar exchange rate, 1990–2007
Source: Irish Central Statistics Office; European Central Bank, authors' own calculations.

significantly against both the sterling and the dollar, appreciably in the latter case. Moreover, in each case, this reverses the trend depreciation of the punt against both currencies in the period prior to entry. Consequently, Ireland witnessed a significant loss in simple price competitiveness in both of its principal non-Euro Area export markets. Just as the 1990s witnessed a significant improvement, so the period since 1999 has seen a significant erosion of simple price competitiveness.

This does not look like good news for the Irish economy. Yet, before drawing the perhaps obvious inference from this data, it is first important to note a few contextualizing complications.

1. Any losses arising from an appreciating currency in external markets need to be offset against the benefits of the elimination of currency transaction costs and exchange-rate uncertainty within newly internal (i.e. Euro Area) markets. It is only if we gauge the relative size of these effects that we can be clear about the net benefits or losses to the Irish economy.

2. Much of the sceptics' discourse is predicated on the assumption that, had Ireland retained the punt, it would have used devaluation as a means to boost its competitiveness in key export markets. That is far from self-evident; indeed, it is extremely unlikely. There is no recent Irish example of the use of such a competitive devaluation strategy.[10]

3. It is dangerous to attribute the appreciation of the euro against both the dollar and sterling solely to factors internal to the Euro Area. Consequently, it is wrong to see a loss of price competitiveness in the UK and US markets as a simple product of EMU. Indeed, as a more detailed consideration of the timing of exchange-rate movements shows, it is far more plausible to see the appreciation of the euro against the dollar since 2001 as a product of exogenous shocks (such as the slowdown in the world economy before and after 9/11 and the Second Iraq War).

Each of these points is an important caveat to any simple reading of Irish EMU entry as responsible for a loss of price competitiveness in key export markets. But it is nonetheless the case that the euro has appreciated against the dollar and sterling in a manner many predicted prior to entry, reversing in so doing a long-term trend depreciation of the punt.

---

[10] Ireland devalued the punt by 10 per cent in late January 1993. It would be wrong, however, to see this as an instance of a strategy of competitive devaluation. The principal objective was to restore the confidence of international markets, following a period of sustained weakness of sterling. It followed an earlier decision not to devalue the currency in the wake of sterling's forcible ejection from the Exchange Rate Mechanism in September 1992. Five thousand million punts were spent by the Irish government on foreign exchanges at that time in maintaining a stable exchange rate with the D-Mark (Leddin and O'Leary 1995).

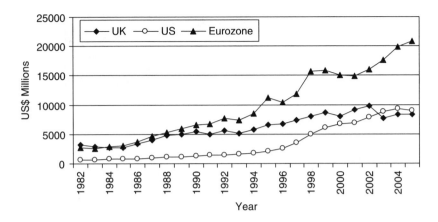

Figure 9.4. Irish exports (at constant 1982 US$ millions)
Source: IMF direction of trade statistics (various years).

This raises a further, crucial, empirical question: what, if any, impact has this had on the geographical character of Ireland's economic interdependence? Has Ireland, for instance, started to shed its historic trade dependence on the UK? And have exports to the USA suffered from a loss of price competitiveness?

To answer these questions, we turn to the Irish trade and direction of trade data.

Figure 9.4 presents data on Irish exports to the USA, the UK, and the Euro Area from 1982 to 2005. It shows strong continued growth in the Euro Area and US markets since 2001. Interestingly, however, it shows some loss in recent years in exports to the UK market. Overall, it suggests a growing export orientation towards the Euro Area.

Figure 9.5 shows the Irish economy's trade balance with the USA, the UK, and the Euro Area. This shows even more clearly that, despite a worsening of simple price competitiveness with the USA since 2001, Ireland merely strengthened its already considerable trade surplus. It also shows that Ireland competed well in the Euro Area market, opening up a very healthy and seemingly ever-growing trade surplus. It does, however, suggest that a combination of a loss of export price competitiveness and the improved price competitiveness of UK imports has contributed to a significant worsening of the trade balance with the UK—which is now in growing deficit. This is perhaps to be expected, since Ireland's ties with the UK are historic and trade between the two economies is rather more intense in traditional, low-technology sectors which tend to be more price-sensitive. Trade with the Euro Area and the USA in particular tends to be is less price sensitive.

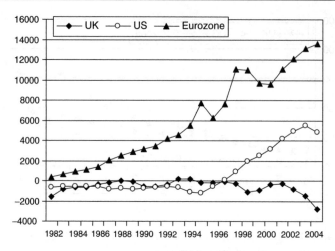

Figure 9.5. Irish trade balance (at constant 1982 US$ millions)
Source: IMF direction of trade statistics (various years).

Finally, in terms of trade, Figure 9.6 presents data on the share of Irish exports destined for the USA, the UK, and the Euro Area. This shows very clearly the long-term decline in exports to the UK market, the steady growth since EMU entry of exports destined for the Euro-Area market and the recent decline in the share of exports destined for the USA. Overall, it shows that, although the USA continues to be a substantial export market for the Irish economy, the period since EMU entry has seen something of a weakening of trade dependence of the Irish economy on the UK and the USA as it has become ever more closely integrated with the Euro-Area economy. This is

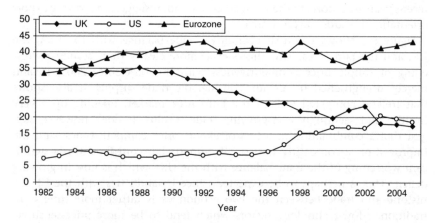

Figure 9.6. Share of Irish exports 1982–2004
Source: IMF direction of trade statistics (various years).

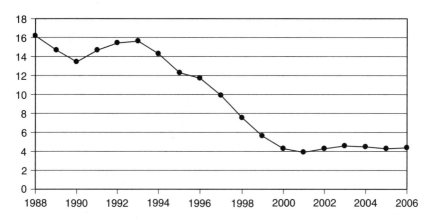

Figure 9.7. Irish (world standardized) unemployment levels, 1998–2006
Source: Irish central statistics.

good news for Ireland's economic stability within the Euro Area, since it is likely to prompt further business cycle convergence. Moreover, this is only reinforced by the modest, but accelerating, growth in intra-industry trade as a share of Ireland's total trade with the Euro Area (Faruquee 2004).

With significant and growing trade balances with its two largest export markets, the Euro Area (taken as a whole) and the USA, it is hardly surprising that Ireland's headline economic performance continues to be excellent.

As Figure 9.7 shows, Irish unemployment is both unprecedentedly low and stable. Moreover, as Figure 9.8 demonstrates, since EMU entry (indeed, for some time prior), Irish growth rates have consistently exceeded the Euro Area

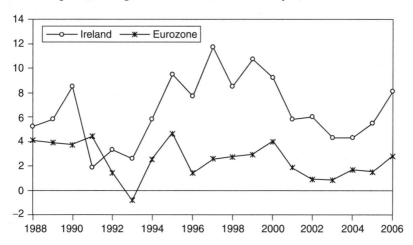

Figure 9.8. Growth of Irish real GDP (constant factor costs), 1988–2006
Source: Irish central statistics office; European Central Bank.

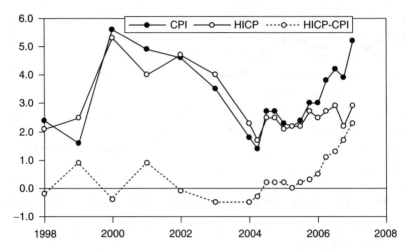

Figure 9.9. Irish inflation, 1998–2007

Source: Irish central statistics office.

average. What is also interesting about this figure, and particularly important for Ireland's long-term stability within the Euro Area, is that it appears to show some convergence in business cycles between the Irish economy and that of the Euro Area more broadly.

This brings us directly the second core aspect of the sceptics' case against EMU entry—namely monetary policy in general and, more specifically, the anticipated sub-optimality of interest rate settings made in Frankfurt to deal with inflationary pressures arising in Ireland. The picture here is both interesting and complex—and here there are certainly some grounds for concern.

Figure 9.9 shows Irish government official inflation data for the period 1998–2007. We show two measures of inflation—the traditional consumer prices index (CPI) and the new EU Harmonised Index of Consumer Prices (HICP) which is the official index of inflation within the Euro Area. Official HICP data show that levels of inflation within the Irish economy since EMU entry have quite consistently exceeded the EMU average, peaking at close to 6 per cent in 2000. Since that time, they have fallen to a low of just under 2 per cent in 2004, but they have risen steadily since (at a time when the Irish growth rate has also risen quite steeply). This is quite consistent with the fears of sceptics (and, indeed, some enthusiasts for EMU entry), who anticipated that interest rates set in Frankfurt for the entire Euro-Area were unlikely to be sufficient to control domestic inflationary pressures. There is plenty of evidence in Figure 9.9 to confirm that supposition.

In this context, two further factors are potentially worrying. The first is that, unsurprising though this is, peaks in Irish inflation within EMU coincide very closely with peaks in rates of economic growth, suggesting that Euro Area interest rates are unable to control the Irish business cycle—and this despite signs, as already noted, that the Irish business cycle has converged since entry on that for the Euro Area in general. Second, and more significantly, perhaps, the relatively brief period between 2001 and 2004 in which Irish inflation was seemingly well contained is potentially misleading. For, as we have noted elsewhere (Hay, Smith, and Watson 2006), it is far more credible to link the deflation of the Irish economy in this period to the consequences of 9/11 and the Second Iraq War for export demand from the USA (and the associated depreciation of the dollar against the euro) than it is to see Euro Area interest rates as having anything to do with it.[11] This can surely only raise concerns that if, as seems likely, Irish growth continues to exceed the EMU average, then Irish inflation will remain uncontrolled by a common monetary policy.

What makes this potentially more alarming still in the growing disparity between the CPI, on the one hand, and the EU HICP, on the other. As Figure 9.9 shows, until about 2004, there was no discernible trend in the difference between the two plots—the plot meanders either side of the baseline. Since then, a clear and ever-growing gap opened up between the CPI and the HICP. If the HICP has not been well-controlled by Euro Area interest rates, then the CPI has scarcely been controlled at all over this period—by 2007 standing at in excess of 5 per cent and rising steeply. Were the HICP merely a more accurate index of inflation, this might be of no great consequence. But this is far from being the case. In fact, the HICP is merely a version of the CPI from which a small list of items (amounting to approximately 10 per cent of the Irish CPI expenditure weighting) are excluded (Central Statistics Office 2007b: 11). What makes these items particularly interesting is that they include the following: mortgage interest payments, household insurance, and building materials—in other words, the principal items in the CPI related to housing. In short, the HICP hides house price inflation—and this, as we argue below, is a crucial element of the Irish experience in the Euro Area.

The Development of Irish 'House-Price Keynesianism' in the Euro Area

There is no denying the gulf that opened between Euro Area interest rates and those necessary to keep Irish retail price inflation in check. It would seem to confirm the fears of the EMU sceptics who were vocal in the public

[11] This is an important point. For, if it is correct, it suggests that the seeming convergence in business cycles observed in Figure 9.8 may well be somewhat spurious—and that such business cycle alignment as we have seen is more a product of coincidence than of structural convergence. That, in turn, would have major implications for the stability and sustainability of the Irish economy within the Euro Area.

debate in Ireland preceding entry (McDowell 1998). It would also seem to confirm academic predictions that a 'one-size-fits-all' monetary policy would impose an inflation penalty on small economies whose stabilization needs were not aligned with those of the Euro Area core (Eichengreen and Wyplosz 1998; Sawyer and Arestis 2006). Yet the details of the Irish case are both more complex and more interesting than this—largely because of the effects on the housing market.

The disparity between the interest rate needs of Ireland and the Euro Area led to Irish mortgage rates falling to a level significantly below what would otherwise have been expected given the state of consumer price rises. Moreover, depressed inflationary expectations in the core Euro Area economies since 1999 mean that this now looks like a step-reduction in the Irish mortgage rate. The effects of an artificially low mortgage rate on mortgage repayments, and hence on consumption potentials, are striking. In 2001, the average price of a new house in Ireland was €181,146. Given that the average mortgage was issued for 90 per cent of the full house price, average initial mortgage debt on new homes was €163,031. The typical mortgage rate in 2001 was 5.7 per cent, so that the household with average initial mortgage debt faced monthly repayments of €1,021. By 2005, the average price of a new house had risen to €272,034 and, with the average mortgage remaining at 90 per cent, average initial mortgage debt was €244,831. The typical mortgage rate now, though, was just 3.3 per cent, leaving the average Irish household purchasing a new house in 2005 with monthly repayments of €1,395 (all figures from Central Statistics Office 2006: 40). Had the typical mortgage rate stayed at the 2001 level of 5.7 per cent, on 2005 house prices the average monthly repayment would have been €1,656. The comparison can be even more starkly drawn when using the 1990 mortgage rate of 11.4 per cent. At that level, the average monthly repayment would have been €2,275.

The difference in monthly outgoings triggered by the EMU-induced mortgage rate of 3.3 per cent, when compared with historical Irish mortgage rates of 5.7 and 11.4 per cent, is €261 and €880, respectively. This is highly significant in terms of the changing character of the Irish growth regime. In 2005, the average price of a new house in Ireland rose by 11.1 per cent (ibid.: 37), a monthly monetary increase of €2,265. The average monthly repayment at 2005 mortgage rates was therefore 61.6 per cent of the price increase. The result is an annual household wealth effect on property assets (price rise minus mortgage repayments) of €10,440. Had the mortgage rate remained at its 2001 level, though, the average monthly repayment in 2005 would have been 73.1 per cent of the price increase. This would have left an annual household wealth effect on property assets of €7,308. And had the mortgage rate remained at its 1990 level, the average monthly repayment in 2005 would have completely wiped out the wealth effects arising from the price increase, freeing up no spare cash for additional consumption. Comparing the two most recent data points, wealth effects arising from the housing market were stimulated by just over 40 per cent due to the fact that Ireland has interest rates set in relation to Euro Area consumer price conditions and not in relation to Irish consumer price conditions.

This is a far from inconsequential figure. When aggregated to the economy as a whole, it has undoubtedly had a major impact on the underlying level of growth. It is usual to associate inflationary conditions with reduced prospects for growth, because consumers are likely to rein back their spending plans in the face of increasing consumer prices. Yet, as the figures presented in previous sections demonstrate, this is not the recent Irish experience. Irish inflation levels have risen above their immediate pre-EMU trend in the period since EMU entry, but underlying levels of economic growth have also been robust. The key to explaining this lies in the fact that the wealth effects arising from a housing market sustained by an artificially low mortgage rate have more than compensated consumers for increases in retail prices. In other words, consumers have been able to maintain or increase levels of consumption despite rising consumer prices, by cashing-in on the wealth effects of house price inflation. In a situation of constantly rising house prices, this release of consumption has been achieved without any loss of net worth linked to the household's growing asset base.

Much therefore now depends on being able to reproduce the recent trajectory of house price increases if the current Irish macroeconomic model is to prove stable. Yet, this is by no means assured. Annual house price increases for the period 2000–5 averaged around 12 per cent. At this rate, the price of the average house doubles every eight years. It is difficult to see how such increases could persist as more than a medium-term phenomenon. The Department of the Environment, Heritage and Local Government devised a simple 'affordability index' by calculating repayments on outstanding mortgage debt as a proportion of net monthly income. In 1994, the figure was a fraction over 20 per cent for the country as a whole, but by 2005 it had grown to almost 27 per cent, even in the context of suppressed Euro Area inflation holding Euro Area interest rates and therefore the Irish mortgage rate significantly below what would have been suitable for Irish inflation conditions. In Dublin, the increase has been even more marked. In 1994, the average household committed almost 24 per cent of net monthly income to mortgage repayments, but by 2005 it was 35 per cent (cited in Central Statistics Office 2006: 48).

This shows just how susceptible the Irish housing market might be to increases in Euro Area interest rates (and hence mortgage rates). It is difficult to think that mortgage repayments can go much higher (as a proportion of net monthly income) than they are at present without significantly undermining confidence in the housing market. But it is this confidence that has done so much to propel the upward trend in house prices in recent years.

Moreover, any fall in house prices amidst future increases in the mortgage rate threatens to bring negative equity to the Irish housing market. Negative equity occurs when the price of the house on the open market falls below the monetary value of the remaining mortgage borrowing. Given the very low level of the Irish mortgage rate in recent years—just 3.3 per cent in 2005—many borrowers have taken out a 100 per cent mortgage advance and many more have taken out a mortgage advance of over 90 per cent. If interest rate increases cause house prices to stagnate, then a high proportion of families who have tried to trade up their housing market position in recent years will be left with negative equity: those with the highest mortgage advances will, in general, be affected most quickly and most severely. And note that this result requires no fall in house prices—merely that interest rates rise. For comparison, during the most recent period of mass negative equity in the UK—the country in the EU with the house price structure closest to that of Ireland—house prices fell in four years by around 30 per cent in money terms from their 1988 peak (Audas and MacKay 1997: 869). This had serious consequences for the consumer economy as households withdrew much of their non-essential consumption. Output fell by at least two percentage points per year throughout the period 1988–92 solely as a consequence of the reverse multiplier effect on consumption as the growth model based on housing market equity release imploded (Pollard 1992: 390–1).

The current Irish macroeconomic model is similarly vulnerable to monetary policy shocks from Frankfurt over which Irish policymakers have no control. These are the well-documented policy constraints of EMU (Buiter, Corsetti, and Roubini 1993; de Grauwe 2005; Fatas 1998), and they will be particularly troublesome for Irish policymakers if they erode the basis of housing market wealth effects. The recent trajectory of house price increases has made a sizeable contribution to a consumer boom in Ireland. The average price paid for a house increased by €27,073 in 2000, €16,325 in 2001, €20,839 in 2002, €37,781 in 2003, €29,838 in 2004, and €35,400 in 2005 (calculated from Central Statistics Office 2006: 37). This compares with average Irish wages in those years of €22,683, €24,490, €26,079, €27,859, €28,692, and €30,206, respectively (Central Statistics Office 2007a). That is, average house prices rose by 119, 67, 80, 136, 104, and 117 per cent of the average wage. Over the six-year period as a whole, house prices rose by 104 per cent of the average wage. For households willing to treat the wealth effects arising from property purchases as additional income, this amounted to an increase in consumption potential equivalent to a doubling of wages. As this suggests, Irish economic activity is now just as dependent on the wealth arising from previous housing market activity as it is on the wages arising from current labour market activity.

Housing market wealth effects are reflected in significant changes in patterns of current savings. Savings rates have diminished appreciably in recent years. In 1995, the average rate of personal credit for the country as a whole rate stood at 47.7 per cent of personal disposable income, but by 2005 it was 132.3 per cent. The steepest increase came in the final two years of that period (Kelly 2006: 82). It is not difficult to see why the housing market might be central to this change. Most personal credit is taken out in the first instance to finance property purchases. Once established on the housing market, further credit can be taken out on the assumption that it can be paid back from the equity release made possible by future house price rises. This latter credit is typically used to feed current consumption.

What, in effect, has happened is the development of a new macroeconomic model in Ireland. Having reviewed the relevant policy documents and parliamentary debates, we can find no evidence that it was consciously constructed. It exists within the framework of the preceding macroeconomic model rather than having replaced it in its entirety. Nonetheless, the foundations of a new growth regime are visible. It is unlikely to be stable as a long-term phenomenon. It takes the form of a regime of 'house-price Keynesianism' in Ireland, whereby personal consumption is tied increasingly tightly to the consequences of using personal credit to secure the household's position on the housing market (see Figure 9.10).

This differs in one very significant respect from the type of Keynesianism that EMU all but precludes: it does not rely on increases in government

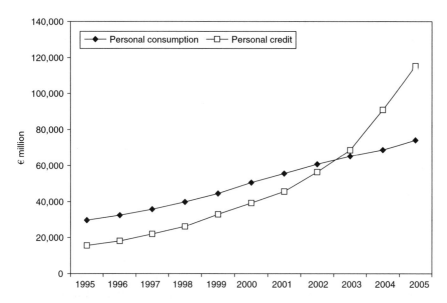

Figure 9.10. Irish personal credit and personal consumption, 1995–2005
Source: Irish central statistics office.

spending made possible by the issue of new public debt. It is a private-sector rather than a public-sector phenomenon, but it might nonetheless be labelled 'Keynesian'. It serves in effect to pump-prime economic activity through generating additional demand for private consumption. This is not achieved, as it was during the so-called golden age, via transfer payments to enhance consumption potential (Pierson 1991). Instead, it is reliant on homeowners enhancing their own consumption potential by trading up in the housing market as a means of expanding their asset-based wealth.

Of course, whenever (global) financial market conditions appear to take a turn for the worse, questions will be raised about the fragility of Irish growth based upon housing market price inflation. These questions are undoubtedly legitimate, because a growth model of this nature remains fragile irrespective of the strength of the financial system. Sudden changes in expectations are all that is required to cause a significant loss in confidence. At such a point, the assumption of fragility may threaten to become self-perpetuating. Our final changes to this chapter were written six weeks into the credit crunch, which began in world financial markets in August 2007. We are in no position to foretell what the future holds. But what the credit crunch has made clear is the relationship between the housing market and inter-bank lending. Banks began to recalibrate their risk exposures as they came to fear that the failure of the US sub-prime mortgage lending market threatened the returns that they could expect from their mortgage business as a whole. The result was an increasing reluctance to lend to other banks, which they suspected of being in the same position. Very quickly, this brought about a cessation of even 'normal' lending conditions in the inter-bank market. The ensuing credit crunch has made it increasingly difficult for mortgage lenders to raise the cash to capitalize new business; and this, in turn, has pushed up the mortgage-lending rate. If this has the effect of suppressing levels of housing equity release in Ireland, as well it might, then, as our analysis has shown, it is likely to impact negatively on economic growth.

Conclusion

In the Irish case, it is difficult to draw definite links between entry into EMU and changes in the standard indicators of micro- and macroeconomic performance (such as exchange rates, price competitiveness, levels of growth, and direction of trade statistics). But a clear EMU effect appears to be evident in the development of what we have termed Irish 'house-price Keynesianism'. The decline in the Irish mortgage rate from 11.4 per cent in 1990 to 3.3 per cent in 2005 contributed massively to the buoyancy of the housing market in that period. For the early part of that period, the trend decline was attributable in the main to Irish economic success. The much-discussed 'Celtic Tiger' phenomenon was centred on a large expansion in production in export-oriented markets (Kirby 2001; Smith 2005; Sweeney 1999). This led to none of the pressure that sustained periods of growth usually bring to bear on the structure of domestic prices. As a consequence, inflation was held in check, allowing both interest rates and the mortgage rate to be gradually reduced, providing a significant confidence boost for the housing market.

It has been in the post-EMU period, though, that house prices have really spiralled. This is no coincidence. The structure of domestic prices has proved to be less stable in this latter period, as the production-oriented growth dynamics of the 'Celtic Tiger' phenomenon have given way, at least partially, to new consumption-oriented growth dynamics. However, heightened inflationary pressures have not shown up in increases in both interest rates and the mortgage rate, as all theories of macroeconomic stabilization predict that they should. This is because of the sub-optimality of a Euro Area interest rate. The result has been to push the Irish mortgage rate still lower, when all monetary indicators suggest that it should be rising. And this in turn has produced a further boost to house prices at a phase in the business cycle when house prices usually stagnate.

It is the EMU effect on the housing market, then, that has fuelled the consumption boom, which has become such a contributory factor to recent Irish growth. But, just as Ireland has inadvertently enjoyed the economic benefits of a more accommodating monetary policy, it is also susceptible to the EMU effects changing in character. There might well come a time at which the Irish economy does not need an interest rate rise but such a rise occurs anyway because of the different monetary demands of the core Euro Area countries. At that moment, the housing market is likely to take a hit. The likely effect would be to wipe out, at a stroke, recent wealth effects and to bring to an abrupt end the recent consumer boom. We have yet to see what would happen to Irish growth in such circumstances, but it is unlikely to be pleasant.

But this is perhaps overly prospective. For whatever the long-term prospects, Ireland's economic performance to date within the Euro Area has been extremely strong. This has undoubtedly contributed to a now well-entrenched governing consensus—shared by all of the major parties and the social partners—on the merits of EMU. It has also contributed significantly to the reputation for economic competence of the Irish government and to Bertie Ahern's longevity as Taoiseach. Finally, precisely because Irish growth has remained strong and the Irish government has not used fiscal policy as an instrument to control inflation, EMU has has little impact on the government's broad economic and social policy latitude. Yet, if our analysis is right, that may not last.

10

Italy: Creeping Towards Convergence

Lucia Quaglia and Paul Furlong

Italy entered the Euro Area at the eleventh hour, after an eventful journey. This chapter examines Italy's first decade in the Euro Area. It focuses on two main themes: the increasing Euro-scepticism amongst national elites, especially political elites, and amongst public opinion; and the Europeanization of core public policies and institutions, as a direct or indirect consequence of Economic and Monetary Union (EMU) and Euro Area membership. Europeanization is identified mainly as a 'top-down' process; it concerns the impact of the European Union on its member states (Boerzel and Risse 2003; Radaelli 2003*a*) or, to be precise, the effects of EU 'output' on their politics, policies, and institutions. We are interested in the domestic effects of EMU in Italy in the past decade and in three key comparative questions. First, how has EMU affected the Italian state, primarily in its capacity to deliver economic change but also in its reputation for economic competence? Secondly, how can we characterize the processes and effects of Europeanization in the policy responses to EMU? Thirdly, since much of the adjustment to EMU was market-driven, how does this affect the functioning of the Italian state?

The second section provides an overview of the 'Italian road' to EMU, on the understanding that Italy's first decade in the Euro Area was deeply affected by the way the country joined in 1999, apparently against the odds. Several of the problems encountered, and either partly or temporarily addressed in approaching EMU, resurfaced once membership was achieved and returned to haunt subsequent Italian governments.

The third section analyses the domestic political context, pointing to the increasing Euro-scepticism amongst national elites (mainly political parties, but also macroeconomic policy elites, such as the central bank) as well as among public opinion.

Section 4 examines the Europeanization of core public policies and institutions directly or indirectly affected by the euro. It argues that Euro Area entry has produced different effects across policies, due to diverse adaptational pressure and different intervening mechanisms: hasty and relatively unstable adjustment in fiscal policy; formal transformation in monetary and exchange-rate policy; inertia, moving towards retrenchment in financial services regulation and supervision; and smuggled-through adjustment in welfare and labour policies. As for institutions, direct and indirect effects of Europeanization are more difficult to detect, except the reform of some macroeconomic institutions, whereas it had limited if any effect on administrative and constitutional issues.

This chapter argues that Italy's adjustment to EMU has been 'patchy': it has been quicker and more effective in policies directly affected by EMU, such as monetary and fiscal policies, than in others, related, for example, to economic competitiveness. Moreover, there is an important dividing line between the period approaching entry (prior to 1999), when pressure to conform to specific EU institutional and policy templates was stronger and more direct, and the period after, when adaptational pressure became less direct, although in economic terms no less important in the medium/long term. In that sense, there is a clear difference between these two phases of Europeanization. In the first, associated with the accession period, the adjustment was political, understood broadly as concerning the political imperatives and dynamics of satisfying the Maastricht criteria. In the second, associated with membership of the Euro Area, the adjustment was mainly economic, indirect, and longer-term.

Before 1999, Italy's failure to adapt sufficiently to the policy regime could be measured by formal convergence criteria and by analysis of central banking legislation. This, and the fact that it could have resulted in Italy's exclusion from the Euro Area, represented powerful external constraints sustaining domestic policy change (Dyson and Featherstone 1999). After the introduction of the euro, insufficient or ineffective national adaptation is less visible: there is no longer a direct threat of 'exclusion from the core Europe'. After all, 'entrare in Europa', which can be translated as joining Europe, was the motto of the centre-left government that oversaw Italy's adoption of the euro. Introduction of the euro was followed by a loss of competitiveness and stagnant economic growth in the national economy. The result was not the major structural reforms that might have been considered necessary. Broadly speaking, inertia predominated. Part of the explanation must be that the lack of strong, direct EU pressure for further domestic reforms weakened the opportunity structure for domestic pro-reform actors in Italy, though other internal factors also weighed heavily.

The Italian Road to the Euro

After the signing of the Maastricht Treaty in 1992, the process of ratification in Italy proceeded smoothly. However, the uncertainty created by the Danish and French referendums unsettled financial markets, triggering speculation against weak currencies in the Exchange Rate Mechanism (ERM). When the Italian lira and the British pound had to leave the system in September 1992, the widespread view in Italy was that the exchange-rate crisis had sanctioned a 'two-speed' Europe, with Italy in the slow lane and unlikely to join the single currency at the outset (Daniels 1993).

The domestic political consensus in favour of European monetary integration came under strain in 1994, with the election of the centre-right government led by Silvio Berlusconi. During its short stay in office, this government adopted more Euro-sceptic stances and implemented a less rigorous fiscal policy, which was far from the fiscal adjustment needed to meet the convergence criteria (Quaglia 2004*b*). The objective of rejoining the ERM also became less important. After taking over from the Berlusconi government in early 1995, the caretaker government led by Lamberto Dini hinted at the possibility of postponing entry into the single currency, in an attempt to 'buy time' for Italy.

The period between 1996 and 1998 was decisive for Italy to be able to qualify for Euro Area membership from the start. The centre-left government, elected in April 1996 and led by Romano Prodi, faced the difficult task of deciding whether or not to join in the first wave (Radaelli 2002). The coalition was divided on the advisability and feasibility of early membership. Even those most committed to Euro Area membership recognized that in early 1996 more draconian fiscal measures would not have been possible without 'killing the country' (interview, Rome, December 1999). The credibility of Italy's adjustment was also an issue for the financial markets and the other member states (Ciampi's parliamentary hearing, 20 June 1996). Italy's reputation for fiscal and monetary management, rightly or wrongly, was not good. Notwithstanding Italy's large primary surplus, and the difficulties of 'core' member states, Italy appeared to be singled out for scepticism about whether it could meet the criteria.

Once the choice in favour of early membership had been made for a variety of internal and external reasons (Radaelli 2002), the government had to devise a workable plan to achieve this goal, which required an economic strategy as well as a diplomatic one. The macroeconomic plan rested mainly on a substantial fiscal adjustment, which had already started in 1992, coupled with drawing on the benefits from the so-called convergence game, based on the reduction of interest rates in the financial market (Spaventa and Chiorazzo 2000) and the lowering of the costs of debt and the operating deficit. Diplomatically, the Italian authorities had to convince the member states most sceptical of Italian membership, such as Germany and the Netherlands, to resist internal pressure for a strict interpretation of the convergence criteria, which would have challenged Italy's ability to qualify. The economic and political circuits were connected, in that economic results were needed to support political statements, whilst the political stances of other member states had economic repercussions for Italy on the financial markets, as they could undermine the 'convergence game'.

The 'European gamble' of Italian policymakers, as an interviewee put it, was in the end successful, making possible—albeit at the last minute and in a rather ad hoc fashion—the fiscal adjustment needed to meet the Maastricht convergence criteria. Since the level of market interest rates converged towards the level of the other member states, this criterion was also met. The lira re-entered the ERM in autumn 1996, and inflation converged towards the level of the 'core' Europe—the other two convergence criteria. Given the fact that several one-off measures, including a special 'Euro-tax', were used by the Italian authorities, the sustainability of the adjustment remained an issue, and not only for sceptical EU policymakers. Some Italian policymakers, for example, the Bank of Italy, were sceptical about Italy's readiness to join the Euro Area (Quaglia 2004b). The resultant worsening of Italy's reputational deficit made the process of adjustment more difficult, in so far as adjustment not only entailed policy change but also required markets to take a positive view of Italy's capacity to join and thereby to achieve the expected economic benefits, especially in terms of interest rates and inflation.

Italy's qualification for first-round entry was approved at the European Council in May 1998, following a decisive presentation by Treasury Minister Carlo Azeglio Ciampi (Governor of the Bank of Italy 1980–93) of Italy's long-term economic and financial adjustment plans. To summarize, the Italian macroeconomic strategy in qualifying for EMU rested on four pillars: first, persistently high primary surplus balances since 1992, which were achieved by increasing total revenue and, to a more limited extent, cutting primary expenditure; second, improved inflationary performance and lower inflationary expectations, both of which were linked to the anti-inflationary incomes policy set in place in 1992–3 and re-confirmed in 1996, within which a renewed strategy of concertation involving government, unions, and employers was central; third, lower interest payments on the public debt as a result of the downward convergence of interest rates; and fourth, the late rejoining of the ERM, which Italy re-entered in November 1996 and which promoted exports, resulting in a positive balance of payments.

Nonetheless, the overall competitiveness of the economy, inextricably linked to labour-market policy and social policy, remained problematic, as became clear once Italy entered the Euro Area. In failing to address these issues, Italy was far from alone, and like other member states, was not directly required to do so within the asymmetrical convergence criteria.

Domestic Politics in the Euro Area

Electoral change, especially in 1992, fatally weakened the power of the ruling Christian Democrats, in part because of corruption scandals but also in ways that indicated serious concerns about Italy's failure to respond adequately to European and global trade change. With no party able to take on the Christian Democrats' pivotal role in government, technocrats had unprecedented scope to direct long-term policy, such as monetary integration. In doing so, they were not operating in a political vacuum. On the contrary, the landscape-changing votes in 1992 and 1994 were clearly influenced by European concerns as well as by the corruption scandals (Golden 2004: 30).

These conditions did not last beyond the Prodi centre-left government elected in 1996. The regionalist Northern League party (*Lega Nord*), which appeared to have successfully captured the normally pro-EU Northern voters as they abandoned the Christian Democrats in 1992 and 1994, changed its strategy after the electoral failure of 1996. By mid-1998, it was both more radically separatist and more anti-European. The last months prior to euro entry saw the resignation of Prime Minister Prodi in September 1998, after passing a Financial Bill that consolidated the fiscal adjustment in Italy. Massimo D'Alema, then leader of the Party of the Democratic Left, was appointed Prime Minister, the first ex-Communist in Italy's history. Financial markets did not react negatively—as they had done in the past—to the government crisis, or to D'Alema's appointment. The lack of reaction suggested that Italy's macro-economic policies had become more credible, especially once embedded in the EMU macroeconomic regime. Credibility was reinforced in 1999 by the appointment of Ciampi as President of the Republic and Giuliano Amato as Treasury Minister. It is reasonable to conclude that the firm prospect of Italy's Euro Area membership stabilized otherwise volatile financial market assessments. Consequently, other critical events, such as the 'early warning' against Italy for an excessive fiscal deficit, the Cirio and Parmalat financial scandals and the Bank of Italy affair, did not produce major effects on the financial markets in the form of increases in the interest rate on Italian public debt.

Within the centre-left coalition, Communist Refoundation, one of the two successors of the former Italian Communist Party (PCI), embodied some Euro-sceptic tendencies, especially compared to the overtly pro-European party of the Democratic Left, which incorporated the bulk of the former PCI (Benedetto and Quaglia 2007). During the Prodi government (1996–8), both parties were essential to the parliamentary majority. This leverage was used by Communist Refoundation to force the hand of the government on issues perceived as politically salient for the party, such as the 35-hour working week, one of the main issues behind Prodi's resignation in autumn 1998.

The centre-left coalition remained in office until the 2001 general elections, won by Berlusconi's centre-right coalition, the 'House of Freedom' (*Casa delle Libertà*), consisting of three main parties and a federation of small Catholic parties and movements that developed out of the fragmentation of the old Christian Democracy.

Italy's EU policy under the first and second Berlusconi governments exhibited a higher degree of Euro-scepticism than in the past, and both were at best lukewarm towards the single currency. In the political parties, Euro-sceptic tendencies showed increasingly in the centre-right coalition, though this trend was not uniform and evolved over time (Quaglia 2005). Evidence of this can be found in the many critical and dismissive public statements made by senior figures in the government coalition, such as Defence Minister, Antonio Martino, Treasury Minister, Giulio Tremonti and Minister for Institutional Reforms, Umberto Bossi. In some respects, perhaps, the most disturbing demonstration of changed priorities was the resignation of the very experienced Foreign Minister Renato Ruggiero in January 2002. The appointment of Ruggiero was widely reported to have been requested by the head of FIAT, Gianni Agnelli, to improve Italy's external credibility, but his position was undermined by his pro-European stance on a wide range of issues, not only on the euro but also on the EU arrest warrant and the Airbus military transport plane project. Another spectacular demonstration of the Berlusconi government's highly instrumental attitude to Europe was the comment of Bossi's deputy, the Minister for Welfare Roberto Maroni, calling for Italy to re-introduce the lira (*La Repubblica* 3 June 2005: 31). This followed the failure of the French and Dutch constitutional referendums, and several years of slow growth or recession, with significant differentials appearing in market rates for government bonds across the Euro Area. The Northern League moved from strongly pro-European attitudes to soft Euro-scepticism in 1998, hardening its stance after returning to office in 2001. In contrast, the National Alliance, led by the Deputy Prime Minister Gianfranco Fini, which had held some Euro-sceptic views, softened these positions following its first government experience in 1994. This process was even more evident after its return to office in 2001.

As for *Forza Italia*, it has always been characterized to some extent by neutrality on Europe. In practical terms, this might express itself in soft euro-scepticism. On more than one occasion, Berlusconi emphasized the need to protect the national interest and expressed preferences for a more intergovernmental Europe. This should not be understood as hostility to Europe, rather that European issues do not figure strongly in its political discourse. In general, in party political terms, opposition to the euro and to the EU in general was fragmented between Left and Right and within and outside the government. It was associated with smaller parties on both sides that were prone to habitual policy opportunism rather than seeking coherent alternatives.

If at the level of elites, especially political elites, 'soft' Euro-scepticism resurfaced from the mid-1990, amongst public opinion it emerged more slowly. In general terms, we might say that whereas for political and economic elites, Europe is seen as a matter of direct self-interest as well as ideology, for the Italian public Europe has been more associated with safety and virtue. In approaching the final stage of EMU, the 'European priority' of the centre-left government of Prodi (or at least of a large part of it) was shared by the vast majority of public opinion, whose permissive consensus made possible the large fiscal adjustment needed in order to join the euro (Sbragia 2001). Under the Prodi government, when the fiscal adjustment was more burdensome, the Italian public remained largely in favour of early membership, up to the point of willingly accepting the Euro-tax, a one-off tax designed by the Prodi government in 1996 to top-up the funding needed to meet the 'deficit-to-GDP' criterion.

Using Eurobarometer data, Figures 10.1–10.4 chart support for the euro and for the EU from 1993 to 2007, and levels of trust in the Italian government and in the EU from 2001 onwards (the 'trust' question was not asked before 2001). Over the longer period, support for the euro peaked in early 1998 and again in early 2002, at which time support for the EU reached highs only exceeded in Italy during the internal crises of 1992–6. From then on, with the onset of the widespread Euro Area stagnation and the strains in the Stability and Growth Pact especially in 2003, levels of support for both fell sharply.

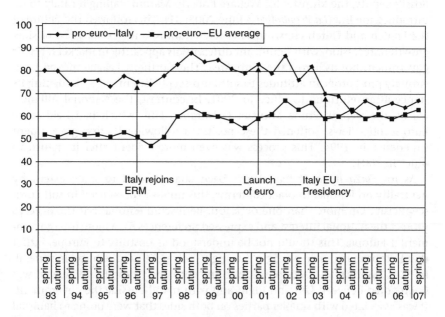

Figure 10.1. Support for the euro: Italy and the EU15 average (%)

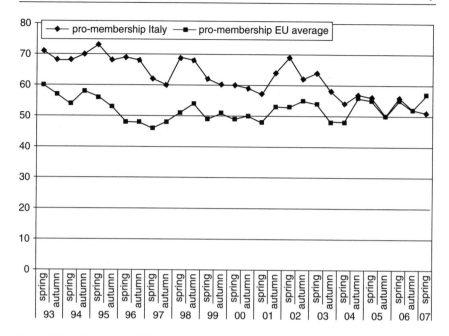

Figure 10.2. Support for EU membership: Italy and the EU-15 average (%)

By mid-2007, they appeared to have stabilized at levels close to the EU-15 average—a reversal of a historic tendency, which seems emphatically to have ended Italy's exceptionalism as unquestioning supporters of the EU.

With the data available, however, it is difficult to relate these changes in public opinion to government policy. At the generic level, trust both in the government and in the EU began to decline from early 2002 on. It is difficult to identify a clear trend, except that in both cases public opinion appears to be converging towards the EU15 norm. In policy terms, as discussed above, the Berlusconi government had already been more critical of the euro and of the EU when coming into office in 2001. This trend was strengthened by the economic difficulties from 2002, perceived as 'side effects' of the euro, such as price increases, reduced purchasing power capacity, low growth, and high unemployment.

Though, among the public, Euro-scepticism (in the sense of diminishing public support for the EU) may have been be triggered by the euro's difficulties, support for the euro remained higher than support for the EU throughout. It appears that the EU suffered unpopularity more than the euro itself. However, after 1996, this trend applied across the EU-15 and was not specific to Italy.

In Italy, the link between Euro-scepticism and Europeanization is strong, especially with reference to EMU, in that, from the late 1990s onwards, the

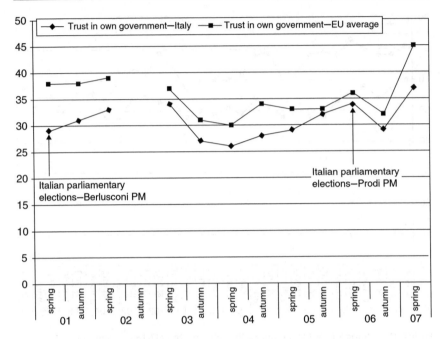

Figure 10.3. Trust in own government: Italy and the EU-15 average (%)

Note: Question not asked Autumn 2002.

former can be considered, to a significant extent, a consequence of the latter, as a response to the domestic impact of the euro. As the rise of the Asian economies began to affect European competitiveness, the well-publicized difficulties of vulnerable sectors in Italian manufacturing also prompted opposition to European trade liberalization.

The 'external constraint' in Italy (Dyson and Featherstone 1999) was used to legitimize much needed and painful domestic policy and institutional reforms in the run-up to the introduction of the euro. However, the governing coalition that steered Italy's entry into the euro was not the one that led the country after entry. In the circumstances, the extent of 'soft' Euro-scepticism may be judged to be relatively limited. It may create electoral opportunities for minor parties, but can hardly be said to be mainstream. The impact is rather that weakening support for the EU and the euro makes difficult reforms even more problematic politically.

Domestic Policies in the Euro Area

Differences in impacts across policy sectors depended on how domestic elites managed and exploited the introduction and implementation of the euro as

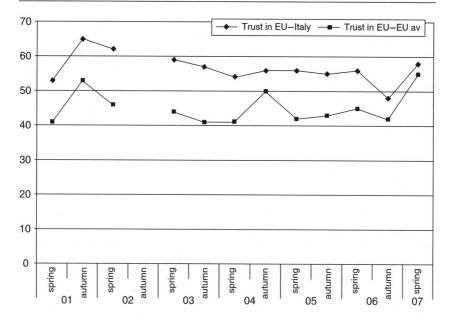

Figure 10.4. Trust in EU: Italy and the EU-15 average (%)

Source: Eurobarometer (1993–2007).

Note: Question not asked Autumn 2002.

an external constraint. From the previous section, it follows that the priorities, capacities, and resources of these elites, and the opposition or support that they encountered, were critical.

Monetary policy in Italy remained relatively tight throughout the 1990s; indeed, the strict monetary policy in 1997 and early 1998 was criticized as being 'too severe' by some Italian and foreign observers. After 1999, the conduct of monetary policy was transferred to the ECB. The Bank of Italy became part of the ESCB and the Eurosystem and, under Governor Fazio, it championed the role of national central banks therein.

The conduct of exchange-rate policy also underwent a major transformation. After the exit from the ERM in 1992 and until 1996, this policy had been characterized by a depreciating lira, which improved the competitiveness of Italian exports, fostering an export-led boom that sustained Italian economic growth in a phase of fiscal retrenchment. After 1999, the conduct of exchange-rate policy was transferred to the authorities of the Euro Area (the ECB and ECOFIN).

The locking in of the exchange rate, together with the sclerotic labour market and other structural constraints, endangered the competitiveness of the Italian economic system, with negative repercussions on the balance of payments. The current account, which had been in surplus for most of the 1990s, turned increasingly negative from 1999. Economic growth remained low, indeed one of the lowest in Europe, together with Germany. In approaching the final stage of EMU, the Italian monetary authorities had expressed some scepticism about whether Italy was really ready to join and to give up the macroeconomic instrument of the exchange rate (Quaglia 2004*b*). The economic trends after 1999 seemed to confirm some of these doubts and at the same time draw attention to the need of urgent structural reforms, especially of the labour market and the welfare state.

Fiscal policy had undergone a major adjustment in the 1990s. From 1992 onwards, Italy had a primary surplus, even though the latter varied in intensity under subsequent governments, for example, declining during the first Berlusconi government. Although there were some remarkable changes in revenues and primary expenditures, what made it possible for the fiscal adjustment to achieve the 3 per cent deficit ratio in 1998 was the reduction in interest payments on the Italian public debt as a result of lower nominal interest rates. Thus, this rapid adjustment was to a large extent dependent on lower interest rates. As discussed above, the robustness of the market's belief in Italian entry was critical, and even endured Italy's announcement in May 1999 that it would breach the agreement made by Treasury Minister Ciampi in 1998 to hold government borrowing to 2 per cent of GDP each year (an agreement undertaken as a sign of Italy's renewed virtue, not strictly necessary under the Stability and Growth Pact).

The bonus of the lower interest payments continuing after joining the Euro Area and during the second Berlusconi government was counterbalanced by a reduction of the primary budget surplus, which produced an upward trend in the public-sector borrowing requirement. Two factors account for this reduction: an increase of public expenditures—for example, the government was committed to major projects (the *grandi opere*), but also to increasing the amount of the minimum retirement pensions; and the decrease in public revenue, due to the attempt to reduce fiscal pressure. The European Commission also criticized Italian fiscal policy for the several one-off or temporary measures.

In 2002, several members of the Italian government issued public statements urging the review of the Stability and Growth Pact, particularly of the 3 per cent ceiling on the budget deficit, or proposed to bypass the maximum by excluding investment expenses from the calculation of the deficit. The centre-left opposition was split in that some leaders, such as former Prime Minister Massimo D'Alema, agreed on a moderate change, whereas other opposition leaders supported 'economic rigour'. At the EU level, the Berlusconi government strongly supported a reform of the Stability and Growth Pact. The Italian Presidency in the second half of 2003 was perceived by many small member states and EU institutions as sympathetic to the suspension of the Pact for France and Germany (cf. Quaglia 2004*a*).

In 2004 Italy faced serious problems in meeting the 3 per cent ceiling and in reconciling Italy's EU obligations with a campaign pledge to cut taxes. Treasury Minister Tremonti resigned in July 2004 following pressure from the National Alliance, which opposed the budget cuts needed to stay within the established threshold. Berlusconi, acting as *ad interim* Treasury Minister, presented an emergency budget package and persuaded Euro Area finance ministers not to accept the Commission's proposal for an 'excessive deficit early warning' against Italy. It was difficult for the other governments to be rigorous about the size of the Italian deficit, after freezing the procedures against Germany and France, which had both exceeded the 3 per cent threshold.

In 2005, after further deterioration of the budgetary situation in Italy, there was a formal warning to Italy by the European Commission. Adaptation of Italian fiscal policy to the requirements imposed by the EU remained problematic. The centre-left Prodi government, appointed in 2006, pledged to address the budgetary imbalance, making several direct references to the need to respect the (reformed) Stability and Growth Pact.

Incomes policy had undergone a major change during the summer of 1992, when the three trade-union confederations and the employers' organization *Confindustria*, under the auspices of the government, signed a tripartite agreement that laid the foundation for a new type of industrial relations, the so-called *concertazione*, and abolished the mechanism of wage indexation (Cazzola 1993). In 1998, the renewal of the *concertazione* procedure by the D'Alema government was heralded as a major support for Ciampi's adjustment package presented to the European Council earlier that year.

The evolution of incomes policy during the Berlusconi government should be seen in conjunction with the trends in social policy, welfare-state reform, and employment policy. Prior to 1998, the draconian fiscal adjustment in order to meet the convergence criteria was accompanied by a limited reform of the welfare state and social policy. Two pension reforms were carried out in 1992 and 1995, directed towards a reduction in benefits, a rise in the retirement age, more restrictive conditions of access to pensions, a lower degree of indexation, and a more harmonized system of different pension funds. Another significant pension reform was carried out during the second Berlusconi government 2001–6 (Natali and Rhodes 2005). The partial nature of these repeated and politically demanding efforts was indicated by the need for the Prodi government to return to the issue yet again in the summer of 2007.

Since the 1990s, there has been an ongoing debate about the reform of the labour market in order to increase its flexibility, which became more pressing once Italy joined the Euro Area in order to restore Italian competitiveness in a period of low economic growth. A first step was taken in 1997 with the so-called Treu law, named after the Labour minister who proposed it, which aimed to increase flexibility and employability (Natali 2008).

The Berlusconi government took two further steps. In 2001, the *White Paper on the Labour Market* was drafted by a group of experts led by Marco Biagi, a professor subsequently killed by the terrorist group, the Red Brigades, in 2002. One of the most important and controversial proposals was the modification of Article 18 (*licenziamento per giusta causa*) of the Workers' Statute, aiming to ease dismissal for redundancy. Despite the fact that the paper contained several references to the EU and the Luxemburg process, pointing to the urgent need to reform the domestic labour market, the content of this reform was not prescribed by 'Europe'. Instead, it targeted at an Italian audience and had the political rationale of diluting the role of the trade unions in central contractual negotiations, and indeed led to a confrontation between the government and the unions. As such, the reform broke with the con-certation procedure. The unions emerged divided and weakened. Following mass protest, a general strike and a referendum, which was lost by those opposing the reform of the workers' statute, the law eventually approved in 2003 introduced some measures to increase flexibility.

The law was flanked by the *Patto per l'Italia*, signed in 2002 by two trade-union confederations (CISL and UIL), *Confindustria* and the government. The main trade-union confederation, CGIL, refused to sign the agreement. The pact contained the pledge to reduce income taxes, increase unemployment benefits, and boost economic growth in Southern Italy. It also contained limited revisions of the workers statute (Natali 2008). Here again, the government engaged in a creative usage of 'Europe', to justify the policy put forward, making reference to EU guidelines and the European Employment Strategy, though the reform was driven by domestic politics (Quaglia and Radaelli 2007).

Indeed, the approach of the centre-right government to the Lisbon agenda seemed to be one-sided, focusing on labour-market flexibility but not on other policies that could promote competitiveness, such as better regulation, reform of the inefficient public administration, and breaking down 'rent' positions in the professions, hence liberalizing these markets. In June 2005, Italy was ranked 20th (out of the EU-25) in the transposition of directives specifically highlighted as crucial to the success of the Lisbon agenda (the so-called Lisbon directives) (Quaglia and Radaelli 2007).

There can be little doubt that *Confindustria* and other employer organiza-tions have become more assertive with entry into the euro, and have been very critical of both the Berlusconi and the Prodi governments. The support for the Social Pacts under both governments are evidence of the assertiveness. The main objective of *Confindustria* however is not to encourage market-led adjustment within Italian private- and public-sector industry and commerce, but rather to push the state to internal reform, arguing as it does as that it is inefficient public administration and high taxes which impede Italian entrepreneurial capacities from making the most of the euro. That the oligopolistic and protectionist structures that have traditionally dominated Italian industry and commerce might also need to adjust, is not part of their concerns, at least not explicitly. Support among employers for the modest liberalizing reforms of the financial services sector proposed by the Treasury Minister Tommaso Padoa Schioppa in 2006 was implicit rather than explicit. However, much some large employers might approve, those who were willing to engage publicly in that debate were few in number.

Institutional Adjustment to the Euro Area

During the 1990s, Italy underwent a process of transition to a new economic and political order. Institutional changes, which simultaneously strengthened and 'hollowed out' the Italian state (Della Sala 1997), were accompanied by a transformation of the party system. The institutional changes of the 1990s were continued or, in some cases, undone in the post-1999 period and affected EMU membership in two main ways. They strengthened certain macroeconomic policymaking institutions, making it possible to comply with the convergence criteria; and they introduced alternation in office, which laid the seeds for a new and the more Euro-sceptic foreign policy that became more evident after 2001 (Quaglia 2004*b*).

Starting with domestic political institutions, in 1993, the electoral system was transformed into a (quasi) majoritarian system, with 25 per cent proportional representation, and the party system was reshaped into a bi-polar format with two main coalitions, centre-left and centre-right. The new system introduced alternation in power and, together with other concurrent causes, such as the *tangentopoli* scandal and the domestic repercussion of the end of the Cold War, reshaped the Italian party system. New political parties emerged and old ones disappeared (Bull and Rhodes 1997).

By the end of 2005, the party system had been consolidated, and the electoral reform had gone through a full circle because the proportional representation system, which had been in place before 1993, was reintroduced towards the end of the legislature by the second Berlusconi government. Notwithstanding that Fini and Berlusconi had supported the majoritarian system in the past, the rationale for the changes of the electoral law was clear. In terms of party competition, the new electoral system was configured in such a way as to limit the electoral success of the centre-left coalition. Indeed, the eminent Italian political scientist Giovanni Sartori called the new law '*Salva Berlusconi*', conceived only in Berlusconi's interest and for the centre-right coalition electoral victory (*Corriere della Sera* 16 September 2005). The law was criticized on the grounds that it did not guarantee a strong and stable majority, as evidenced by the 2006 electoral results, which gave a clear majority in the lower chamber to the Prodi coalition but a bare majority of four senators in the upper chamber. The change of the electoral law was un-related to EU politics and policy, but did not help the process of policy adjustment.

Throughout the 1990s, some institutional changes concerning the conduct of monetary policy were needed in order to adapt the central banking framework in Italy to the institutional and policy templates set up for Eurosystem/ ESCB membership. Such changes mainly concerned central bank independence and were directly imposed and 'locked-in' by EMU. The major institutional change that took place after 1999 was the transfer of monetary-policy and exchange-rate policy competences to the ECB. It is, however, noteworthy that, except for the direct legal changes prescribed by EMU/ECB legislation, and the operational changes needed to take part in the Eurosystem/ESCB, the Italian central bank was the one that exhibited the least adaptation to the EMU framework, prior to 2005.

Central banking governance in Italy was reformed in 2005, when the new saving law (*legge sul risparmio*) was passed, after having been (at times heatedly) discussed since 2002, and after having contributed to cause the resignation of two successive Treasury Ministers. Overall, the change introduced in December 2005 was relatively small, but it was significant precisely because in the past it had been successfully opposed, principally by the Bank of Italy and by some political forces.

The changes approved in 2005 concerned primarily the governance structure of the central bank. First, a term mandate for the Executive Board, including the Governor, was introduced, whereas previously their mandate was unlimited. Secondly, collegial decision-making and greater transparency within the Executive Board were established. Thirdly, the oversight of banking competition policy was to be shared between the competition authority and the central bank, with the former assessing competition issues and the latter evaluating prudential issues. In the past, the central bank was entirely responsible for competition policy in the banking sector, as well as having extensive and discretionary supervisory powers.

It should also be noted that the Italian banking system has undergone a process of privatization and consolidation from the 1990s onwards, partly as a result of the increasing competition in EU financial markets triggered by the introduction of the euro. External pressure for change mounted in Italy in the 2000s, when an increasing number of foreign financial companies, with the backing of the European Commission, which was keen to promote further financial market integration in Europe, tried to penetrate the national banking sector, straining the existing institutional and policy framework in the field of banking supervision and competition policy. The Bank of Italy has generally been seen as a strong institution in a weak state. This has partly been changed by the introduction of the euro, which reduced the functions of the central bank, but also by what might be termed collateral institutional reforms, such as the reduction in its monitoring role, and by a combination of market adjustment and institutional change, such as the increasing role of the competition authority referred to above.

In the 1990s, significant institutional changes had affected the conduct of fiscal policy. They had been needed for the reduction the national deficit and debt, so as to fulfil the EMU fiscal convergence criteria. Hence, they were indirectly imposed by EMU, or rather by the need to adapt to it domestically. In 1996, the Treasury was merged with the Budget Ministry, reducing the fragmentation of the state apparatus dealing with macroeconomic issues and strengthening the grip of the Treasury Minister on the public budget. Continuing this institutional process, in 2001, the Ministry of Finance, in charge of the revenue side of the budget, was merged with the reformed Treasury, creating the 'super-Ministry' for the Economy. The newly created Ministry for the Economy was thus responsible for the revenue and expenditure side of the state budget.

Finally, constitutional reforms were the leitmotiv of much of the 1990s and early 2000s, but after more than decade of debate the extent of real reform was minute relative to the range of and depth of the proposals, and the time spent on them. In November 2005, the centre-right government approved the reform of the second part of the Italian constitution (Vassallo 2005), which was however rejected by a referendum that took place in June 2006. The crux of the reform was to introduce 'devolution', assigning the regions the right to administer and legislate on health service, education and other matters. It also attempted to regulate the relation between the centre and the federal regions, reducing the number of parliamentarians, and ending 'bicameralismo', whereby both chambers have the same legislative power. Furthermore, the reform allowed citizens to choose directly the prime minister and allocated more powers—such as the annulment of ministerial appointment, early dissolution of Parliament—to the Prime Minister. Some changes, such as the introduction of devolution, were strongly supported by the Northern League, whereas other changes, such as strengthening the position of the Prime Minister, were advocated by *Forza Italia*. The constitutional reform was the result of a political compromise within the centre-right coalition, dictated mainly by tactical and strategic political considerations. Although this was a major issue in terms of policy change, there was no direct or indirect influence of the EU, except that the need to modernize Italy's governing arrangements by raising them to European standards was a persistent theme in the debate. This theme was a thread appearing in many of the reform debates of the last decade, like the central banking reform (Quaglia and Radaelli 2007).

Conclusion

One important effect of EMU on domestic politics has been an increase of 'soft' Euro-scepticism amongst political parties and public opinion. The Europeanization of public policies and institutions, directly or indirectly affected by EMU, has had diverse consequences. There has been a hasty and relatively unstable adjustment in fiscal policy; formal transformation in monetary and exchange rate policies; inertia, moving towards retrenchment in financial services regulation and supervision; marginal adjustment in labour-market policy and social policy. Effects of Europeanization are evident in reform of domestic macroeconomic institutions, but seem almost non-existent in administrative and constitutional reform.

Italy's eventful entry in the Euro Area, characterized by a hasty adjustment in order to fulfil the convergence criteria, has been followed by a delayed and limited adaptation to living in the Euro Area. Much-needed economic and institutional reforms have been implemented only partially, if at all. The result has been a worsening of Italian competitiveness in the context of a stagnant national economy: Italy has had one of the worst growth rates in the Euro Area and a deteriorating balance of payments deficit. On the positive side, the exchange-rate environment and associated financial indicators have been stabilized as a result of EMU membership, though the state of the public finances remains difficult.

In comparative terms, it is possible to see similarities with the Greek case analysed by Featherstone, in that Italian political and economic elites clearly used the introduction of the euro as an external constraint to legitimize reform, delayed some major adjustments especially in labour-market structures, which were less open to external pressure, and faced declining levels of public support after 2001. However, the extent of the similarity should not be overstated. The governing elites largely responsible for pushing through the euro strategy did so in conditions that suggested a relative detachment from electoral pressure. Unlike in Greece, the coalition supporting first-round membership of the Euro Area, though narrow, was relatively deep, and could count both on sustained party-political support and on support among economic actors—not only *Confindustria* but also trade-union leaders. It would be difficult on the basis of this to argue for a 'Mediterranean cluster'.

More generally, the impact of the euro-process on the Italian state has been mixed. On the one hand, the success in achieving first-round membership is noteworthy both in itself and even more so in the light of the apparently constant suspicion from northern Europeans about Italy's capacities and intentions, however unjustified that might be, and however much the Italians might feel that the performance of their detractors is even worse—sentiments felt particularly strongly around the crisis of the Stability and Growth Pact in 2003 with regard to Germany and France. On the other hand, trade unions and employers alike have expressed increasing concern about the delayed adjustment in wider economic reform, even to the extent of returning to the language of the 1980s in describing Italy as the 'stalled state'. This clearly does not improve the credibility and capacity of successive governments.

In the Italian case, Europeanization in and of itself has not strengthened the state. The internal and external pressure to join the euro increased support for difficult reforms before entry. After entry, countervailing pressures that had impeded reform in the first place were not sufficiently mitigated by the political and economic advantages of being within the Euro Area, to enable the reform momentum to be maintained. The effect of entry is not to make adjustment less necessary, but rather to make it both more painful, because the external shock is more immediate, and possibly more difficult, because the political context is less supportive.

11

The Netherlands: A Turning Point in Dutch–EU Relations?

Amy Verdun[1]

With some stretch of the imagination one could argue that since the early 2000s events in the Netherlands have only just fallen short of a political revolution—in otherwise a steady pro-European, elite-driven, consensual political system. The political turmoil had at its heart attitudes towards Economic and Monetary Union (EMU) and the euro as well as to the European Union (EU) more generally. These developments marked a clear change from what had gone on before the euro banknotes and coins were introduced in 2002. Thus the analysis of the developments in the Netherlands over the period 2002–7 stand in stark contrast to the developments over the prior five years (Verdun 2002).

Though the Netherlands made gradual moves towards economic and monetary integration in Europe in the 1980s and 1990s (Verdun 1990), the first years of the new millennium turned to be everything but gradual and smooth. Once the euro was introduced many Dutch citizens experienced an increase in prices and attributed blame to the euro. Furthermore, a recession that followed the boom of the late 1990s made Dutch citizens wonder if the euro was a major cause of economic decline. In the midst of all these concerns, the Dutch political system was shaken up by the rise of a new politician, Pim Fortuyn, and his party [Lijst Pim Fortuyn (LPF)], the success of which was cut short when he was murdered in 2002. Another political murder of a documentary maker, Theo van Gogh, in 2004 put into question Dutch policies towards

[1] The research for this chapter was made possible by generous grants from the Social Sciences and Humanities Research Council of Canada (SSHRC Grant: 410-99-0081 and 410-2005-01142). An earlier version of this chapter was presented at the conference 'European States and the Euro: The First Decade', London 23–25 May 2007, generously sponsored by the British Academy. The author thanks the participants of that conference, in particular Benjamin J. Cohen, Mark Hallerberg, Daniel Wincott, and Kenneth Dyson, the editor of this book, for useful comments and suggestions on earlier versions of this chapter.

immigration and multicultural tolerance. Finally, on the eve of the Dutch referendum on the Constitutional Treaty, in spring 2005, amidst a general discussion about the Treaty, a public debate emerged about the pros and cons of the euro, and of membership of the EU. Increasingly, people expressed dissatisfaction with the relationship between the Netherlands and the EU as a whole. The result was a shocking 62 per cent of 'no' votes in the Dutch referendum on the Constitutional Treaty held in June 2005.

These developments in the period 2002–7 took place against the background of a state that had done well from both EMU and from European integration more generally in both the recent and the distant past. Many years a net recipient, the Netherlands benefited from agricultural subsidies, infrastructural funds, and increased trade. Only in recent years has it evolved into the largest per capita contributor to the EU budget. It is a state that has typically been in favour of European integration, generally complacent about EU policymaking, and overall done well throughout five decades since the signing of the European Economic Community (EEC) Treaty in Rome.

This chapter examines how EMU has affected the Netherlands over the past 10 years, in particular the ability of Dutch elites to govern the country. To address this question, a number of issues are examined. The next section provides an overview of the context within which EMU was introduced in the Netherlands. The second through fourth sections explore the euro's effects on the Netherlands, in particular its polity, politics, and public opinion. Section five examines changes in Dutch discourse and policies. The final section draws some conclusions that reflect on the Dutch case and what particular lessons can be drawn from this case about opportunities and constraints for domestic elites and economic and political structures created by the euro. It is argued that EMU was introduced in a period following relative calm but started during a period that led to political soul searching: the introduction of the euro was a catalyst for domestic reform of the political system (parties, party leadership, political communication, connection of the political elites with the citizens) and for a maturation of the Dutch relationship with the EU. Though occurring at the same time, it is argued that the euro did not single-handedly *cause* a change in Dutch attitudes towards the EU. It worked as a catalyst in fuelling the discussion about the pros and cons of EU membership and EMU.

The Context of the Euro

The Netherlands is a small, open trading nation, which is highly dependent on its immediate neighbouring states and on other more distant EU member states. This openness is considered part of its collective national identity. Over decades Dutch policies have been geared towards limiting the differences in monetary policymaking from its most important trading partner, Germany. In fact for many years *De Nederlandsche Bank*, the Dutch central bank, under the leadership of Willem Duisenberg,[2] de facto copied German monetary policies. As such the creation of an EMU based on price stability, and the introduction of the euro, should be seen as part of long-term policies of the Dutch authorities to improve trade and maintain stability. Thus, EMU, and, by extension, the introduction of the euro, can in no way be seen as a break from the policies of the past. Interest rates in the Netherlands were typically close to those in Germany, and were not out of line with those that were needed in the Netherlands in terms of its economic growth. If at any point in the past interest rates were not appropriate (e.g. just after German unification in 1990, when rates were higher than what was deemed beneficial), the Netherlands adjusted through wages and prices.

The Dutch dealt with European integration very proactively. In the 1980s they strongly supported the completion of the single European market. They also favoured progressive policies in such fields as environment, social policy, and justice and home affairs. In policy implementation too the Dutch have a solid record (Falkner et al. 2005). European integration was considered to be a strategy at the heart of the Dutch governmental policies of the Christian-Democratic/Liberal coalitions of the 1980s. When the composition of Dutch coalition governments changed from centre-Right to Social Democratic/Liberal, there was no change in policies towards European integration. The same holds true for the approach to EMU. It was seen as yet another initiative to strengthen the general European integration process as well as the successful monetary policies pursued by the Dutch monetary authorities since the late 1970s. The Dutch have been strong supporters of European integration in general and also the economic and monetary integration process throughout the entire period prior to the introduction of the euro banknotes and coins in 2002.

During the mid- to late 1990s the Netherlands managed to restructure its economy with great success. It was sometimes called the 'Dutch Miracle' (cf. Visser and Hemerijck 1997). Some analysts looked to the Netherlands as a 'model' for successful restructuring. 'The Polder Model', as it was often called in the 1990s, attracted attention from academics, politicians, and the media. There is not a uniform clear definition of the term 'Polder Model', which is used widely and loosely. However, a useful definition is given by Labohm and Wijnker (2000: 5): 'On an institutional level, the Polder Model includes a quasi-permanent dialogue between government and social partners (tripartitism), which is conducive to the creation of a climate in which both employers and trade unions trust each other and are prepared to strike deals

---

[2] Duisenberg was president from 1982 to 1997 after which time he became the first president of the European Central Bank.

Table 11.1. Annual average Gross Domestic Product (GDP) per capita (percentage change on preceding year, the Netherlands compared to Euro Area and EU-27, 1997–2007

	1997–2001	2002–6	2003	2004	2005	2006	2007 projected
The Netherlands	3.1	1.1	−0.1	1.9	1.3	2.9	2.6
Euro Area	2.5	1.0	0.2	1.4	0.9	2.2	2.2
EU-25	2.7	1.6	0.9	2.0	1.3	2.6	2.6

Source: European Commission (2007a: 133, Table 11.4).

that are beneficial to both parties in a long-term perspective.' They go on to explain what policy outcomes the Polder Model has produced:

Within this institutional framework, it has been possible to foster wage moderation and gradual trimming of the welfare state, with positive effects on employment and social spending, thus contributing to the financial sustainability of the welfare state. Other positive effects include the reduction of public spending and budget deficits, as well as the gradual reduction of the public debt/GDP [Gross Domestic Product] ratio. (ibid. 5)

Various commentators wondered to what extent the Dutch model offers a successful formula for other states to adopt in order to deal with external constraints caused by globalization and Europeanization and, of course, EMU. With the slowdown of economic growth in the Netherlands in the early 2000s, the interest in the Polder Model subsided considerably (Table 11.1).

For many years, Dutch political elites have favoured economic and monetary integration. Thus, the introduction of the euro was not politically challenging. However, once the euro was introduced, the perceived level of inflation increased dramatically. Newspapers in February through April 2002 reported inflation rates in the Netherlands at higher than 1.5 per cent above the average for the EU. Especially the prices of hotels and restaurants increased considerably (De Nederlandsche Bank 2002). However, official inflation statistics did not reflect perceived inflation, even though they showed a doubling in the rate of inflation in 2001 to 5 per cent and just below 4 per cent in 2002, returning to just above 2 per cent in 2003, and dropping to below 2 per cent thereafter (Table 11.2).

In 2005 an incident with a Dutch central bank official, who was quoted out of context as saying that the introduction of the euro had occurred at too high an exchange rate, with a commentary that the Dutch lost 10 per cent of their income because of the euro introduction, caused major public unrest and dismay (Het Parool 2005a, 2005b).[3] It led to a period of criticism of the

[3] In an interview with this author, officials within *De Nederlandsche Bank* (DNB) explained that when the interview was given with the official that the transcript of the interview had been reviewed and approved by the DNB, but they had not seen the sensational front page 'header' that was more alarmist than what was merited by the newspaper article (DNB official, interview with the author, Amsterdam, August 2006).

Table 11.2. Dutch inflation rates 2000–6

	Annual percentage change in harmonized consumer price index (HCPI)						Projected 2006
	2000	2001	2002	2003	2004	2005	
The Netherlands	2.34	5.11	3.87	2.24	1.38	1.50	1.65
Euro Area[a]	2.12	2.36	2.26	2.08	2.14	2.18	2.18
EU-27	3.46	3.20	2.54	2.14	2.27	2.28	2.30
EU-25[b]	2.44	2.49	2.13	1.95	2.14	2.16	2.20
EU-15[c]	1.90	2.19	2.08	1.96	1.96	2.14	2.19

[a] Euro area with 12 countries.
[b] Former EU-25.
[c] Former EU-15.
Source: Adapted from European Commission (2007*b*).

euro and lack of trust in political elites, just two months before the Dutch referendum on the EU Constitutional Treaty. Several sources commented that the euro had become one of the key points on which voters would be reflecting when voting in the referendum (NRC Handelsblad 2005).

Aarts and van der Kolk (2005, 2006) examined the reasons behind the Dutch 'no' vote and found that almost 94 per cent of the interviewees 'completely agreed' with the statement 'as a result of the introduction of the euro, prices have gone up in the Netherlands' (ibid. 2006: 245). They also showed a major discrepancy between elite perceptions (measured as party political preference towards the Constitutional Treaty) and those of the voters (whether or not they voted 'yes' or 'no'). All the established political parties recommended a 'yes' vote, whereas the result was a large 'no' majority against. The outcome of the Dutch referendum has been seen by many as signalling a new critical stance about Europe and a lack of public trust in Dutch political elites.

A media content analysis by Kleinnijenhuis, Takens, and Van Atteveldt (2005), covering the 365 days before the referendum, shows that no single issue dominated the media coverage.[4] Their sample suggests the following breakdown of issues: the campaign itself (14.2 per cent); daily matters related to the EU (13.6 per cent, in particular the 'Bolkenstein directive'); general economic, budgetary, and financial matters (11.9 per cent); the euro (6.7 per cent); enlargement (6.6 per cent, of which 4.6 dealt with Turkey); and national identity matters (4.5 per cent) (ibid. 129–30). However, in the final weeks before the referendum, three issues dominated the media: the campaign itself, the referendum, and the euro.

Van der Kolk and Aarts find that many 'no' voters held a negative view on how the euro affected the Dutch (see Table 11.3). Otherwise they were unwilling to spell out their reasons. Many stated that 'it seemed better' (ibid.

[4] They analysed a full year of newspaper articles in national and regional newspapers, in total 1145 articles (Kleinnijenhuis, Takens, and van Atteveldt 2005: 125).

Table 11.3. Opinion on the euro and percentage of voters who voted 'no' in the Dutch referendum

	Completely agree	Neither agree nor disagree	Disagree
The Netherlands was disadvantaged at the transition from the guilder to the euro	73	37	30
The introduction of the euro is beneficial to the Dutch economy	40	53	76
The introduction of the euro has led to price increases in the Netherlands	64	28	20
The introduction of the euro has made payments in foreign countries easier	60	93	75

Source: Aarts and van der Kolk (2005: 199).

2005: 187). They also held a negative attitude about the EU. Their polling found that 92 per cent of 'no' voters held a negative attitude towards EU membership; and 84 per cent agreed that 'European unification had gone too far' (ibid. 2005: 189). In other words, even though the negative perception of the euro was central, a number of other issues played an important role in determining the outcome.

Exploring the Euro's Effects on Dutch Polity

A highly corporatist state, the Netherlands has typically been governed by political elites representing the 'social partners' (Hemerijck 1995). Trade unions, employers' associations, and government representatives are at the heart of wage negotiations, changes in policies and laws, and of informal agreements to keep labour costs under control. Dutch political actors have a long history of tackling problems together.

The Netherlands had already experienced changes to its economy and its political actors during the period following the end of the Bretton Woods system of fixed exchange rates. The major restructuring period occurred in the 1980s. From the late 1970s to the mid-1980s the Dutch economy suffered from what became known as 'Dutch disease', which referred to the worsened competitiveness of its economy. André Szász (1988: 208–9) identifies four factors that caused the 'Dutch disease': first, the tradition of centralized wage bargaining; second, the political preference to increase wages rather than worry about profits; third, the rapidly increasing state expenditures made possible by the high revenue from Dutch natural gas; and, fourth, the rapid increase of general wages due to a number of automatic mechanisms. The decision to follow a strong currency policy put pressure on a number of these practices, and offered a method to combat inflation.

For these reasons the Dutch authorities decided to follow German monetary policies and secure a fixed exchange rate between the guilder and the D-Mark. This policy objective was maintained until the launch of the euro in 1999. By 1999 the Dutch exchange rate with the D-Mark had been the most stable of all ERM currencies over two decades. The Dutch were among the first to decide to follow German monetary policies. It was part of wider political and socio-economic factors supporting a restructuring of the Dutch economy (Jones 1998). The macro-economic adjustments necessary to maintain these fixed exchange rates were spread over a longer period than in a number of other ERM states, notably Italy, Portugal, and Spain.

After coming to terms with the economic decline of the 1970s, the Dutch government had the difficult task of dealing with the consequent economic problems. High wages, high public debt, lack of competitiveness, low economic growth, and high unemployment were among the many problems. The governments of the 1980s chose to focus first on cutting expenditure. The 1980s could be characterized as one long period of *Bezuinigingen* (cuts in public expenditure). It started with the Van Agt government, which announced its *Bestek '81* with as its main aim to reduce public expenditure.

In order to tackle unemployment, during the 1980s the three governments of Ruud Lubbers aimed at 'freezing' wages. Within the neo-corporatist structures of the Netherlands, representatives of trade unions, employers' organizations, and government bargained over labour conditions, wages, and public expenditure. In the 1970s they had only once succeeded in negotiating a collective agreement. A major breakthrough came in 1982 with the so-called 'Accord of Wassenaar'—a general agreement, with recommendations on employment policy. After the Accord of Wassenaar a number of important changes were made (Visser and Hemerijck 1997). The trade unions accepted that the overall profitability of Dutch industry had to improve in order to deal with unemployment. They accepted the employers' proposal that they should refrain from demanding a nominal wage increase in line with inflation. The employers, in turn, agreed to open discussions about reducing the working week for some jobs. Wassenaar also led to a change from a centralized, failing system of collective bargaining to a decentralized, though highly coordinated system.

During the 1980s many automatic wage increases were abolished (Kapteyn 1993). In consequence, the overall wage level in the Netherlands, compared to that in Germany, declined considerably. The strategy of freezing wages appeared for most of the 1980s not to be very beneficial to employment. During the second half of the 1980s, the restructuring of the labour market followed some unconventional methods, not necessarily aimed at this result (de Beus 2004). The Dutch employment disability law was used to fund persons who were unable for medical reasons to continue their jobs. At one point as many as one million people (out of a population of then 15 million) were on disability money, and out of the labour force. By the 1990 it was clear that the employment laws needed to be changed in favour of flexibility, and that an end had to be made to using the disability law to place workers outside the workforce.

In the 1990s the use of temporary employment was 'rediscovered'. The labour market grew increasing more flexible, with jobs being done part-time, more temporary positions created, and an increasing number of women entering the labour market.[5] Whereas in other states, for example Germany, the introduction of flexi-jobs have typically been associated with job insecurity and lack of social safety-net, in the Netherlands this has been less the case. The flexi-jobs and part-time jobs are held by young employees and by women (often as an additional income in the household).

Meanwhile, the government continued on its path of reducing government expenditure, in particular to obtain lower public debt and to reduce the budgetary deficit to around 2 per cent. By the mid-1990s the Dutch economy had restructured itself in two important areas: employment law and government expenditure. Miraculously, by the mid-1990s the Dutch economy seemed to have come out of 15 years of hard restructuring work to face the new reality of above average economic growth, decreasing levels of unemployment, and a higher ratio of employed persons to the total population. The 'Dutch Miracle' had emerged (Visser and Hemerijck 1997).[6] The 'Polder Model' was discovered by analysts as a guide to how to deal with the constraints posed by Europeanization and globalization (Labohm and Wijnker 2000; also Marcussen this volume).

As a mode of governance the 'Polder Model' has the following characteristics. There is strong cooperation between the government, employers' organizations, and trade unions in neo corporatist structures. These 'tripartite' bodies discuss employment issues and restructuring of the welfare state, as well as issues relating to privatization and price-setting. Wage moderation has been used to improve the competitiveness of the Dutch economy (Visser and Hemerijck 1997: 26–7; cf. Blanchard et al. 1993).

Notably, the Dutch government was among the first in Western Europe to deregulate and privatize. Many large state-owned corporations were sold to the private sector. In numerous areas of traditional monopoly competitors

[5] The percentage of female participation in the workforce increased from 34.7 per cent in 1983 to 55.0 per cent in 1996, compared to the EU average of 42.9 per cent in 1983 and 48.4 per cent in 1996 (*OECD Employment Outlook*, July 1997).

[6] Over the period 1991–6 the Dutch economy did much better than the EU average on the important economic indicators. In annual growth of GDP the Dutch performance was 2.2 per cent compared to the EU average of 1.5 per cent; private consumption 2.3 per cent compared to 1.5 per cent; investment 1.3 per cent compared to -0.2 per cent; total employment 1.5 per cent compared to -0.5 per cent; unemployment level 6.2 per cent compared to 11.1 per cent; and employment/population ratio 64.2 per cent instead of 60.6 per cent (Visser and Hemerijck 1997: 11).

entered the market. In the Dutch case marketization happened early, but also in consultation with the tripartite bodies.

However, some critics of the 'Polder Model' argued that it concealed considerable hidden unemployment. A large percentage of the potential Dutch workforce is out of employment on disability payments; many of the 60–65-year olds are on early retirement; and numerous new jobs are part-time. The Netherlands also traditionally has had one of the lowest percentages of female labour participation among EU member states. The new jobs for women and youth are often temporary and/or part-time and do not always offer the workers the full satisfaction that they seek (Jones 1998; OECD 1997).

Changes in Dutch Domestic Politics

The Dutch political system has been calm throughout most of the post-Second World War period, with coalition governments with a combination of mostly two of the following three political groupings in governments: Social Democrats, Liberals, and Christian Democrats. The 'politics of accommodation' (Lijphart 1968)) continued even after the strong 'pillarization' in the Netherlands disappeared. Governing in the Netherlands remained a matter of elite cooperation and contract making prior to starting a four-year governing period.

Major change occurred when Pim Fortuyn took centre stage. His political message and style broke with the tradition of what has been referred to as *'Regentenpolitiek'* (politics of the 'regents'), commonly understood to be elitist, rather boring (technocratic and apolitical), and accommodating to the issues raised by other parties (Bélanger and Aarts 2006). Fortuyn made his points in clear language, making his political message simple, and he did not seek to accommodate differences with other parties. His prominent views were on migration issues, such as bringing a halt to further immigration, and on integrating newcomers into Dutch society. Although he had clear views on many topics, he did not particularly run on a platform of attacking the euro (and the topic was not very salient when he was in the news in 2002). Before the 2002 election he started a political party, Lijst Pim Fortuyn (LPF), which soon became very popular and was set to win a significant share of the vote. However, a week before the elections, he was assassinated—a political circumstance unprecedented in modern Dutch history. Although the murder sent shock waves through the population, the leaders decided to continue with the elections as planned. The result was that the LPF became the second party of the Netherlands (with 17 per cent), following the Christian Democrats. The election results shook the political foundations of the country, as the Christian Democrats had been declining, and the new party (now without leader) had overtaken the Social Democrats and the right-wing Liberals.[7]

A period of political crisis followed. The political impasse was in large part due to the success of the LPF in the elections, but as a party it was totally unprepared to take a seat in government. The CDA (Christian Democrats), LPF, and the VVD (right-wing Liberals) formed a coalition whose term of office started in July 2002 and ended in October 2002. LPF was not prepared to govern. It had lost its charismatic leader; as a group the members had little to no political experience; the party had no internal coherence or structure; and it lacked the general support from the other political parties that was so typical of Dutch politics.

New elections were held in January 2003. This time the outcome was more typical of what had been seen in previous years. The LPF lost spectacularly, and the CDA stayed the largest party. The result was a continuation of a government by the CDA leader, Jan Peter Balkenende, with the right-wing liberals (VVD) and the left-wing liberals (D'66) in the coalition. This second Balkenende government initiated the plan to hold a referendum on the European Constitution, the first major one since 1793. Holding a referendum on major constitutional issues was an important matter for the smallest coalition party, D'66.

Perceptions of EMU and the EU

What were Dutch attitudes towards EMU in the run up to, and in the wake of, the introduction of the euro banknotes and coins? In anticipation of the euro, the Dutch central bank started its own opinion polling in 1995. These polls of the public and businesses—conducted four times per year—showed that business was substantially more favourable to the introduction of the euro than the public. Even so, overall public acceptance levels were at 60 per cent or higher throughout the period 1995–9. The percentage of people in favour of the introduction of the euro started at 60 per cent in 1995, climbed to 73 per cent in September 1996, and then declined to 62 per cent in September 1997. Thereafter, it rose steadily to 80 per cent in March 1999 (Prast and Stokman 1999: 4).

In October 1996 the Dutch Social Democratic Party (PvdA) issued a report *'De Strijd om de EMU'* ('The Battle for EMU'), stating that the convergence criteria and the proposed Stability Pact were too stringent. The report warned against the hard rules, arguing that they led to lower economic growth and higher unemployment (Metten and van Riel 1996). However, and indicative

---

[7] The LPF was dissolved on 1 January 2008.

of the state of Dutch opinion, the report did not lead to a major public debate on this topic.

Interestingly, after years of support for European integration in general, and economic and monetary cooperation in particular, a public debate suddenly emerged in 1997. There had already been some calls by a newly established action group, which claimed to represent small shop owners, for a 'boycott' of the euro. In the view of its spokesperson, EMU would just cost money and would not guarantee a positive outcome. The group was particularly concerned about the lack of serious sanctions to constrain Greece and Italy. The real public debate opened on 13 February 1997, when a leading Dutch newspaper published a declaration, signed by 70 Dutch economists, criticizing EMU—'*Met deze EMU kiest Europa de verkeerde weg*' ('With this EMU Europe is choosing the wrong road') (*De Volkskrant* 1997; Reuten, Vendrik, and Went 1998). Their main concern was that EMU would endanger the welfare state and the social welfare of European citizens. The fear was that, by having government expenditures as the only instrument to deal with economic shocks, it would not be possible to create an economically prosperous and equitable society. At the same time as the Dutch economists' declaration, a prominent Dutch Liberal politician, Frits Bolkestein, also voiced criticism of the EMU project. The result was the first real public debate in the Netherlands on EMU.

However, the reaction of the Dutch Parliament and the government was lukewarm. Some parliamentarians, such as the Social Democrat Rick van der Ploeg, argued that Parliament could not take the criticism seriously, as the moment to discuss EMU had already passed some time ago. Hans Hoogervorst, a Liberal MP, thought that the advice of the 70 economists would lead to higher unemployment—rather than that EMU would have this effect, as they claimed. Parliamentarians also criticized the list of economists and noted that the 'real experts' were not among them (*De Volkskrant* 1997). A week later other politicians voiced the need to increase the amount of information to the public about the introduction of the euro. By March 1997 the central banking community, as well as the more prominent experts on EMU, were expressing their surprise about the newly started debate on EMU.

Though the Dutch central bank opinion polling did not observe a decline in support, Eurobarometer data *did* show a decline in support for the euro by Dutch citizens in 1997. Whereas support in the spring of 1996 had been 66 per cent in favour and 26 per cent against, the numbers in support came down considerably in 1997 (European Commission 1996: 45). In the spring of 1997 those in favour dropped to 52 per cent, and those opposed rose to 42 per cent (European Commission 1997: 28). However, this dip in support was only temporary. The Eurobarometer figures for spring 2000 indicated that the Dutch were back to their earlier levels of support: 67 per cent in favour and 27 per cent against (European Commission 2000*a*: 46).

These Eurobarometer figures suggest that the Dutch reduction in support for the euro in 1997 may have been caused by the new, more critical public debate on EMU. However, no systematic analysis has been made analysing whether this debate had an impact on the general public attitude towards EMU. Moreover, it is possible that other factors also had an effect on Dutch public opinion (such as the voting into power of left-wing governments in Britain and France; and increasing expression of criticism of the EMU project throughout Europe and in the United States). Finally, the two conflicting polls cast some doubt on whether there really was a downward trend in public support for EMU.

In any event, the debate in the Netherlands soon subsided, and after 1997 EMU was no longer debated in these terms until the euro banknotes and coins were actually introduced in 2002. In the five years following the 1997 debate, the media returned to its overall positive reporting of the European integration process. In 1999–2000 the Dutch seemed once again at ease with EMU. The debate about the EU moved on to discuss issues of accountability, legitimacy, and democracy.

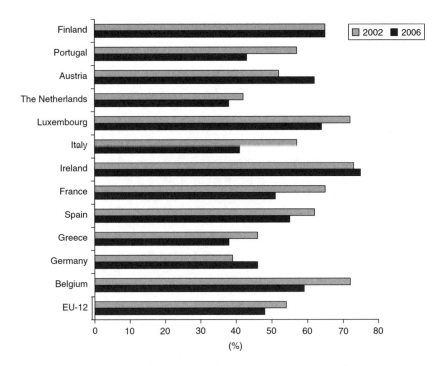

Figure 11.1. Proportion of the public in the EU-12 countries identifying the euro as 'advantageous overall' for their country, 2006

Source: Eurobarometer (2002*a*, 2003, 2004, 2005, 2006).

Table 11.4. Main advantages of the adoption of the euro—public opinion in EU-12, 2006

	More stable prices (% = 'yes')	Reinforce place of Europe in the world (% = 'yes')	Improve employment growth (% = 'yes')	Easier/cheaper to travel (% = 'yes')	Easier to compare prices (% = 'yes')	Lower interest rates, less debt charges (% = 'yes')	Sounder public finances (% = 'yes')
EU-12	11.2	27.2	5.2	45.9	30.2	4.2	4.7
Belgium	14.3	22.5	5.8	60.8	52.1	2.2	1.7
Germany	9.8	17.3	3.9	46.7	33.2	1.0	2.4
Greece	17.8	29.9	8.2	24.6	17.3	1.0	10.6
Spain	9.0	25.0	6.4	51.5	16.9	1.3	4.1
France	5.5	27.9	3.6	37.4	16.3	2.6	2.6
Ireland	22.4	16.8	11.3	63.1	47.5	27.6	18.3
Italy	19.1	35.1	6.4	42.8	39.4	10.9	8.5
Luxembourg	14.3	22.2	7.7	71.8	59.6	2.3	3.7
The Netherlands	7.4	18.4	3.9	34.0	28.9	1.0	2.7
Austria	12.9	16.7	6.9	57.0	51.5	8.1	4.4
Portugal	17.5	25.8	9.7	66.1	53.3	8.1	5.1
Finland	7.4	9.7	1.9	57.6	38.8	8.7	16.1

Source: Eurobarometer (2006: 87–8).

Once the 'Dutch miracle' became visible, and the 'Polder Model' a talking point, economic policies of restructuring became much easier politically, and the reduction of budgetary deficits and public debt a less difficult process. Attitudes to EMU were no longer framed in the context of whether it might have a negative impact on the welfare state. With the Dutch economy performing so well, no one could make a serious claim that the Dutch model was being put under pressure by EMU or market forces. There was an overall sense of well-being. The performance of the Dutch economy appeared even more spectacular against the background of the poor performance of its neighbouring states, in particular France and Germany.

The introduction of euro banknotes and coins had a profound impact on the Netherlands. The so-called 'menu costs' went up, as well as the cost of fruit and vegetables (Centraal Planbureau 2002, 2005). Although the actual official inflation did not rise much, Dutch citizens were unhappy with the increase of prices on goods and services that were very visible (costs of drinks and foods in bars and restaurants). The perceived level of inflation went up much more than what could be shown in official statistics. Throughout the Euro Area this perceived inflation had been considerably higher than measured inflation (see Table 11.2).

By 2006 the Dutch public were among those most critical of the euro (see Figure 11.1). They did not value the contribution of the euro to the economy, ease of travel, or lowering the cost of servicing the debt as of major importance (see Tables 11.4 and 11.5).

Table 11.5. Main disadvantages of the adoption of the euro—public opinion in the EU-12, 2006

	Low interest rates (% = 'yes')	Too rigid for public spending (% = 'yes')	Loss of competitiveness (% = 'yes')	Price rises (% = 'yes')	Loss of sovereignty (% = 'yes')	More unemployment, less growth (% = 'yes')
EU-12	3.0	1.9	5.2	81.4	5.0	7.0
Belgium	4.0	6.6	10.2	89.2	2.6	12.6
Germany	0.6	1.2	4.8	75.9	6.4	4.1
Greece	1.6	0.9	2.5	82.2	2.9	6.0
Spain	0.6	0.8	1.5	85.9	1.2	3.0
France	0.3	0.0	5.1	64.4	6.6	5.0
Ireland	6.6	6.3	6.5	22.1	24.0	58.3
Italy	8.8	3.5	5.3	95.9	3.1	10.6
Luxembourg	2.0	3.0	16.5	85.4	11.0	11.3
The Netherlands	2.1	1.1	5.9	85.7	2.7	4.0
Austria	4.0	4.2	8.2	92.7	7.4	11.7
Portugal	4.7	5.1	16.7	91.8	9.0	22.2
Finland	0.8	5.5	7.4	64.9	16.8	1.5

Source: Eurobarometer (2006: 89–90).

EMU and Changes in Dutch Discourse and Policies

Has EMU led to more Europeanization? Or has Europeanization led to EMU? In the Dutch case one can argue that both happened. It seems that the process swings back and forth between the two, like a pendulum (Wallace and Wallace 1996). In the late 1980s, when EMU was once again put on the agenda, the Dutch accepted it as part of Europeanization and their overall policies. Once EMU was accepted, it became part of the successful policies that one could look to in order to find evidence that Europeanization was happening.

However, following the introduction of euro banknotes and coins the situation changed. The euro was often blamed for having caused too much inflation, and the European project for being too costly for the average Dutch citizen.

Has EMU led to a change in discourse in the Netherlands? Again, the answer is not clear-cut. At the end of the 1980s public debate and domestic politics in the Netherlands had already incorporated the discourse on restructuring or retrenchment and on stability (i.e. reducing debts and deficits) (Marcussen, this volume). The Dutch had kept inflation rates low, so the public debate did not emphasize the need for low inflation. However, with the coming of the EMU and the euro, the language extended to include more monetary-policy-related 'buzzwords' that were now heard more frequently. 'Low inflation', 'price stability', 'convergence criteria', and 'stability pact' were added to vocabulary throughout the 1990s.

It appears that there was no regime shift, but a new specification of the words and concepts being adopted within the regime. In other words, the discourse had changed prior to the time that EMU was put on the agenda. However, with the introduction of EMU the discourse was further strengthened and legitimized (Verdun 2000). At the same time, the perceived increase in prices following the introduction of banknotes and coins, as well as dissatisfaction with the fact that the Dutch were the member state that contributed per capita the largest part to the EU budget, led them to be more critical of the euro and the EU more generally.

How EMU affects Dutch identity is difficult to pin down. The Dutch see themselves as a nation of traders, and realize that they need to cater to this self-image and aim. EMU nicely fits this profile. With the rediscovered success of the Dutch economy, the Dutch started to appreciate that they were considered to be the 'winners' of the game that was being played in Europe. Most people realize that the introduction of the euro is to a certain extent an unknown quantity and that there will be winners and losers. What came out of the public debate in 1997 was this sense that the future was uncertain. When the Dutch economy did well in the late 1990s, whilst their important and considerable larger and richer neighbours Germany and France did less well, the Dutch felt that Europeanization, globalization, and EMU had done their state and economy quite some good.

However, perceptions changed when the economy cooled down. The antipathy was targeted at the euro and European integration in its broader sense. It is striking to note how the Dutch thought about the euro once their economy picked up again in 2005–6. Attitudes towards the euro in the period after the Dutch referendum improved in favour of support. The period from 1999–2007 has been characterized by a more balanced inflation performance (as opposed to the higher inflation in the early years). The result of the improved economic growth is that the Dutch government regained some of the support that it had lost before and after the Dutch referendum in spring 2005. In fact, very few would have predicted that Jan Peter Balkenende would become the winner of the national elections of 22 November 2006. The fourth Balkenende government consisted of the Christian-Democrats, the right-wing Liberals (VVD), and a smaller Christian party (Christen Unie). An openly eurosceptic party, the Socialistische Partij (SP) or 'Socialist Party', made gains, winning 25 seats out of the 150 available. It collected most of the disgruntled voters, many of whom in the past would have voted LPF or other left-wing parties. Yet, the SP did not manage to get into power as a coalition with Christian Democrats (CDA) and the Labour Party (PvdA) proved impossible. Thus, Balkenende started his fourth term with a right-wing coalition.

From the start of 2007 attitudes towards constitutional change, the euro, and European integration improved considerably. The signing of the Lisbon Treaty generated little protest by the general public (even though the SP still presses for a referendum). Attitudes towards the euro also improved. Whether or not the improved attitudes towards the euro may have something to do with the current economic climate, or a general apathy about European matters, will remain speculation. The Dutch are now more sympathetic towards their political elite and towards 'European integration' than when a majority of the Dutch voted 'no' in the 2005 referendum. The Dutch government seemed also not to have suffered too much from the turbulence surrounding the referendum.

Conclusion: A Break with the Past?

The Netherlands has gone through two distinct stages in recent history. The first period from the start of EMU until the introduction of the euro banknotes and coins in 2002 can be characterized as one in which the Dutch generally accepted EMU. European monetary integration was considered to be in line with Dutch policies that focused on maintaining fixed exchange rates with Germany and other EU member states. The Dutch view themselves as a nation of traders, who want their country to do well in an interdependent global world. European economic and monetary integration was accepted as a process that strengthened these fundamental Dutch interests.

In the early-mid 2000s the Dutch underwent a U-turn in attitudes towards EMU and the euro. The high 'menu costs' were seen as important negative aspects. The Dutch turned from pro- to anti-European integration, in particular regarding their opinion on the Constitutional Treaty and the euro. Most citizens did not want to leave the EU, but overall enthusiasm for European integration and the European project clearly declined.

The Dutch approach to EMU is firmly embedded in the Dutch approach to European integration and Europeanization. The construction of Europe remains at the heart of Dutch policies, and EMU is merely another stepping stone on the road to further integration. The Dutch also remained confident that European integration in general, and EMU in particular, will not threaten the Dutch model of governance. On the contrary, the Dutch were more capable than most of maintaining their own model, performing well, and joining EMU without many problems at all.

In the Dutch case EMU was not a causal factor in restructuring the welfare state and the labour market. The pressures for reform preceded the plan to create EMU. The relaunching of the EMU project did, however, add another incentive to step up the process of restructuring, in particular of the public debt and the budgetary deficit. But it would be a serious misrepresentation to state that EMU had very much effect on the Dutch mode of governance in the first period. In the second period the situation changed. The political turbulence created by Pim Fortuyn and the two political assassinations, and the overall dissatisfaction with declining benefits of European integration, the perceived cost of the euro, and the dislike of the Constitutional Treaty, led to a turn-around in the Netherlands that caused a significant change in attitudes. The result was a period of soul searching for the Dutch and even a question of what the Dutch wanted to get out of European integration.

It is difficult to judge how EMU affects Dutch society and identity. Dutch attitudes towards EMU and the euro seem to be correlated to how the economy is doing (even if perhaps by chance). Furthermore, the effects of the euro and EMU are so firmly embedded in Dutch preferences and policy objectives that it is hard to draw the line between those effects and EMU per se. To give an example, the effects of the euro and EMU are to increase competition between the Netherlands and its neighbouring country, to force discipline on budgetary policy, and to accept a 'low-inflation' monetary policy stance. These objectives have traditionally been considered important pillars of good Dutch governance and economic policy. As such the euro and EMU did not change all that much from what was earlier the case.

Moreover, the 'feel-good' factor in the Netherlands—as a result of the economic growth and prosperity since the mid-1990s—and the 'feel-bad' factor in 2002–5 constrain us from making an objective evaluation about what EMU does to the Netherlands. The Dutch are divided about the euro, depending on the period of the past 10 years that one studies public opinion. The most negative period has already passed: economic growth and job creation have resurfaced in the Netherlands and thus the Dutch government is not facing the most politically difficult redistributive questions.

Many critics of EMU stress that the euro, and the specific policy regime chosen for economic and monetary integration in Europe, involves a large number of risks. Various authors identify a lack of legitimacy of the EMU project (Crouch 2000; Minkkinen and Patomäki 1997; Patomäki 1997). With Thomas Christiansen, I argued elsewhere that the way legitimacy of EMU has been created is through 'output' legitimacy (Verdun and Christiansen 2000). The downside of this process of legitimacy building is that once the success of the euro is in question, the legitimacy of the entire project is put into doubt (Verdun and Christiansen 2001). This process occurred in the Netherlands when the euro lost support.

Others scholars have focused on the fact that governments are lacking adequate tools to deal with economic shocks and social inequality (Boyer 2000; Pochet 1998). There have also been lively debates about how a fully symmetrical EMU might work, with both EMU and a *gouvernement économique*, as well as a more fully developed political union (Dyson 2000*b*; Dyson and Featherstone 1999; Umbach and Wessels this volume; Verdun 1996, 1998, 2003). During the Intergovernmental Conferences preparing the Maastricht Treaty in 1991 and in the course of the 1990s, the Dutch emphasized the need for further political integration. These debates consider what role there might be for national and European governance, and whether there might be a need for fiscal transfer payments to deal with any imbalances. The Dutch have shied away from thinking seriously about these matters.

EMU confirmed the belief of the Dutch government and people that neo-liberal policies, conducted within a framework of consensus governance (the 'Polder Model'), served them well in their fundamental aim of remaining a prosperous small trading nation. At first, EMU strengthened the Dutch overall commitment to Europe. In the second period, the euro was cause for distancing from Europe, reflected in rejection of the Constitutional Treaty. By 2007 enduring uncertainty about the consequences, combined with the widening implications of the credit crunch, raised questions about how durable changes to more positive Dutch perceptions of EMU would prove, given the reliance on 'output' legitimacy, and how the might affect perceptions of the broader project of European integration.

There are grounds for thinking that the five years of euro-scepticism in the Netherlands will not have a lasting impact on Dutch attitudes to the EU and

EMU. The political and economic circumstances of the period 2001–6 were sufficiently specific and contingent to suggest that when they have passed the Dutch are likely to return to their permissive consensus on European integration and EMU. These years were characterized by political turmoil and a bout of high inflation and slow growth. At the time of writing political stability has returned, and inflation and growth have normalized. The Dutch are likely to return to a level of acceptance of the euro and EMU similar to when it was first introduced into financial markets in 1999.

Part III

Domestic Political and Policy Contexts in Euro Area 'Outsiders'

12

Baltic States: When Stability Culture is Not Enough[1]

Magnus Feldmann

In August 1991 the Baltic States re-emerged as independent after half a century. The reforms that lay ahead were daunting, as these three states had been fully integrated in the economic and political structures of the Soviet Union and had to build most of the institutions of an independent state from scratch. Many observers were sceptical about their prospects as independent states at the time. Within a few years most of these doubts had dissipated. In 2004 Estonia, Latvia, and Lithuania joined both the EU and NATO, marking the culmination of their transformation and reintegration with the West.

The establishment of national currencies was one of the central planks of their reform programmes. The successful introduction of the Estonian kroon, the Latvian lats, and the Lithuanian litas had great symbolic importance for these newly independent states. All three states chose macroeconomic policy programmes that minimized the scope for discretionary monetary policy—either by adopting currency boards or (in the case of Latvia) by a hard peg that operated in a similar way. This kind of policy environment constituted an excellent fit with the framework embodied in EMU and contributed to rapid disinflation and 'good' fiscal policy outcomes. These macroeconomic policy regimes earned much praise from international organizations, like the IMF, and turned the three Baltic States into pacesetters and likely early joiners of the Euro Area (Feldmann 2006*a*).

This chapter begins by briefly discussing macroeconomic policy in Estonia, Latvia, and Lithuania in the 1990s and some of the main factors leading to a far-reaching consensus on stability culture. I then turn to macroeconomic policy since the Baltic States' accession to the EU in 2004. While the commitment to stability culture is intact, rising inflation has prevented the three

[1] The author thanks the Krupp Foundation and the Minda de Gunzburg Center for European Studies at Harvard University for financial support.

243

states from adopting the euro as fast as most analysts were predicting at the time of accession. The chapter describes the sources of this problem and current challenges. Paradoxically, the factors that ensured a goodness of fit between the Baltic policy regimes and EMU, and that made Estonia, Latvia, and Lithuania front-runners in the first place, also limit their options for combating these problems. The following section offers a political analysis of the policy environment in each of the three states and assesses whether it is conducive to consolidating the Baltic States' position as pacesetters and frontrunners among the new member states in terms of euro entry. While their commitment to stability culture does not seem currently to be in question, it may not be sufficient for ensuring rapid Euro Area entry. Indeed, the Baltic States have been overtaken by Slovenia and Slovakia, which have been using the euro since January 2007 and January 2009 respectively. The final section concludes with some general lessons.

Macroeconomic Policy in the 1990s: Stability Culture Outside the EU

Macroeconomic policy in the 1990s was part of a comprehensive economic reform package that transformed the three Baltic economies from central planning to open, market-based systems. The reform programme included rapid price liberalization, trade liberalization, privatization, and related institutional reforms. Reforms proceeded more rapidly than in the other former Soviet republics, and after a deep recession in the early 1990s Estonia, Latvia, and Lithuania began the path to recovery. The Baltic States have generally privileged market-based governance of the economy and avoided *dirigisme* or ambitious industrial policy programmes. The emerging economic institutions can be characterized as good examples of liberal market economies, notably in the case of Estonia (Feldmann 2006*b*).

In the group of transition states Estonia stands out as the most radical market reformer. The most remarkable policy choice may have been the adoption of unilateral free trade by Estonia in the 1990s, which made the country into a kind of Hong Kong of Europe (Feldmann 2003). Estonia was the first East Central European state to adopt the flat tax, which was later introduced by Latvia and Lithuania and various other transition countries. These radical market reforms helped Estonia, Latvia, and Lithuania rapidly to reorient their external economic relations from Russia and the former Soviet Union to Western Europe.

The choice of macroeconomic strategy fits well within the general policy framework and objective of reintegrating the Baltic economies with world markets. Even though there are some important differences between Estonia, Latvia, and Lithuania, all three states adopted macroeconomic policy

244

frameworks based on currency boards or hard pegs. This minimized the role of discretionary monetary policy and contributed to rapid disinflation (Lainela and Sutela 1994). These pegs have been sustained through the entire transition period. Since the first half of the 1990s the monetary policy regimes in the Baltic States represented a remarkable goodness of fit with the stability culture embodied in EMU (Feldmann 2006a).

Estonia was the first mover among the Baltic States in terms of introducing a national currency, the kroon, in June 1992. The kroon was linked to the D-Mark through a currency board mechanism at the fixed rate 1 DM: 8 EEK. Therefore, the amount of domestic currency in circulation had to be fully backed by foreign exchange reserves, and monetary policy could not be used to finance budget deficits or for activist demand management. The independent central bank, Eesti Pank, was in charge of implementing monetary policy. This removed monetary policy from day-to-day politics and served as a way to tie policymakers' hands. The currency board has been maintained throughout the transition period at the original parity, but the euro has replaced the D-Mark as anchor currency. The monetary policy regime was complemented by an equally stringent fiscal policy. A balanced budget provision was constitutionally enshrined (Article 116 of the Estonian constitution). Since the early 1990s the budget has generally been in balance or even surplus, with the notable exception of the aftermath of the Russian crisis, when revenues fell short of projections. The macroeconomic policy framework has enjoyed high levels of support across the political spectrum (Feldmann 2006a).

Initially, Latvia proceeded somewhat more cautiously towards the introduction of a national currency and launched a temporary currency, the Latvian rouble, in 1992. It was withdrawn in late 1993 after co-existing with the new national currency, the lats, since March 1993. In March 1994 a fixed exchange-rate regime was introduced with the IMF's Special Drawing Rights (SDR) as the anchor at the rate SDR 1: LVL: 0.7997. Given that the Latvian central bank, Latvijas Banka, was highly independent, and that money in circulation was fully backed by foreign exchange holdings, this exchange-rate regime operated de facto like a currency board, and there has not been any independent or discretionary monetary policy. The independence of the central bank also ensured that occasional political pressures (especially in the early years of transition) for using monetary policy to finance budget deficits were not successful (Lainela and Sutela 1994). There is no constitutional provision for balanced budgets, but deficits have generally been low. Prudent fiscal policy is related to practical considerations, such as constraints imposed by the de facto currency board and the limited ability to borrow on international markets (especially in the early years), and also a relatively strong political consensus for stability culture. In terms of economic policy, practically all Latvian parties are located on the centre-right in West European terms. The frequent cabinet crises in Latvia in the 1990s did not affect the general direction of economic policy, in part because of the small differences between party platforms and also because there was significant continuity of parties in government. Most notably, Latvia's Way served in all the cabinets during the 1990s (Nissinen 1999).

Lithuania's introduction of a national currency, the litas, proceeded in similar fashion to the Latvian experience. There was also an interim currency, the talonas (from May 1992 until August 1993), which co-existed with the litas (introduced in June 1993) for a few months. In April 1994 Lithuania replaced the floating exchange rate of the litas with a currency board, but unlike Estonia with a peg to the US dollar at the rate USD 1: LTL 4. In February 2002, the euro replaced the dollar as anchor, now at the parity EUR 1: LTL 3.45. As in the case of Latvia, there is no constitutional provision for ensuring balanced budgets, and there were somewhat greater budget deficits and turnover of central bank governors in the earlier years of transition (Äimä 1998). The consensus in favour of stability culture has at times been weaker in Lithuania, as illustrated by the decision in 1997 to abandon the currency board in early 1999. In the aftermath of the Russian crisis, when the currency board was perceived to have a stabilizing effect, this decision was reversed (Korhonen 2004). Overall the discipline imposed by the currency board and independence of the central bank, Lietuvos Bankas, has ensured that fiscal policy has been relatively prudent regardless of the governing coalition, even though deficits were somewhat greater than in Estonia and Latvia in the early years of transition. As in the other two Baltic States, there has been significant goodness of fit with the stability culture enshrined in the EMU model.

As this overview illustrates, stability culture in the Baltic States preceded EU membership and their aspirations to adopt the euro. The consensus on stability culture has been far-reaching, especially compared with most East Central European states, and was based on a number of pillars. The small size of the Baltic economies, high inflation at the time of independence, the lack of credibility of the new currencies, and the need to reorient trade flows away from Soviet markets (which were in deep crisis in the early 1990s) contributed to a wide appreciation of the merits of openness and a fixed exchange rate or currency board as a nominal anchor (Feldmann 2006a). The consensus was largely home-grown, as for example the IMF expressed reservations about introducing national currencies in the Baltic States in early transition. Nevertheless, technical advice from the IMF and prominent émigré economists (like George Viksnins in Latvia and Ardo Hansson in Estonia) was important in shaping these states' currency reforms. The perception of the currencies as cornerstones of successful economic transition has made the monetary policy regimes popular with the public at large, and for most of the transition period there have hardly been any major political parties opposing this beyond soft Euro-populism (Feldmann 2006a).

In the second half of the 1990s European integration became the main focus of policymaking. Full membership of the EU was the main goal, and most political activity was subordinate to this objective. After the Association Agreements with the EU were signed in 1995, the harmonization of national legislation with the *acquis* became a top priority. Increasingly, Europeanization became a driving force for reform. The disappointment in Latvia and Lithuania when only Estonia was initially invited to start negotiations about EU membership as part of the so-called Luxembourg group of applicants in 1997 served as a powerful wake-up call to them (Lainela 2000). The power of contagion or friendly inter-Baltic competition has been an important mechanism driving reforms, as none of the three states wants to lag behind the others. Given the prevailing macroeconomic policy environment, the importance of Europeanization was primarily as an additional lock-in mechanism of the pre-existing stability culture. Its importance in containing public spending and reducing deficits may have been somewhat stronger in Latvia and especially Lithuania than in Estonia, where there are also constitutional provisions for balanced budgets.

After Accession: Policy Continuity, Inflation, and Delayed Euro Adoption

At the time of the Baltic States' accession to the EU, the smooth adoption of the euro by these states seemed virtually assured. Estonia and Lithuania joined ERM II on 28 June 2004. Given the stability of the long-standing currency boards in the two states, it was felt that the exchange-rate stability criterion would not pose any problems, once the required two-year period in ERM II was completed. In the autumn of 2004 Estonia and Lithuania satisfied all the other Maastricht criteria—on interest rates, public debt, public deficits, and inflation. Therefore, many specialists at the time felt that the two states merely needed to continue their long-standing macroeconomic policy and wait until the summer of 2006 to gain admission to the Euro Area.

The situation in Latvia was slightly different, although the general policy framework reflected a similar commitment to stability culture. The lats was pegged to the euro on 2 January 2005, and Latvia joined ERM II on 2 May 2005. However, inflation was higher in Latvia than in the two Baltic neighbours, and it was above the reference value in 2004. Given that all the other criteria were met, many observers were optimistic that inflation would come down sufficiently in the coming two-and-a-half years to enable Latvia to adopt the euro shortly after the other two Baltic States.

Despite a continuing commitment to fiscal prudence and stability culture, the plan for Estonia and Lithuania to start using the euro at the beginning of 2007 turned out to be unrealistic. By the summer of 2006, when Estonia and Lithuania had been hoping to get the green light for adoption of the euro, inflation had increased in both states. In March 2006 Lithuania submitted a

Table 12.1. Baltic States' inflation

	2001	2002	2003	2004	2005	2006
Estonia	5.6	3.6	1.4	3.0	4.1	4.3
Latvia	2.5	2.0	2.9	6.2	6.9	6.7
Lithuania	1.6	0.3	−1.1	1.2	2.7	3.8

Source: European Commission (2006*a*).

request for a convergence assessment. Annual inflation stood at 2.7 per cent and only barely exceeded the reference value of 2.6 per cent. Given how close Lithuania was to the target, and that none of the other criteria posed any problems, the government was hoping to be admitted to the Euro Area. Lithuania's application was turned down, largely because of concerns about the sustainability of inflation (which was correctly predicted to rise further in coming months) (European Commission 2006*a*). Estonian inflation was over 4 per cent, and therefore no application for euro membership was made. Latvia continued to have the highest rate of inflation among the three Baltic States, with inflation at 6.7 per cent in October 2006. By late 2006 the Baltic States had some of the highest inflation rates in the EU (Vanags and Hansen 2006), and they are unlikely to join EMU until after 2010 (Table 12.1).

The Baltic experience since accession raises a question about what these three states with sound public finances (Table 12.2) and a commitment to stability culture could have done to satisfy the Maastricht criterion for inflation. A full analysis of Baltic inflation is beyond the scope of this chapter, but it is important to consider the main factors that have given rise to high inflation.

The first set of factors causing high inflation relate to external developments over which the governments have virtually had no control. These include rising energy and fuel prices. In 2004 fuel prices increased by 25.1 per cent in Estonia, 23.4 per cent in Latvia, and 17.5 per cent in Lithuania; in 2005 the corresponding increases were 18.0 per cent, 22.8 per cent, and 13.8 per cent (Vanags and Hansen 2006). Fuel prices also contributed to substantial increases in the costs of transportation. The effects were larger in

Table 12.2. Baltic States' general government balance, as a percentage of GDP

	2001	2002	2003	2004	2005	2006
Estonia	−0.3	0.4	2.0	2.3	2.3	2.5
Latvia	−2.1	−2.3	−1.2	−0.9	0.1	−1.0
Lithuania	−2.0	−1.4	−1.2	−1.5	−0.5	−0.3

Source: European Commission (2006*a*).

percentage terms in the Baltic States than elsewhere in East Central Europe, in part because taxes on fuel have been low (ibid.). Another external factor contributing to inflation was a form of accession effect, especially through rising food prices, which resulted from improved access to European markets. Baltic producers started to export more to other EU states, thereby contributing to upward pressure on prices domestically. Accession also led to an inflow of structural funds, which have contributed to an increase in domestic demand.

Rapid economic growth—7.5 per cent in Lithuania and over 11 per cent in both Estonia and Latvia in 2006—has also contributed to inflation. Growth rates have been among the highest in Europe for several years. Much of this growth reflects real convergence and catch-up with Western Europe from a rather low level. Between 1996 and 2005 GDP per capita at PPP in the three Baltic States converged more rapidly to the EU-25 average than in the other East Central European member states (International Monetary Fund 2006a: 4). Given that productivity and price levels are still well below Western Europe, growth in the Baltic States is associated with higher inflation. There is disagreement about the magnitude of the associated Balassa-Samuelson effect, but it has been estimated to be around 1–1.2 per cent of additional inflation per year in the case of the Baltic States (Egert 2005; Vanags and Hansen 2006). To the extent that inflation results from real convergence, it may be an inevitable by-product of a desirable process. This may in turn cast doubt on whether the convergence criteria are appropriate for the new member states (Buiter and Grafe 2004), especially since growth and real convergence may contribute to higher inflation for many years to come.

However, the high growth rates experienced by Estonia, Latvia, and Lithuania in recent years do not just reflect real convergence. As noted by domestic and international observers, including the IMF, there are serious concerns about overheating (International Monetary Fund 2006a; Vanags and Hansen 2007). This illustrates that a commitment to budget balance as defined by the Maastricht criteria is not sufficient to guarantee low inflation in a booming economy. Overheating has partly been fuelled by rapid credit growth and capital inflows, which are partly related to the success of the stability culture and optimistic assessments by international creditors. The associated increase in current account deficits (especially in Latvia) has also affected the vulnerability to a banking or exchange rate crisis. High inflationary expectations further fuel wage growth and consumer demand (Benkovskis and Paula 2007). In states where the scope for discretionary macroeconomic policymaking has been minimized, the tools available to the government to manage demand are limited. In an environment of capital mobility and foreign ownership of banks, attempts to raise reserve requirements may only have a very small effect on credit growth, as the mother banks may continue lending from abroad (a point often made in the Baltic States). Since there is no scope for independent monetary policy, this leaves fiscal policy as the prime instrument of government policy (Allsopp and Vines 2005).

Indeed the IMF and many analysts argue that fiscal policy should be tighter in the Baltic States (International Monetary Fund 2006*a*). In the light of the booming economies, a commitment to stability culture defined as balanced budgets is not enough. Substantial surpluses are required to offset the effect of low interest rates and easy credit. Estonia's current surpluses suggest that even sizeable surpluses may be insufficient to bring down inflation in the short run.

The policy proposals developed in the spring of 2007 in the three Baltic States stress the need to maintain fiscal balance and the commitment to stability culture. The objective is, in the words of the Estonian central bank governor, Andres Lipstok, to move slowly but surely towards the euro (Lipstok 2007). By retaining the focus on stability culture, policymakers argue, Estonia, Latvia, and Lithuania should be in a good position to adopt the euro, once the boom ends and the accession-related effects have dissipated. Moreover, Estonia plans to introduce dramatic increases of excise duties on tobacco, alcohol, fuel, and energy in early 2008. Increasing excise duties is an obligation that the Baltic States assumed upon accession, but Estonia wants to implement more rapidly than required. This is likely to cause inflation to increase in the short run. By raising excise duties quickly and early, Estonia hopes that the effect on inflation will have dissipated by the time when it is ready to be admitted to the Euro Area around 2010 or thereafter (Riikoja and Karnau 2007).

Latvia and Lithuania also developed anti-inflation programmes in the spring of 2007. Latvia decided to impose stricter regulation of bank lending and a tax on speculative real estate deals, as well as to tighten fiscal policy. As inflation is well over the reference value and kept increasing throughout 2007, the Latvian government introduced a budget amendment in September 2007. The new budget envisages a small surplus in 2007, and the government intends to pass budgets with surpluses exceeding 1 per cent of GDP in 2008–10 (TBT Staff 2007). These measures may not prove sufficient in the short run, and most experts concur that euro adoption before 2010 is unrealistic. Lithuania, where inflation is lower than in the other Baltic States, implemented an anti-inflation programme in March 2007. It mainly restates the need to maintain fiscal prudence and addresses the need to raise excise duties, and can be viewed as similar to the Latvian programme.

Understanding Macroeconomic Policy: Business, Polity, Politics, and External Factors

To understand the politics of euro adoption, I shall examine the views of business, polity, parties, and external actors in turn.

The vast majority of Baltic businesses favour fixed exchange rates and the euro, largely given the high trade dependence and integration of Baltic companies into international production networks (Frieden 2002). However, business in the Baltic States has not played a very active role in lobbying for the euro. The most commonly voiced opinion by business representatives is that they are satisfied with the status quo, as long as euro entry is not delayed indefinitely (interviews with business associations). They believe that the adoption of the euro will not imply any major changes for them. The long-standing currency boards in Estonia and Lithuania, and the fixed exchange rate (with a +/−1 per cent band) in Latvia, already tie the currencies to the euro and imply that there is no exchange-rate risk, except for the possible risk of a forced devaluation. Despite some occasional concerns (as in Latvia in March 2007), most analysts and businesses have not taken this risk very seriously, and analysts who dare float this idea are typically rebuked in the media. Mounting current account deficits and high inflation, fuelled by private borrowing and capital inflows, are increasingly pushing this issue onto the agenda (Vanags and Hansen 2007). If these trends continue, a greater risk of a banking and currency crisis may in due course make the euro a higher policy priority.

Some smaller businesses, and in the 1990s also some agricultural producers, occasionally voice concerns about the effects of real appreciation on trade. Compared to the financial sector lobby and bigger trans-national enterprises, their influence is limited. On balance even most small businesses favoured retaining the fixed exchange rate, given the credibility it injected into the Baltic economies since independence.

The persistence of high inflation is causing business to become more active in advocating macroeconomic policy changes, and by the autumn of 2007 there were signs that the business lobbies were beginning to advocate greater fiscal surpluses to prevent overheating and a hard landing for the economy. In an open letter to the Prime Minister and the Ministry of Finance, written at the beginning of October 2007, the two biggest business associations in Estonia explicitly say that they 'can no longer be silent' (Kriis 2007). However, the euro was not mentioned in this letter. This omission suggests that the domestic business cycle and demand management, rather than full membership of the Euro Area, is their prime concern. Businesses have also expressed strong opposition to some radical measures to accelerate the euro adoption process, such as dramatic increases of excise duties (Ojala 2007), and argued for reductions in public spending rather than a fiscal tightening.

Popular opinion is not enthusiastic about the prospect of euro adoption, and the three Baltic States consistently belong to the new member states that are most critical of the prospects of adopting the euro. As Tables 12.3 and 12.4 illustrate, this scepticism is reflected in practically every indicator of the Eurobarometer survey.

Table 12.3. Baltic State perceptions of the euro

	Euro has positive consequences for your country	Generally speaking, are most people you know more against the idea of introducing the euro?	Are you personally happy (unhappy) that the euro could replace the national currency?
Estonia, 09/2006	47	48	32 (57)
Latvia, 09/2006	36	55	26 (64)
Lithuania, 09/2006	43	56	32 (53)
NMS-10, 09/2006	50	42	47 (43)
Estonia, 04/2007	43	50	33 (57)
Latvia, 04/2007	33	52	24 (65)
Lithuania, 04/2007	33	55	31 (55)
NMS-11, 04/2007	52	35	48 (38)

Values are in percentage.
Source: Eurobarometer (2007).

The proportions of the Baltic populations who believe that adopting the euro will be good for their country are among the lowest in East Central Europe. More strikingly still, Estonia, Latvia, and Lithuania are the only states where every poll since 2004 has shown that there is a clear plurality or majority of people who are personally unhappy about the prospects of euro adoption (in Cyprus this has been the case since 2005). Latvia comes out as the most critical: 65 per cent was very or rather unhappy about this prospect in April 2007.

While a plurality tends to believe that EMU will ensure sounder public finances, large shares of the populations are worried about possible price increases (as was the case with many food prices after EU accession) and sceptical about the benefits in terms of lower interest rates. Perhaps most importantly, as evidenced by the fact that significantly more people are personally unhappy about the changeover than sceptical about the consequences

Table 12.4. Baltic States—anticipated effects of the euro: agree/disagree

	Abuses and cheating during changeover	Protection from financial crises	Lower interest rates	Sounder public finances	Improve growth/ employment
Estonia, 09/2006	69 (24)	37 (29)	22 (33)	36 (25)	36 (35)
Latvia, 09/2006	78 (18)	30 (44)	27 (40)	40 (33)	34 (47)
Lithuania, 09/2006	77 (18)	33 (35)	29 (30)	44 (28)	51 (23)
NMS-10, 09/2006	73 (24)	40 (32)	35 (32)	44 (30)	40 (39)
Estonia, 04/2007	65 (25)	43 (26)	21 (38)	32 (31)	35 (35)
Latvia, 04/2007	74 (21)	31 (40)	29 (37)	34 (33)	32 (45)
Lithuania, 04/2007	76 (19)	31 (36)	25 (36)	46 (28)	52 (23)
NMS-11, 04/2007	67 (26)	45 (27)	38 (30)	46 (26)	43 (36)

Values are in percentage.
Source: Eurobarometer (2007).

for the country as a whole, the symbolic value of the national currency should not be underestimated. The successful currency reforms and stabilizations in the 1990s have become important symbols of Estonia, Latvia, and Lithuania as independent states. This identity factor and the key role ascribed to the national currencies and currency boards both in the recovery from the deep transformational recessions in the early 1990s and in weathering the Russian crisis of 1998 relatively smoothly should not be underestimated. It seems to be a key factor accounting for the general lukewarm support for the euro despite the fact that abandoning the national currencies will not lead to major changes in macroeconomic policymaking because of the goodness of fit between the policies pursued in the 1990s and euro requirements. For this reason the relative dissatisfaction with the prospect of using the euro does not translate into dissatisfaction with current economic policy, as stability culture remains popular.

While there is strong support of stability culture, it is difficult to convince the public that sizeable budget surpluses are necessary. In states preparing for EMU membership the Maastricht criteria for debt and deficits serve as a key focal point for expectations. When states satisfy these requirements, it is politically hard to argue for *more* austere fiscal policy. In times of economic boom and ever tighter labour markets, as in the Baltic States, popular demands for wage and pension increases and for lower taxes make further tightening, well beyond the Maastricht norms, a major political challenge. Given the high current account deficits and growth in private borrowing, very high levels of public saving and budget surpluses would be required to offset the lack of private saving and to rein in aggregate demand.

There is remarkably little debate among mainstream political parties in the Baltic States about the euro, and there is hardly any outright opposition to it. It is taken for granted that euro adoption will happen in the near future, and, given the remarkable goodness of fit between the Baltic policies in the 1990s and the EMU model, most politicians have tended to view the process as relatively unproblematic. Challenges are attributed mostly to external factors and short-run problems related to the business cycle and full integration into the single market. Given business preferences and popular opinion, it is hardly surprising that there is a broad consensus among political parties in favour of stability culture, but little support for any draconian measures that would dramatically accelerate euro entry.

In the Estonian electoral campaign in 2007 the euro was barely mentioned, except for some passing references by opposition politicians, mostly from conservative Union of Fatherland and Res Publica, to the government's lack of action in preparing for euro adoption, though generally without making any specific proposals about how to address this. The retention of the currency board and of fiscal prudence is not contested, although there are some differences of emphasis regarding the required levels of budget surpluses. Regarding economic policy, the core debate revolves around the appropriate size of government, the level of taxation, and whether it is desirable to move away from the flat tax to progressive taxation. The Centre Party, the Social Democrats, and the People's Union support a move towards progressive taxation, but their positions on economic policy are moderate and centrist overall, and they would be unlikely to support any radical overhaul of current policies (at least one of them has been in office since the early 1990s). The March 2007 elections consolidated the position of the centre-Right, which has dominated Estonian politics since independence. The governing coalition of the market-liberal Reform Party, the conservative Union of Fatherland and Res Publica, and the Social Democrats agreed to continue a prudent fiscal policy.

In Estonia the commitment to stability culture, which continues to be underpinned by central bank independence and the constitutional requirement of balanced budgets, does not seem threatened. The main factors that might endanger the stability of this policy framework are social concerns, notably the declining population (due to low birth rate and high levels of emigration) and tighter labour markets, which trigger increased pressures for greater social spending. These issues have led even Right-wing parties (like the Union of Fatherland and Res Publica) to make more populist-sounding proposals, like giving all school children free laptop computers. However, so far such proposals have been clearly subordinated to the overarching preference for stability culture, especially among centre-Right parties. With growth rates of around 10 per cent, it has been possible to increase spending in absolute terms even with low levels of taxation.

Many aspects of the situation in Latvia bear a striking resemblance to Estonia. The centre-Right has been very strong throughout the 1990s, even though there has been some turnover in party identities. For the first time since regaining independence, the 2006 election did not lead to the emergence of a new party that gained the largest number of votes. Instead the centre-Right coalition in office was re-elected. Like in Estonia, there is a relatively strong consensus in favour of stability culture in parliament. Concerns about emigration and a falling population are often used to advocate increases in public-sector wages and spending. There has been greater cabinet instability throughout the transition period than in Estonia. In the spring of 2007 the whole party system was rocked by serious allegations of corruption (including the imprisonment of a leading figure of one of the governing parties) and a standoff between the government and the president about a security law. Popular protest against the government's handling of the corruption problem triggered a cabinet crisis, but a new government based on the same coalition parties took office in December of 2007. While these developments suggest that there may be further instability in the party system, there are no major differences in economic policy platforms between the main governing and opposition parties. The main opposition party after the 2006 election, New

Era, is also a centre-Right party. Cabinet instability has typically been caused by personal animosities between leading politicians and has not led to major policy shifts.

Europeanization, along with the imperatives of a strict fixed exchange-rate regime and central bank independence, played a stabilizing and focusing role for policy. The objective of euro adoption may continue to stabilize economic policy in the face of future cabinet instability. It should be noted that the main parties that in the past had 'soft' Euro-sceptical positions—the national conservative For Fatherland and Freedom/Latvian National Conservative Party and the Russian Equal Rights party (now Human Rights in a United Latvia)— adopted more pro-European (i.e. only moderately Euro-populist) stances in the run-up to accession (Mikkel and Pridham 2004). Hence, like in Estonia, the broad consensus in favour of Europeanization is likely to favour retaining stability culture, which will help Latvia prepare for euro adoption in the medium term. As in Estonia, however, a very sharp tightening of fiscal policy remains difficult, as no political party would like to be held responsible for a growth slowdown.

The Lithuanian party system has been different from the other two Baltic States in that it has been divided into Left and Right, like in most East Central European and West European states. The former communists enjoyed a greater degree of legitimacy and support than in Estonia and Latvia and therefore they were able to reconfigure into a Social Democratic Party in the early 1990s. Subsequently, as in many other East Central European states, coalition governments have tended to alternate between Left and Right. However, the main parties—on both Left and Right—have been broadly committed to stability culture. Notably, a government dominated by Social Democrats established the currency board in 1994. There has been some cabinet instability in Lithuania as well, and populist parties have been more influential than in Estonia and Latvia. They include a number of smaller parties and the big winner in the election of 2004, the Labour Party (founded by the Russian businessman Vladimir Uspaskikh), which have had Euro-populist policy agendas. When in government, the imperatives of coalition formation and the disciplines of the currency board and central bank independence (which has operated well since the second half of the 1990s) have contributed to moderating these platforms. The disintegration of the Labour Party, largely caused by criminal charges against its leader, led to a fragile minority government in 2006, which made the prospects for sharp fiscal tightening difficult. Nevertheless, 'bottom-up' Europeanization by leading politicians of the main parties and, to some extent, pressure from the central bank has also been used to counter populist pressures.

In addition to domestic factors, international and EU influence is becoming increasingly important. The rejection of Lithuania's application to adopt the euro in 2006 means that the Baltic States will not make another attempt to join the Euro Area unless they are sure to meet all the convergence criteria. As noted above, Europeanization has served as a lock-in of an essentially home-grown stability culture. It seems to have exercised a moderating effect on budget deficits, especially in Latvia and Lithuania. In the late spring of 2007 the IMF and the EU, notably the Commissioner for Economic and Monetary Affairs Joaquin Almunia, expressed concerns about the high rates of inflation in the three Baltic States.

Similarly, during a visit to Estonia in May 2007, the IMF delegation praised the government's decision to raise excise duties in order to ensure that the effects will have dissipated by the time of possible accession (Postimees 2007). Some other international factors are worth mentioning. While the Baltic States still receive favourable credit ratings by Fitch and Standard and Poor, these agencies have slightly downgraded their assessments in 2007, primarily because of increasing external vulnerability due to large current account deficits. These external pressures have increased the sense of urgency associated with euro entry and serve to empower political forces that have stressed fiscal prudence and stability culture throughout the transition period. It may make it easier to justify a fiscal tightening that might otherwise be politically hard to implement. These factors may therefore increasingly serve as a 'vincolo esterno', or a source of external discipline, which played such an important role for economic policy in Italy and other Euro Area countries prior to the adoption of the single currency (Dyson and Featherstone 1996).

Conclusion

The Baltic States have been fascinating cases of economic policy reform ever since regaining their independence. The currency board arrangements (or, in the case of Latvia, the fixed exchange rate that operates virtually like a currency board) and the commitment to fiscal prudence constitute a good fit with the stability culture in EMU. This contributed to rapid disinflation and to making Estonia, Latvia, and Lithuania early pacesetters in euro entry.

This chapter shows that a long-standing stability culture has not been sufficient to ensure rapid accession to the Euro Area. While the stability culture as such is not under threat, and enjoys support across most of the political spectrum, high inflation forced the three Baltic States to postpone their plans for euro entry and see themselves overtaken by Slovenia and Slovakia. Instead of the target dates 2007–8, euro adoption is likely to happen after 2010. Despite some fiscal tightening and strategic timing of increases of excise duties, Estonia, Latvia, and Lithuania may well have to wait for the business cycle to change. As small and very open economies, the Baltic States' prospects for euro entry depend greatly on external developments. Slower growth in the Baltic States, and relatively better economic performance in some of the main Euro Area states, may make it possible to satisfy the inflation criterion more easily.

The mechanism of tying the governments' hands by adopting currency boards and minimizing the scope for discretionary macroeconomic policy contributed to credibility and disinflation in the 1990s. Yet, the very credibility of this policy framework has also emboldened private actors, such as households and foreign-owned banks, and triggered rapid credit growth, especially in recent years. The high levels of private borrowing have contributed to inflation and booming economies after the Baltic States' accession to the EU. Some of this lending has been used for investment that contributes to real convergence, but it may also have aggravated moral hazard problems and external vulnerability. Should the worst-case scenario of a banking or currency crisis materialize, then this would of course be a great setback to the plans of euro adoption.

The policy environment in the Baltic States also restricts the governments' options to resolve these problems. Under this policy regime the government cannot set interest rates freely to control inflation. Capital account liberalization and foreign ownership of banks also restrict the government's ability to use credit policy. Under such circumstances it is very difficult for governments to rein in private lending, which is a key cause of capital inflows, inflationary pressure, and external vulnerability. The politicians' menu of choices is limited, and the most potent tool at their disposal, fiscal policy, cannot probably resolve the problem. The politics of austerity—where very large surpluses are necessary to offset limited private saving—is likely to be quite different from the politics of stability and therefore harder to sustain. While the commitment to stability culture in the Baltic States has been very strong by East Central European standards, politicians are unwilling to adopt more draconian fiscal policies that go beyond the Maastricht deficit rules.

The Baltic experience also raises questions about the appropriateness of the Maastricht criteria in the transition context (Buiter and Grafe 2004). The lower growth rates and high deficit environment in many West European states in the 1990s meant that these criteria had a very different impact in their context. In booming, rapidly converging, and highly open economies it may not be sufficient to adhere to a set of orthodox principles, especially when private sector borrowing is a key challenge. Tying one's hands and being committed to stability culture may not always secure euro entry in the short term and enable a pacesetter role to be maintained.

13

Britain: The Political Economy of Retrenchment

Jim Buller and Andrew Gamble

The impact of Economic and Monetary Union (EMU) on Britain has continued to differ from most other states in the EU since 2001. Despite expectations in some quarters that Tony Blair might seek membership of the euro early in his second term, he lost his battle with his Chancellor, Gordon Brown, and sterling remained outside the Euro Area. Blair resigned in 2007, and Brown succeeded him, which means there is unlikely to be any move to resurrect the case for Britain joining the euro in the foreseeable future. Instead, the Labour government (and particularly the Treasury) has adopted a more critical tone towards the institutions and policies of the Euro Area. Brown (2004) has drawn adverse comparisons between the growth and employment rates in Continental Europe and the performance of the British economy. Frustrated by ministers' failure to launch a concerted campaign in favour of sterling's membership of the Single Currency, 'Britain in Europe', the organization set up to further this goal, has now been disbanded. In short, EMU has strengthened a process of retrenchment in British economic policy since 2001. By 'retrenchment' we mean domestic resistance to further Europeanization in this area (Radaelli 2001).

In this chapter we outline the discourse and policy of the Blair government since the launch of the euro, focusing particularly on the perceived differences between Labour's own framework and that of the Euro Area. We then analyse the economic structure underpinning decision-making, giving specific attention to the City of London, and its ability to influence the stance of the government. The structure of domestic political competition, and its role in dampening enthusiasm for the euro, is then considered. We argue that retrenchment is the result of a powerful confluence of all these factors. The Treasury continues to resist membership in part because it views the euro as a threat to its own strategy of maintaining control over economic outcomes.

Ministers are able to adopt such a policy because there is little pressure from the City of London, which already sees itself as prospering *within* the euro. This Treasury-City (and Bank of England) nexus (Ingham 1984) is supported by a broader domestic political climate, which shows no enthusiasm for a more pro-European initiative.

The Treasury and the Policy of Retrenchment

Compared with other EU states, Britain has witnessed the 'nationalization' of monetary and fiscal policies since 1997. In other words, the Blair government has relied on domestic institutions and policy instruments to control inflation rather than European structures associated with the euro. On the monetary policy side, the key reform after 1997 was Labour's decision to grant operational independence to the Bank of England. While the Chancellor retains responsibility for formulating objectives (in this case an inflation target of 2 per cent, measured by the Harmonized Consumer Prices Index), a new Monetary Policy Committee (MPC) of independent experts is charged with implementing this goal. This inflation target is symmetrical. Deviation below 2 per cent is perceived to be just as problematic as any overshoot of this reference value.

On the fiscal side, the Treasury has created two rules to limit the ability of politicians to 'pump prime' the economy before elections through the manipulation of tax and spending levels. The 'golden rule' states that, on average, over the economic cycle, the government will only borrow to invest and not to fund current spending. The 'sustainable debt' rule stipulates that debt will be held over the economic cycle at a 'stable and prudent' level (40 per cent of national income). The stipulation 'over the economic cycle' is important in this context. It is designed to give Brown a certain amount of flexibility to vary policy in a way that is commensurate with economic circumstances (Balls and O'Donnell 2002).

Although there are broad similarities between the policy regimes in the UK and in the Euro Area, subtle but important differences exist. While the Bank of England was only granted operational independence by the Blair government, the ECB has 'goal' as well as 'operational' independence and, as a result, greater power. The existence of the ECB derives from the Maastricht Treaty, and Article 105 stipulates that its prime objective is the maintenance of price stability. However, no numerical target was specified by the 12 EU leaders who negotiated the treaty, allowing the Governing Council to define its own asymmetrical reference value of 'below, but close to, 2 per cent' (http://www.ecb.int/mopo/html/index.en.html). The ECB's autonomy is further enhanced by Article 107, which stipulates that European (and national) central bankers are explicitly forbidden to 'seek or take instructions from Community institutions or bodies, from any government of a Member State or from any other body'.

Moreover, while the Stability and Growth Pact contains a number of rules designed to constrain the fiscal policy of member states, differences exist compared to the UK regime. Governments are required to maintain their budgets at 'close to balance' and not exceed 3 per cent of GDP, while ensuring public debt is kept at or below a level of 60 per cent of GDP. The Commission has a formal role in monitoring these rules, chiefly through the 'early warning procedure'.

In 1997 the Treasury ruled out British membership of the euro for the lifetime of the first Labour government after an assessment which took a matter of weeks to complete. However, at the beginning of the second term, it appeared for a brief moment that this policy trajectory might change. In February 2001, Blair announced (without consulting Brown) that a new assessment would take place within two years if Labour were returned to power at the election in June. Such an exercise did take place in June 2003 and was, in the words of one commentator, 'the most ambitious evaluation project it [the Treasury] had ever undertaken...' (Peston 2005: 223). It was preceded by no less than 18 'background studies', which took approximately a year and a half to complete. The final document ran to 1,982 pages, with the cabinet given a mere fortnight to digest and comment on its contents.

For all its comprehensiveness, however, the outcome was the same as six years before. Only one of the five tests was deemed to have been met: it was judged (as it had been in 1997) that the City of London would benefit from euro membership. Although 'significant progress' had been made in meeting the other four tests, a lack of convergence between UK and Euro Area economies continued to exist, especially in areas like the housing market (HM Treasury Cm. 5776, 2003*b*: 39). The government also concluded that more flexibility was needed in Britain's labour and product markets, with emphasis placed on the area of public-sector wages.

The June 2003 assessment is interesting for the light that it throws on the relationship between economic theory and political considerations. While Treasury ministers claimed that the sheer thoroughness of its preparation ensured that the euro decision was taken solely on economic grounds, and hence the national interest, this line of argument generated much contention within establishment circles. As many experts noted, the wording of the tests was so general as to accommodate almost any conclusion (Rollo 2002). Even if the phraseology was clearer, on their own the tests could never have generated a definitive verdict on euro entry (see Hay 2003: 93–5). This was certainly Blair's view, and he is said to have put Brown under 'enormous pressure' to 'fix' the assessment in favour of joining.

Blair's behaviour was influenced, in turn, by his increasingly pro-European sentiments at this time. By 2001 he had become convinced of the 'political' case for participating in the euro. Membership of the Euro Area would help augment national economic sovereignty, increasingly under threat from globalization, while at the same time strengthening Britain's influence at the heart of Europe (Scott 2004). As we shall see, Brown remained unconvinced by these arguments and sought to use the tests as a way of maintaining control of this decision and ultimately, keeping Britain out of the euro. Since taking over from Blair as Prime Minister in June 2007, there are no signs that this policy is about to change.

However, there is more to Brown's policy than political manoeuvring. Since 2001, a subtle policy of retrenchment has taken hold in the Treasury (and beyond), with ministers becoming increasingly vocal in celebrating the performance of their policies. They have argued that, because of the adoption of a new domestic monetary and fiscal framework, Britain has experienced unprecedented financial stability in the last 10 years. In particular, the economy has avoided the downturn that has hit Euro Area states like Germany and Italy. Accompanying this stability has been a less volatile inflation record than other EU states. Britain has also achieved quarter-on-quarter economic growth in every year since 1997 and the third highest per capita GDP rate within the G-7 group of industrialized nations. Finally, the unemployment rate under Labour has been half that of France and Germany (and lower than the United States). So long the 'sick man' of Europe, Britain is said to have entered a new era of prosperity. This conclusion is broadly supported by the IMF and the OECD, which have described the UK as the 'paragon of stability' (e.g. Brown 2005a; International Monetary Fund 2006b; Keegan 2005; OECD 2006b, 2007a). However, most commentators also note that the recovery began under the Conservatives, after the exit from the Exchange Rate Mechanism in 1992.

At the same time, the Treasury has become increasingly critical of the Euro Area's institutions and policies. Brown's dislike of the Commission's judgements on his management of the economy as Chancellor is well documented. In recent years, he made little effort to hide his disapproval of the *non-binding recommendations* issued by Brussels, which asserted that his public spending plans and forecasts for borrowing breached the conditions of the Stability and Growth Pact (*Financial Times*, 26 April 2001, 11 February 2002; Parker 2003, 2004). As Chancellor, Brown also censured the Commission for being the source of red tape, which is increasingly perceived to be hampering the performance of British business (Balls 2006b; HM Treasury 2006).

Brown has expanded on these specific criticisms to develop a broader narrative about the future of the EU and Britain's role within it. The EU (like Britain) now faces the challenge of an increasingly competitive global economy, where patterns of trade and production are shifting towards developing countries such as China and India. If Europe is to succeed against this backdrop, *it has no alternative* but to (*a*) continue to ensure that it promotes flexibility and competitiveness in product, capital, and labour markets through the completion of the Single Market; (*b*) work for the continued liberalization of international trade; (*c*) implement reform of the Common Agricultural Policy and restructure the priorities of the EU budget towards research and development, skills, and training; (*d*) become an outward-looking 'Global Europe' of independent nation states, co-operating where necessary to confront these challenges head on. Britain, whose economy is described as already possessing many of these traits, is presented as the member state ideally placed to lead the way on these reforms (e.g. Brown 2005*b*, 2005*c*).

This Treasury discourse has its critics. According to a recent study by the Centre For Economic Performance, productivity in the UK (measured as output per hour worked) was 13 per cent lower than in Germany, 18 per cent lower than the United States, and 20 per cent lower than in France (Seager 2007), although recent data suggests the gap with Britain's main competitors is narrowing (Giles 2008). While Brown frequently claimed to have ended the 'boom and bust' cycle, such an argument only really applies at the aggregate economic level. Within the UK, growth has been very unbalanced with a buoyant service industry generally outpacing a shrinking manufacturing sector. In December 2006 Britain recorded its largest annual trade deficit (£55.8 billion) since figures began in 1697. Of that total, trade in services showed a record surplus of £28.5 billion, while trade in goods posted a record deficit of £84.3 billion (newsvote.bbc.co.uk/mpapps/pagetools/print/news. bbc.co.uk/1/hi/business/6345...). In 2008, Britain's budget deficit is forecast to rise to 3.4 per cent—the worst performance within the G-7 (Giles and Strauss 2007).

How might we account for these increasingly hostile views towards the Euro Area? In part the answer to this question can be traced back to the events of 16 September 1992 when Britain crashed out of the ERM. The story of 'Black Wednesday', whereby participation in these European institutions caused the Conservative government of John Major to lose control over monetary policy, is now well documented. What is just as important in the context of this chapter is the effect of this crisis on the Labour leadership. Of particular interest is a Fabian pamphlet written by Ed Balls (then a journalist with the Financial Times) entitled, 'Euro-Monetarism: Why Britain Was Ensnared and How It Should Escape'. One of the purposes of this paper was to highlight the future dangers to the Labour Party of hankering after European solutions to domestic economic problems, especially in addressing the question of how it could entrench its anti-inflationary credibility in office. Focusing attention on the process of EMU, Balls accepted British membership would free policy from electoral considerations. However, he also cautioned that the Euro Area lacked the sort of automatic stabilizers that allowed a single currency to function effectively in states like the United States. The EU lacked the labour mobility and an adequate policy of fiscal transfers to mitigate the effects of a recession hitting hard certain states, including the UK. Consequently, the outcome would be persistent unemployment, regional imbalances, and a politicization of the policy regime. In other words, membership of the euro could weaken state power and adversely affect Labour's attempts to achieve a reputation for governing competence—just as the ERM had done (Balls 1992).

Balls became Brown's economic adviser in 1994, and William Keegan (2003: 131–4, 305–10) has argued that the former exerted a significant influence on the latter's thinking, especially in the area of monetary policy. Initially, Brown's enthusiasm for EMU membership did not appear to have diminished in the aftermath of Black Wednesday, despite claims by some commentators that, as Shadow Chancellor, his popularity in the party was temporarily damaged by this episode (Routledge 1998: 172–3). It may have been the case that, until the appointment of Balls, Brown could not conceive of an alternative monetary policy. This part of Brown's portfolio holds less interest for him than supply-side matters. The important role that Balls played in drafting the plan for an independent Bank of England is well documented. After 1994 the Euro-sceptic views of Balls may have filled a gap in Brown's intellectual armoury, although, judging from Brown's pro-euro rhetoric in the aftermath of the 1997 election victory, the influence of these ideas may have taken time to filter through.

Since 2001 an increasing tension developed between the Treasury's desire to retain control over economic management and its perception that Euro Area governance arrangements pose a threat to this position. Take, for example, the 'goal independence' of the ECB. In its response to a House of Lords Select Committee report on the operation of the ECB in practice, the government argued that the ECB's power to both formulate *and* implement the Euro Area's inflation target should be curtailed. This target would be better set by a political body containing democratically elected representatives, thus freeing up the Bank to focus on the technical task of realizing these objectives. Quoting the work of Favero et al. (2000) directly, the Treasury set out the advantages of such a change:

It would also allow democratically elected representatives to change the monetary policy objectives if these differed from those of the public. Favero et al. claim that such a move would also *'contribute to fewer national tensions in policy-making'* ... (original emphasis). (HM Treasury 2004; also Balls 1992: 17–18; Keegan 2003: 159)

This argument is shared by a range of other domestic actors in the policy network surrounding this issue. Representatives of British business, trade unions (House of Commons 187-I, 2003b: 15) as well members of the Monetary Policy Committee (House of Lords 170, 2003: para. 50) suggested that the Euro Area inflation target be set by ECOFIN as a way of boosting the accountability of the system. Such demands coincide with the long-standing position of successive French governments.

The attitude and behaviour of the ECB since 1999 compounded Treasury anxieties about being left in a position of responsibility without control if Britain joined the Euro Area. In evidence to the Lords Select Committee on the European Communities in 2003, the government stated that coordination over policy between the ECB and national governments had 'not worked very well' in practice (House of Lords 170, 2003: 58). It also felt that the ECB viewed its role 'as listening rather than engaging' (ibid.), especially in circumstances where states were struggling to pull their economies out of recession. Ministers have also frequently expressed concern about the ECB's asymmetrical inflation target:

An asymmetrical target could provide policy-makers with an incentive to drive inflation as low as possible to ensure they meet their target comfortably, even if this had detrimental consequences for output and employment. Moreover, it might provide insufficient incentives for fiscal consolidation or structural reforms, as the government does not know that its actions will be met by the easing of monetary policy (House of Commons 1004, 2003*a*: 3; see also HM Treasury, 2003*a*: para. 3.64; Keegan, 2003: 170).

In practice, the ECB has always been much more sensitive to risks of deflation than its formal position would suggest, a point acknowledged by the Treasury (See comments by Ruth Kelly, then Financial Secretary to the Treasury, in House of Lords Paper 170, 2003: 23). However, such action does not appear to have convinced ministers that the potential for a deflationary bias has been reduced. This opinion is shared with representatives of the Monetary Policy Committee (House of Lords 2000: para. 115), the Commons Treasury Committee (House of Commons C 187-I, 2003*b*: 5, 14) and the Trades Union Congress (House of Commons 187-I, 2003*b*: 12; also Peston 2005: 180).

It is in this context that Treasury criticisms of the Stability and Growth Pact should partly be understood. If member states participating in the Euro Area have lost control of monetary policy, but remain responsible to their respective electorates for real economic outcomes, then the role of fiscal policy takes on added significance. During Labour's second term, the Treasury increasingly complained that, in requiring member states to meet the fiscal rules annually, the SGP was 'too mechanistic' (see evidence by Steven Timms in House of Lords Paper 74, 2005: 1). In certain circumstances, governments may be forced into pro-cyclical policies such as cutting spending or raising taxes in the middle of a recession. Instead, Brown as Chancellor produced a number of suggestions designed to allow the Pact to operate more like the UK's fiscal framework. Specific recommendations included that the Euro Area rules be judged over the economic cycle (to be defined by ECOFIN); that states with low levels of debt be allowed to exceed the 3 per cent reference value for budget deficits; and that the Pact exclude investment as opposed to current spending (Brown 2003*a*, 2003*b*, 2004; Brown, Sarkozy, and Eichel 2004; King 2004; Peston 2005: 230). Ironically, as these reforms to the Pact were being devised, the credibility of the Treasury's fiscal rules was increasingly being questioned in Britain. Much of this critical comment centred on allegations that the Treasury has constantly re-defined the length of the economic cycle to suit the government's expansionary public spending programme since 2000 (House of Commons 389-I, 2007; see also Giles 2007*a*).

Finally, having supported France and Germany in their decision to suspend the Pact in November 2003, Brown rejected the revised package of fiscal rules proposed by the Commission in March 2005. Of particular concern is the new medium-term borrowing limit of 1 per cent, which was deemed inconsistent with Labour's second-term plans to boost investment on public services (Blitz and Parker 2005; see also Fifield 2004). These spending plans put the UK's average medium-term borrowing over this reference value at 1.6 per cent GDP (Blitz and Parker 2005). This spending programme formed the core plank of Labour's election campaigns in 2001 and 2005. Had the Blair government joined the euro in its second term, it would have been required to cut its spending on public investment in line with Pact obligations. It is not difficult to imagine how such action would have gone down with Labour members in parliament and public opinion.

Economic Structure, the City of London, and the Policy of Retrenchment

What is the relationship between this policy of retrenchment and the structural configuration of the British economy? Britain has long been recognized for having a distinctive set of economic institutions. This 'Anglo-Saxon' or liberal market model of capitalism is often contrasted with the 'Rhenish' or coordinated market variety (Albert 1993). While the reality is often more complicated, this distinction has persisted. Assuming that these conceptual categories are in some sense meaningful, do Britain's particular economic structures help account for the policy trajectory described above?

The conventional view is that Britain's attachment to the Anglo-Saxon model is one of the main factors that generate a sceptical stance towards the euro. At the heart of this resistance are the City of London and the financial services sector. However, to make such a statement is to raise a paradox. Ever since its political ascendancy in the liberal free-trade era of the nineteenth century, the City has demonstrated a clear preference for a policy regime that could ensure sound money and financial stability through an external discipline exerted by adherence to the gold standard. The dislocation of this regime in the twentieth century, including the forced suspension of the gold standard during the First World War, and again in 1931, was perceived as deeply undesirable, and the Treasury/Bank/City nexus did all it could to prevent this outcome. The belief that British policy was being run in the interests of the financial sector, and not in the interests of manufacturing and the national economy, became deeply ingrained. Following the suspension of the gold standard, however, the normal pattern was disrupted, and the British government pursued a national economic strategy in the 1930s that brought recovery from the deep recession at the beginning of the decade. After 1945, however, the opportunity of resurrecting the liberal world order under US leadership proved too enticing. The familiar conflict between the City and industry resumed, as did the pattern of 'stop-go' economics that pervaded all attempts at Keynesian demand management at this time (Brittan 1971; Ingham 1984).

The failure of economic policy in Britain became so marked in the 1970s that it led to a major doctrinal shift, beginning under the Labour government of James Callaghan, but taken much further by the Thatcher government after 1979. The new policy regime that emerged stripped away a large part of the national protectionism that had been built into the British economy in the 1930s and 1940s, entailing the disappearance of a large part of traditional manufacturing and the employment it supported. A new version of the older classical model of British political economy emerged in its place, one that gave new opportunities to financial services. The ending of exchange controls, followed by the deregulation of the City in the 'Big Bang' in 1986, gave an enormous boost to the financial services industry, and confirmed it as the pivotal area of the UK economy. Although in terms of size it remained a relatively small sector, it regained its key role as the property that best exemplified the British model.

Despite the fact that inflation had been brought down from ~22 per cent in 1979 to 3 per cent by the mid-1980s, the City was again persuaded that entrenching financial stability required an external framework. The early experiments with domestic monetarism had disappointed in the sense that the Treasury had failed to discover a reliable relationship between growth in money supply (£M3) and the level of prices in the economy. In this context, Chancellors Nigel Lawson and then John Major turned to the ERM, as a way of injecting credibility into the government's monetary policy framework, based as it was on the prudent policies of the Bundesbank.

As noted above, the shipwreck of this policy in 1992 had profound effects on British attitudes to the euro. The City also became much less keen on the idea of an external anchor, and instead gave support to the domestic strategy, which was developed first under Norman Lamont, then Ken Clarke, and finally Brown. The main support for euro entry came from other economic sectors, particularly large multinational manufacturing companies with major markets and/or production facilities in the Euro Area.

Since 2001, attitudes hardened so that by 2008 there was little pressure on the Brown government from the City of London to enter the euro. Indeed, there is a perception among City firms that they continue to thrive, despite sterling remaining outside the euro. According to recent estimates, London accounts for more than two-thirds of the global market in international bonds. It contains the largest international market in foreign exchange turnover, up from 31.3 in 2004, to 34.1 per cent in 2007 (Bank for International Settlements 2007). The City remains the largest centre for over-the-counter derivatives, at 42 per cent in 2007. Moreover, London's share of global hedge fund assets has more than doubled from 10 to 21 per cent in the period 2002–6: a performance that has seen it significantly narrowing the gap on New York (Teather 2007). In short, the City of London is not lobbying the Treasury to enter the euro because it already perceives itself to be in the Euro Area and doing rather well (Balls 2006*a*; Brown 2006; Gieve 2007).

These feelings of confidence have been coupled with concerns about the broader direction of policy within the EU financial services market. In the Blair government's first term, the City (in alliance with the Treasury and the British Bankers Association) engaged in a protracted rearguard action against European plans for a withholding tax on the savings and investments of non-EU residents. The Commission proposed this policy as a method of cracking down on tax evasion. The City argued against, claiming that its $3,000 billion international bond business would be threatened as investors sought to relocate to financial centres outside the EU. In the end, the Treasury was successful in persuading Britain's European partners to accept a more informal arrangement, involving an exchange of information. In return, the Blair government put pressure on the Channel Islands, as well as dependent territories in the Caribbean to fall into line with this policy.

More recent plans to regulate the EU's market in financial services have also caused increasing consternation within the City of London. A recent survey of 1,000 Chief Executives by ICM, on behalf of the think tank 'Open Europe', provides a flavour of this growing Euro-scepticism among British business. It was initially hoped that Brussels' proposals for creating a level playing field would focus on Europe's retail financial products, thus leaving the City of London's wholesale markets largely untouched. However, it is feared that measures associated with the Commission's Financial Services Action Plan, such as legislation on capital adequacy, market abuse, investment funds, takeovers, and prospectuses, will have a direct impact on London's operations. Critical comment extended from the content of these proposals to the methods utilized to drive this liberalization process. Rather than setting minimum standards based on the principle of mutual recognition (as was the case with the implementation of the '1992' Single Market programme), the EU attempted to harmonize regulations through the enactment of ever more complex directives and laws. Such an approach fails to make any allowance for the 'light-touch' regulatory regime that governs the City's financial activities. In a sign of increasing dissatisfaction, the Corporation of London recently set up an office in Brussels to act as an 'early warning radar' on these issues (http://www.openeurope.org.uk/businesspres.pdf; Record 2005; Willman 2006a, 2006b).

Finally, in the Blair government's first term, individual multinational companies lobbied Whitehall to adopt a more positive policy on the euro. Japanese and some US firms in particular threatened to relocate investment abroad unless ministers gave a firmer indication that Britain sterling would adopt the euro in the short to medium term. However, this pressure was not sufficient to change government policy. Where it has been able to, under EU rules, the Department of Trade and Industry has offered subsidies in the form of Regional Selective Assistance to entice firms to stay. Such a tactic has worked in certain circumstances, most notably with Nissan and its plans to produce the Micra and Almera cars in Sunderland. But in other cases where capital flight, redundancies, or bankruptcies have taken place, the government has not intervened. Once ministers failed to give a lead in promoting euro membership, the CBI stopped campaigning in favour of this policy. As with British political parties, the euro is a divisive issue for business and any unequivocal stance by the CBI leadership (without 'political cover') risks generating awkward splits within the membership (Duckenfield 2006: 143–84).

Retrenchment and the Constraints of Domestic Party Competition

The structure of British domestic politics has further reinforced this policy of retrenchment towards the euro since 2001. Party competition takes place within the context of public opinion, and the British electorate remains overwhelmingly sceptical towards the euro. During the period 1997–2001, between 55 and 65 per cent of those polled opposed membership. Using data from Mori, these findings can be updated to February 2005 and are reproduced below. Mori has consistently asked three different questions on the subject of British attitudes towards the euro.

Q1: If there was a referendum now on whether Britain should be part of a Single European Currency, how would you vote? (Figure 13.1)

Q2: If the government were to strongly urge that Britain should be part of a Single Currency, how would you vote? (Figure 13.2)

Q3: Which of the following best describes your own view of British participation in the Single Currency?

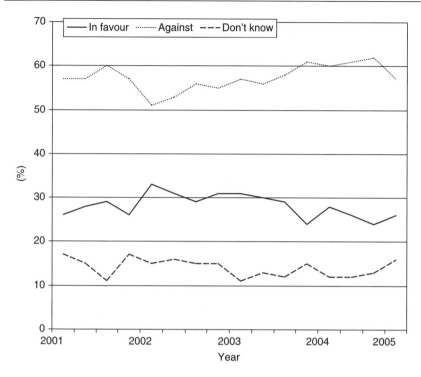

Figure 13.1. How would you vote in a British referendum?
Source: Ipso Mori (http://www.ipso-mori.com).

A. I strongly support British participation

B. I am generally in favour of British participation, but could be persuaded against it if I thought it would be bad for the British economy.

C. I am generally opposed to British participation, but could be persuaded in favour of it if I thought it would be good for the British economy.

D. I strongly oppose British participation. (Figure 13.3)

It is not difficult to see how this survey evidence contributed to the Blair government's non-decision on the euro. As the data in Figure 13.1 demonstrate, approximately two-thirds of the electorate continue to favour the retention of sterling, a trend that remained largely constant during the second term. When asked how they would respond to a government campaign 'strongly urging' euro membership (Figure 13.2), public opinion remained broadly the same, suggesting that the government faced a difficult task persuading voters to take a more pro-European line. These findings have been challenged somewhat by YouGov's 'Euro Tracker' survey. When asked in May 2003 if, '. . . a referendum

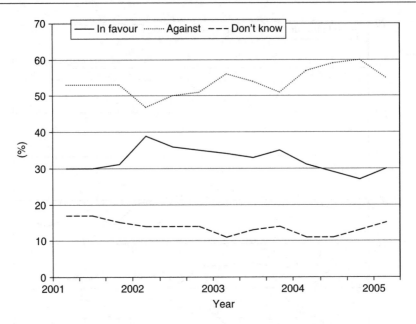

Figure 13.2. How would you vote if the British government were to strongly urge membership?

Source: Ipso Mori (http://www.ipso-mori.com).

were to be held next year or the year after and... were to argue strongly that it would be good for jobs and investment for Britain to join and very risky for Britain to stay out...', 51 per cent supported joining if Brown made such a recommendation, with 47 per cent saying 'yes' if it was Blair. Unlike the Mori data, YouGov's results do at least suggest that a pro-euro campaign might be

	A	B	C	D	DK	A+B	C+D	B+C
May 01	10	23	24	36	6	33	60	47
June 01	13	22	24	31	9	35	55	46
Feb 02	18	24	24	29	5	42	53	48
April 02	19	24	22	29	6	43	51	46
Nov 02	16	23	22	32	7	39	54	45
April 03	15	22	23	33	5	37	56	45
June 03	12	26	26	31	2	38	57	52
Sept 03	14	20	22	38	6	34	60	42
July 04	10	26	24	32	8	36	56	50

Figure 13.3. Views on British participation in the single currency

Source: Ipso Mori (http://www.ipso-mori.com).

boosted if the government gave an explicit lead on the subject, although the evidence is hardly compelling.

Perhaps the only glimmer of hope for any future pro-euro campaign lies in the data presented in Figure 13.3. If one considers the final column (B + C), well over half those surveyed admitted that they could change their views in the face of fresh evidence. Moreover, polls before and after 2001 have also shown that, while voters opposed joining the Single Currency, they fully expected the Blair government to take Britain into the Euro Area in the future. For example, a Mori poll published in July 2003 found that a majority of 74 per cent thought it 'very' or 'fairly likely' that the UK would adopt the euro in the next five years (http://www.ipso-mori.com). It is almost as if the British public has conceded that their views are not important and are willing to accept a 'steer' on this issue. Providing the right (non-party political?) leadership can be found, pro-European groups *may be able* to make up some ground in the future.

Turning to the question of inter-party relations, it is sometimes argued that Britain's two-party system makes it difficult for political leaders to embrace European integration in a more positive way. In particular, the adversarial culture that pervades Westminster frustrates the ability of Prime Ministers to build at least a frontbench consensus on the benefits of EU membership. Since 2001, the Conservative Party's continual drift in a more Euro-sceptical direction has made any cross-party agreement in favour of the euro a virtual impossibility. Ian Duncan Smith's victory over Ken Clarke in the 2001 contest for the Conservative leadership set the tone. Whereas William Hague had ruled out membership of the euro for two parliaments, under Duncan Smith, the replacement of sterling was ruled out indefinitely (a policy that continued under Michael Howard and David Cameron). Kenneth Clarke (who lost two leadership elections because of his pro-European and pro-euro views) admitted that he does not think that Britain's participation in the Euro Area is feasible for the next 10 years (Bale 2006).

That said, although the structure of domestic party debate in Britain continued to move in a Euro-sceptical direction, it is not clear that adopting such a platform at a *general* election is necessarily a vote winner. For example, the Conservatives appear to have accepted their strategy of fighting the 2001 election on the issue of saving the pound did them more harm than good (Cowley and Green 2005: 51). One reason why this stance failed to reap any electoral dividends was because the euro was not a salient issue for voters at this time. In May 2002, a Mori/Sun survey showed that only 5 per cent of the British public rated Europe as an important issue. Likewise, from August 2004 to March 2005 (again according to Mori data) Europe was named as one of the most important issues facing the country by fewer than 10 per cent of respondents. In this context, the Conservatives' increasingly sceptical position on the euro should not necessarily be seen as a manoeuvre to gain extra votes. Instead, it is largely a matter of party management: a ploy to end the continual intra-party bickering on the issue, while protecting the party from a further loss of members to UK Independence Party (Kavanagh and Butler 2005: 28–44; McKay 2006). Ironically then, a tactical consensus *not to talk* about the euro now exists in British politics.

Conclusions

This chapter argues that the Labour Government continues to resist membership of the euro, instead preferring to establish a reputation for anti-inflationary credibility through the construction of an alternative domestic policy regime. Close consideration of speeches, publications, as well as evidence to parliamentary committees, suggests that the Treasury in particular has come to view EMU as a threat to its control over economic management and strategy for promoting an image of governing .competence. The goal independence of the ECB (as opposed to the operational independence of the Bank of England) has led to concerns that European central bankers have too much power over monetary policy. Similarly, the Stability and Growth Pact is perceived as too much of a constraint on the autonomy of decision-makers to 'fine tune' fiscal policy. Put in different terms, Labour politicians are worried they may be left in a position of responsibility without control, especially if the policy needs of the British economy move out of sync with the rest of the Euro Area. The legacy of 'Black Wednesday', not to mention the sterling crises of 1976, 1967, and even 1931, may provide an important historical backdrop to this non-decision.

Furthermore, since 2001 the Blair and Brown governments have been under no pressure to reverse this policy. While some manufacturing companies lobbied for a more positive stance towards the euro in Labour's first term, these efforts have dissipated. More significantly, the City of London sees no reason for a change of direction on this issue. Public opinion remains sceptical and disinterested, while the Labour leadership's preference for not talking about EMU suits the Conservatives, who still find the whole question of Europe inherently divisive. Instead, Britain's 'national' economic framework has won international acclaim for its ability to generate stable, non-inflationary growth. For many commentators in the UK, it remains a viable (even preferable) alternative to Europeanization in this area. In presenting these conclusions, it is not the intention of this chapter to suggest that this policy of retrenchment is permanent or irreversible. If in future, the 'British Model' comes under persistent strain and criticism, advocates of euro membership may find some political space to insert their arguments onto the policy agenda. This is not to say that a pro-euro campaign could then go on and win a referendum. Recent experiences in Sweden suggest that securing a 'yes' vote would remain an uphill task. However, looked at from the perspective of the status quo, a popular plebiscite might be the only chance for a pro-euro campaign to achieve their objectives. At present, the problem with the euro issue is that it remains confined within the suffocating and immobile structures of British parliamentary politics. Shifting this decision to a more open and fluid arena (such as a referendum) may create opportunities for new alliances across a range of political and non-political groups. Such activity would help to broaden the base of a pro-euro campaign (away from Labour leaders). That said, entry would also require a change in the attitude of the City of London and probably of the Conservative Party too. The most likely party to take Britain into the euro is a Conservative Party that has rediscovered its pragmatic, pro-European traditions. None of these developments seems imminent at the time of writing.

14

Hungary and Slovakia: Compliance and its Discontents

Béla Greskovits

Meeting the requirements for euro entry appears to be a harder task for Hungary than for Slovakia. In 2007 Hungary failed to comply with any of the Maastricht convergence criteria and lacked a deadline for entering the Euro Area. Conversely, Slovakia fulfills all entry conditions and is allowed by the EU to introduce the euro in 2009. Hungary delayed the reform of its public sector until 2007. To demonstrate credible commitment to macroeconomic stability, Slovakia radically restructured its welfare state. These differences notwithstanding, since 2006 Hungary and Slovakia share a similarity with each other and, indeed, with many other east European new member states of the EU: the loss of political balance.

This chapter seeks to explain Hungary's and Slovakia's divergence in compliance with the Maastricht criteria, and convergence on political instability, by an interplay of external and domestic factors. Approaching EU membership, both states were exposed to intensifying pressures for compliance. However, their varied records indicate that the Europeanization of fiscal and monetary policies and institutions ultimately depended on what domestic politicians made of the requirements imposed on them. In both states the risky decisions to terminate the social contracts, which hitherto contributed to political stability, have been taken by domestic elites, and mediated and shaped by popular expectations and interest group pressures.

Section two starts with a puzzle. In 2007 Hungarians were rather materialist in their expectations regarding the impact of the euro on their personal lives, whereas Slovaks were more concerned about its consequences for their identity. To explain the difference, the section explores the historical origins of the constraints within which Hungarian and Slovak elites ordered basic policy priorities and institutional changes from the early to late 1990s. It argues that Hungarian elites tried to generate political support for the market society by welfare transfers and appeals to the benefits of a 'return to Europe'. However, political support in the newly independent Slovak state hinged upon a combination of welfare policies with a higher dose of nationalist identity politics that was challenged, after the mid-1990s, by rejection on the part of the EU. The varied means adopted to stabilize the new order led to different political opportunity structures, which constrained the power and coordination of fiscal and monetary authorities.

Section three follows the dynamics of the above political and policy issues in 1998–2007, when impending EU accession in 2004 provoked changes in the material and ideational underpinnings of the new regimes. The Slovak path was redirected dramatically. Capitalizing on fears from authoritarianism at home and isolation in Europe, a new coalition successfully redefined the content of Slovak commitment to nationhood, and turned it into a driving force of Europeanization, competitive economic restructuring, and fast euro entry. Especially after 2002, Slovakia embarked on a radical path of welfare reform and retrenchment that made compliance with the Maastricht criteria easier. The political dynamics of Hungary were different. A consolidating two-party system led to fierce rivalry over the agendas of welfare and Europeanization simultaneously, blocked public-sector reforms, and undermined the prospects for a fast euro entry.

Section four discusses the political backlashes after 2006, which manifested themselves in country-specific patterns of radicalization and apathy. The issues of welfare versus identity continued to be important factors in the paths to the Euro Area in these hard times. The chapter concludes with propositions concerning the impact of preparations for euro entry on state capacity to reform and state power over societal interests.

'Materialist' Hungarians, 'Idealist' Slovaks: Leaving Communism

In spring 2007, 57 per cent of Slovaks but only 49 per cent of Hungarians were happy that the euro could replace their national currencies (Gallup Europe 2007). This difference is unsurprising as Hungary was just starting, while Slovakia had largely completed, a radical and socially costly reform of public administration and welfare in order to comply with the Maastricht criteria. However, the country-specific patterns of public opinion are more puzzling.

To analyse these patterns, the chapter introduces a new tool—*a hope/fear matrix*—constructed from the country scorecards of Gallup Europe (2007). The matrix measures expected identity gains and losses by the normalized share of respondents (new member states' average = 100 per cent) confirming that 'the euro will make people feel more European', versus 'the euro will mean that countries will lose a great deal of their identity'. In turn, perceived gains and

Table 14.1. Hopes and fears about the euro in Hungary and Slovakia

	Hopes (expected gains)	Fears (expected losses)	Average
Hungary			
Identity	50	61	56
Welfare	121	103	112
Slovakia			
Identity	111	106	109
Welfare	93	105	99

Source: author's own calculation based on Gallup Europe (2007), Country Scorecards Hungary and Slovakia.

losses of welfare are measured by the normalized share of those confirming that 'the euro will improve growth and employment', versus 'the euro will increase prices when introduced'.

The finding is that less than half as many Hungarians as Slovaks hope to become more European by having the euro as their official currency. Similarly, only slightly more than half as many Hungarians as Slovaks are afraid that their nation will lose identity. However, while citizens in both states equally fear an initial price shock, many more Hungarians than Slovaks expect faster growth and better job opportunities after euro entry. All in all, Hungarians appear as 'materialist' in the sense that they express *both* their hopes and their fears concerning the impact of the euro in terms of welfare rather than identity. In comparison, Slovaks seem to be 'idealist' as they care more about expected gains and losses in identity than social welfare (Table 14.1).

What are the historical origins of these hopes and fears? Bohle and Greskovits (2007) established that after the collapse of communism Hungary and Czechoslovakia (like Poland and Slovenia) offered both relatively generous welfare transfers to losers of the transformation and protective regulation and subsidies to assist the adjustment of inherited old industries and later the expansion of new, transnational industries.

While the new welfare states and industrial policies had deep roots in the communist past, they did not simply follow from these origins. In principle, Hungary and Czechoslovakia could have opted for the 'pure' neoliberal regimes of the Baltic States, in which radical marketization was less compromised by social protection. At the same time, these initial choices were not overdetermined by the strategic considerations of reform elites. Under the conditions of extreme uncertainty characterizing the early 1990s, the new regimes had been also shaped by unexpected dramatic events.

Hungary: From 'Goulash Communism' to 'Goulash Post-Communism'

Hungary's choice of a new regime had been influenced by its legacy of 'goulash communism' adopted by its communist ruler János Kádár to pacify society after the suppression of the 1956 revolution. To appease the citizenry, Hungarian communists offered a limited compromise: economic reforms, some freedoms of travel and of private life, and modest social protection and welfare in exchange for political quiescence. Pursuing these targets had been costly in terms of recurrent macroeconomic instability: high budget deficits, inflation, and crippling foreign debt. Ultimately, the frustrated efforts to balance an overloaded social, economic, and political agenda, and the resulting loss of macroeconomic control, delivered the *coup de grâce* to Kádárism.

While the inherited instability was a heavy burden on Hungary's first democratic government, led by József Antall, its early attempt at a radical cure, which included a sharp raise in fuel prices in autumn 1990, met fierce resistance: a blockade of Budapest streets by taxi-drivers lasting for several days. The turbulent events activated the historically engrained fears of disruptive social conflict. Once the conflict was settled, 'to avoid upheavals and conflicts' the conservative government opted for a regime that, in Kornai's (1996: 1) view, 'can be aptly called "goulash post-communism"'.

The Antall administration 'divided and pacified' opposition to marketization by extensive welfare provisions, such as liberalized access to disability and early retirement benefits, benefits for the unemployed and families, and encompassing public health care schemes (Vanhuysse 2006). Welfare transfers, however, were not the only means for keeping Hungarians quiescent. Political elites shared a belief in the benefits of a 'return to Europe', and tried to convince Hungarians that social confrontation is 'non-European' as it leads to 'Latinamericanization', a path to be avoided.

Alas, the reincarnation of 'goulash communism' as 'goulash post-communism' reproduced another legacy of the past regime, recurrent macroeconomic instability.

Hungary was forced to 'pay the bill' (Kornai 1996) in 1995, when faced with mounting current account and budget deficits, Gyula Horn's Hungarian Socialist Party (MSZP)-Alliance of Free Democrats (SZDSZ) coalition government launched a stabilization programme named after its architect, Minister of Finance Lajos Bokros. The Bokros package restored macroeconomic stability by a variety of means, including a significant cutback of welfare spending and public employment. Indeed, in the years following the implementation of the package, Hungary partly out-performed Slovakia in fiscal balance and inflation: a remarkable achievement, even if the same years brought about Slovakia's worst performance in macroeconomic stability (Table 14.2).

Slovakia: From Nationally Biased Communism to Paternalistic Nationalism

Similar to Hungary, Czechoslovakia started the 1990s with a radical reform package introduced by Minister of Finance Václav Klaus. The Czech-led transformation frustrated Slovaks as they suffered more from its negative

Table 14.2. Macroeconomic performance, Hungary and Slovakia

	1995–7	1999–2001	2003–5	2006
General government balances (average % of GDP)				
Hungary	−6.2	−4.0	−6.4	−10.1
Slovakia	−2.0	−8.6	−3.2	−2.7
General government debt (average % of GDP)				
Hungary	74.4	55.9	58.7	67.2
Slovakia	24.3	48.9	39.6	35.8
Consumer price index (annual average %)				
Hungary	23.4	9.7	5.0	4.0
Slovakia	7.3	10.0	6.2	4.5

Source: European Bank for Reconstruction and Development (2006).

consequences, such as unemployment and losses in wages and living standards. As a result, they lent increasing support to Vladimir Meciar's Movement for a Democratic Slovakia (HZDS) that dominated political life in the newly independent Slovak Republic from 1993 to 1998. A key to Meciar's success lay in the continuity of his political strategy with that of late Party Chief Gustáv Husák, who restored and consolidated Czechoslovak communism after the Warsaw Pact suppressed the 'Prague Spring' in 1968. When faced with the passive resistance of Czechs, Husák secured the acquiescence of Slovaks by giving preference to their lands' development over that of the Czech part, a policy that resulted in converging industrial output, wages, and living standards.

Meciar drew on this unique historical experience when he 'crafted' independent Slovakia in the new post-communist context. Initially, he tried to negotiate a suitable new deal—less radical reforms, more support from the Czech budget, and more autonomy for the Slovak part—within Czechoslovakia. Only after his attempts faltered on the resistance of Klaus did Meciar accept the 'velvet divorce' in 1993 and foster collective commitment to independent Slovak nationhood. In his own words, '[s]o far no nation lost on having its own state, but many nations lost on not having one' (cited in Lesko 1998: 91).

Once in power, Meciar revived important aspects of the Husák legacy: welfare paternalism, subsidies, and protective regulation for the inherited heavy industries, nationalism, and the east European orientation of foreign policy. His socially inclusive and ethnically exclusive nationalism proved to be popular. Due to relatively generous social transfers and firm subsidies, inequality similar to Hungary could be kept at bay, and large parts of inherited industry afloat. In the high-turnout elections of 1991–8, no single party could garner as strong a support as HZDS. Furthermore, Meciar's role as founding father of

Slovak sovereignty, and his bent for anti-Hungarian rhetoric and policies of ethnic exclusion, secured the support of a radical nationalist ally, Ján Slota's Slovak National Party (SNS), junior member of the HZDS-led block.

How had the Meciar regime performed in macroeconomic terms? While around the mid-1990s the Slovak economy was internationally acclaimed for its low budget deficit, inflation, and general government debt, towards the end of Meciar's rule the macroeconomic situation deteriorated. Nevertheless, Carpenter's (1997: 217) conclusion seems to be correct: above all 'it is the political system that is unhealthy, not the economy'.

During Meciar's rule, Slovak democracy exhibited corruption and authoritarian and sometimes criminal methods of dealing with opponents (Bútora, Meseznikov, and Bútorová 1999). Furthermore, Meciar 'on the international front... attempted to manipulate Russia and the West to vie against each other for his favor' (Mathernová and Rencko 2006: 630). These features impeded international integration. HZDS's rejection of the warnings of the US government and the EU as unacceptable interventions further undermined the regime's reputation. For example, in 1995, the spokesman of HZDS compared a critical resolution of the European Parliament on Slovakia with the logic of the Munich decision of 1938, Czechoslovakia's Nazi occupation in 1939, and the Warsaw Pact intervention in 1968 (Lesko 1998: 170). International isolation peaked in the EU's refusal to include Slovakia in the first group of states with which it started accession negotiations and in the decision of NATO not to offer membership to Slovakia along with its regional peers. The EU grounded its rejection on Slovakia's failure to fulfil the Copenhagen democratic criteria (Kureková 2006).

Consequences for Party Competition and Bureaucratic Politics

As argued above, historically rooted early choices set the course of divergence for the mainstream of Hungarian and Slovak politics. They had lasting consequences for citizens' expectations, party competition, and bureaucratic politics.

The Hungarian routine of buying acquiescence through welfare spending and industry subsidies at the expense of sound finances reflected popular preferences for welfare protection over adherence to the stability culture required by euro entry (Dyson 2002). In relation to the political consequences, the early warning of neoliberal critics about an 'entitlement trap' seems to fit the Hungarian case. '[H]igh and escalating social spending... offers us the real insight into the political dynamics of the region... elections in Eastern Europe have become almost exactly like elections in Western Europe... dominated by interest-group politics' (Sachs 1995: 1). Rival mass parties of the Left and Right responded to the preferences of the electorate.

During election campaigns politicians stressed the intrinsic relationships between economic and welfare protectionism, promised both kinds, and, once in power, tried pragmatically to implement some mix at the expense of fiscal overspending.

This complex and contradictory agenda left its mark on bureaucratic politics. While 'returning to Europe' and later entering the euro required fiscal reforms and an independent central bank, advances on both accounts had been subordinated to *partisan considerations* reflecting domestic electoral risks and opportunities. First, political struggles over control of the Ministry of Finance and the central bank recurred over the 1990s and even later. Second, none of these institutional guardians of sound finances could achieve full hegemony over the 'spending' ministries. Third, the coordination of fiscal and monetary policies proved to be difficult.

Delegation of power for fiscal centralization, rationalization, and adjustment depended crucially on the extent to which prime ministers governed cohesive legislative majorities and perceived finance ministers as brothers-in-arms rather than rivals in politics. Institutional reforms could advance in the former case but were watered or stalled in the latter (Greskovits 2001; Haggard, Kaufman, and Shugart 2001). Similarly, Hungary's muddling towards central bank independence reflected efforts at partisan control, which impaired the coordination of fiscal and monetary policies even after EU accession. Appointments of new presidents of the National Bank of Hungary (NBH) and measures to strengthen central bank independence occurred in a revealing sequence. 'Unreliable' presidents were not allowed to enjoy the longer terms in office, legally better-protected jobs, and enhanced policymaking authority guaranteed by the gradually Europeanized central bank laws. Instead, advances to stronger central bank independence typically favoured and empowered their 'party-loyalist' successors (Greskovits 2006).

In contrast, Slovak politics has been characterized by stronger public support for stability culture and later, at least in the short run, somewhat greater tolerance towards related welfare losses. A number of factors are responsible for this. First, the Husák regime left behind a fairly stable macroeconomy. Unlike Hungary, Czechoslovakia accumulated only moderate foreign debt under communism, partly explaining the lower indebtedness of the Slovak state over the entire period of 1993–2007. Slovakia also inherited the Czechoslovak tradition of price stability and respect for its guardian, the central bank. Indeed, both traditions had deep historical roots. The experiences of Hungary, which had become heavily indebted in the interwar period and had to face hyperinflation after both world wars, had been absent in Czechoslovak history.

Second, after the 'velvet divorce' the legacy of stability culture was reinforced by the popularity of Meciar's grand project, the sovereign Slovak nation state, and its symbol, the stable new national currency. Both HZDS and its rivals were aware of the importance of currency stability for Slovak national pride. This perception strengthened the position of National Bank of Slovakia (NBS) and can partly explain its relative independence even during the Meciar regime. As put by its first governor Vladimir Masar, a 'symbolic milestone on the nation's road to independence was the birth of the Slovak currency, the protection of which is the main duty of the Bank as prescribed by the National Bank of Slovakia Act' (http://www.nbs.sk/BIATEC/MIMORA97/02.HTM).

Some authors claim that Meciar 'attacked the tradition of central-bank independence established between the demise of communism and the divorce with the Czech Republic' (Fish 1999: 48). However, from accounts of Masar and other officials, it seems likelier that even Meciar respected the need for sound monetary policies and currency stability. He empowered the NBS governor to introduce and stabilize the Slovak crown, build up a new professional apparatus and international contacts from scratch, and keep a tight bias in monetary policy. Indeed, as the resident Senior Economist of the IMF recalled, in its effort to stabilize the economy in 1993–5 the NBS 'received significant assistance from fiscal policy which achieved large reductions in fiscal deficit, thus facilitating the tight monetary policy' (http://www.nbs.sk/BIATEC/MIMORA97/02.HTM).

Masar was not forced out of office by the new coalition that took over after Meciar's fall. In striking contrast with the partisan skirmishes around NBH, not only did Meciar's NBS governor serve his full term but also his deputy Marian Jusko was appointed as his successor for the period of 1999–2004 and prepared Slovakia for euro entry.

Heading to the EU, the Euro Area and Political Turbulence in 1998–2007

The varied legacies and early choices defined distinct, largely welfare-driven versus identity-driven political opportunity structures for Hungary's and Slovakia's euro-entry strategy. Though identity politics has certainly not been absent in Hungary, nationalist politicians usually could not reach their constituencies without first addressing their demands for social welfare. Conversely, although welfare has not lacked salience in Slovakia, many Slovaks tended to view the social question through the lenses of national shame or pride. Political opportunities also have been shaped by different demands for macroeconomic stability and critical events, the Bokros package and international isolation, which proved to be *turning points* in Hungary and Slovakia, respectively.

*From the 'Hungarian Model' to 'Transformation
with Welfare' and Euro-populism*

The shock administered by the Bokros package of 1995 proved to be a lasting nightmare for Hungarians, produced loss of trust in Socialists' and Liberals' sensitivity on issues of social welfare, and reinforced the welfarist opportunity structure of political life. Between 1998 and 2006, although nationalist rhetoric was not absent, political competition focused on *social welfare and Europeanization*. The public disappointment with the Left-led government contributed to the Conservative (FIDESZ-MPSZ) electoral victory in 1998, and lent some credibility to Prime Minister Viktor Orbán's claim later in 2001 that his Hungarian model was superior to the Left alternative, even in social welfare. In Orbán's interpretation the model combined growing output, employment, and living standards with improving macroeconomic fundamentals, despite unfavourable external conditions.

The period 1999–2001 was exceptional, as in many of the above terms Hungarian capitalism performed better than ever before or since. To counter international recession, domestic output and consumption were boosted by fiscal measures. The government raised minimum wages twice, by altogether 80 per cent, leading to an economy-wide wage drift. Large-scale development programmes for transport infrastructure, tourism facilities, and public construction were launched. Additional growth stimuli came from generously subsidized loans for residential construction and renovation for middle and upper-middle class home builders, and the 'Széchenyi plan', which combined existing with new incentives for domestic small and medium-sized businesses, local communities, and individuals. Preparing for early euro entry in 2006, NBH allowed the Hungarian forint to float within a 30 per cent band around its central parity against the euro. A policy of inflation targeting was introduced and the exchange rate was used as a tool of disinflation. Yet by 2006 the former pacesetter Hungary became a laggard. The reasons are mainly political.

By 2002 the Hungarian political system consolidated as an essentially two-party democracy, within which both FIDESZ-MPSZ and MSZP had to appear credible on the two issues that seemed important for the majority: social welfare and the issue of EU membership. Thus, even if before the 2002 elections the economy already showed symptoms of strain, MSZP's candidate for premiership Péter Medgyessy felt that his only chance to defeat Orbán and regain lost trust lay in offering yet more of the same desired good: a programme of 'Transformation with Welfare'.

The marginal loss of the 2002 elections to the Left-liberal coalition led FIDESZ-MPSZ to question the legitimacy of the new government. Accusations of electoral fraud, recounting of votes, radical Right-wing rioters blocking a bridge in Budapest, and the public scandal provoked by Medgyessy's previous career in communist intelligence services created an atmosphere of political uncertainty. Losing personal credibility, Medgyessy tried to restore balance by fulfilling his promises of large public-sector salary increases, favours to pensioners, and an extension of subsidized housing loans. However, NBH's president, Zsigmond Járai, former Minister of Finance in the Orbán government, refused to accommodate the consequences of fiscal overspending on the grounds of the central bank's responsibility for meeting the criteria required for the previously envisaged early euro entry.

The issues of social welfare and the appropriate policy strategy for euro entry became heavily politicized. Polarized preferences pitted the opposition against the government on both the desirable timing of euro entry and the desirable policy sequence. On the issue of timing, FIDESZ-MPSZ's original plan for entering the Euro Area as early as 2006 created a straitjacket for the new Left-led coalition government. In committing to ERM II entry in 2004, the plan required fiscal adjustment soon after the election victory, but without the consoling perspective of being able to pacify aggrieved voters by pre-election spending in 2005–6. The early entry date meant that the coalition was compelled to do the 'dirty job' of complying with the Maastricht convergence criteria, and as a consequence risked defeat in the next elections. In this case FIDESZ-MPSZ, the 'free rider' in the hard times of preparation, was going to reap the rewards from the coalition's efforts and introduce the euro in 2006.

On policy sequence, similar considerations of domestic electoral and party competition prevailed. FIDESZ-MPSZ backed NBH president Járai, who made the relaxation of monetary policy conditional on convincing results in fiscal tightening. Otherwise the central bank's disinflation target would be threatened. In contrast, the Left-led government insisted on the opposite conditionality and made fiscal adjustment conditional on relaxed monetary policies. It argued that lower interest rates, a weaker forint, somewhat higher inflation, and less depressed growth could reduce the magnitude of shocks to competitiveness and to welfare, and enhance actors' capacity to gradually adjust.

For these reasons, the stage was set for protracted trench warfare between two major 'advocacy' coalitions competing for power over policy (Sabatier 1991). To lure the government into a trap between unpopular fiscal adjustment and a failure to comply with the Maastricht convergence criteria, the opposition adopted a *euro-populist rhetoric*, which simultaneously attacked the government for lack of sensitivity to social welfare and for incompetence in leading Hungary to euro entry. An increasing range of important Hungarian business associations, core expert elites, opinion-forming intellectuals, holders of non-technical offices, and even various EU-actors were drawn into the battle (Greskovits 2006).

The strong export-orientation of the Hungarian economy helps to understand the mobilization of businesses. Due to the early start in liberalization, as well as to later policy choices, Hungary became a preferred location for foreign transnational corporations, whose operations rapidly turned it into one of the most transnationalized economies of the region and one that was more dependent on the EU business cycle than other post-commmunist states. As a consequence, protracted stagnation in the traditional leading EU economies cut earlier and deeper into output, profits, and employment and resulted in sharper distributional struggles. In this sense Hungary shared older EU members' apparent problems with the EMU straitjacket.

Second, because of Hungary's rapid advance on a labour-intensive manufacturing export path, a relatively powerful transnationally integrated and politically vocal export sector emerged. However, the exhaustion of this kind of export opportunity also affected Hungarian businesses earlier than businesses in other states of the region. Hungarian capital responded to the challenge both by voice and by exit (Hirschman 1970), while none of these responses have been characteristic of Slovakia. On the one hand, Hungarian export businesses vehemently opposed the deflationary policies of the NBH, especially the high exchange rates and interest rates implied. On the other hand, by the 2000s Hungary faced not just threats from foreign transnational corporations, which started to relocate their most labour-intensive operations to lower-wage countries, but also the accelerating outmigration of its largest and most successful domestic businesses, which rapidly transformed themselves into the first transnational corporations of east European origin. The question of whether and how to keep these firms 'loyal' became central for development strategists earlier in Hungary than in Slovakia.

Finally, both Hungarian businesses and policymakers were aware that stretching out the period of preparation for euro entry has its own heavy costs. One important cost, the danger of currency destabilization by recurrent speculative attacks, no less worried exporters, importers, and transnational investors than firms and individuals, who by the mid-2000s accumulated massive debts denominated in foreign currencies.

These domestic struggles had deep impacts on the ensuing volatility, incoherence, and drift of policies. Faced with multiple political and economic pressures, both Medgyessy and Ferenc Gyurcsány, who succeeded him as prime minister in autumn 2004, were inclined to postpone decisions. Medgyessy gave up both the programme of 'transformation with welfare' and comprehensive reforms of the systems of pensions, health care, higher education, and public administration. The reasons included fear of the electorate, reform fatigue, resisting interest groups, and the fiscal burden that such reforms imply in the short term. Under the pressure of worsening macroeconomic performance, and an adverse change in the political climate, the Medgyessy government declared a postponement of the euro entry date to 2008. Faced with the same problems that toppled his predecessor, Gyurcsány put his faith in muddling through the rest of the Socialist-led coalition's term by piecemeal reforms, and further postponed the date of euro entry to 2010. Since during the period 2002–6 Hungary permanently failed to meet most of the targets of its repeatedly revised convergence programmes, it is hard to view euro entry as a serious constraint on economic policy.

Nationalism with a European Face, and Accelerated Euro Entry in Slovakia

International shaming and exclusion brought about a similar turning point for Slovakia as the social shock of the Bokros package for Hungary. Isolation and fiasco in competition with regional peers, the Czech Republic and Hungary, challenged Meciarism at its core as they undermined its capacity to mobilize and harness Slovak national pride for its own political survival. Added to fears of authoritarianism at home, these external pressures opened a new window of opportunity for Meciar's opponents to alter the regime's path.

As much as Hungarian Conservatives could capitalize on Socialists' and Liberals' lost credibility on issues of social welfare, Meciar's rivals questioned his credibility as a true representative of Slovak national interests. In 1998 a heterogenous coalition of Christian Democrats (SDK), former reform-Communists (SDL), and the Party of Ethnic Hungarians (SMK) defeated the HZDS and formed a government under Prime Minister Mikuláš Dzurinda. Their popularity lay in a new definition of Slovak nationhood that was compatible with Europeanization, ethnic inclusion, and competitive economic restructuring. As deputy prime minister for civic and minority rights in the first Dzurinda government, Pál Csáky of SMK asserted: 'We are forming a government now; tomorrow we begin to change the regime' (Fish 1999: 51).

The new regime replaced the old one gradually and in a characteristic sequence. The heterogenous Centre Right/reform-communist coalition of the first Dzurinda government reconquered the international arena for Slovakia. The country did not have to wait long for international recognition, admittance to OECD, NATO, and the group of EU accession countries. 'International integration was the strongest driver for the Dzurinda cabinet and a unifying purpose for the ruling coalition . . . Slovakia would be joining the club that had previously welcomed its neighboring countries' (Mathernová and Rencko 2006: 633).

In economic policy, the government spent 13 per cent of the 2000 GDP to bail out enterprises and near-bankrupt commercial banks (ibid. 634). The banks held sizeable non-performing loans used by the Meciar regime to keep industry afloat. Restructured banks were sold to international strategic investors. The same happened to the large firms, such as the giant East-Slovakian Steel Mills, which were previously used as cash-cows for cronyism and political survival. The massive restructuring effort explains the deterioration of Slovak public finances in 1999–2001. Interestingly, in 2000, when Slovakia was invited to start accession negotiations with the EU, its budget deficit, general government debt, and inflation were twice their level in

1997, the year of Meciar's expulsion from the group of frontrunners for EU membership. Normalization of international and domestic politics appears to have mattered more for the EU than the temporary deterioration of macro-economic fundamentals (Kureková 2006).

After the 2002 election, relying on a more cohesive centre-right coalition, Dzurinda formed his second government, which completed the break with the Meciar legacy. First, the generous flow of subsidies to inherited old industries was redirected in favour of transnational corporations, so that Slovakia could win the 'bidding wars' against regional rivals for major foreign investments in complex export industries, such as the automotive sector. Both Peugeot and Kia invested in Slovakia rather than in neighboring states, and international media began to highlight the 'tiger of the Tatra Mountains'. Second, capital-izing on regained Slovak pride, Minister of Finance Ivan Miklos launched an attack on the welfare-state legacy. Radical reforms relied on the support of the politically included Hungarian minority, but led to social exclusion—with devastating consequences—for the Roma, who suffered both ethnic-based and social marginalization.

In 2002–3 sweeping reforms of pension and health care systems were enacted, the latter of which served as a model for the Hungarian and the Czech reforms of 2007. However, the boldest steps were taken in 2004: Slovakia introduced a flat tax rate, that is a single corporate, income, and VAT rate of 19 per cent. The VAT levied on medicines was among the highest in the EU, and the 9 per cent increase of VAT paid for basic food raised the cost of living for poor families disproportionately. Adding to the stress, the government cut expenditures on family and childcare, and restricted the availability of full unemployment benefits to those actively searching for a new job.

Although dramatic responses promptly followed, their dynamics were very different from the politics of failed compliance in Hungary. Due to the radical and comprehensive public-sector reforms it was easier for Slovakia to meet its EU convergence programme targets. This way the radical reforms paved the way towards early euro entry even if the rhetoric of reformers stressed different advantages: a sustainable rather than wasteful welfare state, dynamic growth, and competitivity. Unlike Hungarian capital, Slovak businesses did not pose resistance to accelerated euro entry either by voice or by exit. Rather, since they gained from lower taxes, social security contributions, and flexible labour markets, businesses backed the new course.

Instead, it was the Slovak population that—in Hirschman's (1970) terms—promptly reacted to welfare retrenchment with *radical voice* and *mass exit* from democratic politics. These responses started in February 2004 with food riots and violent demonstrations in several, mostly Roma-populated, villages and townships of Eastern Slovakia, where unemployment sometimes reached 50 per cent. It took a week before, in the largest domestic security operation since 1989, riot police and the army could restore authorities' control over the region (Slovak Spectator 2004, April 24, Népszabadság Online (NOL) 2004, April 26). Also in 2004, in alliance with trade unions and the radical nationalist SNS, Left-populist leader Robert Fico's opposition party Smer called for a referendum on early parliamentary elections. Although the referendum took place, the turnout did not pass the threshold of validity, which the government viewed as a proof of victory over anti-reform forces (Mathernová and Rencko 2006: 636). Subsequently, however, massive political disaffection has become a permanent troubling feature of Slovak democracy.

When asked about the societal acceptance of his reforms, Minister of Finance Miklos pointed to: 'a schizophrenic state of mind. On the one hand, a majority of the people is critical about the reforms. On the other hand, a majority is against a backlash in reforms. There have been attempts to depose us, but people want reforms. There is no alternative' (interview, Die Welt 2005, September 15). However, the lack of alternative bred disenchantment and apathy that contributed to the reformers' defeat in the 2006 elections. At the 2005 local elections less than 20 per cent of voters turned out. Indeed, even the previously popular project of EU integration failed to raise interest in politics.

Troubled by unpopularity, coalition disintegration, and threatening electoral backlash, the Dzurinda government committed itself to a euro-entry strategy that would tie its successor's hands. Slovakia entered ERM II on 1 January 2006, and confirmed that it would introduce the euro in 2009. Rather than responding to EU pressures, this choice reflected similar domestic political calculations to the Hungarian decision on an early euro entry date back in 2001. Were the Dzurinda coalition re-elected in 2006, it would stay on the radical reform path, and reap the fruits of leading Slovakia to euro entry. In case of an opposition victory, the commitment to stability-oriented policies would increase the international costs of deviation from the reform path.

Reformers Without Mandate?

Mass exit of Slovak citizens from democratic politics predicted, and paved the way for, the victory of radical voices in the June 2006 parliamentary elections. The turnout was at a record low level. Many of those who cast a vote punished the incumbent and deprived reformers of a mandate to continue the radical neoliberal course. A new government under Fico, and formed by Smer, SNS, and HZDS, assumed power. EU-level actors, who were concerned about a revival of Meciarism, resorted to the earlier routine of disciplining Slovak politicians through shaming and isolation. For its coalition with illiberal nationalists, Smer was denied membership in the European Parliament's Socialist party grouping.

Table 14.3. Turnout at Hungarian and Slovakian referenda and elections (%)

	National parliamentary elections			EU referenda 2003	EP elections 2004
	1998	2002	2006		
Hungary	57	74	64	46	39
Slovakia	84	70	55	52	17
New members average	72	68	61	59	32

Source: EuroStat.

Contrary to expectations, Slovakia's stability-oriented policy course has not been significantly altered by the new government so far. Fico's administration enjoyed the fruits of its predecessor's efforts. Rising wages, employment, and living standards due to rapid growth boosted Smer's popularity and mitigated its dependence on populist policies or radical illiberal rhetoric for political support (Malová 2007). Indeed, Slovakia's compliance with the Maastricht criteria is in line with the plan inherited from the Dzurinda government to introduce the euro in 2009. The decision of the EU to allow Slovakia to enter, as the second east European member state (after Slovenia) in 2009 signals that admittance to the Euro Area, unlike to the EU, lacks even informal political conditionality. To allow Slovakia to enter, as the second east European new member state (after Slovenia) in 2009, would signal that admittance to the Euro Area, unlike to the EU, lacks even informal political conditionality (cf. Dyson 2006*c*).

Hungary's muddling towards political destabilization followed a different path. Over the 2000s, Hungarians participated somewhat more actively in democratic politics than Slovaks (Table 14.3). One reason might be that, while Slovak society exhibited striking symptoms of marginalization, commonly viewed as a hotbed for political apathy, welfare spending kept social disparities within safer limits in Hungary. Another factor might be the mobilizing impact of two-party rivalry. During the spring 2006 Hungarian election campaign the opposition launched, and the incumbent joined in, a competition of promises of yet more generous welfare provisions.

Uniquely in Hungary's democratic history, voters granted the incumbent MSZP-SZDSZ coalition a second term, while extremists lost their previous limited support. Hardly were the elections over, however, before the advocacy coalition for stabilization and convergence, supported this time by the entire Hungarian business community, mobilized significant resources—opinion leaders' media campaigns, business associations' petitions, and policy research institutes' blueprints—to convince citizens and the new administration about the urgency of a radical policy shift.

After a month of secretive negotiations, the Gyurcsány government announced a plan that included both a draconian austerity package and a new

EU convergence programme. The former raised existing and introduced new taxes and made expenditure cuts to improve fiscal balances. The convergence programme foresaw comprehensive structural reforms to public administration, education, health care, and pensions to regain credibility on issues of macroeconomic convergence.

As the details of harsh measures became public, the new government's popularity plummeted. The loss of support did not stop there. In September 2006, an (in)famous speech of Premier Gyurcsány, delivered to convince the MSZP parliamentary party about the urgency of reforms, was leaked to media. He admitted: 'Obviously we lied throughout the past one-and-a-half, two years.... Meanwhile, we have done nothing for four years. You cannot tell me of any significant government measures we can be proud of.... I almost died of having to pretend for the past year that we were actually governing' (TIMESONLINE accessed on 19 September 2006 at http://www.timesonline. co.uk/article).

This was not the kind of sincerity that the electorate and especially the angry opposition could appreciate. Thus, unlike their Slovak counterparts, who lost their mandate *after* implementing a neoliberal course, Hungarian reformers had to *start* radical reforms practically without a mandate, as they never asked, and thus lacked public approval, for terminating the social contract. In consequence, from September 2006 to March 2007, the Left-led coalition had to weather massive protests of the opposition, coupled with repeated violent riots by radical Right-wing groups. During the first months of 2007, social protest against the closures of hospitals and high schools made the headlines. Even if political and social mass protest lost momentum, Gyurcsány's government struggled hard, within unfavourable political circumstances, to implement the EU-sanctioned new convergence programme. The new challenge was a series of 'social referenda', initiated by the opposition on a number of symbolically important measures, such as the already introduced fees for visiting general practitioners, using hospital beds, or contributions to the costs of higher education.

Irony of ironies, the business community did not waste time in threatening the government with sabotage of some of its measures. In June 2006, when the new strategy was first presented to business leaders and associations, they predicted investors' mass exit to Slovakia. This was not an empty threat. By March 2006, 7,000 small- and medium-sized Hungarian firms relocated to Slovakia to escape high Hungarian taxes. Large businesses, driven by their quest for foreign markets, followed suit (NOL 2006, March 3).

The flagship firms of Hungary's transnational export industries also used threats of exit. After their unofficial representative, Audi Hungaria, declared that it could not afford paying the so-called 'solidarity tax', and would rather locate new investment projects elsewhere, the government conceded. It allowed all large transnational exporters to deduct research and development expenditures and pay tax on the reduced base. This concession forced the government to try and fill the gap in fiscal revenues with contributions from less powerful actors (NOL 2006, 8 November).

Conclusions

What is the impact of intensifying EU pressures for compliance with the Maastricht criteria on domestic politics, policies, and institutions in the new east European member states? Do such pressures enhance or undermine state capacity for sustainable euro entry? These are complex questions, and the evidence does not support unambiguous answers.

To demonstrate long-term commitment to macroeconomic stability under EMU, these states were urged to reform by reducing the size of their public-sector workforces and welfare states. These measures proved to be difficult, and undermined political stability especially in those states, including Hungary and Slovakia, where neoliberal restructuring had been able to go forward more or less in tandem with democratization, in part because relatively generous compensation appeased losers.

Yet, political instability does not seem to trivially follow from compliance pressures. After all, when preparing for euro entry a decade earlier, older EU democracies were exposed to similar challenges but could meet them at lower political cost. A key to their success was their reliance on special institutions to distribute adjustment costs: established neo-corporatist practices and routines, as well as 'new arrangements involving broad encompassing social pacts between employers, trade unions, and governments striking deals across policy areas from wages to social and employment policies' (Hancké and Rhodes 2005: 1).

Indeed, among the east European newcomers it is only in Slovenia that costly social transfers did not come at the expense of violating the requirements of euro entry. Dominant neo-corporatist institutions, such as legally enforced social partnership, extended collective agreements, and—on the road to EMU—a national social pact, were able to deliver the needed compromises and keep political instability at bay. Neo-corporatism has proven to be Slovenia's asset for building the region's highest state capacity for sustainable euro entry. That tradition made it easier for fiscal, monetary, labour market, and welfare institutions to *accommodate*, in the terminology of Europeanization literature, compliance and share its burden with business and labour. In contrast, in Hungary and Slovakia, where negotiated relationships between management and labour failed to take root beyond the firm level, sharing the burdens of adjustment is entirely left to the process of democratic competition, with troubling consequences for its balance.

As argued above, compliance pressures from euro accession led to varied Europeanization responses in Slovakia and Hungary. In Slovakia identity politics could substitute for the negative balancing impact of welfare spending for some time. At the same time as 'top-down' Europeanization (Dyson 2006c) strengthened the capacity of Slovak central bankers to maintain prudent monetary policy, Europeanized identity politics opened a window of opportunity for Slovak reformers to *radically transform* fiscal, labour market and welfare institutions. Nevertheless, the Slovak experience does not make it easy to separate state power from interest-group power, as reforms there were in line with the preferences of business groups. Finally, since populist nationalism came back with a vengeance on the back of social grievances, it is difficult to predict how long the Slovak state will be capable of meeting the convergence criteria after euro entry.

In relation to euro accession Europeanization, Hungary appears to be a mixed case of *transformation in certain areas and inertia* in others. 'Top-down' compliance requirements affected the competition for power over monetary policy, since they empowered the president of the National Bank of Hungary and allowed him to use the increasingly critical convergence reports of the European Central Bank and the European Commission to buttress his own position. However, struggles over fiscal and exchange-rate policies as well as public-sector reforms have been strongly affected by a divisive process of 'bottom-up' Europeanization, in which domestic actors instrumentalized a variety of European models, such as 'European identity', the 'European social model', or the Lisbon competitiveness agenda, to strengthen their positions. Thus, while compliance pressures enhanced the reform capacity of Hungarian financial technocracy, the political will and skills for public-sector reforms were largely missing until 2006. Finally, the contested efforts at downsizing the state in 2007 resulted in firing altogether 60,000 public servants from administration, health care, and education. The decimation of public-service bureaucracies amidst sweeping and complex institutional restructuring created an atmosphere of uncertainty and chaos inside the public sector and thus challenged state capacity.

15

Poland: From Pacesetter to Semi-Permanent Outsider?

Radoslaw Zubek

This chapter examines the politics of Euro Area accession in Poland in the final stages of EU enlargement negotiations and in the first few years of EU membership.[1] In particular, it explains why Poland's position changed from that of a pacesetter, seeking fast-track euro entry, to that of a semi-permanent outsider, postponing euro entry for the foreseeable future. Two years before EU accession, the government and central bank began to work hand in hand to pave the way for a fast-track euro entry. Within a year the target date for entry was pushed back. This about-face was complete when, in late 2005, prompt accession was ruled out, and the Polish government declined to fix a new date. In abandoning its plans for speedy accession, Poland has joined Hungary and the Czech Republic, two other central European states in which early enthusiasm for euro entry gave way to a general Euro-malaise (cf. Dyson 2006c; Greskovits in this volume).

In explaining the patterns of EU compliance strategies in central Europe, much research has accorded explanatory power to conditionality (Grabbe 2006; Schimmelfenning and Sedelmeier 2005). These 'top-down' perspectives emphasize the role of material and non-material rewards that the EU offers to candidate states in return for compliance with its requirements. The success of Europeanization is thus linked to the determinacy of conditions, size, and speed of rewards, and the credibility of threats and promises (Schimmelfenning and Sedelmeier 2005). Other studies have pointed to the importance of domestic conditions for shaping the patterns of national compliance (cf. Hughes et al. 2004; Zubek 2008a). These 'inside-out' approaches focus on the impact of national institutions and the preferences of key domestic actors.

[1] The author thanks Kenneth Dyson, Bela Greskovits, and Mark Hallerberg and other participants of the British Academy conference on 'European States and the Euro: the First Decade' for their useful comments and suggestions on an earlier version of this chapter.

External incentives have been considered as contextualizing factors that mitigate or reinforce the effect of domestic settings.

This study adopts the 'inside-out' approach. In doing so, it seeks to capture the real-life dynamics of Europeanization through EMU, without prejudging the importance of the EU as the primary causal variable. The first section sets the domestic contexts within which Poland faced the challenges of Euro Area accession. It shows the high integration of Polish trade with the Euro Area, but indicates that a substantial structural deficit is a key obstacle to achieving nominal convergence. The situation is further complicated by divisions among elites, a moderately Euro-sceptic electorate, and a low reform capacity, particularly in fiscal policy. The second section demonstrates how, in the relative absence of strong external incentives, the euro entry strategy in Poland was critically shaped by the economic conditions, the preferences of governing parties and political entrepreneurs, and the nature of the institutional setting. The concluding section teases out the implications of euro entry requirements for Europeanization and for understanding of state capacity.

Euro Entry and Domestic Contexts

Economic and Political Conditions

A strong economic case exists for Poland's prompt entry into the Euro Area. It exhibits general cyclical convergence with the Euro Area. Most research indicates a high correlation of changes in basic macroeconomic indicators, like industrial production and inflation, and of demand and supply shocks (Borowski 2001; National Bank of Poland 2004: 33). Trade integration is also considerable. The Euro Area is Poland's single most important trade partner. In 2005–7, exports to the Euro Area accounted for between 52 and 54 per cent of all Polish exports, while the share of imports stood at between 48 and 50 per cent (GUS 2006, 2007). The euro is also a first-choice currency in most trade transactions. Around 60 per cent of Polish commodity trade is exchanged using euro, and around 45 per cent for payments for services (Gorska et al. 2003). A relatively high cyclical and business convergence with the Euro Area means that Poland is in a good position to reap major benefits from adoption of the single currency. Among the most frequently quoted are the elimination of exchange-rate risk, reduction in transaction costs, enhanced trade and foreign direct investment, and lower interest rates (National Bank of Poland 2004; Pruski 2006; Rybinski 2007).

While Poland stands to gain from EMU entry, some macroeconomic problems impede nominal convergence. A key issue is a large structural budget deficit (Table 15.1), which, in most part, reflects the substantial use of social

Poland

Table 15.1. Structural and cyclical deficits of the Polish central budget

	1995	1996	1997	1998	1999	2000	2001	2002	2003*	2004*
Budget balance	−3.27	−3.33	−2.63	−2.38	−2.03	−2.16	−4.31	−5.10	−4.83	−6.72
Cyclical deficit	0.00	−0.05	0.13	0.50	0.39	−0.22	−0.72	−0.80	−0.66	−0.07
Structural deficit	−2.57	−3.04	−3.00	−3.08	−3.25	−2.12	−3.89	−4.40	−4.69	−6.45

Source: MGPiPS (2003).
* NBP estimates.

transfers to ease the pains of the economic transition (World Bank 2003: 5). In 2001, social security and welfare spending consumed the largest share of government expenditure at 20 per cent of GDP, or 44 per cent of expenditures (World Bank 2003: 15). At the time of EU accession, Poland had the highest proportion of social spending among all the accession states (European Commission 2003c). Being statute-mandated, most of the social expenditures are characterized by high rigidity (Wernik 2005). Budgetary stress is exacerbated by a relatively low share of capital investments and high spending on public-sector wages (Orlowski 2004) and, from 2004, by the need to match EU structural funds with public funds. The delicate fiscal position contributed to speedy nominal divergence from the Maastricht convergence criteria whenever macroeconomic conditions deteriorated. Consequently, there were concerns not just about high wage rigidities and low labour mobility but also about the effective use of fiscal stabilizers under full EMU membership (National Bank of Poland 2004: 30–1).

The Polish elites remained divided on EMU policy. Broadly, there are three major camps—euro-enthusiasts, euro-pragmatists, and euro-rejecters. The differences between the groups relate to the choice of priorities, perception of the single currency, adaptation approach, and entry strategy. For euro-enthusiasts, EMU is a key political priority that should override other policy objectives. It is perceived as an enabling constraint that forces domestic actors to embrace difficult, albeit necessary reforms. Nominal convergence should be achieved mainly through the rationalization of public expenditures, and real convergence will follow under full EMU membership. Euro-enthusiasts prefer a fast-track adoption of the euro, with some even advocating a unilateral euro-ization (Bratkowski and Rostowski 2001). The enthusiasts for entry come mainly from the Polish central bank, commercial financial institutions, and liberal economic institutes. While the views on EMU among Polish parties tend to evolve, the Civic Platform (PO), a liberal-conservative party, is closest to the euro-enthusiastic camp (Karpinski 2005; Niklewicz and Maciejewicz 2005). Table 15.2 outlines the party composition of Polish cabinets in 2001–7.

The euro-pragmatic camp adopts a more cautious position. Their principal priority is short- and medium-term growth, which they perceive as

Table 15.2. Polish prime ministers, finance ministers, central bank governors, and party composition of cabinets (2001–7)

Prime ministers	Finance ministers	Parties	NBP governor
Leszek Miller (2001–4)	Marek Belka (2001–2) Grzegorz Kolodko (2002–3)	SLD, UP, PSL	Leszek Balcerowicz (2000–6)
	Grzegorz Kolodko (2002–3) Andrzej Raczko (2003–4)	SLD, UP	
Marek Belka (2004–5)	Miroslaw Gronicki (2004–5)	SLD, UP	
Kazimierz Marcinkiewicz (2005–6)	Teresa Lubinska (2005) Zyta Gilowska (2005–6)	PiS	
	Zyta Gilowska (2006) Pawel Wojciechowski (2006)	PiS, LPR, Samoobrona	
Jaroslaw Kaczynski (2006–7)	Zyta Gilowska (2006–7)	PiS, LPR, Samoobrona	Slawomir Skrzypek (2007–present)

Source: own compilation.

incompatible with a fast-track euro entry. EMU is perceived as a disabling constraint, which makes industrial and infrastructural upgrading more difficult. With respect to domestic adaptation, some pragmatists advocate achieving nominal convergence through spending cuts in good times; others argue for growing out of deficit on the strength of economic growth alone. Most would like to achieve nominal convergence first, and only then fix the entry date. Euro-pragmatists come from the finance and economic ministries and Left-leaning research institutes. Miroslaw Gronicki, former finance minister, said:

The central bank insists that the faster we adopt the euro, the better. We say—yes, but not at any price. The finance ministry wants to maintain high growth and macro-economic stability and to achieve a gradual fall in unemployment. The bank's main concern is to keep inflation down, while growth is a secondary issue   (Karpinski 2004).

Among Polish parties this view is shared by the majority of the Law and Justice Party (PiS), a socialist-conservative party, and the Alliance of the Democratic Left (SLD), a socialist-liberal party.

The small, though vocal group of euro-rejecters do not see the single currency as a priority. They perceive the single currency as a major threat to national sovereignty. In their view, Poland should retain its own monetary policy, and use it to further its own economic development. The choice of entry strategy is not an issue and should be deferred for the foreseeable future. The hard-line rejecters argue that the decision on the euro should be made only after Poland achieves a level of development similar to the Euro Area; more moderate rejecters call for a national referendum to be held on the issue. There are few economists in this camp, and the rejecters' position holds most sway among the parties of the extreme Right (The League of Polish Families, LPR) and of the populist Left (The Self-Defence). A LPR member explained:

A country that gives up its national currency relinquishes the power to shape its macro politics . . . we will not pursue a policy preferred by the global powers but one which is in line with Polish national interests (Karpinski 2005).

Polish public opinion seems to be broadly in line with the cautious euro-pragmatic camp. The polls indicate a more or less equal share of supporters and opponents. According to Eurobarometer data, in late 2006, 46 per cent were happy that the euro would replace the Polish zloty, while 41 per cent expressed the opposite view (European Commission 2006d). In January 2007, Polish polls gave a slight lead to the opponents of the euro—46 per cent over 44 per cent (CBOS 2007). Public opinion does not favour a fast-track adoption of the euro. The supporters of early adoption account only for 17.5 per cent of the population, while 40.2 per cent and 38.4 per cent prefer adoption after a certain time and as late as possible, respectively (European Commission 2006d). The cautious approach stems from a rather sceptical perception of the consequences of the euro adoption. Thirty-nine per cent believe that they will personally lose on the adoption of the euro, whereas 43 per cent think it will have positive consequences on the personal level (European Commission 2006d). The main fear is price increases. Seventy-five per cent of Poles are afraid of abuses and cheating on prices during the changeover (Figure 15.1; European Commission 2006d).

Institutional Setting

Poland combines high budgetary stress, divided elites, and a moderately euro-sceptic electorate with restricted capacity for maintaining fiscal rectitude. Two points deserve highlighting. Inside the executive the institutional position of the finance ministry is relatively weak, and only limited use is made of binding fiscal targets (cf. Brusis and Dimitrov 2001; Dimitrov et al. 2006; Hallerberg and von Hagen 2006). The finance minister has no veto powers over ministerial spending bids, limited rights to resolve disputes, and the full cabinet may override her or his proposals. Whereas Polish governments set multi-annual fiscal targets, there is no formal requirement to follow them in future years (Hallerberg and von Hagen 2006). These institutional problems contribute to worsening budgetary positions in particular under coalition and minority cabinets. Weak fiscal rules are symptomatic of a more general under-institutionalization of the Polish core executive (Goetz and Zubek 2007; Zubek 2001).

The second point is parliamentary dominance. The Polish executive benefits from few formal agenda-setting and amendment powers in the budgetary process. Once the government has proposed a budget bill, the parliament

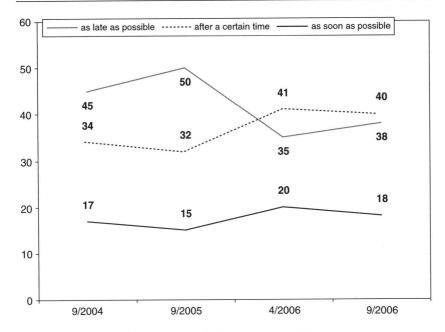

Figure 15.1. Polish public support for EMU membership (%)
Source: European Commission (2006*d*).

is free to revise revenues and to reallocate budgetary expenditures, though it cannot change the overall balance. The government has weak fiscal gate-keeping powers, as non-executive actors may submit tax and spending bills at any time (Goetz and Zubek 2007; Hallerberg and von Hagen 2006). To reinforce its position in parliament, the government must rely mainly on partisan controls, in particular the support and loyalty of the parliamentary speaker and committee chairpersons. Yet, under the conditions of weak party consolidation, such partisan controls provide a relatively ineffective instrument of legislative control. The combination of few formal privileges and ineffective partisan controls provides the foundations of a limited executive capacity to push reforms through the legislature (Zubek 2008*b*).

EU membership has had little reinforcing effect on fiscal institutions. For one thing, EMU prescriptions in this area have been chiefly in the form of ideational templates of good fiscal rules, propagated through technical advice and exchange of experts. Their adoption, including that of the formalized ESA95 accounting standards, was not a formal condition of EU membership. The domestic reform efforts were half-hearted. In 2005, the Marcinkiewicz government introduced a nominal cap on budget deficits but refrained from placing any constraints on expenditures. Domestic economists, including the finance minister, considered the nominal deficit limit as insufficient for alleviating fiscal problems (Jankowiak 2006; Kluza 2006). ECOFIN also recommended that Poland should enhance the institutional framework by introducing a medium-term expenditure rule (Council of the European Union 2006*a*, 2006*b*). But, despite external and domestic calls for new fiscal rules, institutional reforms have remained erratic.

The weakness of fiscal institutions contrasts with the strong independence of the central bank, the National Bank of Poland (NBP). In the first half of the 1990s, the NBP underwent a process of profound anticipatory Europeanization (Epstein 2006; Sobczynski 2002). Modelled on the EU acquis, the constitutional framework granted the Polish central bank the right to formulate and implement monetary policy. It identified price stability as the primary goal of monetary policy, though the bank was to support the government's economic policies insofar as this did not affect inflation. Under the constitution, the central bank's governor is appointed by the parliament for a fixed term of six years and may not be removed from office. The members of the monetary policy council also enjoy independence after appointment.

During the enlargement process, the central bank's financial independence was further reinforced by ensuring that the NBP's accounts were audited by a private auditing firm rather than a government-appointed commission (Polanski 2004: 9). In operational terms, the NBP harmonized its monetary policy instruments with the ECB standards in such areas as required reserve ratios, standing deposit facility, and open market operations (Polanski 2004: 12). The institutionalization of the NBP's and its monetary policy council's independence gave it strong position vis-à-vis the government and facilitated an autonomous monetary policy. However, full institutional convergence with EMU rules was not achieved. The European Commission's and the ECB's convergence reports of 2004 and 2006 noted that a number of major incompatibilities persisted. They included the absence of explicit prohibitions on the NBP seeking outside guidance and on the government influencing central bank policy; the requirement that the NBP governor should present draft monetary policy guidelines to the cabinet; and the excessively broad control prerogatives of the Supreme Audit Office (European Central Bank 2004, 2006*b*).

National adaptation to EMU stalled because of an increasing controversy surrounding the NBP's choice of monetary policy. Following clashes in the mid-1990s, the central bank's stance was openly challenged in 2002, when the SLD-UP-PSL cabinet blamed it for a sharp economic slowdown and weak recovery (Belka 2001; Orlowski 2004). The government publicly called on the bank to reduce rates to support its attempts to stimulate growth. The situation worsened still when, after the 2005 elections, the new PiS-LPR-Samoobrona cabinet set up a committee of enquiry to examine the NBP's role in the privatization of the financial institutions in 1989–2006. The move was widely perceived as a personal attack on Leszek Balcerowicz, NBP governor, and chief architect of the Polish economic breakthrough, by a cabinet that contested the success of the post-communist transition (Karpinski and Smilowicz 2006).

Politics of Euro Entry 2001–7

This section analyses the politics of EMU accession in Poland under four consecutive governments between 2001 and 2007. In doing so, it investigates the factors behind the shift from early enthusiasm to malaise in Polish policy. It shows how the patterns of domestic fiscal and monetary leadership shape the choice of euro entry strategy. It further demonstrates how domestic conditions, and—to a lesser degree—external incentives, provide the context for this leadership.

Planning for Fast-Track Entry in 2007

In the run-up to EU accession, Poland's euro entry strategy was characterized by much enthusiasm. This enthusiasm was particularly apparent in the central bank, which had a strategic preference for fast-track entry (cf. Kokoszczynski 2002). Already in its policy strategy of 1998, the bank's monetary policy council (RPP) declared that 'the EMU's price stability criterion requires that Poland must relatively quickly reduce inflation to a level not exceeding 3 to 5 per cent a year' (RPP 1998: 4). With Poland EU accession, EMU moved to the top of the bank's agenda. Speaking in 2002, Leszek Balcerowicz, its governor, said: 'Poland will be better off adopting the single currency as quickly as possible, that is, in 2006 or 2007' (Slojewska 2002). Consequently, in 2003, the monetary policy council identified monetary convergence as a key priority for its future policy and declared that it wanted Poland to join the euro at the earliest possible date after the 2004 accession, in 2007 (RPP 2003). The monetary policy strategy was thus based on the expectation that Poland would apply to join the ERM II as soon as possible after EU accession.

In mid-2002, the Polish government joined the central bank in pushing for prompt euro entry. The SLD-UP-PSL cabinet formulated an ambitious accession plan (Rzeczpospolita 2002). The key driving force was Finance Minister Grzegorz Kolodko, who persuaded Prime Minister Leszek Miller that early entry would be politically beneficial because it would resolve the problem of restrictive monetary policy maintained by the central bank. The plan envisaged a substantial reduction in the fiscal deficit in 2004 and 2005 and adoption of the single currency in 2007. The Miller–Kolodko accord triggered important preparatory work. The meetings of a working group, established by the finance ministry and the NBP, were intensified to develop a convergence programme. In October 2002, the group announced that 'It is a joint intention of the government and the central bank to conduct macroeconomic policy in such a way as to ensure that Poland meets the nominal convergence criteria of the Maastricht Treaty in 2005' (Ministerstwo Finansow 2002).

The bid for a fast-track euro entry collapsed in mid-2003. Kolodko had received little support from domestic business associations and trade unions. His comprehensive package in March 2003 envisaged the lowering of the fiscal deficit mainly through a combination of restrictive tax policy, spending cuts, and extraordinary revenues (Bien and Lesniak 2003). As the proposal came at a time of relatively low economic growth, Polish business and trade unions were united in calling for lower taxation and higher deficits, even if that meant a delayed euro entry (cf. Jablonski et al. 2003). Also, Kolodko was not fully backed by the central bank. The relations between the finance ministry and the NBP had been strained since the Miller cabinet blamed the bank for the sharp economic slowdown in 2000–1 (Zubek 2006: 202–3). Once Kolodko's package was announced, the NBP objected to plugging the budget shortfall with extraordinary revenues from the dissolution of the bank's revaluation reserve (cf. Slojewska 2003).

But, perhaps most critically, Kolodko clashed with his cabinet colleagues, who were concerned that spending cuts would reduce the already low approval ratings of the government and that a restrictive tax policy would suppress nascent growth. Economics and labour minister, Jerzy Hausner, led internal cabinet opposition. He criticized the finance minister for his desire to lower the deficit at a time when growth, employment, anti-poverty measures, and support for the absorption of EU funds should have been the government's top priorities (Solska 2003). The economics minister believed that 'Poland should not rush its EMU entry. Nominal convergence (including convergence with fiscal criteria) may make it difficult to implement structural adaptations in the Polish economy that are more important for delivering lasting economic growth' (Gazeta Wyborcza 2003). Hausner proposed an alternative economic programme which, on its revenue side, was clearly contrary to Kolodko's and, on its spending side, proposed only selective cuts to be undertaken when the economy reached a higher growth rate (Bien and Lesniak 2003).

While domestic considerations played a key role, Kolodko's bid was also undermined by limited external empowerment. In response to his plans for quick convergence, both the European Commission and the ECB discouraged the Polish government from seeking rapid euro entry. Both these institutions were concerned that, once Euro Area members, Polish decision-makers would not show sufficient commitment to lower inflation, and in particular that Poland needed higher growth to catch up with the old member states (Slojewska 2002). The lack of EU pressures for early entry meant that the finance minister did not find external allies in his push for fiscal convergence. Given the combination of such unfavourable domestic and external conditions, Prime Minister Miller withdrew his support for the finance minister and sided with the rest of the cabinet, a decision that was tantamount to delaying Poland's euro entry.

The Promise of a (Slightly) Delayed Entry in 2009

The failure of Kolodko's bid for fast-track entry amounted to a slippage of two years in the official timetable for Euro Area accession. On EU accession, Poland promised to stabilize its public finances by 2007, so as to clear the way for euro entry in 2009 (Rada Ministrow 2004). But the achievement of this goal hinged on the successful implementation of a comprehensive fiscal stabilization package, known as the 'Hausner plan'. The package was adopted by the Miller government in early 2004, in response to a fast growing public debt. It envisaged a reduction in social spending of some 30 billion zloty or almost 4 per cent of GDP over four years between 2004 and 2007 (Blajer 2004a). In July 2004, ECOFIN accepted Poland's plans and recommended that the fiscal position should be brought under control by 2007, in particular by applying the measures incorporated in the Hausner plan.

It soon transpired, rather unexpectedly, that the viability of entry in 2009 relied on the resolution of a statistical dispute. The Polish public accounting system classified funded pension schemes as part of the general government balance, but in 2004 Eurostat declared the practice incompatible with ESA95. The change in the classification increased Poland's deficit by around 1.5 per cent. To remain within the convergence plan, the government pushed for an exemption during the renegotiation of the Stability and Growth Pact. Finance Minister Miroslaw Gronicki attempted to secure a majority in ECOFIN for the idea of introducing special provisions for how pension reforms with measurable effect on short-term deficit should be classified in the calculation of the budget deficit (Slojewska 2005a; Soltyk 2005). After protracted talks, Poland succeeded in securing an important concession. ECOFIN agreed that the cost of the pension reform could be considered, whenever the deficit reached a level close to 3 per cent. In the latter case, Poland would be able to reduce its deficit in the five consecutive years between 2005 and 2009 by 100, 80, 60, 40, and 20 per cent of the cost of pension reform, respectively (Slojewska 2005b).

But while the government was successfully diffusing adaptation pressures at the EU level, the Hausner plan was failing on implementation in the domestic arena. In 2004 alone, the government backed away from one-third of the expected reductions in social spending (Blajer and Sadlowska 2004). The main reason for the fiasco was a major crisis that had enveloped the SLD party. By supporting Hausner, Miller came into conflict with the core of the SLD party (Olczyk and Ordynski 2003). A regional party leader put it bluntly: 'The Hausner plan is good for Poland but disastrous for the SLD' (Olczyk 2003). Rationalization of public expenditure was likely to be painful for many voters of the SLD, stood in stark contrast to the party's election pledges, and brought the SLD into conflict with the trade unions. It was also certain to hurt the SLD in the European Parliament elections scheduled for June 2004.

The SLD began to suspect that, in the face of plummeting popularity, Miller was fighting for his place in history, without consideration for the fate of the party. This mood quickly translated into calls for Miller to step down as leader and prime minister (Smilowicz 2004). The internal opposition to the Hausner plan within the SLD undermined party discipline within parliament and forced the formally minority coalition to make concessions on issues such as the reduction of sickness pay and pre-pension benefits (Binczak and Blajer 2004).

The SLD party was also labouring under the strain of major corruption scandals that involved senior SLD ministers and party leaders and that the Polish media exposed in 2003–4. Miller's refusal to acknowledge responsibility for these irregularities hurt the approval ratings of the government and eventually led to a split in the party, when a group of party members set up a new party, Polish Social Democrats (SdPL) (Paradowska 2004). The fragmentation of the SLD forced Miller's resignation as prime minister and the formation of a new cabinet under a former finance minister, Marek Belka. To be voted into office, Belka had to make further concessions on the Hausner plan, promising to withdraw proposals for new rules on disability benefits, which accounted for about one-tenth of the expected savings (Blajer 2004*b*; Gottesman 2004). Faced with volatile and fragmentary support in parliament, the Belka cabinet was not able to push through important rationalization measures. Perhaps more importantly, the approaching general elections pushed the parliament to initiate and adopt numerous bills with far-reaching expenditure implications, which undermined the fiscal position even further (Blajer 2005).

Towards a Semi-Permanent Outsider?

The 2005 general elections brought a fundamental revision of the Polish euro entry strategy. The new Law- and Justice-led (PiS) government declared that it would not seek euro entry in the foreseeable future. Prime Minister Kazimierz Marcinkiewicz said: 'We see no reason to adopt the euro in this parliament. This issue will be left to our successors' (Niklewicz 2005). The newly elected PiS president, Lech Kaczynski, concurred: 'Poland is not ready for the euro yet' (Gazeta Wyborcza 2006). Moreover, the government pledged to hold a referendum on the adoption of the single currency. Having delayed euro entry until an unspecified date, the Marcinkiewicz (and later Kaczynski) government planned to bring the budget deficit under 3 per cent only in 2009, which implied overshooting by at least two years the deadline fixed in the 2004 ECOFIN recommendation. Significantly, unlike under previous governments, the achievement of nominal convergence with the budgetary criteria was no longer synonymous with seeking euro entry and no date was fixed.

The decision to delay entry was caused, in large part, by new political priorities of the governing parties. The PiS campaigned on a manifesto that heavily stressed social equality and solidarity, which were pitted against the liberalism of the Civic Platform (PO). Once in government, the PiS entered into a political pact and then into a formal coalition with two populist parties—the League of Polish Families (LPR) and the Self-Defence (Samoobrona), both of which supported increased public spending. Encouraged by high economic growth, the PiS-LPR-Samoobrona government embarked on implementing its spending programmes, including subsidies for farmers' petrol, birth premiums, pay rises for teachers, and higher disability benefits and pensions. It also had plans to reinvigorate public investments on roads and the rail network and to improve the functioning of courts and law enforcement. All in all, the governing parties had a strong preference for using the economic good times to achieve improvement in living standards and infrastructural upgrading rather than for undertaking politically sensitive fiscal rationalization (see Jankowiak 2006; Krzak 2005).

More importantly, the change in euro entry strategy stemmed from the perception of EMU as a threat to national sovereignty among the new governing elites. Unlike the Miller and Belka governments, which brought together euro-enthusiasts and euro-pragmatists, the PiS-LPR-Samoobrona coalition was composed of euro-pragmatists and euro-rejecters. Both the LPR and the Samoobrona strongly oppose the relinquishing of national monetary policy and consider EMU as an instrument of foreign control over the Polish economy (Karpinski 2005). In such circumstances, keeping EMU off the political agenda in the 2005–7 parliament can be interpreted as a key factor in ensuring the survival of the governing coalition. The new position on euro entry was also part of a larger shift in Polish EU policy. The Kaczynski cabinet was perhaps the most Euro-sceptic Polish government since 1989. It had a penchant for intergovernmental diplomacy, was unenthusiastic about attempts to reopen talks on the EU constitution, and adopted a strongly pro-American stance in its foreign policy. Hence, the government was naturally inclined to explore domestic room for manoeuvre on the date for euro entry.

The strongly populist and Euro-sceptic views of the PiS-LPR-Samoobrona cabinet brought it quickly into conflict with the NBP. After the 2005 elections, the governing majority set up a committee of enquiry to examine the NBP's role in the privatization of financial institutions since 1989. The move was widely perceived as a personal attack on Leszek Balcerowicz, the NBP governor, and chief architect of the Polish economic breakthrough, by a cabinet that contested the success of the post-communist transition (Karpinski and Smilowicz 2006). The government also wanted to use the committee to put pressure on the NBP governor in his capacity as chair of the banking sector regulator. This latter challenge was, however, frustrated by the Constitutional Court, which ruled the committee's brief to be unconstitutional. In early 2007, when Balcerowicz's term as governor ended, President Kaczynski nominated Slawomir Skrzypek, his close associate, as the new NBP governor. Soon after the confirmation of the appointment by the PiS-led majority, Skrzypek expressed major caution about Euro Area accession.

This policy reversal occurred in the absence of strong EU-induced incentives for Poland to enter the Euro Area. As a member state with a derogation, Poland was officially committed to euro entry, but the choice of strategy was firmly in the hands of the national government. Meanwhile, the constraints of the Stability and the Growth Pact (SGP) proved largely ineffective in inducing fiscal convergence and, hence, in bringing Poland closer to euro entry. Since May 2004, Poland has been subject to the Excessive Deficit Procedure (EDC) and required to bring its deficit below 3 per cent of GDP by 2007. It has had to submit annual convergence programmes and has been liable to sanctions in case of non-compliance with European Commission recommendations and ECOFIN decisions. Such sanctions typically range from public 'naming and shaming' to limiting access to EU funding. Indeed, Poland has been subjected to some form of sanction. After the Kaczynski government updated its convergence programme in January 2006, the Commission concluded that the new deficit reduction path clearly deviated from that advocated in the Council's 2004 recommendations. As a result, in November 2006, ECOFIN chastened Poland in public for taking inadequate measures to correct the excessive deficit within the deadline fixed by the Council.

At the same time, the SGP regime provided sufficient manoeuvring space for the PiS-led government to pursue its preferred fiscal policy (Glapiak and Jablonski 2006). The cabinet tried to undermine the ECOFIN decision on initiating the EDC by using legal arguments. It argued, among other things, that in 2004 the Council had no legal basis for initiating the procedure because it could only rely on fiscal data from before membership. In 2006, the government planned to ask ECOFIN to invoke the new rule in the SGP pact (negotiated by Gronicki in 2005), which allowed Poland to deduct a share of the cost of the pension reforms provided that the general government deficit was close to 3 per cent. Seeking to stay below 3.5 per cent—a value accepted by the Commission to be a cutting point in measuring the 'closeness' to the reference value—the Polish government promised to reduce the deficit to 3.4 per cent by 2007 in the convergence programme presented in November 2006.

The prospects for Poland's EMU membership improved somewhat when the early elections of autumn 2007 had cut short the term of the Kaczynski government. The new cabinet under Donald Tusk, sworn into office in November 2007, relied on a coalition of the Euro-enthusiastic Civic Platform (PO) and the Euro-pragmatic Polish Peasants Party (PSL). The prime minister appointed a well-known advocate of prompt EMU accession, Jacek Rostowski, as finance minister. Yet, judging from the initial statements in late 2007, the new cabinet is far from embracing a fast-track EMU entry. In its programmatic statement to the parliament, Prime Minister Tusk identified euro entry only as one of many priorities, and placed strong emphasis on the need to make the path to EMU 'safe' and 'least problematic'. In his first public address, the finance minister ruled out euro entry during the term of the 2007–1 parliament and was reluctant to specify any target dates (cf. Glapiak 2007).

Conclusion

This chapter offers three lessons for the study of the politics of EMU accession in Central Europe. First and foremost, it underscores the importance of domestic leadership in shaping national euro entry strategies. The decision to join is more likely, if both the finance minister and the central bank perceive membership of the single currency as a strategic policy goal. This coming together of minds occurred in 2002–3, when the Polish cabinet joined forces with the NBP to lay the groundwork for fast-track accession. If, however, domestic leadership is absent or divided, the process of Euro Area accession grinds to a halt. The effects of the Kaczynski cabinet's stance on euro entry serve as an illustration. The shaping power of domestic leadership should not come as a surprise. Membership of the Euro Area brings benefits that are long-term and diffuse, while political competition rewards policies that produce immediate and concentrated effects. The EMU challenge thus locks domestic actors in a collective dilemma. The presence of policy entrepreneurs is thus a key condition that increases the likelihood that the dilemma is solved and euro entry ensues (Zubek 2008a).

The second lesson is that national leaders on euro entry can be more or less successful depending on the constellation of domestic contexts. The Polish case demonstrates the significance of voter preferences. In 2002–3, Finance Minister Kolodko and the NBP received limited support for a fast-track euro entry, because the Polish electorate was largely unconvinced of the net benefits. The scepticism also extended to key social and business organizations. The chapter further illustrates the critical impact of domestic party political configurations on the room for manoeuvre of domestic leaders on euro entry. The disintegration of the SLD in 2004–5 frustrated Economics Minister Hausner in implementing the fiscal stabilization package, while the entry of euro-rejecter parties into the coalition supporting the Kaczynski government removed euro entry from the political agenda. Finally, the Polish story identifies the institutional setting as a crucial factor in determining the success of national leaders in euro entry. The limited agenda-setting and gate-keeping rights of Polish cabinets made it possible for members of parliament to water down fiscal reforms and to pass new spending legislation. In contrast, the high institutionalization of the central bank's independence reinforced its leadership in monetary convergence.

Third, the chapter shows that external constraints had a limited shaping influence on the domestic politics of euro entry. Before EU membership, the European Commission emphasized general macroeconomic stability and compliance with EU rules on central bank independence. At the same time, both the Commission and the ECB were highly reluctant to endorse a fast-track strategy for entry into the Euro Area. External incentives may have reinforced the NBP's independence and provided support to some of the domestic reform efforts. However, they had little impact on state fiscal capacity and provided limited empowerment to champions of Poland's fast-track euro entry. After EU accession, Poland has been officially bound to join the euro at some point, but the choice of the entry strategy has been in the hands of the national government. While the SGP framework has offered some inducements for fiscal convergence, it has also allowed sufficient manoeuvring space for the government to openly defy ECOFIN recommendations and pursue its preferred policies.

16

Sweden: Stability without Europe[1]

Johannes Lindvall

For more than three decades, ever since the collapse of the Bretton Woods system in 1971–3, Sweden has faced a strategic political and economic choice: to align its economic policies with the European core—represented by the 'Snake' (1972–9), the European Monetary System (1979–99), and the Euro Area (1999 onwards)—or to develop its own macroeconomic policy regime. Sweden made brief attempts to participate in both the Snake (in 1973–7) and the EMS (as a de facto member in 1991–2, when the krona was unilaterally pegged to the ecu). However, on both occasions the country ended up in economic crisis after a few years, and politicians abandoned the 'European' strategy in favour of other arrangements: a trade-weighted exchange-rate index (1977–91) and a floating exchange rate (1992 onwards).

By the early 2000s, the main political parties on both left and right were persuaded that the time had come to enter Stage Three of EMU, and hence to seek a more permanent alignment with the European core. But in a referendum on 14 September 2003, a large majority of voters rejected euro membership. Soon afterwards, the government declared that this issue would not be raised again in the foreseeable future. As in the United Kingdom (see Chapter 13 by Buller and Gamble), the euro has since virtually disappeared from public debate. In Sweden's most influential newspaper, *Dagens Nyheter*, the abbreviation EMU appeared 478 times in the year 2000, 275 times in 2001, 463 times in 2002, and 991 times in 2003—but only 160 times in 2004, 78 times in 2005, 40 times in 2006, and 27 times in 2007 (results generated from the database Presstext on 27 December 2007).

Why has Sweden alternated between a European and a domestic focus for economic policy? Why were Swedish governments initially reluctant to

[1] The author wishes to thank Carl Dahlström, Kenneth Dyson, Karl Magnus Johansson, Lars Jonung, Martin Marcussen, Daniel Naurin, and Åsa Vifell for their helpful comments on previous versions of this chapter.

participate in Stage Three of EMU? And why, when the Social Democratic government and the main opposition parties finally decided to seek membership, did they fail to convince the voters? The literature on European integration suggests two competing interpretations of this sequence of events. One interpretation is that Sweden is a peripheral European state whose governments have gradually been drawn closer to the European core through the economic, institutional, and ideological pull of 'Europeanization'—but remains an EMU-outsider due to the Euro-scepticism of its electorate. Another interpretation is that Swedish governments have only turned to Europe when that was seen as the most effective way to meet domestic political objectives, but turned away from Europe when the European option proved too constraining. This chapter argues that the evidence supports the second interpretation.

Sweden has only aligned its economic policies with the European core in periods when the major political parties and interest groups have agreed that economic policies required an external constraint in order to achieve domestic stability. In the late 1990s and early 2000s, when Swedish politicians deliberated on euro entry, this agreement did not exist. The failure of the ecu peg in 1991–2 was still fresh in everyone's minds, and Sweden was in the process of institutionalizing a new economic policy regime through a series of domestic reforms. The apparent success of the new regime explains the hesitation and conflicts over euro entry within the political elite. This hesitation and these conflicts contributed to the referendum outcome.

Unlike Britain and Denmark, Sweden is not formally exempt from the Maastricht Treaty's provisions on EMU (for a history of Sweden's relationship to the EU and the EMU in the 1990s and 2000s, see Table 16.1). During the negotiations on EU membership in 1993–4, the Swedish minister for European affairs declared that Sweden wished to join Stage Three of EMU in principle, but would only do so if and when circumstances allowed. Moreover, Sweden's participation in Stage Three would be conditional on the approval of the Swedish parliament. Swedish politicians have generally assumed that this declaration removes any legal obligation for Sweden to enter Stage Three. The legal relevance of the declaration is debated (see Bernitz 2000, 2002: chs. 2–3). However, as the Treaty does not give a specific date when states must enter or actively seek entry, the European Commission does not take action against member states that fail to prepare for Stage Three, or choose not to do so. When he learned of the Swedish government's 1997 decision not to enter Stage Three from the start, the Dutch Prime Minister Wim Kok—who was then chairman of the European Council—said that although he 'would have preferred another decision', the EU would not 'be calling out the police or firemen' to make Sweden comply (Agence Europe 7 June 1997).

According to all convergence reports issued in the late 1990s and early 2000s, Sweden fulfils three of the four Maastricht criteria, but not the criterion

Table 16.1. Important Swedish dates, 1990–2006

1990: 26 October. The Social Democratic government declares that it will apply for membership in the European Community.

1991: 17 May. The Swedish central bank pegs the krona to the ecu. 1 July. Sweden applies for membership in the European Community. 15 September. The parliamentary election results in a centre-right majority.

1992: 19 November. The central bank allows the krona to float.

1993: 1 February. Membership negotiations between Sweden and the EU member states commence. 9 November. The Swedish minister for European affairs declares that the final decision on entering Stage Three of the EMU will be made by the Swedish parliament.

1994: 30 March. Sweden and the EU member states reach agreement on the terms of membership. 24 June. The Accession Treaty is signed. 18 September. Elections return the Social Democrats to office. 13 November. Sweden holds a referendum on EU membership. The 'yes' side wins with a 52.3–46.8 majority.

1995: 1 January. Sweden joins the EU.

1996: 4 November. The main report of a major government commission of inquiry into the EMU issue, the Calmfors report, recommends a 'wait-and-see' policy. The commission regards the economic benefits of joining as uncertain.

1997: 4 December. The Swedish parliament decides that Sweden will not enter Stage Three of the EMU at its start.

2002: 29 November. The leaders of the parties represented in the Swedish parliament declare that a referendum will be held on Stage Three of the EMU.

2003: 14 September. The 'no' side wins the referendum on the euro with a 55.9–42.0 majority.

2006: 17 September. A centre-right government is elected. The new government soon reaffirms the previous government's declaration that no new referendum will be held in the foreseeable future.

---

of exchange-rate stability, which is natural given that Sweden has a floating exchange rate and remains a non-member of the Exchange Rate Mechanism, ERM II. There is no doubt that Sweden is economically prepared for euro entry. Sweden's decision to remain outside is a political choice. This chapter identifies the historical and political conditions of this choice.

European Integration and the State

Students of the European Union have long debated whether European integration should be explained with reference to the desire of member states to solve particular collective action and commitment problems, or with reference to European-level institutional and ideological dynamics that have pulled member states towards closer union. This chapter shows that in the area of monetary cooperation, Swedish political elites have been guided by domestic concerns, either because they want to or because they must in order to remain legitimate in the eyes of the voters.

In short, Swedish governments have only aligned exchange-rate policies with the European core when that was deemed necessary to maintain domestic economic stability. This behaviour fits well with the analysis of Alan

Milward (1992), who argues that there is no contradiction between national autonomy and European integration, since integration has in fact strengthened state capacity, at least in comparison with a counterfactual history of Europe without any European Community. In the immediate post-war period, which Milward is primarily interested in, the EC safeguarded a particular conception of the state and helped to secure a 'consensus' that governed politics in European countries in the first decades after the Second World War.

Sweden's path to EU membership and its relationship to European monetary cooperation are highly interesting cases from the point of view of this theory. As Milward (1992: 43) points out: 'The combination of welfare state and employment policy in Sweden represents the apogee of the concept of the nation as the improver of man's lot.' In other words, Sweden had an extreme version of the state model that European integration was meant to protect. But Sweden did not take part in the Second World War, and consequently required no support from any European political entity for post-war reconstruction. From a Swedish perspective, membership in the EC was not regarded as a source of support for the post-war consensus, but rather as a threat to the particular version of that consensus that emerged in Sweden—consensus around the 'strong state' (Lindvall and Rothstein 2006).

Sweden's policy of neutrality was one important reason for Sweden's reluctance to join the EC before the end of the Cold War. But so was a widely shared belief that Sweden's solutions to economic, social, and political problems were superior to the solutions of other states (Stråth 1993). After Bretton Woods, things changed somewhat, as Sweden came to depend more on its neighbours, but the idea that Sweden has 'a lot to be proud of' compared to other countries—as Göran Persson (prime minister 1996–2006) put it in a speech in 1996—still influences Swedish political discourse, especially when it comes to Europe (Höjelid 1999: 241).

My argument implies that the power of Europeanization is limited. Though a term with many meanings, political scientists commonly use 'Europeanization' to describe the effects of European integration on the politics and policies of European states (Olsen 2002: 934–5). European integration may have both 'direct' effects, such as legal requirements on states to change their policies, and 'indirect' effects (Hix and Goetz 2000: 10–11). The 'indirect' effects, in turn, may be divided into 'thin' and 'thick' effects (Dyson 2000a: 646–7), where thin effects manifest themselves through institutions and electoral alignments and thick effects involve the 'collective understanding of actors' (Cowles, Caporaso, and Risse 2001: 4). An analysis of Sweden's relationship to European monetary cooperation shows that while all these factors were active to some extent, the Swedish polity, politics, and policies remain defined by domestic political conflicts.

The European Option

In the Bretton Woods era until the early 1970s, Sweden was a part of a global system of exchange-rate cooperation, with fixed but adjustable rates. Sweden's exchange-rate regime in 1977–91 was also an attempt to maintain a 'global' focus with fixed—but as it turned out very adjustable—rates. The krona was pegged to an exchange-rate index, or 'basket', which contained all currencies that accounted for more than 1 per cent of Sweden's foreign trade, with the US dollar given a double weight since many of the goods Sweden traded in were denominated in dollars. From 1992 to 2007, Sweden's exchange-rate policy has been based on a floating exchange rate and inflation targeting.

In two other periods, Sweden's exchange-rate policy has had an exclusively European focus: 1973–7, when Sweden participated in the Snake, and 1991–2, when the krona was pegged to the ecu. Euro entry would have meant a return to this type of policy, albeit in a more permanent form.

When Sweden joined the Snake in 1973, the main reason was that Bretton Woods had provided stability for more than two decades, and European exchange-rate cooperation was regarded as an imperfect substitute. But a few years later, Swedish governments came to regard the Snake as too restrictive: in 1977, the newly elected centre-right government reached the conclusion that a large devaluation was necessary to improve the competitiveness of Swedish business, and to preserve full employment, which was a political objective of paramount importance at least until the late 1980s. As a result, Sweden left the Snake in the autumn of 1977, and devalued the krona by 10 per cent. Another two 'competitive' devaluations followed in 1981 and 1982 (Lindvall 2004: chs. 2–3; Lindvall 2006).

At the time of the October 1982 devaluation, key advisers to the government wanted to simultaneously change the exchange-rate regime, pegging the krona to the D-Mark. But on this occasion the politicians did not choose the 'European option'. When the finance minister, Kjell-Olof Feldt, presented this idea to the party leadership and the leadership of the main union confederation, LO, they believed that this policy would be too constraining, as Sweden would not be able to maintain low unemployment in the long run. Furthermore, they expected that the new Social Democratic government would be able to control inflation through income policies and a firm fiscal policy. At this time, there was thus no elite consensus around a European strategy.

In the spring of 1991, Sweden returned to the European fold, pegging its currency to the ecu. Although the ecu peg was unilateral—Sweden has never been a member of ERM I, or ERM II for that matter—this move was a way for the government to manifest Sweden's determination to join the EC. But it was also, importantly, a result of a previous decision to change domestic economic policies, making low inflation the main objective of economic policy. The ecu peg reaffirmed the government's commitment to this policy change.

In an interview with the author, Gunnar Lund—a state secretary in the Finance Ministry at the time and one of the ecu peg's chief advocates— describes the policy change as part of an overall economic policy shift: 'pegging irreversibly to the ecu' was about 'putting an end to all that we thought had characterized economic policy for too long—devaluation cycles and general sloppiness'. Swedish monetary authorities thus used Europe as an external constraint to impose stability on the domestic economy. There was broad political agreement on this policy. The economic research unit of the largest trade union had expressed some doubts about the government's 'hard currency policy' (LO 1990), but they were heavily criticized for this initiative, and soon fell silent.

Although inflation declined rapidly in the early 1990s, the attempt to maintain a fixed exchange rate failed. Sweden withstood initial attacks on the krona during the ERM crisis in the summer and autumn of 1992, but on 19 November, facing a new round of speculation, the central bank was forced to adopt a floating exchange-rate policy, which Sweden has followed from November 1992 until the present.

Stability Without Europe

The failed attempt to shadow the ecu in 1991–2 had important effects on Sweden's policies vis-à-vis euro entry. The exchange-rate crisis was associated with a deep financial and macroeconomic crisis, as open unemployment increased from less than 2 to more than 8 per cent of the labour force, and GDP growth was negative for three consecutive years (1991–3). This was a macroeconomic disaster. After 1960, there have been only two other examples of negative growth three years in a row in the 20 OECD countries that have been democracies since the Second World War: Finland (in the early 1990s) and New Zealand (in the late 1970s) (data source: Armingeon et al. 2006). It is quite natural that economic strategies based on a closer association with Europe were regarded with some suspicion in many quarters in the first years following this dramatic event.

Another important explanation for Sweden's EMU policies in the 1990s and 2000s is that the macroeconomic regime that was established in the 1990s was widely regarded as successful and legitimate. There was thus no need to turn to Europe to solve Sweden's macroeconomic problems.

After the floating of the krona on 19 November 1992, the government at first assumed that Sweden would soon return to a fixed exchange rate. The very next day, Carl Bildt, the prime minister, wrote an e-mail message to the finance minister, Anne Wibble (Bildt 1992). In the message, Bildt said that 'the "next step" is ERM-affiliation, and no intermediate steps are considered anymore. In my opinion, we should declare that it is our intention to peg to the ERM in order to become successful in the EMU. This gives long-term stability to economic policy' (translation by the author).

Two weeks later, on 3 December, the finance minister presented parliament with a programme for price stability, saying that 'in due course, we will return to a fixed exchange rate' (quoted in Andersson 2003: 243). The central bank governor Bengt Dennis—who later opposed euro entry in the 2003 referendum campaign—also assumed that a fixed exchange rate, within a European framework, was the natural option for Sweden. In a speech in March 1993, he took for granted that when Sweden joined the EU, it would participate in the ERM (Andersson 2003: 261). Thus, leading Swedish decision-makers were set on participation in European monetary cooperation as a way of institutionalizing the 'hard currency policy' they had pursued in the early 1990s. However, waiting for the situation in Europe to settle after the ERM crisis, Sweden developed its own macroeconomic regime, which has proven resilient.

The first element of the new regime was a new monetary policy strategy. Monetary policy was the most important macroeconomic instrument now that the exchange rate was floating, and in January 1993—two months after the fixed exchange rate was given up—the central bank introduced an inflation target of 2 ± 1 per cent, defined as a yearly increase in the Consumer Price Index, to replace the earlier intermediary exchange-rate target. This target has guided monetary policy since, even if the bank's methods of making monetary policy developed in the second half of the 1990s and in the early 2000s (for an overview of this period, see Heikensten 2003: 338–9).

The central bank measures inflation expectations and sets interest rates on the basis of prognoses that rely on these measurements (for an overview of the theory and practice of inflation targeting, see Truman 2003: chs. 2–3). The floating exchange rate and the policy of inflation targeting sets Sweden apart from its Scandinavian neighbour, Denmark. Although Denmark remains a non-member of the EMU—being exempt from the relevant provisions of the Maastricht Treaty—from a macroeconomic policy perspective, Denmark is a de facto EMU member, in the sense that its krone is pegged to the euro, and the government and the central bank behave as if Denmark were a part of the Euro Area (Marcussen 2002).

The inspiration and impetus for Sweden's monetary policy regime were not primarily European. The central banks that the Riksbank had most contact with regarding the new monetary policy regime were not the central banks of the EU member states in the ERM, but those of Canada and New Zealand, from whose policies it sought to learn, and the Bank of England, which was in a situation similar to Sweden's after Britain left the ERM in September 1992 (Andersson 2003: 246–7). And there are important differences between the monetary policies of Sweden (and Britain) and the policies of the ECB. The monetary policy of the ECB still has monetarist elements, but monetarism is regarded as substandard by the experts who advise on monetary policy in Sweden.

The general perception within Sweden is that the new monetary policy regime has worked well—not least when it comes to stabilizing wage bargaining, which was a constant concern for economic policymakers in the 1970s and 1980s. Before the 2003 referendum, many economists (notably Svensson 2002) declared that, while they were in favour of euro entry for political reasons, they believed that the Swedish Riksbank's organization and policies were superior to the organization and policies of the ECB.

The second element of Sweden's new macroeconomic regime was central bank independence. Sweden's Riksbank has traditionally been relatively dependent on the executive, although formally, it accounts to the parliament rather than the government. In practice, due to the positions of the finance ministers in this period, it became much more independent from the government in the course of the 1980s and 1990s. However, in legal terms the central bank only gained full independence in 1999. An amendment to the constitution states that no external authority is allowed to instruct the central bank in matters of monetary policy.

Central bank independence is the only major element of Sweden's macroeconomic regime that can to some extent be attributed to Europeanization. A government commission of inquiry concluded in 1993 that the central bank should be made more independent, but the Social Democratic members of the commission filed a dissenting opinion. After Sweden became a member of the EU, the Social Democrats supported constitutional reform, since an increase in central bank independence was required by the Maastricht Treaty. Some Social Democratic members of parliament and government ministers—including Prime Minister Göran Persson—were in favour of increased central bank independence because of its perceived economic and political benefits, not because of treaty obligations. But the internal opposition in the party would probably have made it difficult to push through any constitutional amendments if Sweden had not been under legal obligations to the EU. Thus central bank independence was partly, but not primarily, a result of 'direct' Europeanization.

The third element of the new macroeconomic regime was a set of budgeting procedures that were gradually introduced between 1992 (when this issue was first raised inside the Ministry of Finance) and 1997 (when the new Budget Act came into force) (Hallerberg 2004: 160–3; Molander 2001: 32–40). The new budget legislation is an illustrative example of the limited role of Europe in domestic reform processes. This important piece of legislation was introduced to improve the government's control of national-level budgeting, and to avoid excessive spending. With regard to influence from Europe, the bill introducing the new budget procedures (Prop. 1995/6: 220) mentions that 'rules increasing budget discipline' will make it easier for Sweden to meet 'obligations regarding public sector finances that follow from membership in the EU'. However, this remark is made at the very end of a section on the need for a more stringent budgeting process. It is preceded by arguments about the general benefits of such rules and regulations, and about Swedish experiences in the early 1990s. Domestic institutional reforms were thus mainly undertaken for domestic reasons, and EU concerns were only a minor part of the story.

Mark Hallerberg's comparative investigation of budget legislation in EU member states confirms that the fiscal policy changes in Sweden were not related to the EU or EMU membership. In fact, he argues that politicians deliberately avoided making the European connection explicit in the debate on these policy changes. Comparisons with other European states—showing that Sweden's budgeting procedures were weaker than most others—were important when the issue was first raised in 1992 (Hallerberg 2004: 167), but, overall, Sweden's budgetary reforms were a response to perceived domestic failures in economic policymaking.

With regard to the intensive reforms of its economic policy architecture in the mid- to late 1990s, Sweden has much in common with Britain, another EU member state that chose to remain outside the Euro Area (see Chapter 13 by Buller and Gamble). In both states, the failure of ERM entry/ecu pegging in the European currency crisis of 1992 led to an economic as well as a political crisis, which both states attempted to overcome by defining a new model of monetary policymaking, by making their central banks independent, and by introducing 'fiscal rules' to govern budgeting. But there are also important differences. In Britain, political and economic elites are more deeply divided over Europe, not only in general but also with reference to the euro specifically. So there is stronger 'retrenchment' in the British debate over Europe.

The Limits of Europeanization

With the possible exception of central bank independence, there is thus little evidence that the Swedish economic policy reforms in the 1990s were a result of Europeanization, either in the direct or in the indirect sense. Clearly, Sweden's economic policies have become more European in the sense that many of the more distinctive policies that Sweden pursued in the 1970s and 1980s have been abandoned, particularly when it comes to the very strong emphasis that governments used to place on full employment. But there is little evidence that Sweden changed policies because of pressure from EU institutions, a flow of economic ideas from Europe, or a desire to become a 'normal' European partner.

When it comes to policies outside macroeconomic policy proper, it is equally hard to identify any effects of EMU-related Europeanization. The discourse on welfare state reform in Sweden focused either on fiscal consolidation (mid-1990s) or on the argument that welfare programmes diminish labour supply due to overuse of the social insurance system (late 1990s–2000s). Political actors rarely point to Europe as a source of inspiration for domestic reform. In her study of Sweden's implementation of the European Employment Strategy, Åsa Vifell (2006: ch. 4) demonstrates that Swedish labour-market policymaking is 'decoupled' from the EU level. The negotiations with Sweden's EU partners are managed by a small group of civil servants in the ministries of finance and industry, whereas domestic policymaking is managed by other civil servants and by the national Labour Market Board. The reason for this decoupling, Vifell (2004: 25) argues, is that 'EU and European influence on Swedish employment policy was not a legitimate concept at the national level.'

As we shall see later, the prospect of joining the euro is often regarded as a threat to domestic institutions and practices. In the 2003 referendum campaign, opponents of euro entry argued that participation would lead to a homogenization of European welfare policies. The position of euro advocates, on the other hand, was that entry was a minor economic adjustment and a manifestation of Sweden's commitment to European integration (for an overview of the debate on the euro, as conducted in mass media, see Wallin 2004). It is to the referendum, the latest episode in Sweden's debate over the European option in economic policy, that we will now turn.

Elite Conflicts and the Politics of EMU

As a result of the failure of the ecu peg in 1992 and the institutional developments described in the previous section, there was no elite consensus in the early 2000s that Sweden needed Europe to sustain a stable economic policy regime. The situation was therefore very different from the two previous instances when Sweden aligned its exchange-rate policy with the European core, the mid-1970s and the early 1990s.

Politicians and economic experts hesitated for a long time when it came to euro entry. The outcome of the fixed exchange-rate policy in the 1980s and 1990s made the European strategy seem risky, and the government commission of inquiry that prepared the report on EMU, which formed the basis for the parliament's 1997 decision to 'wait and see', referred specifically to the crisis of the early 1990s. It argued that Sweden remained vulnerable and that it was desirable to retain the option of adjusting to asymmetric shocks by means of the exchange rate, at least for the time being. Meanwhile, as we have seen, there was increasing faith in the new domestic policy regime. It seems likely

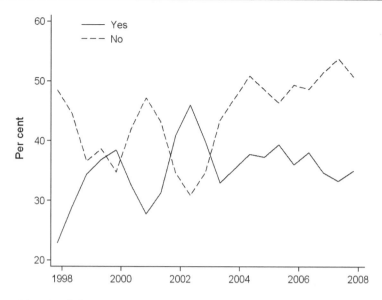

Figure 16.1. Swedish attitudes to EMU entry (adopting the euro), 1997–2007
Source: Statistics Sweden, *Partisympatiundersökningen*.

that hesitation and conflicts within the elite contributed to the common perception that EMU is a high-risk project with uncertain economic benefits, for
as John Zaller has pointed out (1992: 267), 'resistance to persuasion depends
very heavily on the availability of countervalent communications, either in
the form of opposing information or of cueing messages from oppositional
elites'.

The hesitation and conflicts within the elite were manifest on many levels.
First of all, although the referendum outcome is often described as a clash
between a euro-friendly elite and a euro-sceptic electorate, this characterization must be qualified. At the time of the referendum, a wide gap had
emerged between elites and masses, but this is mainly true for the period
immediately preceding the referendum. As Figure 16.1 shows, public opinion
has fluctuated since measurements started in the mid-1990s, and the solid 'no'
majority only emerged in 2002–2003. Meanwhile, politicians have become
more positive to the euro over time. Shortly before the 2003 referendum, 73
per cent of all members of parliament declared that they would vote for euro
entry, but this was a fairly recent phenomenon. For example, the proportion
of convinced 'euro-positives' in parliament increased from 45 per cent in
1996 to 58 per cent in 2002 (Brothén 2004: 68, 73). The Prime Minister,
Göran Persson, himself had genuine doubts about the EMU and took several
different positions over time—he was very sceptical only a few years before
the referendum (Fichtelius 2007: ch. 10; cf. Höjelid 1999: 293–4).

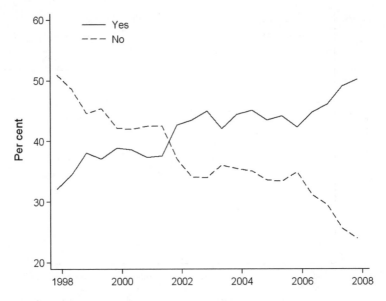

Figure 16.2. Swedish attitudes to EU membership, 1997–2007
Source: Statistics Sweden, *Partisympatiundersökningen*.

As Figure 16.2 shows, increasing public opposition to the euro is not a result of increasing opposition to the EU as a whole. A majority of Swedes is now in favour of Sweden's EU membership. In consequence, Lindahl and Naurin (2005) claim that, after the referendum, a *modus vivendi* has emerged in Sweden with regard to EU and the EMU. While politicians accepted the result of the referendum, and the government declared that there will be no new referendum in the foreseeable future, most Swedes have 'come to terms with the country's status as a full EU member' (Lindahl and Naurin 2005: 67). This interpretation is also consistent with survey-based research, which shows that, while attitudes to deeper European integration—such as the move to a more 'federal' Europe—are strongly correlated with attitudes to the euro (cf. Oscarsson, 2004), there is a weaker correlation between attitudes to EMU and attitudes to Sweden's remaining in the EU (as Figures 16.1 and 16.2 show). Swedes have come to accept EU membership, but resist further moves towards a 'federal' Europe.

Returning to the hesitation and conflicts within the political elite, several of the political parties are internally divided, both within the party leadership and among members and voters. Swedish politics is organized along a strong left-right dimension (cf. Oscarsson 1998), and the seven parties in parliament are divided into two distinct ideological blocs. But the EMU issue has split both blocs, as well as the parties themselves. The Left Party and the Green Party are both opposed to the euro, but the Social Democrats—the largest party in the left-wing bloc—are in favour. In the right-wing bloc, the Liberals, the conservative Moderate Party, and the Christian Democrats are for the euro, but the Centre Party, a former agrarian party, is against.

All parties are internally divided, but some parties are more divided than others. Among supporters of the Social Democrats and the Christian Democrats, only a minority voted for the euro (Holmberg 2004b: 83–6). Divisions over the euro placed some parties—notably the traditional Swedish 'party of government', the Social Democrats—under great strain. In their internal evaluation of the election in 2006, which they lost, the Social Democrats do not single out conflicts over the euro as a major explanation of the result. However, the report says that the underlying conflict between the 'EU-positive' party leadership and the 'Euro-sceptic' rank and file is a long-term problem that the party must address in the future (Socialdemokraterna 2007: 150). Furthermore, several ministers in the Social Democratic government at the time of the referendum—including the minister of industry Leif Pagrotsky, formerly a close associate of the prime minister—were openly opposed to euro entry.

Another important factor during the referendum campaign was that the Social Democrats and the main trade union confederation, LO, failed to reach agreement. Since euro entry would entail a loss of control over monetary policy, LO refused to support membership if the government did not create a central fund that would improve the effectiveness of fiscal policy as a macroeconomic instrument in the event of a deep economic crisis. The Social Democrats refused, since the government feared that voters on the right would be worried that this fund might be used for some sort of 'socialist experiment' (Fichtelius 2007: ch. 10). The lack of support from LO, which remained neutral, was important, as LO normally places substantial resources at the disposal of the Social Democrats in election campaigns. Furthermore, the split between the party and the unions was another signal to voters that the economic benefits of EMU are contested (Rothstein 2004).

Yet another elite-level conflict—and this was an important difference between the EU referendum in 1994 and the euro referendum in 2003—emerged within the business community. In 1994, very few business leaders opposed EU membership, which was expected to benefit most sectors of the Swedish economy as it opened up European markets. Although the main business organizations campaigned aggressively for euro membership in 2003, a number of high-profile business leaders voiced their opposition to the monetary union. One example was Rune Andersson, the chairman of Electrolux, a world-leading manufacturer of household appliances and one of Sweden's largest firms. In media coverage during the referendum campaign, 'entrepreneurs' (*företagare*) featured in 5 per cent of the 'yes' campaign's news space and in 4 per cent of the 'no' campaign's news space, so there was little difference. In contrast, official 'business representatives' (*näringslivsföreträdare*) were predominantly pro-euro: they represented 4 per cent of the 'yes' campaign's coverage but only 1 per cent of the 'no' campaign's coverage (Asp 2004: 47–9).

In the absence of an elite consensus that alignment with Europe was necessary to achieve general economic stability, different groups of voters evaluated the economic consequences of EMU very differently, which was one of the crucial factors behind the referendum outcome (Holmberg 2004a; Oscarsson and Holmberg 2004: 458–60). These different evaluations can be attributed to economic sectors (tradeables versus non-tradeables, private versus public) and the distribution of various assets (income, education, etc.) among individuals (Jonung 2004; Jonung and Vlachos 2007).

The absence of an elite consensus on the benefits of the euro also meant that domestic political conflicts were activated by the euro referendum campaign. Attitudes to European integration are more strongly associated with the left-right dimension in Sweden than in other member states. The reason is that deeper European integration is regarded as a threat to the welfare state (Oscarsson 2006). According to referendum study data, among voters who believe that welfare spending should be cut, the 'yes' side won 65–35. Among voters who believe the welfare state should remain or even expand—a much larger group—the 'no' side won with an equally large majority. Kumlin (2004) argues that differences in voting behaviour between the EU referendum in 1994 and the euro referendum in 2003 can be explained with reference to the fact that voters have come to associate Europeanization with a perceived decline of the welfare state.

The remarkable thing about the resolution of the euro issue is that, for all the political conflict surrounding it, its impact on Swedish party politics is small. Politicians have successfully kept this issue out of electoral competition. The two general elections in the 2000s (in 2002 and 2006) were fought over other issues. According to exit polls (see Hernborn, Holmberg, and Näsman 2006), only 20 per cent of voters in 2006 said that their position on the EU and EMU was important for their party choice—down from 28 per cent in 1998 and 2002, and lower than any other issue included in the poll (this was also the case in 2002). Party competition has a strong domestic orientation.

Conclusion

This chapter identifies the failed, unilateral attempt to achieve domestic stability by means of an ecu peg in 1991–2 as a turning point with regard to Sweden's relationship to EMU and European exchange-rate cooperation more broadly. In the late 1980s and early 1990s, Swedish governments had decided to change domestic economic policies, by de-emphasizing the full employment target and placing low inflation first on the list of economic policy objectives. Sweden turned to Europe—which at this time meant Germany—in order to manifest its commitment to this economic policy change, which governments elsewhere in Europe had already implemented up to 15 years earlier. If this strategy had not failed—if the European exchange-rate system had not all but collapsed in the early 1990s—Sweden might well have been set on a path where domestic political actors rallied around the new 'European' regime as a source of domestic stability.

Instead, Sweden developed its own monetary and fiscal policy regime in the mid- to late 1990s, with increasingly broad support among domestic actors. Labour-market organizations trusted the central bank to reach its inflation target, which provided for stable wage formation, while politicians gradually came to terms with the division of labour between the central bank, the executive, and the legislature. Thus, unlike in 1994, when the Swedish electorate was persuaded to join the EU in the midst of a severe economic crisis and when it appeared that Swedish institutions and economic policies had failed (Oskarson, 1996: 148), there was no sense of crisis in 2003. Like Britain, Sweden did not need Europe to achieve stability.

It could be argued that the 2000s were different from the 1970s and early 1990s since the government favoured an alignment with the European core because of a more Europe-centred political approach, not because the 'European option' was seen as an economic necessity. Prime Minister Göran Persson's development from EMU-critic to enthusiastic supporter is a case in point, since his arguments for the euro in the early 2000s focused on Sweden's place in Europe and the role of monetary cooperation in the wider process of European integration. Yet even if individual politicians were socialized into a more Europe-centred approach it was impossible for them to achieve their aims, for the historical and political reasons described in this chapter.

The role of the state in contemporary Sweden is different from the period Alan Milward (1992) referred to when he noted that the combination of welfare state and employment policy in Sweden 'represents the apogee of the concept of the nation as the improver of man's lot'. The 'strong state' that developed after the Second World War has been weakened, but the Swedish state still relies on its own capacity for reform and progress, not on European institutions. Or rather, it is a state whose legitimacy depends on domestic capabilities.

Part IV

Sectors, States, and EMU

17

Banking and Financial Market Regulation and Supervision

Huw Macartney and Michael Moran

Patterns of Financial Politics

A similar chapter in the volume which is the ancestor of the present one (Moran 2002) identified three critical entanglements that shaped the politics of finance and banking in the transition to the euro. Our chapter investigates how far they continue to be critical in the age of the euro itself.

The first entanglement concerns the *governance of financial markets*. Despite great national and regional variations, there is a consistent pattern to governance over the last quarter of the century, at least in the markets of the advanced capitalist world. On the one hand, there was a sustained crisis of the dominant institutions of prudential regulation and supervision, manifested in a continuing series of regulatory failures. The upshot of that crisis was the dismantling of dominant institutions of self-regulation, and their replacement by specialized regulatory agencies of a legal, or quasi-legal, character. On the other hand, this spread of public control over regulation was counterbalanced by a radical shift in the governance of central banking: by the rise of central bank independence, which largely meant the insulation of key decisions—notably control of short-term interest rates—from the influences of majoritarian democracy. This tendency was part of the wider rise of non-majoritarian institutions in economic government (Thatcher 2005; Thatcher and Coen 2005).

The second entanglement concerned *competitive practices* in financial markets. The age of the introduction of the euro was also the age of the financial services revolution: a revolution in competitive practices which saw, worldwide, the dismantling of barriers to market entry, to price competition, and to product innovation. The origins of that revolution lay in the United States, notably in bursts of innovation that originated as far back as the 1960s. By the

1990s, it was beginning to engulf the markets of the European Union, with London as a major 'router' of revolutionary shock waves. This tendency was naturally bound up with the changing governance of markets, both because forms of governance were an important source of competitive advantage and disadvantage and because the revolution in competitive practices was responsible for many of the prudential crises that forced the reconstruction of regulatory institutions (some of the wider global context is examined in Chapter 2 by Cohen).

The third entanglement was with the *'high' politics of European integration.* The 'road to Maastricht' and then 'the road to the euro' were elitist projects with numerous complex skeins, many of which are explored in separate chapters of this volume. One critical skein involved the management of the competitiveness of the EU as an economic system—a skein that, at the highest level, involved debates about whether a particular 'model' of capitalism was needed for the new economic space. That in turn was inseparable from issues to do with competitive practices in financial markets, for they lie at the heart of any 'high politics' vision of the future of the economy of the EU.

In the 'ancestor' chapter to this present contribution a key theme underlying these substantive issues was a procedural one: the separation between what might be called 'public politics' and the more technical 'esoteric' politics of financial government: the former engages actors in democratic politics, the latter is dominated by private interests. We use this as a simple framework to organize the substance of the chapter, concentrating in the first instance on the esoteric politics of the 'Lamfalussy Process'.

The Road from Lamfalussy: Building the 'Infrastructure of the Infrastructure'

The birth of the euro marked a renewed political impetus to achieve the single financial market as the infrastructure for European champions in nascent global markets. The accompanying Lisbon agenda then locked in the two interconnected strategies (one favouring stability, the other competition), which have driven the financial market project (see Chapter 5 by Marcussen). This section examines the development of the single financial market since 2000/1 to posit two related claims: first, the 'high' politics of financial integration is increasingly characterized by non-majoritarian technocracies and dominant financial elites; second, amidst a renewed competitive drive, historical differences fundamentally shape the politics of financial integration. Put differently, financial market elites increasingly share a common interest in a liberalized, integrated market yet are divided by their underlying business strategies. Thus, our answer to a critical question that runs through this volume—are we witnessing convergence or divergence?—is that we are witnessing both simultaneously. In developing our argument we consider first the 'Lamfalussy Process' and the Markets in Financial Instruments Directive (MiFID).

The single most important recent development in EU financial markets is the establishment of the Lamfalussy Process (for the historical and institutional context see Quaglia 2007*a*, 2007*b*). Its importance derives less from its legislative successes than from the deeper convergence that it signals. In essence, the Lamfalussy Process marks a *variegated neo-liberal* convergence. This embryonic trend has centred on the increasing acceptance by financial elites of greater capital market competition, though markedly more so in the lead up to the euro and immediately following its inception.

This convergence has been fuelled by the transnationalization of financial elites and recent moments of crises. The inception of the euro has heightened problems of unemployment and sluggish growth, notably in the leading economies of the Euro Area, whilst championing the cause of 'first-movers' such as the UK. Simultaneously and related, transnational investment service providers have both expanded cross-border business and, in turn, been compelled to lower transaction costs by similar developments elsewhere. A common liberal economic interest between transnational elites has therefore emerged.

The concept of variegated neo-liberalism rejects pre-defined categories which associate and tend to conflate Anglo-American arrangements with a liberal market economy (Hall and Soskice 2001) and which implicitly assume a monolithic, univariant conceptualization of neo-liberalism. Instead, financial market reform is best conceived as a *process* of neo-liberalization wherein neo-liberalism is *defined by* its diversity (Peck and Tickell 2002: 387). We argue that a common neo-liberal interest is apparent, whilst still allowing for path dependencies that engender conflicts in EU negotiations. Implicit in the chapter is the notion that the pro-competitive convergence evidenced in financial markets justifies the application of the term 'neo-liberal'. Set within this context the trajectory of the Lamfalussy Process can now be mapped.

From Cecchini to Lamfalussy

Since 2000 the single financial market has been characterized by a 'new' degree of consensus over opening and integrating financial markets and by ongoing conflicts over embedded market practices and underlying business strategies. The political impetus for both the Lamfalussy Process and the Financial Services Action Plan came at the Lisbon Council of 2000. From the outset they clearly represented a (re)commitment by the most significant member states to promote the integration project. Under the auspices of Baron Alexandre Lamfalussy a Committee of (twelve) Wise Men (*sic*) convened to examine the state of the EU financial market. Lamfalussy himself was emblematic of the cosmopolitan elite that shaped outcomes: he was of Hungarian descent but resided in Belgium; formerly a member of the Delors Committee, General Manager of the Bank for International Settlements (BIS) and the first President of the European Monetary Institute. His fellow Wise Men represented a similar elitist group, senior financial officials from the most influential member states. Thus the sociology of the group faithfully reflected the sociology of the elite that had propelled states along the road to the euro, as discussed in Moran's earlier chapter (2002).

Their findings highlighted many of the flaws previously recognized by both Commission reports (Commission of the European Communities 1988; Single Market Review 1997) and scholarly analysis in the 1990s (Steil 1995). Aside from overt protectionism the Report focused primarily on the technical, fiscal, and legal barriers that remained (Lamfalussy 2001: 14, 18–19). In addition, the timing of the Report coincided with the acknowledgement of the failures of several key pieces of financial services legislation (Capital Adequacy Directive I, Investment Services Directive). The proposals eventually adopted at the Stockholm Council (March 2001) sought to overcome these difficulties by strengthening the legislative capabilities of technical experts. This has further reinforced forms of Madisonsian 'governance' in EU institutions (Majone 1991, 1994, 1998, 1999).

The Lamfalussy Process, as it became known, stipulates that only framework directives need be approved by Parliament and Council before the technical details are 'filled-in' by a Committee composed of national regulators, the Committee of European Securities Regulators (CESR). The streamlined passage of legislation was intended to allow not only for the rapid passage of 'first-time' legislation but also for the simplification of subsequent amendments (see Figure 17.1). Already though, the Final Report of the Wise Men signalled the nascent 'consensus' amongst political and financial elites on the necessity and socio-economic benefits of an integrated, liberalized financial market (Lamfalussy 2001: 7–8).

Whilst the Process was initially limited to securities market regulation, the Wise Men advised that, if successful, it be extended to banking and insurance sectors. Two other committees have since been established; the Committee of European Banking Supervisors (CEBS) and the Committee of European Insurance and Occupational Pensions Supervisors (CEIOPS). This time, struggles over geographical locations and embedded market traditions were apparent. These conflicts largely involved market participants and political actors in Paris, the City of London, and Frankfurt who were concerned that the location of the committees would allow privileged access for interests in the given location. The result was a compromise which saw the CESR positioned in Paris, the CEBS in London, and the CEIOPS in Frankfurt, respectively. Significantly then, the Lamfalussy Process already signalled a new era of consensus and renewed political struggles.

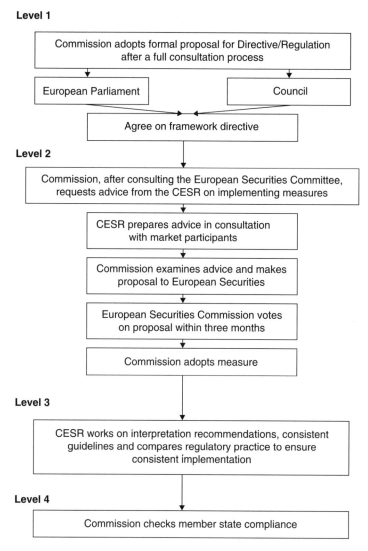

Figure 17.1. The 'Lamfalussy process'
Source: Lamfalussy 2001:6.

Under the Lamfalussy Process there are two significant consultation periods wherein dominant market elites formatively influence legislation (see Figure 17.1). This 'intimacy' between regulator and market participant, combined with the expertise and involvement of a non-majoritarian technocracy in the legislative process, has fuelled criticism of a democratic deficit. This assertion stands in contradistinction to those accounts which tend to emphasize the beneficial effects of closer industry involvement (Christiansen and Larsson 2007; Quaglia 2007*a*). Instead, our account argues that Lamfalussy consultation processes display an institutionalized structural bias towards the formidable resources of transnational financial elites (Macartney 2007). As we will see, these consultation periods have been focal points for the new stage in consensus and ongoing rivalries between these elites.

Since its inception the Process has contributed to the passage of over 42 Directives and has been hailed an overwhelming success (see McCreevy 2006). Its first seven years, however, have been beset by controversies and achievements that reveal the above nascent consensuses, ongoing path dependencies, and the inadequacy of conceptual 'models' of capitalism in a new era of transnational class solidarity and internal conflict.

These controversies, achievements, and path dependencies can be concretely illustrated by one particularly important example: the Markets in Financial Instruments Directive (MiFID) (Commission of the European Communities 2004). We choose this case because it has been the single most comprehensive piece of legislation within the Financial Services Action Plan. An updated version of the Investment Services Directive (Directive 93/22/EEC), the MiFID sought to provide the single passport for investment service providers and enhance competition between exchanges, multilateral trading facilities, and systematic 'internalizers' (banks and firms trading on account). According to Internal Market Commissioner Charlie McCreevy (2006), 'MiFID is a ground-breaking piece of legislation. It will transform the landscape for the trading of securities and introduce much needed competition and efficiency. It is good news for investors because it will both increase their level of protection and give them greater choice.' Given that increased competition will lower the cost of capital with the goal of stimulating growth and employment, the enabling effect of the MiFID in promoting competition between service providers cannot be underestimated. The passage of the directive, however, shows the complex connection between the pressure for liberalization and defence of particular, geographical interests—variegated neo-liberalism, in other words.

The historic conflict that underpinned the earlier Investment Services Directive was between investment firms and stock exchanges (Underhill 1997). The liberal environment within the City of London has been attractive historically (in the nineteenth century and the 1970s) to internationally mobile merchant banks and investment firms (Moran 1991; Polanyi 1944). In contrast, financial provision on the continent was typically dominated by credit institutions; typically this was mediated by the state (France) or through direct banking involvement (Germany) with industry (Zysman 1983). The contemporary financial services revolution rewrote these traditional distinctions, though French, German, and Italian 'big bangs' typically resulted in the expansion of domestic stock exchanges as providers of equity capital and the growing centrality of domestic credit institutions in the securitization of debt. As a result, the late 1990s continued to be characterized by transnational investment firms' dominance in UK markets and stock exchanges' dominance in continental Europe.

Two developments have dominated the progress of the MiFID: the concentration principle and the conflicts over price transparency clauses. The main protagonist of 'concentration' has traditionally been France, owing to the fact that the principle restricted trading to stock exchanges. This afforded exchanges a de facto monopoly and meant that even transnational firms (not physically located in the host country) seeking to gain access to French markets (remote access) were compelled to operate through host firms 'on-exchange'.

During the consultation process, however, it became clear that to facilitate a 'level playing field' both investment firms and stock exchanges would need to be able to compete for orders. In abolishing concentration MiFID therefore signalled a victory for foreign firms seeking to access continental European markets previously dominated by exchanges. It has effectively proven a monumental turnaround in financial market integration. Conceptually though, the abolition of concentration of orders is not simply reducible to the triumph of Anglo-American over Continental capitalism. This is evidenced by the fact that French financial elites chose to pitch their battle on another contentious issue. A close textual analysis of responses by the French Banking Federation (FBF) and the Association Française des Entreprises d'Investissements (AFEI) reveals surprisingly little contestation over the abolition of concentration and instead a focus on both pre- and post-trade price transparency clauses (Articles 21, 25, 27–30 MiFID). The details of the relevant clauses were contested at Level 2 (see Figure 17.1) and reveal the importance of the Lamfalussy Process to financial elite struggles.

In the words of the FBF, 'in order to respect the principles of transparency and non-discriminatory access to the different systems of order execution . . . the obligations of pre- and post-trade price transparency of internalisers (*read investment firms*) must be specified' (French Banking Federation 2005). Translated into the specifics of the two clauses the demands of French finance elicited the traditional conflicts between French/Italian and Anglo-American elites, suggesting the continued relevance of these conflicts within the broader emerging consensus.

The basic contention of French finance was that, '(a)nything other than (pre-trade transparency) would create pockets of liquidity known to only a privileged few with information not available to other investors. Not only would this interfere with equal access to information . . . but it would probably create a vicious circle whereby order internalisation contributes to wider spreads on regulated markets and MTFs. This in turn would make internalisation easier and more advantageous' (AFEI 2002). The 'market' rationale is therefore apparent; whilst competition between regulated market and 'internalizer' is essential, a lack of transaction information would provide 'internalizers' with an unfair competitive advantage. Understandably however, Anglo-American financial interests did not share this conviction; they argued that the inclusion of the price transparency clauses was an overt attempt to privilege already dominant regulated markets. The actual wording of the clause appeared to justify their contention.

Significant lobbying efforts were made by French finance, amounting to 'no fewer than thirty-six meetings...with twenty-seven MEPs' throughout 2002, as well as continuing their 'active efforts to raise awareness at the Council of Europe and the Commission' (AFEI 2002) concerning the necessity of stringent price transparency clauses. The results appeared to favour the French. In 2003 the CESR draft Directive implied that, at the time of the transaction, systematic 'internalizers' would be required to publish a 'firm bid-offer spread', a term which essentially meant declaring an agreed price for the securities at time of execution. The clause alarmed financial elites in both Frankfurt and London, who remonstrated that the legislation would allow the market to move against the 'internalizer'. Elites contended that, if prices are disclosed either before a trade is transacted or immediately after a 'larger' (relative to standard market size) trade is executed (i.e. before the full amount of shares can be sold on), then the investment firm risks other market actors making decisions in response to the disclosed price. In essence the investment firm would lose out as 'the market moved against the firm' (Steil 1995; ZKA 2005). The implication is clear; French and Italian elites had agreed to the increased competition between firms and exchanges only on the condition that transparency clauses were implemented that would avoid conceding a competitive advantage to firms. The exchange, unlike the firm, does not enter into a risk position itself and hence is not adversely affected by changes in the price of the security.

By 2005 the Directive had reached a compromise which looked set to satisfy Anglo-American and German elites more than it did French and Italians, having determined that transparency clauses are to vary in stringency according to the size of the order (AFEI 2005). These legislative details point to two key features in the ongoing revolutions in financial markets and the accompanying political controversies in the EU.

The first is that the high politics of European financial market integration are increasingly characterized by non-majoritarian technocracies and dominant transnational business elites; our brief study of the Lamfalussy Process substantiates this claim. Whilst democratically elected officials are engaged at Level 1, 'the devil' has *truly* been in the detail at Level 2. Here the Committee of European Securities Regulators and the institutionalized interests of transnational business tend to dominate debate. The resultant MiFID legislation typifies these intra-elite struggles.

The second related point is that new axes of allegiance are being realized whilst historical axes of conflict remain. Processes of neo-liberalization fuelled by recent economic crises and the transnationalization of business have given rise to increasingly shared interests in the single financial market. Nonetheless, embedded market traditions and divergent underlying business strategies remain enduringly significant. Talk of full-scale capitulation to Anglo-American investment and institutional investors is misplaced (Clift 2004).

These twin themes are simultaneously fuelling convergence and path dependencies. This analysis sits uneasily with certain monolithic, univariant varieties of capitalism theses and instead argues for an understanding of capitalisms as variegated; as defined by their diversities (Peck and Tickell 2002). Variegated neo-liberalism thus allows us to conceptualize the elite formations and intra-elite conflicts that are shaping the integration process under EMU.

The Road from the Euro: Patterns of Financial Governance

The essence of our argument is that the technical politics of financial reform in Lamfalussy show a complex pattern, which we have summarized as variegated neo-liberalism: a complex mix shaped by material and ideational forces. If we now turn to the 'public' politics of financial governance in the age of the euro, we find that they are shaped by equally complex forces. Three are especially important: the power implications of the government of financial markets; the links between 'Euro Area' governance and the wider global governance of financial markets; and the links with the 'high politics' of European economic integration.

At the core of all these questions lies a more straightforward one: how far in the period since the introduction of euro can we see any patterns of convergence or divergence in the government of financial markets? The question is central because the issue of convergence or divergence, either within the Euro Area or between the Euro Area and other groups, has formed a major theme in this volume.

The first theme to be examined is the power consequences of the establishment of the Euro Area system, and notably of the establishment of the European Central Bank itself. The earlier chapter (Moran 2002) argued that the process of institution formation, the shape of the institutions themselves, and the intellectual assumptions underlying the responsibilities of the new ECB amounted to what another observer has more recently called a central bankers' 'coup' (Wyplosz 2006: 230).

The coup represented a break from much of the development of central banking in the 1990s, which had seen the simultaneous assignment of independent functions to central banks, accompanied by a growth in the transparency and accountability of their operations, including for the performance of the newly endowed independent functions (see McNamara 2002). To what extent has that 'coup' been successfully pursued in the realm of policy practice in the intervening years?

The record is mixed. On the one hand, comparative evidence indicates that the ECB at foundation was designed as one of the least accountable of the 'big' central banks, and one most focused, because of its original policy mandate, on the 'sound money' ideology that guided its formation.

That accountability record continues to distinguish it, as it did at foundation, from the accountability practices of its big counterparts. Transparency as marked by details of the policy debates that lead to interest-rate decisions remain well below those available, for instance, from the Bank of England, still the Federal Reserve. More generally, in the words of Wyplosz (2006: 243):

Formally, (the ECB) reports to the European Parliament, but this is a weak form of accountability. The quarterly reporting sessions of the Chairman to the Parliament's Economic and Monetary Committee—in principle the Chairman is only bound to appear once a year—are accurately called 'Monetary Dialogue'. They certainly do not resemble the tough questioning of the Fed Chairman by the relevant committees of the US Congress.

Institutionally, therefore, the 'coup' has proved highly successful in practice: the practicalities of accountability have left the ECB strikingly independent of democratic political actors.

But the history of the core of the ideological compact that marked the 'coup' has been another matter entirely. Two features are striking and they both arise out of examination of the history of the Growth and Stability Pact, the 'policy' core of the 'bankers' coup'. The first, as well documented in other chapters, is that there have been striking divergences in the performance of individual national economies in the face of the Growth and Stability Pact; larger economies have breached the Pact, and got away with breaching it. The ability to enforce the 'sound money' terms, and thus the ideological foundations of the coup, has been fatally compromised by the behaviour of, especially, a number of the larger national economies—a compromising that led, in 2005, to a substantial dilution of the terms of the pact (Annett 2006).

We have seen that the record on what might be called the practicalities of policy implementation of the 'banker's coup' is a mixed one. What of supervision and regulation? The essential background is the continuing story of structural change in markets. The Vice President of the ECB summarizes these economically:

Four developments can be mentioned. . . . First, banks have considerably expanded their cross-border banking activities in Europe, especially in the wholesale and capital markets. For example, in 2005 cross-border interbank loans account for 30 per cent of total interbank loans and the share of cross-border bank holdings of non-bank securities in the total holdings of such securities by banks is more than 45 per cent; in 1997, however, both figures stood at around 20 per cent. Second, a number of large and complex institutions spanning several jurisdictions have emerged. Some of them are akin to pan-European players. The 14 largest of these cross-border banking groups already account for almost one-third of total banking assets in the EU. Third, large foreign establishments with a significant market share in host countries have become more prevalent, especially, but not exclusively, in the new Member States. Finally, cross-border banking groups are increasingly centralising key business functions such as credit risk and liquidity management, often cutting across separate legal entities in different countries (Papademos 2005*a*).

Against this background, four particularly important features have marked out the experience of the politics of banking supervision in the age of the euro.

The first—already alluded to above—is the incorporation of the process of policy change into the Lamfalussy Process. This development is best interpreted as a way of shaping the politics of supervision and regulation so as to enclose it in a space where market actors could exercise most control, to the exclusion of democratic political actors. To that end, the participation of the European Parliament in the process is minimal. As the Annual Report of the European Central Bank (2006*a*: 123) said in describing its response to the Commission's Green Paper on Financial Services:

In its contribution to this consultation, the Eurosystem underlined that an improvement to the EU framework for financial supervision should seek to exploit the potential of the Lamfalussy framework to the greatest extent possible. The Eurosystem also expressed its preference for a further rationalisation of financial rules through use of the main elements of the Lamfalussy framework. A clearer distinction could be made between core principles (Level 1 legislation) and technical details (Level 2 legislation).

The second is the failure of the ECB to expand its supervisory responsibilities to match its central banking duties. This is not the same as its supervisory expertise: as Quaglia (2007*b*) shows there we see significant investment of institutional resource. There are two good reasons for this failure. The first is that the emergence of the ECB coincided with an important change in the distribution of regulatory responsibilities at national level in many of the most important national members, not only of the Euro Area but also of the wider EU. In the UK and Germany there emerged specialized financial supervisory institutions.

Though there were contingent reasons in each case—such as the massive prudential crisis that led to the collapse of Barings in the UK—the development signalled an important paradigm shift in the world of financial supervision. It involved an abandonment of the historically engrained notion that central bankers had primary responsibility for managing the prudential safety of a financial system, at least in a European setting.

The development of specialist supervisory agencies at national level had a second important impact: it created a set of institutional interests standing in the way of any appropriation of supervisory responsibilities by the new central bank. That helps explain why the framework for the development of supervision is heavily intergovernmental in character—dominated by committees like the CEBS (see Committee of European Banking Supervisors 2006).

In one sense, therefore, the 'weight' of supervisory power is weighted to the national level. In another sense, it is weighted to levels that transcend not only the Euro Area but also the whole of the Union. The important developments in prudential supervision in recent years have reflected global rather than European negotiations. In the words of the Commission of the European Communities (2005a: 15):

Increasingly, standards and best practices are set and defined at global level, for example on accounting, auditing and banking capital requirements. Considering the size of the EU market, and Europe's experience in pragmatically uniting the legitimate call for harmonised rules and the diverging needs of different markets/cultures/players, the EU must have a leading role in standard setting at global level.

The most important instances of this process are the results of the workings of the Basel-based Bank for International Settlements, for over 30 years the main institutional arena for the negotiation of international prudential banking supervision arrangements. Its most important recent product is the development of a system of capital measurement and capital standards commonly abbreviated as Basel II (Bank for International Settlements 2006). What it striking is the extent to which the Euro Area is a 'taker' of these standards. As the European Central Bank (2006a: 123; also 2006c) noted:

At the European level, Basel II has been introduced into EU legislation by amending the Codified Banking Directive and the Capital Adequacy Directive. The European Parliament and the EU Council adopted the final legislative texts in September and October 2005 respectively. Member States will have to amend national law to incorporate the new rules, which will become applicable from 2007 onwards. In addition, at the end of 2005 the BCBS undertook a fifth quantitative impact study (known as the 'QIS5') of the new capital rules.

The reason is fairly obvious, and links to our fourth and final factor in the supervisory equation. The prominence of the Basel process takes us back to one of the key arguments of the original chapter: that everything happening within the system of financial governance in the EU as a whole, and in the Euro Area, had to be viewed through the reflective lens of the worldwide global financial services revolution. A similar process occurred in the related regulatory domain of accounting (European Central Bank 2006a: 124). This is partly a matter of emphasizing how far the institutional arenas, and the policy choices, available to regulators are set and constrained by this wider global setting—because that setting is a key source of opportunities and problems. But it is also a matter of something else: it is a key link between the esoteric business of financial regulation and supervision, and the wider domain of high politics: the domain created by the continuing debate about European responses to the global challenges of competitiveness.

This takes us full circle in this chapter, for the Lamfalussy Process, as we noted at the outset, was a central part of the Lisbon Strategy—that part which attempted to create 'the infrastructure of the infrastructure' which would equip the members states of the EU with economies capable of meeting the challenges of global competitiveness. It thus remains central to a 'strategy' mired in immobility. The 'relaunch' of the Strategy at the 2006 European Council was a recognition of the problems, evident even in the restrained language of the Commission of the European Communities (2005d) in its review of the strategy:

Today, we see that progress has at best been mixed. While many of the fundamental conditions are in place for a European renaissance, there has simply not been enough delivery at European and national level. This is not just a question of difficult economic conditions since Lisbon was launched, it also results from a policy agenda which has become overloaded, failing co-ordination and sometimes conflicting priorities.

State Power, Convergence, and the Euro

The 'ancestor' chapter to this contribution ended on a questioning note: would the attempt to resurrect the spirit of Montagu Norman prove successful? In other words, could monetary government be controlled by an integrated financial oligarchy, coordinated by a central bank? In two senses, it has proved successful, in two important senses not.

Our discussion of securities regulation portrays a world where elites united by a commitment to economic liberalism manoeuvre varying forms of this liberalism (hence variegated neo-liberalism) in a highly technical discourse in a world of esoteric politics, well cut off from democratic politics. And our discussion of the institutional practices of the ECB in the Euro Area shows that the institutional template for a central bank powerfully insulated from democratic politics has indeed been realized.

But there are two big complications to this relatively straightforward account of policy as shaped by elitist epistemic communities. The history of the Stability and Growth Pact has shown that the attempt to convert this central bank hegemony into the fiscal sphere has met with limited success faced with the pressures on national governments that do indeed have to respond to the demands of democratic politics (see Chapter 4 by Bridwell and Hallerberg).

The second complication is more fundamental. The original chapter was drafted and published before the major accessions to the Union of the former Soviet colonized states of eastern Europe. Nevertheless, a serious shortcoming was its failure to recognize the very different patterns of financial politics that were already at work in this sub-set of accession states. These patterns of financial politics have become of central importance not only to the Union but also to the Euro Area and to its financial politics, since accession. The complexity of financial politics here is striking, and hard to condense in summary form (see Dyson 2006c).

A predominant (though not universal) pattern of the 1990s was a kind of 'wild-west' politics. Banking supervision and control, either at systemic level or at the level of individual enterprises, was primitive or non-existent. Corrupt or semi-corrupt modes of privatization had produced banking systems that were uniquely unstable. Banking crises, and their consequences for the wider populations, meant that supervision became highly politicized. In the accession phase the imposition of control on this chaotic world involved three processes. First, banking ownership has been transformed through the domination of the system by foreign institutions: By 2003, over 70 per cent of banking sector assets in eight of the new accession states were foreign-owned (Nagy 2006). The unambiguous conclusion in Nagy's survey is that this late burst of foreign-owned privatization has significantly raised the quality of prudential control at the level of the individual enterprise.

Second, and even more important, there has been an extension both of the institutional 'reach' of the ECB and of the epistemic world of central banking in the Euro Area. Since that epistemic world is an extension of the wider world institutionalized in the Bank for International Settlements and the 'Basle' processes, this process means an extension of the global epistemic banking regulatory community. The substantive consequence is the extension (from 2006) of the supervisory world encapsulated in the Basle II (Bank for International Settlements 2006). We saw earlier that, despite lack of clarity over the institutional allocation of responsibilities for financial supervision in the Euro Area, the ECB has built and consolidated its resources of prudential capacity and expertise. These resources were further strengthened by its role in stabilizing markets in 2007 in the wake of the crisis caused by the problems of 'sub-prime' mortgage lending in the United States. In consequence, it has acted as a significant agent of institutional and policy transfer of central banking supervisory expertise and, in addition, of ECB institutional support for embattled central bankers in the accession states (see Chapters 14 and 15 by Greskovits and Zubek). This support has been necessary because the attempt to extend the epistemic central banking community has in some individual national cases confronted the raw politics of economic and political change in states still attempting to make a painful transition to democratic capitalism. Though experience differs significantly across individual states, Johnson summarized the wider limits of the project as follows:

Post-communist central banks have changed radically since 1989, making institutional transformations from command economy cash cows into independent guardians of price stability... The post-communist central bankers now share the trans-national central banking community's belief that protecting price stability and central bank independence is the key to economic development in democratic states. However, this recent, externally driven transformation process means that these central banks had converged ideologically and institutionally with EU norms without the need to develop significant political support or economic credibility among domestic actors. East Central European politicians and publics accepted independent central banks as an EU requirement and as a symbol of economic modernization and sovereignty, not because they believed deeply in the institution and its core goals. As a result, in the post-accession period the central bankers have found themselves politically embattled and undermined because other domestic actors often did not share their policy priorities and did not always see the central banks as credible and trustworthy actors.

(Johnson 2006: 363)

In a volume on European *states* and the euro issues of convergence are naturally central, for they impinge directly on the kind of experience that individual members have of the integration process. Much of this volume is taken up with making sense of those individual national experiences (as is Dyson's 'companion' volume, 2006c). In a synthetic account of a sector, of the kind offered in this chapter, much of that individuality of experience is lost. In addition, 'convergence' is itself a notion with many layers of meaning: of process, of policy substance, and of outcome. The last is particularly important because, in the final analysis, integration is about market outcomes. Yet the bias of this chapter is about the first layer of meaning, and for a particularly important reason: process is both critical to substance and outcomes, and is in turn joined reflexively to those two other levels. As the European Central Bank (2006c: 66) says, in speaking of the progress of financial integration:

While the euro has generally acted as a major catalyst for the integration of the euro area financial markets, the degree of integration differs from market segment to market segment, with integration being more advanced in those segments that are closer to the single monetary policy, above all the money market.

In short, what we get is not a one-dimensional pattern of integration, but a complex, changing mosaic.

We have to give a similarly conditional answer to another key question that concerns this volume: what these changes and processes have done to state power. There can be little doubt that a key institutional consequence of the introduction of the euro has been to create a significant new public power, in the form of the ECB. Despite scepticism about its role as a global

339

currency manager (see Chapter 2 by Cohen), the ECB is emerging, as we saw above, as a major shaper of the transnational epistemic community of financial regulators, especially of banking regulators. Yet our account of the processes of negotiating regulatory change under Lamfalussy makes it hard to speak of any simple language of the public and the private: the highly technical world of financial politics is one where the nominally private and the nominally public are inextricably entwined. Nor, even, can we speak of the world only of the Euro Area. Our picture of variegated liberalism also dissolves some other conventional distinctions, such as that between 'London-centred' and 'Frankfurt-centred' coalitions. Perhaps the greatest consequence of the first decade of the euro is to make us rethink these well-established nation-based categories.

18

Wages and Collective Bargaining

Nick Parsons and Philippe Pochet

Since the introduction of the euro on 1 January 1999, monetary policy is no longer the preserve of national governments or central banks but of the European Central Bank (ECB). Although fiscal policy remains under the aegis of national governments, European budgetary constraints are present in the form of the Stability and Growth Pact (SGP). Essentially, Euro Area governments can no longer increase the money supply through interest rates or public spending in the hope of soaking up unemployment. In addition, a single European currency deprives national governments of the recourse to currency devaluation as a tool for improving economic competitiveness. Furthermore, a single currency enhances the transparency and comparability of wage levels across the Euro Area states. An additional problem is that the product and financial market integration at the heart of EMU is not mirrored by any federalist fiscal approach. Euro Area states cannot rely on the transfer of funds from one part (state) of the monetary union to another in order to secure adjustment to asymmetric shocks (which affect some states or regions but not the Euro Area as a whole). Given linguistic and cultural obstacles, labour migration is also unlikely to play an adjustment role in a near and medium term, as it can in optimum currency areas (Mundell 1961). Therefore, competitive wage levels and unit costs compared to other states become all the more important for national economic growth and employment.

Prior to the introduction of the euro many feared that adjustment would take place through 'regime competition' (e.g. Rhodes 1998). In other words, harsh neo-liberal policies of tax reduction, welfare state retrenchment, employment flexibility, wage moderation, and a downwards spiral in working conditions would be implemented in order to provide the most advantageous conditions for retaining and attracting the internationally mobile investment capital necessary for job creation in an increasingly internationalized economy (Martin 1999). On the other hand, coordinated wage bargaining could counter such pressures. The pressures on wage bargaining are of differing natures: objective, as wage increases beyond productivity can no longer be compensated by a national currency devaluation, and socially constructed as different possibilities exist (multiple equilibria) to offset this change (Dyson 2000a; Natali and Pochet 2007). Changes in wage bargaining will, therefore, be a function not only of the new economic environment of EMU but also of the interaction between multiple actors within this new environment.

Here, we first review some theoretical arguments concerning actors' strategies with respect to wage bargaining. We then present and evaluate the two main dynamics at work, social pacts at national level and wage coordination at EU level. The third part briefly presents the challenges linked to the ongoing enlargement of the Euro Area. Part four analyses recent developments, with respect to their timing and fit/misfit in terms of inflation, and the strategies of the actors.

Which Wage Policy Regime Under EMU? Actors' Strategies

Where a strong independent bank is present, as in Germany before EMU, labour-market actors, and particularly unions, have a strong incentive to reach non-inflationary pay deals in the knowledge that the central bank would react by increasing interest rates, thereby provoking a rise in unemployment, should they fail to do this. Under EMU, however, wage settlements in one state (with the possible exception of Germany) will not have an impact upon ECB policy, which is supposed to cover the whole of the Euro Area. The incentive for national wage moderation could therefore decline as ECB reactions to national pay settlements and their potential negative externalities are no longer internalized by unions. The shift is towards a *de facto* 'de-coordination' of pay bargaining in the Euro Area. On the other hand, the risk that inflationary wage settlements will cause a rise in unemployment could lead to 'beggar-thy-neighbour' strategies to preserve jobs. This is an important argument for coordinating national wage bargaining systems and actors (see Crouch 2002; Janssen and Watt 2006).

For employers, more intense international competition, a desire for greater flexibility linked to changes in work organization, and a desire to limit the role of unions as national actors may see them push for more decentralized wage bargaining. Furthermore, the internationalization of companies means that they will be less likely to accept national wage policies. EMU is certainly not the main driver of such developments, but it provides export firms with an incentive to reduce unit labour costs and thereby improve competitiveness by pushing for structural reforms of fiscal, welfare state, labour market, and wage policies. Changing economic structures are also important. Increasing service-sector specialization means that this sector now accounts for over half of employment and value added in all Euro Area states. The dominance of small- and medium-sized companies in the sector (Urbanski 2007) along with below-average unionization rates can be expected to increase pressures for decentralized wage bargaining while reducing the unions' capacity for coordination.

Under EMU, the state still has a central role, particularly in promoting reforms and strategies aimed at the control of inflation in order to cope with the new monetary regime (Hancké and Soskice 2003). Theoretically, this could be achieved by collective wage restraint or by linking pay and pay increases to individual productivity. On the one hand, then, this means supporting wage decentralization. On the other hand, the state has to ensure stability in the case of adverse economic circumstances, which means supporting wage centralization/coordination. We could, accordingly, expect the state to follow an ambiguous policy, but in any case to try to keep control of the variables left at national level.

From a strategic choice perspective, then, we could expect four possibilities: more decentralization (the preference of the employers); more social pacts at national level (the preference of the state and 'second best' for the employers and trade unions); more coordination (the ambiguous preference of the unions); and a renewed diversity within a multi-level governance framework. The position of the state is more ambiguous: while decentralization could promote wage restraint and competitiveness, a perceived need to control the economic variables remaining at national level could also result in preferences for coordinated wage bargaining at the national level.

Of the four possibilities, we will not analyse in depth the decentralization possibility. This is an ongoing, long-term perspective embedded in a global context (Calmfors 2001; Visser 2002), whereas in the short and medium terms, collective bargaining has remained multi-level, with the sector level dominant in most EU-15 states (Visser 2004: 38–9). Neither will we develop the multi-level approach, which provides a general descriptive framework but does not allow us to distinguish the main underlying dynamics at work.

The Dynamics at Work: Social Pacts and EU Coordination

According to Fajertag's and Pochet's analyses (1997, 2000), the process of wage setting became *more* centralized in Belgium, Greece, Italy, Spain, and Portugal over the course of the 1990s, while 'at the national level, new tripartite approaches were taken in 11 Member States' (European Commission 2000*b*: 2), a phenomenon related to the conclusion of social pacts.

This has, indeed, been the most significant development and an increasingly widespread phenomenon since the early 1990s as far as collective bargaining is concerned, although two landmark agreements—the Dutch Waasenaar Agreement of 1982 and the Irish 'National Recovery Programme' of 1987—date back earlier. In line with the Dutch precedent, wage moderation is central to these pacts. Indeed, in all the social pacts signed in the 1990s—in Belgium, Finland, Greece, Ireland, Italy, and Portugal—agreement was found on wage increase formulae. Four agreements (Belgium, Ireland, Italy, and Portugal) explicitly mentioned EMU as a motivating factor in the conclusion of the agreements (European Commission 2000*b*).

However, the sustainability of social pacts under EMU has been questioned. First, in the 1990s, social pacts were most prevalent in those states believed to be facing the greatest difficulties in meeting the Maastricht criteria of low inflation, a stable currency, and reduced public debts. Once they qualified for EMU, such constraints were attenuated, along with the hard sanction of non-entry, alleviating the need for national concertation, particularly with the SGP being less constraining than anticipated. In addition, the launch of the single currency coincided with a more favourable macro-economic context of higher GDP growth, declining inflation and unemployment, and improved national finances in a number of EU states, giving governments a wider margin for manoeuvre within which to operate while still meeting their commitments in their stability or convergence plans (Hancké and Rhodes 2005; Natali and Pochet 2007).

Furthermore, social pacts depended upon a consensus between the state and the social partners about the risks associated with EMU in the qualification period. However, tensions re-emerged over wage moderation, labour flexibility, welfare reform, and further decentralization of bargaining after 1999. In Germany, in 2003, the tripartite national forum, the Alliance for Jobs, set up in 1998, broke up after the unions withdrew their support over the issue of pay moderation (Dyson 2006*a*). In Portugal, the government failed to reinvigorate social pacts on welfare policy, labour-market regulation, and incomes policy, as employers preferred decentralized wage setting. In Italy, the 2002 Pact for Italy was not signed by the CGIL, which opposed certain labour-market reform measures, while national social dialogue broke down completely in 2004 when the union refused to discuss a decentralization of the country's collective bargaining structure. Even where social pacts appear to have become an institutionalized mechanism for pay setting and wider reform, tensions have appeared since 1999 in states like the Netherlands (2004), Finland (2004), Belgium (2005), and Greece (2005). In Belgium the cross-sectoral agreement was rejected by the unions over the questions of flexibility and pay but was implemented by the government. In Greece the unions prematurely ended the 2004 agreement with a strike over pay and conditions in 2005, with no new agreement signed until April 2006 following intense conflict (EIRO 2006*a*).

Nevertheless, social pacts have proved remarkably resilient under EMU. Indeed, new national agreements on incomes policy have been signed for the first time in Spain since the introduction of the euro, while cross-sectoral agreements or pacts have continued to be signed on a regular basis in Belgium, Finland, Greece, Ireland, and the Netherlands (see Table 18.1). This resilience is related to some features that social pacts share across states despite the inevitable national variations in form and content.

While wage moderation is central to these pacts, they are not 'hard', centralized incomes policies, but a form of 'soft' coordination or regulation. Indeed, the pacts signed in all states provide wage guidelines or recommendations and allow for lower-level negotiation of concrete wage rises, with the exception of Ireland. Even in the Irish case, though, there is room for flexibility in the system, with 'inability-to-pay' clauses protecting companies in difficulty.

More generally, Table 18.1 shows that social pacts link wage moderation to wider issues such as economic growth, employment, labour-market flexibility, vocational training, and social security reform. Again, though, they usually provide framework agreements for wider reform rather than concrete prescriptions for change. Exceptions generally occur when quantified tax cuts and/or social security contribution reductions may be proposed by government in order to facilitate an agreement (e.g. in Finland). In these cases, wage moderation is compensated by an increase in the real wage once social security and tax payments are taken into consideration. However, qualitative and welfare issues are dealt with through the setting of targets and/or devolution to further negotiations and/or working groups. Furthermore, the focus of reform in these areas is also oriented towards greater economic competitiveness and tends to focus on supply-side issues such as vocational training and more flexible working time, with welfare spending linked to 'activation' programmes rather than income redistribution (Donaghey and Teague 2005: 483). Social pacts are thus aimed at creating employment by reducing overall labour costs and are oriented towards competitiveness, low inflation, and the control/reduction of public debts in order to satisfy the stability and convergence criteria of EMU.

As a result, in the years following the introduction of the euro, trends towards moderation and convergence appear to have continued (European Commission 2003*b*: 100–7). Furthermore, the EU Broad Economic Policy Guidelines (BEPGs) appear to have been respected as far as wage developments reflecting price stability and productivity gains are concerned (European Commission 2003*b*: 103, EIRO 2006*b*: 8). The result is a trend towards declining real unit labour costs within the Euro Area, the EU-15, and the wider EU (Table 18.2).

However, wage rigidity is still seen as a problem by the Commission and the ECB. The Commission's biannual industrial relations report (European Commission 2004*a*: 47) notes that 'The problem of limited nominal wage adjustment has come up in a number of euro states...Employees are not yet ready to accept downward flexibility of wages, even if low wages are

Table 18.1 Social pacts in EU-15 member states 1999–2006

Country	Year	Wage guidelines	Other major themes
Belgium	1998	Two-year intersectoral agreement for the private sector sets maximum 5.9% for 1999–2000, on the basis of a recommendation by the Central Economic Council which takes into account wage increases in France, Germany, and the Netherlands	Vocational training, lower labour costs, job creation, work sharing, equal opportunities
	2000	Two-year agreement sets indicative pay 'norm' of 6.4% for 2001 and 2002	Working time, training, older workers, reduction of employers' social contributions, harmonization of white- and blue-collar worker status
	2003	Two-year agreement sets indicative 'norm' of 5.4% for 2003 and 2004	Promoting employment and training, reduction of employers' social contributions, harmonization of white- and blue-collar worker status
	2005	Pay norm of 4.5% set for the private sector for 2005–6	Investment in innovation, overtime (flexibility), low pay, redundancy
	2006	Pay norm of 5% set for 2007–8. Minimum wage increased	'Active ageing', outplacement, tax cuts, reductions in overtime costs, vocational training, and paid leave for training
Finland	1997	Two-year intersectoral framework incomes policy agreement based on the 1995 agreement of the national tripartite incomes policy commission that wages should rise in line with inflation targets and productivity growth	Working groups to examine working time, equal opportunities and local bargaining, tax and social security cuts
	2000	Two-year agreement, to be implemented by sectoral agreements: rise of 3.1% in 2001 and 2.2% in 2002	Working time, holidays, unemployment benefit, labour-market issues, training, employment legislation, low pay, tax cuts
	2002	Two-year agreement (2.9% increase in 2003 and 2.2% in 2004)	Working time, training, partial care leave, worker representatives, gender equality, foreign worker rights, increased unemployment benefit, tax cuts
	2004	Two-and-a-half year agreement: 2.5% increase in 2005 and 2.1% in 2006	Greater income differentiation, improved redundancy protection, income tax cuts, particularly for low pay, gender equality, training and education, improved status for workplace representatives
Greece	1998	Two-year national collective agreement for the private sector, based on 1997 Confidence Pact which recommends that wages should rise in line with inflation and national productivity growth	Working time, especially reduction, bargained over at all levels, paid annual leave
	2000	Two-year agreement setting minimum increases	Framework for lower-level bargaining, annual leave, maternity leave, social insurance, profit sharing
	2002	Two-year agreement giving rises of 5.4% in 2002 and 3.9% in 2003	Working time, redundancy compensation, annual leave, parental leave
	2004	Two-year agreement giving minimum rises of 6% in 2004 and 5.5% in 2005	Increased severance pay for blue-collar workers, new forms of special leave, older workers, working time referred to further negotiations
	2006	Staggered increase in minimum wage (2.9% on 1.1.06 and 1.9.06, 5.1% on 1.5.07)	Severance pay, telework, vocational education and training, family support, and promoting female employment

Country	Year		
Ireland	1997	Partnership 2000: 9.25% over 39 months	Improve competitiveness, fulfil Maastricht criteria for EMU, tax relief measures, employee share ownership
	2000	Programme for Prosperity and Fairness: 15.8% increase over 33 months	Improved public investment, fulfil 'European stability pact', profit sharing, minimum wage, 'family friendly' policies, tax cuts, social welfare, and equity measures
	2003	Sustaining Progress: pay to rise by 7% over 18 months (8.9% in the public sector)	Compliance measures, improved statutory redundancy pay, increase in minimum wage, worker representation, public sector modernization
	2004	Second half of the pay element of Sustaining Progress negotiated: 5.5–6% over 18 months	Increased maternity benefit, benchmarking public sector pay, working group on pensions
	2006	Towards 2016: 10% increase over 27 months	Public service modernization, pensions, new employment rights, workplace learning and partnership, health care, childcare, redundancy, and job displacement
Italy	1998	National tripartite agreement confirms the 1993 agreement that sectoral wage developments should be in line with the planned inflation rate while company-level bargaining should recognize the company's performance	Benchmark is the European rate of inflation; reduce labour costs and tax (especially for business), reinforce concertation, vocational training, public investment for employment
	2002	Pact for Italy: reiterates the 1998 agreement on a two-tier (sectoral and company) bargaining system and wage guidelines	Tax cuts for the low paid and business, employment, training, welfare to work and increased unemployment benefit, pensions, social protection, public investment for development of southern Italy, talks on new Work Statute
The Netherlands	1999	National bipartite agreement within the Labour Foundation recommends wage moderation	Improved competitiveness via PRP, qualifications, training, leave
	2002	Tripartite 'social agreement' for pay increase limit of 2.5% for 2003 (first such centrally agreed wage ceiling for a decade)	Tax and social security contribution reductions
	2003	Pay freeze agreed for 2004	Early retirement, 'life-span leave' arrangements, government waters down or postpones welfare cuts
	2004	Tripartite 'social agreement' for pay restraint over three years	Early retirement, 'life-span leave' arrangements, occupational disability and unemployment insurance, childcare, government withdraws proposals for abolition of extension of pay provisions of collective agreements
Portugal	1996–9	'Strategic Concertation Pact': wage guidelines recommend that increases should be no more than one half of the increase in productivity	Increasing employment, improving competitiveness, productivity, working conditions, education and training, reforming social protection, the tax system, and public administration
Spain	2001–7	National agreement on pay moderation for 2002, taking into account inflation, productivity, and the specific situations of companies and sectors. Updated annually with guidelines for pay moderation	Usually linked to a range of social issues, especially employment (stability in exchange for flexibility), qualifications, health and safety, equal treatment and discrimination

Source: Adapted from EIRO country publications.

Table 18.2. Real unit labour cost growth (annual percentage change)

	1995	1996	1997	1998	1999	2000	2001	2002	2003	2004	2005	2006
EU (27 countries)	:	-0.7	-0.8	-0.4	0.3	0.2	0.2	-0.5	-0.3	-0.1	-0.6	-0.1
EU (25 countries)	:	-0.7	-0.9	-0.6	0.2	0.2	0.2	-0.4	-0.4	-0.1	-0.6	-0.7
EU (15 countries)	:	-0.7	-0.9	-0.4	0.2	0.3	0.2	-0.3	-0.4	-0.9	-0.4	-0.7
Euro area	:	-0.7	-1.2	-1.1	0.2	-0.3	-0.2	-0.2	-0.3	-1.0	-0.8	-0.8
Euro area (13 countries)	:	-0.8	-1.2	-1.0	0.1	-0.3	-0.2	-0.2	-0.3	-1.0	-0.8	-0.8
Euro area (12 countries)	:	-0.8	-1.2	-1.0	0.1	-0.3	-0.2	-0.2	-0.3	-1.0	-0.8	-0.8
Belgium	-2.6	0.0	-0.7	-0.8	1.0	-1.5	2.2	0.3	-1.0	-2.6	0.3	-0.8
Bulgaria	:	-13.6	-8.0	18.4	-2.2	-15.9	2.7	2.7	1.2	-4.0	-1.3	-3.4
Czech Republic	:	2.8	1.2	-3.2	0.4	0.7	1.0	3.1	2.7	-1.5	-0.9	:
Denmark	0.2	0.3	-0.6	2.1	0.5	-2.4	1.9	0.9	0.6	-1.4	-2.2	0.2
Germany	0.0	-0.5	-1.4	-0.4	0.1	1.3	-0.4	-0.6	-0.3	-1.3	-1.7	-1.5
Estonia	-2.6	-6.7	-1.8	-0.8	4.7	-8.8	-2.4	-1.5	4.7	2.2	-3.8	-0.4
Ireland	-6.3	-2.3	-4.3	-1.6	-3.6	-2.0	-0.9	-3.5	0.2	3.5	0.6	:
Greece	:	:	:	:	:	:	:	:	:	:	0.4	:
Spain	-4.2	0.1	-0.3	-0.7	-0.7	-0.6	-1.0	-1.2	-1.2	-1.4	-1.8	-1.1
France	-0.4	-0.3	-1.0	-1.0	0.9	-0.2	0.3	0.6	-0.1	-0.5	0.0	-0.4
Italy	-3.3	0.3	0.3	-4.6	-0.3	-1.5	0.3	-0.2	0.5	-0.4	0.8	0.6
Cyprus	:	1.5	0.6	-3.5	6.3	-3.9	-1.5	3.9	4.2	-1.7	-1.1	2.7
Latvia	:	4.4	1.6	-3.1	-1.7	-6.9	-3.9	-4.2	2.0	-0.6	4.6	0.2
Lithuania	-3.4	6.5	1.2	2.5	2.7	-8.9	-3.3	1.6	1.8	0.7	-2.3	-5.7
Luxembourg	-11.7	0.1	2.0	-0.5	-4.2	0.6	6.7	-0.0	-2.4	1.2	-1.9	0.0(f)
Hungary	-8.7	-2.6	-2.3	-1.8	-4.0	-0.7	3.2	0.2	0.6	1.3	0.8	-3.0
Malta	:	:	:	:	:	:	5.6	-2.1	2.9	-0.8	-4.2	-1.4
The Netherlands	-1.5	-0.9	-1.3	0.8	-0.5	-1.2	-0.1	0.9	0.2	-0.9	-2.4	:
Austria	:	:	:	:	:	:	:	:	:	:	:	-2.0(f)
Poland	-6.0	2.7	0.2	-1.1	-1.4	-2.4	2.9	-4.4	-3.6	-6.0	-2.3	-1.1(f)
Portugal	:	1.4	-0.5	3.8	7.0	0.9	-0.1	-0.1	0.2	-1.3(f)	-0.4(f)	:
Romania	:	:	:	:	-7.6	21.7	-1.1	-5.6	-2.6(f)	-0.8(f)	0.5(f)	-1.5(f)
Slovenia	4.3	-3.4	-2.8	-2.1	-2.6	3.3	0.4	-1.3	-2.2	0.3	0.1	-0.9
Slovakia	2.2	-2.0	3.0	3.4	-3.6	-0.6	-1.5	-0.3	1.1	-2.6	-1.8	-1.8
Finland	-2.7	0.5	-3.2	-2.1	-0.1	-1.6	0.5	-0.1	1.5	-0.4	2.0	-2.1
Sweden	-3.0	4.0	-0.6	-0.1	-1.9	4.1	3.2	-0.6	-1.0	-1.1	-0.5	-2.1
UK	-1.2	-2.4	-0.1	1.3	0.4	1.6	1.3	-1.1	-0.3	-0.3	1.5	-0.3

(:) Not available.   (f) Forecast.
Source: Eurostat (2007*a*).

compensated for by public subsidies.' For example, although focused on wage moderation with explicit referral to the requirement of stability in the EMU, the Spanish central agreement in 2003 rejected a downward adjustment of wages. Instead, it saw working time as a key adjustment variable, through shorter working hours and reduced overtime. In addition, the agreement advised lower-level bargainers to promote increased employment stability in exchange for more flexible working time. As well as in Spain, extended and/or more flexible working time arrangements were on the bargaining agenda of many states in 2006, including Belgium, Finland, France, Germany, Italy, the Netherlands, and Portugal (EIRO 2007: 14–15).

Thus, while wage moderation is an explicit part of social pacts, it is no longer part of a bigger package deal, and in only very few instances do trade unions receive anything concrete in return. Rather, the promise is of further discussion of reform, and where reform is labour-friendly, as in the case of increases in unemployment benefits, it tends to be linked to 'activation' measures. In other words, the question of wages becomes decoupled from wider social welfare issues (e.g. pension reforms) where unions have little to win (Hassel 2003). When wages increase too quickly, fuelled by inflation, as in the Netherlands in 2002–3, the government can threaten the unions with radical reforms to force a wage freeze (Natali and Pochet 2007). As a result, wage moderation seems to have been integrated into trade union behaviour. This process can be explained either by the new phase of globalization, which affects not only industrial sectors but also large parts of the service sectors, and involves the internalization of the new rules of the game, or by the incapacity on the part of the unions to develop an alternative communicative discourse. On the other hand, unions remain embedded in their national context and may respond to signals from their domestic economy as much as from the ECB or EU-wide economic developments. Wage claims are still sensitive to the domestic economic cycle, and tensions over wage moderation appeared in Austria, Belgium, Denmark, Finland, France, Germany, the Netherlands, and Sweden in 2006, in readiness for bargaining rounds in 2007 (EIRO 2007: 12–14).

Nevertheless, faced with the risk that cross-national differences in unit costs in a single currency area could lead to competitive underbidding, trade unions in some states have recognized the need for some, at least minimal, coordination of wage setting on a cross-national basis. Confronted with the 1996 law on competitiveness—which links domestic wage increases to the weighted average of those in the neighbouring states of Germany, France, and the Netherlands—the Belgian unions took the lead in 1997 in establishing the Doorn Agreement. Signed by the metalworking unions in these states, this agreement establishes a joint cross-national approach to wage bargaining in these states, along with Luxembourg.

Following this, the European Metalworking Federation (EMF) established a 'European coordination rule' by which unions should negotiate for wage rises in line with inflation plus 'a balanced participation in productivity gains' (cited in European Commission 2000*b*: 55). The inflation plus productivity formula was taken up by the European Trade Union Confederation (ETUC) in its 1999 Congress as the basis for a cross-national coordination of collective bargaining. For the ETUC, this would result in a 'solidaristic wage policy', in which wages are taken out of competition at the European level, thus avoiding further wage dumping (Schulten 2004: 3). Soon almost all European industry federations (EIFs) were producing wage-bargaining guidelines, as well as establishing common positions on non-wage issues such as working time and training (ibid. 12).

The effects of these efforts are difficult to discern. On the one hand, initiatives like Doorn could lead to the regional fragmentation of bargaining in the Euro Area rather than its Europeanization. On the other, the experiment in cross-national coordination undertaken at Doorn has not been replicated elsewhere, suggesting that such close cooperation relies upon strong union organization and pre-existing close cross-border ties in sectors exposed to intense international competition. Such conditions are rarely found in cross-border regions in the EU.

Second, coordination in well-organized sectors may not lead to Euro Area-wide 'pattern' bargaining—the process whereby a leading sector in a national economy, usually exposed to international competition, sets the benchmark for wage rises in other sectors thereby ensuring national economic competitiveness—if there is no spill-over to other sectors. In this respect, the increasing weight of the service sector may present an important barrier to the effective spread of pattern bargaining, particularly given union weakness there, and the fact that 'wage-plus-productivity' formulae are difficult to apply to the service sector due to the difficulties of calculating productivity gains. Finally, it is unclear whether coordination rather than merely *ex post* monitoring of bargaining rounds is really occurring under these initiatives (Dufresne 2002).

Indeed, there are several obstacles to a European level of coordination for collective bargaining, not least high coordination costs and institutional, cultural, and linguistic diversity (Visser 2002: 74–5; Calmfors 2001: 21–2). Furthermore, neither the EIFs nor the ETUC have any legal or political power over their affiliates and can offer no sanctions to enforce adherence to any coordination rules (Schulten 2004: 16). Compliance rests on voluntarism and moral suasion.

Moreover, in a multi-level bargaining system such as that emerging in the EU, different pressures appear with differing intensities at different levels of the system (Marginson and Sisson 2004). Thus, the coordination approach at

EU level can conflict or be complementary with coordination at the domestic level. In the first scenario EU-wide coordination aims at a 'solidaristic' wage policy on an EU-wide basis, but national coordination remains geared towards national competitiveness. In the second scenario, coordination at national level is a prerequisite for broader coordination at EU level.

For this reason, national union strength remains of paramount importance to the unions' capacity to resist arguments in favour of competitive wage moderation for employment and growth at the domestic level and thereby avoid concession bargaining. However, this capacity is in retreat everywhere. Unions often lack the political leverage to fulfil the terms of European bargaining formulae. Thus, 'the coordination initiatives of the European trade unions have hardly had any discernable bearing on national collective bargaining disputes so far' (Schulten 2004: 18). Moreover, domestic competitive pressures need influence only one affiliate to abandon the European coordination rule for others to have an increased vested interest to do the same (Traxler 2003: 196–7).

The lack of effective sanctions and the internalization in practice of wage moderation represent considerable obstacles to the 'governability' of a putative European collective bargaining system. Indeed, the lack of credibility of the coordination processes so far has also had an impact upon the Macro-Economic Dialogue between the ECB, Commission, employers, and unions, which was seen as the basis of the German economic and monetary success story and 'uploaded' to the EU as the Cologne process under the German Presidency in 1999.

The Macro-Economic Dialogue was intended to provide direct contact between the ECB and the social partners so that a signalling process between the bank and the unions could be established, similar to that which had existed in Germany between the Bundesbank and the German unions. This process of 'dialogue' would enable the unions to adapt their wage demands to the monetary policy of the ECB, thereby avoiding inflationary pay demands that could fuel unemployment.

The importance of this signalling process can be questioned on several grounds. First, there is the problem of a coordinated union response on a pan-European level due to the de facto decentralization of bargaining along national lines following the introduction of the euro, let alone other pressures for decentralized bargaining mentioned above. Second, unions in sectors exposed to international competition have to take this external dimension into consideration anyway when formulating pay demands. As such sectors are often the pacesetters for pay awards, it could be argued that wage moderation will occur, with or without signals from the ECB. Third, there is the reality of collective bargaining processes. Even when the relatively powerful German unions reject wage moderation at the national level and IG Metall asks for a 5 per cent wage rise, as in 2006, this move is only an opening gambit. Following compromise bargaining at the sectoral level and concession bargaining to adjust to competitive pressures at the enterprise level, collectively bargained wages across the German economy rose by only 1.5 per cent (ETUC 2007).

Last, the ECB is concerned with Euro Area macro-economic policy, and takes little account of national pay trends, considering that increases that are too high in one country will affect that country, rather than the whole Euro Area, through high inflation and a loss of competitiveness (Pochet 2002: 19). As argued earlier, wage discipline will then be restored through a dose of unemployment. In other words, in a multi-level system, competitive pressures at the sectoral and company levels will affect actual wage increases more than ECB signals due to their immediate and visible impact on the employment of groups of workers.

The Euro and Enlargement

The 10 states that joined the EU on 1 May 2004 and the two—Romania and Bulgaria—that joined on 1 January 2007 are committed to eventually adopting the euro by the terms of their accession. To date only Slovenia, Cyprus, and Malta have achieved entry.

As with several of the Euro Area states, Slovenia implemented social pacts to do so (in 2002, 2003, 2004, 2006). This was possible due to the highly centralized nature of the Slovenian industrial relations system with (until 2006) its obligatory membership of the Chamber of Commerce for Slovenian companies, national tripartite bargaining in the Economic and Social Council, and a history of social pacts dating back to 1994. These pacts have associated formula-based wage moderation with welfare and macro-economic reform, echoing developments in other Euro Area states.

Elsewhere, national-level tripartite consultation on a range of economic and social issues has been a characteristic of the industrial relations systems of these states since the transition from communism. However, while a minimal institutional setting is in place, weak unions are still dominated by former communist unions and do not have the capacity to coordinate wage bargaining at sectoral and cross-industry level, while tripartism is mostly formal. In such circumstances, there is little hope for a repetition of the 1990s social pacts' story (Benczes 2006).

Indeed, apart from the minimum wage, national agreements regulating wage increases are rare. Where they occur (e.g. in Poland and Hungary), they are only non-binding guidelines or recommendations for lower-level bargaining. The impact of these national agreements on actual wage settlements is weaker than in Euro Area states due to the poor governability of the system, with deviations from agreed increases frequent in both directions (EIRO 2004: 6–12).

There is a tension between, on the one hand, the need for wage levels in new member states to catch up with those in the rest of the EU and, on the other, the need to maintain competitiveness in economies that are open and integrated with EU trading partners and to meet the Maastricht criteria of low inflation and balanced budgets. While unions can argue for the former, based on substantial increases in productivity, employers argue for the latter. With the notable exception of Hungary from 2000 to 2003 (see Chapter 14 by Greskovits), governments have generally backed employers and sought to curb inflation and government debt through wage moderation, citing the external constraints of the Maastricht criteria and EMU. Unions, too, have generally accepted wage restraint in order to increase employment (EIRO 2004: 10–11).

Hence, in spite of high nominal wage increases compared to EU-15 states, wage moderation is the norm as wage increases are generally pitched below productivity gains. As a result, although unit labour cost growth declined more sharply in Euro Area states than in the EU-25 as a whole from 1996 to 2001, since 2002 reductions in labour costs have fallen by similar proportions in both (Table 18.2).

Thus, the new member states have engaged in a process of wage moderation, with any catching up with EU-15 states through higher nominal wage settlements based upon productivity gains and on average higher inflation rates. This has not, however, been achieved through a high level of coordination of bargaining. Rather, as in EU-15 states, through the external constraints of the Maastricht criteria for EMU and more general competitive pressures, decentralized wage determination has become fundamentally deflationary and aimed at competitiveness through its impact on unit costs. However, labour shortages due to economic growth and emigration following enlargement may put a strain on this moderation (Meardi 2007).

Clustered Convergence or Domestically Mediated EU Pressures?

In analysing recent trends, we have to consider three sets of variables. The first is temporal. Some states were in a *quasi de facto* EMU around the D-Mark before Maastricht. For these states—Austria, Belgium, France, Luxembourg, and the Netherlands—changes have to be traced back to the 1980s. In Ireland, too, change first occurred in the 1980s with the signing of the National Recovery Programme in 1987. Finland, Italy, Portugal, Spain (and later Greece) are members of a second group, which changed their national policies in parallel with EMU. Germany is also a member of this second group as it had to adapt to a change of level on losing its 'anchor' role. Even if monetary policy is still conducted in Frankfurt, it is by an institution other than the Bundesbank. Finally, Slovenia and the future members have to respect the Maastricht criteria after the birth of the euro.

What is striking about the evolution of the first 'D-Mark' group is that they followed very different paths to adapt to the euro. Two states followed their previous policies: coordination by the state and the minimum wage in France, coupled with competitive disinflation; and traditional neo-corporatism in Austria. Two states departed from their previous paths: from corporatism to coordinated decentralization in the Netherlands and from decentralization to centralization in Ireland. Finally, Belgium did not find an agreed national solution and adopted a law on competitiveness to try to solve the coordina-tion problem (in a way this is also a departure from the previous path, but unstable).

The evolution of the members of the second group can be divided into two periods: pre- and post-selection for euro entry. All were successful in the first period, innovating by adopting new social pacts for the Southern states (less true for Greece) and 'buffer funds' for Finland.[1] During the first period, there was no discussion about the selection of Germany as it constituted the benchmark. Since selection, Germany, Italy, and Portugal have struggled to find a new long-term equilibrium. Both the Italian and Portuguese economies are in trouble, and social pacts were not fully embedded. Germany is another story, but the Alliance for Jobs and other attempts at coordination were not a success (Dyson 2006a). Finland and Spain seem to have found more stable national arrangements. Once again both are going in diverse directions: more coordination in the Spanish case, and more decentralization in the Finnish case. For Slovenia, it is too early to draw any conclusions.

Time, then, seems to matter. One explanation is that early alignment to the D-Mark was internally politically driven by elites in France, the Netherlands, and Belgium due to the failures of previous policies. The same is true for the decision to sign social pacts in Ireland after decades of economic failure and migration. It was less the case for the Southern states, for whom the decision to enter the Euro Area was often guided more by political reasons (to remain at the heart of the EU dynamic) than by strictly economic ones. They used EMU as a *vincolo esterno* for national changes (Dyson and Featherstone 1996). Pressures from the Maastricht Treaty (until 1998) were much more stringent than those from the single currency since 1999. Thus, the rise, then decline, of concerted actions in some states in recent years can be explained in terms of a less pressing obligation 'from without' (Fajertag and Pochet 2000).

[1] Negotiated by the central social partners in 1997, buffer funds aim to protect workers against asymmetric shocks under EMU by building up reserves in the occupational pension and unemployment insurance schemes. Basically, employers and employees pay higher social security contributions than necessary in economic upturns and use the 'buffer' created in downturns so as to avoid increased contributions to pay for higher social security costs.

For the new member states, labour reforms were undertaken before EMU. With the exception of Slovenia (already in), the flexibilization of the labour market and of wage setting is in line with the BEPGs recommendations and the ECB mantra, but has not led to the conclusion of social pacts. In Cyprus and Malta, too, wage bargaining is decentralized, with tripartite national-level consultation over a range of social and economic issues but no social pacts. Given their entry into the Euro Area on 1 January 2008, the most recent states to enter are the first less-/non-coordinated market economies of the Euro Area.

However, time tells us nothing about the direction of reforms and the new complementarities found in the new monetary regime. Broadly, two groups can be discerned. Some states have developed what appears to be a stable institutional framework (Austria, Finland, Ireland, the Netherlands, Spain, and, to a lesser extent, France), while others have a very unstable one (Greece, Italy, Portugal). Germany appears to have recently moved from the second to the first group as wage restraint has been achieved through a measure of decentralization linked to change in institutional practice, that is the role of works councils in company-level wage setting. In both groups, some states have engaged in path-dependent change, others in non-path-dependent change towards both greater and lesser centralization. The first group (with the exception of France) has a good macro-economic performance and low levels of unemployment. The second has a poor macro-economic performance and increased unemployment. Germany is now recovering after years of wage restraint.

This brings us to the second variable: the 'fit/misfit' approach. As far as EMU constraints are concerned, in line with the 'fit/misfit' argument, states where the 'problem load' was particularly important in the run-up to EMU (e.g. 'high inflation states' like Italy) would have more adjustment problems, and therefore more incentive to engage in social concertation (see also Hancké and Rhodes 2005). This should explain why, in the same European context, some states experienced concerted agreements while others did not.

However, 'core/periphery' and 'fit/misfit' variables would not seem to be of any greater explanatory power than time. Some states from the old 'D-Mark Zone' have established social pacts, while others, including Germany, have not. While there would appear to be a correlation between seeking EMU entry and using social pacts for those states needing to institutionalize domestic stability cultures, this broke down once entry had been gained in the case of Portugal and Italy, while other states continued to sign national social pacts on a regular basis.

These examples also give some salience to the 'bottom-up' argument for structural change: relatively powerful domestic company actors have managed to moderate wage rises in these states without the need for recourse to national coordination, while where pacts have been signed they have had to take into account 'bottom-up' pressures for a decentralization of collective bargaining. However, change in this area is not always path dependent, as the example of Ireland demonstrates.

Finally, politics matter, as the new generation of Europeanization studies shows (Falkner et al. 2005). This finding echoes the new generation of neo-institutionalist studies (Streeck and Thelen 2005*b*), which emphasizes the importance of actors in shaping and reshaping institutions, and presents more diverse institutional arrangements than the classic 'varieties of capitalism' literature (Hall and Soskice 2001). From this perspective, we expect a less coherent new framework but more innovation, failures, and inefficiencies.

This line of reasoning suggests that the constraints of Euro Area accession have created pressures for a national coordination of collective bargaining. However, these pressures are mediated by domestic institutions, structures, concerns, and interests. Thus, where social pacts have been signed, variations among them reflect national differences in economic and bargaining structures, as well as differences among labour-market actors, their strategies, power, and interests. Where they have not been signed, moves towards national coordination have been undermined in Germany by the trade unions' opposition to the politics of austerity and a strongly embedded system of 'pattern' bargaining; in Portugal by employer opposition; in Austria by the existence of well-established institutions for policy concertation; and in France because of the impossibility of coordination in a situation of profound union fragmentation. Thus, EMU may create pressures towards a national coordination of bargaining, but to what extent this happens, and in what manner, still depends upon a complex interaction of domestic variables.

Conclusion

Wage developments since the introduction of the euro have been broadly in line with the tight monetary policy regime of the ECB and the Commission's BEPGs. There are several possible explanations for this. The first is that wage bargainers are receptive to ECB signals and act accordingly. While recent developments suggest that unions have internalized the new rules of the game, including wage moderation, calls for higher settlements in several states over 2006–7 suggest that this is coming under strain after several years of restraint. It also suggests that the national economic situation is still important in wage determination.

A second, more realistic, explanation, therefore, is that collective bargaining actors are internalizing signals from their own national governments and engaging in wage moderation in the light of policies of competitive disinflation enacted at the national level. These domestic policies aim to promote national competitiveness within the constraints of the single currency and the tight monetary regime associated with it.

This explanation does not, however, address the issue of compliance at the company level in a context where bargaining is increasingly decentralized and where the 'free-rider' problem is most acute. As local wage bargainers have less incentive to internalize the externalities of wage bargaining, the implication must be that companies are using increased competition as a justification for moderate wage settlements.

Under the pressure of external constraints, change in wage and collective bargaining has occurred in both path-dependent and non-path-dependent ways. The general trends are towards coordinated wage bargaining in the forms of social pacts or 'pattern' bargaining in the West, and decentralized bargaining in the east. However, social pacts are complimentary, not contradictory, to the continued decentralization of collective bargaining under the pressures of increasing globalization, the shift to service-sector employment, and the individualization of the employment relationship. Pacts may provide a coordinating framework for wage bargaining, but actual wage developments are a function of company-level pressures and the national economic and labour-market context.

On the other hand, in many cases Euro Area accession was the trigger for social pacts, but after 1999 they endured as they provide states with some leverage over labour-market developments, and provide legitimacy for tough labour-market and welfare reforms when other policy tools have been lost. As with 'pattern', or decentralized, bargaining, however, the focus is on the competitiveness of the bargaining unit (nation, sector, or company) rather than of the Euro Area as a whole.

Under such circumstances, given its economic weight in the EU, and despite its economic upswing since 2004, continued wage moderation in Germany will in all likelihood act as a pacesetter for other states, either directly (e.g. for the Benelux states and perhaps France) or indirectly, through its effect on the Euro Area inflation rate. Rather than cross-national coordination, however, we are witnessing the mobilization of cross-national benchmarking and comparison in the name of national competitiveness. In the absence of cross-national coordination, as Hancké (2002a) argues, employer concerns for competitiveness and the deflationary macro-economic environment of the Euro Area mean that wage setting has become a function of competitiveness and therefore takes place on employers' terms. The result is falling labour costs in a fundamentally and structurally deflationary wage-setting system, inflation acting as the floor for wage settlements and productivity the ceiling.

Unions have an incentive to follow the new rules of the game. Social pacts give them some input into policymaking on a wide range of issues when they otherwise risk being sidelined in an era of retrenchment. Even without social pacts, competitive pressures mean that it is hard for them to find an alternative discourse to wage moderation. The 'technocratization' of wage setting, involving cross-national benchmarking and comparison, reinforces such difficulties and lends justification to the wage moderation discourse. Nevertheless, unions must also retain their legitimacy in the eyes of their members and so will demand higher settlements if they perceive the national context as justifying them. As the case of Germany demonstrates, however, competitive pressures will mediate such calls when actual wage settlements are negotiated.

Despite these pressures and the Commission's perceived need for greater wage responsiveness to asymmetric shocks in the Euro Area, a certain amount of wage rigidity has prevailed. Nominal wages have not moved down in any state of the Euro Area, even where unemployment has remained high (e.g. France) or has risen (e.g. Germany). Indeed, wage cuts appear acceptable only when the survival of a firm is at stake (Calmfors 2001: 3). Macro-economic adjustment is therefore likely to take place via other mechanisms such as shorter contract periods, adjustments to working hours, increased labour flexibility, changes in taxation and welfare benefits and, most worryingly, through a greater volatility of employment.

In the long-term, the 'governability' of this system may be problematic. Agreement on the desirability of price stability does not preclude the possibility of distributional tensions or conflict. First, the impact of moderate wage settlements on macro-economic performance is deleterious through its impact on consumption, resulting in sub-optimal growth and continually high levels of unemployment across the Euro Area. Second, as wage earners see a greater share of value added going to company profits, they may reject wage moderation. As national business cycles coincide under the impact of the euro, such tensions may be felt simultaneously across the Euro Area, and beyond, creating additional pressure for change as convergence occurs despite a lack of coordination. Such a scenario may be made more likely by the increasingly technocratic nature of wage setting at the national and cross-national levels, which tends to alienate the wage earner from the wage policy of her or his union at these levels.

19

Welfare Reform

Daniel Wincott

Convergence is a keyword of European monetary union. At least since the Maastricht 'convergence criteria', EMU's sponsors have pressed for national economic policies and performance to become more similar across Europe. Moreover, EMU seemed to rest on convergence towards a particular substantive orthodox vision, focused on stable, sustainable public finances and sound money, with the welfare state typically depicted as burden. In contrast, Martin Rhodes's striking and provocative 'welfare state' chapter for *European States and the Euro* suggested that EMU might prove 'good' for the welfare states, emphasizing EMU's (perhaps paradoxical) potential to *strengthen* both states' welfare capacities (focusing particularly on 'social pacts') and EU-level policy coordination, thereby 're-embedding' European liberalism rather than imposing neo-liberalism. Rhodes (2002: 309) also hinted that today's welfare state was best understood from a revisionist perspective on post-war embedded liberalism, or the 'Keynesian welfare state'. Particularly in its third section, this chapter re-addresses these questions in the light of the implementation and operation of EMU—as well as EU enlargement—and asks whether this subsequent experience has caused European welfare states to converge.

First, however, I address the concept of convergence in the context of EMU, as well as offering observations on the complexity of 'welfare states'. I seek to deepen Rhodes's perspective on revisionism and states' social capacity, arguing that the 'social purpose' (echoing Ruggie 1982) of 'the welfare state' has always been a matter of compromise, accommodation, and contestation; of 'puzzling' as well as 'powering' (Heclo 1974). If social policies are increasingly complex, they are much less esoteric than finance (Chapter 17 by Macartney and Moran): social policy remains more directly connected to democratic—or at least public—debate. Nevertheless, set in revisionist perspective, little-noticed domestic reforms over a longer period begin to come into focus, particularly in Bismarckian states, alongside more widely recognized recent reform tendencies and discourses (such as social pacts and 'activation' reforms).

Second, the singularity of social purpose for EMU and the European Union (EU) is equally contentious, as debates about the 'European Social Model'— and how it relates to EMU—suggest. My (tentative) claim is that we see some convergence, if not of 'social purpose', at least of socio-economic discourse across key EU-level governance institutions. This analysis places Rhodes's concern with EU-level coordination in a novel, and updated, perspective. The new coordinative 'architecture for welfare'—perhaps 'designed to ensure that social policy does not become subordinate to finance ministers and economic affairs' (Rhodes 2002: 328–9)—is still in flux. While economic priorities and actors gained strength through mid-term reforms of 'Lisbon', ECB officials—who have traditionally remained allusive on state policy concerns—have begun to advocate 'Lisbon' and to celebrate the (iconographically social democratic) 'Nordic model'. Here, Marcussen's 'Lisbon' discourses of stabilization, redistribution, and competitiveness may become somewhat interwoven, rather than remaining largely distinct and competing.

Conceptualizing Convergence and the Welfare State

During the process of euro-membership qualification, the convergence criteria were perceived as undercutting social priorities by putting pressure on public finances. Many of EMU's neo-liberal supporters still advocate welfare retrenchment to improve public finances and enhance (especially labour) market efficiency. Together with the ultra-orthodox blueprint for EMU—with a stronger constitutional commitment to price stability and larger measure of independence than any comparable central bank—the impact of the convergence criteria fuelled criticism of its 'new constitutional', 'disciplinary neo-liberalism' (Gill 1998). While some subsequent neo-Gramscian analysis stressed the 'variegations' of national responses (Carfuny and Ryner 2007), the general story remains one of EMU restricting national policymakers to choices from a neo-liberal menu. Together with states' raft of ongoing social policy commitments, these variegations may motivate the apparently oxymoronic idea of 'embedded neo-liberalism' (van Apeldoorn 2002), suggesting that across Europe neo-liberalism's disembedding logic has become entrenched within a series of particular social arrangements.

Discretionary macroeconomics and social policy are often seen as aspects of a single concept: the Keynesian welfare state. By suggesting that states had an alternative to balancing their budgets during recessions, Keynesians may have generated some capacity for governments to protect and stabilize social policy spending. Social spending might be singled out as a means of reflation. Conversely, EMU's anti-Keynesian character (but see Clift 2006) might increasingly squeeze the capacity of states to maintain their established welfare commitments. So, EMU finally interred the already weakened body of Keynesianism, particularly insofar as it represented the defeat of proposals for a continental, Europe-wide Keynesian strategy (Grahl 2001). To the extent that monetary union was a decisive defeat for Keynesianism, the Keynesian welfare state concept implies that social policy also suffered. Traditionally, many analysts have regarded the welfare state as an essentially national domain, with little role for the EU (Majone 1998). So, if EMU curtailed the autonomy of these welfare states, it moved the EU onto new terrain.

As critical perspectives gained strength through the late 1990s it became easy to assume that monetary union's clear and singular 'social purpose' (Ruggie 1982) was neo-liberal convergence. Yet there were always empirical and conceptual contraindications, especially in relation to the welfare state. Much of the drive towards monetary union came from non-neo-liberal sources. Informed by the disastrous French experience with 'Keynesianism in one country', some actors saw EMU as insulation for national social and economic policies from financial market pressures and a means of shifting European monetary politics from German to supranational control. A focus on EMU's ultra-orthodox blueprint may neglect its implementation, which fell short of the orthodoxy. Germany's failure to meet the (strict) convergence criteria scuppered Bundesbank plans for a small-scale monetary union of 'stability culture' states. For critics of EMU's 'new constitutionalism' the Stability and Growth Pact entrenched disciplinary neo-liberalism, rather than being an attempt to control the unexpected inclusion of inflation-prone economies in a larger-scale monetary union. Ironically, then, the left critics' 'reality' might describe the *aspirations* of the neo-liberals: the Pact's subsequent fate suggests that these aspirations have been (partly) frustrated (Clift 2006).

Alternatively EMU might re-embed liberalism in a new global setting. Rhodes (2002) sees EMU as potentially good for the welfare state, particularly by creating pressure for reforms to be based in social pacts. But, once states achieved membership, this pressure may have dissipated (Hancké and Rhodes 2005, but see Donaghey and Teague 2005). Others, by contrast, argue that the embedding of euro-liberalism within the diverse specificities of domestic policy regimes (Jones 2002) occurs *after* euro qualification as states' fiscal/social policy autonomy increases (especially from foreign exchange markets).

Important conceptual difficulties lurk behind these arguments. First, it is commonplace to note that convergence is a slippery concept. What, precisely, is converging requires specification: political objectives, policies (policy instruments, policy regimes), or outcomes? Many discourse analysts observe that policy (and policy change) is discursively constructed; they include 'policy' and 'implementation' within 'discourse' rather than treating them as somehow 'extra-discursive'. Nevertheless, it remains the case that patterns of policy continuity and change may be masked or hidden by the terms of political debate. Equally, similar policy patterns may be articulated quite differently within distinct contexts and narratives. In distinct contexts shared discourses may, first, resonate differently and, second, a common political narrative might be linked to different strategies for policy change. Moreover, common pressures—even similar policies—may produce quite different consequences, depending on their timing and sequence, or refraction through distinct institutional frameworks and policy legacies. These difficulties are magnified when the 'object' of convergence is as complex and contested as 'the welfare state' (Veit-Wilson 2000; Wincott 2001).

A preliminary stylized depiction of the conventional (but not uncontested) wisdom might look something like this: a prior diversity of (three or more) 'golden-age' 'welfare (state) regimes' is increasingly squeezed by neo-liberalizing and globalizing pressures. Esping-Andersen's (1990) 'conservative', 'liberal', and 'socialist' regimes have mutated into 'Nordic', 'Anglo-Saxon', 'Continental', and 'Mediterranean' models in recent EU-related discourse (especially Sapir 2005, 2006). Neo-liberalizing tendencies, perhaps including European integration and monetary union, may trigger convergence on a neo-liberal, residualist 'Anglo-Saxon' model. The main variation merely attributes a dull, unchanging character to the welfare state, famously characterized as an 'immoveable object' (Pierson 1998; Swank 2002), rather than repudiating the basic 'neo-liberal pressures' narrative. Welfare states have proven difficult to change, particularly when the interests of public-sector professionals align with citizens' entitlements. There is, however, much more to the recent history of welfare provision than sullen inertia and neo-liberalizing pressures.

The elements of this stylized account require close interrogation. Even (perhaps especially) influential comparative analysts deploy an unclear conception of the welfare state. Clarity will not be achieved by definitional fiat, especially if the complex connotations and associations attached to this concept are ignored (Veit-Wilson 2000; Wincott 2001). The welfare state is (at least implicitly) assumed to be a distinct form of the state—a 'redefinition of what the state is all about'—evoking T. H. Marshall's notion of social citizenship (for many 'the core idea of a welfare state'). In 'a genuine welfare state the majority of its daily routine activities must be devoted to servicing the welfare needs of households' (Esping-Andersen 1990: 21, 20, 1999: 34). Unfortunately, this sort of definition runs into an immediate problem; its criteria are so demanding that few, if any, states ever qualify as welfare states: 'no state can be regarded as a real welfare state until the 1970s, and some that we normally label as welfare states will not qualify' (Esping-Andersen 1990: 20). On this account, the emergence of the 'real' welfare state coincides with the end of the 'golden age'! Ironically, then, close interrogation of states' current failure to live up to demanding discriminating criteria for 'welfare statehood' may create a false impression of neo-liberal 'convergence': if these standards never were achieved, current configurations could equal past realities.

Conventional analysis depicts limited variation within regime-clusters, downplaying historic differences between, say, the 'activation' of Swedish labour-market policy and relative passivity in Denmark. Moreover, while mainstream analysis tends to assume that a welfare state is internally consistent and coherent, some state theorists depict state unification as a *tendential political accomplishment*. Hay (1999: 327, 331, 338) echoes T. H. Marshall's (1992 [1950]: 49) classic characterization of social citizenship as 'a stew of paradox' from which 'a human society can make a square meal...without getting indigestion—at least for quite a long time' (Wincott 2004). We might, then, find features of different regime types present within any particular state's social policies. Different branches of a state may also serve distinct, and sometimes mutually contradictory, purposes. For example, many Bismarckian states have parallel ('Beveridge-style'?) benefits, financed from general taxation for those outside the social insurance system. While the importance of these 'assistance' systems tended to wane from the late 1960s, their importance often increased again starting in the 1980s—in some cases representing a partial return to the *status quo ante*. Seeleib-Kaiser and Fleckenstein (2007: 429, 432–3) compare the 1969 German employment promotion law with changes from the 1980s.

These problems multiply if the Keynesian welfare state is the object of analysis. The connections between Keynesianism and the welfare state may be weaker, comparatively and historically, than is usually supposed: their wholesale fusion—the Keynesian welfare state—requires careful scrutiny (Notermans 2000; Rhodes 2002: 309). For example, even before the Bundesbank subverted the brief German flirtation with 'Keynesian' fiscal expansion in the early 1970s, this macro-economic philosophy enjoyed little support within the previously dominant Christian democratic CDU/CSU. Nonetheless, Germany developed as one of Europe's most robust (and expensive) social states. More generally, 'sound public finance' is not inimical to sustaining—or even expanding—welfare commitments, at least if taxpayers are prepared to fund them. Reducing public debt *will* pose difficulties for state welfare (and restricting public deficit levels reduces a welfare state's short-term room for manoeuvre). High public indebtedness also imposes strains on any state's capacity to sustain welfare commitments or pursue Keynesian policies. Swank's (2002: 94) sophisticated quantitative analysis suggests that (only) 'when budget deficits become high' does 'capital mobility engender(s) cuts in social welfare effort'.

Similar conceptual problems attach to contemporary changes in welfare discourses and provision—which seem to be occurring despite welfare 'inertia' narratives. Beyond the changes to Bismarckian states, 'new' social policy discourses, which accent 'activation' and 'social investment', are widely deployed across western Europe, although both their novelty and how far they penetrate into social provision remain unclear. 'Activation' requires (or in some forms offers opportunities for) 'performance' from claimants in place of passive reception of benefits, while 'social investment' strategies seek to change the emphasis of policy from compensating individuals for bad outcomes to reducing risks as well as increasing opportunities and individual resilience. These 'new' discourses are often associated with 'neo-liberalization' and 'recommodification', with subjugating welfare to the imperatives of the economy. Yet they were particularly closely associated with Swedish social policy in its heyday: arguably the state that most closely approximated to Esping-Andersen's definitions. In fact, these welfare themes can take a variety of forms, some of which are characteristically social democratic, while others are neo-liberal, or even neo-conservative (Wincott 2003*a*, 2003*b*).

Moreover, if a *general* change is taking place—if 'the welfare state' is changing into something else (competition state, regulatory state, workfare regime...)—the states concerned will not necessarily become more similar: we may still have three or more 'worlds' under the new meta-concept. Recall that while comparative welfare theory (Esping-Andersen 1990) emphasized variety, it was a diversity of something *shared*: all states are presented as *types* of *welfare state (regime)*. We must remain alert to the potential for a common discourse to serve a variety of purposes, or trend take distinct forms, in different contexts.

EMU and the European Social Model

Just as with the welfare state, the social purpose of monetary union has always been contested, as has that of the EU more generally. It is too easy 'to identify the EU . . . as ordered, coherent and consistent, [as] providing a clear basis from which to develop claims' about convergence or Europeanization (Wincott 2003*b*). For example, if standard welfare historiography stresses decline after a golden age, a similar, partly parasitic, stylized narrative attaches to the EU, the European social model and the Union's putative fall from 'social' grace. The European social model invokes a past in which Europe had a distinctively generous and encompassing public commitment to social provision. The roles of the Union and European states within the European social model are somewhat occluded. Official Commission discourse describes the European social model as a common, distinctive, feature of European states, while insinuating that the EU itself has made a substantial contribution to its development and defence (Wincott 2003*b*). Some analysts detect a change in 'Brussels' in the late 1980s and early 1990s, from being 'more oriented towards the development of public social policies in the 1980s' towards the 'discourse of . . . economically-oriented actors' which 'has become more similar to the discourse of international financial organizations': these analysts rightly point out the ambiguous character of the European social model, at once widely 'proclaimed...but not sustained...through explicit policies' (Guillén and Palier 2004: 206, 208). Social policy clearly occupied a lowly place on the policy agenda in 'Brussels' during the late 1980s and early 1990s. Instead, political attention concentrated on two issues: EMU and the collapse of the Soviet bloc.

Thus, social policy concerns were almost completely absent from the criteria set in Copenhagen in 1993 for east central European applications to the Union (as Guillén and Palier 2004: 208 rightly note; also Ferge and Juhász 2004: 234; Lendvai 2004: 322–3; Potùèek 2004: 263–5). This absence suggests that key EU actors did not view welfare state considerations as an essential feature of the EU. These initial criteria structured the relationship between the prospective members and the Union: they have had a continuing influence on most of these states, setting the terms on which they relate to EMU. Only Slovenia has proven able to institutionalize something like a 'continental' model of social partnership, industrial relations, and social welfare (Bohle and Greskovits 2007; Feldmann 2006a, 2006b), building on a prior 'Yugoslavian' tradition of decentralized co-operative systems of economic management and its small and homogeneous population. By contrast, the Visegrad countries still seem to face the same sharp choice between equity and efficiency initially presented to them by the Washington institutions. Even so, Bohle and Greskovits (2007) argue that these states have proven unable to repudiate welfare, instead repeatedly having recourse to *ad hoc* compensation packages for particular groups. Strikingly, these analysts see 'no clear division of labour between Left and Right' in this ad hocery: 'all parties that hoped for mass popular support usually stressed the intrinsic relationship between economic and welfare protectionism, promised both kinds at once and, once in power, tried pragmatically to implement some mix' (ibid. 2007: 454). This equation of economic and welfare protectionism contrasts sharply with the idea of social policy as a potentially 'productive factor'. Instead, it confirms the neo-liberal 'choice' between equity and efficiency.

If advocates of 'social' Europe accurately identify the weakness of these themes in the accession process, they may also perpetuate fallacies about the European social model. This discourse largely post-dates the 1980s, having grown out of the concept of the 'European model of society', which Commission President Jacques Delors espoused at an earlier time and which enjoyed a brief vogue in Commission documents, notably the 1993 Social Policy Green Paper (European Commission 1993a: 33). It seems to mutate into the European social model in official Commission documents during the early and mid-1990s. Thus, the European social model discourse emerged fully *after* the Copenhagen criteria were set. Strictly speaking, then, the European social model could not be 'sustained' (compare Guillén and Palier 2004: 208) by criteria that were formalized before its full emergence. Arguably, the European social model was most salient *after* the 2000 Lisbon European

365

Council (certainly scholarly concern is a twenty-first century phenomenon, with only one ISI citation prior to 2001, after which references explode).

Crucially, the stylized European social model narrative may confound aspirational Commission-based social discourses from the 1980s with the poorly developed character of EU social policy at this time. Rather than describing a concrete historical 'model' inscribed in EU policies, the European social model might be best seen as a defensive discourse, a counter-weight to dominant economic ideas. This might account for its proponents' tendency to focus on 'western' Europe and their general failure to engage with eastern enlargement. While the 1993 White Paper on Growth, Competitiveness, and Employment is widely seen as a decisive moment in the European Commission's (1993b) shift towards a more economically oriented ideology (Rosamond 2002), it can also be read as Delors' final throw of the political dice after his 'Russian Dolls' strategy—of nesting a 'social dimension' within the single market programme—failed. In it Delors placed his main bet on 'sustainable development' as a means of embedding market liberalism; the European social model was only a minor theme.

Yet, the European social model's importance in the political discourses of European integration subsequently grew: social policy actors within the Commission seized on it as a major theme of their own White Paper (European Commission 1994). Perhaps the most important new influence was exercised by the growing number of Nordic member states. In particular, Sweden brought in its tradition of linking employment with social protection— precisely the connection Delors had sought to highlight. Ongoing concerns with high long-term unemployment and low employment participation rates in much of EU-Europe helped Swedish officials and politicians (led by Allan Larrson) to assume leadership within the European Employment Strategy (Johansson 1999; Wincott 2003a). Propitious timing of a British general election in 1977 brought a broadly supportive Labour government to power just as the Amsterdam Treaty formalized these policies.

Two features of employment as a major EU theme are particularly relevant here. The first concerns the complex mix of 'relative autonomy' for social policy within the institutional framework of the EU and the general emergence of EU 'policy coordination' during the 1990s (see Chapter 3 by Umbach and Wessels). While outside commentators sometimes expressed concern about the relatively 'soft' character of social policy governance instruments in the employment field, these policymakers seemed palpably excited about becoming involved in an important aspect of the European political economy— arguably previously equalled only by gender policy. If the ability of socially oriented actors to develop this policy depended partly on the existence of EU institutional capacities and sites for social policymaking, the emergence of the European Employment Strategy was also facilitated by a general turn towards new 'strategies' and 'processes' concerned with social and economic policy, typically associated with particular meetings of the European Council. For a period during the 1990s, almost every one of its meetings seemed to generate a new 'process', most of which can be interpreted as efforts to galvanize the rather moribund European economy in preparation for stage three of EMU. So, though the European Employment Strategy was partly a product of relatively autonomous social policy actors and institutions at the EU level, it also always had a link to EMU. The attempt to knit social concerns together with economic performance, which was already evident in the 1993 White Paper, continued to animate the European Employment Strategy throughout the 1990s.

Second, it is easy to misunderstand the role of Swedish actors and ideas in the European Employment Strategy. While social and employment policies in Sweden are famous (or notorious) for their generosity, they have also long linked social protection to economic adjustment in the light of structural change. From the 'solidaristic wage policy' to the 'active labour-market policy', adjustment was as much a leitmotif of Swedish policy, as was the eschewal of nationalizing industry. As Ryner (2002) notes, these features of the vaunted 'Swedish model' are systematically ignored in much discussion of 'old social democracy', [especially in Giddens's (1998) particular reading of the British experience, which privileges his 'third way']. A richer engagement with Swedish experience suggests that social policy, often associated with redistribution, is interwoven with discourses of innovation and competitiveness. As Marcussen argues in this volume, the Swedish 'model' plays a key role in EU 'redistributive' discourses. But historically it is also strongly connected to 'Schumpeterian' themes of innovation and structural change.

After the Amsterdam European Council in 1997, swept along by the euphoric effects of the 'dot.com' boom (later exposed as a 'bubble') and by a tide of 'new social democratic' electoral successes across Europe, EU political leaders again sought to knit social themes together with the promotion of innovation. The March 2000 Lisbon special European Council (ironically just at what later turned out to be the very peak of the 'dot.com' bubble) came to symbolize this effort. Rather than repudiating the European social model as a fetter on economic performance, it was to be 'modernized' in the context of the 'new' 'knowledge-based economy'. Even if 'dot.com' investment became more sober, Europe simply lacked the institutional prerequisites for an entrepreneurially driven 'knowledge-based economy', issues that the 'Lisbon' process did not address effectively (Watson 2001). Arguably the hold of the 'knowledge-based economy' idea on these leaders at Lisbon was due, at least in part, to the promise of rapid economic growth to ease the pressures of 'stabilization' (Mullineux and Ryan 2002) including on state welfare; it seemed able to integrate stabilization and welfare through innovation.

Be that as it may, in practice Lisbon set two distinct policy dynamics in motion, for the European social model and for innovation and competitiveness, respectively. After Lisbon, the European Council's various policy coordination forums were (partially) reformed, redeveloped, and (certainly) relabelled as the 'Open Method of Coordination'. Some 'economic' Open Methods of Coordination developed after Lisbon, but 'socially oriented actors' seized on it with alacrity, and social policy Open Methods of Coordination proliferated. During this initial phase, Lisbon was arguably primarily associated with social policy, especially as the gloss rapidly came off its 'knowledge-based economy', 'dot.com'-influenced strand.

Again, east central European accession provides an indication of Lisbon's importance for European social policy. In 2002, when the Lisbon agenda was presented to the accession states, 'social policy moved to the top of the EU political agenda of enlargement' (Potůček 2004: 263), and 'poverty, social inclusion and exclusion have acceded to the... political agenda' of many CEEC states ('thanks to... the Open Method of Coordination', according to Ferge and Juhász 2004: 234). This occurred nearly a 'decade after setting up the Copenhagen criteria' at a stage when, ironically, the preparation of the new member states for membership in 2004 'had just finished' (Potůček 2004: 263). While there was some supervision of the candidate countries adoption of the EU social *acquis* from the mid-1990s (Ferge and Juhász 2004: 246–9), Lisbon as a 'new political initiative' focused on the ' "social fabric" of contemporary societies' (Potůček 2004: 263). Even so, this was a one-way influence, from west to east. 'Western' Europe continued to be taken as the relevant universe in most EU social policy debate, with new member states seen mainly as source of pressure on Western 'models' (see Sapir 2005, 2006).

Until about 2004, Lisbon was closely associated with social policy. At this stage, however, economically oriented actors began to heap criticism on the Open Method of Coordination's ineffectiveness and lack of focus, before it could possibly have impacted on Europe's deeply rooted social policy configurations. The Sapir (2003) and Kok (2004) reports prepared the way for the Commission's 'mid-term review', which refocused 'Lisbon' on the economy. The review threatened the social applications of the Open Method of Coordination, which survived—in 'streamlined' form—only after intense lobbying by non-governmental organizations and other social policy advocates. Of course, the Stability and Growth Pact was loosened—perhaps weakening the EU's 'stabilization' discourse—alongside this refocusing of 'Lisbon'. In this context, the appropriation of 'Lisbon' by ECB officials from about 2004 is particularly striking, perhaps indicating an increasing concern with economic reform and innovation, in the light of their difficulties in maintaining the 'stabilization' orthodoxy.

While this use of 'Lisbon' by ECB officials reflected and reinforced the 'rightward' shift of its increased emphasis on 'economic reform', these officials also deployed elements of the 'innovation' discourse. Thus, in September 2005

ECB vice-president Lucas Papademos eulogized 'Schumpeterian "creative destruction" '. More strikingly, unlike Marcussen, who divides Denmark from Sweden as examples of 'innovation' and 'redistribution', respectively, ECB officials link these states in discussing the 'Nordic EU countries' (Trichet 2006a, 2006b), Sweden and Denmark (Papademos 2004: 10), or the 'Scandinavian Model' (Noyer 2005) in laudatory terms. They focused particularly on Nordic-type measures to raise employment, including those 'aimed at reconciling motherhood with professional life, such as the provision of child care' (Trichet 2006a; also Papademos 2004: 10). For all that the Lisbon agenda shifted to the right, ECB officials seem keen to celebrate these states *as a group* and because of the manner in which they *combine* innovation, high rates of employment, and social concerns. Papademos (2005b) is illustrative:

To plead for all this is not 'to dream the impossible dream'. That it can be done successfully is shown in the Nordic countries, which have undergone such structural reforms in the past decade—and have done so without abandoning the basic features of what we call the European social model. These countries are now reaping the benefits of these reforms in terms of growth, employment and technological excellence.

Strikingly, ECB officials are praising cases—the 'Nordic EU countries'—most of which are outside the Euro Area. Finland, the only Nordic Euro Area state, is also the state least likely to be mentioned by them. This official lauding of non-Euro-Area states as reformist exemplars begs important questions about the detailed impact, if any, of Euro Area membership on state welfare provision. It is directly to this question that we now turn.

Clusters and Convergence

Analysis of the impact of EMU on national welfare provision in Europe faces some empirical difficulties. The most relevant quantitative data are available for a subset of relevant states and are currently available only for the initial years after the euro's introduction: social expenditure data run to 2003 and cover few of the most recent EU members (generally those with the strongest social and economic performance). Thus, these data shed only a limited light on our concerns. (Figure 19.1)

Jones (2002) argues that euro entry reduces subsequent pressure on the (social) budgets of states. The change from gradual decline during the 1990s to growth after 2000 among Euro Area states might lend him some support. However, the sharper turnaround—from a steeper fall to more rapid growth—occurred among non–Euro-Area EU states and raises a question: how important are currency markets—which Jones emphasizes—since they could continue to monitor and discipline social spending in non–Euro-Area states? By contrast, if the recovery of social spending after 2000 had a more general

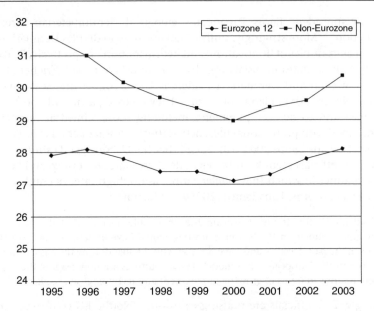

Figure 19.1. Social expenditure as percentage of EU-15 GDP by Euro Area membership

cause, perhaps the ECB and/or the Stability and Growth Pact did retain *some* capacity to discipline Euro Area members, in spite of the Pact's apparent weaknesses (see Chapter 4 by Hallerberg and Bridwell). Where we do have evidence for newer EU member states, social expenditure levels appear fairly stable; they show less evidence of decline than Western European countries did during the euro entry qualification period.

Social expenditure data have been sharply criticized as a measure of welfare effort, notably by Esping-Andersen (1990: 19): 'expenditures are epiphenomenal to the theoretical substance of welfare states'. Social spending typically increases as welfare problems increase, and may do so even as entitlements are reduced (if welfare demands increase more quickly). His 'decommodification index' replaced spending with a measure of their quality (income replacement, qualifying criteria, waiting times, etc.) for pensions, unemployment, and sickness benefits. However, expenditure data also cover other welfare provisions, including social services, which Esping-Andersen's index does not embrace, but may also have 'decommodifying' effects (Room 2000). If discursive emphasis on 'social investment' is having a policy impact, then European states' welfare effort may be growing in these other areas, even as (or if) classic transfer benefits are retrenched.

Nevertheless, Esping-Andersen's (1990) conceptualization and operationalization of 'decommodification' remains a vital point of reference for welfare analysts. Sadly, the data that he used are not in the public domain, and the index was only calculated for a single year—1980. Recently, however, Scruggs and Allan (2006) have used publicly available data to replicate—and develop a critique of—these results, and ultimately to generate a decommodification or 'welfare benefit generosity' time-series. Unfortunately, these data currently end marginally earlier than the social expenditure data, and is not available for most southern or any eastern member states. There are, moreover, analytical risks in placing too much weight on a single measure, especially one that purports to capture a multi-dimensional concept like 'the welfare state' in a single number for each state in every year. Nevertheless, by opening a window on welfare dynamics, they improve on the widely-used, single-year measure of decommodification.

Aggregating state 'welfare benefit generosity' indices into three state-categories—Euro Area, non-Euro-Area, and non-EU—shows a strikingly similar pattern for each group. The common pattern is of relatively fast growth through the 1970s and into the mid-1980s, followed by a second 'plateau' period, with some slight decline towards the end of the time-series. These results may derive from the particular combination of states that each group brings together. For example, the non-EU states include Norway, which managed to sustain a high and unparalleled level of 'welfare benefit generosity' throughout the latter part of the period for which we have data, as well as Switzerland, which shows a surprisingly high peak on this measure—high, that is, in relation to the expectations of the Swiss expressed in the comparative literature, but then an equally sharp decline. (Figure 19.2)

This overall pattern suggests that, while the welfare state may have 'grown to limits' during the 1970s and 1980s, it has subsequently proven to be relatively robust. The similarity of these aggregate results might suggest that EMU—and even EU membership itself—had only a relatively minor and indirect impact on 'welfare benefit generosity'. Investigation of the disaggregated patterns shown by key states within the EU reinforces this impression, while also throwing up some unexpected results. Because no 'Continental' or 'Mediterranean' states remain outside EMU, it is impossible to find empirical evidence of what difference membership might make within these clusters. Nonetheless, examination of the data for Germany and Italy remains helpful. The German data start at a relatively high level, but then show remarkable stability throughout the relevant 30-year period, albeit with some limit evidence of decline in the most recent period. Contrary to its reputation as a hotbed of resistance to globalization, France shows a comparatively sharp decline, whereas Austria, Belgium, and the Netherlands generally show more sustained 'welfare benefit generosity' than Germany. The standard view of Italy is as a state that used euro entry to achieve public-sector retrenchment that it might have been impossible to obtain otherwise. In contrast, these data

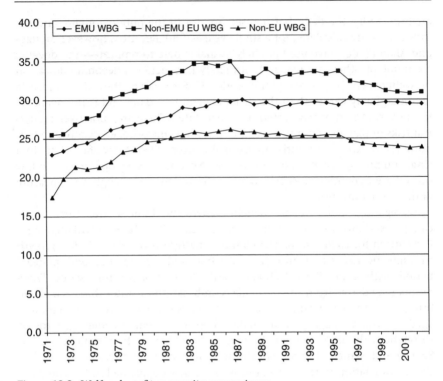

Figure 19.2. Welfare benefit generosity comparisons

suggest that Italy has experienced recent growth in the generosity of welfare benefits, which achieved their overall highest level towards the end of the period for which we have data.

The 'Anglo-Saxon' and 'Nordic' clusters include Euro Area members and non-members, so here we have the requisite variation to explore membership impacts. The putatively 'Anglo-Saxon' states show surprising results from the perspective of comparative welfare theory, each displaying growth in 'welfare benefit generosity' since the mid-1990s. Ireland's improvement in this respect is partly a matter of catching up from a relatively low base, and also reflects the benefits of very high growth together with a rather un–'Anglo-Saxon' pattern of social partnership. In this context, seeking qualification for euro entry did not prevent a step-growth in 'welfare benefit generosity' from 1995–6. Equally, while Britain has remained resolutely outside the Euro Area, it has also been able to improve its 'welfare benefit generosity' (at least according to this measure), achieving its highest score right at the end of the time-period. For all the dissonance that it might engender with standard discourses of British exceptionalism, this result partly reflects changes introduced by the post-1997 Labour governments, which

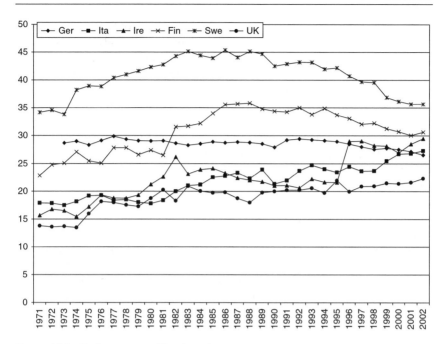

Figure 19.3. Six key cases, welfare benefit generosity

seem poorly understood across Europe (Figure 19.3; Hopkin and Wincott 2006).

The Nordic states also show an unexpected pattern. The comparative literature suggests that these states have ridden out retrenchment pressures relatively well, a characterization only partly endorsed by 'welfare benefit generosity' data. These states clearly remain the most generous providers of welfare benefits in the world, but except for oil-rich Norway they show marked patterns of decline in benefit generosity, albeit from remarkable peaks. Crucially, Denmark, Finland, and Sweden share a common recent pattern (although Finland's rise to welfare generosity was comparatively late). This unexpected evidence raises questions about the lauded Nordic ability to reconcile economic efficiency and social equity. Perhaps recent retrenchment has been their key to avoiding punishment by international financial markets; if so, can it be sustained? Here we should recall that the 'welfare benefit generosity' index is only concerned with certain transfer benefits; it does not touch on the wide range of other social benefits and services—such as childcare provision—which are widely held particularly to distinguish the Nordic states. For present purposes, however, we note that being in the 'Nordic' cluster seems to be more important than Euro Area membership for these states.

The existence of this Nordic cluster stands in clear contrast to the lack of other evidence of clustering in the 'welfare benefit generosity' data, whether along traditional regime-types or those of Euro Area membership. If a pattern is detectable for the most recent years of the index, it seems to be one of 'catch-up' for the traditionally least generous European states—Britain, Ireland, and Italy. Together with the Nordic decline, this evidence shows an overall pattern of convergence, although one that seems hard to attribute to European monetary union. In continental Europe the general pattern is of continuity during the period for which data are available, although there is a bit more evidence of retrenchment for the larger states—France and Germany—than for the smaller ones. A good deal of concern has been expressed about the perceived sluggishness of these larger states, which have traditionally been at the heart of the European economy. Ironically, the 'failure' of these states to display rapid economic growth has been attributed to the alleged weakness of domestic retrenchment-oriented structural reform in France and Germany. For example, Mayer and Folkerts-Landau (2005: 1, 4) of the Deutsche Bank have attributed low growth in 'Germany—and other European economies' partly to the apparent impossibility of converting 'unemployed coal miners ... into "Hamburger flippers".'

Yet, close analysis of recent welfare trajectories in Germany and France shows more evidence of change than many neo-liberals seem prepared to acknowledge. In France, ongoing reform has been partly obfuscated by widespread repudiation of Anglo-Saxon 'ultra-liberalism', including among established politicians. German neo-liberals have used sluggish economic growth as an indicator that social reforms have not yet gone far enough. Ironically, the public reaction to these claims, in combination with changing business practices (see Chapter 1 by Dyson) and reforms that have chipped away at historic entitlements themselves, slowed economic recovery, for example by increasing personal saving rates. In keeping with a growing scholarly emphasis on the potentially cumulative impact of incremental reforms (Streek and Thelen 2005a, 2005b), both cases have seen a layering of new social provisions targeted at 'excluded' groups and often funded from general taxation over their traditional 'Bismarckian' social insurance systems (Mabbett and Schelkle 2005: 17; Palier 2005; Seeleib-Kaiser and Fleckenstein 2007). Without it ever being directly repudiated, then, these states may have started 'departing from the path of Conservative Welfare' or Bismarckianism (Seeleib-Kaiser and Fleckenstein 2007: 430) through a series of seemingly small steps.

Equally strikingly, however, these accounts of change concentrate on domestic politics, largely to the exclusion of the European level, if not explicitly arguing that EMU has not been causal in determining policy change. Thus while Palier (2007: 15) sometimes suggests that 'European (Union) economic policies channel and bind welfare reforms, especially in Bismarckian countries', he has also analysed French reforms solely in terms of domestic politics

(Palier 2005), sometimes even suggesting that Paris led and shaped the EU agenda for social and labour-market policies more than the other way round (Coron and Palier 2002: 113, 129). Seeleib-Kaiser and Fleckenstein (2007: 437) argue even more directly that the cause of pressure on German policy was 'the fiscal conservatism of German policy-makers' not 'European integration as such'.

Conclusion

The headline aggregates for European states' social expenditure show no major reversal over EMU's lifetime, although there is some evidence that its pace of increase was slower for Euro Area states after 2002. Thus far, then, the aggregates provide little support for strong versions of the 'disciplinary neo-liberal' thesis, at least for Western Europe. While what evidence we have does not suggest a dramatic decline in social commitment for the new EU member states, the comparative data here is very patchy. Social policy discourses remain strikingly distinct in Eastern and Western Europe: the poor integration of the new member states into EU social policy, patterns of coordination, and debates about the 'European Social Model' emerges clearly from this analysis. Western Europe states seem to have significantly greater resources to resist neo-liberal welfare discourses than do those in east-central Europe; Slovenia aside, the latter are faced, it seems, with a sharp choice between efficiency and equity.

Beneath the aggregates, social policy seems to be undergoing complex processes of change, even in Western European heartland. In contrast to comparative theory's expectations of inertia, the evidence—from a diversity of sources—for welfare state change is growing. While radical critics rightly draw attention to the degrading of some established entitlements, this is not simply a story of hidden retrenchment. Many European states are also developing new social discourses and new forms of policy. Even when we consider measures of 'decommodification' or benefit generosity for the traditional core of welfare transfers, unexpected patterns emerge. While Nordic generosity remains unparalleled, these states—which arguably attained 'decommodificatory' status between the late 1970s and early 1990s—have recently recorded the sharpest decline. Matched with a measure of 'catch-up' from erstwhile welfare laggards, the result has been a measure of welfare convergence in (mostly north-western) Europe, but one unrelated to Euro Area membership.

A second look at continental Europe's reputedly frozen Bismarckian landscape shows a complex pattern of change, elements of which often began a surprisingly long time ago. Examples include the French *revenu minimum d'insertion*—a non-insurance minimum income benefit which dates from

1988- and the increasing role of social assistance in Germany. Many such moves pre-date stage three of EMU, and often began even before Maastricht: even more recent developments of this kind are often, that is, rooted in domestic politics, with EMU serving as an additional conditioning factor rather than a primary cause of change. They often concern problems of post-industrialization that are faced in welfare states that have been traditionally focused on industrial workers. They support my contention that individual states show features typically associated with multiple ideal-regimes. Ironically, the historic success of its manufacturing industry base may mean that Germany now faces a late and particularly intractable post-industrialization process. Together with absorbing the eastern *Länder*, this lag provides important elements to explain its economic sluggishness and role as laggard in welfare reforms in the 1990s and early 2000s. However, even where new policies seek solutions to emerging social problems, they may unsettle established welfare configurations: complexity, while hardly as 'esoteric' as the politics of financial regulation, does make welfare reform proposals difficult to digest in democratic polities, potentially with complex and surprising results, perhaps particularly where the extent of reform has been obfuscated in both domestic and European debate. In this vein the impact of 'Community Method' rules on health services or insurance markets may eventually have a bigger impact on state welfare than EMU or the Open Method of Coordination.

Within the complex politics of welfare reform EMU has often served as a convenient symbol of neo-liberalism for many opponents of welfare retrenchment. While the evidence of direct policy-impacts is at best patchy, EMU has been an important element of the context for European welfare politics. And recently ECB officials seem to have become more engaged in the discursive politics of European welfare reform. The detail of their chosen themes is hardly new—as our discussion of relatively unnoticed continental reforms implies. However, at first glance, the celebration of the Nordic states' 'productive' social policy (focused on activation and, albeit less emphasized, social investment) might appear surprising. It seems to represent a discursive convergence—a shared socio-economic 'model' at the EU level— from the Open Method of Coordination, by way of the Commission, to the ECB. ECB officials are relatively recent converts to this vision. Rather than 'leading', they took up this discourse *after* it had been adopted in many (western) member states and spread through other EU institutions. Nevertheless adoption by the ECB may consolidate the discourse and alter its political meaning.

European central bankers' celebration of the 'Nordic model' coincided with their deployment of 'Lisbon' as a means of pressing for structural reform. They tend to stress the ability of the Nordic states to facilitate large-scale formal participation by women in the labour market, rather than traditional transfer benefits. Even if this discourse may, in principle, be consistent with a variety of welfare policy configurations, ECB officials may be making subtle strategic use of it. They deploy Nordic experience to suggest that structural reform *need* not imply a large-scale dismantling of a state's social agenda. In other words, ECB officials may have been addressing these remarks to policymakers, or even the mass publics, in the Franco-German Euro Area core (which helps to explain the absence of any attempt to address this discourse to east central Europe). Instead, attempting to reassure French and German policymakers and electors about the possibility of reconciling economic reform with social concerns may prove a more effective means of motivating politically controversial reforms that reconfigure and transform state capacities. Ultimately, ECB advocacy of the Nordic model—together with ongoing domestically based welfare changes and other 'community Method' pressures—may help to twist the kaleidoscope of European politics and produce a pattern that undermines state social policy capacities; while the condition of European welfare states remains unsettled, this paradoxical outcome seems to have been avoided, at least so far.

20

European States and the Euro Area: Clustering and Covariance in Patterns of Change

Kenneth Dyson

In the light of the preceding 'country' and thematic chapters, this chapter asks whether patterns can be identified in the effects that the Euro Area is having on European states, with respect to their institutional characteristics, policies, and politics. Its central argument focuses on the need to embed Europeanization research—on how European economic governance and policies, especially the euro, affect states and their activities—in a broader political economy analysis. This approach to analysing change incorporates the preferences of firms—how they respond to changing market circumstances, consequent on the euro, in turn altering the context of state action. The chapter focuses principally on Euro Area member states.

In terms of Europeanization the simplest and basic starting point is different 'clusterings' of states as defined by their strategic positions in relation to Euro Area accession and membership. By 2009 there were 16 Euro Area member states ('insiders'); nine temporary 'outsiders'—mostly in east central Europe—which are distinguished by having their own euro entry strategies with road maps and dates; and at least three semi-permanent 'outsiders' (Britain, Denmark, and Sweden) that attach no date to euro entry and have no entry strategy (Table 20.1). This formalistic pattern highlights contrasting Europeanization experiences of states: for 'insiders', living with Euro Area membership; for temporary 'outsiders', meeting adjustment challenges from tough accession conditionality including ERM II entry (the Maastricht convergence criteria); and, for semi-permanent 'outsiders', managing the opportunities and constraints of retaining independent monetary and exchange-rate policies. The declining credibility of frequently deferred and ultimately abandoned domestically set entry dates acts as an indicator of transition from temporary

Table 20.1. Euro Area insiders and outsiders

Insiders	Temporary outsiders	Semi-permanent outsiders
Austria	Bulgaria	Britain
Belgium	Czech Republic	Sweden
Cyprus	Estonia	
Finland	Hungary	
France	Latvia	
Germany	Lithuania	
Greece	Poland	
Ireland	Romania	
Italy		
Luxembourg		Denmark?
Malta		
The Netherlands		
Portugal		
Slovakia		
Slovenia		
Spain		

to semi-permanent 'outsider' status. For instance, in 2007 the new Czech government declared the 2012 target date to be unrealistic and did not set a new deadline; whilst in January 2008 the Czech central bank president suggested 2019 as a possibility.

However, this formalistic analysis masks subtle and dynamic processes. In the case of east central European temporary 'outsiders' Dyson (2006*b*, 2007*a*) provides a more differentiated analysis of 'clustered' convergence. The three Baltic States sought to lock in a pre-existing domestic regime of economic stability by accelerated euro entry; the Czech Republic, Hungary, and Poland were disposed to defer entry in favour of investment in industrial restructuring and of social policies to support social solidarity and ease domestic tensions; whilst Slovenia entered in 2007 on the basis of a gradual transition, negotiated through social partnership, that reconciled economic stability with industrial modernization and social solidarity. Denmark was also difficult to categorize. It had no date for entry but, unlike Britain and Sweden, was an ERM II member and had a government in 2007 keen to revive euro entry. Conversely, some east central European states looked as if they might slip into the semi-permanent 'outsider' category as their doubts about ERM II entry and revised dates for entry put their status in question.

There is also evidence of some institutional differentiation inside the Euro Area, notably in representation in its structures. It is possible to identify an inner core. The six-member ECB directorate has displayed a continuing presence of former French, German, Italian, and Spanish central bankers. These four central banks had, in turn, a leading role in developing and operating a core infrastructure of the Euro Area, the TARGET2 electronics payment system. Post-Euro Area enlargement, the ECB Governing Council will differentiate between a nucleus of large states (defined by a combination of GDP and financial assets) with lower rotation of voting rights than for other states. This pattern suggests a shadow of G-7 in the working of the Euro Area, leaving aside Spain. Nevertheless, the shadow was faint. There was no evidence of a Euro Area 'directorate'. In 2007 the chairs of the Economic and Financial Committee and of the Economic Policy Committee were respectively French and British, but the president of the Euro Group was a Luxembourgian. The open question was whether with continuing Euro Area enlargement there would be a strengthened tendency towards differentiated representation in the Euro Area's institutional structures.

In seeking to map the effects of the euro we face the serious difficulties identified in Chapter 1 by Dyson: specifying the independent variable, handling the 'nested' character of EMU, identifying the timing of regime change, tracing and interpreting processes of change and their effects over time, dealing with the scope of the dependent variable (policies, polities, and politics), and incorporating 'soft' data, for instance about discourse and identities that are not readily measurable, often not available, and yet crucial to answering the question. These difficulties complicate the search for underlying patterns, are by no means easy to manage, and resist being 'solved'. The difficulties mount with the 'reach' of political analysis: as one extends it beyond policies (or just a narrow subsection of policies, say fiscal and wages) to both politics and polities. They also grow if one seeks to go beyond narrow 'snapshots', which lack temporal context, and offer a more wide-angled 'moving picture' of the Euro Area in time.

'Clustered' Convergence?

The central question requires clearer specification. First, are there discernible spatial and temporal patterns; second, if so, do these patterns tend to 'cluster' or display covariance, suggesting perhaps random processes; and, third, what are the implications of any patterns for the sustainability of the Euro Area?

In response to the first and second questions, the chapter argues that over the first decade some spatial and temporal patterns seem to reinforce each other—though there is no implication that they will endure. They yield three clusters within the Euro Area; two clusters amongst temporary 'outsiders' (Baltic and three of the Visegrad states); whilst the three semi-permanent 'outsiders' defy much more than formalistic categorization (Table 20.2). States from each cluster are represented in this volume.

Within the Euro Area, the persistence of a distinct core 'D-Mark-Zone' cluster is suggested by a combination of patterns—continuing German economic hegemony, path dependence, early timing of entry into *de facto* monetary

Table 20.2. Three Euro Area clusters

D-Mark-Zone	Mediterranean	Small, neo-corporatist
Austria	Greece	Austria
Belgium	Italy	Cyprus
France	Portugal	Finland
Germany		Ireland
Luxembourg		Luxembourg
The Netherlands		Malta
		The Netherlands
		Slovenia
	Spain?	

union, assertive firm-led strategies to enhance competitiveness by reducing unit labour costs, and the so-called 'gravity' effects. Improved German economic performance post-2005 imparted a new confidence to this cluster (see Chapter 11 by Verdun) and to the Euro Area. In the period of economic weakness of this core cluster between 2001 and 2005, however, public support for the euro and the wider integration process eroded, notably in the Dutch case.

In addition, there appears to be a distinct 'small-state' cluster (though one to which not all small states belong). This cluster is characterized by small size, cultural homogeneity, and a neo-corporatist bias in economic policy. These states lack overall economic weight in GDP and financial assets but punch well above their economic weight based on economic reform capacity and performance. This small-state cluster comprises Austria, Finland, Ireland, and Luxembourg plus Cyprus, Malta, and Slovenia. Minus these three latter states, for which comparable data were not available, it displays an above average positive public assessment of the euro. On average 67 per cent view it as 'advantageous overall', compared to an Euro Area-12 average of 48 per cent and a D-Mark-Zone cluster average of 53 per cent (Gallup Europe 2006: 30). Austria and Luxembourg are in both the D-Mark-Zone and small-state clusters. However, Greece and Portugal are in neither.

A third 'Mediterranean' cluster is defined by distinctive domestic governance (weak state capacity for coordinated economic policymaking), firm-led strategies that focus on protection of domestic markets, late timing of entry into *de facto* monetary union, and geographic distance from the D-Mark-Zone core: Greece, Italy, and Portugal (Spain is problematic because on balance its firm-led strategies differ and state capacity is stronger). These states have been characterized by weak economic performance, especially in unit cost development and in unemployment and in fiscal conditions, and by declining public support for the euro. Average positive public assessment of the euro (including Spain in the calculation) dropped from 56 per cent in 2002 to 44 per cent in 2006. Conversely, those seeing the euro as 'disadvantageous overall' climbed from 23 to 39 per cent (Gallup Europe 2002: 32, 2006: 30).

By 2006 for Greece and Italy the same public opinion survey recorded net negative assessments of 6 and 7 per cent, respectively. They had net positive assessments of 22 and 28 per cent in 2002.

However, these Euro Area 'insider' clusters are also cross cut, dynamic over time with signs of randomness (witness Spain), and, in consequence, not always clearly defined. For instance, the 'D-Mark-Zone' cluster is internally differentiated by size, cultural homogeneity/segmentation, domestic governance mechanisms, domestic path dependencies, and domestic political strategies for temporal management of change. Mediterranean states vary too, not just in size but also in internal variegation linked to differences in 'gravity' and in cultural and governance characteristics. For instance, the weight of Catalonia in Spain and of the North in Italy is associated with sharp internal contrasts. States are not always easily pigeonholed; Spain has participated more strongly in trade effects of the euro than other members of the Mediterranean cluster and enjoys more positive public attitudes to the euro.

Covariance applies especially in processes of domestic reform to fiscal, financial, and labour-market policies and in strengthening firm competitiveness consequent on the euro. In Austria, Finland, and Ireland major 'top-down', politically led reforms by governments, often in anticipation of euro entry, *co-existed* with active 'bottom-up', firm-led change to improve competitiveness. In Germany, by contrast, assertive firm-led change *compensated* for deficits in 'top-down' structural reforms. In Greece and especially Portugal painful 'top-down' reforms were paramount, especially in fiscal policies, and *compensated* to some extent for weak 'bottom-up' processes of firm-led change.

The answers to the first two questions are complex and yield neither one single pattern nor simple 'clusters' into which states can be neatly and indefinitely slotted. In response to the third question, the combination of a persisting but weakened core D-Mark-Zone cluster with crosscutting patterns, of an even weaker Mediterranean cluster, and of a small-state 'high-performing' cluster had paradoxical consequences for the sustainability of the Euro Area. The relatively poor economic growth and employment performance of this traditional core (in comparative and historical terms), at least until 2006, created tensions and conflicts with small states like Austria, Finland, and the Netherlands (inside and outside the core). Similarly, Germany's intense unit cost reduction placed new competitiveness pressures on states in the Mediterranean cluster. On the other hand, the superior growth and employment performance of many small, culturally homogenous, neo-corporatist states defused potential tensions by diffusing power and broadening the benchmarking of policies and performance away from the traditional German 'hegemon'.

The problems focus on those Mediterranean states that are outside the 'small state' and D-Mark-Zone clusters and are vulnerable to declining competitiveness. As Eichengreen (2007) has shown, these states also face profound disincentives to contemplating Euro Area exit. Hence, they face a formidable long-term challenge of competitive disinflation. Even so, the location of Euro Area problems can shift, not least as a consequence of mistaken domestic political and policy choices in previously successful states. As Marcussen stresses, success is contingent, economic models short-lived. Ireland and Spain, for instance, have provided much of Euro Area growth, but their consumption-led expansion remains vulnerable to over-commitment to their housing and construction sectors.

A Kaleidoscope of Patterns

In recognition of these difficulties in identifying EMU as an independent variable, in tracing cause-effect relations, in interpreting limited data, and in contextualizing the euro, the chapter focuses on developing a set of hypotheses around intervening variables. It considers hegemony, size, cultural homogeneity, domestic governance mechanisms, geographic distance ('gravity'), comparative advantage, initial conditions, and political strategies for temporal management of economic reform. The chapter seeks to tease out—in a provisional and tentative way at this early stage—some underlying spatial and temporal patterns in the complex relations between European states and the euro. Its working assumptions are, first, that space and time matter in understanding how these relations are evolving and, second, that states and their governments matter, but in a limited and conditional way.

The chapter outlines two sets of 'spatial' and 'temporal' hypotheses. It proceeds on the basis of inference from limited data and trying to weave together different bits of evidence into plausible patterns. What emerges is a kaleidoscope of patterns. This complexity raises the question of whether these patterns—like hegemony, size, gravity, domestic governance mechanisms, timing of entry, and misfit on entry—reinforce each other to exhibit a clear 'clustering' or crosscut each other and display covariance and illustrate randomness across space and over time.

Before this analysis the chapter considers how the answers to these questions relate to the wider literature on comparative political economy and comparative politics, specifically on 'varieties of capitalism', on types of democracy, and on comparative advantage. In both cases answers are difficult because there is no consensus on how to categorize states and because states defy neat 'timeless' categorization. On closer political economy analysis states look like evolving neo-liberal hybrids rather than pure types of capitalism (Dyson and Padgett 2006). Moreover, there remains a tendency to limit analysis to the old EU-15 and to a time period before 1998. With the exception of Slovenia, and to a lesser extent Slovakia, the institutional conditions for corporatism are absent in east central Europe; they are also diminishing in the old EU-15. In addition, since the late 1990s, if not earlier, Austria and the Netherlands have been less recognizable as 'consensus' democracies (Lijphart 1999).

Varieties of Capitalism and the Euro

Using Hall and Soskice's (2001) dichotomy of models of capitalism, and assuming persisting German hegemony and a D-Mark-Zone cluster, the Euro Area seems *prima facie* closer to the model of 'coordinated' market economy than 'liberal' market economy. Seen this way, the Euro Area exhibits a bias towards non-market forms of coordinated capitalism in areas like industrial relations, vocational training, technology transfer, and, above all, wage bargaining. However, this conclusion is heavily qualified both by the general relative lack of capacity for effective non-market coordination outside the old D-Mark-Zone cluster (e.g. in Greece and Italy), by the Irish 'Anglo-Saxon' case, and by market liberalization processes within the D-Mark-Zone cluster (including Germany itself).

This problem is partly circumvented by Sapir's (2005) more complex categories. In this perspective, the Euro Area comprises four clusters: a 'D-Mark-Zone' cluster of 'Rhineland' capitalism, with three contrasting outliers—'Anglo-Saxon' (Ireland), Mediterranean (Greece, Italy, Portugal, and Spain), and Nordic (Finland and, oddly, the Netherlands which is slotted into this category). Sapir's definition of 'Rhineland' capitalism combines relatively low employment participation rates with an emphasis on policies to promote social solidarity. The result is high non-wage labour costs and fiscal strains. However, this 'Rhineland' core seems to be endogenously eroding and reconfiguring as a hybrid (Dyson and Padgett 2006).

The 'varieties of capitalism' literature has some heuristic value in highlighting differing macro-economic institutional problems of fitting EU states to the requirements of Euro Area membership. However, it has been slow to accommodate east central Europe. Drawing on Dyson (2007a) and Bohle and Greskovits (2007), three clusters emerge. Baltic capitalism—with its priority to macro-economic stabilization—was strongly focused on rapid Euro Area entry but far removed from the 'Rhineland' model of social solidarity. The Visegrad states—the Czech Republic, Hungary, Poland, and Slovakia—were much closer to the 'Rhineland' model in this respect, but lacked its organizational capacity (with weak employer and trade-union organizations) and, with the notable exception of Slovakia, were more inclined to hesitate on euro entry. Slovenia was a Rhineland capitalism outlier that was the first to enter the Euro Area in 2007.

Types of Democracy and the Euro

Similar problems of discrimination and mutability arise with the political science literature on different types of democracy in trying to shed light on patterns in the relationship between European states and the euro. Lijphart's (1999) classic distinction between 'majoritarian' and 'consensus' or 'negotiation' democracies rests on 10 variables in two clusters. It includes contrasts between 'first-past-the-post' and proportional representation electoral systems, single-party and coalition governments, executive and parliamentary dominance, unicameral and bicameral parliaments, and pluralist and corporatist patterns of interest accommodation. However, Lijphart's indices for categorizing and measuring, his attempts to link these types of democracy to policy performance, and his conclusions on the superiority of the 'consensus' type present a number of difficulties. In practice, using these indices, most states are hybrids, shift over time (as with Ireland), and—like Greece—defy neat categorization. There is no clear linkage between economic performance and type of democracy.

Prima facie 'consensus' democracies, with their complex sharing of powers amongst actors, are vulnerable to an inbuilt bias to a slower speed of policy innovation when problems mount and to consequent populist mobilization against government inefficiency and perceived elite collusion, corruption, and failure. Austria and the Netherlands are examples. However, this conclusion invites two qualifications. First, the key issue seems to be whether features of 'consensus' democracy are accompanied by ideological and party fragmentation at the level of political elites. The resulting centripetal or centrifugal party system tendencies, and their effects on policy performance, shape the difference between Austria, Finland, Germany, the Netherlands, and Slovenia, where cabinet and ministerial duration in office is relatively high, and the Baltic States, Italy, Poland, and Romania, where it is low. Consensus democracies with ideological and party fragmentation are at greater risk from both cabinet and ministerial instability and from populist mobilization against governmental inefficiency and perceived elite collusion, corruption, and failure. Second, neo-corporatist forms of arranging relations between organized interests and the state are not synonymous with 'consensus' democracy. Both neo-corporatism and central bank independence may be more relevant to policy performance than the governance devices normally attributed to 'consensus' democracy. Ireland is a case of new forms of neo-corporatism and central bank independence without 'consensus' democracy.

Comparative Advantage and the Euro

The effects of the euro on EU states are bound up in the nature of their economic structures, their specific comparative advantage, and variations in the endogenous capacity of firms and sectors to lead or inhibit processes and patterns of change associated with EMU. Strategies to exploit comparative advantage—whether in global finance, in low-tech, or in high-tech manufacturing—lead firms to press states not just for different kinds of policy positions on euro entry but also for different types of domestic institutional arrangements in wage bargaining. The combination of a powerful globally oriented, technologically sophisticated, highly innovative financial sector in the City of London with a relatively small-scale, low-tech manufacturing sector (which feared 'importing' higher-cost business practices) produced a British corporate sector that was biased towards a sceptical 'wait-and-see' attitude on euro entry. In contrast, high-tech export manufacturers in Germany were not just in favour of Euro Area membership to extend their market scale; they also supported domestic sector-level coordination of collective bargaining in the interests of protecting their investment in a skilled labour force. In the British and German cases different types of assertive large firms, embedded in different economic structures, were able to seek out and use a freedom of manoeuvre, with different results for the way in which EMU relates to domestic change.

East central Europe offered a variegated economic structure that led to different kinds of firm strategies across states. For instance, in the Baltic States the low-tech manufacturing sector of smaller firms sought to retain cost advantage by supporting a macro-economic strategy that locked in economic stability through accelerated euro entry. At the same time their preference for flexibility in firm-level wage bargaining and for very low tax and social security obligations made fiscal consolidation for early euro entry relatively easy. In the Visegrad states cross-national, high-tech firms engaged in intra-industry trade generated more demands both for public spending (that hindered fiscal consolidation) and for early euro entry (which required fiscal consolidation). The result was more ambivalent positions on euro entry and domestic reforms. In short, firm strategies have very different implications for euro entry and for domestic reforms.

Spatial Hypotheses

Spatial hypotheses about the Euro Area have to contend with the presumption—based on longer historical experience of European monetary integration—that the 'old' D-Mark-Zone cluster would come to define the underlying pattern for how the Euro Area would affect member states. Quite simply, there would be a 'periphery' of Euro Area states, whose reform agendas would be driven by a German-centred core cluster, and a set of 'supplicant' Euro Area accession states that would—sooner or later—join and be driven by the same agenda. In practice, the patterns that have emerged display covariance. The D-Mark-Zone cluster remains discernible but represents a 'softened' core of the Euro Area.

Hegemony Matters

The first hypothesis suggests that 'hegemony matters'. *The direction, content, and pace of domestic reforms across the Euro Area are set by the hegemon.* Any claim to a hegemonic role as responsible leader lies with Germany. This claim rests on a traditional set of indicators: Germany's absolute GDP size, its relative economic performance, its traditional 'anchor' role in European exchange-rate regimes and hence pacesetting role in monetary policy, and its effectiveness in 'uploading' German institutional and policy templates into the design of the Euro Area (notably of the European Central Bank). In combination, they define an inherited 'D-Mark-Zone' cluster, comprising six current Euro Area states—Austria, Belgium, France, Luxembourg, and the Netherlands (potentially also Slovenia), and defined by German leadership.

German leadership is both ideational and material. It has been reflected in the prestige of 'Rhineland' capitalism within this Euro Area 'core'. The influence of this 'German model' into the 1990s was underpinned by an intensifying trade relationship within this emerging 'family' of 'cooperative' market capitalism based on a high valuation of social solidarity. Its material manifestations included a much closer intra-industry trade and cyclical syn-chronization of economies around Germany than elsewhere in the EU. In 2006 the D-Mark-Zone cluster accounted for 62.3 per cent of the Euro Area's GDP (purchasing power parity); Germany, for 27.5.

A series of developments undermined the capacity of Germany to play this hegemonic role in the Euro Area. First, before the Euro Area, German unifi-cation led to the de-synchronization of the German economy. The hegemon was shaken from within; it emerged as a fiscally and economically 'burdened state' destabilizing its 'cluster' members. This problem appeared to have been ameliorated by 2006. Second, with the Euro Area Germany lost its role as the anchor of monetary policy: the ECB, and no longer the Bundesbank, 'ruled Europe', notionally according to German rules but crucially by territorial reference to the Euro Area and not to Germany. Third, the political decision to opt for a larger Euro Area rather than a 'mini' D-Mark-Zone cluster Euro Area reduced the German share in total GDP and aggravated the potential for a German 'misfit' with ECB interest rates. At 2006 prices, it would have accounted for 44.1 per cent of a Euro Area comprising the six D-Mark-Zone cluster (instead of 27.5).

Finally, in consequence of these developments, Germany lost credible claims to be a model around which the direction and content of Euro Area reforms could be driven. Its performance, especially in GDP growth, fell well below the Euro Area average, as well as its own historical and declining average. Between 2001 and 2005 its average GDP growth was under half the Euro Area average; even Italy and Portugal delivered slightly better performances. Correspondingly, the German share of Euro Area GDP declined, from 34.2 per cent in 1996 to 27.5 per cent in 2006.

The result of this erosion of German hegemony was new stresses and strains within the old D-Mark-Zone cluster and a diminished capacity for leadership. Within this cluster only tiny Luxembourg (3.7 per cent) outperformed Britain and Sweden in average GDP growth between 2001 and 2005; over the period 1996–2000 only Luxembourg and the Netherlands had achieved this distinction. Hence, there was a loss of reputation and influence within the wider EU debates on economic reform. Within the Euro Area the outstanding performers (other than Luxembourg) in average GDP growth between 2001 and 2005 were Greece (4.4 per cent), Finland (2.5), and Ireland (5.3), far removed from the old geographic core.

However, a distinction needs to be drawn between deterioration in relative economic performance, on the one hand, and absolute GDP size and per capita income and wealth, on the other. Even in relative performance, the German economy manifested a sustained capacity for unit cost reduction that restored its competitive trading position vis-à-vis its Euro Area competitors. In absolute size Germany continued to represent the Euro Area core. As we shall see, 'gravity continues to matter' through geographical proximity to the state with the highest combination of population size with per capita income, financial assets, capital exports, and trade. In this sense, at least, there was continuity.

But in the sense of coherent and persuasive ideas to shape and guide domestic reforms something had been lost that neither the variegated Euro Area 'periphery' nor the heterogeneous 'outsiders' like Britain, Denmark, and Sweden—or the 'new' mosaic of post-2004 member states—could provide. Whatever coherent organization the ECB could deliver was, paradoxically given its Germanic origins, a 'misfit' with German requirements. Germany was part of the problem of economic reform rather than the provider of solutions. On the other hand, its success in unit cost reduction was a source of new adjustment problems for its trading partners and of intensifying pressures for domestic changes.

Size Matters: Economic Openness

The second hypothesis suggests that 'size matters'. *EMU has activated and empowered the economic policy role of small EU states as models of structural reforms to a greater extent than large states, irrespective of whether or not they are Euro Area members.* As with the Common Foreign and Security Policy, there appears to be a differential empowerment of member states, with stronger activism by small states. Denmark, Finland, and the Netherlands scored highly in OECD measures of 'structural reform intensity', especially in labour markets (where they were the top three) (Duval and Elmeskov 2006). Similarly, the 'ambitious' public expenditure reformers were Belgium and the Netherlands in the 1980s, then Finland and Sweden in the 1990s. They made large cuts in transfers, subsidies, wages, and public employment, and reformed domestic fiscal institutions (Hauptmeier, Heipertz, and Schuknecht 2006). With respect to fiscal institutions to strengthen domestic budget discipline, Austria, Belgium, Ireland, and Portugal led in implementing reforms, Germany did not—at least till federal reforms in 2006–8 (Enderlein 2004). This picture of differential empowerment runs counter to the earlier expectation that a hegemonic Germany would lead processes of structural reform across the Euro Area.

The rationale offered for this 'superior' small state performance in reforms is their trade openness and dependency. On the one hand, small states benefit disproportionately from the deepening of market integration because of their higher degree of openness to intra-Euro Area trade—measured as the average of exports and imports over total demand. They also gain more from income risk sharing through their access to larger more liquid financial markets. On the other hand, openness is linked to greater vulnerability and an incentive to assume joint responsibility for managing change and cushioning its effects, notably through the welfare state (Cameron 1978). The result is that EMU offers greater incentives—through gains from trade creation, income risk sharing, and increased higher external vulnerability—and hence lower political costs for small states than for large states to simultaneously engage actively in, and offer compensation for, radical labour-market, welfare-state, and product-market reforms. In consequence, they are better placed to adjust swiftly to asymmetric shocks (Hoeller, Giorno, and de la Maisonneuve 2004). Duval and Elmeskov (2006) stress the marginal effects of the euro on structural reforms in large states. If anything, on OECD measures, the pace of structural reforms in the large states seemed to slow down after 1998/9, suggesting a weakening of incentives consequent on the loss of monetary policy autonomy (Duval and Elmeskov 2006).

This conclusion echoes the argument of Alesina and Spolaore (2005) that globalization 'tilts' the balance of advantage to small states through the higher marginal economies of market scale that it offers them compared to large states. However, the globalization/small state argument also suggests that small European states may benefit from an incentive to structural reforms whether or not they are Euro Area members or have intensive trade with the Euro Area. Small Euro Area outsiders like Denmark and Sweden have benefited more than many insiders from its trade effects, which have been equivalent to unilateral trade liberalization by the Euro Area (see Baldwin 2006a, 2006b). Conversely, Finland, a Euro Area insider, has gained disproportionately from extra-Euro Area trade.

The argument that 'size matters' seems to apply also to public opinion surveys. According to Gallup Europe (2006: 30, 75), the percentage viewing the euro as 'advantageous overall' after five years was over 60 in Ireland, Finland, Luxembourg, and Austria (in descending order), with Belgium next at 58; whilst the figure was over 70 per cent for those 'personally happy that the euro has become our currency' in Luxembourg, Belgium, Ireland, and Finland (in descending order). However, to complicate the picture, small states figured at the other end of the scale: the two lowest on 'advantageous overall' were Greece and the Netherlands (both 38 per cent); whilst Austria (39 per cent) and the Netherlands (37 per cent) were behind only Germany (though well behind) in the percentage 'unhappy that the euro had become our currency'.

The 'size matters' hypothesis loses some of its robustness in the face of the next three spatial hypotheses. Measures of openness to Euro Area trade do not seem to correlate too well with 'structural reform intensity'. Finland—a model of 'structural reform intensity'—is more comparable with Greece—a laggard on reforms—in intra-Euro Area trade; Belgium—not usually seen as a pacesetter in reform intensity—leads all others in openness to Euro-Area trade. Moreover, in the 1990s Belgium shifted from 'ambitious' to 'timid' public expenditure reformer. At least up to 2006–7 Hungary proved as timid on expenditure reform as Italy. More seriously, both Austria (though on the borderline to 'ambitious') and Denmark counted as 'timid' expenditure reformers, compared to larger states like Britain and Spain (Hauptmeier, Heipertz, and Schuknecht 2006). These complications suggest that Alesina and Spolaore as well as Duval and Elmeskov neglect the role of domestic political culture and governance mechanisms and evolving political dynamics.

Small and Homogenous Matters: Domestic Political Culture and Governance Mechanisms

The robustness of the 'size' hypothesis is questioned by a third set of hypotheses that focus on classic political science variables of domestic political cultures and governance mechanisms. A first hypothesis is that: *EMU has activated the economic policy role of culturally 'homogenous' small states, like Ireland and the Nordic states, to a greater extent than traditionally culturally 'segmented' small states, like Belgium and the Netherlands.* This hypothesis highlights domestic patterns of socio-political cleavages and suggests that political culture and related modes of democratic governance matter more than size (cf. Lijphart 1980 and 1999). The Euro Area is associated with a differential empowerment amongst small states, which is to be explained by reference to these domestic intervening variables, notably power-sharing arrangements. Small states are not all the same (cf. Katzenstein 1985).

Political culture studies identify 'segmented' small states, which are characterized by historically sensitive, and sometimes reinforcing, social and political cleavages. They juxtapose potentially fractious communities, whether on class, religious, linguistic, and/or ethnic lines. For some periods, in some cases (like Austria, Belgium, the Netherlands, and Switzerland), these segmented political cultures have been managed by skilful, consensus-seeking elite behaviour. Their 'accommodative' modes of 'non-majoritarian' or 'negotiation' democracy are associated with a distinctive set of governance mechanisms for promoting inclusiveness through power sharing and carefully negotiated change. They include grand coalition governments or complex, broad-based coalitions, detailed coalition commitments (including fiscal contracts), party proportionality in making public appointments, and minority veto (Lijphart 2002).

This type of small state has been variously characterized as 'consensual' or 'consociational' democracies and seen as efficient at managing change through collective sharing of its costs. They are associated with a lower tolerance for income disparities and large redistributive welfare states. In terms of domestic reforms, they are seen as slower in forming governments, as potentially more time-consuming in effecting change, as less effective in political innovation, and as less transparent in decision processes than 'majoritarian' democracies (Schmidt 2002). In short, to the extent that the Euro Area represents a 'step' change in economic reforms towards market liberalization, the euro exposes the weaknesses of 'consensual' democracies and raises questions about the polity as a whole.

A particular strength of 'consensual' democracies, not recognized in conventional definitions, lies in a greater capacity to pursue informal party political collusion or 'cartelization' as a strategy for 'blame avoidance' with voters in pursuing economic and welfare-state reforms (Blyth and Katz 2005). The incentive to restrict party competition about policy alternatives—thus to collude in reform, short of formal grand coalition—is increased where two or more parties are ideologically committed to defending social solidarity. Pension reforms provide an example of this type of strategy to avoid electoral failure (Hering 2005). The risk of this 'blame avoidance' through party cartel-like behaviour is encouragement of anti-system populist politics, seen in Austria, Belgium, and the Netherlands, as well as the Baltic States.

This type of political explanation for differential performance in economic reform suffers from problems of treating political cultures as historical 'givens' and of failing to capture the hybrid, evolving character of political systems. Most democratic systems offer particular, varying combinations of consensual and majoritarian governance mechanisms: Germany, for instance, is characterized by power-sharing arrangements, but has strong majoritarian features. Hence, attempts to shoehorn particular states into 'consensual' democracies, and then use them to explain how a particular type of domestic governance mechanism is related to economic performance, are rarely convincing.

Domestic governing mechanisms in segmented societies are contingent and fragile, especially in the face of the pressures from rising structural unemployment and consequent rising costs of collective sharing of burdens. In these circumstances, as in Belgium and the Netherlands in the 1970s and again from the mid-1990s, and in Austria after 2000, 'consensus-seeking' mechanisms erode, structural reforms prove more politically contested, and anti-establishment populist politics gathers strength. Simultaneously, as the experiences of Austria, Belgium, and the Netherlands reveal, the boundaries for reform are opened and the constraints on reform made transparent.

This hypothesis of link between cultural homogeneity and domestic reform performance seems to be confirmed by the small state cases of Cyprus, Denmark, Ireland, Finland, Malta, Slovenia, and Sweden. They served as central role models of structural reforms since 1998. They are relatively homogenous in socio-political structures, exhibit high levels of social trust and hence their elites have a greater incentive to support cooperative policy processes and outcomes. They find it easier to bind coalition governments to credible commitments on structural and especially fiscal reforms, without frequent defections. An interesting variation is states that are segmented but behave as if culturally homogenous. Instances include Slovakia, with its Romany population, and the Baltic States, with their even larger Russian minorities especially in Estonia and Latvia. They score highly on reform indicators (though concealing substantial exclusion and potential for domestic conflict) but eschew collective sharing of costs (thereby exhibiting a lack of social trust). In contrast, Belgium, and to a lesser extent Austria, occupied a secondary position in structural reform league tables. Their relative decline in reform performance was associated with more competitive elite behaviour and elite defensiveness in the face of populist politics. Hence, it seems plausible to argue that domestic consensus building around structural reforms has proved easier in the more homogenous Nordic states, Cyprus, Ireland, Malta, and Portugal, as well as in the 'virtually' homogenous Baltic States and Slovakia, than in Belgium and the Netherlands.

Despite this qualification to the 'size' hypothesis, even segmented small states with more competitive elite behaviour like Austria, Belgium, and the Netherlands outpaced the larger states, especially France, Italy, and Spain, on most measures of 'structural reform intensity' (Duval and Elmeskov 2006: 23). This result also applies in fiscal policy reforms, where the large states—France, Germany, and Italy—fell into the 'timid' category compared to Finland, Ireland, and the Netherlands (Hauptmeier, Heipertz, and Schuknecht 2006).

A different variant of the domestic governing mechanism hypothesis focuses on neo-corporatism, in which the emphasis is on negotiated change involving employer and employee representation and participation: *EMU's effects are mediated by the domestic intervening variable of neo-corporatism*. There is an area of overlap between 'consensual' democracies and neo-corporatism. Both can be seen as expressing a high cultural valuation on power sharing and joint responsibility, as opposed to the 'winner-take-all' mentality; both are linked to large welfare states as instruments for compensating losers. Hence in Austria and the Netherlands 'consensus' democracy and neo-corporatism have tended to complement each other in what appears a 'syndrome of closely related traits' (Lijphart 2002). However, they are not identical (Armingeon 2002; Vergunst 2004). In particular, neo-corporatism can flourish in non-consensual democracies, like Ireland and Sweden.

Neo-corporatism offers a strategic political response to the existence of powerful domestic veto players in small states that are sharply exposed to international trade and competition. The incorporation of trade unions and of employer organizations in joint responsibility for macro-economic policies offers a framework for wage moderation and control of unit costs to reconcile high employment with price stability. As a domestic governing mechanism, neo-corporatism is to be found in culturally homogenous states like Denmark, Finland, Ireland, Luxembourg, and Sweden: all of which have an above-average record in structural reforms. Indeed, it is tempting to see neo-corporatism as a more characteristically small state pattern than 'consensual' democracies (which reflect the particular circumstances of cultural segmentation). Greater economic openness increases a state's social risks; the inducement to neo-corporatism and large welfare states as compensatory instruments for losers comes from the search for buffers against external vulnerabilities (Cameron 1978). In consequence, one might combine the two previous hypotheses into one: *small states that are culturally homogenous and neo-corporatist tend to excel in domestic reforms and in Euro Area performance.*

As with 'consensual' democracies, however, neo-corporatism is conditional and contingent rather than an historic 'given'. Though small states have a bias to neo-corporatism based on the vulnerabilities of economic openness, neo-corporatist practice varies over space and time. Ireland has shifted from non-corporatist to corporatist with Euro Area accession; Austria and Sweden have altered over time. Euro Area accession is a powerful catalyst to domestic neo-corporatism. However, not all small states have the domestic institutional capacity in employer and trade-union organizations to make neo-corporatism an attractive and feasible option, for instance in most of east central Europe. Neo-corporatist mechanisms of economic reform have not been practical politics in new member states like the Baltic States, the Czech Republic, Hungary, and Poland.

More broadly, a range of factors led to a decline in the political incentive to embrace and rely on neo-corporatism. In an era of faster rate of change in products, services, and processes, it proved less effective in economic innovation; employer and trade-union organizations were diminishing in membership and inclusiveness in representing business and employees in old as well as new member states and thus had legitimacy problems; whilst Euro Area membership was a less powerful inducement to neo-corporatism than accession. German-centred unit cost reduction induced new perceptions of competitive risk and strengthened the attractions of joint responsibility. It was, however, less clear that neo-corporatism could deliver a similar macro-economic performance in growth and employment as in the past (cf. Eichengreen 2006; Phelps 2005).

A focus on domestic governance mechanisms allows us to penetrate behind the broad concepts of 'consensual' democracies and 'neo-corporatism' to more specific variables like whether, and in what ways, domestic institutional arrangements privilege certain veto players. In Euro Area accession states national central banks are privileged vis-à-vis domestic political elites; governing parties are dependent on them for support in promoting growth and employment. Similarly, in Europe—though not necessarily elsewhere—federalism may serve to protect welfare states from the effects of fiscal consolidation consequent on the euro (cf. Obinger, Leibfried, and Castles 2005). In Austria and Germany the territorial dimension of state power safeguards egalitarian fiscal outcomes; in a more attenuated way, decentralized structures in Belgium, Italy, and Spain act in the same way. The more effective fiscal reforms in Austria than in Germany attest to the greater relative strength of the governing parties in relation to the federal system (cf. Obinger 2005).

In a further hypothesis, political mobilization around a set of domestic hegemonic political values, and the institutional arrangements that embed them, matters: *the direction and speed of domestic reforms consequent on the euro depends on whether domestic political hegemony rests on the idea of the state as the provider of social solidarity.* European states differ in the extent to which the state is attributed a role as guarantor of social solidarity, whether by Catholic social teaching, Republican ideas of the 'one and indivisible' nation, or class-based political organization around social democratic parties, trade unions, and neo-corporatist arrangements (Dyson 1980). Where one or a combination of these three streams of political ideas is prevalent, as in Austria, Belgium, and the Netherlands, preferences for egalitarian outcomes will privilege income transfer policies in processes of adjustment to the Euro Area. In short, though the euro might act as a catalyst for market liberalization, strongly embedded collectivist values ensure that the state retains a strong redistributive function. Domestic capacity to mobilize around hegemonic values of social solidarity cuts through the small/large state distinction. There are small states that fall outside this category, like the Baltic, and small states that are inside, like Slovenia; whilst large states like France, Germany, and Italy fall firmly inside.

A further domestic governance hypothesis assumes that partisanship matters: that *Right-wing parties have a stronger inclination to cut deficits and debt.* The political variable of partisanship, defined in terms of the different fiscal preferences of Left-wing and Right-wing parties, seem to offer little explanation for processes of economic reform. There was no discernible Left/Right divide between states on the merits of euro entry. Euro entry meant that two traditionally Left/Right divisive issues—exchange rate and monetary policies—became redundant. Instead, partisanship became focused on fiscal policy preferences and shifts. However, fiscal policy behaviour, especially tolerance for deficits and debt, in states with fixed electoral terms showed a less clear relationship to partisanship of governments than to domestic political business cycles, with a broad preference across Left and Right for relaxing fiscal policy in the face of elections (Sadeh 2006: 74–7). The Euro Area was not dominated by either Left-wing or Right-wing parties of government. There was a slight bias to the Left in 1998–99 and to the Right in 2006/7, but there were no clear effects on the direction and speed of fiscal consolidation or economic reforms.

More plausible is the hypothesis that *cabinet and ministerial duration affects capacity for domestic economic reforms*. Short-term, unstable periods of office, resulting from ideological and party fragmentation, are associated with high incentives not to challenge special interests. Party fragmentation, whether intra-party or inter-party or both, created a particular problem for fiscal consolidation and economic reforms in Italy, Poland, and Romania. The German Grand Coalition's inability to agree a fiscal contract binding ministries and its more general difficulties in agreeing economic reforms derived in substantial part from intra-party factionalism. However, intra-party factionalism did not translate into low cabinet duration. More seriously for the hypothesis, relatively high cabinet and ministerial duration in Germany did not lead to a high reform performance. In contrast, greater cabinet and ministerial duration in Austria, Finland, Ireland, Luxembourg, the Netherlands, Slovenia, and Britain was associated with bolder measures of fiscal and economic reforms. As in France, the Baltic States, and Bulgaria, ministerial reshuffling can prove a more persistent problem than cabinet duration: witness the rapid succession of French and Polish finance ministers. The Euro Area creates an incentive to strengthen the durability of cabinets and ministers: whether by providing a focal point for domestic negotiation and agreement or by offering an opportunity for blame shifting. However, continuing failure to strengthen cabinet and ministerial durability undermines domestic adjustment capacity and reputation for governing competence (Sadeh 2006: 79–89). Intra-party and inter-party fragmentation is toxic for economic reform processes.

Gravity Matters

The robustness of the 'size' hypothesis is further tested by the fourth hypothesis: *EMU's effects in activating the economic policy role of small states are diluted by the 'gravity' variable of geographic distance* (Anderson 1979). The gravity variable

395

highlights a centre-periphery characteristic to the Euro Area, more specifically the domestic effects of the unequal spatial distribution of trade effects and of business cycle synchronization. Euro Area states with the greatest incentive to engage in active and intense structural reforms are those closest to its geographic 'core'. This core is defined not by relative growth rates but by absolute GDP level, typically a combination of GDP per capita with population size, and by scale of financial assets. It tends to place Germany at the core. Trade gravitates towards the largest market, and trade intensity increases incentives for structural reforms (Duval and Elmeskov 2006).

States that are more distant from this core are less likely to participate in the market deepening effects of EMU and to gain from its trade effects because of continuing higher transaction costs (Baldwin 2006a: 49). They are also less likely to benefit from high and growing levels of intra-industry trade and hence from a closer synchronization of their business cycles with the Euro Area (Baldwin 2006a, 2006b; Boewer and Guillemineau 2006: 32–3). The result is a lower incentive for structural reforms. Examples are provided by Greece and Portugal, which are geographically distant and characterized more by trade specialization than intra-industry trade.

The impact of the 'gravity' variable is manifested not just in trade intensity but also in asymmetries in growth and inflation developments and in asymmetric demand and supply shocks. Asymmetry in output and price movements correlates poorly with size and well with proximity to the core. The most asymmetry is displayed by Ireland, followed by Finland, Greece, and Portugal; whilst Austria, Belgium, and the Netherlands exhibit the least asymmetry. Well before currency union, Bayoumi and Eichengreen (1993) concluded that a core around Germany, France, Austria, Belgium, and the Netherlands exhibited a stronger correlation of structural demand and supply shocks than 'peripheral' states (including Britain, Italy, and Spain). As a consequence, for these core states in the Euro Area the potential costs of a loss of monetary autonomy were more limited, even without structural reforms to labour and product markets. In addition, Baldwin (2006a, 2006b), following Rose (2000) and Frankel and Rose (2005), shows that there is a core in which close trade linkages through prolonged ERM membership is associated with more tightly synchronized economic activity. Sueppel (2003) suggests that some east central European states—notably the Czech Republic, Hungary, and Poland—are more closely synchronized with the Euro Area economy than existing Euro Area members like Finland, Greece, Ireland, and Portugal.

The 'gravity' hypothesis highlights not so much 'size' as the inner core of the D-Mark-Zone cluster, which is based on tighter integration in intra-industry trade, in symmetrical shocks, and in output and price movements. Hence it approximates much more closely to an Optimum Currency Area (McKinnon 1963; Mundell 1961). The effects are exhibited in the phenomenon of persisting inflation differentials that distinguish the Euro Area from the United States as a monetary union.

In practice, however, the effects of 'gravity' on domestic reforms may be less straightforward, casting doubt on the robustness of the hypothesis. Small states may benefit disproportionately from presence in, or proximity to, the core, notably through trade intensity. However, their lack of vulnerability to asymmetric shocks as a consequence of being in or close to the 'core' may paradoxically act as a disincentive to active structural reforms. One could recast the 'gravity' hypothesis in a radically different way: *the more remote a European state is from the geographic core, the greater the incentive to compensate by pursuing active structural reforms.*

This recast 'gravity' hypothesis appears robust in the cases of the Baltic States (in the vanguard for euro entry) and Finland. They are geographically distant from the core, but have an above average record for structural reforms. Finland outpaces Austria and Belgium, and the Baltic States excel most of the four Visegrad states in measures of structural reforms. It may also fit the Irish and (increasingly) the Greek and Portuguese cases.

Small States Push Large States

According to this hypothesis, *the more visible the symptoms of economic stagnation and of reform 'trap' in the larger states, the stronger are the incentives for the small states to push at EU level for an acceleration of domestic reforms in larger states.* The incentive springs, in part, from frustration with their dependence on the larger states in order to realize the full market benefits from their own difficult domestic reforms and, in part, from the search for internal political rewards from a strong external profile on an EU-wide reform agenda. For the large states the incentive to listen stems from the threat of exit by firms to small states that offer lower-cost, more flexible conditions and from rising costs to their credibility and reputation and consequent influence in EU negotiations. States like Austria, Estonia, Denmark, Finland, Ireland, Slovakia, and Sweden have been able to punch well above their weight in EU-level debates about economic reform. The overriding priority of the Merkel Grand Coalition to fiscal policy consolidation was in substantial part about restoring German reputation and influence, not least amongst the increasing number of smaller EU states that are important for effective EU consensus building by Germany.

The flow of ideas and influence has been less from a hegemonic D-Mark-Zone core to the periphery than from a variety of small states towards the core. Examples include Nordic ideas of 'flexicurity', in which increasing labour flexibility is matched by generous welfare support, and Baltic and central European corporate taxation policies. In particular, relatively high unit labour costs in the core have been an incentive to look at new ways of financing welfare states that reduce burdens on business. On fiscal consolidation and the Stability and Growth Pact crisis of November 2003, small D-Mark-Zone cluster states like Austria and the Netherlands were pitted against larger D-Mark-Zone states like France, Germany, and Italy.

However, pressuring and persuading is not a one-way process from small to large states. The 'gravity' factor acts simultaneously as a disincentive for firms to move too far from low-cost access to the largest markets and as an incentive to climb the quality ladder in products and services. In consequence, it offers some room for manoeuvre to large states, and more broadly the D-Mark-Zone cluster, to retain higher tax and spending policies, along with more stringent labour-market regulation. Moreover, firms in the core state of Germany pursued a strategy of reducing unit labour costs that had important spillover effects on other large states as well as on some smaller D-Mark-Zone cluster states. Belgium, Italy, and Spain lost export market share to Germany, creating an incentive to find new ways of reducing unit labour costs. Similarly, small states were vulnerable to each other in retaining a comparative advantage. Ireland, which had pursued an FDI-based development strategy, was forced to reflect anew on the domestic economic policy implications of its vulnerability to the deflection of FDI flows to east central European states (some on the cusp of euro entry).

Comparative Advantage and the Endogenous Capacity of Firms Matters

According to this hypothesis, *EMU's effects on European states are to be explained not just through the 'top-down' process of governmental economic reforms but also through 'bottom-up', firm-driven processes of change that are rooted in competitive advantage*. This hypothesis is rooted in political economy and the effects of differences in comparative advantage. In one variant, it highlights the role of large, export-oriented firms, which are active across borders in intra-industry trade, able to credibly threaten exit, and possess the capacity to reorganize domestic political economies on their own terms in order to strengthen export competitiveness (cf. Hancke 2002*b*). These firms act as drivers of institutional change 'from within'. Their increased incentives to act in this way derive from various sources: globalization, the single European market, and EU enlargement. EMU adds to this cocktail the ingredient of changes in wage bargaining, working conditions, and labour markets to speed adjustment to real exchange-rate changes and competitive processes of unit cost reduction within the Euro Area that can no longer be ironed out by traditional exchange-rate policies. Firms use the threat of costs in lost jobs, tax revenues, and investment from their exit, and outsourcing to seize the initiative in speeding industrial change. The effects are conditioned by competitive advantage (Herrmann 2005).

The hypothesis stands in contrast to OECD attempts to formally measure structural reform 'intensity' (Duval and Elmeskov 2006), with their problematic choice of weights to attach to scores in individual policy categories of labour and product-market reforms. It argues that they fail to capture much of the dynamics of change. In practice, economic reforms often serve to ratify and legitimate what firms and employees are already doing. In short, behavioural change precedes public policy change (Dyson and Padgett 2006). Thus German labour markets are *de facto* more deregulated and flexible than a reading of employment and labour relations law suggests. Similarly, wage moderation and changes in structures of wage bargaining do not necessarily depend on major top-down economic reforms, as Germany again shows.

The main 'bottom-up' mechanism of change is the active use by firms of exit (or its threat) from employer organizations, from collective bargaining arrangements, and from domestic markets unless wage and working conditions are changed. In addition, employees exit, or threaten to exit, trade unions. These processes lead either to new institutional practices (like more use of 'opt-outs' from wage agreements or greater resort to employee profit-sharing schemes) or to the 'reinvention' of institutions, which remain formally the same but function differently (as in the changed use and relationship between 'area-wide' collective bargaining and works councils in Germany) (Dyson and Padgett 2006; Hall and Thelen 2006). Institutions are, in short, malleable and work in various ways. In particular, German firms pursued a more effective strategy of reducing unit labour costs than 'top-down' governmental reforms to health, pensions, and unemployment insurance for this purpose, and reflected in resurgent German exports. Delay in 'top-down' reforms can mask major structural changes as firms renegotiate and reshape traditional institutional arrangements in response to EMU and related Single Market and EU enlargement developments.

States differ in the nature of their corporate elites, reflecting their various sources of comparative advantage. Firms—and the sectors that they represent—differ in their endogenous capacity to drive or conversely to inhibit change. The key variables are exposure to export market competitiveness and market scale; whether firms represent high-quality, high–value-added activities, requiring continuing innovation and skilled employees; and whether they engage in cross-national, intra-industry trade. Where a state is strongly characterized by this type of economic structure, economic change is likely to reflect a strong shaping influence for 'institutional entrepreneurs' at the corporate level, beyond the narrow confines of the state (Crouch 2005).

Correspondingly, states cluster according to how comparative advantage mediates the effects of the euro and whether 'bottom-up', firm-led change plays a relatively more or less important role. Amongst 'temporary' outsiders in east central Europe this mechanism of change is stronger in the Visegrad states than the Baltic States, reflecting the greater presence of intra-industry trade. Amongst semi-permanent 'outsiders', British reforms suggest a strong shaping influence for City firms (the financial sector was the only one to be chosen as a test for euro entry). Euro Area members can be clustered by comparative advantage and the strategic responses of firms. Austria, Finland, France, Germany, Ireland, Luxembourg, the Netherlands, and Slovenia exhibit strong firm-led adjustment, even if to varying degrees. Greece, Italy, Portugal, and, to a lesser extent, Spain form a different kind of cluster in which there is a higher representation of firms seeking state protection of domestic markets. Economic structure helps to explain differences in endogenous capacity of firms to drive change. Once again, this variable cuts across small states (cf. Greece and Ireland) and even through states like Italy and Spain where key firms in Lombardy and in Catalonia seek to gain from more forceful market liberalization. It also draws attention to the high potential for 'bottom-up' change in Britain and in the Nordic states.

Temporal Hypotheses

Temporal hypotheses are of two types. The hypotheses that deal with the euro as 'politics in time' derive from historical institutionalism and stress initial conditions, 'path dependence' and persistence in patterns of change (Pierson 2004). Scope for reform is defined by past choices and temporal legacies. The hypotheses that focus on the euro as the 'politics of time' derive from rational-choice institutionalism and see time as a scarce strategic resource whose often opportunistic use by actors shapes the dynamic patterns in reform strategies that emerge (Goetz 2006). The 'politics in time' hypotheses assume that history matters. The 'politics of time' hypotheses attribute more significance to how actors manage time and consequent variegation over time. Both sets offer accounts of the Euro Area as a 'moving picture' rather than a series of one-off 'snapshots' (cf. Pierson 2004).

Path Dependence Matters

This 'politics in time' hypothesis focuses on how the direction of change in the Euro Area is the outcome of a 'causal chain' over an extended time period: *the direction of change derives from self-reinforcing processes that are generated by initial conditions: by the nature of the actors first mobilized by the process of EMU and their entrenched institutional position, by their policy beliefs, and by the institutional 'rules of the game' and policy legacies.* In short, 'initial' conditions matter.

The significance of initial conditions is highlighted by comparison of the Werner Report of 1970 and the Delors Report of 1989 on EMU. The Werner

Report identified two equally important centres of co-ordinated decision in EMU—economic and monetary—and gave little importance to central bank independence. The Delors Report focused on the principle of an independent European central bank as the basis for institutional design of EMU. This difference reflects the influence of timing of EMU on design: in the Werner Committee case, the context was the continuing ascendancy of the Keynesian economic paradigm, in which explicit macro-economic co-ordination and tools of demand management were seen as central; in the Delors Committee case, the context was the monetarist paradigm of stability-oriented policies.

The direction of the effects of the Euro Area on domestic change reflected the circumstances of the timing of the creation of EMU in the late 1980s: vivid memories of the 'great' inflation in the 1970s and beyond, persisting inflationary threats, enlarged public debts from years of deficit financing, and—in this context—the appeal of monetarist ideas of firm rules to ensure smooth, sustainable growth and anchor stable expectations of low inflation amongst economic agents. The circumstances of temporally distant events and processes retained causal significance for the direction of change in the Euro Area. Self-reinforcing processes at work in the Euro Area help explain 'stickiness', even inertia, in policy development, for instance in matters of macro-economic policy co-ordination. Not least, the legacies of the 1970s and 1980s included a fiscally burdened Euro Area, with consequent loss of manoeuvre for many states to compensate losers from reforms (Dyson 2008*a*).

In particular, the direction of change can be seen as the outcome of a conjuncture of events. EMU represented the coming together of, on the one hand, a political decision to pursue the next stage in European political integration after the Single Market and the ERM—including 'locking in' Germany after unification in 1990—and, on the other, a response to the continuing shared policy problems of securing economic stability and sustainable growth in Europe. The result of this historic conjunction was a victory for stability-oriented policy ideas over alternative ideas for more discretionary processes of macro-economic policy co-ordination in the design of the Euro Area. This victory was embedded in the institutional arrangements of the Euro Area: an extreme model of central bank independence (the ECB having 'goal' as well as 'instrument', 'personnel', 'financial', and 'institutional' independence), a rules-based approach to fiscal policy discipline, and no institutional arrangements for *ex ante* macro-economic policy co-ordination of monetary with other policies. The French-inspired notion of a European economic 'government' was kept off the agenda.

Temporal sequencing reinforced 'path dependence' in change. EMU followed on from the ERM, which in turn was anchored on the D-Mark. In consequence, the Bundesbank was the central reference point for domestic monetary policies of those states that sought a 'hard' exchange-rate peg. Hence the variant of monetarism that prevailed in institutional design was German Ordo-liberal ideas of 'sound' money and finance, focused on tightly controlled discretion. In a formal sense the key training ground was the 'hard' ERM and the trainer was the German Bundesbank. In a substantive sense the formative historical experience for this training was the even more temporally remote experience of the acute economically and politically damaging consequences of German hyperinflation in the 1920s and 1940s. It led to a post–war German preoccupation with inflation over deflation in EMU policy development, manifested in later critiques of 'asymmetry' in the ECB definition of its monetary policy objective.

This combination of timing and sequencing with path dependence highlights the long-term historical process at work in EMU. The resulting institutional arrangements are, however, associated with different patterns of domestic political debate about the euro. These patterns are shaped by historically conditioned, deeply rooted differences in 'fit' or 'misfit' with beliefs amongst domestic actors and the institutional structures that embody these beliefs. 'Fit' is more apparent where these domestic beliefs focus on identity as a trading nation (like the Netherlands); and more problematic where ideas of social solidarity are institutionally anchored (as in Sweden). Notably, in France core Republican political beliefs continue to stress the centrality of the sovereign nation in institutional design and hence the primacy of politics. Political 'misfit' is experienced in Britain, where the domestic traditions of Parliamentary sovereignty and ministerial accountability sit awkwardly with the notion of 'goal' independence for the central bank and more broadly with ideas of supra-national integration. In short, notions about what constitutes the legitimate boundary between democratic politics and technocracy remain contested and variable and shape different patterns of relationship to the euro. Domestic traditions have the potential to resurface, as in French debates about an 'economic government' for the Euro Area and about 'economic patriotism'. Domestic politics either co-exist or exist in incipient tension and conflict with the Euro Area.

Timing of De Facto Entry Matters

This 'politics in time' hypothesis states that *the longer the period of time in which a state has been part of a* de facto *monetary union (through fixing its exchange rate to the D-Mark and aligning market expectations behind a credible commitment), the more likely it is that the state will have a lower challenge of adjustment on Euro Area entry and hence be under less pressure to reform.* In the case of states that share this initial condition—in effect, the old D-Mark-Zone cluster—the challenges of euro entry have been addressed over a longer time period, for instance in fiscal institutional reforms and wage policy reforms (like de-indexing of wages). In addition, they benefited disproportionately from the trade-creation effects of the euro after 1998 (Baldwin 2006a: 49). They also displayed a greater capacity for policy 'shaping' in the design of EMU and thereby minimizing potential 'misfit'. However, this hypothesis does not account for the 'misfit' that may originate from the creation of a larger and more heterogeneous Euro Area (see the 'misfit on entry' hypothesis below).

Fixing the (differing) timing of a state's *de facto* accession to monetary union matters, in particular in relation to whether and to what extent a domestic 'stability culture' had already become institutionally embedded not just in monetary but also in fiscal and wage policies before *de jure* monetary union in 1999. This variable identifies as important the 'hard' ERM as a 'training ground' for EMU, often for a decade and longer: in effect, the old D-Mark-Zone cluster. However, ease of adjustment to the ERM might reflect even earlier domestic adjustments, especially by small states like Austria and the Benelux states or the way in which a traditionally centralized form of state—as in France—reduces the pressure for domestic reforms to better coordinate fiscal institutions. Belgium and the Netherlands converged on German inflation norms even before the ERM. In this way temporal analysis can uncover the limits of explanations centred on Europeanization, let alone EMU.

This hypothesis helps in identifying different patterns of sequencing in state accommodation to stability culture. There are states with highly developed stability cultures well before the creation of the Euro Area—like Austria, Benelux, France, Germany, and Denmark, a non-member. Once again, the 'timing of entry' hypothesis highlights the D-Mark-Zone cluster. Second, there are states for which there was a correlation between seeking entry into the Euro Area and institutionalizing domestic stability cultures—like Greece, Ireland, Italy, Spain, Portugal, and the new member states in 2004. In these cases EMU serves as an external discipline for importing stability and highlights problems in political strategies for the temporal management of euro entry (which, as we see below, produce different patterns) (Dyson 2006b, 2007a). Finally, Britain and Sweden represent states where domestic monetary stability was established independently of the ERM and EMU.

In the first cluster of states the Euro Area was a less central ideational reference point for domestic reforms—the pattern was one of relatively peaceful co-existence. In the second cluster, the 'misfit' was greater, given that the states had been policy 'takers' rather than 'shapers' in designing EMU. The pattern of relationships to the euro ranged from consensual structural reforms, to capture the potentially high payoffs from Euro Area accession and membership, to conflict over the social and regional distribution of costs of reforms. It was reflected in varying temporal strategies for entry that distinguished pace-setters (like Slovenia, Slovakia and earlier the Baltic States) from laggards (like Poland and increasingly Hungary), those accommodating EMU from those

403

exhibiting inertia on entry (Dyson 2006c). In the third cluster the pattern of relationship to EMU gravitated between inertia and retrenchment. Britain and Sweden shifted to a politics of retrenchment in the context of a domestic economic performance superior to that of the Euro Area.

A variant of this hypothesis states that *given the long time-lag effects of monetary and currency union, after a period of a decade and more within the Euro Area, 'non–D-Mark-Zone' states will capture more fully the trade-creation effects of the euro and make the institutional and policy adjustments to membership.* This hypothesis of 'lagged' adjustment must remain speculative at this stage. However, the 'gravity' variable of geographic distance suggests that this process is likely to remain weak for states, like Greece and Portugal, because the trade effects are less strong than in the geographic core, and more pronounced more quickly in east central Europe.

Misfit on Entry Matters: Hypothesis One

According to Enderlein (2004): *the greater the 'misfit' between the nominal Euro-Area-wide interest rate set by the ECB and the domestic business cycle, the more likely it is that Euro Area entry will trigger pressures for intensive economic reforms by states (subject of course to domestic intervening variables).* In this 'time' hypothesis, the critical variables are the 'one-size-fits-all' monetary policy and the 'real' interest rates that states face on entry in relation to domestic output growth, employment, and price developments. Timing remains important, but the focus is on 1998–9 and the inception of the single monetary policy. The direction of the economic reforms depends on the nature of this 'misfit': whether real interest rates are too high or too low.

The hypothesis suggests different clusters of states. First, there are states where nominal Euro Area interest rates are consistent with low inflation and trend growth. This cluster is difficult to identify. Secondly, there is a cluster in which lower real interest rates boost domestic consumption and growth, underpin persisting inflation problems, and create the risk of destabilizing asset price bubbles especially in housing and construction. It includes Greece, Ireland, Portugal, and Spain. A third cluster faces the challenge of high real interest rates that restrict output growth and threaten persistent excess capacity (the old D-Mark-Zone cluster including Belgium, France, and Germany, but minus the Netherlands). Finally, there are states for which the effects are more complex—given a combination of output contraction with increasing inflation—and appropriate domestic policy responses less clear: Italy and the Netherlands.

Each cluster requires different mixes of economic reform responses. States with output growth and employment problems have to seek new ways to boost demand in place of lost monetary or exchange-rate policies (e.g. developing a low-wage sector with fiscal incentives and export growth through unit labour cost reduction). States with persisting inflation problems have to focus on restraint by fiscal, wage, and labour-market reforms. By 2005–6 a combination of continuing wage moderation with labour-market reforms to ease part-time, temporary, and agency work helped Germany shift away from its initial condition of 'misfit' with an ECB restrictive monetary policy. In contrast, the different initial 'misfit' expressed in a persisting inflation differential continued to offer challenges to Greece, Ireland, Portugal, and Spain.

Misfit on Entry Matters: Hypothesis Two

According to this hypothesis: *the creation of a large and heterogeneous Euro Area in 1998–9 (and the prospect of its further enlargement) produced a bigger problem of interest-rate 'misfit' for the old 'D-Mark-Zone' cluster and hence heightened its problems of domestic adjustment.* Until at least 1996–7, the widespread assumption was that the Euro Area would start as a small group of 5/6 states, in effect gathering together the D-Mark-Zone cluster and excluding Italy. These states were seen as more closely approximating an 'optimum currency area' (Bayoumi and Eichengreen 1993). However, agreement of the Stability and Growth Pact in 1997—toughening the excessive deficit procedure— opened up political opportunities to agree a larger Euro Area extending to the Mediterranean states. This late timing of change was at the root of a lack of anticipation of potential 'misfit' amongst key German policymakers. The assumption had been that ECB monetary policy for the Euro Area would give a greater weight to Germany and the D-Mark-Zone cluster than actually materialized.

This 'time' hypothesis highlights size and heterogeneity of the Euro Area as a key initial condition. The effects were especially problematic for the old D-Mark-Zone cluster, notably in reinforcing output growth and unemployment problems. Euro-Area–wide monetary policy, confronted with persistent inflation differentials outside this cluster, proved overly restrictive for Germany in particular (Aherne and Pisani-Ferry 2006; Angeloni and Ehrmann 2004). A spectrum of domestic political effects materialized in the old D-Mark-Zone cluster, ranging from inertia and resistance to retrenchment. Adverse shifts in public opinion towards the euro were notably apparent in the Netherlands. Not least, in Germany expectations of welfare-state retrenchment alongside a restrictive monetary policy reinforced uncertainty, provided incentives for precautionary savings, and helped to inhibit consumption as a driver of aggregate demand.

Temporal Sequencing of Reforms Matters

According to this 'politics of time' hypothesis: *the scale of the problems of domestic political management of conflict and the effects of the euro on perceptions of the effectiveness and credibility of governments are a function of how domestic policy elites use time, sequence, and pace structural reforms.* This hypothesis highlights the temporal management of domestic political elites as a variable in differentiating states. In stressing strategic leadership in timing reforms (whether brought forward in good times or in bad), in sequencing reforms (which reforms first?), and in the speed of reforms, it introduces a greater degree of domestic political dynamics in explaining processes and effects of the euro.

Structural reforms are in general politically costly because they challenge vested 'insider' interests, whether in welfare-state programmes, in particular product-market structures, or in wage setting and labour-market participation. They threaten negative distributional effects and create uncertainty about prospective outcomes (Debrun and Pisani-Ferry 2006). Characteristically, costs are short-term and specific; benefits are longer-term and more diffuse (Olsen 1965). As losers are more clearly defined than beneficiaries, they have a greater incentive to mobilize politically.

Though the barriers to change are broadly high, the challenge of managing reforms varies across states. It depends on how the choice of particular reforms distributes costs and benefits over time, on the opportunities that domestic political institutions offer to veto players, on how domestic ideologies shape preferences between equity and efficiency, on how reforms impinge on domestic electoral cycles (which are in turn often complex, as in German federalism), and on whether there is fiscal scope to provide compensation to losers (Dyson 2008a).

The Euro Area has shifted the locus for overcoming resistance to reforms from pressure of exchange-rate crisis (as in Britain, Denmark, France, the Netherlands, and Ireland in the 1980s and Finland and Sweden in the 1990s) to domestic strategic skills in timing, sequencing, and pacing reforms. Moreover, the combination of the Stability and Growth Pact with a legacy of constrained room for fiscal manoeuvre generally discouraged labour-market reforms because of the absence of opportunities for budgetary compensation for losers (Debrun and Annett 2004; Dyson 2008a). Many of the characteristic problems of temporal management of reforms, notably under Chirac and Schröder, were caused by tough and ideologically challenging labour-market reforms, alongside fiscal consolidation, in 'hard' times when growth, employment, and fiscal conditions deteriorate. Domestic strategies for timing and accelerating economic reform in 'hard' times proved highly costly for governments in the D-Mark-Zone cluster and in the Mediterranean cluster. In 'good' times changes in income distribution are less visible, labour can more easily shift across sectors, and losers can be compensated through smart fiscal policy (Debrun and Pisani-Ferry 2006: 3). From 2001 to 2005 'good times' were not on offer.

Despite the injunctions of the Stability and Growth Pact and general evidence of its association with greater restraint, there is strong empirical evidence to link fiscal policy outcomes to domestic electoral cycles (Buti and van den Noord 2004). The political cycle, and the opportunities that it offers to special interests, seems to trump the business cycle as a point of reference in fiscal policy, with potentially perverse pro-cyclical macro-economic outcomes (Solow 2002). Governments are induced to shift between procrastination and short-term activism. Domestic electoral calendars shape temporal discourse about 'windows of opportunity' and the sequencing and pace of structural reforms. One might, accordingly, expect states to dynamically re-cluster as their governments change their temporal positions in the electoral calendar, correspondingly varying timing, sequencing, and tempo of reforms. The behaviour of governments seems less motivated by their ideological composition (say, social democratic-led being more tolerant to relaxing public expenditure and to higher budget deficits) than by opportunism in seeking to boost voter welfare shortly before elections (Clark and Hallerberg 2000).

An analysis of political timing, sequencing, and pace of reforms suggests two clusters of states. First, in France, Germany, and Italy political leaders proved timid in expediting public expenditure reforms during good times, whereas, in bad times, they opted to prioritize labour-market and welfare-state reforms alongside fiscal consolidation. This temporal conjunction of belated and comprehensive reforms involved notably high domestic political costs in the face of deep-seated ideas about social solidarity and of vested interests, especially of public-sector workers. Reforms took place in a temporal context in which there was no fiscal room to compensate potential losers (Dyson 2008a). Ambitious and failed French reform plans in 1995, and the price that Chirac paid in the 1997 Assembly elections, induced a subsequent hesitancy and procrastination over reforms during his Presidency.

Similarly accumulating fiscal problems coincided with an increased tempo of labour-market and welfare-state reforms in Germany with Schröder's Agenda 2010 of March 2003. The immediate effect was to reinforce precautionary savings by anxious German households and to reduce the potential for consumption to serve as a stimulus to growth, employment, and tax revenue. It also created serious internal party problems, and a terminal set of electoral defeats, both for the Schröder government and for the ambitious reform agenda of opposition leader Angela Merkel in the September 2005 federal elections. In consequence, the Grand Coalition exhibited greater caution about labour-market and welfare-state reforms, despite the emergence of 'good times'.

A second cluster of states comprise those that sequenced less politically costly fiscal policy and product-market reforms before more difficult labour-market and welfare-state reforms and thereby increased the benefits from these later reforms (Blanchard and Giavazzi 2003). This sequencing reduced domestic political difficulties of reforms. As Finland, Ireland, and Sweden demonstrate, along with Britain and more recently Spain, ambitious fiscal expenditure reforms, resulting in budgetary surpluses and low indebtedness, provide greater opportunities to compensate losers and buy off domestic opposition to reforms (Dyson 2008a; Hauptmeier, Heipertz and Schuknecht 2006; International Monetary Fund 2004). Ambitious expenditure reformers correlate with effectiveness in broader reforms in labour and product markets. From this perspective, the decision of the Merkel Grand Coalition to prioritize fiscal consolidation appears politically rational. Similarly, product-market reforms (as in energy and telecommunications), service market reforms (as in private job placements and retail distribution), and financial market reforms offer more direct stimuli to growth and employment. Britain provided an example of a state that sequenced product, services, and financial market reforms, and fiscal consolidation, so as to serve as catalysts for labour-market changes and offer means of absorbing adjustment costs. Similarly, Denmark's 'flex-security' model offered an insurance against costs of more flexible labour markets.

Using Time Devices Matters: Hypothesis One

This 'politics of time' hypothesis argues that *the timing and tempo of domestic reforms is shaped by the use that EU member state elites make of time devices like 'road maps', calendars, and deadlines*. Here, the emphasis is on varying the discipline of time in making domestic adjustments. The result is a complex picture of political dynamics that is more resistant to a clear clustering of states.

Domestic finance ministers have an incentive to 'invite' clear and specific 'road maps' for euro entry and tight deadlines to correct fiscal imbalances as a way of underlining their executive authority and putting ministerial colleagues under pressure to expedite 'overdue' reforms and honour commitments. On the other hand, they have an incentive to take political credit for having won extra time under the Stability and Growth Pact for painful domestic adjustments. Either way—depending on the domestic political opportunity structure—they can use time devices to consolidate their domestic political positions. How this dilemma is resolved depends on problems of fit between euro entry calendars and domestic electoral calendars, grounded in complex calculations of payoffs that include domestic party, coalition, and electoral interests. These calculations led three of the Visegrad states—the Czech Republic, Hungary, and Poland—to delay projected entry to 2010 and beyond.

Clustering is discernible in temporary outsiders, who face the challenge of Euro Area accession timing by meeting the conditions spelt out in the Maastricht convergence criteria. In the first place, there are states that seek an early date for entry, typically by speedily joining ERM II. They can in turn be (sub-)clustered according to their motives in using this time device. States may seek to bring forward and legitimate structural reforms and to increase reform tempo by a voluntary 'binding of hands'. Their elites seek to import external discipline, following the Italian example, as with Slovakia. Alternatively, they may attempt to 'lock-in' a pre-established domestic stability regime (e.g. the Baltic States). More generally, the motive can be to make a rapid escape from the 'tough' stage of accession 'conditionality' (the convergence criteria, including the ERM II) into the less rigorous framework of Euro Area membership.

A second type of cluster comprises states that use prolongation of the entry timetable to create extra political space in which to make difficult reforms to fiscal policy, welfare states, and labour markets in a manner tailored to domestic political exigencies (as in the Czech Republic, Hungary, and Poland). In short, patterns are not simply structurally determined. Domestic elites can use various temporal strategies to shape processes of structural reform, and states can be categorized in these terms and can jump categories over time. Thus, Hungary moved from pace-setter to laggard on euro entry (Dyson 2006, 2006*b*, 2006*c*).

Using Time Devices Matters: Hypothesis Two

According to this 'politics of time' hypothesis: *the effectiveness of EMU as an external constraint depends on how EU policymakers, in particular the ECB and the European Commission, use the time device of lengthening the period of Euro Area accession or of persuading member states to enter into a set of firm, binding commitments to complementary economic reforms.* This hypothesis highlights the use of strictly defined accession conditionality or of membership commitments to deliver on specific product, service, or financial market reforms as a device for strengthening domestic temporal management of reforms.

Prolongation of the euro accession process, especially through a restrictive interpretation of the Maastricht convergence criteria, maximizes the potential of the ECB and the Commission to use the 'conditionality' requirements to raise and sustain external 'top-down' pressures for domestic reforms (as with the decision to exclude Lithuania in 2006). In addition, early and politically easier cases of exclusion can be used to send signals and set precedents for other states, like Poland, that could prove more complex and difficult. Agreement to Euro Area accession—that a state has met the convergence criteria in a sustainable manner (itself a temporal variable)—is an instrument (and variable) that enables supra-national actors to increase and sustain Europeanization pressures on states.

However, the tough EU-level use of conditionality is by no means predictable in its political effects. It may create space for populist politicians to mobilize anti-EU and anti-euro sentiment and produce new political patterns of inertia and retrenchment amongst non-Euro Area member states. Similar anxieties about negative political spill-back and loss of domestic political control have led Euro Area member states to shy away from making specific commitments to complementary domestic reforms in financial, product, and service markets. In consequence, Euro Area reforms have lacked coherence.

Conclusion: Clustering and Covariance

This chapter has highlighted variations in the robustness of spatial and temporal hypotheses for explaining emerging patterns in the relationship between European states and the euro. In particular, it questions the over-reliance in recent literature (notably Duval and Elmeskov 2006) on 'hard' data like size and measures of 'top-down' structural reforms. Cultural homogeneity and neo-corporatism appear as significant as size—indeed, their combination seems decisive in explaining differences in distribution of both economic reform performance and favourable public opinion towards the euro. Domestic governing devices and political culture, including hegemonic values, matter. Similarly, variation in the endogenous capacity of firms and sectors to lead economic adjustment, and the bias towards market opening or protection that they impart to that adjustment, assumes a great significance in explaining the nature, scale, sequencing, and pace of economic change. Comparative advantage matters, as do corporate elites. In addition, political leadership in the temporal management of reforms matters.

The enduring importance of temporality and path dependence is confirmed in the continuing impact of timing of entry into *de facto* monetary union with Germany on persistence of policies. Conversely, exogenous change is captured in the impact of initial conditions of *de jure* monetary union, specifically how the relatively large size and heterogeneity of the Euro Area created 'misfit' for the D-Mark-Zone cluster. It meant that 'misfit' was no longer defined as a problem just for those who had not learnt to adapt to this core cluster. However, though weakened, the German hegemony hypothesis retains value, especially given the endogenous capacity of German firms to drive industrial change through reducing unit costs.

The spatial and temporal hypotheses do not yield a single unified pattern in the relations between Eurosystem 'insider' states and the euro. However, there is some evidence of 'clustering' and not just of complex overlapping patterns.

Clustering around the old 'D-Mark-Zone' is confirmed by research on trade-creation effects (Baldwin 2006*a*, 2006*b*) and on business cycle synchronization (beginning with Bayoumi and Eichengreen 1993). Various hypotheses suggest a continuing plausibility to the notion of German hegemony and centrality of the D-Mark-Zone cluster: path dependence, the timing of entry, 'misfit' on entry, the gravity variable, and the endogenous capacity of firms to drive change and lead processes of competitive unit cost reduction. Equally, a cluster of small, culturally homogenous states with a neo-corporatist bias is identifiable. Most problematic is the Mediterranean cluster. Conversely, there does not seem to be a single east central European cluster but three: the Baltic States, the Visegrad states (minus Slovakia), and Slovenia (Dyson 2006*c*, 2007*a*).

In this sense the Euro Area is part of an evolving historical process, displaying both substantial continuity and change. The change is in part endogenous to the German hegemon (notably long-term unification effects) and in part exogenous to Germany and related both to the nature and to the direction of the real interest rate 'misfit' on euro entry and to the size and heterogeneity of the Euro Area. It also reflects the way in which the D-Mark-Zone cluster has been crosscut by differences in size, in temporal sequencing of domestic change (especially the difference between fiscal deficit and surplus states), and even in real interest rate effect (where Dutch experience differs, at least in part). In turn, small size is crosscut by cultural homogeneity/segmentation within states and by gravity. The result is a paradoxical combination of clustering with crosscutting patterns and varying degrees of weakness of 'fit' of states to clusters.

In particular, the Euro Area seems to have empowered a positive role for small states that are culturally homogenous and have a neo-corporatist bias: Austria, Finland, Ireland, Luxembourg, and Slovenia. Though this cluster is crosscut by gravity, it suggests that gravity, understood as distance from the economic core of the Euro Area, is a second-order variable. Greece and Portugal remain excluded not so much by gravity (and certainly not lack of cultural homogeneity) as by their possession of domestic governance mechanisms that are weak. In consequence, the states in this particular small-state cluster punch well above their economic weight in the Euro Area.

The emerging patterns of differentiation throw light on Europeanization processes. These patterns bear little relationship to formal membership. The differences amongst Euro Area member states in trade effects and in business cycle synchronization are often greater (notably between the D-Mark-Zone cluster and the Mediterranean cluster) than between the D-Mark-Zone cluster and some temporary 'outsiders' like the four Visegrad states and even semi-permanent 'outsiders' like Britain, Denmark, and Sweden. Moreover, by drawing on variables in political economy, the hypotheses escape a narrow reliance on a state-centric political analysis of Europeanization. They highlight 'bottom-up' mechanisms of change and structural variables like gravity, comparative advantage, and the endogenous capacity of firms and sectors. Politics matters, not least governance mechanisms to manage conflict, electoral calendars, and the use of time devices as a resource of leadership in managing change. However, the effective assessment of changes consequent on the euro requires contextualization of politics and especially of 'top-down' reforms of governments.

A central question is whether these patterns support the literatures on 'families of nations' (e.g. Castles 1993) and 'varieties of capitalism' (e.g. Hall and Soskice 2001). The results seem to support the 'politics in time' hypothesis of path dependence: the persistence in patterns of change across related groups of states (Pierson 2004). In particular, the old D-Mark-Zone cluster might be seen as a 'family' that shares an underlying value commitment to economic stability and social solidarity, has some common institutional patterns and identities (for instance in cooperatively managing industrial relations and wage setting), engages in substantial mutual cross-national policy transfer and learning (in fiscal institutional reforms, for instance), and exhibits commonalities in substantive policy outcomes (notably a preference for defending high social benefits). From the perspective of path dependence, the D-Mark-Zone cluster comprises a shared set of institutional specificities that channel liberalization pressures into different substantive outcomes from those in the Baltic, Mediterranean, Nordic, or English-speaking 'families'.

However, other crosscutting patterns are apparent. 'Bottom-up' processes of firm-led change are eroding the family identity of the D-Mark-Zone cluster; the functions of institutions are changing (especially in industrial relations and wage setting); and cross-national policy transfer and learning processes are more promiscuous as internal 'family-based' benchmarking seems less relevant to problem solving for growth and employment. Accordingly, it seems less plausible to claim that the D-Mark-Zone cluster is exporting or privileging the model of 'Rhineland' capitalism within the Euro Area, let alone that the creation of the Euro Area has strengthened this process. The states that are seen as its exemplar—notably Germany itself—are changing into complex hybrids of market liberalization. They manifest internal variegation across sectors and firms, for instance in liberalization outcomes, depending on external economic exposure and the behaviour of firms (Dyson and Padgett 2006).

More broadly, the spatial and temporal hypotheses about European states and the euro offer an opportunity to critically re-examine the claims of the literatures on 'families of nations', 'varieties of capitalism', and types of democracy. By highlighting the multi-dimensionality of change, the complex varieties of patterns and covariance, these hypotheses help us to see that states are not statically trapped within one or more clusters. Taken together, they help us towards a moving picture rather than series of 'timeless' snapshots of how political economies relate to the euro (Pierson 2004). In particular, hypotheses about 'bottom-up' mechanisms of change (exit from, and re-invention of, institutions) and of the 'politics of time' (differences in the way time is managed, contingent for instance on electoral calendars) capture the role of corporate and political elites in 'instrumentalizing' the euro to change domestic institutions, policies, and practices. They help us to gain a stronger sense of the flexibility and dynamism in patterns of change within European capitalism and to avoid shoehorning domestic elites into simplistic one-dimensional and temporally static models (Campbell 2004; Crouch 2005). A stress on institutional and policy continuity within the Euro Area may mask discontinuity in their functioning and outcomes as actors, not least in the corporate sector, exploit the emerging freedom of manoeuvre that a currency union allows (Dyson and Padgett 2006).

The Euro Area remains a work in progress, on which many hands are active. As a work in European unification, it rests on the supple but uncertain foundations of a 'fuzzy' EU polity that lacks the protective umbrella of a European sovereign power; as a work in Europeanization, its fate is bound up with problematic domestic political ownership and the dense thickets and contingencies of domestic politics through which economic reforms must be adjusted; and as a work in forging a new political economy it is subject both to endogenous effects through trade creation, firm strategies to capture trade gains or protect against losses, and financial risk-sharing and to exogenous shocks for which its 'fuzzy' character and problematic and varying domestic leadership capacities may leave it ill-prepared. Much depends on whether exogenous shocks and leadership failures expose the stronger or the weaker parts of its economic and social foundations that were outlined in Chapter 1 by Dyson and on how powerful endogenous effects turn out to be.

References

Aarts, K. and van der Kolk, H. (eds.) (2005). *Nederlanders en Europa: Het Referendum over de Europese Grondwet*. Amsterdam: Bert Bakker.

Aarts, K. and van der Kolk, H. (2006). 'Understanding the Dutch 'No': The Euro, the East, and the Elite', *PS: Political Science and Politics*, 39(2): 243–6.

Aeschimann, E. and Riché, P. (1996). *La guerre de sept ans: histoire secrète du franc fort, 1989–1996*. Paris: Calmann-Lévy.

AFEI (Association Francaise des Entreprises d'Investissements) (2002). Rapport Annuel. http://www.afei.com/pj/GB/D0000060.pdf (accessed 1 June 2005).

——— (2005). 'Implementing Measures for the Markets in Financial Instruments Directive (MiFID). Second consultation paper', March. AFEI's observations. http://www.afei.com/pj/FR/D0000843.pdf (accessed 31 May 2005).

Ahern, B. (2001). 'Moving Towards a Truly Fair, Equal and Inclusive Ireland', in Department of Finance', *Budget 2001: An Information Update from the Department of Finance*. Dublin: Department of Finance.

Aherne, A. and Pisani-Ferry, J. (February 2006). *The Euro: Only for the Agile*. Brussels: Bruegel.

Äimä, K. (1998). 'Central Bank Independence in the Baltic States', *Review of Economies in Transition*, 4: 1–37.

Albert, M. (1993). *Capitalism Against Capitalism*. London: Whurr.

Alesina, A. and Spolaore, E. (2005). *The Size of Nations*. Cambridge: MIT Press.

Allsopp, C. and Vines, D. (2005). 'The Macroeconomic Role of Fiscal Policy', *Oxford Review of Economic Policy*, 21(4): 485–508.

Alphandéry, E. (2000). *La réforme obligée sous le soleil de l'Euro*. Paris: Grasset.

AMECO (Annual Macroeconomic Database, European Commission). (Various Years). Luxembourg: Eurostat.

Andersen, A., Egelund, N., Jensen, T., Krone, M., Lindenskov, L., and Mejding, J. (2001). *Forventninger og færdigheder—danske unge i en international sammenligning*. København: Socialforskningsinstituttet.

Anderson, J. (1979). 'The Theoretical Foundations for the Gravity Equation', *American Economic Review*, 69: 106–16.

Andersson, K. (2003). 'Utformningen av inflationsmålet och den penningpolitiska analysramen', in L. Jonung (ed.), *På jakt efter ett nytt ankare*. Stockholm: SNS Förlag, pp. 223–79.

Androsch, H. (2007). 'Wisdom from the Greybeards', *The International Economy*, 21(1): 48–51, 62.

References

Angeloni, I. and Dedola, L. (May 1999). 'From the ERM to the Euro: New Evidence on Economic and Policy Convergence Among EU Countries', European Central Bank Working Paper No. 4. Frankfurt am Main.

—— and Ehrmann, M. (September 2004). 'Euro Area Inflation Differentials', ECB Working Paper No. 388. Frankfurt am Main.

Annett, A. (2006). 'Enforcement and the Stability and Growth Pact: How Fiscal Policy Did and Did Not Change Under Europe's Fiscal Framework', IMF Working Paper No. 06/116. Washington, DC: International Monetary Fund.

Arghyrou, M. (2006). 'The Accession of Greece to the EMU: Initial Estimates and Lessons for the New EU Countries', *Liverpool Quarterly Economic Bulletin*, 27(4): December.

Armingeon, K. (2002). 'The Effects of Negotiation Democracy: A Comparative Analysis', *European Journal of Political Research*, 41: 81–105.

—— Leimgruber, P., Beyeler, M., and Menegale, S. (2006). *Comparative Political Data Set, 1960–2004*. University of Berne: Institute of Political Science.

Arrowsmith, J., Sisson, K., and Marginson, P. (2004). 'What Can "Benchmarking" Offer the Open Method of Co-ordination?', *Journal of European Public Policy*, 11(2): 311–28.

Artis, M. and Zhang, W. (1999). 'Further Evidence on the International Business Cycle and the ERM: Is There a European Business Cycle?', *Oxford Economic Chapters*, 23: 120–32.

—— Krolzig, H.-M., and Toro, J. (2004). 'The European Business Cycle', *Oxford Economic Chapters*, 56: 1–44.

Asp, K. (2004). *Jordskredssegern*. Göteborg: Institutionen för journalistik och masskommunikation.

Audas, R. and MacKay, R. (1997). 'A Tale of Two Recessions', *Regional Studies*, 31(9): 867–74.

Baker, T. et al. (1996). 'Economic Implications for Ireland of EMU', Policy Research Series Paper No. 28. Dublin: ESRI.

Baldassarri, M., Castiglionesi, F., and Modigliani, F. (1996). *Il Miracolo Possibile*. Bari: Laterza.

Baldwin, R. (2001). 'The ECB's Numbers Problem', *Financial Times*, 4 December: 15.

—— (2006a). 'The Euro's Trade Effects', ECB Working Paper No. 594. Frankfurt am Main.

—— (2006b). *In or out: Does It Matter? An Evidence-Based Analysis of the Euro's Trade Effects*. London: Centre for Economic Policy Research.

Bale, T. (2006). 'Between a Soft and a Hard Place? The Conservative Party, Valence Politics and the Need for a New "Euro-Realism"', *Parliamentary Affairs*, 59(3): 385–400.

Balleix-Banerjee, C. (1999). *La France et la Banque Centrale Européenne*. Paris: PUF.

Balls, E. (1992). *Euro-Monetarism: Why Britain was Ensnared and How It Should Escape*. London: Fabian Society.

—— (2006a). 'The City as the Global Finance Centre: Risks and Opportunities', Speech by the Economic Secretary to the Treasury at Bloomberg, 14 June.

—— (2006b). 'Why We Must Not Gold Plate European Directives', *Financial Times*, 13 July.

—— and O'Donnell, G. (eds.) (2002). *Reforming Britain's Economic and Financial Policy: Towards Greater Economic Stability*. Basingstoke: Palgrave.

416

Bank for International Settlements (2006). *Basel II: International Convergence of Capital Measurement and Capital Standards: a Revised Framework*. Basel: Bank for International Settlements. http://www.bis.org/pub/bsbsca.htm (accessed 26 April 2007.)

—— (2007). *Triennial Central Bank Survey: Foreign Exchange and Derivatives Market Activity in 2007*. http://www.bis.org/publ/rpfxf07t.pdf.

Bank of Greece (1995). *Annual Report of the Governor*. Athens: Bank of Greece.

—— (2001). *Summary of the Annual Report 2001*. Athens: Bank of Greece.

—— (2007). *Summary of the Annual Report 2006*. Athens: Banks of Greece.

Barry, F. (2001). 'Fiscal Policy in EMU', in E. Pentecost and A. van Poeck (eds.), *European Monetary Integration*. Aldershot: Edward Elgar.

Bartolini, S. (2007). *Restructuring Europe: Centre Formation, System Building and Political Structuring Between the Nation State and the European Union*. Oxford: Oxford University Press.

Bayoumi, T. and Eichengreen, B. (1993). 'Shocking Aspects of European Monetary Integration', in G. Torres and F. Giavazzi (eds.), *Adjustment and Growth in European Monetary Union*. Cambridge: Cambridge University Press, pp. 193–229.

Becker, U. and Schwartz, H. (eds.) (2005). *Employment 'Miracles'. A Critical Comparison of the Dutch, Scandinavian, Swiss, Australian and Irish Cases versus Germany and the US*. Amsterdam: Amsterdam University Press.

Begg, I. (2007). 'Contested Meanings of Transparency in Central Banking', *Comparative European Politics*, 5: 36–52.

—— Buti, M., Enderlein, H., Pench, L., Schelkle, W., and Weale, M. (2004). 'Reforming Fiscal Policy Co-ordination Under EMU: What Should Become of the Stability and Growth Pact?', *Journal of Common Market Studies*, 42(5): 1047–59.

—— Hodson, D., and Maher, I. (2003). 'Economic Policy Coordination in the European Union', *National Institute Economic Review*, 183, London.

Bélanger, E. and Aarts, K. (2006). 'Explaining the Rise of the LPF: Issues, Discontent, and the 2002 Dutch Election', *Acta Politica*, 41(1): 4–20.

Belka, M. (2001). 'Czy to już kryzys?', *Polityka*, 34.

Belke, A. (2003). 'The Rotation Model is Not Sustainable', *Intereconomics*, 38(3): 119–24.

—— Herz, B., and Vogel, L. (2005). *Structural Reforms and the Exchange Rate Regime*. University of Hohenheim/University of Bayreuth, 3 August, mimeo.

Benczes, I. (2006). 'Social Pacts: A Helping Device in Euro Adoption?', *Transition Studies Review*, 13(2): 417–38.

Benedetto, G. and Quaglia, L. (2007). 'The Comparative Politics of Communist Euro-Scepticism in France, Spain and Italy', *Party Politics*, 12, at proof stage.

Benkovskis, K. and Paula, D. (2007). *Inflation Expectations in Latvia: Consumer Survey Based Results*. Riga: Bank of Latvia.

Berger, H. (2006). 'Unfinished Business? The ECB Reform Ahead of Euro Area Enlargement', *CESifo Forum*, 4: 35–41.

Bergsten, C. F. (2005). 'The Euro and the Dollar: Toward a "Finance G-2"?', in A. Posen (ed.), *The Euro at Five: Ready for a Global Role?* Washington: Institute for International Economics, pp. 27–39.

Bernanke, B. (2005). 'The Euro at Five: An Assessment', in A. Posen (ed.), *The Euro at Five: Ready for a Global Role?* Washington, DC: Institute for International Economics, pp. 179–90.

References

Bernau, P. (2007). 'Alles wird teuer—zumindest fuehlt's sich so an', *Frankfurter Allgemeine Sonntagszeitung*, 11 November.

Bernitz, U. (2000). 'Folkomröstning om EMU—svenskt fördragsbrott?', *Europarättslig tidskrift*, 3(2): 281–92.

—— (2002). *European Law in Sweden*. Stockholm: Faculty of Law.

Bertuch-Samuels, A. and Ramlogan, P. (2007). 'The Euro: Ever More Global', *Finance and Development*, 44(1): 46–9.

Beus, J. de (2004). 'The Netherlands: Monetary Integration and the Polder Model', in G. Ross and A. Martin (eds.), *Euros and Europeans: Monetary Integration and the European Model of Society*, pp. 174–200.

Bien, K. and Lesniak, G. (2003). 'Kierunkowa zgoda rzadu dla programu Kolodki', *Rzeczpospolita*, 20 March.

Bildt, C. (1992). 'Riksbanken', e-mail message to Anne Wibble, 20 November, in Anne Wibble's papers, National Archives of Sweden.

Binczak, H. and Blajer, P. (2004). 'Rozmiekczanie planu Hausnera', *Rzeczpospolita*, 5 February.

Bini Smaghi, L. (2004). 'A Single EU Seat in the IMF?', *Journal of Common Market Studies*, 42(2): 229–48.

Blajer, P. (2004a). 'Mniejsze oszczednosci zatwierdzone', *Rzeczpospolita*, 28 January.

—— (2004b). 'Budzet zaplaci za wotum zaufania', *Rzeczpospolita*, 26 June.

—— (2005). 'Hojnosc parlamentarzystow', *Rzeczpospolita*, 4 August.

—— and Sadlowska, K. (2004). 'Fiasko planu Hausnera', *Rzeczpospolita*, 16 December.

Blanchard, O. and Giavazzi, F. (2003). 'The Macroeconomic Effects of Regulation and Deregulation in Goods and Labour Markets', *Quarterly Journal of Economics*, 118(3): 879–909.

—— and Landier, A. (2003). 'The Perverse Effects of Partial Labour Market Reform: Fixed-Term Contracts in France', *The Economic Journal*, 112, June: 214–44.

—— Muet, P., Gridli, V. and Vial, P. (1993), 'Competitiveness through Disinflation. An Assessment of the French Macroeconomic Strategy', *Economic Policy*, 8(16): 12–56.

Blitz, J. and Parker, G. (2005). 'Brown Hints New Pact Could Stop UK Joining Euro', *Financial Times*, 22 March.

Blyth, M. and Katz, R. (2005). 'From Catch-All Parties to Cartelization: The Political Economy of the Cartel Party', *West European Politics*, 28(1): 33–60.

Boerzel, T. and Risse, T. (2003). 'Conceptualizing the Domestic Impact of Europe', in K. Featherstone and C. Radaelli (eds.), *The Politics of Europeanization*. Oxford: Oxford University Press, pp. 57–80.

Boewer, U. and Guillemineau, C. (February 2006). 'Determinants of Business Cycle Synchronisation across Euro Area Countries', ECB Working Paper No. 587. Frankfurt am Main.

Bohle, D. and Greskovits, B. (2007). 'Neoliberalism, Embedded Neoliberalism and Neocorporatism: Towards Transnational Capitalism in Central-Eastern Europe', *West European Politics*, 30(3): 443–66.

Boissonnat, J. (1998). *La révolution de 1999. L'Europe avec l'Euro*. Paris: Sand.

Borowski, J. (2001). 'Podatnosc Polski na szoki asymetryczne a proces akcesji do Unii Gospodarczej i Walutowej', *Bank i Kredyt*, 11–12.

Bratkowski, A. and Rostowski, J. (2001). 'Why Unilateral Euroization Makes Sense for (some) Applicant Countries—A Response, with Particular Reference to Poland', in

Finance Ministry, *The Polish Way to the Euro*, Conference Proceedings, 22–23 October, Falenty, Poland.

Brettschneider, F., Maier, M., and Maier, J. (2003). 'From D-Mark to Euro: The Impact of Mass Media on Public Opinion', *German Politics*, 12(2): 45–64.

Brittan, S. (1971). *Steering the Economy: The Role of the Treasury*. Harmondsworth: Penguin.

Brothén, M. (2004). 'Bristande förankring', in H. Oscarsson and S. Holmberg (eds.), *Kampen om euron*. Göteborg: Department of Political Science, pp. 61–80.

Brown, G. (2003a). *Speech to CBI National Conference*, Birmingham, 18 November. http://www.ht-treasury.gov.uk/newsroomandspeeches/press/2003.

—— (2003b). *Speech by the Chancellor of the Exchequer at the Wall Street Journal Europe, CEO Summit*, Four Seasons Hotel, London, 24 November. http://www.ht-treasury.gov.uk/newsroomandspeeches/press/2003.

—— (2004). 'Europe Must Meet the Challenge of Reform', *Financial Times*, 10 September.

—— (2005a). Speech at the British Chambers of Commerce Annual Conference, 25 April.

—— (2005b). 'Global Britain, Global Europe: A Presidency Founded on Pro-European Realism', Speech at the Mansion House, London, 22 June.

—— (2005c). Global Europe: Full Employment Europe. http://www.hm-treasury.gov.uk/093/BF/global_europe_131005.pdf.

—— (2006). 'The Right Way to Help the City Thrive', *Financial Times*, 18 October.

—— Sarkozy, N., and Eichel, H. (2004). 'Europe Must Seek Reforms if It Wants to Speed Up Growth', *Financial Times*, 21 May.

Brusis, M. and Dimitrov, V. (2001). 'Executive Configurations and Fiscal Performance in Post-Communist Central and Eastern Europe', *Journal of European Public Policy*, 8(6): 888–910.

Buiter, W. and Grafe, C. (2004). 'Patching up the Pact', *Economics of Transition*, 12(1): 67–102.

—— Corsetti, G., and Roubini, N. (1993). 'Excessive Deficits: Sense and Nonsense in the Maastricht Treaty', *Economic Policy*, 8(1): 58–100.

Bull, M. and Rhodes, M. (1997). 'Between Crisis and Transition: Italian Politics in the 1990s', *West European Politics*, 24(3): 1–13.

Bulmer, S. and Paterson, W. (1987). *The Federal Republic of Germany and the European Community*. London: Allen & Unwin.

Bundesregierung (1991). *Regierungserklärung von Bundeskanzler Kohl am 30. Januar 1991 vor dem Deutschen Bundestag*. Bonn: Deutscher Bundestag Plenarprotokoll 12/5, 30.01.

Bundesverband deutscher Banken (2001). *Demoskopie*, 13, November: http://www.bankenverband.de/index.asp?channel=133610&art=1312&ttyp=3&tid_. Source: Mannheim Forschungsgruppe Wahlen 'Polibarometer'.

Burnes, B., Katsouros, M., and Jones, T. (2004). 'Privatization and the European Union: The Case of the Public Power Corporation of Greece', *International Journal of Public Sector Management*, 17(1): 65–80.

Buti, M. and van den Noord, P. (2004). 'Fiscal Discretion and Elections in the Early Years of EMU', *Journal of Common Market Studies*, 42(4): 737–56.

Bútora, M., Meseznikov, G., and Bútorová, Z. (1999). *The 1998 Parliamentary Elections and Democratic Rebirth in Slovakia*. Bratislava: Institute for Public Affairs.

References

Calmfors, L. (2001). 'Wages and Wage Bargaining Institutions in the EMU—A Survey of the Issues', Seminar Paper No. 690. Stockholm University: Institute for International Economic Studies.

Cambadélis, J.-C. (1999). *L'avenir de la gauche plurielle*. Paris: Plon.

Cameron, D. (1978). 'The Expansion of the Public Economy: A Comparative Analysis', *American Political Science Review*, 72: 1243–61.

Campbell, J. (2004). *Institutional Change and Globalization*. Princeton: Princeton University Press.

Carfuny, A. and Ryner, M. (2007). *Europe at Bay: In the Shadow of US Hegemony*. Boulder: Lynne Rienner.

Carpenter, M. (1997). 'Slovakia and the Triumph of Nationalist Populism', *Communist and Post-Communist Studies*, 30(2): 205–20.

Castles, F. (ed.) (1993). *Families of Nations: Patterns of Public Policy in Western Democracies*. Aldershot: Dartmouth.

Cazzola, G. (1993). 'L 'Accordo di Luglio: l' Ultima Concertazione della Prima Repubblica', *Il Mulino*, 49(3): 941–51.

CBOS (2007). *Opinie o wprowadzeniu euro*. BS/14/2007, Warsaw: Centrum Badania Opinii Spolecznej.

Centraal Planbureau (2002). 'Prijsstijgingen in de Horeca', CPB Notitie, 11 September.

—— (2005). 'Geen uitverkoop van de Gulden', CPB, Memorandum, 19 May.

Central Statistics Office (1999). *External Trade*. Cork: CSO.

—— (2006). *Construction and Housing in Ireland*. Dublin: Stationery Office.

—— (2007*a*). 'Irish Earnings Data'. http://www.cso.ie/px/pxeirestat/database.

—— (2007*b*). *Consumer Price Index: January 2007*. CSO: Dublin.

Cerny, P. (1997). 'Paradoxes of the Competition State: The Dynamics of Political Globalization', *Government and Opposition*, 32(2): 251–74.

Chirac, J. (2000). *Notre Europe*. Speech given by Jacques Chirac, President of the French Republic, Berlin, 27 June. http://www.elysee.fr/cgi-bin/auracom/aurweb/search_all/file?aur_file=discours/2000/ALLE0003.html.

Christiansen, T. and Larsson, T. (eds.) (2007). *The Role of Committees in the Policy-Process of the European Union—Legislation, Implementation, Deliberation*. Cheltenham: Edward Elgar.

Ciampi, C. (1996). *Un Metodo per Governare*. Bologna: Il Mulino.

Clark, W. and Hallerberg, M. (2000). 'Mobile Capital, Domestic Institutions, and Electorally Induced Monetary and Fiscal Policy', *American Political Science Review*, 94(2): 323–46.

Clift, B. (2004). 'The French Model of Capitalism: Still Exceptional?', in J. Perrino and B. Clift (eds.), *Where Are National Capitalisms Now?* Basingstoke: Palgrave, pp. 91–110.

—— (2006). 'The New Political Economy of Dirigisme: French Macroeconomic Policy, Unrepentant Sinning, and the Stability and Growth Pact', *British Journal of Politics and International Relations*, 8(3): 388–409.

Cohen, B. (2000). 'Beyond EMU: The Problem of Sustainability', in B. Eichengreen and J. Frieden (eds.), *The Political Economy of European Monetary Unification*. Boulder: Westview, pp. 179–204.

—— (2003). 'Global Currency Rivalry: Can the Euro Ever Challenge the Dollar?', *Journal of Common Market Studies*, 41(4): 575–95.

—— (2004). *The Future of Money*. Princeton, NJ: Princeton University Press.

—— (2006). 'The Macrofoundations of Monetary Power', in D. Andrews (ed.), *International Monetary Power*. Ithaca, NY: Cornell University Press, pp. 31–50.

Collignon, S. (2007). 'The Three Sources of Legitimacy for European Fiscal Policy', *International Political Science Review*, 28(2): 155–84.

Commission of the European Communities (1988). *Cecchini Report*. Brussels: Commission of the European Communities.

—— (2004). Directive 2004/39/EC.

—— (2005a). *White Paper: Financial Services Policy 2005–2010*, SEC(2005) 1574. Brussels: Commission of the European Communities.

—— (2005b). 'Working Together for Growth and Jobs. A New Start for the Lisbon Process', COM(2005) 24, 2 February. Brussels.

—— (2005c). Communication to the Spring European Council. Working Together for Growth and Jobs: A New Start for the Lisbon Strategy. http://ec.europa.en/growthandjobs/pdf/com2005_en.pdf (accessed 30 August 2006.)

—— (2005d). 'Working Together for Growth and Jobs. Next Steps in Implementing the Revised Lisbon Strategy', SEC(2005)622/2, 29 April. Brussels.

Committee of European Banking Supervisors (2006). http://www.c-ebs.org/ (accessed 29 August 2006).

Coron, G. and Palier, B. (2002). 'Changes in the Means of Financing Social Expenditure in France Since 1945', in C. de la Porte and P. Pochet (eds.), *Building Social Europe through the Open Method of Co-ordination*. Brussels: P.I.E.- Peter Lang.

Council of the European Union (2005a). *Improving the Implementation of the Stability and Growth Pact*, 7423/05, UEM 97, ECOFIN 104, Brussels.

—— (2005b). *Council Regulation (EC) No 1056/2005 of 27 June 2005 Amending Regulation (EC) No 1467/97 on Speeding Up and Clarifying the Implementation of the Excessive Deficit Procedure*, Official Journal of the European Union L 174, 5–9.

—— (2006a). *Council Opinion of 14 March 2006 on the updated Convergence Programme of Poland, 2005–2008*, 7383/06, 14 March.

—— (2006b). 'Presidency Conclusions, March 2006', mimeo. http://ue.eu.int/ueDocs/cms_Data/docs/pressData/en/ec/89013.pdf (accessed 30 August 2006).

Cowles, M., Caporasa, J., and Risse, T. (eds.) (2001). *Transforming Europe: Europeanization and Domestic Change*. Ithaca: Cornell University Press.

Cowley, P. and Green, J. (2005). 'New Leaders, Same Problems: The Conservatives', in A. Geddes and J. Tonge (eds.), *Britain Decides: the British General Election 2005*. Basingstoke: Palgrave.

Crouch, C. (1993). *Industrial Relations and European State Traditions*. Oxford: Clarendon Press.

Crouch, C. (ed.) (2000). *After the Euro: Shaping Institutions for Governance in the Wake of European Monetary Union*. Oxford: Oxford University Press.

Crouch, C. (2002). 'The Euro and Labour Market and Wage Policies', in K. Dyson (ed.), *European States and the Euro: Europeanization, Variation and Convergence*. Oxford: Oxford University Press, pp. 278–304.

—— (2005). *Capitalist Diversity and Change. Recombining Governance and Institutional Entrepreneurs*. Oxford: Oxford University Press.

Cullen, M. (1998). Speech given in the Dáil Éireann, 1 April 1998.

Daniels, P. (1993). 'Italy and the Maastrict Treaty', in S. Hellman and G. Pasquino (eds.), *Italian Politics: A Review*. Bologna: Il Mulino, pp. 178–91.

de Grauwe, P. (2005). *Economics of Monetary Union*. 6th edn. Oxford: Oxford University Press.

de la Porte, C. and Pochet, P. (2003). 'A Twofold Assessment of Employment Policy Coordination in Light of Economic Policy Coordination', in D. Foden and L. Magnusson (eds.), *Five Years' Experience of the Luxembourg Employment Strategy*. Brussels: ETUI, pp. 13–67.

——— and Room, G. (2001). 'Social Benchmarking, Policy-Making and New Governance in the EU', *Journal of European Social Policy*, 11: 291–307.

De Nederlandsche Bank (2002). 'Smooth Euro Changeover, Higher Prices? Results of a Survey Among Dutch Retailers', DNB Research Memorandum 682.E.

De Volkskrant (1997). 'Met deze EMU kiest Europa de verkeerde weg', 13 February.

Debrun, X. and Annett, A. (2004). 'Implementing Lisbon: Incentives and Constraints', in *Euro Area—SelectedIssues*. Washington, DC.: IMF Country Report 04/235.

—— and Pisani-Ferry, J. (November 2006). *Economic Reforms in the Euro Area: Is There a Common Agenda?* Brussels: Bruegel.

Della Sala, V. (1997). 'Hollowing out and Hardening the State: European Integration and the Italian Economy', *West European Politics*, 20(1): 14–33.

Delors Report (1989). *Report on Economic and Monetary Union in the European Community*. (Committee for the Study of Economic and Monetary Union) Luxembourg: Office for Official Publications of the EC (April).

Deutsche Bank (2001). *The Two-pillar Strategy of the ECB: A First Assessment*, €MU Watch 92/2001. http://www.dbresearch.com/PROD/DBR_INTERNET_EN-PROD/PROD0000000000036543.pdf.

Deutsche Bundesbank (2006). 'A Disaggregated Framework for Analysing Public Finances: Germany's Fiscal Track Record between 2000 and 2005', *Monthly Report*, March: 61–76.

Deutsche Bundesbank (2007). 'Advances in Strengthening the Economy's Growth Potential', *Monthly Report*, October: 35–45.

—— (2007a). 'Upturn with a Bright Outlook', *Monthly Report*, February: 40–1.

—— (2007b). 'German Intra-Euro-Area Trade: Cyclical Effects and Structural Determinants', *Monthly Report*, March: 35.

Diamandouros, N. (1993). 'Politics and Culture in Greece, 1974–91', in R. Clogg (ed.), *Greece, 1981–89: The Populist Decade*. London: Macmillan, pp. 1–25.

—— (1994). 'Cultural Dualism and Political Change in Post-authoritarian Greece', Working Paper No. 50. Madrid: Instituto Juan March.

Die Welt (2005). 'Man muss bereit sein', interview with Ivan Miklos, 15 September.

Dimitrov, V., Goetz, K., Wollmann, H. (2006). *Governing after Communism: Institutions and Policy-making*. Lanham: Rowman & Littlefield.

Donaghey, J. and Teague, P. (2005). 'The Persistence of Social Pacts in Europe', *Industrial Relations Journal*, 36(6): 478–93.

Duckenfield, M. E. (2006). *Business and the Euro: Business Groups and the Politics of the EMU in Germany and the United Kingdom*. Basingstoke: Palgrave.

Dufresne, A. (2002). 'Wage Co-ordination in Europe: Roots and Routes', in P. Pochet (ed.), *Wage Policy in the Eurozone*. Brussels: PIE-Peter Lang, pp. 79–109.

Duval, R. and Elmeskov, J. (2006). 'The Effects of EMU on Structural Reforms in Labour and Product Markets', ECB Working Paper No. 596. Frankfurt am Main.

Dyson, K. (1980). *The State Tradition in Western Europe*. Oxford: Blackwell.

—— (1994). *Elusive Union. The Process of Economic and Monetary Union in Europe*. London: Longman.

—— (2000*a*). 'EMU as Europeanization', *Journal of Common Market Studies*, 38(4): 645–66.

—— (2000*b*). *The Politics of the Euro Zone. Stability or Breakdown?* Oxford: Oxford University Press.

—— (2002). 'The German Model Revisited: From Schmidt to Schröder', in S. Padgett and T. Poguntke (eds.), *Continuity and Change in German Politics: Beyond the Politics of Centrality?* London: Frank Cass, pp. 135–54.

—— (ed.) (2002). *European States and the Euro: Europeanization, Variation and Convergence*. Oxford: Oxford University Press.

—— (2005). 'Economic Policy Management: Catastrophic Equilibrium, Tipping Points and Crisis Intervention', in S. Green and W. Paterson (eds.), *Governance in Contemporary Germany: The Semi-Sovereign State Revisited*. Cambridge: Cambridge University Press, pp. 115–37.

Dyson, K. (ed.) (2006). *Enlarging the Euro Area: External Empowerment and Domestic Transformation in East Central Euro*. Oxford: Oxford University Press.

Dyson, K. (2006*a*). 'Binding Hands as a Strategy for Economic Reform: Government by Commission', in K. Dyson and S. Padgett (eds.), *The Politics of Economic Reform in Germany: Global, Rhineland or Hybrid Capitalism?* London: Routledge, pp. 110–33.

—— (2006*b*). 'Euro Area Entry as Extreme "Accession" Europeanization and "Clustered" Convergence: Political Strategies for Temporal Management in East Central Europe', in A. Agh and A. Ferencz (eds.), *Deepening and Widening in an Enlarged Europe*. Budapest: Research Centre of the Hungarian Academy of Sciences.

—— (2006*c*). 'Euro Entry as Defining and Negotiating Fit: Conditionality, Contagion and Domestic Politics', in K. Dyson (ed.), *Enlarging the Euro Area: External Empowerment and Domestic Transformation in East Central Europe*. Oxford: Oxford University Press, pp. 7–43.

—— (2007*a*). 'Euro Area Entry as Paradoxical Europeanization and 'Clustered' Convergence: Political Strategies for Temporal Management in East Central Europe', *West European Politics*.

—— (2008*a*). 'Economic and Monetary Union: A Hard and Stony Path', in P. Phinnemore and A. Warleigh-Lack (eds.), *Reflections on European Integration*. London: Palgrave.

—— (2008*b*). 'Crisis in Economic Statecraft? Policy Misfit, Institutional Gridlock, and Firm-Led Adjustment', in A. Miskimmon, W. Paterson, and J. Sloam (eds.), *The German Crisis and the 2005 Elections*. Basingstoke: Palgrave.

—— and Featherstone, K. (1996). 'Italy and EMU as "Vincolo Esterno": Empowering the Technocrats, Transforming the State', *South European Politics and Society*, 1(2): 272–99.

—— and Featherstone, K. (1999). *The Road to Maastricht: Negotiating Economic and Monetary Union*. Oxford: Oxford University Press.

Dyson, K. and Padgett, S. (eds.) (2006). *The Politics of Economic Reform in Germany*. London: Routledge.

References

Dyson, K. and Quaglia, L. (2007). 'Committee Governance in Economic and Monetary Union: Policy Experts and their Images of Europe', Report of the FP 6 INTUNE PROJECT, Cardiff/Sussex, unpub. paper.

——Featherstone, K., Michaelopoulos, G. (1994). 'Reinventing the French State, Construction européenne and the Development of French Policies on EMU', European Briefing Unit Report No. 2. University of Bradford: Department of European Studies.

Easton, D. (1965). *A System Analysis of Political Life*. New York: John Wiley.

Eckstein, G. and Pappi, F. (1999). 'Die öffentliche Meinung zur europäischen Währungsunion bis 1998: Befund, geldpolitische Zusammenhänge und politische Führung in Deutschland', *Zeitschrift für Politik*, 46: 298–334.

ECOFIN (2003). 'The 2546th Economic and Finance Ministers', Council Meeting. Press Release: Brussels (25.11.03), Nr. 14492/03.

Égert, B. (2005). 'The Balassa–Samuelson Hypothesis in Estonia: Oil Shale, Tradable Goods, Regulated Prices and Other Culprits', *The World Economy*, 28(2): 259–86.

Eichengreen, B. (2006). *The European Economy Since 1945: Co-ordinated Capitalism and Beyond*. Princeton: Princeton University Press.

——(2007). *The Euro: Love It or Leave It?* 19 November. http://www.voxeu.org/index.php?q=node/729.

——and Wyplosz, C. (1998). 'Stability Pact: More than a Minor Nuisance?', *Economic Policy*, 13(1): 67–113.

Eijffinger, S. (2006). 'Change at the ECB Executive Board', *Intereconomics*, March/April: 93–9.

EIRO (2004). *National-level Tripartism and EMU in the New EU Member States and Candidate Countries*. http://.eiro.eurofound.europa.eu/eiro/2004/03/study/tn0403101s.html.

——(2006a). *New National Collective Agreement Signed for 2006–2007*. http://www.eiro.eurofound.ie/2006/05/articles/gr0605019i.html.

——(2006b). *Pay Developments—2005*. http://www.eiro.eurofound.ie.int/2006/06/update/tn0606101u.html.

EIRO (2007). *Industrial Relations Developments in Europe 2006*. Luxembourg: Office for Official Publications of the European Communities.

Employment Taskforce (2003). *Jobs, Jobs, Jobs. Creating More Employment in Europe*. Brussels: European Commission.

Enderlein, H. (2004). *Nationale Wirtschaftspolitik in der Europäischen Währungsunion*. Frankfurt am Main: Campus.

Epstein, R. (2006). 'Cultivating Consensus and Creating Conflict: International Institutions and the (De)Politicization of Economic Policy in Post-Communist Europe', *Comparative Political Studies*, 39(8): 1019–42.

Esping-Andersen, G. (1990). *The Three Worlds of Welfare Capitalism*. Cambridge: Polity.

——(1999). *The Social Foundations of Post-Industrial Economies*. Oxford: Oxford University Press.

ETUC (2007). 'The Euro Area Can Afford Higher Wages for German Workers!', *Collective Bargaining Bulletin*, 2007/2, Brussels: ETUC.

Eurobarometer (July 2001a). 'Qualitative Study on the Preparation of Citizens to the Changeover to the Euro'. http://ec.Europa.eu/ public_opinion/quali/ql_Euro0701_en.pdf.

—— (2001*b*). *Flash Eurobarometer No. 98/2: Euro Attitudes (Wave 2): Euro Area*. Brussels: European Commission.

—— (2002*a*). *Flash Eurobarometer No. 139: The Euro, One Year Later*. Brussels: European Commission.

—— (2002*b*). 'Qualitative Study on EU Citizens and the Euro in the Months Following its Introduction', http://ec.Europa.eu/public_opinion/quali/ql_Euro0502_en.pdf, May.

—— (2003). *Flash Eurobarometer No. 153: The Euro, Two Years Later*. Brussels: European Commission.

—— (2004). *Flash Eurobarometer No. 165: The Euro, Three Years Later*. Brussels: European Commission.

—— (2005). *Flash Eurobarometer No. 175: The Euro, 4 Years After the Introduction of Bank Notes and Coins*. Brussels: European Commission.

—— (2006). *Flash Eurobarometer No. 193: The Euro, 5 Years After*. Brussels: European Commission.

—— (2007). 'Introduction of the Euro in the New Member States: Summary', *Flash Eurobarometer 207*, Brussels: European Commission.

European Bank for Reconstruction and Development (2006). *Transition Report*. London: EBRD.

European Central Bank (2004). *Convergence Report. Economic and Legal Assessment. Poland*. Frankfurt am Main: ECB.

—— (2005*a*). 'Trends in Euro Area Potential Output Growth', *Monthly Bulletin*. Frankfurt am Main: ECB, July: 46–54.

—— (2005*b*). 'A Longer-Term Perspective on Structural Unemployment in the Euro Area', *Monthly Bulletin*. Frankfurt am Main: ECB, August: 46–9.

—— (2005*c*). *Competitiveness and the Export Performance of the Euro Area*. Occasional Paper 30. Frankfurt am Main: ECB, June.

—— (2006*a*). *Annual Report 2005*. Frankfurt am Main: ECB.

—— (2006*b*). *Convergence Report. Economic and Legal Assessment. Poland*. Frankfurt am Main: ECB.

—— (2006*c*). 'The Contribution of the ECB and the Eurosystem to European Financial Integration', *ECB Monthly Bulletin*, May: 61–74.

—— (2007*a*). 'The EU Arrangements for Financial Crisis Management', *Monthly Bulletin*, February: 73–84.

—— (2007*b*). *Annual Report 2006*. Frankfurt am Main: ECB.

—— (2007*c*). *Review of the International Role of the Euro*. Frankfurt am Main: ECB.

—— (2007*d*). *Financial Integration in Europe*. Frankfurt am Main: ECB.

—— (2007*e*). 'Measured Inflation and Inflation Perceptions in the Euro Area', *Monthly Bulletin*, Frankfurt am Main: ECB, pp. 63–72.

European Commission (1985*a*). *Euro-Barometer: Public Opinion in the European Community*, p. 24.

—— (1985*b*). *Euro-Barometer: Public Opinion in the European Community*, p. 23.

—— (1990). *Eurobarometer: Public Opinion in the European Community*, p. 34.

—— (1993*a*). *European Social Policy—Options for the Union: A Green Paper* COM(93) 551 17 November.

References

European Commission (1993*b*). *Growth, Competitiveness, Employment—The Challenges and Ways Forward into the 21st century: A White Paper* COM(93) 700 5 December.

—— (1994). *European Social Policy—A Way Forward for the Union: A White Paper* 27 July COM(94) 333.

—— (1995). *Eurobarometer: Public Opinion in the European Commission*, p. 43.

—— (1996). *Eurobarometer: Public Opinion in the European Community*, p. 45.

—— (1997). *Eurobarometer: Public Opinion in the European Community*, p. 47.

—— (2000*a*). *Eurobarometer: Public Opinion in the European Community*, p. 53.

—— (2000*b*). *Industrial Relations in Europe, 2000*. Luxembourg: Office for Official Publications of the European Communities.

—— (2001*a*). *Commission Recommendations for the 2001 Broad Guidelines of the Economic Policies of the Member States and the Community*. Brussels: European Community.

—— (2001*b*). *Eurobarometer: Public Opinion in the European Union*, p. 54.

—— (2002). *Commission Sets out Strategy for Economic Policy Coordination and Surveillance*, Brussels IP/04/35.

—— (2003*a*). *Communication from the Commission to the Council, the European Parliament, the Economic and Social Committee and the Committee of the Regions: The Future of the European Employment Strategy (EES) 'A Strategy for Full Employment and Better Jobs for All'*, COM(2003)6 final, 14.1.

—— (2003*b*). *Employment in Europe, 2003: Recent Developments and Prospects*. Luxembourg: Office for Official Publications of the European Communities.

—— (2003*c*). *European Economy: Public Finance in EMU*.

—— (2004*a*). *Industrial Relations in Europe, 2004*. Luxembourg: Office for Official Publications of the European Communities.

—— (2004*b*). *Public Finances in EMU*. Brussels: Directorate-General for Economic and Financial Affairs.

—— (2005*a*). *Integrated Guidelines for Growth and Jobs (2005–2008) including a Commission Recommendation on the Broad Guidelines for Economic Policies of the Member States and the Community (under Article 99 of the EC Treaty) and a Proposal for a Council Decision on Guidelines for the Employment Policies of the Member States (under Article 128 of the EC Treaty)*, COM(2005)141 final, 2005/0057 (CNS), Brussels, 12 April.

—— (2005*b*). *Communication from the Commission to the Council and the European Parliament, Common Actions for Growth and Employment: The Community Lisbon Programme*, COM(2005)330 final, [SEC(2005)981], 20.7.

—— (2006*a*). 'European Economy: Convergence Report', *Commission Services Working Paper* (December). Brussels: European Commission.

—— (2006*b*). *Development of the EES*, DG Employment and Social Affairs. http://ec.europa.eu/employment_social/employment_strategy/develop_en.htm.

—— (2006*c*). *Eurobarometer: Public Opinion in the European Union*, p. 64.

—— (2006*d*). *Introduction of the Euro in the New Member States*, Flash Eurobarometer No. 191.

—— (2007*a*). 'Economic Forecast', Spring. http://ec.europa.eu/economy_finance/publications/european_economy/2007/ee207en.pdf. (accessed on 24 August 2007).

—— (2007*b*). 'Economic Forecasts—Fall', *European Economy*, p. 7.

—— (2007*c*). 'Harmonised Index of Consumer Prices', made available by the Commission services DG Ecfin in March.

—— (several years). *Public Finances in EMU*. Brussels: European Commission.

European Convention (2002). *French-German Contribution on Economic Governance*, CONV 470/02, http://register.consilium.eu.int/pdf/en/02/cv00/00470en2.pdf, 22 December.

European Council (2005). *Presidency Conclusion, Spring European Council, 22 and 23 March 2005*, 7619/1/05, REV 1, CONCL 1, Brussels.

—— (2007). *Presidency Conclusion, Brussels European Council*, 14 December, 16616/07, CONCL 3, Brussels.

Eurostat (2004). *Report by Eurostat on the Revision of the Greek Government Deficit and Debt Figures*, 22 November, Brussels: Eurostat.

—— (2005). 'The European Constitution: Post-referendum Survey in France'. Flash Euro-barometer EB171, http://ec.europa.eu/public_opinion/flash/fl171_en.pdf. Accessed 27 November 2007.

—— (2007*a*). *Real Unit Labour Cost Growth*. http://epp.eurostat.ec.europa.eu/portal/page?_pageid=1996,39140985&_dad=portal&...(accessed 11 July 2007).

—— (2007*b*). 'Euro-Indicators', *News Release*, 22 October, p. 142.

—— (2007*c*). *Economy and Finance* [cited 26 November 2007b]. http://epp.eurostat.ec.europa.eu/portal/page?_pageid=0,1136173,0_45570701&_dad=portal&_schema=PORTAL.

Fajertag, G. and Pochet, P. (1997). *Social Pacts in Europe*. Brussels: OSE/ETUI.

—— —— (2000). *Social Pacts in Europe. New Dynamics*. Brussels: OSE/ETUI.

Falkner, G., Treib, O., Hartlapp, M., and Leiber, S. (2005). *Complying with Europe: EU Harmonization and Soft Law in the Member States*. Cambridge: Cambridge University Press.

Faruquee, H. (2004). 'Measuring the Trade Effects of EMU', *IMF Working Papers*, No. 154.

Fatas, A. (1998). 'Does EMU Need a Fiscal Federation?', *Economic Policy*, 13(1): 165–203.

Favero, C., Freixas, X., Persson, T., and Wyploz, C. (2000). *One Money, Many Countries: Monitoring the European Central Bank 2*. London: Centre for Economic Policy Research.

—— (2003). 'Greece and EMU: Between External Empowerment and Domestic Vulnerability', *Journal of Common Market Studies*, 41(5): 923–40.

—— and Papadimitriou, D. (2007). 'Manipulating Rules, Contesting Solutions: Europeanization and the Politics of Restructuring Olympic Airways', *Government and Opposition*, 42(1): 46–72.

—— and Papadimitriou, D. (2008). *The Limits of Europeanization*. Houndmills: Palgrave Macmillan.

—— Kazamias, G., and Papadimitriou, D. (2000). 'Greece and the Negotiation of Economic and Monetary Union: Preferences, Strategies, and Institutions', *Journal of Modern Greek Studies*, 18: 393–414.

Feldmann, M. (2003). 'Free Trade in the 1990s: Understanding Estonian Exceptionalism', *Demokratizatsiya*, 11(4): 517–33.

—— (2006*a*). 'The Baltic States: Pacesetting on EMU Accession and the Consolidation of Domestic Stability Culture', in K. Dyson (ed.), *Enlarging the Euro Area: External Empowerment and Domestic Transformation in East Central Europe*. Oxford: Oxford University Press, pp. 127–44.

References

Feldmann, M. (2006*b*). 'Emerging Varieties of Capitalism in Transition Countries: Industrial Relations and Wage Bargaining in Estonia and Slovenia', *Comparative Political Studies*, 39(7): 829–54.

Ferge, Z. and Juhász, G. (2004). 'Accession and Social Policy: the Case of Hungary', *Journal of European Social Policy*, 14(3): 233–52.

Fianna Fáil and Progressive Democrats (2002). *An Agreed Programme for Government Between Fianna Fáil and the Progressive Democrats*. Dublin: Fianna Fáil and Progressive Democrats.

Fichtelius, E. (2007). *Aldrig ensam, alltid ensam*. Stockholm: Norstedts.

Fifield, A. (2004). 'Adviser Urges Pact to Reflect Brown's Regime', *Financial Times*, 24/25 January.

Financial Times (2006). 29 September.

——(2007*a*). 'Europeans' Low Expectations of Eurozone Prove Widespread', 29 January: 8.

——(2007*b*). 21 May.

——(2008). 'Clement Attacks 'Lethal' Policies', 14 January.

Fischer, J. (2000). *Vom Staatenverbund zur Föderation—Gedanken über die Finalität der Europäischen Integration*. Speech on 12 May, Humboldt-University Berlin, http://www.auswaertiges-amt.de/4_europa/index.htm.

——Jonung, L., and Larch, M. (2006). '101 Proposals to Reform the Stability and Growth Pact. Why So Many?', Manuscript.

Fish, S. (1999). 'The End of Meciarism', *East European Constitutional Review*, 8(1–2): 47–55.

Fitoussi, J.-P. (1992). *La désinflation compétitive, le mark et les politiques budgétaires en Europe*. Paris: OFCE and Editions du Seuil.

——(1995). *Le Débat interdit*. Paris: Editions du Seuil.

Fitz Gerald, J. (2001). 'Managing an Economy Under EMU: The Case of Ireland', *The World Economy*, 24(10): 1353–71.

Fondation Robert Schuman (2007). *The Lisbon Treaty. 10 Easy-to-Read Fact Sheets*, http://www.robert-schuman.eu/doc/divers/lisbonne/en/10fiches.pdf.

Frankel, J. (2006). 'Comment' on 'The Euro's Trade Effects' by Richard Baldwin. In Baldwin, R., *ibid*, 2006a.

——and Rose, A. (1998). 'The Endogeneity of the Optimum Currency Area Criteria', *Economic Journal*, 108: 1009–25.

——and Rose, A. (2005). 'An Estimate of the Effect of Common Currencies on Trade and Income', *Quarterly Journal of Economics*, 117: 437–66.

Frankfurter Allgemeine Zeitung (2007). *Europäische Zentralbank fürchtet um ihren Status. Präsident Trichet fordert Änderung am EU-Reformvertrag*, 15 August: 12.

French Banking Federation (2005). 'Directive Marchés des Instruments financiers (MIF): Pour une application cohérente', http://www.fbf.fr/web/internet/content_presse.nsf/(WebPageList)/Marche+des+capitaux+en+Europe/$File/Directive_MIF_pour_une_application_coherente.doc.

Frieden, J. (2002). 'Real Sources of European Currency Policy: Sectoral Interests and European Monetary Integration', *International Organization*, 56(4): 831–60.

——(2004). 'One Europe, One Vote? The Political Economy of European Union Representation in International Organizations', *European Union Politics*, 5(2): 261–76.

Friedman, B. (2005). *The Moral Consequences of Economic Growth*. New York: Alfred Knopf.

Gallup Europe (2002). *The Euro, One Year Later*. Flash Eurobarometer 139, November.

—— (2005). *The Euro, Four Years after the Introduction of the Banknotes and Coins*. Flash Eurobarometer, November.

—— (2006). *Five Years after the Introduction of Euro Coins and Banknotes: Analytical Report*. Flash Eurobarometer 193, November.

—— (2007). *Heading to the Euro-Zone. Hopes and Fears about the Euro in the New Member States*. http://ec.europa.eu/public_opinion/flash/fl183-en.pdf.

Gamble, A. and Kelly, G. (2002). 'Britain and EMU', in K. Dyson (ed.), *European States and the Euro*. Oxford: Oxford University Press, pp. 97–119.

Garganas, N. (2007). 'Does One Size Fit All? Monetary Policy and Integration in the Euro Area', speech given at the Bank of Chile, Santiago, 12 October.

Gazeta Wyborcza (2003). 'Bedzie plan Hausnera', *Gazet Wyborcza*, 28th March.

—— (2006). 'Prezydent Kaczynski: Referendum o euro w 2010', *Gazeta Wyborcza*, 9 October.

Giannone, D. and Reichlin, L. (March 2006). 'Trends and Cycles in the Euro Area. How Much Heterogeneity and Should We Worry About It?', ECB Working Paper No. 595. Franfurt am Main.

Giddens, A. (1998). *The Third Way: The Renewal of Social Democracy*. Cambridge: Polity.

Gieve, J. (2007). 'The City's Growth: The Crest of a Wave or Swimming with the Stream?', Speech to the London Society of Chartered Accountants, 26 March. (www.bankofengland.co.uk/publications/speeches/2007).

Giles, C. (2007a). 'Time to Overhaul the Two Fiscal Rules, Report Concludes', *Financial Times*, 24 April.

—— (2007b). 'Inflation Shock Set to Lift Rates', *Financial Times*, 18 April.

—— (2008). 'UK Reports Slow but Steady Rise in Productivity Growth', *Financial Times*, 15 January.

—— and Strauss, D. (2007). 'Record Deficit Heads Wave of Bad Data', *Financial Times*, 21 December.

Gill, S. (1998). 'European Governance and New Constitutionalism: Economic and Monetary Union and Alternatives to Disciplinary Neoliberalism in Europe', *New Political Economy*, 3(1): 5–26.

Glapiak, E. (2007). 'Euro musi poczekac', *Rzeczpospolita*, 26 November.

—— and Jablonski, P. (2006). 'Tanie panstwo nie moze byc tandetna taniocha: rozmowa z Zyta Gilowska, wicepremier i ministrem finansow', *Rzeczpospolita*, 11 December.

Goetz, K. (2006). *The Politics of Time: The Temporality of EU Enlargement and Europeanization*. Potsdam, mimeo.

—— and Zubek, R. (2007). 'Government, Parliament and Lawmaking in Poland', *Journal of Legislative Studies*, 13(4).

Golden, M. (2004). 'International Economic Sources of Regime Change: How European Integration Undermined Italy's Post-War Party System', Estudio/working paper 2004/207 June. Madrid: Instituto Juan March de Estudios e Investigaciones.

Goodman, J. (1992). *Monetary Sovereignty: The Politics of Central Banking in Western Europe*. Ithaca: Cornell University Press.

References

Gorska, A., Jakubiec, S., Lezanska, H., and Siemaszko, M. (2003). 'Analiza wplywu wprowadzenia euro na polski system bankowy', *NBP Materialy i Studia*, No. 169.

Gottesman, K. (2004). 'Wzloty i upadki planu Hausnera', *Rzeczpospolita*, 28 July.

Government of Ireland (2006). *Towards 2016: Ten-Year Framework Social Partnership Agreement, 2006–2015*. Dublin: The Stationery Office.

Grabbe, H. (2006). *The EU's Transformative Power: Europeanization Through Conditionality in Central and Eastern Europe*. Basingstoke: Palgrave Macmillan.

Grahl, J. (2001). 'Globalised Finance: The Challenge to the Euro', *New Left Review*, 8: 23–47.

Green, S. and Paterson, W. (eds.) (2005). *Governance in Contemporary Germany: The Semisovereign State Revisited*. Cambridge: Cambridge University Press.

Greskovits, B. (2001). 'Brothers-in-Arms or Rivals in Politics? Top Politicians and Top Policy Makers in the Hungarian Transformation', in J. Kornai, S. Haggard, and R. R. Kaufman (eds.), *Reforming the State. Fiscal and Welfare Reform in Post-Socialist Countries*. Cambridge: Cambridge University Press, pp. 111–41.

——(2006). 'The First Shall Be the Last? Hungary's Road to EMU', in K. Dyson (ed.), *Enlarging the Euro Area*, pp. 178–96.

——(2007). 'Economic Woes and Political Disaffection', *Journal of Democracy*, 18(4): 40–6.

Gros, D. (2003). 'An Opportunity Missed!', *Intereconomics*, 38(3): 124–9.

Guillén, A. and Palier, B. (2004). 'Does Europe Matter? Accession to EU and Social Policy Developments in Recent and New Member States', *Journal of European Social Policy*, 14(3): 203–9.

Gunlicks, A. (2007). 'German Federalism Reform: Part One', *German Law Journal*, 8(1): 111–32.

Gunther, H. (2004). 'Eurostat Takes Issue With Former Greek PM on Reasons for the Revision of Economic Data', *Financial Times*, 28 December.

GUS (2006). *Obroty handlu zagranicznego ogóşem i wedşug krajów I–XII 2006*. Warsaw: GUS.

GUS (2007). *Obroty handlu zagranicznego ogóşem i wedşug krajów I–IX 2007*. Warsaw: GUS.

Haggard, S., Kaufman, R. R., and Shugart, M. (2001). 'Politics, Institutions, and Macroeconomic Adjustment: Hungarian Fiscal Policy Making in Comparative Perspective', in J. Kornai, S. Haggard, and R. R. Kaufman (eds.), *Reforming the State*, pp. 75–110.

Hall, P. and Soskice, D. (eds.) (2001). *Varieties of Capitalism: The Institutional Foundations of Comparative Advantage*. Oxford: Oxford University Press.

——and Thelen, K. (2006). *Institutional Change in Varieties of Capitalism*. 15th International Conference of the Council for European Studies, Chicago, 29 March–2 April.

Hallerberg, M. (2004). *Domestic Budgets in a United Europe: Fiscal Governance from the End of Bretton Woods to EMU*. Ithaca, NY: Cornell University Press.

——and von Hagen, J. (2006). *Budget Processes in Poland: Promoting Fiscal and Economic Stability*, A report prepared for the Ernst & Young Better Government programme in Poland.

——Strauch, R., and von Hagen, J. (2009). *Fiscal Governance: Evidence from Europe*. Book Manuscript.

Hancké, B. (2002a). 'The Political Economy of Wage-Setting in the Eurozone', in P. Pochet (ed.), *Wage Policy in the Eurozone*. Brussels: PIE-Peter Lang, pp. 131–48.

——(2002b). *Large Firms and Institutional Change: Industrial Renewal and Economic Restructuring in France*. Oxford: Oxford University Press.

——and Rhodes, M. (2005). 'EMU and Labor Market Institutions in Europe. The Rise and Fall of National Social Pacts', *Work and Occupations*, 32(2): 196–228.

——and Soskice, D. (2003). 'Wage-Setting and Inflation Targets in EMU', *Oxford Review of Economic Policy*, 19(1): 149–160.

Hardiman, N. (2000). 'Social Partnership, Wage Bargaining and Growth', in B. Nolan, P. O'Connell, and C. T. Whelan (eds.), *Bust to Boom? The Irish Experience of Growth and Inequality*. Dublin: Institute of Public Administration.

Hasse, R. H. and Hepperle, B. (1994). 'Kosten und Nutzen einer Europäischen Währungsunion', in R. Caesar and H.-E. Scharrer (eds.), *Maastricht: Königsweg oder Irrweg zur Wirtschafts- und Währungsunion?* Bonn: Europa Union Verlag, pp. 165–93.

Hassel, A. (2003). 'The Politics of Social Pacts', *British Journal of Industrial Relations*, 41(4): 707–26.

Hauptmeier, S., Heipertz, M., and Schuknecht, L. (May 2006). 'Expenditure Reform in Industrialised Countries: A Case Study Approach', ECB Working Paper No. 634. Frankfurt am Main.

Hay, C. (1999). 'Crisis and the Structural Transformation of the State: Interrogating the Process of Change', *British Journal of Politics and International Relations*, 1(3): 317–44.

——(2003). 'Macroeconomic Policy Coordination and Membership of the Single European Currency: Another Case of British Exceptionalism?', *Political Quarterly*, 74(1): 91–9.

——(2007). *Why We Hate Politics*. Oxford: Polity.

——and Smith, N. (2005). 'Horses for Courses? The Political Discourse of Globalisation and European Integration in the UK and Ireland', *West European Politics*, 28(1): 125–59.

——Smith, N., and Watson, M. (2006). 'Beyond Prospective Accountancy: Reassessing the Case for British Membership of the Single European Currency Comparatively', *British Journal of Politics and International Relations*, 8(1): 101–26.

Hazareesingh, S. (1994). *Political Traditions in Modern France*. Oxford: Oxford University Press.

Heclo, H. (1974). *Modern Social Politics in Britain and Sweden: From Relief to Income Maintenance*. New Haven: Yale University Press.

Heikensten, L. (2003). 'Bakom Riksbankens tjocka väggar', in L. Jonung (ed.), *På jakt efter ett nytt ankare*. Stockholm: SNS Förlag, pp. 331–75.

Heipertz, M., and Verdun, A. (2004). 'The Dog that Would Never Bite? What We Can Learn from the Origins of the Stability and Growth Pact', *Journal of European Public Policy*, 11(5): 765–80.

——and Verdun, A. (2005). 'The Stability and Growth Pact—Theorizing a Case of European Integration', *Journal of Common Market Studies*, 43(5): 985–1008.

Heise, A. (2006). 'European Economic Governance: Policy-Making Beyond the Nation-State?', in E. Hein, A. Heise and A. Truger (eds.), *European Economic Policies. Alternatives to Orthodox Analysis and Policy Concepts*. Marburg: Metropolis, pp. 303–27.

References

Hemerijck, A. (1995). 'Corporatist Immobility in the Netherlands', in C. Crouch and F. Traxler (eds.), *Organized Industrial Relations in Europe: What Future?* Aldershot, UK: Avebury.

Hering, M. (2005). *Welfare Restructuring without Partisan Cooperation: The Role of Party Collusion in Blame Avoidance.* SEDAP Research Paper 142. Hamilton, Ontario: McMaster University.

Héritier, A. and Knill, C. (2001). 'Differential Responses to European Policies: A Comparison', in A. Heritier, D. Kerwer, C. Knill, D. Lehmkuhl, and M. Teutsch (eds.), *Differential Europe: The European Union Impact on National Policymaking.* Douillet: Rowman & Littlefield, pp. 257–94.

Hernborn, H., Holmberg, S., and Näsman, P. (2006). *Valu i allmänhetens tjänst.* Stockholm: SVT.

Herrmann, A. (2005). 'Converging Divergence: How Competitive Advantages Condition Institutional Change Under EMU', *Journal of Common Market Studies,* 43(2): 287–310.

Het Parool (2005a). 'Het laatste wat DNB wilde, was onrust; Directeur Brouwer: "De gulden was ondergewaardeerd"', 30 April.

——(2005b). 'De Nederlandsche Bank hield kaken op elkaar; Gulden te goedkoop de Euro in', 30 April.

Hirschman, A. O. (1970). *Exit, Voice, and Loyalty.* Cambridge: Harvard University Press.

Hix, S. and Goetz, K. (2000). 'European Integration and National Political Systems', *West European Politics,* 23(4): 1–26.

HM Treasury (2003a). *Government Response to the Thirteenth Report of the House of Lords Select Committee on the European Union, Session 2002–03* (http://www.parliament.uk/ parliamentary_committees/s_comm_a/s_comm_a_reports_and_publications.cfm).

HM Treasury Cm. 5776 (2003b). *UK Membership of the Single Currency: An Assessment of the Five Economic Tests.* London: HM Treasury.

HM Treasury (2004). *Government Response to the 42nd Report of the House of Lords Select Committee on the European Union, Session 2002–03 (HL Paper 170).* (http:// www.parliament.uk/parliamentary_committees/s_comm_a/s_comm_a_reports_and_ publications.cfm).

——(2006). *Davidson Review: The Implementation of EU Legislation.* London: HMSO.

Hodson, D. and Maher, I. (2004). 'Soft Law and Sanctions: Economic Policy Co-ordination and Reform of the Stability and Growth Pact', *Journal of European Public Policy,* 11(5): 798–813.

Hoeller, P., Giorno, C., and de la Maisonneuve, C. (2004). *One Money, One Cycle? Making Monetary Union a Smoother Ride.* Paris: OECD.

Höjelid, S. (1999). *Politiskt beslutsfattande och EMU.* Lund: Studentlitteratur.

Holmberg, S. (2004a). 'It's the Economy, Stupid!', in H. Oscarsson and S. Holmberg (eds.), *Kampen om euron.* Göteborg: Department of Political Science, pp. 447–55.

——(2004b). 'Ännu inte marginaliserade partier', in H. Oscarsson and S. Holmberg (eds.), *Kampen om euron.* Göteborg: Department of Political Science, pp. 81–99.

Honohan, P. (2000). 'Ireland in EMU: Straitjacket or Skateboard?', *Irish Banking Review,* Winter.

——and Leddin, A. (2006). 'Ireland in EMU: Less Shocks, more Insulation?', *Economic and Social Review,* 37(2): 263–94.

Hopkin, J. and Wincott, D. (2006). 'New Labour, Economic Reform and the European Social Model', *British Journal of Politics and International Relations*, 8(1): 50–68.

House of Commons 1004 (2003*a*). *Government Response to the Committee's Sixth Report on the UK and the Euro (HC 187)*. London: HMSO.

House of Commons 187-I (2003*b*). *6th Report of the House of Commons Treasury Committee, Session 2002–03: The UK and the Euro*. London: HMSO.

House of Commons 389-I (2007). *House of Commons Treasury Committee: the 2007 Budget: Fifth Report of the Session 2006–7*, Volume 1. London: HMSO.

House of Lords (2000). *18th Report of the House of Lords Select Committee on the European Union, Session 1999–2000: How is the Euro Working?* (http://www.parliament.uk/parliamentary_committees/s_comm_a/s_comm_a_reports_and_publications.cfm).

House of Lords Paper 170 (2003). *42nd Report of the Select Committee on the European Union, Session 2002–03: Is the European Central Bank Working?* London: HMSO.

House of Lords Paper 74 (2005). *7th Report of the House of Lords European Union Committee, Session 2004–05: Evidence From the Financial Secretary on the Proposed Reforms of the Stability and Growth Pact*. London: HMSO.

Howarth, D. (2001). *The French Road to European Monetary Union*. Basingstoke: Palgrave.

—— (2002). 'The European Policy of the Jospin Government: A New Twist to Old French Games', *Modern and Contemporary France*, 10(3): 353–70.

—— (2004). 'Rhetorical Divergence; Real Convergence? The Economic Policy Debate in the 2002 French Presidential and Legislative Elections', in J. Gaffney (ed.), *The French Elections of 2002*. Aldershot: Ashgate, pp. 200–21.

—— (2005). 'Making and Breaking the Rules: French Policy on EU 'Gouvernement économique' and the Stability and Growth Pact', *European Integration online Papers (EIoP)*, 9(15): 1–16.

—— (2007). 'Making and Breaking the Rule: France and EU "gouvernement économique"', *Journal of European Public Policy*, 14(7): 1061–78.

—— (2008 forthcoming). 'The Banque de France: A Quite Force for Stability', in K. Dyson and M. Marcussen (eds.), *Central Banks in the Age of the Euro*. Oxford: Oxford University Press.

Hughes, J., Sasse, G. et al. (2004). 'Conditionality and Compliance in the EU's Eastward Enlargement: Regional Policy and the Reform of Sub-National Government', *Journal of Common Market Studies*, 42(3): 523–51.

IBEC (1999). *Ireland's Transition to the Euro*. Dublin: IBEC.

—— (2000). *EMU—The Implications for Ireland*. Dublin: IBEC.

Ingham, G. (1984). *Capitalism Divided: The City and Industry in British Social Development*. Basingstoke: Macmillan.

Insee (*Institut National de la Statistique et des Études Économiques*) (2007). 'Temps partiel et durée du travail hebdomadaire dans l'Union européenne'. http://www.insee.fr/fr/ffc/chifcle_fiche.asp?ref_id=CMPTEF03204&tab_id=252update ed August 2007. Accessed 22 April 2008.

International Monetary Fund (2000). *IMF Survey*, 10 January. Washington, DC.: IMF.

—— (2004). *Fostering Structural Reforms in Industrialised Countries*. Chapter III in *World Economic Outlook*. Washington, DC.: IMF.

International Monetary Fund (2006*a*). *Republic of Estonia: Selected Issues*. Washington DC: World Bank, November.

International Monetary Fund (2006b). 'Interview With Susan Schadler and James Morsink: UK Policy Frameworks Prove Their Mettle', *IMF Survey*, 35(6): 86–7.

—— (2007a). *Concluding Statement of the IMF Mission on Euro-Area Policies*. Washington, DC.: IMF (May 30).

—— (2007b). 'Greece: Selected Issues', *Country Report No 07/27*. 25 January.

Jablonski, P., Lesniak, G. et al. (2003). 'Wojna programow czy osobowosci', *Rzeczpospolita*, 11 April.

Jankowiak, J. (2006). 'Mity i troche faktow o finansach publicznych', *Rzeczpospolita*, 3 November.

Janssen, R. and Watt, A. (2006). *Delivering the Lisbon Goals: The Role of Macroeconomic Policy*. Brussels: ETUI-REHS.

Jessop, B. (1998). 'The Rise of Governance and the Risk of Failure: The Case of Economic Development', *International Social Science Journal*, 155: 29–45.

Johansson, K. (1999). 'Tracing the Employment Title in the Amsterdam Treaty: Uncovering Transnational Coalitions', *Journal of European Public Policy*, 6: 85–101.

Johnson, J. (2006). 'Two-Track Diffusion and Central Bank Embeddedness: The Politics of Euro Adoption in Hungary and the Czech Republic', *Review of International Political Economy*, 13(3): 361–86.

Jones, E. (1998). 'The Netherlands: Top of the Class', in E. Jones, J. Frieden, and F. Torres (eds.), *Joining Europe's Monetary Club. The Challenges for Smaller Member States*. New York: St. Martin's Press, pp. 149–70.

—— (2002). *The Politics of Economic and Monetary Union: Integration and Idiosyncrasy*. Lanham: Rowman & Littlefield.

Jonung, L. (2004). 'The Political Economy of Monetary Unification: The Swedish Euro Referendum of 2003', *Cato Journal*, 24(1–2): 123–49.

—— and Vlachos, J. (2007). 'The Euro—What's in it for Me?'. SIEPS Report 2007: 2.

Jospin, L. (1999). *Modern Socialism*. London: Fabian Society.

Juel, K., Bjerregaard, P., and Madsen, M. (2000). 'Mortality and Life Expectancy in Denmark and in Other European Countries. What is Happening to Middle-Aged Danes?', *The European Journal of Public Health*, 10(2): 93–100.

Juppé, A. (2000). 'Pioniergruppe als Übergang. Ein Gespräch mit Alain Juppé über das Europa von morgen', *Frankfurter Allgemeine Zeitung*, 8 July: 7.

Kapteyn, P. (1993). *Markt Zonder Staat*. Bussum: Coutinho.

Karpinski, S. (2004). 'Im dşu£ej bez euro, tym gorzej', *Rzeczpospolita*, 5 November.

—— (2005). 'Euro dzieli polskich politykow', *Rzeczpospolita*, 29 June.

—— and Smilowicz, P. (2006). 'Na klopoty kolejna komisja', *Rzeczpospolita*, 13 March.

Kathimerini (2007a). 26 January.

—— (2007b) 27–28 January.

Katzenstein, P. (1985). *Small States in World Markets: Industrial Policy in Europe*. Ithaca: Cornell University Press.

Kavanagh, D. and Butler, D. (2005). *The British General Election of 2005*. Basingstoke: Palgrave.

Keegan, W. (2003). *The Prudence of Mr Gordon Brown*. Chichester: John Wiley & Sons.

—— (2005). 'On the Euro, Brown is Right—For Once', *The Observer*, 27 November.

Kellermann, C. and Rattinger, H. (2006). 'Economic Conditions, Unemployment and Perceived Government Accountability', *German Politics*, 15(4): 460–80.

Kelly, J. (2006). 'The Net Worth of Irish Households', *Quarterly Bulletin*, 3: 79–92.

King, M. (2004). *The Institutions of Monetary Policy—The Ely Lecture*, Lecture to the American Economic Association Annual Meeting, San Diego, 4 January.

Kirby, P. (2001). *The Celtic Tiger in Distress: Growth with Inequality in Ireland*. Basingstoke: Palgrave.

——(2004). 'Globalization, the Celtic Tiger and Social Outcomes: Is Ireland a Model or a Mirage?', *Globalization*, 1(2): 205–22.

Kleinnijenhuis, J., Takens, J., and Van Atteveldt, W. (2005). 'Toen Europa de dagbladen ging vullen', in K. Aarts and H. van der Kolk (eds.), *Nederlanders en Europa: Het Referendum over de Europese Grondwet*. Amsterdam: Bert Bakker, pp. 123–44.

Kluza, S. (2006). 'Potrzebna nam druga kotwica budzetowa', *Gazeta Wyborcza*, 22 September.

Koenig, T. (2006). 'The Scope for Policy Change after the 2005 Election: Veto Players and Intra-Party Decision Making', *German Politics*, 15(4): 520–32.

Kok, W. (2004). *Facing the Challenge: The Lisbon Strategy for Growth and Employment*. Luxembourg: Office for Official Publications of the European Communities.

Kokoszczynski, R. (2002). 'Poland before the Euro', *Journal of Public Policy*, 22(2): 199–215.

Korhonen, I. (2004). 'Some Implications of EU Membership on Baltic Monetary and Exchange Rate Policies', in V. Pettai and J. Zielonka (eds.), *The Road to the European Union (Vol. II): Estonia, Latvia and Lithuania*. Manchester: Manchester University Press.

Kornai, J. (1996). 'Paying the Bill for Goulash-Communism. Hungarian Development and Macro-Stabilization in a Political Economy Perspective', Discussion Paper 23. Budapest: Collegium Budapest/Institute for Advanced Study.

Krägenau, H. and Wetter, W. (1994). 'Europäische Wirtschafts- und Währungsunion (EWWU)—Vom Werner-Plan bis Maastricht', in R. Caesar and H. E. Scharrer (eds.), *Maastricht: Königsweg oder Irrweg zur Wirtschafts- und Währungsunion?* Bonn: Europa Union Verlag, pp. 58–88.

Kriis, T. (2007). *Festi Tööandjate Keskliidu pöördumine 2008.a. riigieelarve eelnõu osas*. Tallinn: Estonian Employers' Association.

Krzak, M. (2005). 'Euro odlozone na polke', *Rzeczpospolita*, 11 October.

Kumlin, S. (2004). 'Välfärdsmissnöje och euroskepticism', in H. Oscarsson and S. Holmberg (eds.), *Kampen om euron*. Göteborg: Department of Political Science, pp. 385–412.

Kunstein, T. (2007). *Die Auseinandersetzung zur Unabhängigkeit der Europäischen Zentralbank. Eine Diskursanalyse der Berichterstattung in Deutschland, Großbritannien und Frankreich von 1998 bis 2006*, masters thesis, unpublished manuscript, Cologne.

Kureková, L. (2006). 'Electoral Revolutions and their Socio-Economic Impact. Bulgaria and Slovakia in Comparative Perspective', MA Thesis. Budapest: Central European University, Department of International Relations and European Studies.

Labohm H. and Wijnker (eds.) (2000). *The Netherland's Polder Model: Does It Offer any Clues for the Solution of Europe's Socio-Economic Flaws?* Amesterdam: De Nederlandsche Bank.

Lainela, S. (2000). 'Baltic Accession to the European Union', *Lituanus: Lithuanian Quarterly Journal of Arts and Sciences*, 46(3): 74–92.

——and Sutela, P. (1994). *The Baltic Economies in Transition*. Helsinki: Bank of Finland.

References

Lamfalussy Committee of Wise Men on the Regulation of European Securities Markets (2001). Final Report, 15 February. Brussels: Commission of the European Communities, http://ec.europa.eu/internal_market/securities/docs/lamfalussy/wisemen/final-report- wise-men_en.pdf.

Landler, M. (2004). 'In Eastern Europe, Skepticism Over the Euro', *The New York Times*, 6 December: C3.

Lane, P. (2006). *The Real Effects of EMU. IIIS Discussion Paper no. 15*. Dublin: Trinity College Dublin.

Lastra, R. (2003). 'The Governance Structure for Financial Regulation and Supervision in Europe', *Columbia Journal of European Law*, 10(1): 49–68.

Lavdas, K. (1997). *The Europeanization of Greece: Interest Politics and the Crises of Integration*. London: Macmillan.

Leddin, A. and O'Leary, J. (1995). 'Fiscal, Monetary and Exchange Rate Policy', in J. O'Hagen (ed.), *The Economy of Ireland: Policy and Performance of a Small European Country*. Basingstoke: Palgrave-Macmillan.

——and Walsh, B. (1998). *The Macro-Economy of Ireland*. Dublin: Gill & Macmillan.

Lees, C. (2002). ' "Dark Matter": Institutional Constraints and the Failure of Party-Based Euroscepticism in Germany', *Political Studies*, 50(2): 244–67.

——(2005). *Party Politics in Germany: A Comparative Politics Approach*. Basingstoke: Palgrave Macmillan.

——(2006). 'The German Party System(s) in 2005: A Return to *Volkspartei* Dominance', *German Politics*, 15(4): 361–75.

Le Heron, E. (2007). 'The New Governance in Monetary Policy: A Critical Appraisal of the FED and the ECB', in P. Arestis, E. Hein and E. Le Heron (eds.), *Aspects of Modern Monetary and Macroeconomic Policies*. Basingstoke: Palgrave, pp. 146–71.

Lendvai, N. (2004). 'The Weakest Link? EU Accession and Enlargement: Dialoguing EU and Post-Communist Social Policy', *Journal of European Social Policy*, 14(3): 319–33.

Lesko, M. (1998). *Meciar és a meciarizmus* (Meciar and Meciarism). Bratislava and Budapest: Balassi Kiadó and Kalligram Könyvkiadó.

Lijphart, A. (1968). *The Politics of Accommodation: Pluralism and Democracy in the Netherlands*. Berkeley: University of California Press.

——(1980). *Democracy in Plural Societies: A Comparative Exploration*. New Haven: Yale University Press.

——(1999). *Patterns of Democracy: Government Forms and Performance in Thirty-Six Countries*. New Haven: Yale University Press.

——(2002). 'Negotiation Democracy Versus Consensus Democracy: Parallel Conclusions and Recommendations', *European Journal of Political Research*, 41: 107–13.

Lindahl, R. and Naurin, D. (2005). 'Sweden: The Twin Faces of a Euro-Outsider', *Journal of European Integration*, 27(1): 65–87.

Lindvall, J. (2004). *The Politics of Purpose*. PhD Thesis, Göteborg University.

——(2006). 'The Politics of Purpose', *Comparative Politics*, 38(3): 253–72.

——and Rothstein, B. (2006). 'Sweden: The Fall of the Strong State', *Scandinavian Political Studies*, 29(1): 47–63.

Linsenmann, I. and Meyer, C. O. (2003). 'Eurogruppe und Wirtschafts- und Finanzausschuss', in W. Weidenfeld and W. Wessels (eds.), *Jahrbuch der Europäischen Integration 2002/2003*. Berlin/Bonn: Europa Union Verlag, pp. 123–8.

Lipstok, A. (2007). 'Rahulikul, aga kindlal sammul euroni', *Postimees*, 24.01.

Litfin, K. (1997). 'Sovereignty in World Ecopolitics', *Mershon International Studies Review*, 41(2): 167–204.

LO (1990). *Ekonomiska utsikter hösten 1990*. Stockholm: LO.

Loriaux, M. (1991). *France After Hegemony*. Ithica: Cornell University Press.

Lundvall, B-Å. and Tomlinson, M. (2002). 'International Benchmarking as a Policy Learning Tool', in M. J. Rodrigues (ed.), *The New Knowledge Economy in Europe*. Cheltenham: Edward Elgar, pp. 203–31.

Mabbett, D. and Schelkle, W. (2005). 'Bringing Macroeconomics Back in to the Political Economy of Reform: the Lisbon Agenda and the 'Fiscal Philosophy' of the EU'. http://www.eu-newgov.org/protected_pages/DOCS/P19a_D04_Mabbett_Schelkle_2005.pdf.

Macartney, H. (2007). 'Transnationally Oriented Fractions of Capital, Variegated Neo-Liberalism and EU Financial Market Integration'. Unpublished PhD thesis. University of Manchester: Centre for International Politics.

MacCoille, C. and McCoy, D. (2001). 'Smoothing Adjustment through Modified Bargaining', *Irish Banking Review*, Winter: 15–27.

——— (2002). 'Economic Adjustment Within EMU: Ireland's Experience', *Economic and Social Review*, 33(2): 179–93.

McCreevy, C. (2006). 'Recent Regulatory and Structural Developments in the EU Financial Sector', EU-China Dialogue on Macroeconomic and Financial Regulatory Issues Beijing.' At http://europa.eu.int/rapid/pressReleasesAction.do?reference=SPEECH/06/303&format=HTML&aged=0&language=EN&guiLanguage=en (accessed 17 May 2006.).

McDowell, D. (1998). 'Speech to the Irish Parliament on EMU', 1 April.

McKay, D. (2006). 'The Reluctant European: Europe as an Issue in British Politics', in J. Bartle and A. King (eds.), *Britain at the Polls 2005*. Washington: CQ Press.

McKinnon, R. (1963). 'Optimum Currency Areas', *American Economic Review*, 53: 717–25.

McNamara, K. (1998). *The Currency of Ideas: Monetary Politics in the European Union*. Ithaca: Cornell University Press.

——— (2002). 'Rational Fictions: Central Bank Independence and the Social Logic of Delegation', *West European Politics*, 25: 47–76.

——— (2006). 'Managing the Euro. The European Central Bank', in J. Peterson and M. Shackleton (eds.), *The Institutions of the European Union*. Oxford: Oxford University Press, pp. 169–89.

——— and Meunier, S. (2002). 'Between National Sovereignty and International Power: What External Voice for the Euro?', *International Affairs*, 78(4): 849–68.

Maier, J., Brettschneider, F., and Maier, M. (2003). 'Medienberichterstattung, Mediennutzung und die Bevölkerungseinstellungen zum Euro in Ost- und Westdeutschland', in F. Brettschneider, J. van Deth, and E. Roller (eds.), *Europäiche Integration in der öffentliche Meinung*. Opladen: Leske & Budrich, pp. 213–33.

Majone, G. (1991). 'Cross-National Sources of Regulatory Policymaking in Europe and the United States', *Journal of Public Policy*, 11(1): 79–109.

——— (1994). 'The Rise of the Regulatory State in Europe', *West European Politics*, 17(3): 77–101.

——— (1996). *Regulating Europe*. London: Routledge.

References

Majone, G. (1998). 'Europe's 'Democracy Deficit': The Question of Standards', *European Law Journal*, 4(1): 5–26.

—— (1999). 'The Regulatory State and its Legitimacy Problems', *West European Politics*, 22(1): 1–24.

Malová, D. (2007). 'Instability and Extremism in the New Member States: The Slovakian Case', paper presented at conference 'Political Turbulences in Central Europe: Symptoms of a Post-Accession Crisis?', Friedrich Ebert Stiftung, Budapest, 25–27 February.

Mamou, Y. (1987). *Une machine de pouvoir: La direction du Trésor*. Paris: Editions La Découverte.

Marcussen, M. (2000). *Ideas and Elites: The Social Construction of Economic and Monetary Union*. Aalborg: Aalborg University Press.

—— (2002). 'EMU: A Danish Delight and Dilemma', in K. Dyson (ed.), *European States and the Euro*. Oxford: Oxford University Press, pp. 120–44.

—— and Kaspersen, L. (2007). 'Globalization and Institutional Competitiveness', *Regulation and Governance*, 1(3): 183–96.

Marginson, P. and Sisson, K. (2004). *European Integration and Industrial Relations*. Basingstoke: Palgrave Macmillan.

Marian, M. (1999). 'Lionel Jospin, le socialisme et la réforme', *Esprit*, March–April: 112–21.

Marshall, T. H. (1992 [1950]). 'Citizenship and Social Class', in T. H. Marshall and T. Bottomore (eds.), *Citizenship and Social Class*. London: Pluto Press.

Martin, A. (1999). 'Wage Bargaining Under EMU: Europeanization, Re-Nationalization, or Americanization?', *DWP 99.01.03*. Brussels: OSE/ETUI.

Mathernová, K. and Rencko, J. (2006). ' "Reformology": The Case of Slovakia', *Orbis*, 50(4): 629–40.

Mayer, T. and Folkerts-Landau, D. (2005). 'Structural Reform: Liberalise Markets!', *Structural Reform Special: Global Markets Research—European Economics 4*, February. London: Deutsche Bank.

Mayntz, R. (1993). 'Governing Failure and the Problem of Governability: Some Comments on a Theoretical Paradigm', in J. Kooiman (ed.), *Modern Governance. New Government–Society Interactions*. London: Sage, pp. 9–20.

Meardi, G. (2007). 'More Voice After More Exit? Unstable Industrial Relations in Central Eastern Europe', *Industrial Relations Review*, 6 November.

Metten, A. and van Riel, B. (1996). 'De Strÿd om de EMU'. Amsterdam: Wiardi Beckman Stichting.

MGPiPS (2003). *Raport: Racjonalizacja wydatkow spolecznych*. Warsaw: Ministerstwo Gospodarki, Pracy i Polityki Spolecznej.

Michas, T. (2002). *Unholy Alliance: Greece and Milosevic's Serbia*. College Station: Texas A&M University Press.

Mikkel, E. and Pridham, G. (2004). 'Clinching the 'Return to Europe': The Referendums on EU Accession in Estonia and Latvia', *West European Politics*, 27(4): 716–48.

Milesi, G. (1998). *Le Roman de l'Euro*. Paris: Hachette.

Milward, A. (1992). *The European Rescue of the Nation State*. London: Routledge.

Minc, A. (1994). *La France de l'an 2000 (rapport au premier ministre de la commission présidée par Alain Minc)*. Paris: Odile Jacob.

Ministerstwo Finansow (2002). *Komunikat dotyczacy prac Miedzyresortowej Grupy Roboczej ds Interacji Polski z Unia Gospodarcza i Walutowa*. Warsaw: MF.

Ministry of Finance, Estonia (2007). 'Valitsus arutas maksuküsimusi', Press release, 10.05.2007, accessible at http://www.fin.ee/index.php?id=77529.

Ministry of Interior (2007). *National Elections 2007*. [cited 14 October 2007]. Available from http://www.ekloges.ypes.gr/pages/index.html.

Minkkinen, P. and Patomäki, H. (1997). 'Introduction: The Politics of Economic and Monetary Union', in P. Minkkinen and H. Patomäki (eds.), *The Politics of Economic and Monetary Union*. Boston, Dordrecht and London: Kluwer, pp. 7–18.

Molander, P. (2001). 'Budgeting Procedures and Democratic Ideals', *Journal of Public Policy*, 21(1): 23–52.

Mongelli, F., Dorrucci, E., and Agur, I. (2005). *What Does European Institutional Integration Tell Us about Trade Integration?* Frankfurt am Main: ECB, 9 March, mimeo.

Moran, M. (1991). *The Politics of the Financial Services Revolution*. London: Macmillan.

—— (2002). 'Politics, Banks and Financial Market Governance in the Euro-Zone', in K. Dyson (ed.), *European States and the Euro: Europeanization, Variation and Convergence*. Oxford: Oxford University Press, pp. 257–77.

Morris, R., Ongena, H., and Schuknecht, L. (2006). 'The Reform and Implementation of the Stability and Growth Pact', *European Central Bank Occasional Paper*, No. 47, June.

Mullineux, A. and Ryan, C. (2002). 'The EMU after Lisbon', in A. Arnull and D. Wincott (eds.), *Accountability and Legitimacy in the European Union*. Oxford: Oxford University Press.

Mundell, R. (1961). 'A Theory of Optimum Currency Areas', *The American Economic Review*, 51(4): 657–65.

—— (2000). 'The Euro and the Stability of the International Monetary System', in R. Mundell and A. Cleese (eds.), *The Euro as a Stabilizer in the International Economic System*. Boston: Kluwer Academic, pp. 57–84.

Nagy, P. (2006). 'Financial Market Governance: Evolution and Convergence', in K. Dyson (ed.), *Enlarging the Euro Area: External Empowerment and Domestic Transformation in East Central Europe*. Oxford: Oxford University Press, pp. 237–60.

Natali, D. (2008). 'Rekabulierung von Sozialprogrammen und Flexibilisierung der Arbeitsmarktpolitik: Das italienische Wohlfahrtssystem', in K. Schubert, U. Bazant, and S. Hegelich (eds.), *Europäische Wohlfahrtssysteme. Ein Handbuch*. Wiesbaden: VS Verlag, pp. 333–54.

—— and Pochet, P. (2007). *The Evolution of Social Pacts in the EMU Era: A Case of 'Uneven Institutionalisation'*, Paper presented at the IIRA conference, Manchester, 3–6 September.

—— and Rhodes, M. (2005). 'The Berlusconi Pension Reform and the Double Cleavage of Distributive Politics in Italy', in C. Guarnieri and J. Newell (eds.), *Italian Politics. Quo Vadis?* Oxford: Berghahn, pp. 172–89.

National Bank of Poland (2004). *Raport na temat Korzysci i Kosztow Przystapienia Polski do Strefy Euro*. Warsaw: NBP.

Niklewicz, K. (2005). 'Polska europowolna', *Gazeta Wyborcza*, 5–6 November.

—— and Maciejewicz, P. (2005). 'Poltora miliona powodow, by mowic o euro', *Gazeta Wyborcza*, 2 September: 25.

References

Nikolacopoulos, I. (2005). 'Elections and Voters, 1974–2004: Old Cleavages and New Issues', in K. Featherstone (ed.), *Politics and Policy in Greece: the Challenge of 'Modernization'*. London: Routledge, pp. 38–58.

Nissinen, M. (1999). *Latvia's Transition to a Market Economy*. Basingstoke: Macmillan.

Nol (Népszabadság Online) (2006). Accessed on 3 March 2006 at http://nol.hu.

Norman, P. (2003). *The Accidental Constitution. The Story of the European Convention*. Brussels: EuroComment.

—— (2007). *Plumbers and Visionaries*. London: John Wiley.

Notermans, T. (2000). *Money, Markets, and the State: Social Democratic Economic Policies Since 1918*. Cambridge: Cambridge University Press.

Noyer, C. (2005). 'Interview with Christian Noyer', *Financial Times*, 11 July.

NRC Handelsblad (2005). 'Burger gaat alsnog stemmen over de Euro; Bij referendum speelt "Euro-kwestie" hoofdrol', 19 May.

Obinger, H. (2005). 'Strong Parties in a Weak Federal System', in H. Obinger, S. Leibfried, and F. Castles (eds.), *Federalism and the Welfare State: New World and European Experiences*. Cambridge: Cambridge University Press.

—— Leibfried, S., and Castles, F. (eds.) (2005). *Federalism and the Welfare State: New World and European Experiences*. Cambridge: Cambridge University Press.

O'Donnell, R. (2001). *Future of Social Partnership in Ireland: A Discussion Paper*. Dublin: National Competitiveness Council.

OECD (1997). *Employment Outlook*, July.

—— (2005a). 'Economic Survey of Ireland, 2005', *Policy Brief*, March. Paris: OECD.

—— (2005b). 'Economic Survey of the Netherlands, 2005', *Policy Brief*, December. Paris: OECD.

—— (2006a). 'Economic Survey of Denmark, 2006', *Policy Brief*, May. Paris: OECD.

—— (2006b). *OECD Factbook 2006: Economic, Environmental and Social Statistics*. Paris: OECD.

—— (2007a). *OECD Economic Outlook 81: Statistical Annex Tables* [cited 13 November 2007]. Available from http://www.oecd.org/document/61/0,2340,en_2825_32066506_2483901_ 1_1_1_1,00.html.

—— (2007b). *OECD Statistics database* [cited 13 November 2007]. Available from http://stats.oecd.org/wbos/default.aspx?DatasetCode=ULC_QUA.

—— (several years). *Country Survey, France*. Paris: OECD.

Office of Management and Budget (2006). 'The Nation's Fiscal Outlook.' http://www.whitehouse.gov/omb/budget/fy2006/outlook.html Accessed on 3 October 2007.

Ojala, A. (2007). 'Kaubanduskoda ja tööandjad soovitavad valitsuskulusid vähendada', *Äripäev*, 21 May.

Olczyk, E. (2003). 'Plan Hausnera dobry dla Polski, zly dla SLD', *Rzeczpospolita*, 17 October.

Olczyk, E. and Ordynski, J. (2003). 'Wojna palacow zawieszona', *Rzeczpospolita*, 3 November.

Olsen, J. P. (2002). 'The Many Faces of Europeanization', *Journal of Common Market Studies*, 40(5): 921–52.

Olson, M. (1965). *The Logic of Collective Action*. Cambridge: Harvard University Press.

Olson, M. (1990). *How Bright are the Northern Lights?* Lund: Lund University Press.

Organisation For Economic Co-operation and Development (2006). *Economic Survey of the United Kingdom*. Paris: OECD.

—— (2007). *Economic Survey of the United Kingdom*. Paris: OECD.

Orlowski, W. (2004). *Optymalna sciezka do euro*. Warsaw: Scholar.

Oscarsson, H. (1998). *Den svenska partirymden*. PhD thesis, Göteborg University.

—— (2004). 'Ideologi fällde euron?', in H. Oscarsson and S. Holmberg (eds.), *Kampen om euron*. Göteborg: Department of Political Science, pp. 299–319.

—— (2006). 'The Ideological Response: Saying No to the Euro.' Unpublished manuscript, Department of Political Science, Göteborg University.

—— and Holmberg, S. (2004). 'Kampen om euron', in H. Oscarsson and S. Holmberg (eds.), *Kampen om euron*. Göteborg: Department of Political Science, pp. 457–69.

Oskarson, M. (1996). 'Väljarnas vågskålar', in M. Gilljam and S. Holmberg (eds.), *Ett knappt ja till EU*. Stockholm: Norstedts Juridik, pp. 124–48.

Padgett, S. and Poguntke, T. (eds.) (2001). *Continuity and Change in German Politics: Beyond the Politics of Centrality?* London: Frank Cass.

Pagoulatos, G. (2003). *Greece's New Political Economy: State, Finance and Growth from Post-War to EMU*. Oxford St. Antony's Series. London and New York: Palgrave Macmillan.

—— (2004), 'Believing in National Exceptionalism: Ideas and Economic Divergence in Southern Europe', *West European Politics*, 27(1): 45–70.

—— (2005). 'The Politics of Privatization: Rewarding the Public–Private Boundary', in K. Featherstone (ed.), *Politics and Policy in Greece: The Challenge of 'Modernization'*. London: Routledge, pp. 136–58.

Palier, B. (2005). 'Ambiguous Agreement, Cumulative Change: French Social Policy in the 1990s', in W. Streeck and K. Thelen (eds.), *Beyond Continuity: Institutional Change in Advanced Political Economics*. Oxford: Oxford University Press.

—— (2007). 'The Politics of Reforms in Bismarckian Welfare Systems'. Paper prepared for the EUSA Tenth Biennial International Conference, Montreal, Canada 17–19 May.

Panic, M. (January 2007). 'Does Europe Need Neo-Liberal Reforms?', *Cambridge Journal of Economics*.

Papademos, L. (2004). 'Determinants of Growth and the Role of Structural Reforms and Macroeconomic Policies in Europe'. 2004 Ludwig Erhard Lecture Delivered at the Lisbon Council.

—— (2005*a*). 'Banking Supervision and Financial Stability in Europe.' Speech by Lucas Papademos, Vice-President of the ECB, delivered at the Conference 'Supervision of International Banks: Is a Bank Crisis still Possible in Europe?', Organized by the European Banking Federation, Brussels, 28 October, at http://www.ecb.int/press/key/date/2006/html/index.en.html (accessed 28 August 2006.).

—— (2005*b*). 'Growth and Competitiveness in Euro Area Economies'. Speech at the General Assembly of the Hellenic Chamber of Industry and Commerce, Athens, 22 September.

Pappi, F. and Thurner, P. (2000). 'Die Deutschen Wähler und der Euro: Auswirkungen auf die Bundestagswahl 1998', *Politische Vierteljahresschrift*, 3: 435–65.

Paradowska, J. (2004). 'Sojusz wyprowadzic!', *Polityka*, 13.

Parker, G. (2003). 'Brown in EU Clash Over his Spending', *Financial Times*, 19 February.

—— (2004). 'Brussels Let's UK Off the Hook Over Budget Deficit', *Financial Times*, 26 January.

References

Patomäki, H. (1997). 'Legitimation Problems of the European Union', in P. Minkkinen and H. Patomäki (eds.), *The Politics of Economic and Monetary Union*. Boston/ Dordrecht/London: Kluwer, pp. 162–204.

Pébereau, M. (2005). *Le rapport Pébereau sur la dette publique*. Paris: Documentation française.

Peck, J. and Tickell, A. (2002). 'Neoliberalizing Space', *Antipode*, 34(3): 380–404.

Peers, S. (2007). *Statewatch Analysis. EU Reform Treaty Analysis no. 3.4: Revised Text of Part Three, Titles VII to XVII of the Treaty Establishing the European Community (TEC): Other Internal EC Policies*, Essex. http://www.statewatch.org/news/2007/oct/eu-reform%20treaty–part-three-tec–internal-market-3–3–2.pdf.pdf.

Peston, R. (2005). *Brown's Britain*. London: Short Books.

Phelps, E. (2005). 'Understanding the Great Changes in the World: Gaining Ground and Losing Ground Since World War II', World Congress of the International Economics Association, September.

Pierson, C. (1991). *Beyond the Welfare State? The New Political Economy of Welfare*. Cambridge: Polity Press.

Pierson, P. (1998). 'Irresistible Forces, Immovable Objects: Post-Industrial Welfare States Confront Permanent Austerity', *Journal of European Public Policy*, 5(4): 539–60.

—— (2004). *Politics in Time: History, Institutions and Social Analysis*. Princeton: Princeton University Press.

Pisani-Ferry, J. and Sapir, A. (2006). 'Last Exit to Lisbon'. Brussels: Bruegel, press release 14 March.

Pochet, P. (1998). 'The Social Consequences of EMU: An Overview of National Debates', in P. Pochet and B. Vanhercke (eds.), *Social Challenges of Economic and Monetary Union*. Brussels: European Interuniversity Press, pp. 67–102.

—— (2002). 'Introduction', in P. Pochet (ed.), *Politique salariale dans la zone euro*. Brussels: PIE-Peter Lang, pp. 17–39.

Polanski, Z. (2004). 'Poland and the European Union: The Monetary Policy Dimension. Monetary Policy Before Poland's Accession to the European Union', *Bank I Kredyt*, May.

Polanyi, K. (1944). *The Great Transformation*. Boston: Beacon Press.

Pollard, S. (1992). *The Development of the British Economy, 1914–1990*. 4th edn. London: Edward Arnold.

Postimees (2007). 'IMF: Eesti vajab nüüd tugevamat majanduspoliitikat', *Postimees*, 14.05.

Potůček, M. (2004). 'Accession and Social Policy: The Case of the Czech Republic', *Journal of European Social Policy*, 14(3): 253–66.

Prast, H. and Stokman, A. (1999), 'The Euro in the Netherlands: Results of the Eight DNB Euro Surveys'. Amsterdam: De Nederlandsche Bank.

Programme for Prosperity and Fairness (2000). EIRO 'Rescuing Ireland's Social Pact', 28 December.

Pruski, J. (2006). 'Droga Polski do Euro', in *Perspektywy Wejscia Polski do Euro*, Zeszyty BRE Bank-Case Nr. 85.

Puetter, U. (2007). 'Providing Venues for Contestation: The Role of Expert Committees and Informal Dialogue Among Ministers in European Economic Policy Coordination', *Comparative European Politics*, 5(1): 18–35.

Quaglia, L. (2004*a*). 'The Italian Presidency of the European Union in 2003', *Journal of Common Market Studies Annual Review*, 42(4): 53–6.

—— (2004*b*). 'Italy's Policy Towards European Monetary Integration: Bringing Ideas Back In?', *Journal of European Public Policy*, 11(6): 1096–111.

—— (2005). 'Europe and the Right in Italy: An Ambivalent Relationship', *South European Society and Politics*, 10(2): 277–91.

—— (2007*a*). 'The Politics of Financial Services Regulation and Supervision Reform in the European Union', *European Journal of Political Research*, 46(1): 269–90.

—— (2007*b*). 'Committee Governance in the Financial Sector in the European Union'. Brighton: Sussex European Institute Working Paper.

—— and Radaelli, C. (2007). 'Italian Politics and the European Union', *West European Politics*, 30(4): 924–43.

Radaelli, C. (2000). 'Whither Europeanization? Concept Stretching and Substantive Change', Paper presented to the annual Conference of the Political Studies Association, London, 10–13 April.

—— (2001). 'Conceptualising Europeanisation: Theory, Methods and the Challenge of Empirical Research', Paper Presented to the Europeanisation Residential Easter School, University of York, 24–25 March.

—— (2002). 'The Italian State and the Euro: Institutions, Discourse and Policy-Regime', in K. Dyson (ed.), *European States and the Euro—Europeanization, Variation, and Convergence*. Oxford: Oxford University Press, pp. 212–37.

—— (2003*a*). 'The Europeanization of Public Policy', in K. Featherstone and C. Radaelli (eds.), *The Politics of Europeanization*. Oxford: Oxford University Press, pp. 27–56.

—— (2003*b*). 'The Open Method of Coordination. A New Governance Architecture for the European Union'? *Preliminary Report no. 1*. Stockholm: Swedish Institute for European Policy Studies.

Rada Ministrow (2004). *Convergence Programme*. Warsaw: Rada Ministrow.

Record, N. (2005). 'Europe is Dragging Britain into the Mire', *Financial Times*, 6 January.

Reland, J. (1998). 'France', in A. Menon and J. Forder (eds.), *The European Union and National Macro-Economic Policy*. London: Routledge, pp. 85–104.

Reuten, G., Vendrik, K., and Went, R. (eds.) (1998). *De Prijs van de Euro. De Gevaren van de Europese Monetaire Unie*. Amsterdam: Van Gennep.

Rheinhardt, N. (1997). 'A Turning Point in the German EMU Debate: The Baden-Württemberg Regional Election of March 1996', *German Politics*, 6(1): 77–99.

Rhodes, M. (1998). 'Globalisation, Labour Markets and Welfare States: A Future of "Competitive Corporatism"?', in M. Rhodes and Y. Mény (eds.), *The Future of European Welfare: A New Social Contract?*. London: Macmillan, pp. 178–203.

—— (2002). 'Why EMU Is, or May Be, Good for European Welfare States', in K. Dyson (ed.), *European States and the Euro*. Oxford: Oxford University Press, pp. 305–33.

Riikoja, H. and Karnau, A. (2007). 'Valitsus tahab aktsiiside seljas mõne aastaga euroni ratsutada', *Postimees*, 15 May.

Rochon, L-P. and Rossi, S. (2006). 'The Monetary Policy Strategy of the European Central Bank. Does Inflation Targeting Lead to a Successful Stabilisation Policy?', in E. Hein, A. Heise, and A. Truger (eds.), *European Economic Policies: Alternatives to Orthodox Analysis and Policy Concepts*. Marburg: Metropolis, pp. 87–110.

References

Rollo, J. (2002). 'In or Out: The Choice for Britain', *Journal of Public Policy*, 22(2): 217–29.

Room, G. (2000). 'Commodification and Decommodification: A Developmental Critique', *Policy and Politics*, 28(3): 331–51.

—— (2005). 'Policy Benchmarking in the European Union', *Policy Studies*, 26(2): 118–31.

Rosa, J.-J. (1998). *L'erreur européenne*. Paris: Grasset.

Rosamond, B. (2002). 'Imagining the European Economy: 'Competitiveness' and the Social Construction of 'Europe' as an Economic Space', *New Political Economy*, 7(2): 157–77.

Rose, R. (1993). *Lesson-Drawing in Public Policy*. Chatham: Chatham House Publishers, Inc.

Rose, A. (2000). 'One Money, One Market: Estimating the Effect of Common Currencies on Trade', *Economic Policy*, 30: 9–45.

Rothstein, B. (2004). 'Det terminologiska misstaget', in H. Oscarsson and S. Holmberg (eds.), *Kampen om euron*. Göteborg: Department of Political Science, pp. 121–32.

Routledge, P. (1998). *Gordon Brown*. London: Pocket Books.

RPP (1998). *Sredniookresowa strategia polityki pienieznej na lata 1999–2003*. Warsaw: National Bank of Poland.

—— (2003). *Strategia polityki pienieznej po 2003 roku*. Warsaw: National Bank of Poland.

Rürup, B. (2007). 'Merkel macht die gleichen Fehler wie *Schröder'*, *Die Welt*, 8 November.

Ruggie, J. (1982). 'International Regimes, Transactions, and Change: Embedded Liberalism in the Post-War Economic Order', *International Organization*, 36(2): 379–415.

Rybinski, K. (2007). *The Euro-Adoption: Assessing Benefits and Costs*, paper prepared for a panel discussion at the American Chamber of Commerce, Warsaw, 17 January.

Ryner, M. (2002). *Capitalist Restructuring, Globalisation and the Third Way: Lessons from the Swedish Model*. London: Routledge.

Rzeczpospolita (2002). 'Kryteria do spelnienia', *Rzeczpospolita*, 18 November.

Sabatier, P. (1991). 'Toward Better Theories of the Policy Process', *Political Science and Politics*, 24(2): 147–56.

Sabethai, I. D. (2000). 'The Greek Labour Market: Features, Problem and Policies', *Bank of Greece Economic Bulletin*, 16: 7–40.

Sachs, J. (1995). 'Postcommunist Parties and the Politics of Entitlements', *Beyond Transition. The Newsletter About Reforming Economies*. Washington, DC.: The World Bank Group.

Sadeh, T. (2006). *Sustaining European Monetary Union: Confronting the Costs of Diversity*. Boulder: Lynne Rienner.

Salverda, W. (1998). 'Is There More to the Dutch Miracle than a Lot of Part-Time Jobs?', unpub. manuscript. Netherlands: Faculty of Economics, University of Groningen.

Sapir, A. (2003). *An Agenda for a Growing Europe: Making the EU Economic System Deliver*. Brussels http://www.euractiv.com/ndbtext/innovation/sapirreport.pdf.

—— (2005). *Globalization and the Reform of European Social Models*. Brussels: Bruegel.

—— (2006). 'Globalisation and the Reform of European Social Models', *Journal of Common Market Studies*, 44(2): 369–90.

Sawyer, M. and Arestis, P. (2006). 'What Type of European Monetary Union?', in P. Whyman, M. Baimbridge, and B. Burkitt (eds.), *Implications of the Euro: A Critical Perspective from the Left*. London: Routledge.

Sbragia, A. (2001). 'Italy Pays for Europe: Political Leadership, Political Choice and Institutional Adaptation', in J. Caporaso, M. Green Cowles, and T. Risse (eds.), *Transforming Europe: Europeanization and Domestic Change*. Ithaca: Cornell University Press, pp. 79–96.

Schäfer, A. (2005). *Die neue Unverbindlichkeit. Wirtschaftspolitische Koordinierung in Europa*. Frankfurt/New York: Campus.

Scharpf, F. (1994). 'Games Real Actors Could Play. Positive and Negative Coordination in Embedded Negotiations', *Journal of Theoretical Politics*, 6(1): 27–53.

——(1998). *Governing in Europe: Effective and Democratic?* Oxford: Oxford University Press.

——(2001). 'Notes Towards a Theory of Multilevel Governance in Europe', *Scandinavian Political Studies*, 24(1): 1–26.

——(2006). Nicht genutze Chancen der Föderalismusreform. MPIfG Working Paper 06/2, Mai. Köln: Max-Planck-Institut für Gesellschaftsforschung.

Schäuble, W. and Lamers, K. Pressedienst CDU/CSU Fraktion im Deutschen Bundestag (eds.) (1994). *Neuer Schwung für Europa*. Bonn: Deutscher Bundestag, 1 July.

Schelkle, W. (2005). 'The Political Economy of Fiscal Policy Coordination in EMU: From Disciplinarian Device to Insurance Arrangement', *Journal of Common Market Studies*, 43(2): 371–91.

Schill, W. and van Riet, A. (2000). 'Europäische Zentralbank', in W. Weidenfeld and W. Wessels (eds.), *Jahrbuch der Europäischen Integration 1999/2000*. Bonn: Europa Union Verlag, pp. 103–6.

——and Willeke, C. (2001). 'Die Europäische Zentralbank', in W. Weidenfeld and W. Wessels (eds.), *Jahrbuch der Europäischen Integration 2000/2001*. Bonn: Europa Union Verlag, pp. 103–8.

Schimmelfenning, F. and Sedelmeier, U. (eds.) (2005). *Europeanization of Central and Eastern Europe*. Ithaca: Cornell University Press.

Schinasi, G. (2003). 'Responsibility of Central Banks for Stability in Financial Markets'. Working Paper WP/03/121. Washington, DC.: International Monetary Fund.

——(2005). 'Financial Architecture of the Eurozone at Five', in A. Posen (ed.), *The Euro at Five: Ready for a Global Role?* Washington, DC.: Institute for International Economics, pp. 117–22.

Schmidt, M. (2002a). 'Political Performance and Types of Democracy: Findings from Comparative Studies', *European Journal of Political Research*, 41: 147–63.

Schmidt, V. (2002b). *The Futures of European Capitalism*. Oxford: Oxford University Press.

Schor, A.-D. (1999). *Economie politique de l'euro*. Paris: La documentation française.

Schuknecht, L. (2004). 'EU Fiscal Rules: Issues and Lessons from Political Economy', *European Central Bank Working Paper*, No. 421.

Schulten, T. (2004). 'Foundations and Perspectives of Trade Union Wage Policy in Europe', *WSI Discussion Paper*, No.129, August, Dusseldorf.

Schuman, R. (1950). *Declaration of 9 May 1950*. http://europa.eu./abc/symbols/9-may/decl_en.htm.

Schumann, S. (2003). 'Persönlichkeitseigenschaften und die Einstellung zur Einführung des Euro', in F. Brettschneider, J. van Deth and E. Roller (eds.), *Europäische Integration in der öffentlichen Meinung*. Opladen: Leske & Budrich, pp. 235–49.

445

References

Schwarzer, D. (2007). *Fiscal Policy Coordination in the European Monetary Union.* Baden-Baden: Nomos.

Scott, D. (2004). *Off Whitehall: A View From Downing Street by Tony Blair's Adviser.* London: I B Tauris.

Scruggs, L. and Allan, J. (2006). 'Welfare-State Decommodification in 18 OECD Countries: A Replication and Revision', *Journal of European Social Policy*, 16(1): 55–72.

Seager, A. (2007). 'UK Productivity on the Rise', Guardian.co.uk/business/2007/july/02/manufacturing.ukeconomy.

Seeleib-Kaiser, M. and Fleckenstein, T. (2007). 'Discourse, Learning and Welfare State Change: The Case of German Labour Market Reforms', *Social Policy and Administration*, 41(5): 427–48.

Selmayr, M. (2002). 'Die Europäische Zentralbank', in W. Weidenfeld and W. Wessels (eds.), *Jahrbuch der Europäischen Integration 2001/2002.* Bonn: Europa Union Verlag, pp. 111–16.

——(2003). 'Die Europäische Zentralbank', in W. Weidenfeld and W. Wessels (eds.), *Jahrbuch der Europäischen Integration 2002/2003.* Bonn: Europa Union Verlag, pp. 117–22.

——(2006). 'Europäische Zentralbank', in W. Weidenfeld and W. Wessels (eds.), *Jahrbuch der Europäischen Integration 2005.* Baden-Baden: Nomos, pp. 123–8.

——(2007). 'Die Europäische Zentralbank', in W. Weidenfeld and W. Wessels (eds.), *Jahrbuch der Europäischen Integration 2006.* Baden-Baden: Nomos, pp. 121–6.

——(2008). 'Europäische Zentralbank', in W. Weidenfeld and W. Wessels (eds.), *Jahrbuch der Europäischen Integration 2006.* Baden-Baden: Nomos, pp. 99–102.

Simitis, C. (2004). 'Greece's Deficit Revision Damaged Europe', *Financial Times*, 22 December.

——(2005). *Policy for a Creative Greece 1996–2004 [Πολιτική για μια Δημιουργική Ελλάδα].* Athens: Polis.

Slojewska, A. (2002). 'Poczekajcie dluzej na euro', *Rzeczpospolita*, 11 December.

——(2003). 'Minister nie chce zrezygnowac z pieniedzy NBP', *Rzeczpospolita*, 11 April.

——(2005a). 'Nie karac naszego kraju za reforme', *Rzeczpospolita*, 19 January.

——(2005b). 'Euro w Polsce w 2009 roku', *Rzeczpospolita*, 21 March.

Smilowicz, P. (2004). 'Dostali palec, chca dloni', *Rzeczpospolita*, 20 February.

Smith, G. (1976). 'West Germany and the Politics of Centrality', *Government and Opposition*, 11(4): 387–407.

Smith, N. (2005). *Showcasing Globalisation? The Political Economy of the Irish Republic.* Manchester: Manchester University Press.

——and Hay, C. (2007). 'Mapping the Political Discourse of Globalisation and European Integration in the UK and Ireland Empirically', *European Journal of Political Research*, forthcoming.

Sobczynski, D. (2002). *Euro: historia, praktyka, instytucje.* Warsaw: KiK.

Socialdemokraterna (2007). 'Valet *2006*'. Stockholm: Socialdemokraterna.

Solow, R. (2002). *'Is Fiscal Policy Possible? Is it Desirable?'.* Cambridge: MIT Press, September, mimeo.

Solska, J. (2003). 'Obnizam, czyli podnosze: Reforma finansowa wicepremiera Kolodki bolesnie uderzy w podatnikow', *Polityka*, 13.

Soltyk, R. (2005). 'Do euro pozniej o rok', *Gazeta Wyborcza*, 18 February.

Spaventa, L. and Chiorazzo, V. (2000). *Astuzia o Virtu? Come Accadde che l'Italia fu Ammessa all'Unione Monetaria*. Roma: Doninzelli.

Stéclebout-Orseau, E. and Hallerberg, M. (2007). 'Sending Signals Under the Stability and Growth Pact', *European Economy*. April.

Steil, B. (1995). *Illusions of Liberalization: Securities Regulation in Japan and the EC*. London: Royal Institute of International Affairs.

Stråth, B. (1993). *Folkhemmet mot Europa*. Stockholm: Tiden.

Strauch, R. (1998). *Budget Processes and Fiscal Discipline: Evidence from the US States*. Working paper. Bonn: Zentrum für Europäische Integrationsforschung.

Streeck, W. and Thelen, K. (2005a). 'Introduction: Institutional Change in Advanced Political Economies', in W. Streeck and K. Thelen (eds.), *Beyond Continuity: Institutional Change in Advanced Political Economics*. Oxford: Oxford University Press.

——and Thelen, K. (2005b). *Beyond Continuity: Institutional Change in Advanced Political Economies*. Oxford: Oxford University Press.

Sueppel, R. (2003). *Comparing Economic Dynamics in the EU and CEE Accession Countries*, ECB Working Paper 267, September. Frankfurt am Main: ECB.

Sustaining Progress: Social Partnership Agreement 2003–05, Republic of Ireland.

Svensson, L. (2002). 'Sweden and the Euro'. Briefing paper for the Committee on Economic and Monetary Affairs of the European Parliament. http://www.princeton. edu/svensson/.

Swank, D. (2002). *Global Capital, Political Institutions, and Policy Change in Developed Welfare States*. Cambridge: Cambridge University Press.

Sweeney, P. (1999). *The Celtic Tiger: Ireland's Continuing Economic Miracle*. Dublin: Oak Tree Press.

Szász, A. (1988). *Monetaire Diplomatie. Nederlands Internationale Monetaire Politiek, 1958– 1987*. Leiden/Antwerpen: Stenfert Kroese.

TBT Staff (2007). 'Latvian Lawmakers Amend 2007 Budget, Kalvitis Vows Bigger Surplus in Future', *The Baltic Times*, 26 September.

Teather, D. (2007). 'London Doubles its Share of Global Hedge Fund Assets', *The Guardian*, 16 April.

Ten-Year Framework Social Partnership Agreement (2006–2015), Towards (2016). Republic of Ireland.

Thatcher, M. (2005). 'The Third Force? Independent Regulatory Agencies and Elected Politicians in Europe', *Governance*, 18(3): 347–74.

——and Coen, D. (2005). 'The New Governance of Markets and Non-Majoritarian Regulators', *Governance*, 18(3): 329–46.

Thompson, H. (2008). *Might, Right, Prosperity and Consent: Representative Democracy and the International Economy, 1919–2001*. Manchester: Manchester University Press.

Traistaru-Siedschlag, I. (2007). 'Macroeconomic Adjustment in Ireland Under the EMU', *Quarterly Economic Commentary*, Spring. Dublin: ESRI, pp. 78–92.

Traxler, F. (1995). 'Farewell to Labour Market Associations? Organized Versus Disorganized Decentralization as a Map for Industrial Relations', in C. Crouch and F. Traxler (eds.), *Organized Industrial Relations in Europe: What Future?* Aldershot: Avebury, pp. 3–19.

References

Traxler, F. (2003). 'Co-ordinated Bargaining: A Stocktaking of its Preconditions, Practices and Performance', *Industrial Relations Journal*, 43(3): 194–209.

Trichet, J.-C. (2006a). 'Why Europe Needs Structural Reforms', Speech Delivered at the Council on Foreign Affairs, New York, 24 April.

——(2006b). 'Structural Reforms in Europe', Speech Delivered at the OECD Forum, Paris, 22 May.

——(2007). *Letter to Manuel Lobo Antunes, President of the Council of the European Union on the Clarification of the Institutional Status of the ECB*, 2 August, Frankfurt.

Truman, E. (2003). *Inflation Targeting in the World Economy*. Washington, DC: Institute for International Economics.

——and Wong, A. (2006). 'The Case for an International Reserve Diversification Standard'. Working Paper WP 06–2. Washington, DC: Institute for International Economics.

Tsebelis, G. (2002). *Veto Players: How Political Institutions Work*. Princeton, NJ: Princeton University Press.

Tsoukalis, L. (1997). 'Beyond the Greek Paradox', in A. T. Graham and K. Nicolaïdis (eds.), *The Greek Paradox: Promise vs. Performance*. Cambridge, Mass. and London: The MIT Press, pp. 163–74.

Umbach, G. (forthcoming). *Intent and Reality of a New Mode of Governance: 'Get Together' or 'Mind the Gap'?—The Impact of the European Employment Strategy on the Europeanization of National Employment Policy Co-ordination and Policies in the United Kingdom and Germany*. Baden-Baden: Nomos.

UNCTAD (2005). *World Investment Report 2005*. New York: United Nations.

——(2006). *World Investment Report 2006*. New York: United Nations.

Underhill, G. (1997). 'The Making of the European Financial Area: Global Market Integration and the EU Single Market for Financial Services', in G. Underhill (ed.), *The New World Order in International Finance*. London: Macmillan, pp. 101–23.

United Nations (2005). *World Economic and Social Survey*. New York: UN.

Urbanski, T. (2007). 'Main Features of the Services Sector in the EU', *Statistics in Focus*, 19/2007. Luxembourg: Eurostat.

Vanags, A. and Hansen, M. (2006). *Inflation in the Baltic States and Other New EU Member States*. Riga: BICEPS.

——— (2007). *Inflation in Latvia: Causes, Prospects and Consequences*. Riga: BICEPS.

van Apeldoorn, B. (2002). *Transnational Capitalism and the Struggle over European Integration*. London: Routledge.

Vanhuysse, P. (2006). *Divide and Pacify: The Political Economy of Welfare State in Hungary and Poland, 1989–1996*. Budapest: Central European University Press.

Vassallo, S. (2005). 'The Constitutional Reforms of the Center-Right', in C. Guarnieri and J. Newell (eds.), *Italian Politics. Quo vadis?* New York: Berghahn Books, pp. 117–35.

Veit-Wilson, J. (2000). 'States of Welfare: A Conceptual Challenge', *Social Policy and Administration*, 30(1): 1–25.

Velasco, A. (1990). Naar een Economische en Monetaire Unie (1970–1990): een analyse van de politieke beleidsruimte in Nederland. (Towards an Economic and Monetary Union (1970–1990): an Analysis of the Political Room for Manoeuvre in the Netherlands). University of Amsterdam (unpub. manuscript).

Verdun, A. (1996). 'An "Asymmetrical" Economic and Monetary Union in the EU: Perceptions of Monetary Authorities and Social Partners', *Journal of European Integration/Revue d'Integration européenne*, 20(1): 59–81.

—— (1998). 'The Institutional Design of EMU: A Democratic Deficit?', *Journal of Public Policy*, 18(2): 107–32.

—— (2000). *European Responses to Globalization and Financial Market Integration: Perceptions of Economic and Monetary Union in Britain, France and Germany*. Houndmills: Macmillan/New York: St. Martin's Press.

—— (2000a). 'Debts and Deficits With Fragmented Fiscal Policymaking', *Journal of Public Economics*, 76: 105–25.

—— (2002b). 'The Netherlands and EMU: A Small Open Economy in Search of Prosperity', in K. Dyson (ed.), *European States and the Euro*. Oxford: Oxford University Press, pp. 238–54.

—— (2003). 'La nécessité d'un "gouvernement économique" dans une UEM asymétrique. Les préoccupations françaises sont-elles justifiées?', *Politique Européenne*, 10: 11–32.

—— and Christiansen, T. (2000). 'Policy-Making, Institution-Building and European Monetary Union: Dilemmas of Legitimacy', in C. Crouch (ed.), *After the Euro: Shaping Institutions for Governance in the Wake of European Monetary Union*. Oxford: Oxford University Press, pp. 162–78.

—— —— (2001). 'The Legitimacy of the Euro: An Inverted Process?', *Current Politics and Economics of Europe*, 10(3): 265–88.

Vergunst, N. (2004). 'The Impact of Consensus Democracy and Corporatism on Socio-Economic Performance in Twenty Developed Countries', Working Papers Political Science 2004/02, ISSN 1569–3546, University of Amsterdam.

Vifell, Å. (2004). '(Ex)Changing Practices: Swedish Employment Policy and European Guidelines'. SCORE working paper 2004: 11.

—— (2006). *Enklaver i staten*. PhD thesis, Stockholm University.

Visser, J. (2002). 'Unions, Wage Bargaining and Coordination in European Labour Markets—The Past Twenty Years and the Near Future', in P. Pochet (ed.), *Wage Policy in the Eurozone*. Brussels: PIE-Peter Lang, pp. 41–85.

—— (2004). 'Patterns and Variations in European Industrial Relations', in European Commission, *Industrial Relations in Europe, 2004*. Luxembourg: Office for Official Publications of the European Communities, pp. 11–57.

—— and Hemerijck, A. (1997). *A Dutch Miracle*. Amsterdam: Amsterdam University Press.

Voltmer, K. and Eilders, C. (2003). 'The Media Agenda: The Marginalization and Domestication of Europe', in K. Dyson and K. Goetz (eds.), *Germany, Europe and the Politics of Constraint*. Proceedings of the British Academy 119. Oxford: Oxford University Press, pp. 173–97.

Von Hagen, J. (1992). 'Budgeting Procedures and Fiscal Performance in the European Communities', *Economic Papers*, p. 96.

—— and Harden, I. (1994). 'Budget Processes and Commitment to Fiscal Discipline', *European Economic Review*, 39: 771–9.

Wallace, H. and Wallace, W. (eds.) (1996). *Policy-Making in the European Union*. 3rd edn. Oxford: Oxford University Press.

References

Wallin, U. (2004). 'Den långsiktiga pressbevakningen', in H. Oscarsson and S. Holmberg (eds.), *Kampen om euron*. Göteborg: Department of Political Science, pp. 153–74.

Wanlin, A. (2006). *The Lisbon Scorecard VI. Will Europe's Economy Rise Again?* London: Centre for European Reform.

Watson, M. (2001). 'Embedding the 'New Economy' in Europe: A Study in the Institutional Specificities of Knowledge-Based Growth', *Economy and Society*, 30(4): 504–23.

Wehner, J. (2007). 'Budget Reform and Legislative Control in Sweden', *Journal of European Public Policy*, 14: 313–32.

Wernik, A. (2005). 'Fiskalne przeszkody na drodze do euro', *Nowe Zycie Gospodarcze*, No. 15.

Wessels, W. (1994). 'Die Wirtschafts- und Währungsunion. Krönung der Politischen Union?', in R. Caesar and H.-E. Scharrer (eds.), *Maastricht: Königsweg oder Irrweg zur Wirtschafts- und Währungsunion?* Bonn: Europa Union Verlag, pp. 107–24.

—— (2005). 'Keynote Article: The Constitutional Treaty—Three Readings from a Fusion Perspective', *Journal of Common Market Studies*, 43/Annual Review: 11–36.

—— and Faber, A. (2007). 'Vom Verfassungskonvent zurück zur 'Methode Monnet'? Die Entstehung der 'Road Map' zum Reformvertrag unter deutscher Ratspräsidentschaft', *Integration*, 4: 370–81.

—— and Linsenmann, I. (2002). 'EMU's Impact on National Institutions: Fusion Towards a, Gouvernance Économique' or Fragmentation?', in K. Dyson (ed.), *European States and the Euro. Europeanization, Variation, and Convergence*. Oxford: Oxford University Press, pp. 53–77.

Wildavsky, A. (1975). *Budgeting*. Oxford: Transaction Publishers.

Willman, J. (2006a). 'Board Room Sentiment Turns Against Brussels As Frustrations Grow', *Financial Times*, 16 October.

—— (2006b). 'Optimism Eroded by Costly Regulatory Burden', *Financial Times*, 4 December.

Wincott, D. (2001). 'Reassessing the Foundations of Welfare (State) Regimes', *New Political Economy*, 6(3): 409–25.

—— (2003a). 'The Idea of the European Social Model: Limits and Paradoxes of Europeanization', in K. Featherstone and C. Radaelli (eds.), *The Politics of Europeanization*. Oxford: Oxford University Press, pp. 279–302.

—— (2003b). 'Beyond Social Regulation? New Instruments and/or a New Agenda for Social Policy at Lisbon?', *Public Administration*, 81(3): 533–53.

—— (2004). 'Policy Change and Discourse in Europe: Can the EU Make a 'Square Meal out of a Stew of Paradox?', *West European Politics*, 27(2): 354–63.

World Bank (2003). *Poland: Towards a Fiscal Framework for Growth, A Public Expenditure and Institutional Review*. Washington, DC.: World Bank.

—— (2006). *Doing Business in 2006*. Washington, DC.: The World Bank.

World Economic Forum (2006). *Global Competitiveness Report, 2006–2007*. World Economic Forum.

Wüst, A. and Roth, D. (2006). 'Schröder's Last Campaign: An Analysis of the 2005 Bundestag Election in Context', *German Politics*, 15(4): 439–59.

Wyplosz, C. (1999). 'An International Role for the Euro?', in J. Dermine and P. Hillion (eds.), *European Capital Markets with a Single Currency*. New York: Oxford University Press, pp. 76–104.

Wyplosz, C. (2006). 'European Monetary Union: The Dark Sides of a Major Success', *European Policy*, April: 207–61.

Zaller, J. (1992). *The Nature and Origins of Mass Opinion*. Cambridge: Cambridge University Press.

Zestos, G. (2006). *European Monetary Integration: The Euro*. Mason, OH: Thomson South-Western.

ZKA (2005). 'Comments of the Zentraler Kreditausschuss on Working Document ESC/20/2005-rev 1 on implementing measures for articles 22(2), 27 to 30, 40 and 44 to 45 of Directive 2004/39/EC of the European Parliament and of the Council', 16 August 2005.http://www.bankenverband.de/pic/artikelpic/082005/sp0508_vw_zka-finanzinstr_en.pdf (accessed 2 September 2005).

Zubek, R. (2001). 'A Core in Check: The Transformation of the Polish Core Executive', *Journal of European Public Policy*, 8(6): 911–32.

——(2006). 'Poland: Unbalanced Domestic Leadership in Negotiating Fit', in K. Dyson (ed.), *Enlarging the Euro Area: External Empowerment and Domestic Transformation in East Central Europe*. Oxford: Oxford University Press, pp. 197–214.

——(2008a). *Core Executive and Europeanization in Central Europe*. Basingstoke: Palgrave Macmillan.

——(2008b). 'Parties, Rules and Executive Legislative Control in Central Europe: The Case of Poland', *Communist and Post-Communist Studies*, 41(2).

Zysman, J. (1983). *Governments, Markets and Growth: Financial Systems and the Politics of Industrial Change*. Ithaca: Cornell University Press.

Index

and Euro Area financial crisis 42
and Europeanization 19
and financial crises 12
and financial market integration 336
and France 115–16, 130
and Hungary 280
and independence of 7, 325, 333–4
and Italy 218
and power of 20
and Slovakia 281
and Sweden 314
and United Kingdom 259
see also Bundesbank; European Central Bank
  (ECB)
Centre for Economic Performance 262
China 13, 14
Chirac, Jacques 117, 119, 122, 124, 126,
  127
Christian Democratic Union (CDU,
  Germany) 134
Christian Democrats (CDA, Netherlands) 230,
  231, 237
Christian Democrats (Italy) 208
Christian Social Union (CSU, Germany) 134
Christodoulakis, Nikos 168, 181
Ciampi, Carlo 207, 208, 214
Civic Platform (PO, Poland) 294, 303, 304
Clarke, Ken 266, 271
Clement, Wolfgang 134, 143
Clinton, Bill 100
coalitions, and fiscal governance 75
collateralized debt obligations (CDOs) 12
collective action problems, and Euro Area 7
Cologne process 90
Committee of European Banking Supervisors
  (CEBS) 328
Committee of European Insurance and
  Occupational Pensions Supervisors
  (CEIOPS) 328
Committee of European Securities Regulators
  (CESR) 328
Communist Party (KKE, Greece) 172
Communist Refoundation (Italy) 208
comparative advantage 385–6
  and economic reform 398–400
competitiveness:
  and benchmarking:
    problematic usefulness of 94–6
    ranking of countries 94–5
  and regime competition 341
  and social pacts 345
  and state models 95–6
Confederation of British Industry (CBI) 268
Confindustria 215, 216, 220
Conseil national du patronat français
  (CNPF) 117
consensus democracy 385, 391

Conservative Party (UK) 271–2
consociational democracies 391
contagion, and Euro Area 41
convergence:
  and benchmarking 93
  and clustered convergence 380, 410–11
    D-Mark-Zone 380–1, 411
    Mediterranean cluster 381–2
    small-state cluster 381
    variations within 382, 410–14
  and covariance 382
  and definitional difficulties 361–2
  and Economic and Monetary Union 30,
    359
  and the euro 19, 21
  and financial markets 326–7, 333
  and neo-liberalism 360
  and Open Method of Coordination 91
  and welfare state:
    conventional analysis of 362
    definitional difficulties 361–2
    welfare benefit generosity indices 374
  see also financial market integration
coordinated market economy, and Euro
  Area 384
corporate profits, and Euro Area 2
credit creation, and financial markets 12
credit default swaps (CDSs) 12
Csáky, Pál 285
currency crises, and removal of national 5–6
Cyprus 2
  and small-state cluster 381
  and wage bargaining 355
Czech Republic 2, 379
Czechoslovakia:
  and economic legacy of 280
  and post-communist reform 277–8

D'Alema, Massimo 208, 214
Delors, Jacques 43, 166, 365, 366
Delors Report (1989) 400–1
democracies, and types of 385
Democratic Left (Italy) 208
Denmark 2
  and economic success 94, 97
  and education expenditure 99
  and Lisbon process 97
    incomplete criteria 98
  and research and development
    expenditure 98–9
  and social service expenditure 99
Dennis, Bengt 313
Deutsche Volksunion (DVU) 156
Dimocratiko Koinoniko Kinima (DIKKI) 173
Dini, Lamberto 206
disintermediation 11
disposable income, and Euro Area 2